THE
WHO'S WHO
OF GOLF

Keep Swinging!

THE WHO'S WHO OF GOLF

PETER ALLISS

with research by Michael Hobbs

ORBIS PUBLISHING · LONDON

First published in Great Britain by
Orbis Publishing Limited, London
1983

Printed and bound in
Great Britain by R. J. Acford, Chichester

Phototypeset by Tradespools Ltd, Frome, Somerset

ISBN 0–85613–520–8

Frontispiece:
Dai Rees and his caddie, 'Little Mac', with Gene
Sarazen.

ACKNOWLEDGMENTS
The author and his publishers would like to thank the
following organizations who have assisted with
information in the preparation of this book: the Royal
and Ancient Golf Club of St Andrews, the Professional
Golfers' Association, the PGA European Tour, the
United States Golf Association, the United States
Professional Golfers' Association, the Tournament
Players' Association of America, the Ladies'
Professional Golf Association of America, the Asia
Circuit.

CONTENTS

Foreword by Arnold Palmer   7

Introduction   9

North America   11

Great Britain & Ireland   203

Europe   314

Australia & New Zealand   328

South Africa   348

Africa   357

Asia   359

South & Central America   363

Index   369

Photographic Acknowledgments   381

FOREWORD

I am happy that Peter Alliss has asked me to write this foreword for the first comprehensive who's who of world golfers. Peter and I have known each other for many years. We first met at the Centenary Open at St Andrews, Scotland, in 1960. We met again in the 1961 Ryder Cup at Royal Lytham and St Annes, England, where we had one of the best singles matches ever on the morning of the second day. It was close all the way and ended in a half.

Many are the talks we have had about golf and other things at Ryder Cup matches, the British Open and when Peter competed at Augusta National in the Masters.

Today, of course, he has stopped competing on the professional circuits of the world but travels as widely as ever, commenting on TV in the US, Europe, Australia and elsewhere. In this field, his contribution has been as great as when a tournament player.

I was interested to see how detailed the coverage of my own career is in this book but every golfer that I have ever heard of seems to have found a place: from Horace Rawlins, who won the first US Open at Newport, Rhode Island, in 1895, including early Scottish players at the dawn of the British Open and earlier down to those just beginning to make a mark in 1982.

The book gives prominence to major championship performances and I believe this is right. Certainly my wins in the 1954 US Amateur, my Cherry Hills Open in 1960 and then my Birkdale and Troon British Open wins in 1961 and 1962 were personal highlights.

However, not everyone can win an Open and I have found this book well balanced in its treatment of about 1,000 golfers, men, women, amateur and professional, who have made a contribution to golf's long story.

I think that anyone interested in golf will find much information and entertainment in these pages. It will also be an essential reference source for many years to come for experts and enthusiasts alike.

Arnold D. Palmer

ARNOLD PALMER

Latrobe, Pennsylvania, USA, March 1983

INTRODUCTION

This who's who of golfers attempts to include all who have achieved considerable success at the game. The time span is from approximately the middle of the last century to the end of the 1982 US and European seasons. This means that the earliest golfer included is Allan Robertson, who was born in the year of the battle of Waterloo and died in 1858, a couple of years before the Open Championship was first played. The best player of his day, he is the first known to have broken 80. At the other end of the time span are such players as 1982's US and European Rookies of the Year, Hal Sutton and Gordon Brand Jnr; first-time professional winners Tim Norris and Ronan Rafferty; or Juli Inkster, who in 1982 extended her winning sequence in the US Women's Amateur to three and then turned professional at the end of the season.

Golf, unlike baseball and cricket, for instance, has not been much obsessed with statistics because so much depends in a round of golf on course and weather conditions. A 62 when everything is in favour of good scoring may not represent as good a performance as a 76 in icy rain and high winds. One of Jack Nicklaus's best achievements may have been to play the first nine at Pebble Beach in the 1967 Bing Crosby Pro-Am in 39. Nothing outstanding there, you might well think, but a hurricane was in progress at the time and other well-known names had scored into the 50s for the nine before play was abandoned....

The main statistics you will find in these pages, therefore, are money winnings and tournament wins and about both a word of caution is in order. Ben Hogan, indisputably one of the three greatest golfers of all time, won $207,779 in a career of about 30 years, while Tom Watson topped $530,000 in the 1980 season alone. Similarly, Hal Sutton won more than Hogan's career total in his first season, 1982. Yet Hogan won 13 tournaments on the US Tour in 1946 to Watson's six in 1980 and Sutton's one in 1982. In present-day money terms, Hogan's year might have been worth $2 million. Numbers of tournament wins seem a better guide to achievement, but even here there are problems. The early US Tour was largely a matter of winter tournaments only, while in Europe tournaments were few and far between. Earlier players, then, had much less opportunity to pile up victories, for the tournament schedules expand year by year in every part of the world where competitive golf is played. Even the tournaments themselves are often of different status for there is as yet no such thing as a world Tour – nor is there likely to be – in which all the best players compete.

That is why so much weight has been given to performance in the major championships, the US and British Opens, the Masters and US PGA or, for amateurs, the US and British Amateur Championships; a golfer winning any of these has always earned a kind of immortality. Much the same applies to the equivalent events in the totally separate world of women's golf. To finish in the top groupings in such championships is a higher achievement than to win a lesser tournament because the competition consists of a high proportion of the world's best. In this book, only outstanding winners of major championships have their achievements listed at the beginning of their biographies. All players for whom figures are available have their tournament wins and money winnings in different parts of the world detailed after their biographies.

Statistics have mainly been obtained from the various golfing organizations noted in the Acknowledgments. 'US money' and 'Europe money' refer, for example, to the respective American and European PGA money winnings, as announced annually. The figures for world money winnings come from Mark H. McCormack's *Dunhill World of Professional Golf 1983*, published by Springwood Books, 22 Chewter Lane, Windlesham, Surrey, GU20 6JP. These include certain events, such as the Sun City $1 Million Challenge and the Suntory World Matchplay, which are not included in the statistics of other golf organizations. When individual tournaments were not recognized by the appropriate professional golfers' associations, the author has made a subjective judgment as to whether or not that event should be included as a win in particular players' records. Such an event would not normally feature amongst, for example, European or US official money winnings. The judgment has been based mainly on the quality of the competitive field. US money winnings are given to the end of the 1982 season, as are world money winnings. In the case of European winnings, these are also given to the end of the same season. Such winnings also include amounts won in PGA-approved pro-ams but, at the time of going to press, 1982 pro-am totals were available only for those on the all-time Top 60 list.

Players are listed alphabetically within the geographical region which was their 'home' base. Emigrants, for example to the USA, are usually listed under whichever area they played their most successful golf, which in most cases became their adopted country. Cross-references are given for borderline cases, for example those who played equally successful golf in two different countries. Women golfers have, of course, sometimes competed under more than one name as a result of marriage(s). In these cases, the entry will be found under the familiar name (e.g. Glenna Collett and Joyce Wethered rather than Mrs Edwin H. Vare or Lady Heathcoat-Amory). Other names under which they competed are given as cross-references. Names beginning 'de', 'da', 'di', 'von', 'van' etc. are listed under the initial of the main name following.

I would like to record my thanks to my editor, Stephen Adamson, and to Richard Williams, for their guidance, help and enthusiasm throughout the preparation of this who's who of golfers. Finally, my warm thanks must go to Michael Hobbs for all his patience and hard work in helping to prepare this book. His eye for an odd fact and his persistence in hunting down elusive details have cast a bright light on many hitherto dark corners of golf history; nevertheless the responsibility for any errors or omissions is entirely my own.

NORTH AMERICA

AARON, Thomas Dean   USA
b. Gainesville, Georgia 1937

Tommy Aaron at one time well earned the nickname of 'the Bridesmaid'. In the 1961–9 period he was indeed a champion runner-up, finishing in that position no less than nine times. The label perhaps derived from 1963, when he twice lost US Tour play-offs – to Tony Lema and Arnold Palmer. Victory eventually came in a prestige tournament, the 1969 Canadian Open, and this time Aaron won a play-off, against J.C. Snead. The next year, he managed his first victory on the US Tour, the Atlanta Classic. Even so, by the end of the 1972 season he had increased his number of second-place finishes to 14, including the US PGA, and in that year also won $100,000 for the first and only time. Tommy had had an excellent amateur career, dominating amateur golf in Georgia, starting his habit of second-place finishes in the US Amateur of 1958, beaten by Charlie Coe, and winning a Walker

Tommy Aaron

Cup place in 1959. (Later, he was to be one of the few also to represent his country in the Ryder Cup, which he did in 1969 and 1973.) In 1960 he turned professional and went on Tour the following year. He immediately made the Top 60, which exempts a player from pre-qualifying the following season, and remained there without interruption until the end of 1973. He remained a consistent money-winner until 1980. His best placings in the money list were 13th in 1963 and 1969 and ninth in 1972, when he also won the Lancôme in France and the individual prize in the USA versus Japan contest. Tommy's greatest occasion was the 1973 US Masters. He birdied the first two holes of the championship and at the end of the round held the lead with his 68. He was joint leader after the second round but then fell behind Peter Oosterhuis. A final round of another 68, however, saw him home by 1 stroke from J.C. Snead. Aaron's worst occasion also came in the US Masters, this time in 1968. For it was he that made the error of marking down a 4 to Roberto de Vicenzo for the 71st hole, when Roberto had a birdie 3. After the Argentinian had failed to notice, Aaron's scoring had to count and Goalby became the outright winner.

US wins 2 (1970–73)
US money $897,464 (1961–82) (43rd all-time)
Overseas wins 3
World money $1,074,475 (1961–82) (48th all-time)

ADAMS, Lynn   USA
b. Kingsville, Texas 1950

Lynn Adams first considered a career as a professional tennis player, a game she taught as well as being a school teacher. She qualified for the US Tour in 1978 and since then has shown considerable promise, leading the 1981 US LPGA by two after a first-round 66, and in 1982 she won $65,283 to double what she had won in the previous three and a half seasons. She is one of the longest drivers in women's golf, averaging some 240 yards.

US money $123,796 (1978–82)

ADAMS, Sam   USA
b. *Boone, North Carolina 1946*

After turning professional in 1969 Adams joined the US Tour in 1972, a year in which he finished equal second in the Canadian Open. The following year he won his first event, the Quad Cities Open, with a 13-under-par score of 72, 64, 64, 68. Remarkably, this was only the second US Tour event to be won by a left-hander. Thereafter, he achieved little.

US wins 1 (1973)
US money $84,401 (1972–8) (250th all-time)

AHERN, Katherine   USA
b. *Pittsburgh, Pennsylvania 1949*

Highly successful as a teenager, Kathy Ahern won the Texas Public Links at the age of 15, and the following year, 1965, the full and junior Texas titles. At 17 she won the Western Open and was runner-up for the US Junior, she then became one of the youngest players to turn professional. Thereafter her career did not fully live up to early promise. She was, however, in the Top 60 on the US Tour from 1967 to 1980. She won her first tournament in 1970, and 1971 and 1972 were her best years. In the first of these years she was 12th on the money list. In 1972, comfortably her best season, she was sixth and won twice, including the US LPGA.

US wins 3 (1970–2)
US money $214,287 (1967–81)

ALBERS, Roberta (later Speer)   USA
b. *Tampa, Florida 1946*

Winner of the 1965 National Collegiate and the Trans-Mississippi the same year, Roberta Albers had earlier achieved the considerable feat of reaching the semi-finals of the US Amateur in 1961 at the age of 14 years 8 months. In 1968 she was a member of the Curtis Cup team but did not seek a golf career immediately on graduating; instead she became director of marketing with a toy manufacturer. She tried the US Tour from 1973 but has had back problems.

US money $66,269 (1973–82)

ALCOTT, Amy   USA
b. *Kansas City, Missouri 1956*

Currently one of the leading US professionals, Amy Alcott won the US Junior in 1973 and the following year was second in the Canadian Amateur behind Marlene Stewart. With a 70, she also beat Babe Zaharias's record for Pebble Beach. As a professional she had to wait only five weeks for her first Tour victory in the Orange Blossom Classic of 1975, and in 21 events in her first year was only once placed outside the top 20. Her $26,798 was then a record for first-year earnings and she finished fourth in the Vare stroke-average rankings and 15th on the money list. She was Rookie of the Year. Amy has won at least once each year since then, two victories coming in major championships. In 1979 she won the Peter Jackson Classic, and the following year the US Open. In this latter event she dominated throughout, her scores of 70, 70, 68, 72 putting her 9 strokes ahead of Hollis Stacey in second place, while her 280 was a record for the championship, though lasting for only a year until Pat Bradley beat it. On the US Tour Amy has never finished worse than 15th on the money list but so far her peak has been the years 1979–80. In 1979, she won four times, won $144,838, and was third on the money list with a stroke average of 72.43. She did better still the following year, with four wins, $219,887, third place on the money list and the Vare Trophy for an average of 71.51

Amy Alcott

(second lowest in Vare history). She also broke 70 in tournaments 25 times, an LPGA record.

US wins 16 (1975–82)
US money $904,993 (1975–82) (7th all-time)

ALEX, Janet (later Anderson)   USA

b. *West Sunbury, Pennsylvania 1956*

Coming into professional golf after managing a golf shop, Janet Alex qualified for the US Tour in 1978, when she ended as Rookie of the Year and in 61st place on the money list. She made a big stride forward in 1980, coming 25th, and she was 16th in 1981. However, she did not fully become a name player until 1982 with victory in the US Open. She began 70, 73, 73 and her closing 68 then took her home to a 6-stroke victory. This has been her only Tour victory.

US wins 1 (1982)
US money $222,890 (1978–82) (47th all-time)

ALEXANDER, Stewart   USA

b. *Philadelphia, Pennsylvania 1918*

After some success as an amateur in the 1930s which included his being medallist at one US Amateur (the medallist is the man who returns the lowest score in the final qualifying rounds for the matchplay stages), 'Skip' Alexander turned professional shortly before the US entry into World War II. He was a Ryder Cup player in 1949 and then was involved in a light plane crash in which he broke both ankles and was badly burnt. After this he found it difficult to feel the grips of his clubs. Despite his handicap, he fought his way back within a year and again played in the 1951 Ryder Cup. In this match, he demolished John Panton by 8 and 7 in the singles. A few years later he retired from tournament golf and became solely a club professional.

US wins 3 (1946–54)

ALLEN, Donald   USA

b. *Granville, New York 1938*

A Walker Cup team member in 1965 and 1967, Donald Allen was the winner of six New York State titles. Otherwise, he had a good run in the US Amateur, reaching the quarter-finals in 1964, being third the following year and sixth in 1966. He was also second amateur in the 1965 US Masters.

ALLIN, Brian   USA

b. *Bremerton, Washington 1944*

After spending 16 months in the Vietnam War and being four times decorated, 'Buddy' Allin may have found the US Tour less rigorous than some. Quickly he qualified and went on the circuit in 1970. The following year he had his first victory in the Greater Greensboro' Open and was in the Top 60 from 1971 to 1976. His most dominating performance came in the 1973 Florida Citrus Open when he recorded 66, 65, 67, 67. He was in the lead after two rounds, increased it to 4 after three rounds and finished 8 ahead, the best performance of the year. His final 265 meant he was no less than 23 under par. The following year he won two tournaments, having a 63 in the course of his Byron Nelson Classic win, and was ninth in the money list, easily his highest placing and the only time he exceeded $100,000. He had two more good years and then faded out of sight, apart from a sudden win in the 1976 Pleasant Valley Classic and again in 1980 when he took the New Zealand Open.

US wins 5 (1971–6)
US money $563,587 (1970–82) (80th all-time)
Overseas wins 1 (1980)

ANDERSON, Janet: see Alex

ANDERSON, William   USA

b. *North Berwick, Scotland 1878; d. 1910*

Willie emigrated to America in about 1895 (at the time the game was just beginning to take off over there) with his father, an ex-greenkeeper at North Berwick. After a couple of years, he began to establish a record in the US Open that has never been bettered. He was fifth three times, fourth twice, third once and second once. More important, he is of that select company (the others are Jones, Hogan and Nicklaus) who have won it four times. There are many who claim that he could not have been of the stature of those great names that were to follow after World War I, and indeed it is impossible to judge; but Fred McLeod, who saw them all, put him on an equal level with Jones and Hogan. His sequence of Open wins began in 1901 and then he won three in a row from 1903 to 1905, the only golfer to accomplish this feat in the US Open. His scores do not bear comparison with those of later years but neither do clubs, balls and, most important of all, the condition of golf courses.

In Britain, Opens were being played on long-established courses at that time, while every course Willie Anderson played on in America was, at best, in its early years. So his best winning score in an Open was 303, an average of around 76 and good enough to give him victory by 5 strokes. All other tournaments of the day, with one exception, were somewhat hastily arranged minor events, usually of local interest only. The exception was the Western Open. Willie won this four times, his victory in 1908 establishing a scoring record of 288 for a standard golf course, which in this case measured 6,108 yards, with rounds of 71, 73, 72, 72. These are scores that look good even today. In the Open he set the one-round record at 73 in 1904 and lowered it to 72 the following year. This stood for several years until Tom McNamara broke 70 in 1909. Willie had a flat swing, bent his left arm and had a very full hip turn – as was standard at the time. He reckoned his greatest strength was with the driver, but opponents thought the best shot in his locker was his imperturbable temperament, something that would have stood him in good stead in any era. One week in 1910 he played three 36-hole matches, then suddenly died. The cause is thought to have been arteriosclerosis, despite malicious rumours spread by his detractors that he died of the demon drink.

ARCHER, George William   USA
b. San Francisco, California 1939

At 6 feet 5¼ inches, George Archer is one of the most impossibly tall players to have made a considerable name for himself. In my youth, it was generally felt that medium height was best for golf and though our ideas have modified since then (6 feet might now be thought the right height), few indeed have been successful at George's distance from the ground. He is currently the tallest player on the US Tour. As an amateur George won the 1963 Trans-Mississippi and reached the semi-finals of the US Amateur. He then turned professional and finished 50th in the money list in his first year. Thereafter he did not finish worse than 31st on the US Tour until 1973, and since that time his best finishes have been 20th in 1977 and 31st in 1981. He was fourth in the money list in both 1968 and 1971, and third in 1972. He has topped $100,000 six times. Relatively little was heard of him between 1973 and 1980 (though he had a good year in 1977) because he was seldom fit, undergoing both

George Archer

back and left wrist surgery, but he is now said to be fully well. Putting has been the backbone of George's game. He crouches low over the ball, also gripping well down the shaft, and makes a slow stroke at it, the left hand guiding, he says, and the right providing the pace. As a putter I rank him third among those playing in the last 35 years, behind only Locke and Charles. It is fitting that he broke the US Tour record over 72 holes when he took only 94 putts in the 1980 Heritage Classic, an average of only 23½ per round! His greatest career moment came in 1969. Having won the Crosby (despite ending his third round double bogey, triple bogey!) he opened up in the Masters with a first-round 67. Although he did not score as well again, he took the championship by one stroke as Knudson, Coody, and Casper, particularly, threw it away. He named his daughters Elizabeth Taylor and Marilyn Monroe 'because they are the two most beautiful girls in the world'. All right when you are in your pram, but I dare say both now conceal their second names as teenagers!

US wins 12 (1965–76)
US money $1,249,965 (1964–82) (22nd all-time)
World money $1,467,848 (1964–82) (25th all-time)

ARMOUR, Thomas Dickson USA

b. Edinburgh, Scotland 1895; d. 1968

Known as 'the Silver Scot', Tommy Armour was undoubtedly one of the few golfers to become a legend in his lifetime. He played most of his golf with the aid of only one eye, having been wounded in World War I and, so the story goes, having leapt out of his tank with eight pieces of shrapnel in a shoulder and killed a German officer with his bare hands. Certainly in later life the Armour hands were legendary and he was said to be able to hold a billiard cue by the tip at arm's length with thumb and forefinger only. Such strength is undoubtedly highly useful to the golfer, enabling him to grip the club firmly without tension. Armour first began to earn a name for himself when he took second place in the 1919 Irish Open. The following year he won the French Amateur and went off to the USA on the same boat as Walter Hagen. Later that year he tied for the Canadian Open before being defeated in a play-off, and back in Britain he represented his country in the 1921 match against the USA. The following year Armour stayed in the USA and played in the 1922 Walker Cup. He then spent a couple of years as social secretary at the Westchester-Biltmore Club (at the then massive salary of $10,000 a year), after which he turned professional. As an amateur golfer he had as yet achieved comparatively little, but that was to change when he began playing golf for a living. Soon he was winning tournaments on the winter tour in the USA, and then there came his first substantial win in the 1927 US Open. In this he knew what he had to do, as 'Light-Horse' Harry Cooper was in with a total of 301. Armour was a shot to the bad after he reached the turn in 39. He then recorded double bogeys at two of the next three holes with a birdie in between. Yet his finish was memorable, for he played the last six holes in 2 under par. This included being on the last tee of a 460-yard hole needing a birdie to tie Cooper. Armour hit a 3-iron to 10 feet and holed the putt. In the play-off, Cooper had established a lead of 2 with six holes to go. Again, Armour put in a fine finish as he birdied the 13th and 15th holes to be level. The title became his when Cooper then dropped two shots on the 16th. By this time, Armour had the reputation of being a master with the irons and it remained with him. In fact the reputation was the result of a publicity stunt, a sports writer having suggested, without opposition from Armour, that he should continually refer in print to Tommy's mastery of iron shots.

Armour himself considered his greatest strength was accurate driving which usually left him in the fairway with the best line in to the green. By this time, Armour was a consistent winner on what US Tour there then was – basically winter events when the professionals could be away from their home clubs. He took one event in 1925 and seven in 1927, four in 1928 and two, including the Western Open, in 1929. In 1930, he won his second major, the US PGA, beating Sarazen in the final. He was again a finalist in this event in 1935, losing to Johnny Revolta. By now, the British Open, an event in which he had never featured strongly, was Armour's prime target. At Carnoustie, Armour played steadily for two rounds and then had a 77 in the third that left him five shots behind José Jurado and two behind Macdonald Smith. Armour played almost flawless golf that final afternoon until on the 71st green he missed a short putt. On the last hole, he was then faced with a short putt for a 71 which would leave a reasonable target for those pursuing him to face. Armour later described how he got the ball into the hole: 'I took a new grip, holding the club as tightly as I could and with stiff wrists. From the instant the club left the ball on the backswing I was blind and unconscious.' In fact, quite a normal reaction for a golfer undertaking a putt for a major championship! As his golf career slowly waned thereafter, Armour increasingly concentrated on other fields and seems to have been successful in almost everything he attempted. The most famed teacher in America, he was said to charge the then enormous sum of $50 a lesson, and his skill at setting the odds in money matches, and winning,

Tommy Armour

was legendary. This despite the fact that his putting was gone. Armour invented the term 'the yips' which he described as 'that ghastly time when, with the first movement of the putter, the golfer blacks out'. (It looks as if he had yipped the ball into the hole on the last at Carnoustie.) He was also extremely successful as a golf instruction writer who is read to this day, and it may be that some of this writing holds the record for length of time in print. His two books were: *How to Play Your Best Golf All the Time* and *A Round of Golf with Tommy Armour.*

ARMSTRONG, Walter   USA
b. *New London, Connecticut 1945*

After being an All-American choice in 1966, Wally Armstrong qualified for the Tour in 1973. He was in the Top 60 for three years – 1975–8.

US money $355,779 (1973–82) (131st all-time)

ASHLEY, Jean (later Crawford)   USA
b. *Chanute, Kansas 1939*

Jean Ashley first reached the final of the US Amateur in 1960, when she was the 6 and 5 victim of JoAnne Gunderson. She was there again in 1965 and this time defeated Anne Quast by 5 and 4. She once more reached the final, in 1967, this time losing to Mary Lou Dill. Jean Ashley was in the Curtis Cup teams from 1962 to 1968 and was non-playing captain in 1972.

AUCHTERLONIE, Laurie   Scotland & USA
b. *St Andrews 1868; d. 1948*

A semi-finalist in the British Amateur in 1895, Laurie was one of a small host of Scotsmen who sought fame and fortune in the USA at the turn of the century as the game began to develop fast. He was fourth in the US Open in 1900, fifth the next year and then won it in 1902. He had become the first man to break 80 in every round and did so with scores of 78, 78, 74, 77 for a total of 307 with the Haskell ball.

AUSTIN, Deborah   USA
b. *Oneida, New York 1948*

On the US Tour since 1968, Debbie Austin was always in the top 40 in the period 1968–81, becoming a leading player by 1973 when she was

Debbie Austin

13th, her first top 20 position which she has repeated from 1974 to 1978 and in 1981. However, she did not become a winner until 1977 with the Birmingham Classic. She then went on to win four more times that year to climb to sixth place in the money list with a stroke average of 73.19 and winnings of $86,392. This has been easily her best season, though she has had two other victories, in 1978 and 1981. She is a long hitter and good iron player, putting sometimes being a weakness.

US wins 7 (1977–81)
US money $466,749 (1968–82) (17th all-time)

AUSTIN, Michael Hoke   USA
b. *1910*

In the US National Seniors in 1974 at Las Vegas this 64-year-old hit a drive of 515 yards which carried 450 yards in the air. This feat, which defies belief, was accomplished with the aid of a tailwind of some 35 mph.

BAIRD, Butch   USA
b. *Chicago, Illinois 1936*

At one time a Caribbean specialist, winning six events between 1967 and 1969, Baird turned professional in 1959 and was in the Top 60 the following year and in 1962. He did not appear there again until 1975, and in 1976 he was 46th and earned over $58,000. He also came fourth in the US Open that year.

US wins 3 (1961–76)
US money $329,789 (1960–82) (139th all-time)

BALDING, Albert Canada

b. Toronto, Ontario 1924

Although never competing in amateur golf, or indeed being either a member of a golf club or working at one, Al Balding is one of those rare examples of a player who has taken to the game late in life and achieved outstanding success at the highest level. Together with Stan Leonard and George Knudson, he dominated Canadian golf of the 1950s and 1960s. Turning professional in 1950, he soon made an impact in Canada, winning the Canadian Matchplay in 1952, a victory he was to repeat three times between 1954 and 1961. He first won the Canadian PGA in 1955 and then again in 1956, 1963 and 1970. Meanwhile he had begun to play on the US Tour, and in 1955 he became the first Canadian ever to win there when he took the Mayfair Inn Open. Playing more frequently, Balding won three times on the US Tour in 1957: the Miami Beach and West Palm Beach Open and the Havana Invitational. Balding was not to win again on the Tour but he did tie four times in all, losing the play-offs. In 1963 he took the Mexican Open, and then in 1968, at the age of 44 achieved his greatest triumph. With scores of 68, 72, 67, 67, 14 under par, he was leading individual in the World Cup and, together with his partner George Knudson, took Canada to the team victory. Shortly after this he settled down to the life of a club professional and later became based in Florida.

Canada wins 8 major (1952–70)
US wins 4 (1955–7)
US money $166,977 (205th all-time)

BARBER, Jerry USA

b. Woodson, Illinois 1916

At 5 feet 5 inches, Jerry Barber is one of the shortest players to have become a golfer of distinction. After being second in the 1959 US PGA he took it two years later in unlikely fashion. With three holes to play he lay 4 strokes behind Don January but then holed putts of 40 feet, 40 feet and 60 feet to draw level. He won the play-off with 67 to 68. He was named Player of the Year and Ryder Cup captain that same year. Barber was eight times in the Top 60 in his US Tour career, which began in 1948, with 17th in 1960 being his best placing. He was also in the 1955 Ryder Cup team.

US wins 8 (1952–63)
US money $177,848 (200th all-time)

BARBER, Miller USA

b. Shreveport, Louisiana 1931

Barber is nicknamed 'Mr X' and 'Mr Consistency', the first derived from his habits of wearing dark glasses and disappearing rapidly at the end of the day's play and the second from his habit of being a regular money-winner. He was never out of the Top 40 from 1963 to 1978 and never worse than 95th between 1959 and 1981. Six times he topped $100,000, while he was sixth in the money list in both 1971 and 1973 and eighth in 1977 – at the age of 46. He was 12 times in the top 25. As late as 1979, he equalled the US Masters record with a 64 in the second round. Oddly, he seldom featured strongly in a major championship, one of his few chances coming in the 1969 US Open when he led by 3 with one round to go and fell away to a 78 and sixth place, which he also achieved a year later. Between 1967 and 1974, however, he never failed to win a Tour event each year and one of these was the 1973 World Open, which carried the then record first prize of $100,000. He took it despite the fact that everyone was rooting for the new super-star, Ben Crenshaw. Another win was the 1971 Phoenix Open in which he scored 65, 66, 67, 65 for 261, the lowest on Tour since Souchak's record of 1955. Miller Barber has a very strange swing indeed, one of the first that comes to mind when oddities that win are discussed. He takes the club

Miller Barber

back very much on an outside line, right elbow projecting strongly, and loops it around and into the ball. He qualified by age for the Senior Tour in 1981 and topped the year's money list with $83,136, winning three events, one of which was the US PGA Seniors which he won by 2 shots from Arnold Palmer. He was a Ryder Cup player in 1969, when he beat Maurice Bembridge by 7 and 6, and in 1971. He has won six events on the Senior Tour, the most of any, and was also 1982's top money-winner.

US wins 11 (1964–78)
US money $1,577,220 (1959–82) (13th all-time)
World money $2,068,608 (1959–82) (13th all-time)

BARNES, James M.   USA
b. Lelant, England 1887; d. 1966

Long Jim Barnes (he was 6 feet 4 inches tall) was brought up in Cornwall and was a club assistant professional from 1902 to 1904 before emigrating to San Francisco. He later took out US citizenship, but remained attached to his native country, frequently returning to play in the British Open. In this event, he was in the top 8 seven times between 1920 and 1928. In 1922 he was equal second and won at Prestwick in 1925. This was the famous occasion when the crowds hooting for Macdonald Smith were later said to have cost him the championship. Barnes put in a last-round 74 against Smith's 82 and beat him by 3 and Compston and Ted Ray by 1. Barnes had had troubles of his own, for although he had opened with a 70 he had then fallen away to 77, 79 in the middle rounds. In the US Open, his record was equally good, and from an earlier date. At his second attempt in 1913 he came fourth and did so again two years later, improving to third in 1916. In 1920 he was sixth and then in 1921 at the Columbia Country Club in Maryland he won it by the record margin of 9 strokes. Barnes scored 69, 75, 73, 72 and left Walter Hagen and Fred McLeod far behind in joint second place with the next man another 4 strokes in arrears. The US PGA Championship was first played in 1916; Jim Barnes beat Jock Hutchison in the final. Because of World War I it was next played in 1919. Barnes won again, defeating Fred McLeod by 6 and 5. In 1921, he was the beaten finalist, losing to Walter Hagen, a result repeated in 1924. By winning each of the major titles then available (the US Masters was first played in 1934), Barnes is one of only eight golfers to do so. He is also credited with a

further 17 wins in the USA, and this in the days before a regular Tour was built up in the 1930s. Yet he remains a relatively little-known figure, probably because he was a quiet man who did not seek to project his personality. He preferred to lope round the course in almost complete silence, often with a sprig of clover or grass clamped tightly between his teeth.

BARNETT, Pamela   USA
b. Charlotte, North Carolina 1944

Pam Barnett twice won the North Carolina Junior and once the Women's before turning professional in 1966. Her best year on Tour was 1971, when she was eighth on the money list and won the Southgate Open. In 1972 she was placed second in the US Open.

US wins 1 (1971)
US money $108,979 (1966–76)

BARR, David   Canada
b. Kelowna, British Columbia 1952

Dave Barr turned professional in 1974 and qualified to play on the US Tour three years later. In 1981 in a five-way play-off and at the 8th extra hole he won the Quad Cities Open and a cheque for $36,000. This sum about equalled the money he had won in other US events during his career. He has, however, won five Canadian events and the 1977 Order of Merit. In the US he has only once been within the top 100 – in 1981 as a result of his Quad Cities win and a year in which his next best finish was 30th.

US wins 1 (1981)
US money $98,270 (1978–82) (243rd all-time)

BARRETT, Sharon   USA
b. San Diego, California 1961

One of the current promising players of the US Tour, Sharon was an outstanding junior golfer, winning the first five collegiate events she entered and the California and World Junior titles in both 1978 and 1979. She left college to play professional golf and in her first two years had low rounds, but she could not produce a good score in a whole event. However, she began to emerge from the ruck in 1982, with a joint second place in the Lady Michelob.

US money $41,586 (1980–82)

BARRON, Herman — USA
b. Port Chester, New York 1909

One of relatively few top Jewish golfers, Barron had his nearest approach to glory in the 1946 US Open. After three rounds of 72 he lay a few strokes behind the leaders and then with a couple of holes to go seemed headed for a 67, which would have given him the title. But he failed to par these holes and finished 1 stroke out of the three-way tie for first place. However, he did win two other tournaments that year, and had one other high placing in the US Open – fifth in 1941. Otherwise, his best achievements were to win the 1942 Western Open and play for the US in the 1947 Ryder Cup. In 1963 he won the PGA Seniors with a record score of 272.

BARROW, Barbara — USA
b. Chula Vista, California 1955

As an amateur Barbara Barrow won the Trans-National and the 1975 National Collegiate, being runner-up in the latter the next two years. She played in the 1976 Curtis Cup team. She joined the US Tour in 1977 and had her best season in 1980, when she finished in 26th place for $46,633 and won a Tour event, the Birmingham Classic.

US wins 1 (1980)
US money $150,301 (1977–82)

BASTANCHURY, Jane: see Booth

BAUER, Alice — USA
b. Eureka, South Dakota 1927

A founder and charter member of the US LPGA with her sister Marlene Hagge, Alice Bauer was one of the attractions of the early US Tour in the 1950s. At one stage she continued competing when eight months pregnant. She said that the condition made her adopt a more upright stance and improved her game, and indeed she finished seventh in her last entry at that time. Alice won the South Dakota Amateur at the age of 15 and the Long Beach Invitational every year from 1944 to 1949, after which she turned professional. She won no Tour events, but once tied and lost the play-off.

BAUER, Marlene: see Hagge

BAUGH, Laura Zonetta (later Cole) — USA
b. Gainesville, Florida 1955

A youthful prodigy at golf, Laura Baugh was winning important titles at the age of 15, taking the Southern Amateur in 1970 and again in 1971. She reached the quarter-finals of the US Amateur in 1969 and 1970 and the next year, at 16 years 2 months 20 days, became the youngest winner of that event. After being one of the stars of the 1972 US Curtis Cup team she turned professional and joined the US Tour as soon as she qualified to do so by age in 1973. She made a strong start, leading her first tournament and eventually finishing second. Since that time she has not managed to win but has several times been second, and was in the Top 60 from 1973 to 1980, 12th in 1974 being her best finish. Voted *Golf Digest*'s 'Most Beautiful Golfer' in 1972, she was well placed to make a high income from endorsements alone and was said to be earning $300,000 a year from these sources by 1975, the highest of anyone. She gave her name to a line of sportswear, and endorsed a brand of toothpaste; but she turned down a *Playboy* offer to appear in their centrefold. She is outstandingly popular in Japan and is married to South African golfer Bobby Cole, her second of two marriages in a single year, 1980. She did not play on Tour in 1982, having given birth to a daughter in 1981.

US money $268,666 (1973–82) (36th all-time)

Laura Baugh

BAXTER, Rex, Jnr　　　　　　　USA
b. *Amarillo, Texas 1936*

Winner of the 1953 US Junior Championship, Baxter took the NCAA Championship four years later and represented the US in the Walker Cup. Two years later he turned professional but had little success on the US Tour, though he did record one victory in the 1963 Cajun Classic.

BAYER, George　　　　　　　USA
b. *Bremerton, Washington 1925*

One of the most massive men ever to have been a top golfer, Bayer was 6 feet 5 inches tall and broad to match, weighing around 250 lb. It is little surprise that he was the longest hitter of his day and would be high on anyone's all-time listing. His average drive was close to 300 yards and two drives of his on the US Tour were measured at 420 yards, while in an Australian tournament it is claimed that he drove about 530 yards at a 589-yard par-5 hole. This long hitting to some extent had a bad effect on the rest of Bayer's game, for in tournaments he was always surrounded by crowds who merely wanted to see him hit the ball vast distances. Despite this distraction, he did manage to organize the rest of his golf well enough to win a few times, one such victory being in the 1957 Canadian Open. He was in the Top 60 from 1955 to 1964 with a best placing of 14th in 1962, a year in which he also achieved his best placing in a major championship – equal third in the US PGA. He now plays on the Senior Tour.

US wins 4 (1957–60)
US money $188,868 (194th all-time)

BEAN, Thomas Andrew　　　　　USA
b. *Lafayette, Georgia 1953*

At 6 feet 4 inches and weighing well over 200 lb, Andy Bean might be expected to be a very long hitter. But he has also earned the reputation of being a straight one as well and having excellent touch on and around the greens. Bean first went on the US Tour in 1976 after a good amateur career in which he won the Eastern, Falstaff and Western Amateurs and reached the semi-finals of the US Amateur Championship. He made little or no impact the first year, finishing 139th on the money list, but the following year won his first event, the Doral-Eastern Open and moved dramatically up to 12th in the money list and passed the $100,000

mark. In 1978 he reached major status, winning $267,000 and achieving third place in money winnings. He took three events, including the Western Open. In each of the years 1978–80 he passed the $200,000 mark and would doubtless have done so in 1981 but for a wrist fracture that put him out of action for about half the season. Even so, he was tenth in the scoring averages and sixth best at hitting greens in regulation figures. The previous year, he had scored the most birdies. Bean's upbringing was a little unusual: when he was 15 his father bought a Florida golf course and no doubt Andy had unrestricted use. . . . Two of his tournament wins have been achieved with supreme dominance. When he won the 1979 Atlanta Classic, he included a 61 (over a course measuring over 7,000 yards) with a back nine in 29 and seven birdies. In the four rounds he claims to have missed just two greens, but these he three-putted. His total was 265 and his winning margin of 8 was the highest of the year. Later, in the 1981 Bay Hill Classic, he finished 18 under par for 266, including a round of 62, and left Tom Watson in second place 7 strokes behind. Bean competes fairly frequently overseas and has one victory, in the 1978 Dunlop Phoenix in Japan. He has supported British charities generously, contributing electric wheelchairs for the disabled.

US wins 7 (1977–81)
US money $1,196,982 (1976–82) (24th all-time)
Overseas wins 1 (1978)
World money $1,345,159 (1976–82) (32nd all-time)

BEARD, Frank　　　　　　　USA
b. *Dallas, Texas 1939*

'I didn't do anything. I just got well.' Thus spake Frank Beard in rejecting the Ben Hogan Trophy, awarded for those who have fought back against debilitating injury or disease. Beard had suffered encephalitis and felt that recovering from inflammation of the brain is what most of us would quite naturally wish to do and therefore not worth a trophy in a wall cabinet. This reaction was typical of Beard's approach to golf as a job to be done: to him, going to the course was an exact equivalent of going to the office or factory bench. Such feelings led to his being labelled 'as colourless as putty'. This was an injustice to him for he was and is a man of some insight: his book about the US Tour, *Pro*, is certainly the most revealing of any written on tournament golf and he now writes a perceptive

Frank Beard

column in *Golf Digest*. In his book he recalls that after his first win, the 1963 Frank Sinatra Tournament, his host evidently wished that someone of more glamour had won the event. It is in keeping with the image Beard had in the late 1960s and early 1970s that he should have been the first man to win $100,000 in a season without a Tour win. This was in 1968, one of a sequence of years from 1967 to 1971 in which he topped $100,000, while he was never worse than 12th in the money list between 1966 and 1971. In 1969 he was leading money-winner and was selected as a Ryder Cup team member, a choice repeated two years later. Beard joined the Tour in 1962 and by the following year was in the Top 60, a position he retained until 1975 but then has never achieved again, not even managing the top 100 from 1976 onwards. Beard's game was based on an excellent putting stroke and the ability to move the ball consistently from right to left. After a successful 1971 season he decided that there was more consistency still in a left to right flight of shot but he could neither master this nor, when he later tried, return to his reliable draw of earlier years. Frank had one last moment of glory, in 1975. Prior to the US Open that year, he had failed to make the 36-hole cut in 16 of 20 tournament entries, including 13 consecutively. In the Open he began 74, 69, 67 and with a round to go held a lead of 3 over Tom Watson, who had

recorded a 78 in the third round at Medinah. Things were looking promising. The next day it was a 77 for Watson and a 78 for Beard, but the others began pressing him. He finished in equal third place and, despite the 78, just 1 stroke behind the play-off between Lou Graham and John Mahaffey. He was also third in 1965. Among his later wins he twice took the Tournament of Champions. At the end of 1972 he stood eighth in the all-time US money list.

US wins 11 (1963–71)
US money $1,018,442 (1962–81) (36th all-time)
World money $1,112,966 (1962–81) (47th all-time)

BELL, Margaret Anne (née Kirk)   USA
b. Findlay, Ohio 1921

Three times a winner of the Ohio State title, Peggy Kirk took the International Four-ball with Babe Zaharias as partner in 1947, and in 1949 won the North and South and the Titleholders' at Augusta with professionals in the field. The following year she won the Eastern Amateur and was a Curtis Cup choice. At the end of the year she turned professional and was a charter member of the LPGA but played little competitively, preferring to concentrate on teaching. After her marriage in 1953 she owned and ran a country club in partnership with Julius Boros and others. She became one of the leading women teachers in America and was voted Teacher of the Year in 1961. In 1966 she published *A Woman's Way to Better Golf*.

BEMAN, Deane R.   USA
b. Washington DC 1938

Beman has one of the best amateur records amongst US golfers since World War II. Four times each he represented the US in the Americas Cup, the Eisenhower Trophy and the Walker Cup. He also won the Eastern Amateur four times. He took three of amateur golf's major championships, beginning with the 1959 British Amateur Championship and then the US equivalent in both 1960 and 1963. He is one of nine players to have won both championships. At the rather advanced age of 29 he turned professional in 1967. Money was not the prime object, for Beman had a flourishing insurance business. Rather, he wanted to prove himself in the premier arena of world golf, and that undoubtedly is the US Tour. In some ways Beman was not well equipped. He has a flat backswing, caused in part by opening the clubface, and also fails to achieve a full shoulder turn. The movement into the ball involves a heave with the shoulders. With his height of 5 feet 7 inches and a defective method, it is not surprising that Beman is a short hitter, and many felt that lack of length would prevent his achieving much as a professional. However, he did bring to the professional game one of the best of putting strokes, and to a considerable extent he made up for his lack of length by expertise with the fairway woods, with which he was soon reckoned to be the most effective amongst players of his time. Beman's career lasted from 1967 to 1973. In his first year he came 76th in the money list, but for the next five years he was never worse than 49th, finishes of 20th, 22nd and 21st in 1969, 1971 and 1972 being his best achievements. In his final season, Beman was troubled by a wrist injury. On 1 March 1974, he was apponted Tour Commissioner in succession to Joe Dey; his serious playing days were over. Although Beman won four Tour events in a relatively brief career, his best memory may well be his performance in the 1969 US Open. After finishing sixth in the 1967 event, Beman led in 1969 with opening rounds of 68, 69 and kept up the pressure with rounds of 73, 72. All not quite enough and he finished 1 behind Orville Moody in second place. Beman has also shown himself an excellent thinker about golf with a series of articles dealing with 'mutually exclusive factors' in the golf swing. His main point is that while you may be able to tolerate various peculiarities in your swing, some may work against each other and the result is then potentially disastrous. An incidental proof of Beman's excellence as a putter is that he has recorded the second fewest in a US Tour event: 19 only in the 1968 Haig Open.

US wins 4 (1969–73)
US money $369,648 (123rd all-time)

BERG, Patricia Jane USA
b. Minneapolis, Minnesota 1918

In 1935 Patty Berg reached the final of the US Amateur in her first entry, where she joined two generations by meeting and being defeated 3 and 2 by Glenna Collett. Two years later she was there again, this time losing to Estelle Lawson Page by 7 and 6; but she made no mistake against the same opponent the following year, becoming champion by 6 and 5. In her amateur career she won 40 tournaments before she was signed to a professional contract by Wilson's in 1940. There was

no professional Tour but she did win the 1941 Western Open for a first prize of $100. In 1942 she had her knee smashed in an accident and it was set so badly that the bones had to be re-broken and set a further three times, and she had months of strengthening exercises before she began to play golf again. In 1943 she won twice, and was then on war service. In 1948 Fred Corcoran, manager of Babe Zaharias, decided the time was ripe to attempt a women's Tour and the first members were Zaharias, Patty Berg and Betty Jameson. From that year until 1959 Patty won events each year. One event of 1951 which attracted much attention was a visit to Britain of the US women professionals to play their British equivalents. To no one's surprise they won easily, and General Critchley then arranged a match for them at Wentworth against a team of good men amateurs, which included Leonard Crawley and Gerald Micklem, both Walker Cup players, and some internationals. At lunch there were a few jokes at the expense of the two British foursomes pairs who had 'only' halved their

Patty Berg

matches. Out they all went in the afternoon for the singles, all played level off the men's tees, no strokes given. The women won every match. The legend grew that the ladies had beaten the British Walker Cup team – not true, but perhaps they might have done. During those first 11 years of the US Tour Patty Berg won 39 tournaments, and had won the first Women's Open, at matchplay for the only time, in 1946. She was leading money-winner in 1954, 1955 and 1957, won the Vare Trophy for lowest stroke average in 1953, 1955 and 1956, her best average being 74.47, about a stroke a round better than Babe Zaharias managed in her winning year, 1954. In 1952 she set the record at 64 for a tournament round at Richmond, California, which stood for 12 years until Mickey Wright lowered it to 62. Patty also won the World Championship from 1953 to 1955 and in 1957 and continued a consistent winner until 1959, taking six events in both 1953 and 1955. In 1971 she underwent cancer surgery which cost her some of the strength of her 5-foot 2-inch frame, but she continued to compete for part of the Tour until 1981. She is estimated to have won 83 professional tournaments, about half of which count as official victories and was the first woman to reach $100,000 in career money winnings. In later years she concentrated on giving golf clinics, and is said to have given more than anyone else in golf history. During her main career, she maintained a stroke average of about 75½, and this only rose by about three strokes a round after her 1971 operation.

US wins 41 (1940–62) (6th all-time)
US money $190,760 (56th all-time)

BERNING, Susan (née Maxwell)   USA
b. *Pasadena, California 1941*

The first woman to get a golf scholarship to Oklahoma City University, Susie Berning justified the university's outlay by being good enough to play on the men's team. In 1964 she went on the US Tour and was selected Rookie of the Year at the end of her first season. The following year Susie took her first tournament, added another later and was eighth on the money list. From 1964 to 1973 she was only twice not in the top 20, with a best money list placing of seventh in 1969. However, her outstanding achievements came in the US Open. She won in 1968 and then twice in a row (one of four women to have done so) in 1972 and 1973. A mother of two, she played the Tour full-time only from 1965 to 1967 and now her appearances are only occasional.

US wins 11 (1965–76)
US money $208,679 (1964–82) (50th all-time)

BERTOLACCINI, Silvia: see South & Central America

BESSELINK, Albert Cornelius   USA
b. *Merchantville, New Jersey 1924*

The son of an immigrant Dutch artist, the handsome Al Besselink turned professional in 1949 and went on the US Tour in 1950, where he quickly earned a reputation as a convivial partygoer, often in association with Doug Sanders and Ray Floyd. Besselink won six events between 1952 and 1964, including the 1953 Tournament of Champions.

US wins 6 (1952–64)
US money $114,439 (231st all-time)

BIES, Donald William   USA
b. *Cottonwood, Idaho 1937*

Turning professional in 1957, Don Bies largely confined himself to the life of a club professional and did not win any money on Tour until 1961, and then it was a mere $115. In the years that followed he was not once in the top 100 and on one occasion only went on Tour because his home club, Seattle, was closed for renovations. In 1968, however, he finished fifth in the US Open and in just 15 tournaments made it into the Top 60. As this meant he did not have to pre-qualify the following year, he decided to play full-time and was thereafter in the top 100 until 1978, consistently making good annual sums. He now competes infrequently. His best years were 1974 to 1976, when he was 32nd, 29th and 28th in the US money list, earning a career best of $92,450 in 1976. One career highlight came in the first round of the 1972 Matchplay Championship when, after eight holes played, he stood 4 up on Arnold Palmer and went on to win by 5 and 4. He eventually went out in the semi-final to Jack Nicklaus. Later, in 1975, he scored 65, 66, 67, 69 in the Greater Hartford Open, 17 under par; even this score was not good enough to win outright; but it did earn a play-off with Hubert Green. This Bies won for his only Tour victory, though he five times took the Washington State PGA.

US wins 1 (1975)
US money $535,929 (1961–82) (85th all-time)

BILLOWS, Raymond E. USA

b. *Fond-du-Lac, Wisconsin 1914*

Ray Billows had the galling experience of reaching the finals of the US Amateur Championship three times and each time being defeated. He did, however, win the New York State title seven times and was twice a Walker Cup selection, in 1938 and 1949.

BISHOP, Stanley E. USA

b. *1923*

Stan Bishop played in two US Walker Cup teams: 1947 and 1949. The previous year he had stood 3 down in the final of the US Amateur Championship but recovered to win on the first extra hole.

BLALOCK, Jane USA

b. *Portsmouth, New Hampshire 1945*

One of the most consistent players on the US Tour for a dozen years, Jane Blalock as an amateur won the New Hampshire title four years in a row, and also the 1968 New England title. As a professional she was an immediate success, being Rookie of the Year in 1969, and the following year she won her first tournament and cut three strokes off her average for the season. By 1971 she was third in the money list and then had a run of never being out of the top 9 until 1981. So consistent was Jane Blalock that at the close of the 1980 season she had played 299 events consecutively without missing a cut, while her stroke average shows the same qualities: never higher than 73.59 from 1971 to 1981, and with a low of 71.98 in 1978. She had her first win in 1971, won five times in 1972, four in 1974, 1978 and 1979, and was second on the money list in 1972 and 1974. She was the first woman to win more than $100,000 in four consecutive seasons, which she did between 1977 and 1980. At the beginning of 1981 she stood second on the all-time money list and was one of those favoured to be the first to reach $1 million career winnings, although she had not yet achieved this total at the end of 1982. A woman of strong opinions, Jane was suspended for alleged cheating in the early 1970s and sued the US LPGA for deprivation of livelihood; they counter-sued. She received $4,500 in the resultant settlement. Later,

when a photograph of Jan Stephenson reclining on an unmade bed was published in *Fairway*, magazine of the LPGA, she was strongly critical.

US wins 27 (1970–80) (10th all-time)
US money $976,067 (1969–82) (4th all-time)

BLANCAS, Homero USA

b. *Houston, Texas 1938*

'What a terrible shot!' So said Henry Longhurst in his TV commentary on a Blancas topped iron shot that nevertheless reached a par-3 hole. Longhurst later claimed to have unwittingly started a new trend in US TV commentary, for such frank language had seldom previously been used and 'He hit that one a little low on the club' would have been the norm. Homero, using a short fast backswing, did not top all that many, however, as is shown by his record, which includes the lowest known round of golf: a 55 shot in 1962 on a 5,002-yard course at Longview, Texas. Perhaps encouraged by this, he turned professional in 1965 and after the US Tour season of that year was named 'Rookie of

Jane Blalock

the Year'. He had finished in 38th place in the money and won the Mexican Open. He remained in the Top 60 until 1975. He was 16th in 1970 and 15th in 1973, the year he won the Ryder Cup place. On the US Tour his lowest round was a 61 at Phoenix in 1973; it was the lowest of the year. In 1973 he also came equal fourth in the US Open and equal fifth in the Masters. His best placing in a major championship was fourth in the 1972 US Open.

US wins 4 (1966–73)
US money $665,380 (1965–82) (68th all-time)

BOLT, Thomas   USA
b. Haworth, Oklahoma 1918

Some judges credit 'Thunderbolt' with the best swing golf has ever seen, and almost all place him foremost amongst those of unsunny tempers. In the latter category, stories about him are legion. In one tournament Bolt snapped a 6-iron across his knee when short of the green with his approach; his caddie retaliated with exact appropriateness; he snapped Bolt's 5-iron in like manner and departed the course. The truth of this next tale should be judged in that context. Here we have Bolt asking another caddie what iron he should take to a particular green. Caddie: 'An easy 2, Mr Bolt.' Tommy: 'Hell, son, I can reach that with a 9, maybe a wedge.' Caddie: 'There's only the 2 left in the bag, Mr Bolt.' On yet another occasion, Tommy whirled his driver around his head before releasing it far out into a lake after he had duck-hooked a tee shot. Horror then came into his eyes: the club was a favourite, perhaps irreplaceable. A boy plunged in, swam out and retrieved it and reappeared clambering up the bank, club aloft in triumph. Tommy advanced with a warm smile, hand ready with dollar bills. The boy glanced around, then darted away into the crowd. After all, it was a very good driver. Finally, in the 1957 Ryder Cup, he was drawn to play Eric Brown, himself not noted for exceptional calmness of temperament. As teeing-off time approached, it was asked where the two rivals were. The answer came from Jimmy Demaret: 'They're throwing clubs at each other from 50 paces.' True or not, Brown certainly politely informed Bolt that Tommy was to play the first shot by saying: 'Your beat, sucker.' He won by 4 and 3. Tommy Bolt turned professional in 1946 and did not go on Tour until 1950, at the fairly advanced age of 32. Having a buoyant arrogance that made

Tommy Bolt

him think himself better than anyone, he was almost immediately successful. In 1951 he was in the Top 60 and had won his first tournament, the North and South Open. He remained in the Top 60 until 1962, and got back again in 1963, 1964, 1966 and 1967. He continued to win tournaments, four of them in 1955, while his best year was 1958, when he was seventh in the money list and, more importantly, won his sole major championship, the US Open, by 4 from Gary Player. Earlier he had come close to the 1952 Masters. Level with Sam Snead with four holes still to play, Tommy three-putted three of the last four greens, leaving Snead well ahead and himself tied for third. He once had a round of 60 in 1954 at Wethersfield Country Club, Hartford, Connecticut, en route to winning the Insurance City Open, and in the same year set the two-round record for the US Tour at the Cavalier Yacht and Country Club, Virginia Beach, when he began 64, 62. Tommy's swing lasted well, as may still be seen. As late as 1971, at the age of 53, he finished third in the US PGA, and his record in Senior competition is formidable. The National

Seniors Association Open he took five times in a row from 1968 to 1972 and in 1969 took the US PGA Seniors, which qualified him to represent the US against what is in effect the rest of the world. He beat the other qualifier, John Panton, on the 39th hole. In 1978 and 1979 he competed effectively in Britain, and in both years made forays to Australia to capture their Seniors title.

US wins 15 (1951–61)
US money $320,792 (141st all-time)

BOOTH, Jane (née Bastanchury)   USA
b. *Los Angeles, California 1948*

National Collegiate Champion in 1969, Jane Booth won the Trans-Mississippi in 1967, 1969 and 1971, the Western in 1969 and 1970, the Doherty Cup in 1972 and 1973, and the North and South in 1972. She also was five times in the winning pairing for the International Four-ball between 1968 and 1974. With this kind of record she might have been expected to have won the US Amateur, but a semi-final place in 1970 was her best result; while in the US Open she was twice leading amateur, in 1971, when she was third, and 1972. She played in three Curtis Cup teams between 1970 and 1974, and in the World Team Championship between 1968 and 1972, in 1970 having the lowest individual score.

BOROS, Julius Nicholas   USA
b. *Fairfield, Connecticut 1920*

Of Hungarian extraction and nicknamed 'The Moose', Julius Boros remained for long at the top of world golf, demonstrating that excellent golf can be played into the 50s by those blessed with an easy rhythmic swing. In his prime, he was one of the most consistent golfers in the US Tour, as is shown by the fact that he was eight times in the first five in the US Open between 1951 and 1965. In 1958 and 1960 he was third, and he won in 1952 and 1963, when at 43 he was the second oldest to win this championship, after Ted Ray. When he won the 1968 US PGA he became the oldest player to win both that and one of the major championships. He finished the event with a 69 after going to the first tee saying that he had little chance of winning. Sam Snead, at 52, is the oldest winner of a US Tour event. In the 1975 Westchester Classic Boros began 70, 66, 70 to be 5 strokes off the lead. Then he played the final 18 holes in 65 to tie for the lead with Gene Littler, himself no stripling at 45. In the sudden-death play-off he lost on the first extra hole

– all this at the age of 55. Afterwards he was asked when he planned to retire. Boros replied: 'Retire to what? I already play golf and fish for a living.' Boros had been an accountant until he turned professional in 1950 and joined the US Tour. In two years he had become US Open Champion, Player of the Year and leading money-winner. He was again Player of the Year in 1963 and leading money-winner in 1955. In the US money list his worst finish between 1951 and 1969 was 44th, and in the same period he was seven times in the top seven and 13 times 23rd or better. Considering that he did not compete until he was 30 years old, his record is difficult to better: for a quarter of a century he was never out of the top 90. Boros had an exceptionally casual-seeming wristy swing and appeared to stroll up to the ball, place his feet quickly and then swing. Relaxed it may all have seemed, but Boros himself has said that if he had not played virtually without pause he would have been likely to have frozen for all eternity over the ball! Boros is acknowledged to have been perhaps the best player of wedge shots ever, and his consistent record was achieved with little of the practice so often considered essential. He suffered from numerous ailments and seldom felt fit enough to subject his body to the extra stress that practice imposes. He was four times a Ryder Cup player and in 1967 became the second oldest US player to be chosen. He won the US PGA Seniors in 1971 and 1977 but was beaten in the World Seniors on both occasions by Kel Nagle and Christy O'Connor.

US wins 18 (1952–68)
US money $1,004,861 (1950–79) (38th all-time)
World money $1,292,836 (1950–82) (34th all-time)

BOURASSA, Jocelyne   Canada
b. *Shawinigan South, Quebec 1947*

An all-round athlete, Jocelyne was on the University of Montreal teams for track, skiing, volleyball and basketball. Already, she was an outstanding golfer on the Canadian scene, having won the Quebec Junior from 1963 to 1965, and the full title as early as 1963, then in 1969, 1970 and 1971. She also took the Eastern Province from 1967 to 1970 and the 1971 Ontario. She won the Canadian Open title in 1965 and 1971, and in the latter year also won the New Zealand title. In 1972 she turned professional on the US Tour, and was Rookie of the Year and 19th on the money list, her $16,098 being the highest winnings for a first-year player at that time. In 1973 she won La Canadienne which, as the Peter Jackson Classic, has later come to be recognized as one of the three major championships. Thereafter, she did not fully justify early promise, although she was 16th on the money list in 1975. She later went into TV work and public relations.

US wins 1 (1973)
US money $69,524 (1972–6)

BOYKIN, Gerda (née Schleeh, later Whalen)
Germany & USA

b. *Worms, Germany 1938*

It is one thing to become a professional golfer; another is to find someone to play with you. Though normally this is not a problem, it was when Gerda turned professional in 1955. She was the first German woman professional and had therefore to play with men. Perhaps because there were not many of those either, she did well, coming fourth in the German PGA of 1958. In 1960 she was professional to Hanau Golf Club, and coach to German women teams. In 1961 she went to the USA and played a little on the Tour with no real success until she tied fourth in a 1967 tournament; then she was much encouraged by finishing third in the 1968 US LPGA. She became a Tour regular for about a decade. She never won a tournament but had three second-place finishes and three thirds. She was 19th in the money list in 1970 and 20th in 1968, a year in which she played just two tournaments.

US money $97,248 (1961–76)

BRADLEY, Patricia   USA

b. *Westford, Massachusetts 1951*

As an amateur, Pat Bradley was successful mainly in state golf, taking the New Hampshire title in 1967 and 1969 and following up with the New England in 1972 and 1973, and the Massachusetts in 1972. A professional from the opening of 1974, she was 39th in her first year but improved dramatically in 1975, lowering her stroke average by 2 and moving up to 14th on the money list. In Australia, with birdies on three of the last four holes, she took her first tournament, the Colgate Far East. The following year she won for the first time in the USA and fully established herself as a leading Tour player at sixth place in the rankings. In the period 1976–81 eighth was her worst finish,

while she was second in 1978 and third in 1981. From 1978 to 1981 she won well over $100,000 each year, with a high of $197,050 in 1981. She won three events in 1978, and has taken two of the major championships for women: the 1980 Peter Jackson Classic and the 1981 US Open. In the Open she began 71, 74 to be 6 strokes behind leaders Kathy Whitworth and Bonnie Lauer, but then she finished crushingly with 68, 66, to beat Beth Daniel, who had herself closed with 69, 68, by a single stroke. Pat Bradley's 279 set a new Open record and was also a record as the most under par. It won her the extra $25,000 offered by *Golf Digest* for the Open record aggregate. Her 66 was one of the lowest scores recorded in an Open (65 being the record) and was the best finish by a champion, as was her final 36-hole score. Undoubtedly this was Pat Bradley's finest achievement, but she shares another record. Only four players have had 29s for nine holes, and Pat Bradley has done it twice – in the 1978 California Golden Lights and the 1979 New York Golden Lights. In 1980 she took the J & B Gold Putter award, given to the best putter on the Tour: the formula is complex and involves tabulating both putts per round and birdies during the year, followed by a 'putt-off' among the leaders in these categories.

US wins 9 (1976–81)
US money $966,134 (1974–82) (6th all-time)

BRADY, Michael Joseph   USA

b. *Brighton, Massachusetts 1887; d. 1972*

Mike Brady was one of the first home-bred professionals to feature on the US scene and, although he never won the US Open, he was a major figure in the event for a good many years. Twice he tied for first place and then went on to lose play-offs – in 1911 and 1919. Mike seemed unable to produce a good final round, and indeed it was not until as late as 1926 that he bettered 74 over the last 18 holes. In 1911, playing with just six clubs, he faced Johnny McDermott and George Simpson in the play-off, but it was Johnny who became the first native-born American to win. The following year Mike stood 4 ahead of the field after three rounds but finished tied for third when he had a 79 to McDermott's 71. In 1914 he finished fifth, and sixth the following year. His worst experience was just ahead of him. In the 1919 championship Brady was 5 better than Walter Hagen with one round to play. Brady then went round in 80 and was summoned

Mike Brady

and then and there made up her mind that she might as well be one. She first played on Tour the following year, 1958, and from that year till 1980 was never placed worse than 49th in the money list, this despite the fact that the commitments of motherhood have restricted her tournament entries at times. She is one of several players whose first victory has been in the US Open. As Lindstrom she won in 1962 by 2 strokes from Ruth Jessen and JoAnn Prentice. With many players an Open victory has been a flash in the pan; but Murle won other Tour events in 1962, 1967 and 1969, and in 1979 she won the J.C. Penney four-ball, an unofficial event, with Dave Eichelberger. Her highest place in the rankings was eighth in 1969, while she was inside the top 20 in the years 1959–62, 1967–9 and 1974.

US wins 4 (1962–9)
US money $260,649 (1958–82) (37th all-time)

BREWER, Gay   USA
b. Middleburn, Ohio 1932

Gay Brewer broke an elbow at the age of seven and this was responsible for one of the strangest swings that golf has seen, but nevertheless an effective one. Brewer himself describes it as a 'figure of eight': the club is taken out and up, the right elbow flying free, and then is looped round before coming down to the ball, at which point everything has become orthodox. There is perhaps a difference of as much as a couple of feet between the upswing and downswing planes. It has been said that an unusual swing can be an aid to consistency: if the club is put into highly eccentric positions, the golfer is more easily able to 'feel' what has gone wrong with the mechanism. Certainly Brewer was consistent. He joined the Tour in 1956 and did not fall from the top 100 until 22 years had elapsed, and from 1957 to 1973 he missed the Top 60 only once. Seven times between 1961 and 1973 he was in the top 25 on Tour and three times, 1961, 1966 and 1967, he was ninth or better with fifth in 1966 being his peak placing. As his game waned in effectiveness it was not his swing that let him down, but putting. Brewer himself has said that it first 'went' in 1961. He still appeared to be afflicted by the twitch on the final green of the 1981 US Masters. Here the veteran had a placing in the first ten within his grasp, putted up to 2 feet and took three more nervy stabs at it. Years earlier putting had actually cost Brewer a Masters title. Again on that last green he

by Hagen from the clubhouse to watch him hole his final putt for a 75 and a tie. In the play-off that followed, a Hagen shot finished half buried in mud on the 17th. He requested permission for a free drop and, when this was refused, asked if he might identify his ball. When Walter had done this, the ball was far more easily playable and soon Brady found himself the loser by 78 to 77. Brady did not feature strongly in the US Open again, seventh in 1925 being his best finish, but he did win the 1917 North and South and the 1922 Western Opens. He was twice second in the Canadian Open and was elected to the PGA Hall of Fame in 1960. He spent many years as professional at Winged Foot.

BREER, Murle (née Lindstrom) USA
b. St Petersburg, Florida 1939

Murle Lindstrom, as she then was, had an odd beginning to her professional career. Playing in a competition, she was announced as a professional,

Gay Brewer

needed two putts to win, putted close and missed the next. He was next day eclipsed by Jack Nicklaus in the play-off – 70 to 78. However, it was all very different the following year. He came to Augusta with the confidence of having just won the Pensacola Open with a score of 262, which, at 26 under par, is still the second lowest score returned in a recognized US Tour event. Brewer began the final round two behind Bobby Nichols, Julius Boros and Bert Yancey. He went to the turn in 33, despite missing five greens, and was still not in the lead until the 13th. Putts kept on dropping and Brewer won by a single shot, having single-putted ten greens that last day for his 67. At the end of the year he picked up the then vast sum of £23,000 when he beat Billy Casper in a play-off for the Alcan Golfer of the Year title, one of those events which strove to become a fifth major championship before fading away. At Royal Birkdale, in foul weather, Brewer did it again the following year. Later he showed himself even more an international golfer by taking the 1972 Taiheiyo Pacific Masters in Japan. These three wins netted him some $175,000 and were instrumental in causing US golfers to be less bound to their own Tour – Brewer never topped $100,000 in a year at home. As a youngster, Brewer had won the 1949 Junior title and had added the Southern Open before turning professional but he had to wait until his sixth season on the US Tour for his first victory. That hurdle done with, he then won twice more in 1961 and was a fairly regular winner until the 1967 Masters. His next win after that was not

until 1972, in the Canadian Open. Brewer played in the 1967 and 1971 Ryder Cup teams. An infrequent competitor on the US Tour today, he should prosper on the growing Senior circuit, for which he qualified by age in 1982.

US wins 11 (1961–72)
US money $791,670 (1956–82) (56th all-time)
Overseas wins 3 (1967–72)
World money $1,172,555 (1956–82) (42nd all-time)

BRITZ, Jerilyn   USA
b. Minneapolis, Minnesota 1943

Jerilyn Britz came quite late to professional golf, working for some years as a physical education teacher. She is also a pilot. She joined the US Tour in 1974 and was in the Top 60 from 1974 to 1978. Then she had an important year in 1979. She began the US LPGA with a 64 and held on to finish second, and in the US Open she recorded her first Tour win, her 284 being a record at the time. She has had one other attempt at a major championship, finishing joint second in the 1981 LPGA. On the US Tour as a whole her best years were 1979 and 1980, when she was 16th and 14th on the money list. Her US Open victory made her the oldest woman, at 36, to become a first-time winner.

US wins 2 (1979–80)
US money $288,771 (1974–82) (31st all-time)

BROWN, Mrs Charles S.   USA

At Meadow Brook in 1895 Mrs Brown won the first ever US Women's Championship by 2 strokes from a Miss N.C. Sargeant. This was the only time the event has been settled by strokeplay; she had 69, 63 against the field of just 13 competitors. Although her scoring looks good, this by no means represents two 18-hole rounds but two of nine.

BROWN, Peter   USA
b. Port Gibson, Missouri 1935

Pete Brown turned professional in 1954 and went on the US Tour in 1963. The following year he became the first black golfer to win a US PGA tournament with the Waco Turner Open. Earlier, he had won the Negro National Open in both 1961 and 1962. He was in the US Tour Top 60 three times, with a best placing of 35th in 1970.

US wins 2 (1964–70)
US money $214,413 (1963–81) (179th all-time)

BROWNE, Mary Kimball   USA
b. Ventura, California 1891; d. 1971

Mary Browne won the US tennis championship from 1912 to 1914, the Doubles in 1913 and 1914 and the Mixed Doubles from 1912 to 1914 and in 1921. In 1924 she reached the semi-finals of the US tennis singles; but she did better at golf. In the semi-finals she defeated former and future champion Glenna Collett, but then she went down to Dorothy Campbell in the final. Mary Browne reached the quarter-finals the following year. She is the only example of any player (man or woman) reaching the final of a US national championship at both tennis and golf, although her feats do not fully compare with those of Lottie Dod in England, as detailed in her entry.

BRUCE, Louise: see Parks

BRYANT, Bonnie   USA
b. Tulare, California 1943

A left-hander is a rarity at the highest levels of golf, and Bonnie Bryant is the only woman left-hander to have taken a US Tour event. She did it in 1974 in the Bill Branch Classic. Bonnie Bryant did not turn professional until 1971; before this she had been a semi-professional for five years of fast-pitch softball. At golf she was in the Top 60 in the years 1972–6 and 1979–80, her best placing being 22nd in 1974.

US wins   1 (1974)
US money $132,168 (1971–82)

BUDKE, Mary Anne   USA
b. Salem, Oregon 1953

One of the youngest winners of the US Women's Amateur, Mary Budke defeated Cynthia Hill in the 1972 final by 5 and 4 and got to the quarter-finals the following year, where she was put out by the eventual champion, Carol Semple. She was also Intercollegiate Champion in 1974 and a championship winner in the north west of the US. She played on the 1974 Curtis and World Team Championship teams.

BULLA, John   USA
b. Newell, West Virginia 1914

When Johnny Bulla won the 1941 Los Angeles Open it caused a stir: for promotional reasons, he was using a 35-cent ball when 75 cents was the norm. Surprisingly, it was the only important event he was to win, for his record in major championships was good. He reached the last eight of the US PGA in 1948 and 1951 and led the 1939 US Open after three rounds before falling to sixth place with a final round of 76. He was equal third in 1941 and fourth in 1952. In the US Masters he was equal second when his closing rounds of 69, 69 were bettered by Sam Snead's 67, 67. He competed in the British Open in 1939 and began with a 77, yet finished in second place, only 2 strokes behind the champion, Dick Burton. In 1946, he worked strenuously to persuade Sam Snead to enter and, as the Wilson Sporting Goods firm also felt it would benefit sales of their Snead-endorsed clubs, the great man reluctantly agreed. Snead won, Bulla was second. In the following two years Bulla was sixth and seventh in the British Open. A right-hander, he putted from the left side, and may have been the first to do so.

Johnny Bulla

BURFEINDT, Elizabeth   USA
b. *New York 1945*

On the US Tour since 1969, Betty Burfeindt is one of the longest hitters among women, but she has been much afflicted with ill health. Her peak was emphatically 1972–3. In 1972 she brought her stroke average down some 4½ strokes from the previous year, won two tournaments, was in the top 3 on eight occasions and 20 times out of 28 was in the top 10. She was third in the Vare averages and fourth in the money list and won again. Thereafter, she has been relatively ineffective except for another good year in 1976. She was seven times in the top 10 but, more importantly, won the US LPGA Championship by a stroke from Judy Rankin.

US wins 4 (1972–6)
US money $286,516 (1969–82) (32nd all-time)

BURKE, A.J.   USA

On the 6,389-yard Normandie course in St Louis, Missouri, in 1970, Bill Burke scored a 57, with a remarkable 25 over the back nine.

BURKE, Jack, Snr   USA
b. *Philadelphia, Pennsylvania 1888; d. 1943*

The father of the 1956 Masters and PGA Champion had his greatest moment when in a tie for second place in the 1920 US Open at Inverness he finished 1 behind Ted Ray with Harry Vardon, Jock Hutchison and Leo Diegel. In 1941 he won the PGA Seniors.

BURKE, Jack, Jnr   USA
b. *Forth Worth, Texas 1923*

The magnificence of Byron Nelson's feat in winning 11 consecutive US Tour events is highlighted by Jack Burke's achievement. Between 14 February and 9 March 1952 he won the Texas, Houston, Baton Rouge and St Petersburg Opens. The sequence is the second best after Nelson's record. Jack Burke turned professional in 1940 and joined the Tour in 1950. He made the Top 60 in his first season and remained there until the end of 1963, winning frequently. In 1952 he won the Vardon Trophy and was second in the US Masters, a 69 in the last round making him the only one to break 70 in the high winds of the final two days (Snead's closing 77, 72 lost him little if any ground). In the 1956 Masters, Burke achieved another memorable finish. With one round to go, amateur Ken Venturi led him by 8 strokes. Burke then went round in 71 in poor conditions; Venturi took 80. The final turning point was the par-4 17th, which Burke birdied and where Venturi took 5. His 289 is the highest winning score. Burke took the US PGA the same year and was voted Player of the Year. He holds the dubious distinction of being the only losing US Ryder Cup captain since World War II. At Lindrick in 1957 the US team collapsed, Burke himself being defeated by 5 and 3. However, this was his only defeat in the five Ryder Cups he played from 1951 to 1959. He was again captain in 1973. Although he seldom competed overseas, he won the 1958 Japan Open. His most remarkable scoring feat was 260 (67, 65, 64, 64) in the 1960 Texas Open. A hand injury was a factor in cutting short Jack Burke's career. He later built the Champions Club with Jimmy Demaret near Houston, Texas. Both the US Open and the Ryder Cup have been staged there.

US wins 15 (1950–63)
US money $260,746 (1940–63) (168th all-time)

BURKE, William   USA
b. *Naugatuck, Connecticut 1902; d. 1972*

Billy Burke was the first winner of the US Open to use steel shafts and he did it in 1931, the first year that Bobby Jones was not in the field. This Inverness event was extraordinary for the play-off that concluded it. George Von Elm and Burke tied on 292 and the play-off was a lengthy one: 36 holes. After that, both had recorded 149. Out they had to go again and it was very nearly another tie, with Burke ousting Von Elm by a single shot – 148 to 149. In the same year Burke also reached the semi-finals of the US PGA and was third in the US Masters in both 1934 and 1939. Sixth in 1934 was his best other placing in the US Open. Burke won the North and South Open in 1928 and was a Ryder Cup team member in 1931 and 1933.

BURKEMO, Walter   USA
b. *Detroit, Michigan 1918*

A Ryder Cup player in 1953, Burkemo took the US PGA that year, part of a sequence of four years in which he three times reached the final. Because of this run of matchplay success, Burkemo's thoughts on this form of golf are worth notice. Most have claimed that they play the course, not the man (Jones was emphatic about this). Burkemo felt that the doings of an opponent must be reacted to: if he strikes an iron near the pin, you must rule out thoughts of getting safely on the green; if he drives out of bounds, you play for safety. Burkemo was medallist in the 1938 Public Links Championship and then spent the war as an infantry sergeant – which accounts for his nickname on Tour of 'Sarge'. He turned professional in 1944, and went on Tour in 1950, winning the Mayfair Inn Open in 1957. He was equal fourth in the 1957 US Open and fifth the next year.

BURNS, George, III   USA
b. Brooklyn, New York 1949

In the 1981 US Open Burns began 69, 66, 68 at Merion, brilliant scoring which set a 54-hole US Open record of 203, bettering by 1 Nicklaus's record set the previous year. The question was, would this player just a rung below the highest class be able to hold his position? In the final round, Burns usually took an iron from the tee, but repeatedly put his ball in the left rough. Despite this, he usually managed to save par and completed his round in 73, having begun with a 4-stroke lead over Bill Rogers and 3 over David Graham. Alas for George, Graham played one of the great US Open rounds of 67 and won by 3 over Burns and Rogers. Burns had gone to the University of Maryland intent on excelling at football but he soon concen-

George Burns

trated on golf, though he had by no means an exceptional college golf career. Success came soon afterwards with a win in the 1973 Canadian Amateur, and in 1974 he took five important amateur events, including the North–South, the Porter Cup and the New York State. He lost to eventual champion Pate in the US Amateur. In 1975 he was chosen for the World and Walker Cup teams, and shortly after turned professional. Happening to be in Europe at the time he made the most remarkable start by winning two tournaments, the Scandinavian Open and the Irish Kerrygold. Back in the US for the 1976 season, he finished 30th in the money list and since that time has not been worse than 38th, winning more than $100,000 on five occasions and in 1980 $219,928 for seventh place in the money list. Burns has a flailing swing with a flying right elbow, but it works. He has an excellent short game and US Tour statistics rated him the second best putter in 1980 and sixth the following year.

US wins 2 (1979–80)
US money $874,274 (1976–82) (46th all-time)
Overseas wins 2 (1975)

BURROWS, Gaylord   USA
b. 1944

An expatriate American who has played mainly on the Asian Circuit since 1974, he has won the Indonesian Open (1977) and the Indian Open (1979). He was the first American to win twice on this circuit.

BYERS, Eben M.   USA
b. Allegheny, Pennsylvania 1880

At 5 feet 4 inches, Eben Byers was one of the shortest men to win an important championship. This came with his victory in the 1906 US Amateur, in which he beat George S. Lyon, a man who was eight times Canadian Champion. Byers had twice reached the final previously, in 1902 and 1903, losing to Walter Travis in 1903.

BYMAN, Robert   USA
b. Poughkeepsie, New York 1955

Bob Byman won the 1972 US Junior Championship; in the same year he was the youngest ever to qualify for the US Open. He turned professional in 1976, after a successful collegiate career at Wake Forest, Arnold Palmer's *alma mater*. Twice he then failed to qualify for the US Tour and, after winning a few times on mini-tours, decided to try his luck and increase his experience overseas. This he did to some effect, winning the New Zealand, Scandinavian and Dutch Opens in 1977 and the latter in 1978 also. He was fourth in the European Order of Merit in 1977. With this kind of success under his belt he was able to get through the spring US qualifying school, as did his brother Ed. Bob found the US Tour a sterner test, winning only $14,000 in his first season. The following year he improved greatly to 39th in the money list, with $94,000 and his first win – the Bay Hill Citrus Classic. Byman is a student of the golf swing and his bibles are the writings of Ben Hogan. Despite this he fell from grace after 1979, with a 26th place being his best finish in the succeeding two seasons. However, 1982 saw improved performances on the US Tour, and he again won the Scandinavian Enterprises Open.

US wins 1 (1979)
US money $160,373 (1978–82) (209th all-time)

BYRD, Samuel Dewey   USA
b. Bremen, Georgia 1907; d. 1981

Few players have successfully transferred from one sport to another: youthful dedication seems essential and this is particularly true of golf, where most good players note that they first started swinging a golf club while in short trousers. Sam Byrd was an exception. He was seriously injured while playing major league baseball in 1935 after being an understudy to Babe Ruth. With that career closed to him, Sam took to golf and had a successful career. He was third in the 1941 US Masters and fourth the next year after opening with a pair of 68s. He also reached the final of the 1945 US PGA. Winning the Victory Open in Chicago in 1943 was perhaps his career high, but he is also unofficially credited with 23 tournament wins.

CALDWELL, Rex   USA
b. Everett, Washington 1950

After obtaining his US Tour card in 1974 Caldwell has struggled for success, winning money but little glory. Undoubtedly his best tournament performance was in the 1979 US PGA. In this he began 67, 70, 66 to go into the final round 2 ahead of Ben Crenshaw. He played Oakland Hills in 71 in the last round, hardly a score to indicate he might have

cracked in the unaccustomed limelight, but Crenshaw turned in a 67, while David Graham went round in 65 and won the play-off. Caldwell was alone in third place. He has yet to win on the US Tour but did win the 1978 California Open, a non-Tour event. His best money placing was 36th in 1979 for $96,088 and he was 42nd the previous year, the only other occasion when he made the Top 60. In 1982 this happy-go-lucky golfer showed improved form and finished third in both the Crosby and Bob Hope Desert Classic, finding a putting stroke with all movement coming from the shoulders which worked well for him.

US money $369,745 (1975–82) (122nd all-time)

CALLISON, Carole Jo (née Kabler, formerly Skala)   USA
b. Eugene, Oregon 1938

Carole Callison's career falls into several sections. First she was US Junior champion in 1955 and then a semi-finalist in the 1957 US Amateur. She has seven consecutive Oregon state wins from 1955 to 1961. In 1958 she married and, after having three children, was next heard of nationally when she won the Trans-Mississippi in 1968; she was runner-up the following year in both that and the Western. These successes encouraged her to attempt the professional Tour in 1970 at the advanced age of 32. On Tour she has always played limited schedules, but she was in the top 50 from 1970 to 1977 and again in 1982. Her best year was 1974 when she won three times, including the Peter Jackson Classic, and was placed eighth on the money list. She had another good year in 1975 for 13th place, and also had a successful 1982 at the age of 44, losing a play-off for the Sun City Classic.

US wins 4 (1973–4)
US money $202,647 (1970–82) (52nd all-time)

CAMPBELL, Dorothy Iona (later Hurd)   Scotland & USA
b. Edinburgh, Scotland 1883; d. 1945

A formidable golfer of the first quarter of this century, Dorothy Campbell was one of three players to win the British and US Amateur Championships in the same year, a feat she accomplished in 1909. For long she was the only player to have won all three titles of Britain, Canada and the US before Marlene Stewart duplicated the feat. She began her golf career at North Berwick and took the Scottish title in 1905, 1906 and 1908; she was runner-up in 1907 and 1909. In the British title she was runner-up in 1908 and won in 1909 and 1911. She moved to live in Canada in 1910 and took the national title there from 1910 to 1912 before going on to live permanently in the USA. There, beside her 1909 victory, she won again in both 1910 and 1924 and was runner-up in 1920. She was also successful in state events, taking the Pennsylvania title at the late age of 51.

CAMPBELL, Joseph   USA
b. Anderson, Indiana 1935

Cigar-smoking Joe Campbell was a Walker Cup choice in 1957 and turned professional the following year. In a fairly short career, curtailed by back trouble, he won three tournaments, with a highspot of winning $50,000 for a hole in one at the 1966 Palm Springs Classic.

CAMPBELL, William Cammack   USA
b. Huntington, West Virginia 1923

In 1982, Bill Campbell became President of the USGA, culmination of a participation in both golf and political administration (he served in the West Virginia legislature from 1949 to 1951). As a top amateur golfer his swing endured from the late 1940s to the mid 1970s; he qualified for the US Amateur a record 37 times and played in 15 US Opens and 18 Masters. He was a Walker Cup player from 1951 to 1957 and again in 1965, 1967, 1971 and 1975. He had an outstanding record in his eight singles, only one British player, Ian Hutcheon in 1975, taking as much as half a point from him, while he once beat the greatest British amateur of the era, Michael Bonallack, by 6 and 5. At the highest level of amateur golf, his results were good rather than outstanding. Once he reached the final of the British Amateur, being beaten in the 1954 final by Australian Doug Bachli at Muirfield. In the US Amateur, he reached the semi-finals in 1949 and 1973 – a 24-year gap – and took the event in 1964, beating Ed Tutwiler in the final. His record in regional golf is awesome, including three wins in the West Virginia Open and 14 in the state's amateur event. He also won the North and South four times, the Mexican Amateur in 1956, and was three times runner-up in the Canadian Amateur. He was five times a choice for the Americas Cup team

and once for the Eisenhower Trophy. Campbell first made a name in college golf. After serving as an infantry captain in World War II he went to Princeton and there played 22 consecutive victorious matches. Three and a half decades later, he is still a considerable player, winning the 1979 and 1980 US Seniors Championship and being runner-up in the 1980 Seniors Open. He has played in 37 US Amateurs, 33 consecutive from 1941 to 1977. Only Chick Evans, with 40, played in more.

CAPONI, Donna (formerly Young)   USA
b. Detroit, Michigan 1945

Turning professional in 1965 after being quite successful in junior golf, Donna Caponi has only once been out of the top 30 on the US Tour in the years 1965–82. She had a quiet first few seasons and really came to the fore with her 1969 victory in the US Open. She won by a stroke from Peggy Wilson in unusual circumstances. With a hole to play, a thunderstorm suspended the competition for 15 minutes but Donna Caponi then birdied for victory. In 1970 she then became only the second player (Mickey Wright was the other) to win the title in successive years. In 1976, she took the Peter Jackson Classic and won the US LPGA in 1979 and 1981. With these five major championships, she has a higher total than anyone else still playing. Donna Caponi has been equally formidable as a tournament-winner during her career. The US Open was her first tournament win and since then she has added another 23 officially with four wins in 1976, and five in both 1980 and 1981. On the money list she was in the top 10 in the years 1968–71, 1974–6 and 1978–81. In 1980 and 1981 she had more victories than any other Tour player. Besides these successes Donna won the 1975 Colgate European Open and the 1976 Australian Open, the latter by a margin of 9 strokes. She holds what is thought to be a Tour record of playing 50 holes before dropping a stroke, achieved during her 1979 US LPGA victory. She has four times topped $100,000 in a season and in 1981 became the third player after JoAnne Carner and Kathy Whitworth to exceed $1 million in career winnings, this despite the fact that she has never been leading money-winner. However, she has twice been runner-up, once third and a further four times in the top 5. Donna's swing tempo is slow and measured and her left-hand grip is very strongly positioned, as often with leading women players, though it leads to a shut face at the top of the backswing – and also frequent lower-back problems.

US wins 24 (1969–81) (14th all-time)
US money $1,099,156 (1965–82) (3rd all-time)

CARNER, JoAnne (née Gunderson)   USA
b. Kirkland, Washington 1939

One of the greatest players in the history of women's golf (many would rate her among the top three or four), JoAnne Carner, often known as 'Big Momma', has had a brilliant record as both an amateur – for a dozen years – and professional since 1970. She reached the final of the US Amateur in 1956, losing to Marlene Stewart of Canada, but won the US Junior title, having been runner-up in the previous year. In 1957 she became the second youngest at the time, after Beatrix Hoyt, to win and did so by the emphatic margin of 8 and 6 in the final. She won again in 1960 and 1962 (by 9 and 8 on this occasion) before being runner-up to Barbara McIntire in 1964. In 1966 she faced Marlene Stewart again, but this time came through to win on the 41st hole, the longest final in the history of the event. She completed her series of wins in 1968, when she defeated Anne Quast. Her five wins are exceeded only by Glenna Collett. There is little doubt in the light of JoAnne's later career that she would have beaten Collett's total of six had she not turned professional. She played in the Curtis Cup from 1958 to 1964 and her competitive successes included such top events as the Intercollegiate (1960), the Western Amateur (1959), the Eastern (1968), the Trans-Mississippi (1961), the Pacific Northwest (1958 and 1959), the Southwest (1960), the Northwest (1967) and the Doherty Challenge Cup (1969). In 1969, while still an amateur, she won a US Tour event, the Burdine's Invitational. A professional the following year, she won again during her first season, was Rookie of the Year and finished 11th on the money list. Since that time she has finished in the top 6 money-winners eight times, being leading money-winner in 1974 and 1982 and second in 1975, 1977 and 1981. By 1971, she had won her first of two US Opens (the other followed in 1976), and by this victory became the only woman to have won the US Junior, Amateur and Open. Her decision to turn professional was probably delayed by the relatively low prize money available during JoAnne's 20s; but things have changed drastically since, and she is now the leading money-winner of all time with $1,352,944, and was one of three players in 1981 to reach $1 million in career winnings. In 1982 alone she won $310,399, easily a record, was US LPGA Player of the Year and also won the Vare Trophy. She has yet to win the US LPGA but has twice, in 1975 and 1978, won the Peter Jackson Classic in Canada. An event dating only from 1973, this is one of three major championships for women. On the US Tour she had six wins in 1974, four in 1975 and 1976, five in 1980 and four in both 1981 and 1982, by which time she had totalled 37. JoAnne Carner is one of the longest hitters of all time among women and, with Mickey Wright, is sometimes said to be the only woman who has been able to hit long-irons with the authority of the best men players. She is one of not a few great right-handed golfers who are basically left-handers. During 1982 she had 25 rounds in the 60s, equalling Amy Alcott's record.

US wins 37 (1970–82) (8th all-time)
US money $1,352,944 (1970–82) (1st all-time)

CASPER, William Earl, Jnr   USA
b. San Diego, California 1931

Recognition of Billy Casper as one of the great players of modern times was slow to come. Ben Hogan, for instance, is credited with having once unkindly remarked to him: 'If you couldn't putt,

JoAnne Carner

you'd be selling hot dogs outside the ropes.' Casper was indeed one of the great putters of his or any other age and the most unorthodox of them all. Because of the presumed importance of not letting the right hand overtake the left, most have partially or totally eliminated wrist action and relied mainly on arm or shoulder movement. Not so Casper. With him, the ball is given a wristy rap, with little movement of anything other than the wrists. For many years, the result was that the ball went into the hole more consistently than his rivals could manage. In the 1959 US Open, which he won, for example, he needed only 112 putts throughout the four rounds. All in all, he is recognized as being amongst the best half a dozen putters of modern times. But Casper was far more than merely a superb putter; he had all the shots in his armoury and foremost amongst them was consistency. This is shown, for instance, by the fact that he was in the Top 60 every year between 1955 and 1976; even more so that he was 11 times in the top four between 1958 and 1970. As a winner of tournaments, there have been few to approach him on the US Tour. There he first won in 1956 and continued to win every year except one until 1976. His total was 51. Eight times he topped $100,000 and once passed the $200,000 mark. He was the second man – after Arnold Palmer – to reach $1 million on the US Tour. He is one of just ten players in US Tour history to win three times in a row, which he accomplished in 1960. His five awards of the Vardon Trophy during the 1960s are a record for that or any other decade and his average of 69.82 in 1968 was the last to better 70 until Trevino in 1980. Oddly, Jack Nicklaus has never secured the Vardon, and this is additional evidence of Casper's achievements. Casper was also leading money-winner in 1966 and 1968, second in 1958 and 1970 and chosen US PGA Player of the Year in 1966, 1968 and 1970. Yet despite this record of success, Casper himself will probably now feel that he did himself less than full justice in the major championships. He did not, for instance, win the US PGA, although he was second in 1958, 1965 and 1971. He also had little success in the British Open, a fourth place in 1968 being his best result. However, he first competed only in 1968, when he led going into the last round, and occasionally thereafter. The Masters was not an event that suited his play strategy, a mixture of caution and boldness. Through the green, he was concerned, to a considerable degree, to keep the ball in the fairway, lay

Billy Casper

up short of bunkers, water hazards and other perils and then play for safe lines into the green rather than go for the flag. So far, caution; thereafter boldness, for once on the green Casper did not dribble the ball gently holewards but gave it a sharp rap, confident that if he missed, the return putt would succeed. The Masters tournament did not suit this strategy: fast and undulating greens at Augusta mean that there is little chance of a birdie unless the shot to the green finishes quite near the hole, and the water hazards guarding greens on par 5s mean that a player faces triumph or disaster with his second shot. Casper tended to play conservatively short of the hazards. In 1969 he qualified for the 13th time to play in the Masters and dominated the headlines with a start of 66 followed by a pair of 71s. But on the last day he went out in a daunting 40. Although he came home in a fine 34 this was only enough for equal second place. In 1970 he began with a 72 and followed up with a pair of 68s. On the final day the lead fluctuated but Casper eventually tied with Gene Littler on 279. In the play-off, two conservative players matched, he won easily with 69 to 74. His finest hour, however, had already come in the 1966 US Open, one of the most memorable of all and remembered best, perhaps, not because Casper won but because Palmer lost. With nine holes to play, Casper was 7 strokes to the bad from a dominant Arnold Palmer, but as Casper plugged away trying to secure second place, Palmer committed virtual suicide in the home stretch at the Olympic Country Club in San Francisco. They tied and in the resultant play-off Palmer led after nine holes by 4, but then fell away and Casper was US Open Champion a second time. What Palmer felt about this turn of events he has himself recorded. Sure of victory, he had been aiming at a new record score for a US Open – and had been beaten by a man playing cautiously for second place. Years later there was a kind of revenge for Palmer. He defeated Casper in a play-off for the US Seniors title. Casper stands very high in the list of all-time winners on the US Tour. His 51 victories have been exceeded only by Snead, Nicklaus, Hogan, Palmer and Nelson, in that order. Thereafter, there is a considerable gap before the 37 wins of Cary Middlecoff. But Casper was also an international player, though much of his career came in a period when Americans paid little attention to competition outside the USA. However, he twice took the Brazilian Open, the 1974 Lancôme, the 1975 Italian Open and the 1977 Mexican. In the Ryder Cup he represented his country every year between 1961 and 1975, a record number of US appearances, and captained his country in 1979. His failure to dominate the major championships was one flaw in his career; another was his lack of colour. People were passionately concerned in the doings of, say, Palmer. Not so with Casper. He earned respect but no adulation. Indeed, in Casper's great years, press coverage centred on two things: his food allergies, which caused him at one time to eat buffalo steaks and little other meat, and his membership of the Mormon religion and resulting church activities. It was also commented that he had the record number of children for a US Tour player: 11, six of whom were adopted. Casper always made the game of golf appear undramatic. He would decide on his shot before he reached the ball, pull out a club, take a quick, light practice swing and then hit the ball. His grip was strong

with the left hand and all his full shots had the impression of a wristy pull in them, while he dragged his right foot, like Britain's Neil Coles, in the course of each shot. However, if his concentration was disturbed, Casper would interrupt the ritual even to the extent of replacing his club in the bag, and then start the sequence again. His most unbelievable victory came in the 1968 Alcan, Trevino's most famous defeat. While Casper birdied the last four holes and finished in 66, Trevino dropped a shot on the 16th hole and then on the par-3 17th hit his tee shot into a greenside bunker, took two to get out and three-putted – a 6 against Casper's 2. Casper is now active on the Senior Tour, where he won two 1982 events.

US wins 51 (1956–75)
US money $1,684,728 (1955–82) (9th all-time)
Overseas wins 5 (1958–77)
World money $2,306,555 (1955–82) (10th all-time)

CERRUDO, Ronald　　　　　USA
b. Palo Alto, California 1942

In 1967, Ron Cerrudo was defeated finalist in the British Amateur and a Walker Cup player. He turned professional the same year. In 1968 he won his first US Tour event, the Cajun Classic, and in 1970 he won again – the Texas Open. In 1968 and 1969 he placed in the Top 60 of the US money list. Afterwards he achieved little.

US wins 2 (1968–70)
US money $226,568 (176th all-time)

CHAPMAN, Richard Davol　　　　　USA
b. Greenwich, Connecticut 1911

Dick Chapman's career reached a peak before World War II and continued well into the 1960s. He was in fact a significant force between 1930 and 1967, his game frequently rejuvenated by variations to his swing, always, for club and major golfers alike, a source of new hope. His first significant success was to reach the semi-finals of the US Amateur in 1938 and then to win the event in 1940. After service as a major in the US Army Air Corps in World War II, he was the defeated finalist in the 1947 British Amateur to Willie Turnesa, after being 4 up after the first nine holes. Again in 1950 he reached the final but was annihilated 8 and 6 by Frank Stranahan at St Andrews. The following year, things went better: he reached the final at Porthcawl and defeated Charlie Coe by 5 and 4. His last major success was to win the Italian Open Amateur in 1960, while earlier he had taken the 1949 Canadian Amateur, won the French Amateur in 1939 and 1952 and had four times been a Walker Cup choice for the USA from 1947 to 1955. Playing in the 1948 British Amateur at Sandwich, he once went to the turn in 29. He is the only man to have won the British, US and Canadian amateur championships.

CHENEY, Leona (née Pressler)   USA
b. Stockton, Missouri 1904

The first American to play in three Curtis Cup matches, Leona did it in the period from 1932 to 1936. She won two singles and all her foursomes. A prominent figure in the US Amateur in the late 1920s and early 1930s, she was often in the late stages but only once reached the final, in 1929 when she was beaten by Glenna Collett 4 and 3.

CHENEY, Mary: see Porter

CHERRY, Donald R.   USA
b. Wichita Falls, Texas 1924

If Bing Crosby was the best-known singer who happened to play golf, Don Cherry, though a lesser singer, was the superior golfer. He has some popular music successes to his name, too, foremost being 'Band of Gold'. He played three times for the USA in the Walker Cup – 1953, 1955 and 1961 – winning every match in which he was involved. His singles record was particularly formidable: he beat Norman Drew 9 and 7, Joe Carr 5 and 4 and finally David Blair 5 and 4. He also twice represented the USA in the Americas Cup, in 1954 and 1956. In championship golf his best achievement was to take the 1953 Canadian Amateur, while he reached the semi-final of the 1952 US Amateur and the quarters two years later. He turned professional in 1962, but is also a successful cabaret performer.

CLAMPETT, Robert Daniel   USA
b. Monterey, California 1960

Tom Watson, as a youngster, went into the final round of the 1974 US Open with a narrow lead and finished with a 79. For a while it gave him the reputation of being a 'choker'. So what of Bobby Clampett? His start of 67, 66 in the 1982 British Open was the most glittering in a major championship since Henry Cotton's start of 67, 65 at Sandwich in 1934. At the end of the second day the question was: 'Who can catch Clampett?' The answer seemed to be that no one could unless Clampett destroyed himself. He was 11 under par and his closest rival, South Africa's Nick Price, was 5 behind. The favourite, Tom Watson, was 7 strokes back. Although Clampett was only a couple of months or so past his 22nd birthday he was already quite rich in experience. As an amateur he had been an All-American three times (1978–80), had twice been given the Fred Haskins award for the best collegiate player, and was medallist in the 1978 World Team Championships. He had won his state title and both the Western and Sunnehanna Amateurs. He was low amateur in the 1978 US Open and the following year had shown that he was not overawed by the big occasion. Playing as a card-marker on the final day, he decided to entertain his gallery by playing tee shots from his knees and putting with a wedge. The USGA were not amused and Clampett was ordered off. Bobby atoned a little the following year, when he finished 37th and second low amateur. A month later, he turned professional and soon qualified for the US Tour without having to pass the qualifying school test: he had passed the minimum of $8000 that now earns exemption. In 1981 he began his move to the fore of US golf. Four times he was second in the

Bobby Clampett

38

Westchester Classic and the Greater Hartford Open, while he lost play-offs to John Cook in the Crosby and to Hale Irwin in the Buick Open. He had a 64 in the final round of the Greater Hartford and was medallist in the USA versus Japan matches. At the end of the season he stood 14th on the US money list, with earnings of $184,710, the second highest earned by a player in his second season, despite the fact that in all but name this was Clampett's first season. Clampett, a fluent French speaker, soon showed himself interested in the international scene, unusually for a player in his early days on the US Tour. He lost a play-off for the 1981 Italian Open and finished equal second in 1982. In fact he has compiled a fairly remarkable sequence of second places, extending this with another in the US Spalding Invitational when he finished 4 behind winner Jay Haas yet six ahead of the third-place man. In the 1982 US Open he was contending throughout, eventually finishing third equal with Dan Pohl and Bill Rogers, behind Nicklaus and Watson. And so to Troon for the British equivalent. In his third round at Troon he came to the 6th tee 12 under par, having just holed an enormous putt for a 2. Then disaster, as on the par 5 he twice hit bunker lips, hooked into long grass, and thinned an approach. At the end of it all he was quite relieved that it was no worse than an 8. He stuck his tongue out in mock insult of his competence, yet, cocky though the gesture was, Clampett was now subject to doubt. Strokes began to leak away and he ended the day with a 78, his lead cut to one over Nick Price, Watson lurking only 3 back now. If the disasters were lesser ones on the final day, the result was much the same: 77. Clampett finished in tenth place. A pair of 75s would have seen him Open Champion. His first tournament win came at the end of 1982, in the Southern Open, and was long overdue. He also represented the USA in the 1982 World Cup.

US wins 1 (1982)
US money $379,500 (1980–82) (117th all-time)

CLARK, Clarence　　　　　　　　　USA
b. Burlington, Kansas 1907

This little-known golfer had one moment of near glory. In the 1936 US Open at Baltusrol he was in contention throughout after opening with a 69. Like 'Light-Horse' Harry Cooper, he was eclipsed by Tony Manero's unexpected final 67. Clark also won occasionally on Tour.

CLARK, Judith　　　　　　　　　　USA
b. Akron, Ohio 1950

A player to watch for, Judy Clark has been on the US Tour since 1978 and has improved each year. She has been in the top 50 from 1979 to 1982 and won more than $40,000 in both 1981 and 1982.

US money $152,535 (1978–82)

CLARKE, Douglas　　　　　　　　　USA
b. California 1960

A Walker Cup player in 1979, Doug Clarke had won the 1976 Trans-Mississippi and the 1977 Southern California. In both 1977 and 1978 in the US Amateur he lost by 1 down in the fourth round to eventual champions John Fought and John Cook.

COCHRAN, Robert E.　　　　　　　USA
b. St Louis, Missouri 1912

Bob Cochran had a remarkably long career. In 1931, he won the Western Junior, and after 40 more years of golf he was still winning local events and was medallist in the 1971 USGA Seniors. A winner of numerous regional titles, Cochran had one of his best achievements in reaching the final of the 1960 British Amateur at the age of 47, but then, alas, he was eclipsed 8 and 7 by Irishman Joe Carr. He won the 1945 Tam o' Shanter World Amateur and was once a Walker Cup choice – in 1961, when he won his foursomes and was not asked to play in the singles.

COE, Charles Robert　　　　　　　USA
b. Ardmore, Oklahoma 1923

Although Charlie Coe had a highly successful career in amateur golf, his sharpest memories may be of the US Masters, a tournament he now helps to run. Six times he finished as low amateur, was sixth in 1959 and ninth in 1962. His finest entry came in 1961: he began 72, 71 and then closed with a pair of 69s. Those last rounds gained him 5 strokes on Gary Player and 6 on Palmer. Player was champion by a stroke; Palmer tied for second place with Charlie Coe, whose 281 was, and is, the best score ever returned by an amateur. Only Billy Joe Patton, Ken Venturi and Frank Stranahan have come as close to winning the Masters as amateurs. Coe played six times in the Walker Cup between 1949 and 1963, taking 3½ points out of 6 in foursomes and 2½ out of 6 in singles. He played six times in the Americas Cup and also in the World Amateur Team Championship. Coe once reached the final of the British Amateur, being beaten by Dick Chapman. His record in the US Amateur is better. He won in 1949, annihilating Rufus King by 11 and 10, and in 1958, when he overcame Tommy Aaron, experiencing one of his numerous second-place finishes in competition, by 5 and 4. The following year there came an epic final of cut and thrust with Nicklaus in which neither was able to establish dominance. The emerging giant came through by 1 hole.

COLBERT, James Joseph   USA
b. Elizabeth, New Jersey 1941

Jim Colbert won the Kansas Junior precociously at 11 years old. He went to Kansas State College on a football scholarship, and the resultant loss of his front teeth may have persuaded him to concentrate on golf: he finished second in the 1964 NCAA Championship. He turned professional the following year and qualified for the US Tour. He did not make a mark until 1969 with a win in the Monsanto Open, but since then has been a consistent performer if seldom in the spotlight, though he won a tournament each year from 1972 to 1975. Between 1969 and 1981 he only twice missed finishing in the Top 60, and in both 1974 and 1980 he was 21st in the money list. In 1980 he topped $150,000 and had his other $100,000 year in 1981, apparently improving with age (which he tries to conceal with what must rank as the worst hairpiece on the US Tour). His best performances in major championships have been to finish third in the 1971 US Open and fourth in 1974, combined with a fourth place in the 1974 Masters, three behind Gary Player's remarkable finish. A minor achievement is that he shares the US Tour record for the fewest putts over a nine-hole stretch – 8 in the 1967 Greater Jacksonville Open.

US wins 6 (1969–80)
US money $1,006,777 (1966–82) (37th all-time)
World money $1,141,008 (1966–82) (45th all-time)

COLE, Laura: see Baugh

COLES, Janet   USA
b. Carmel, California 1954

Anyone wanting the facts on the differences between the male and female golf swing could do worse than consult Miss Coles. She took a BSc in Kinesiology at UCLA, the subject of her thesis being the comparison of muscular activity. Highly athletic, Janet Coles was on the UCLA basketball team, is a downhill and cross-country skier and likes to run a few miles daily. She has been on the US Tour since 1977 and always in the Top 60 (though that is less of a feat than on the men's Tour), with progress each year. She has one win, in the 1978 Lady Tara Natural Light Classic after a play-off, and her best money list placing has been 17th with $58,377 in 1980. She had another good year in 1982, topping $60,000.

US wins 1 (1978)
US money $249,587 (1977–82) (40th all-time)

COLLETT, Glenna (later Vare)   USA
b. New Haven, Connecticut 1903

The greatest American amateur of the 1920s and 1930s, Glenna Collett has a record which has since been approached only by JoAnne Carner. As a child she was a keen baseball player, but first tried golf at 14 and began playing more frequently, mainly because her mother considered the former game unladylike. At about this age she watched some great young players such as Bobby Jones and Alexa Stirling, and later took a long course of lessons from former US Open Champion Alex Smith. At the age of 18 and 5 feet 6 inches tall, she hit a measured drive of a little over 300 yards, which was thought at the time to be a record for a woman. In 1921 she had her first taste of success when she defeated the great British player Cecil Leitch in an 18-hole match. The following year she won her first US Amateur. She then won the Canadian Amateur in 1923 and 1924, and took the US title again in 1925 beating Alexa Stirling 9 and 8. In 1924 in the semi-finals, she had suffered a particularly unlucky defeat. Playing the last hole, when she was 1 up, her opponent, tennis champion Mary K. Browne, hit a tree with a wood shot but the ball was redirected onto the green and the match went into extra holes. On the first of these – at a time when balls were not allowed to be marked on greens – Mary's long putt hit Glenna's ball and went into the hole for victory. In 1925 she made her first entry for the British title and interest was intense as the great American player was now in a miscellany that included the great British rivals, Cecil Leitch and Joyce Wethered, whom she met in an early round,

Glenna Collett

seeding not then being in operation. Glenna played well, but Joyce produced some of her best golf and won. The trip was, however, worth while, for she took the French Championship. Glenna attempted the British title again in 1927, and in 1929 reached one of the classic finals of the history of women's golf. Facing Joyce Wethered at St Andrews, she went out in 34 to be 5 up but her lead was cut to 2 holes by lunch. In the afternoon Joyce won 6 of the first nine holes and all seemed over, but Glenna cut the lead to 2 holes before eventually losing on the 35th. The following year she again reached the final (no Wethered this time) and there faced the young Diana Fishwick, relatively unknown at the time but good enough to win and, much later to commemorate the feat by naming a daugher Glenna. In the USA Glenna Collett continued to carry all before her and the late 1920s probably saw her at her best. In 1928 she defeated Virginia van Wie by what was then the record margin of 13 and 12 in the final, and was victorious again in 1929. In 1930 the van Wie final was repeated by a reduced margin of 6 and 4. She reached the final again in 1931, when she had won the USGA record sequence of 19 matches, but then she was defeated. Again a finalist in 1932, she faced Virginia van Wie once more, and this time the tables were decisively turned, Virginia winning by 10 and 8. One more major achievement remained. In 1935 she was in her last

final against a new generation, in the person of Patty Berg, who went under by 3 and 2. Beside these national titles, Glenna also won the Eastern seven times and the North and South on six occasions. In all, she is thought to have won 49 championships in her career. She was runner-up in the 1962 Senior Womens' (US). She played in the Curtis Cup each year from 1932 to 1948 and was non-playing captain in 1950 but her greatest claim to fame remains her record six wins in the US Championship. Some of her success in golf stemmed from the fact that she had early played other sports with her family and was naturally athletic. Consequently she attacked the ball with vigour, employing a long backswing with full shoulder turn but the restricted hip turn that had begun to come in under the influence of J. Douglas Edgar in the early 1920s. Her long hitting, however, was mainly the result of rhythm and smooth acceleration, not brawn, and she is sometimes claimed to be the first woman who always played for the flag rather than the green. Although not as much the centre of adulation as Bobby Jones, she was easily his nearest equivalent in the field of women's golf. The two were attractive and had both the will to win and the ability to lose with grace – the latter an experience they seldom had to suffer in their best years.

COLLINS, William   USA
b. Meyersdale, Pennsylvania 1928

The 6-foot 3½-inch, bulky Bill Collins turned professional in 1951 but did not attempt the US Tour until he was 30. He won four US tournaments in 1959–62, the 1959 Barranquilla Open and the 1973 PGA Matchplay. In 1961, he was a Ryder Cup choice, losing his singles. Collins was a particularly steady player and would undoubtedly have achieved more had he not been plagued by back trouble. He now plays the Senior US Tour.

US wins 4 (1959–62)
US money $189,331 (193rd all-time)

COMMANS, Ronald R.   USA
b. Los Angeles, California 1959

Ron Commans was an All-American choice in 1981, NCAA Champion, and reached the semi-finals of the Western Amateur. He qualified for the US Tour for 1982, after playing in the 1981 Walker Cup.

CONGDON, Charles W.   USA
b. *Blaine, Washington 1909*

Some of Chuck Congdon's best years were lost to World War II. His highest achievement was to win the 1948 Canadian Open at Vancouver, British Columbia, and a US tournament in 1947.

CONLEY, Peggy Shane   USA
b. *Seattle, Washington 1947*

By a few days – at 16 years 2 months 14 days – Peggy Conley became the youngest finalist in 1963 in the US Amateur. To get there she had beaten three Curtis Cup players and faced Anne Quast Welts in the final, which she lost by 2 and 1. In a sense that was the peak of her career, but there were considerable achievements yet to come. She was, for instance, a highly successful Curtis Cup player, winning three and halving one of the singles she played in during the 1964 and 1968 Curtis Cup matches. In 1964 she was US Junior champion and a semi-finalist in the Women's in 1967. She also won several regional titles in the Northwest and won the 1966 Western of which she was runner-up in 1975. During this period she had worked at a number of jobs: freelance photographer, dental assistant, teacher and skiing instructor amongst them – so why not professional golf? This she did, having tied for 17th as an amateur in the 1976 US Open, giving up a job as head of a school art department to do so. She was in the Top 60 from 1978 to 1980, 31st in 1979 being her best money list placing, and in the same year she tied for third in a tournament.

US money $95,246 (1977–81)

CONNER, Frank Joseph   USA
b. *Vienna, Austria 1946*

Golf is a demanding art which must be pursued intently. A majority of today's players seem to have first played before the age of 10, and to have settled on the game before 20. But Frank Conner's early love was tennis: he was National Junior Champion at 17 and later three times qualified to play in the US Open at Forrest Hills. He did not swing a golf club until the age of 24. In 1970 he decided that he was not going to progress further in tennis and that he had better give golf a try. For a while he continued coaching tennis and competing on golf mini-tours and he failed the US Tour qualifying school four times. By 1975 he was qualified, but he

did not break into the top 100 until 1979. His first year in the Top 60 came in 1981, when statistics rated him as the third best putter. He has yet to win a tournament but tied second in the 1979 New Orleans Open and in 1981 had two second places. In 1982 he went one better, only losing the Heritage Classic to Tom Watson in a play-off, and then winning the King Hassan Trophy in Rabat. He and Ellsworth Vines are the only men to qualify for both the US golf and tennis Opens.

US money $280,514 (1975–82) (160th all-time)
Overseas wins 1 (1982)

CONRAD, Joseph W.   USA
b. *San Antonio, Texas 1930*

Joe Conrad played some of his most successful golf as a lieutenant in the USAF. After winning state and regional amateur titles in the USA in the 1950–54 period, he had a very good year in Britain in 1955. There he won the Amateur Championship, beating Alan Slater 3 and 2 in the final, and was also low amateur in the Open at St Andrews. In the same year he played in the Walker Cup. In 1956 he reached the quarter-finals of the British Amateur and repeated his 1954 appearance in the Americas Cup. He turned professional in 1957 and tried the US Tour but, partly because he was a short hitter, had little success. He soon concentrated on the life of a club professional. In 1981 he finished third in the World Seniors.

COODY, Billy Charles   USA
b. *Stamford, Texas 1937*

Although pre-eminently a steady player who quietly keeps the ball in play and misses few 36-hole cuts, Charles Coody has known what it is both to finish a tournament in convincing style and to meet disaster. On the US Tour, for instance, he went into the last three holes of the L & M Open with a 3-stroke lead. He bogeyed the 16th, dropped 2 on the 17th and another on the last. That was a fifth-place cheque for Charles. Again, in the 1969 US Masters he held a lead of 1 with three holes to go – and dropped a shot on each hole to finish in fifth place. Coody bounced back to win the Cleveland Open the following week. Two years later he won the Masters itself. His finish was more than adequate: two birdies and two pars. This time it was another player who faltered. With four holes to go, Johnny Miller held a 2-stroke lead on Coody but fell away

Charles Coody

to finish in joint second place, 2 behind him. In 1973 Coody had an outstanding September in Britain. At King's Norton near Birmingham, on baked fairways, he was in contention throughout and birdied the last three holes to win by a shot from Jack Newton. The feature stroke came on the last hole. Coody bunkered his second shot 80 yards from the green and then played a running third to about 3 feet, holing the putt for victory. His win qualified him for the rich John Player Classic at Turnberry at the end of the month. On the second day, there were more scores in the 80s than 70s. The wind was a steady 70 mph, gusting up to 120 mph. The tented village was blown to pieces, but Coody went round in 74. After a 70 in the third round he was firmly in the lead and in bad weather again on the last day his 77 was good enough to keep him 3 ahead of Jacklin, the only player to challenge. Coody was, however, primarily a US Tour player. There he won just three times, plus the 1971 World Series; but he was a most consistent performer. He was four times in the top 20 on the money list and 14 times made the Top 60, including a run from 1965 to 1977. His best placing was 16th in both 1967 and 1971, the year he was a Ryder Cup choice. Charles Coody came to professional golf after a fine career in Texan amateur

golf, in which he won some 30 tournaments and also reached the semi-finals of the US Amateur in 1962.

US wins 3 (1964–71)
US money $1,127,905 (1963–82) (29th all-time)
Europe wins 2 (1973)
World money $1,331,422 (1963–82) (33rd all-time)

COOK, John Neuman   USA
b. Toledo, Ohio 1957

John Cook had what has now come to be the usual short, successful amateur career of a future US Tour star. His first success was to win the 1974 World Junior title from Gary Hallberg, and four years later he won the US Amateur. The next year he again reached the final but was this time defeated by Mark O'Meara, now a fellow Tour player. By this time he had been three times an All-American choice and was in the 1979 US World Amateur team. He then turned professional and is now recognized as one of the best young strikers of a golf ball on the Tour. In his first season he came 78th on the money list and then improved in 1981 to 25th. In the Crosby he tied with Hale Irwin, Barney Thompson, Ben Crenshaw and Bobby Clampett. Cook came through the play-off for his first win. He also tied for fourth place in the US Open later in the season, 6 behind champion David Graham. His Crosby play-off performance was particularly to his credit. Anyone might have lost concentration after the unfortunate incident which occurred: his playing partner, actor James Garner, was provoked by a spectator and retaliated with a punch, but Cook never wavered. Garner later won the handicap section of the Bob Hope Classic at Moor Park, showing that his accurate hitting was not confined to spectators!

US wins 1 (1981)
US money $228,407 (1980–82) (174th all-time)

COOPER, Harry E.   England & USA
b. Leatherhead, England 1904

'Light-Horse' Harry – so nicknamed because of his speed about a golf course – was one of that band of unfortunate players who never quite succeeded in winning a major championship. He was second in the 1936 Masters by 1 stroke to Horton Smith after holding the three-round lead with a sequence of 70, 69, 71 that declined to 76 and equal second two years later behind Henry Picard. He was also twice

Harry 'Light-Horse' Cooper

fourth. His experience was similar in the US Open, though perhaps more extreme. In 1927 he failed to win because he three-putted the last hole while Tommy Armour got a 10-foot putt in; he then lost the play-off. He was twice third, once fourth and in 1936 broke the previous Open scoring record by 2 strokes, only to have Tony Manero come in 2 better still. He did less well in the US PGA: reaching the semi-finals of the 1925 event was the closest he came to winning. In tournaments his record was more convincing. Despite having the reputation of always coming second (an estimated 28 times) he also won frequently, and as a modern player would have been a prodigious money-winner, certainly past the $1½ million mark. At the age of 18 he won the Texas Professional Open, repeated this the following year, and took his first important tournament in 1926, the first time the Los Angeles Open, one of the oldest US Tour events, was played. Wins occurred regularly over the years, but his greatest season was 1937, when he piled up nine wins, was leading money-winner, and took the Vardon

Trophy for stroke average the first year it was awarded. Although he won seldom thereafter, in 1942 he took the first Crosby. As some compensation for not taking a major, Cooper won the Canadian Open in both 1932 and 1937. In 1938 he tied and then lost a play-off to Sam Snead, another man who failed to win the US Open. In 1958 he won the First Quarter Century Seniors.

US wins 20 to 32 (various official figures) (1926–42)
US money $76,000

COOPER, Peter　　　　　　　　　USA
b. Gainesville, Georgia 1914

Pete Cooper turned professional in 1938 and joined the US Tour in 1944, in due course earning himself the title 'King of the Caribbean', as a result of some ten successes on that circuit. On the US Tour he first won in 1949 and had occasional victories up to 1958. In 1976 he won the US PGA Seniors but in the match for the world title was beaten 2 and 1 by Christy O'Connor.

US wins 5 (1949–58)
US money $63,681

CORNELIUS, Katherine　　　　　　USA
b. Boston, Massachusetts 1932

Now one of the oldest competitors on the US Tour, Kathy Cornelius won the Southern Amateur in 1952 and was twice runner-up for the Intercollegiate Championship. She turned professional in 1953 but did not attempt the US Tour until 1956. It went well, for she won the US Open that year and one other tournament. Later there came five other tournaments up to her last win in 1973. Between 1957 and 1977 she was only once placed worse than 48th on the money list and was no less than 12 times 18th or better, her best result being ninth in 1959 and eighth in 1973. She was never on the bad side of 16th from 1961 to 1965. She has by no means always played a full season, either. Her daughter Kay, at the age of 14 in 1981, became the youngest winner of the US Junior Girls'.

US wins 8 (1956–73)
US money $228,199 (1956–81) (46th all-time)

COUPLES, Frederick Stephen　　　　USA
b. Seattle, Washington 1959

An as amateur, Fred Couples was an All-American in 1978 and 1979 and was low amateur in the 1978

US Open. He turned professional in 1980 and qualified for the US Tour. During his first season, Couples twice tied for second place on Tour and finished 53rd in the money list, while US Tour statistics show that he was the second longest driver that year, averaging 277.6 yards, behind Dan Pohl. During one tournament he drove a 317 par 4 in all four rounds. He won $78,939, the highest earnings by a new player. During the 1982 PGA he had six consecutive birdies in his first round and closed with a 66. No one could hope to catch Floyd, but there was a short period when Couples seemed a possibility. He finally tied for third place.

US money $156,545 (1981–2) (210th all-time)

COURTNEY, Charles   USA
b. Minneapolis, Minnesota 1940

Chuck Courtney's first year on the US Tour was 1964, and during it he won his first tournament and finished 38th in the money list, his highest placing. Consistency was something he never quite managed to achieve, though he twice won again before his retirement towards the end of the 1970s.

US wins 3 (1964–9)
US money $310,820 (1964–76) (142nd all-time)

COWAN, Garry   Canada
b. Kitchener 1938

Garry Cowan reached the final of the Canadian Amateur five times in the years 1959–68 yet won only once, in 1961. He was perhaps more successful in the US, taking the important North and South Amateur in 1970 and winning the US Amateur twice, in 1966 and 1971. His 1966 victory was the first success by a non-American player since Ross Somerville in 1932. He was also low amateur in the 1965 US Masters and played for Canada in the World Amateur Team Championship from 1960 to 1966.

COX, Wilfred H.   USA
b. Brookline, Massachusetts 1897; d. 1969

'Whiffy' Cox was a tournament player whose successes were mainly confined to the 1930s. Playing with a wide stance and three-quarter swing, his best year was 1931, when he won five events. He was a Ryder Cup choice that year and won both of his matches. He had a creditable record in the US Open, four times finishing in the top five in the years 1931–5, with third in 1934 being his best finish, two behind the winner, Olin Dutra.

CRAWFORD, Jean: see Ashley

CREAVY, Thomas   USA
b. Tuchahoe, New York 1911; d. 1979

Tom Creavy had a brief career at the top of US golf, cut short by a near-fatal illness. As a virtually unknown 20-year-old he won the US PGA, and to do it beat three Open champions of Britain or the US. The following year he reached the semi-finals and in 1933 the quarters, when he also took the San Francisco Matchplay Open. In 1934 he finished equal eighth in the US Open at Merion after a final round of 66, the only one under 70 in the event. The rest is silence.

CREED, Clifford Ann   USA
b. Alexandria, Louisiana 1938

Winner of her state championship six times, as an amateur she also won the Southern Amateur in 1957 and 1962 and in the latter year the South Atlantic and North and South also. She played in that year's Curtis Cup. Turning professional shortly after, Clifford Ann Creed played one tournament and came in third. In her first full year, 1963, she was fifth on the money list, her first wins, three, coming in 1964 when she was eighth. She had more wins between 1965 and 1968, but has not won since. On the money lists she was not worse than eighth from 1963 to 1968; from then on she remained a healthy money-winner up to 1982, being in the Top 60 until 1979.

US wins 11 (1964–8)
US money $281,608 (1962–82) (34th all-time)

CRENSHAW, Ben Daniel   USA
b. Austin, Texas 1952

As an amateur, Ben Crenshaw was seen as arguably the most promising since Jack Nicklaus. He was an All-American choice between 1971 and 1973 and in the same period three times won the NCAA Championship, perhaps second only to the US Amateur in prestige. In 1972 he was runner-up in the US Amateur and in 1973 won both the match and medal events of the Western Amateur and the Sunnehanna Amateur. In this final year, he averaged 69.9 strokes over 42 competitive rounds. He

Ben Crenshaw

nine entries he had won some $76,000 and was firmly in the Top 60 in 34th place. His US Tour performance since then has been very consistent, only dropping below his first-year placing in 1982. From 1976 to 1981, he always topped $100,000 and in 1976, 1979 and 1980 he was well past $200,000. He was second on the money list in 1976 and fifth in 1979 and 1980. Despite this record of solid achievement, Crenshaw has fallen far short of what both he and others expected. The money has piled up and he now approaches $1½ million on the US Tour alone, but his US and World victories are relatively few. He has also failed to win a major championship, though he has had several chances and a number of high finishes. The closest was the 1979 US PGA. Over the testing 7,000-yard Oakland Hills course he broke 70 in every round – 69, 67, 69, 67; yet that was only good enough to tie David Graham's 69, 68, 70, 65. In the play-off Graham saved himself with putts for halves on the first two holes and won the next as Crenshaw faltered. Crenshaw was again second in a major less than a month afterwards, in the British Open, where he made errors towards the end of his final round. The British Open is probably the title which he most covets, partly because of his interest in the history and traditions of golf. When Crenshaw makes his annual pilgrimage to the British Open he also usually takes time to visit historic courses and collect books, clubs and other memorabilia. His collection has been said to be worth $500,000 – perhaps an exaggeration, even though the value of such things is rising fast. His record in the Open is excellent, though without victory. In 1977 at Turnberry he was equal fifth but he was the only player who for three rounds nearly matched the epic golf of the Nicklaus–Watson duel. At St Andrews in 1978 he finished equal second behind Nicklaus and was again equal second at Lytham the following year, three in arrears of Severiano Ballesteros. Muirfield, 1980, saw a dominant performance from Tom Watson and Crenshaw played very consistent golf for 70, 70, 68, 69, to be 6 behind and in third place. For 1981 he persuaded his friend Bill Rogers to enter. Crenshaw looked a likely winner after two rounds but then faded down the list. Rogers won. The prime strength of Crenshaw's game is his putting: his fellow players consider him the best on the US Tour though Crenshaw himself thinks Watson his peer. He sets himself up with a slightly open stance and then strikes the ball with what appears to be solely an arm movement. For the long

also tied for third in a US Tour event, the 1972 Heritage Classic. He played in the 1972 World Amateur Team Championship, and would have been a 1973 Walker Cup choice had he not turned professional towards the end of the year. As a professional, much was expected of him, but his beginnings were so startling that many began to talk of him as a rival to Jack Nicklaus. He played his first professional round on 1 November 1973 at San Antonio in the Texas Open. It was a 65. He followed that with 72, 66, 67. After leading throughout he won by 2 strokes for a start of $25,000 and about as much publicity as it is possible for a young golfer to get. A few days later he was at Pinehurst for the ill-fated World Open, which carried a top prize of $100,000 and was played over no fewer than eight rounds. After five rounds he was 18 strokes behind leader Tom Watson; but a 64 pulled him well up the field, and in the end he finished firmly in second place behind the far less glamorous figure of Miller Barber. Nevertheless, that was another $44,000 for Crenshaw. By the end of a very short season, in

shots, he has a very long backswing – well beyond the horizontal – and a wide arc, both of which compensate for his lack of inches. He has been voted the best recovery expert, but this implies that Crenshaw has often been wild with his driver. However, in more recent years he has cut the length of his backswing a little and now driving gets him into wild country less often. With his excellent putting it is not surprising that Ben has had his share of low rounds. During the 1981 US Open at Merion, for instance, he equalled the course record with a 64; while en route to winning the 1979 Phoenix Open he had a 61, which included a run of nine birdies in 11 holes. Yet the enigma remains that he is an outstanding performer in major championships without yet being a winner. Sometimes Crenshaw has beaten himself, as in the 1975 US Open at Medinah Country Club, when he put a shot into the water on the 71st and came in third, 1 stroke behind the Mahaffey–Graham play-off. In the 1976 US Masters Crenshaw scored 70, 70, 72, 67 for 279, a good enough total to win most years – but not when Ray Floyd is busy equalling the Masters scoring record. Another second for Crenshaw, 8 behind Floyd. Crenshaw has, however, won two national Opens: the 1976 Irish, said to be his first experience of a links course, and the 1982 Mexican Open. In 1982 he had the unusual experience of being statistically the US Tour's best putter, yet came only 83rd among the money-winners with a little over $50,000.

US wins 8 (1973–80)
US money $1,376,445 (1973–82) (16th all-time)
World money $1,721,752 (1973–82) (21st all-time)

CROCKER, Helen: see South & Central America

CROCKER, Mary Lou (née Daniel)   USA
b. Louisville, Kentucky 1944

In 1962 Mary Lou Daniel won both the US and Western Junior titles and the full Kentucky title in 1965. She played the US Tour from 1966 and was in the Top 60 from 1966 to 1977 in all but one year. Her highest ranking was 24th in 1977 and she had one victory, in 1973. She now competes infrequently.

US wins 1 (1973)
US money $100,246

CRONIN, Grace: see Lenczyk

CROSBY, Harry Lillis   USA
Tacoma, Washington 1904; d. 1977

The 16th at Cypress Point is certainly the most photographed hole in golf and perhaps also the most famous. All you have to do is hit a ball 200 yards or so over the Pacific Ocean to a green set on a peninsula and two-putt for a par. Many have been the scores, even by seasoned professionals, that have soared into the teens as golfers have watched their tee shots find the ocean. Only two men have holed in one. Bing Crosby was one of them, accomplishing the feat in 1947. Otherwise, he was a man with no great achievements to his name as a player of the game. Once he reached the sectional qualifying round for the US Amateur and in 1950 appeared in the British. Here, at St Andrews, he began with a pair of birdies and a gallery of an estimated 20,000. He lost by 3 and 2. But Crosby also began what has grown to be one of the best loved tournaments on the US Tour, the Crosby Pro-Am. It began in 1937 when he sponsored an 18-hole event and, when it proved popular, decided to continue. It expanded first to 36 holes then, after World War II, to 54 and, from 1958, to 72, eventually being played over three famous courses: Spyglass Hill, Cypress Point and Pebble Beach. Crosby first played golf as a teenager in Spokane, Washington and then took it up again in 1930 during the filming of *King of Jazz* with Paul Whiteman, when some of the cast would gather after shooting to play at Lakeside, Los Angeles. Thereafter, he was a typical golfer for fun, in low single figures which rose as the years passed, but always a good partner to have in a four-ball. It was after just such a four-ball in Madrid, which included Manuel Pinero, that he suddenly died in the club locker room as the post-game talk was beginning – an end he might well have chosen.

CROSBY, Nathaniel   USA
b. Hillsborough, California 1952

To be born the son of Bing Crosby must mean that a youngster has opportunities in plenty to learn the game of golf and play the variety of courses that many consider essential to the development of one's game. By his late teens, Nat Crosby had become a sound player with a putting style very reminiscent of the Crenshaw 'arms only' action and a distinct pause at the top of the full swing. Many have felt that such a pause rules out the possibility of producing the rhythm essential to a golf swing –

but there is the successful example of Cary Middlecoff to remember. When Crosby competed in the 1981 US Amateur at Olympic Country Club in San Francisco his previous record was such that no one gave him a serious chance of the title. However, Crosby fought through to the final, finding himself 4 down with eight holes remaining. Later, he was 2 down with three to go, won the next two holes and then took the championship on the first extra hole. This was not accomplished without a great deal of facial contortion and punching of the air after successful shots. Some felt that this added to the drama of the occasion; others that it was contrary to the spirit of golf – especially in matchplay. He was 33 over par for the 120 matchplay holes and 12 over for the 36 holes of qualifying strokeplay. Whether Crosby can maintain this level of achievement is doubtful, for his US Amateur win flattered his abilities. His experiences in Britain in 1982 could have done little to encourage him. He was knocked out in the first round of the British Amateur at Deal and in the Open at Troon compiled the highest score of any qualifier (82, 84) before bowing out. Yet he was low amateur in the 1982 US Open and had the lowest round, a 68, in the 1982 World Amateur Team Championship. After the death of his father he has become progressively involved in the running of the Crosby tournament, and in this capacity the aura of championship will do him no harm at all.

CRUICKSHANK, Robert Allan
Scotland & USA

b. Grantown-on-Spey, Scotland 1894; d. 1975

In the period 1971–3, 'Wee Bobby' matched or bettered his age no fewer than 12 times in US PGA events. Although it is always impossible to compare the champions of today with those of an earlier age, to score in the mid to high 70s when approaching 80 years of age is evidence of a lasting method. Similarly, competing in the 1950 US Open, the 5-foot 5-inch Bobby finished equal 25th at the age of 55. As a younger man, Bobby compiled a good record in the US Open although he won neither it nor any other major championship, one of the best golfers ever to fail to do so. After he emigrated to the USA in 1921, he came in the first four five times between 1923 and 1937, and was involved in the final stages of one of the most renowned US Opens of all, the Open of 1923 – a part of golf legend, in which Bobby Jones 'broke through'. At Inwood Country Club, the two were tied after 72 holes, with Jones having finished, he said, 'like a yellow dog', with bogey, bogey, double bogey. In the 18-hole play-off they matched each other shot for shot until on the last Jones hit a 1-iron from a sandy lie over water to 6 feet from the flag. Jones had arrived; Cruickshank never had a major so nearly in his grasp again. In other majors his best placings were fifth in the 1929 British Open and fourth in the 1936 US Masters, but he took part in one of the most remarkable matches seen in the US PGA or anywhere else. On the 6th hole in the second round of the 36-hole match Al Watrous conceded him a 6-foot putt out of pure kindness of heart. After all, Al was 9 up with 13 to go. On the next, Bobby holed from some 20 feet, Watrous missed from 8. Cruickshank then took the next two and the lead was becoming less impregnable. When they reached the 18th, Watrous was only 1 up and Cruikshank was 6 under par for the back nine. He then holed a long birdie putt and they went into extra holes. The first three were halved. On the fourth, Bobby was outside Watrous in two and then three shots and thought of gracefully conceding as Watrous was nearly dead from his tee shot. However, he holed out for a 4; Watrous knocked his 2-footer just past – and then missed the return. A couple of holes later it was all over as Watrous three-putted.

US wins 16

Bobby Cruickshank

CUDONE, Carolyn   USA
b. *Oxford, Alabama 1918*

Though never the winner of a national title, Carolyn Cudone won the 1960 Eastern and the 1958 North and South, and the Metropolitan five times between 1955 and 1965. She won the New Jersey title no less than 11 times in 16 years. She reached the semi-finals of the US Amateur in 1953 and played on the 1956 Curtis Cup team, being non-playing captain in 1970. Later she became equally formidable as a senior golfer, taking the national championship in the five years 1968–72, a record for any USGA national event. She was runner-up in 1974 and 1975.

CULLEN, Elizabeth   USA
b. *Tulsa, Oklahoma 1938*

Betsy Cullen won the Oklahoma Junior three times and the Women's in 1954, 1955 and 1961. She became a school teacher for a while and was then a golf professional before playing the US Tour from 1965. She was in the top 40 from 1965 to 1976 and was five times in the top 20, with 12th in 1972 her best money list placing. She won her first event in 1972, the Sears Classic, and had two other victories in a competitive career that ended in 1980. Now she has one of the best addresses in American golf as teaching professional at Sweetwater.

US wins 3 (1972–5)
US money $181,738 (1965–80)

CUMMINGS, Edith (later Munson)   USA
b. *Chicago, Illinois 1899*

Winner of the US Women's in 1923, Edith Cummings defeated Alexa Stirling in the final. The previous year she had reached the semi-final where she was defeated by Glenna Collett, who went on to take her first of six titles. In 1924 she won the Western, and reached the semi-final of the US again in 1925, when she was again bested by Glenna Collett. Edith Cummings dropped out of tournament golf not long after. Apart from her golf prowess, she won much admiration for her beauty.

CUPIT, Jacky D.   USA
b. *Longview, Texas 1938*

One of four brothers in professional golf, Jacky Cupit had one of the stranger swings once to be seen on the US circuit: there was an extravagant loop at the top. He joined the US Tour in 1961 and was soon successful, taking a near major, the Canadian Open, and the following year the Western Open, one of the more coveted tournament titles. His greatest moment came in 1963 at Brookline Country Club. In the highest-scoring US Open since Sam Parks's win in 1935, Cupit had 70, 72, 76, 75 for 293 and a tie with Arnold Palmer and Julius Boros. In the 18-hole play-off, it was Boros who came through with 70 to Cupit's 73 and Palmer's 76. Cupit enjoyed a few more successful years, but little was heard of him after his late 20s.

US wins 4 (1961–6)
US money $244,204 (1961–72) (170th all-time)

CURL, Rod   USA
b. *Redding, California 1943*

Rod Curl is three-quarters Wintu Indian, and has a tribal name very appropriate for a golfer: 'Yoso', which means 'Johnny come from behind'. He turned professional in 1968 and went on Tour the following year, at 5 feet 5 inches perhaps the shortest player. It was some time before he was able to pay his way, but from 1973 to 1981 he was always in the top 100 and five times made the Top 60. His best year was 1974, when he finished 17th on the money list for $120,154. That year he also took his first and only tournament, the Colonial National Invitational. In 1977 he also won the World Indian Open, a non-PGA event. Like Snead, Curl was a player who saw the solution to his problems on the greens to be a between-the-legs putting style, until this was outlawed.

US wins 1 (1974)
US money $612,318 (1969–82) (77th all-time)

CURTIS, Harriot   USA
b. *Manchester-by-the-Sea, Massachusetts 1881; d. 1974*

With her sister Margaret, Harriot played in an international match for the USA against a British team at Cromer in England early in the century. They were to be instrumental in starting the Curtis Cup from 1932 and presented the original trophy. Harriot won the US Championship in 1906 and lost the title in the final the following year to her sister. She reached the semi-finals in 1913, where she was beaten by Marion Hollins. Later she became active in the Civil Rights movement and in higher education.

Harriot and Margaret Curtis

Beth Daniel

CURTIS, Margaret   USA

b. *Manchester-by-the-Sea, Massachusetts, 1883; d. 1965*

Margaret Curtis won the US Amateur in 1907, unkindly beating her sister by 7 and 6 in the final, and was also champion in 1911 and 1912. She had been beaten finalist in 1900 and 1905. Margaret was also an excellent tennis player, US Doubles Champion in 1908. During World War I she helped set up food centres for children in war-torn parts of Europe, and was active in the Red Cross.

DANIEL, Elizabeth Ann   USA

b. *Charleston, South Carolina 1956*

Perhaps the best woman currently playing in the USA , Beth Daniel has, some say, won more than $200,000 in each of her last three seasons (1980–2). As an amateur she took the US title at her first attempt in 1975 when still 18, beating both Nancy Lopez and defending champion Carol Semple en route to the final, where she beat Donna Horton, who was to be 1976 winner. In 1977 she won again, this time defeating Cathy Sherk (1978 champion) in the final. She played on the 1976 and 1978 Curtis Cup teams, and also occasionally on the Furman University men's team. She qualified for the US Tour in early 1979 and soon won the so-called 'World Ladies' Championship' in Japan, a title she won once in her first season, the Patty Berg Classic

and the Rookie of the Year award was just about automatic for her tenth on the money list with $97,027. In 1980 she became the first player ever to win more than $200,000 in a season (something now accomplished three times) and won four events, including the World Championship of Women's Golf, a parallel event to the men's World Series. Incredibly, in her last 18 tournaments that year she only once finished out of the top 5. She was named Player of the Year; her stroke average was 71.59. Her 1981 was scarcely less successful. She was again leading money-winner and took the World Championship and one other event, being the quickest woman player to reach $½ million in career winnings. With Tom Kite, she also won the J.C. Penney Four-ball. In 1982 she won five times, taking the Columbia Savings with a last-round 64 while in the WUI she began 68, 68, 67 and then coasted to an 8-stroke victory with a last-round 73. Beth Daniel is a long hitter and excellent putter – she won the 1982 J & B Gold Putter – but her main strength is reckoned to be the mid-irons.

US wins 12 (1979–82)
US money $758,640 (1979–82) (12th all-time)

DANIEL, Mary Lou: see Crocker

DARBEN, Althea: see Gibson

DAVIES, Richard D.   USA

b. Pasadena, California 1930

Richard Davies was a surprise winner of the 1962 British Amateur when he beat John Povall in the Hoylake final. Previously he had been runner-up in the 1957 and 1958 Mexican Amateurs. After finishing as leading amateur in the 1963 US Open he was a Walker Cup choice that year, but lost both his singles.

DeARMAN, Marlene: see Floyd

DECKER, Anne: see Quast

DEMARET, James Newton   USA

b. Houston, Texas 1910

One of the best players not to win the US Open, Jimmy Demaret came tantalizingly close. In 1946, he finished sixth, but only 2 strokes behind the winner, Lloyd Mangrum; and then in 1948 at the Riviera Country Club, Los Angeles, he set a new US Open record at 278. Alas for Jimmy, Ben Hogan had 276 and pushed him into second place. In 1953 Demaret was fourth but this time 11 behind Hogan. Then came his last chance at the age of 47 in 1957: he was third, just 1 stroke behind the Mayer/Middlecoff play-off. Less successful in the US PGA, though he reached the semi-finals four times, Demaret was a US Masters specialist. In 1940 he opened with a 67, helped in no small measure by a second nine in 30, which equalled the all-time record for nine holes on a championship course. Even so, he was 3 strokes behind Lloyd Mangrum who set an Augusta record for a round that has since only been equalled. For the remainder of the championship, however, Demaret outscored Mangrum, who finished second, in every round and won by the record margin at the time of 4 strokes. After being sixth in 1942 and fourth in 1946, Demaret in 1947 became only the second man to win the Masters twice, pushing Byron Nelson and Frank Stranahan into second place by 2 strokes. In 1950 Jimmy became the first man to win three times. After the first three rounds Australian Jim Ferrier was 4 strokes ahead and then with 6 holes to play in the last round had increased his lead to 5. Demaret played those final holes in 2 under par, while Ferrier was 5 over. He was round in 69 to Ferrier's 75. Demaret, one of nine children of a carpenter, became one of three golf professional

brothers in the early 1930s. The US Tour was not then a great attraction – risks were high, rewards low – so he confined his competitive play to Texas, winning the state's PGA five times consecutively from 1934 to 1938. In this final year he decided to try himself out against the field and went on the US Tour full-time. He won that year and took the Los Angeles Open the following year. Besides the US Masters, 1940 was a peak year for him, for he took six other events and three in 1941, including the Argentine Open. Perhaps 1947 was his best season: he took six events, won the Vardon Trophy for lowest stroke average and was leading money-winner. His winnings totalled $27,936 – a comment on the way prize money has inflated in later years: in 1947 total prize money was $352,000, over $1 million by 1958, $7 million in 1971 and $14 million in 1981. In today's terms, Demaret's 1947 earnings would have been worth over $300,000. Demaret played in the Ryder Cup three times between 1947 and 1951, and won every time. In the twilight of his career he represented the US in the 1961 World Cup, being a member of the winning pair. For a time a band singer in night clubs, Demaret maintained his rapport with the public in tournament golf and became well known for his wisecracking and very colourful clothing; but he knew how to concentrate on the business in hand and hit the ball with a low boring flight. One of the few people to have a close relationship with the austere Ben Hogan, with whom he played sometimes in four-ball events, Demaret wrote the book *My Partner Ben Hogan*, after Ben's severe road accident in 1949. Demaret was elected to the PGA Hall of Fame in 1960 and is credited with 44 tournament wins, not all of which are recognized by the US PGA. With Jack Burke, he now owns the Champions Club at Houston, Texas.

US wins 31 (1938–57) (9th all-time)
US money $173,982 (202nd all-time)

DENENBERG, Gail: see Toushin

DENT, James L.   USA

b. Augusta, Georgia 1942

At 6 feet 2 inches and weighing over 225 lb, the powerful black Jim Dent is one of the longest drivers in golf history. As a teenager on his home course it is said that he would regularly drive the greens on two par-4s: one was 360 yards downhill; the other 312 uphill. In 1974 he won the US PGA long-driving contest at 324 yards and Jack Nicklaus, after playing a tournament round with him, is said to have declared that he had never been outhit by so much. But perhaps Nicklaus broke 70 and Dent 80, for at this time, although he was getting a length of 350 yards and more, it was not always in predictable directions. He earned the reputation of being wild off the tee and having a poor short game, perhaps not helped by the fact that galleries tend to flock to big hitters and spur them on to ever more prodigious efforts. Dent has once broken into the US Tour Top 60 when he was 59th in 1974, winning $48,486. He won the Florida PGA in 1976, 1977 and 1978.

US money $361,840 (1970–82) (127th all-time)

DEROUAUX, Catherine: see Reynolds

DICKINSON, Gardner   USA
b. *Dothan, Alabama 1927*

Dickinson held Ben Hogan in great reverence. He once flew 6,000 miles for a lesson from the Master, played in a white cloth cap and was even said to walk with the limp of the post-accident Hogan. Behind his back, some of his fellow touring pros nicknamed him 'Chicken Hawk' and 'Sparrow Hawk', a reference to Hogan's 'the Hawk'. But Dickinson was as hard and tough as Hogan himself and, thanks to his very strong arms and hands, hit the ball with every bit as much venom, though he did not have the all-round game of Hogan. Dickinson went on Tour after turning professional in 1952 and won money in 24 of his first 25 events. He first won in 1956 and occasionally thereafter up to 1971. He was in the Top 60 in the periods 1953–9, 1961–9 and finally in 1971. He was 16th in 1968. At about this time he was the mastermind of the breakaway of US touring professionals from their PGA, and remained a figure in the dispute until it was eventually settled by the establishment of the Tournament Players Division (now Association). He was a Ryder Cup player in 1967 and 1971 and won nine of the ten matches in which he was involved, while one of his best scoring streaks came in the 1968 Alcan at Royal Birkdale. In the final round he went to the turn in 29 and finished in 67 for equal third place, an unexpected result after his opening 77.

US wins 8 (1956–71)
US money $534,348 (1952–80) (88th all-time)

DICKSON, Robert B.   USA
b. *McAlester, Oklahoma 1944*

Bob Dickson had a very good two years in 1967 and 1968. A Walker Cup choice in 1967, he won each of the three matches in which he was involved, including beating Peter Oosterhuis by 6 and 4, and he was also a member of the winning US Americas Cup team. Better still, he took both the British and US Amateur. In the British, he beat Ron Cerrudo in a close-fought match by 2 and 1 with estimated rounds of 71, 67, this despite being unhappy enough with his driving to play his tee shots with a 3-wood off the turf. He then decided to turn professional, and won the US Tour spring qualifying school event. In his first season, he finished 37th in the money list and also won the Haig Open. In 1969 he made a good start by coming second in the Crosby. But then he 'lost his swing' and dropped out of the Top 60. He returned to form in 1973, winning the San Diego Open and having his best Tour placing of 28th in the money list. He raised his total of Top 60 years to four in 1975 but left the Tour during the later 1970s. He was given the Bob Jones Award in 1968 'for distinguished sportsmanship in golf'.

US wins 2 (1968–73)
US money $296,639 (1968–77) (147th all-time)

DIDRIKSON, Mildred: see Zaharias

DIEGEL, Leo   USA
b. *Detroit, Michigan 1899; d. 1951*

'In a way the greatest golfing genius I have seen.' So wrote Bernard Darwin about Leo Diegel; but that 'in a way' severely qualifies his assessment. Diegel had a superb array of talents but was never able to make anything like full use of them. For example, he finished in the top eight on 11 occasions in US or British Opens and finished in the first four seven times. The problem was nerves, seen at their worst when Diegel was joint leader in the 1933 British Open. He came to the last green with a short putt to tie, but yipped it a foot wide. Earlier at the 1929 British Open, it was pointed out to Walter Hagen, who was enjoying a convivial evening before the final day of the event, that Diegel was leading him by 2 strokes and was safely in bed. 'Yes,' responded Hagen, 'but he won't be sleeping.' Diegel finished 82, 77 for third place, but that was 7 behind Walter. Diegel added a second-place finish the following

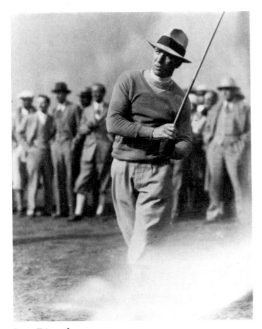

Leo Diegel

year at Hoylake, behind Bobby Jones. In the US Open he was equal second in 1920, third in 1926, third in 1931 and fourth in 1932. At the end of all these attempts, Diegel said: 'They keep trying to give me a championship but I won't take it.' However, he did manage two majors, the 1928 and 1929 US PGAs, and was also dominant in the Canadian Open, which he won in 1924, 1925, 1928 and 1929. So highly strung a player was he that he would rush down the fairway after each shot and would often be thinking about his next but one shot rather than the problem in hand. Obviously he thought long and deeply about how to conquer nerves on the greens and eventually he came up with an individual solution: he spread his legs wide and pointed out both elbows parallel with his chest, while his chin was near to touching the top of his putter shaft. For a while the method was successful and a new verb was coined, 'to diegel', as many club golfers gave it a try. In the end it failed for Diegel and most of the others, though it did have the merit of making the putting stroke very much a shoulder and arms movement. Diegel was a Ryder Cup player four times in the period 1927–33 and won 31 tournaments during his career. An estimated number of those that ought now to be recognized is given below.

US wins 20 (1920–34)

DIEHL, Terrence Jeffrey   USA
b. Rochester, New York 1949

Terry Diehl won the 1969 New York State Amateur and was second in the NCAA Championship. After no other major successes as an amateur he turned professional in 1972 and qualified for the 1974 US Tour season. He then, for nearly every tournament, had to attempt to pre-qualify – and failed on no less than seventeen occasions, in itself by no means an unusual experience for first-year players, many of whom anyway do not go on for a second year. By the last event of the season, he had won just $1,900, with 54th his best position. He qualified for the Texas Open with a 73, then when the tournament proper began opened with a 68 and followed up with 65, 65. The startled Diehl found himself with the lowest 54-hole total of the year and, better, a lead of 4 strokes into the last round. He faltered a little then but still finished with a 71, victory by 1 – and the knowledge that he would not have to pre-qualify (because he was a Tour winner) for the following year. Since that opening season Diehl has won useful sums of money each year, though he has not again set the wires humming. He has only twice made the Top 60 – in 1976 and 1980, with 50th in 1976 being his best money-list position. He has twice again been close to winning: he lost a play-off to Tom Kite for the 1976 IVB-Philadelphia Classic and in 1980 finished second in the Texas Open, 1 stroke behind Lee Trevino.

US wins 1 (1974)
US money $369,183 (1974–82) (124th all-time)

DILL, Mary Lou   USA
b. Eastland, Texas 1948

Winner of the US Amateur in 1967, beating Jean Ashley 5 and 4 in the final, Mary Lou was in the 1968 Curtis Cup team. After college she turned professional, but went into golf instruction rather than tournament play.

DILL, Terrance   USA
b. Fort Worth, Texas 1939

Six-foot 4-inch Terry Dill's best performance as an amateur was to win the 1960 South West Conference title. He turned professional in 1962, going on the US Tour the same year. Dill was a very long driver, hitting a high ball. He was in the Top 60 for 1964, 1966, 1967, 1969 and 1970. He left the Tour in 1971 but returned again in 1974 and made the

Top 60 one more time, in 1975, before leaving again. He went to Britain for a short three-tournament spell in 1966 and won £3,000, good in days of much lower prize money. Many felt that the play of this relatively unknown golfer demonstrated the gulf between the US and British Tours at that time.

US money $237,134 (1962–76)

DOUGLAS, David   USA
b. Philadelphia, Pennsylvania 1918

Dave Douglas played a key role in one of the closest of all Ryder Cup matches, played at Wentworth in 1953. It was won by the USA by 6½ to 5½. In partnership with Ed 'Porky' Oliver, Douglas won the leading foursomes against Harry Weetman and Peter Alliss, and then faced a young Bernard Hunt in the singles towards the bottom of the draw. Hunt came to the last hole 1 up but three-putted; Douglas did not. Douglas won two events on the US circuit, including the 1953 Canadian Open.

DOUGLAS, Findlay S.   Scotland & USA
b. St Andrews 1875; d. 1959

After emigrating to the USA, Douglas was quickly on the fledgeling US golf scene when he reached the semi-finals of the US Amateur the very next year. He then won the event in 1898 and was beaten finalist the next two years, on the second occasion to the redoubtable Walter J. Travis. Douglas reached the semi-finals once again, in 1901; but the competition was getting hotter and his day was done. He was president of the USGA from 1929 to 1930. Two years later he showed that he was still a golfer of quality by taking the USGA Seniors at the age of 57.

DOUGLASS, Dale   USA
b. Wewoka, Oklahoma 1936

Though now a spent force for several years, Dale Douglass was a good enough player to make the 1969 Ryder Cup team in the match at Royal Birkdale, which ended in a memorable tie. Douglass played in one four-ball and one singles and lost in both. This year was in fact a peak of his career, for he won two of his three US Tour events and finished 12th on the US money list with over $91,000, the only time he was inside the top 20. He was in the Top 60 in 1966, from 1968 to 1971 and in 1974. He has not been in the top 100 since 1975,

but is still a regular tournament player. He may also be remembered for taking a 19 at Pebble Beach in 1967.

US wins 3 (1969–70)
US money $542,472 (1963–82) (82nd all-time)

DUDLEY, Edward Bishop   USA
b. Brunswick, Georgia 1901; d. 1963

Ed Dudley had one of the purest golf swings yet seen – or so thought Chick Evans, who rated it with Vardon's, and Henry Cotton, who said it was the most beautiful he had seen. Despite this, Dudley's successes did not quite live up to the quality of his swing; though he won a good share of tournaments. He once looked a likely winner of the US Open after a 70, 70, 71 start in 1937, but a final round of 76 dropped him down the field to fifth place. He had also finished fifth in 1928. In the British Open in 1933 he led after 36 holes, but then fell away to seventh. Perhaps his best major championship performances were reserved for the Masters, appropriate as Dudley was later for some 20 years

Ed Dudley

professional at Augusta. Here he six times finished in the top six between 1934 and 1941, and was third in 1937. Six times he reached the quarter-finals of the US PGA , but only once got to the semi-finals. Probably his best tournament year was 1931, when he took two of the few prestige events of an undeveloped US circuit – the Los Angeles Open and the Western Open. In all he won 22 events in the 1925–42 period, of which some nine or ten would now earn recognition by the US PGA . Dudley was three times a Ryder Cup choice: 1929, 1933 and 1937. He won two of his three foursomes and the only singles in which he played, when he beat Alf Perry in the 1937 match. When his active golf career was over Dudley was prominent in the US PGA , serving as its president from 1942 to 1948.

DUNLAP, George T., Jnr   USA
b. Arlington, New Jersey 1908

Lawson Little was one of the most prodigious amateurs in the years that followed the reign of Bobby Jones, and would have given even him a good run for his money. But George Dunlap defeated Little in the semi-final of the 1933 US Amateur before going on to dismiss a previous winner, Max Marston, in the final. The same year he had also reached the semi-final stage of the British Amateur. A member of the famous Grossett and Dunlap publishing family, he had previously won the NCAA Championship in 1930 and 1931, and was to total seven wins in the North and South Amateur. Although 1933 was certainly Dunlap's best year, he made three Walker Cup appearances. In 1932 his results were outstanding. After taking his foursomes by 7 and 6, he then moved into an even higher gear, in the course of the match shot a 66 and eventually won by 10 and 9.

DUNN, William, Jnr: see Gt Britain & Ireland

DUTRA, Mortimer   USA
b. Monterey, California 1899

The less talented brother of Olin, Mortie is more known as a teacher. He did, however, reach the semi-finals in the 1925 US PGA , and in 1931 was seventh in the US Open. He won only one tournament of note, but compensated in 1955 when he took the US PGA Seniors and then the World event.

DUTRA, Olin   USA
b. Monterey, California 1901

Olin Dutra proved the virtues of both practice and early rising: as a teenager, for several years he used to get up at dawn and play before going to work in a shop. He was to have two major successes. He won the US PGA in 1932, beating Frank Walsh, in the final, and had a memorable victory in the 1934 US Open. After the first two days Gene Sarazen held a 5-stroke lead on him, but on the morning of the final day Dutra counter-attacked with a 71 to Sarazen's 73 and followed with a 72 to a 76. He was third in the US Masters the next year. Dutra was a Ryder Cup choice in 1933 and 1935. In the first year he lost his singles to Abe Mitchell by 9 and 8; but he compensated in 1935, beating Alf Padgham by 4 and 2. Dutra's game lasted well enough for him to shoot a 61 at his home course, Jurupa Hills, at the age of 60. During his active career Dutra won 21 tournaments, of which some eight might today be recognized as of Tour status by the PGA .

EDWARDS, David Wayne   USA
b. Neosha, Missouri 1956

Unlike his brother Richard (Danny), David has yet to make the Top 60 on the US Tour, but shared victory with him in the 1980 Walt Disney Team Championship. They opened with a better-ball score of 60 and held on to the lead this gave them throughout. David was twice an All-American choice – in 1977 and 1978, the year he won the NCAA and qualified for the US Tour. So far his best performance has been a start in the 1980 Bing Crosby National Pro-Am of 67, 69, 72, at which point he held a 2-stroke lead on Larry Nelson and Gil Morgan before he faltered to a 75 at Pebble Beach and finished in seventh place.

US wins 1 (1980)
US money $198,373 (1979–82) (186th all-time)

EDWARDS, Richard Dan   USA
b. Ketchcan, Alaska 1951

One of a pair of brothers on the US Tour, Danny Edwards has four times finished in the Top 60 – in 1977–8, 1980 and 1982 – with a best showing of 28th in 1977, the year he won the Greater Greensboro' Open. With his brother David, he also took the 1980 Walt Disney World National Team Championship. He was an outstanding college golfer, being an All-American choice in 1972 and 1973, and in 1972 won both the North–South and South-eastern Amateurs. He was rewarded with a Walker Cup place the following year, when he also finished leading amateur in the British Open at Troon. (He was the only amateur to qualify for the last round, an increasingly rare achievement in the modern era.) In both these years he also took the Big 8 Conference titles. A steady money-winner every year since he joined the Tour in 1975, he may have been impeded by a passion for Formula Ford racing. After he finished 120th on the money list in 1979 he decided that golf would receive his maximum attention in the future. In 1981 he won the Toshiba Taiheiyo Club Masters in Japan and in 1982 the Greater Greensboro' Open for the second time.

US wins 3 (1977–82)
US money $490,333 (1975–82) (96th all-time)
Overseas wins 1 (1981)

EGAN, H. Chandler USA
b. *Chicago, Illinois 1884; d. 1936*

A long and often wild hitter, Chandler Egan was a leading US amateur in the first decade of the century, and one of the very few to win the US Amateur in consecutive years (1904 and 1905). He dominated both finals to win by 8 and 6 and 6 and 5. Four years later he was runner-up to pole-vault record holder Bob Gardner. Shortly afterwards he went to live in Oregon and found further achievements thwarted conclusively by the fact that there was not a golf course within 300 miles. But Chandler Egan was by no means done for. By 1929 he was back in golfing country and reached the semi-final stage of the US Amateur at the age of 43, and was a Walker Cup player in 1934 at 50. He is credited with remodelling perhaps the USA's greatest seaside course, Pebble Beach, venue for the 1972 and 1982 US Opens.

EGGELING, Dale (née Lundquist) USA
b. *Statesboro, Georgia 1954*

After being runner-up in the Eastern Amateur and a semi-finalist in the Doherty Cup, Dale became a full-time US Tour player in 1977. She won the 1980 Boston Five Classic and was in the top 60 from 1979 to 1982, 23rd in 1981 being her best season.

US wins 1 (1980)
US money $190,936 (1976–82) (55th all-time)

EHRET, Gloria Jean USA
b. *Allentown, Pennsylvania 1941*

Winner of the Connecticut title as an amateur and also the International Four-ball, Glo Ehret was on the US Tour from 1965 to 1979, retiring early in 1980. Her greatest achievement was to win the 1966 US LPGA, beating Mickey Wright by 3 strokes. She had one other win, in the 1973 Birmingham Classic. She was in the top 40 from 1965 to 1978, was 12th in 1966 and 14th in 1972 and 1973.

US wins 2 (1966–73)
US money $235,758 (1965–80) (43rd all-time)

EICHELBERGER, Martin Davis USA
b. *Waco, Texas 1943*

A long hitter and excellent iron player, Dave Eichelberger has been less consistent with the putter and this has led to many ups and downs in his quite long career. As an amateur he reached the semi-final stage of the 1964 US Amateur, and the following year represented his country in both the Americas and Walker Cup. In the latter event, he defeated the British champion, Michael Bonallack. Dave qualified for the US Tour in 1967, but for a few years was by no means successful. His breakthrough came in 1971, during which he played 20 consecutive rounds in par or better and, more important, won his first event, the Greater Milwaukee Open. Together, these achievements took him above the $100,000 mark for the year and to ninth place on the money list when his previously best position had been no better than 88th. Since then he has four more times finished in the Top 60 and has once topped $100,000, though never approaching his 1971 level of performance. He again won the Greater Milwaukee in 1977, and followed with wins in the 1980 Bay Hill Classic and the 1981 Tallahassee Open. Paired with Murle Breer, he also won the 1979 J.C. Penney mixed team event.

In 1981 he finished third in the US Tour statistics for birdies and the previous year recorded 16 eagles. This put him in first place and prompted the query 'How many eichels does Eichelberger have?' The achievement he is least proud of is finishing 33rd in the 1978 Atlanta Classic after closing rounds of 77 and 74. Dave had led by 3 after beginning 62, 69.

US wins 4 (1971–81)
US money $721,753 (1967–82) (61st all-time)

ELDER, Robert Lee   USA
b. *Dallas, Texas 1934*

Lee Elder leapt to fame after beating Peter Oosterhuis in a play-off for the 1974 Monsanto Open. The win itself was not particularly newsworthy, but it automatically qualified him for the US Masters. It had long been asked of Clifford Roberts, longstanding dictator of the championship, why, though all the caddies were black, none of the golfers were. Roberts's custom was to retort that no black player had proved himself good enough, a doubtful proposition in view of the achievements of Charlie Sifford. Over the years, however, though the Masters remained a purely invitational event, strict qualifications were imposed for all categories, one being that any current US Tour winner received an automatic invitation. The appearance of a black face on the fairways of Augusta National became inevitable in time. That face was Lee Elder's but, alas for drama, he failed to survive the halfway cut. A professional since 1959, Lee had had a long wait for his first win on Tour, twice coming close by losing play-offs, including one that went to the fifth extra hole against Jack Nicklaus, in 1968, his first year on the full Tour. Before qualifying for the Tour in 1967 Lee had played on the minor United Golf Association Tour and had recorded a sequence of 21 wins in 23 starts. On the US Tour proper from 1968 to 1978 he was only twice out of the Top 60 and his best year was 1978 when he was 13th on the money list with over $150,000. This led to another first by a black man when he was selected for the Ryder Cup team, at 45 one of the oldest to play in the match. His first important win had come when he took the 1971 Nigerian Open. At Gary Player's invitation, he also played in South Africa. Lee has won four times on the US circuit, twice in 1978. In the Greater Milwaukee of that year he took part in the second-longest sudden-death play-off, beating Lee Trevino on the eighth extra hole, and followed this by victory in one of the richest US tournaments, the Westchester Classic, where he birdied the final hole to edge out Mark Hayes by a single shot. Lee Elder was beyond argument the best black American golfer until the 1982 surge of form from Calvin Peete, who had the most successful single season of a black golfer.

US wins 4 (1974–8)
US money $909,908 (1968–82) (42nd all-time)
World money $1,069,039 (1968–82) (49th all-time)

Lee Elder

von ELM, George   USA
b. *Salt Lake City, Utah 1901; d. 1961*

Three times a Walker Cup player – in 1926, 1928 and 1930 – before eventually turning professional, George von Elm was one of several talented US amateurs whose deeds were considerably obscured by the dominance of Bobby Jones, his almost exact contemporary. Jones crushed him at Merion in 1924 by 9 and 8 in the final of the US Amateur, but two years later they faced each other again in the final at Baltusrol. This time von Elm came through by 2 and 1 against the then current US and British Open Champion. In 1930 he helped establish the record for the most extra holes played in the US Amateur, before losing. Von Elm also featured strongly in Open Championships, finishing third in the 1925 British, fourth in the 1928 US Open and fifth the following year. In 1931 at Inverness, the longest play-off that we are ever likely to see in a major championship took place. Von Elm tied with Billy Burke on 292 and a 36-hole play-off in one day was then the norm. The two tied again on 149 so off they had to go once more. Von Elm again recorded 149 but Burke took the title with one stroke less.

ENGLEHORN, Shirley   USA
b. Caldwell, Idaho 1940

As an amateur Shirley Englehorn won the Idaho Open four times, the state championship in 1956 and 1957 and the Pacific Northwest in 1959. Thereafter she played as a professional in a career that lasted from 1959 to 1980. She first won in 1962 and had an exceptional spell in 1970 during which she won four tournament entries successively, including the US LPGA. From 1962 to 1970 she was only once not in the money list top 10, while her most effective years were 1969 when she was fourth, and 1970 when she was third. She was not higher than 40th thereafter, but her entries had become spasmodic as she spent increasing time in teaching; she was named LPGA Teacher of the Year in 1978. Another award that she won, in 1957, was the Ben Hogan, given for her achievement in returning to winning golf after a serious car smash in 1965 (as Hogan himself had returned). In the early 1970s she also had to recover from ankle surgery.

US wins 11 (1962–70)
US money $181,134 (1959–80)

ESPINOSA, Albert R.   USA
b. Monterey, California 1894; d. 1957

The winner of several US tournaments from the mid 1920s and of the Mexican Open when in his mid 50s, Al Espinosa represented the USA in both the 1929 and 1931 Ryder Cup matches. He also reached the final of the 1928 US PGA after reaching the semi-final the year before. It is, however, for his performance in the 1929 US Open that he is most remembered. Bobby Jones had opened a dominating lead during the final round and then began to fritter strokes away to finish in 79, even that achieved at the last gasp by one of the best putts he ever made, a curling 12-footer on the last green. This tied him with Al, who had finished with a 75. The play-off was over 36 holes and Jones requested that the start be delayed to allow Espinosa, a Roman Catholic, to attend mass. Jones then went into overdrive, coming in with 141 and leaving Espinosa no less than 23 strokes in his slipstream – perhaps the heaviest play-off defeat ever recorded.

EVANS, Charles, Jnr   USA
b. Indianapolis, Indiana 1890; d. 1979

Chick Evans was a competitor for 50 years, as late as 1961 competing in the US Amateur at Pebble Beach and qualifying for the US Open in 1953. After he took the Western Amateur in 1909, an achievement he was to repeat on seven other occasions, including four consecutively, he was soon recognized as a major player, but his first championship victory was to be delayed a few years. In 1911 he was for the third time in a row defeated in the semi-finals of the US Amateur, and then in 1912 he reached the final only to lose by 7 and 6 to Jerry Travers after he had held a 3-up lead. However, in 1911 he had won the French Amateur after James Braid had persuaded him to change from the baseball grip to the Vardon; and even before this in 1910 had won the Western Open against a full professional field. In 1914 he came close to winning the US Open, finishing just 1

Chick Evans

stroke behind Walter Hagen, champion for the first time. In 1916 came his finest hour. He led the US Open all the way and with a total of 286 set a record that was to last for 20 years, winning by 2 strokes from Jock Hutchison. To do it, he only used seven clubs: brassie, spoon, jigger, mid-iron, lofter, niblick and putter. He is also said to have kept three putters in reserve, some comment on the fact that this was the weakest part of a game that was based on a simple rhythmic swing and excellent iron play. As he aged, he was wont to experiment, and adopted a 46-inch driver to increase clubhead arc as his muscles grew less supple. At last in 1916 he also took the US Amateur in dominating style, preceding his 4 and 3 win over the defending champion Bob Gardner in the final by two of 10 and 9 and 9 and 8. He had become the first man to win the US Amateur and Open in the same year and is still the only man apart from Bobby Jones to have done so. He took the US Amateur again in 1920, crushing Francis Ouimet in the final by 7 and 6, and twice more reached the final, in 1922 and 1927, this last time being defeated by Jones, who had a spell of seven 3s in 11 holes.

FAIRFIELD, Donald   USA
b. Wichita, Kansas 1929

After turning professional at the age of 18, Don Fairfield joined the US Tour in 1954, and two years later had his first victory in the Pensacola Open. Later he won the St Paul and also the Oklahoma City Opens. He now plays on the US Senior Tour.

US wins 3 (1956–63)
US money $142,435 (1954–81)

FARRELL, John J.   USA
b. White Plains, New York 1901

At his best in the late 1920s to the early 1930s, Johnny Farrell was three times a Ryder Cup player and featured strongly in both British and US Open Championships. In 1929 he finished second behind the inevitable Walter Hagen at Muirfield, and he was fourth to Tommy Armour in the 1931 Carnoustie Open. In the US Open he was fifth in 1923 and then equal third in both 1925 and 1926. At Olympia Field Country Club, Illinois, in 1928, came arguably his greatest achievement: he faced Bobby Jones in a 36-hole play-off for the title. Sinking a 7-foot putt on the last hole made Farrell the champion by 143 to 144. Although Johnny had a graceful swing the ball did not go very far, but he was as

good a putter as anyone. This, at least in part, may account for his winning money in every start in 1923 and 1924 and his eight wins in 1927, including seven in sequence. This bettered his five wins of the previous year. He became a member of the Golf Hall of Fame in 1961.

FAULK, Mary Lena   USA
b. Chipley, Florida 1926

Mary Faulk won the US title in 1953, beating Polly Ann Riley in the final, and the same year reached the semi-final of the British Ladies'. In 1954 she reached the semi-final of the US Amateur where she was defeated by Mickey Wright; she went on to represent the US in the Curtis Cup. She then turned professional and was on the US Tour from 1955, finishing joint second in the US Open her first season. She first won in 1956 and her best year was 1961, when she had four victories.

US wins 10 (1956–64)

FAZIO, George   USA
b. Norristown, Pennsylvania 1912

In recent years, George Fazio has become well known as a golf-course designer in partnership with his brother. He has been responsible for changes to several US Open courses. As a professional golfer he was at his best after World War II into the early 1950s, though his greatest achievement in 1950, to tie for the US Open at Merion, was totally overshadowed by the mass interest in Ben Hogan, making his comeback after a serious road accident. When Hogan, Mangrum and Fazio played off, the latter two did little to disturb a fairy-tale ending and Hogan became Open Champion by 4 over Mangrum and 6 over Fazio. Fazio was later to finish fifth and fourth in the US Open; but his most important success was a win in the 1946 Canadian Open, which he won after a play-off with Dick Metz. The following year he was joint winner of the Crosby with Ed Furgol.

FERGON, Vicki   USA
b. Palo Alto, California 1955

An all-round sportswoman, Vicki Fergon came a little late to golf and in consequence did not have a substantial record of achievement when she turned professional. She qualified for the US Tour in the summer of 1977 and in the competition for places finished 9 strokes ahead of Nancy Lopez, who was to become the leading player so soon afterwards. Playing full-time from 1978, Vicki Fergon had her best season to date in 1979, finishing 18th in the money list and taking her first tournament, the Lady Stroh's. She was also within the top 50 in the following two seasons. She is one of the longer hitters in the Tour and outstanding with the long irons.

US wins 1 (1979)
US money $160,886 (1978–82)

FERGUS, Keith Carlton   USA
b. *Temple, Texas 1954*

One of the multitude of US Tour players who have come via the collegiate route, Keith Fergus was for three years an All-American choice (1974–6) and was runner-up in the 1975 US Amateur. Deciding to turn professional in 1976, he was medallist at the qualifying school by a clear 10 strokes. His progress on Tour has been steady as he has worked his way up the money list from 84th in his first year to 21st in 1981. He has made the Top 60 each year from 1978. By 1980 he was looking a possible major player and his consistency meant that he achieved the unusual feat of not once failing to make the 36-hole cut that year. Additionally, he completed 14 consecutive rounds in par or better that year, the best on Tour, and finished fifth in the stroke averages with 70.75. Three times he was third, including the US Open, and his consistency took him past $100,000 for the first time. By the end of the season he was regarded as the best Tour player without a win. That was put right in 1981 when he won the Jack Nicklaus Memorial Tournament at Muirfield Village, an event that has rapidly established itself as only just below the major championships in prestige, and played over one of America's most demanding courses. At the end of the season he had passed $150,000. This included $1,617 won in the US Masters, despite having been penalized six strokes for twice mistakenly picking and dropping from a fairway crossing-point. In 1982 he won the Atlanta Classic and had winnings of over $100,000 for the third year running. He looks to have many more tournament successes ahead of him. Keith is considered one of the best strikers on the Tour and a straight driver, but his putting is less impressive.

US wins 2 (1981–82)
US money $575,048 (1976–82) (78th all-time)

FERRARIS, Janis Jean   USA
b. *San Francisco, California 1947*

Winner of numerous California junior golf titles, Jan Ferraris took the national event also in 1963 and was named the state's Golfer of the Year at that time. She turned professional in 1966 and was Rookie of the Year. Thereafter she was in the top 40 on the money list from 1966 to 1972; her best placing has been 16th in 1970. She was in the Top 60 until 1977. Jan also won twice on Tour, the 1971 Orange Blossom Classic and the 1972 Pepsi. She also took the unofficial 1973 Japan Classic.

US wins 2 (1971–2)
US money $160,593 (1966–82)

FERREE, Purvis Jennings   USA
b. *Pine Bluff, North Carolina 1931*

Now active on the relatively new US Senior Tour, Jim Ferree turned professional in 1956 and joined the Tour the same year. Never a big-name player, he did win four events including the Jamaica, Panama and Maracaibo Opens. His best year was 1959, when he finished 22nd on the money list.

US wins 1 (1958)
US money $107,719 (236th all-time)

FETCHICK, Michael   USA
b. *Yonkers, New York 1922*

After turning professional in 1950, Mike Fetchick joined the Tour in 1952, and his first win followed three years later. The Western Open has now declined in prestige, but it is the oldest US tournament and had not lost its aura in 1956 when Mike won after an 18-hole play-off with three other competitors: he beat them by 5 clear strokes. He is now a member of the Senior Tour.

US wins 4 (1955–64)
US money $44,648

FEZLER, Forrest Oliver   USA
b. *Hayward, California 1949*

Forrest Fezler is recognizable from billowing hair and a luxuriant moustache, and his name is one that is heard from time to time, though less frequently during the last few years. He turned professional in 1969 and went on Tour three years later, rapidly coming to be regarded as a player with an extremely promising future. By 1974 he had been second five times, once in the most important event of them all, the US Open, when he finished one behind Hale Irwin in 1974. However, late in the year he took one of the less prestigious events, the Southern Open, shooting a last-round 65 to do so. He was in the top 50 from 1973 to 1976, his best year being 1973, when he won $106,390 to finish 12th in the money list.

US wins 1 (1974)
US money $476,188 (1972–82) (98th all-time)

FINSTERWALD, Dow USA
b. Athens, Ohio 1929

It has been said of Finsterwald that he was too cautious a player, too unwilling to risk the bold approach direct to the flag if water or bunker threatened. Instead he preferred to play for safe parts of greens, so the birdies were fewer than they might have been. But this very conservatism made him one of the most consistent scorers of his era, so much so that at one time he held the record for the most consecutive survivals of the halfway cut. Among his fellow Tour players, Dow was also thought of as one of the finest contemporary shot-makers, able to cut and draw the ball at will, and

Dow Finsterwald

one of the straightest hitters from the tee. He was also a very reliable putter. Dow joined the Tour in 1952, not discouraged by the fact that he had taken no fewer than 11 on the par-3 12th hole in the previous year's Masters – there had been more than one visit to water. His peak covered the years 1955–63, but 1956–60 in particular. In that spell of five years he was always in the top three on the money list and second in both 1956 and 1958. From 1960 onwards his game faded in effectiveness and he played very little in the 1970s. In 1956 he won the Canadian Open, the following year he was second in the US PGA and a year after he won it. His best placing in the US Open was third in 1960. The Masters in 1962 saw a triple tie of Finsterwald, Palmer and Player, but that was a time when Palmer was winning almost at will and he duly took the 18-hole play-off. Among other honours, he was once named PGA Player of the Year, and won the Vardon Trophy for the year's lowest stroke average in 1957. He was selected for the US Ryder Cup side on every occasion between 1957 and 1963 and was later non-playing captain.

US wins 12 (1955–63)
US money $402,102 (112th all-time)

FIORI, Edward Ray USA
b. Lynwood, California 1953

Ed Fiori is one of those golfers whose short and frankly fat body makes non-aficionados of the game believe that golf does not require much in the way of athleticism. When the aficionado sees him swing a club, he is apt to wince at the lack of charm in the performance. Fiori crouches over the ball, his grip well down the shaft, and as the man himself says: 'I don't watch myself on TV for fear of picking up even more bad habits!' He was chosen All-American in 1977 and tried the qualifying school that autumn, finishing as medallist. His first win came in 1979 with the Southern Open and he was in the Top 60 in 1980, 1981 and 1982. In 1981 he won the Western Open and passed $100,000 for 36th place in the money list. In the 1982 Hope he reeled off rounds of 70, 65, 66, 67, 67, which was good enough only to tie with Tom Kite. On the first play-off hole, Kite struck an iron 4 feet from the flag while Ed was a woeful 40 feet away. Fiori sank the monster putt and Kite's confidence was dented enough for him to miss.

US wins 3 (1979–82)
US money $360,872 (1978–82) (128th all-time)

FISCHER, John William   USA

b. Cincinnati, Ohio 1912

One of the few players to win a sequence of Walker Cup singles (1934, 1936 and 1938), Fischer was US Amateur Champion in 1936. In this final he confronted Jack M'Lean, the first British player to reach the final in many a long year. With three holes to go, Fischer was 1 down. On the 34th hole he laid M'Lean a stymie to halve the hole and then birdied the last from 12 feet to save the match. On the first extra hole, Fischer went one better, this time holing out from some 20 feet for another birdie, and the title was his. John Fischer had first come to attention in 1932 when he took the NCAA Championship and, incidentally, beat Lawson Little in the first round of the US Amateur, something few were to do during his dominant career as an amateur. He was also twice medallist in qualifying for the matchplay stages of the US Amateur and his 141 in 1933 set a record for the time. He was non-playing Walker Cup captain in 1965.

FITZSIMMONS, Pat   USA

b. Coos Bay, Oregon 1950

In the last two or three decades, the clothing of tournament golfers has attracted more than its share of attention. The trend in the early 1980s has been away from multicoloured trousers and funny hats and towards quiet matching outfits that usually tone in with sky, sand, heather and fairway. The Doug Sanders and Faulkners are no more, though many of the trousers sported still might look better with a pyjama top. Pat Fitzsimmons was a trend-setter in a different way. An earlier generation had felt, particularly in Britain, that golf was a game played in rain and mud and that the appropriate attire was what one might choose to wear when making an asparagus bed (Vardon and Taylor, for instance, played off for an Open wearing working-men's boots). Fitzsimmons adopted the modern equivalent: scruffy jeans and dishevelled hair. As an amateur he won both the Northwest and Oregon Opens and qualified for the Tour in 1972. His outstanding achievement and only tournament win came three years later when he took the prestige Los Angeles Open, much helped by a 64 in the third round, and pushed eternal runner-up Tom Kite into second place. A year earlier, he had almost decided to leave the Tour, but happened to play a round on his home course with a representative of grass growers Penncross Manhattan. Pat breezed round in 58 and the firm decided to put up sponsorship money for him to continue. In 1975 he featured strongly in the US Open, being in second place with a round to go, and again in the Westchester Classic and World Open. The end of the year saw him in 20th place with $86,181 after previous years of 225th, 118th and 143rd – small wonder he had considered quitting. But alas, this was the one year that Pat made the Top 60 and soon he was playing only spasmodically on Tour.

US wins   1 (1975)
US money $149,298 (1972–82) (215th all-time)

FLECK, Jack   USA

b. Bettendorf, Iowa 1921

Jack turned professional in 1939 but it was not until as late as 1954 that he first decided to pit himself against the boys on the US Tour. The results were not encouraging and when he turned up at the Olympic Country Club in San Francisco for the 1955 US Open his confidence could not have been improved by practice rounds that were said to have gone into the 80s. At that time all eyes continued to be upon Ben Hogan and the question everyone was asking was 'Will Ben Hogan beat the record by taking his fifth US Open?' There were a few also hoping to see Sam Snead get his first. It is not likely that anyone watched Jack Fleck till the four rounds were nearly over. Olympic was a very tough test that year. There are always trees in plenty there, but the rough had been allowed to grow into the fairways and was so dense that if you hit into it it was highly risky to take anything other than a lofted iron to get yourself out again. So although Hogan's total of 287 may seem unimpressive it was ahead of everybody else, and few players were still out on the course. (This was, of course, in the days before the leaders were sent out last.) Congratulations on Hogan's fifth win were showered upon him and though he pointed out that the tournament was not over he was doubtless sure that he had become the first to win five times. A rumour began to spread that there was a man with three or four holes to play that did have a chance. The name of Fleck was mentioned; few had heard of him. Jack came to the last needing a birdie 3 for a 67 to tie Hogan. He hit a good drive just off the fairway, a 7-iron a few feet from the hole and in due course, down went the putt. Quite a surprise. Of course, Hogan would crush him in the play-off the next day. Hogan came to the last hole the next day 1 in arrears. He then hooked his drive sharp left into the longest patch of rough on the whole course. His first attempt to move the ball failed but after two more tries he regained the fairway. It was a minor miracle that he took only a 6 after an iron to the green a long way from the hole and a huge putt. But the contest was over already. Jack Fleck had a steady 4 and was in with a 69 to Hogan's 72. Those four days are just about the whole story of Jack Fleck's golfing life. He did not make a million, and indeed returned to his former obscurity. There were a couple more tournaments won and he did feature in the Top 60 from 1955 to 1957 and 1959 to 1963 with a creditable 18th in 1960. That year he again threatened to win the US Open, finishing equal third and thwarted by Arnold Palmer's famous last-round 65. Later, in 1979, he took the World and US Seniors.

US wins 3 (1955–61)
US money $129,898 (1954–81) (226th all-time)

FLECKMAN, Marty   USA
b. Port Arthur, Texas 1944

Marty is one of that quite large band of golfers who sparkle as striplings, are about to achieve great things – and then are gone. Winner of the NCAA Championship in 1965, he joined the Tour in 1967 and caused a sensation by winning the Cajun Classic, the first tournament he entered. This was, however, not entirely a surprise. He had earlier led the US Open by 2 after one round and after three rounds was still 1 in the lead, the first amateur since Johnny Goodman in 1933 to be ahead at so late a stage. Alas, there followed an 80, and Marty came in 18th equal.

US wins 1 (1967)
US money $162,455 (207th all-time)

FLEISCHER, Bruce   USA
b. Union City, Tennessee 1948

In 1968 Bruce was the NCAA junior college champion and, as an unknown, US Amateur Champion. The next year he represented the USA in the World Amateur Team Championship and the Walker Cup. In the latter he had a famous encounter with Michael Bonallack, winning five holes in a row to square his singles. As an amateur he was arrogant and a figure of some glamour. Great things were predicted for him when he turned professional the following year. However, Bruce has never made the

magic Top 60. He came closest in 1981: 64th, with winnings of $69,221.

US money $230,680 (1972–82) (172nd all-time)

FLENNIKEN, Carol: see Sorenson

FLOYD, Marlene (later DeArman)   USA
b. Fayetteville, North Carolina 1948

The sister of Ray, Marlene is a successful Tour player and one of the best putters. While working as a hostess for United Airlines she won the Hawaiian Women's in 1974 and 1975, this in spite of not having tried golf until she was 19. She broke 100 at her first attempt and in her first competition, when playing off an 8 handicap, reached the final of the North Carolina State Championship. She then played little golf for some time. Before the Hawaiian experience she had also competed in national events. In 1976 she began to play the US Tour, successfully after her first season, and has been in the top 60 in 1977–81, her best years being 1979 and 1981, when she was 24th on the money list. She has yet to win a tournament but has had third places. Commercially she is very successful, having her own line of golf clothes and endorsement contracts with several companies. In 1980 she had the lowest average of putts per round, 29.80; and after a play-off she was runner-up for the J & B Gold Putter award.

US money $185,754 (1976–82) (58th all-time)

FLOYD, Raymond Loran   USA
b. Fort Bragg, North Carolina 1942

Ray 'Pretty Boy' Floyd, since his debut on the Tour in 1963, has never been out of the top 80 and in a 19-year career has only twice been out of the Top 60. For the past eight years, his best, he has always been in the top 30 with a highest finish of second in 1982, a year in which he won a monumental $386,809. Floyd's start on Tour was hardly encouraging as he missed the halfway cut in nine of the first ten events for which he entered, but then there was a sudden and unexpected jackpot as he won the St Petersburg Open; at a mere 20 years 5 months old he was the third youngest winner of all time on Tour. Despite this early success Ray did not become a major force in US and world golf until the mid 1970s. Since 1974 he has just once failed to top $100,000 on the US Tour. His dominance of the 1976 US Masters, in which he led from start to finish and won by a record 8 strokes (from Ben Crenshaw) and equalled the Nicklaus 271 record, established him finally as one of the biggest names in contemporary golf, a man whose prospects are always now assessed prior to one of the four major championships. Perhaps full commitment was what Floyd most lacked for many years. Golf came a poor second to night-life. In the 1960s Floyd was quoted as saying that the colour of his eyes was 'usually pretty red' and 'If there's anything better than women I don't know what it is.' Three or four in the morning was his bedtime, though during a tournament he might reform sufficiently to get his head down by a mere hour after midnight. During this period his closest companions were the carousing Doug Sanders and Al Besselink. Ray also had an unusual business on the side: he managed 'The Ladybirds', who claimed to be the first topless band. After that first win in 1963 Floyd won again in 1965 and had his first outstanding year in 1969, when he topped $100,000, came eighth on the US money list and won three tournaments. One of these was highly significant – the US PGA. Ray promptly relaxed and did not win again until as late as 1975. Then came that career best performance in the 1976 Masters which led hosts of Americans to purchase a 5-wood. Floyd had decided that the greens on the Augusta par 5s needed to be attacked with a higher trajectory of shot than that of the long irons. Mainly using this club, he was no less than 13 under par on them for the tournament, while his rounds of 65, 66, 70, 70 meant that, besides equalling the Nicklaus record, he had also set up his own for the best 36- and 54-hole totals. He had 21 birdies and an eagle. His putting was also formidable during the event and temporarily brought into vogue the 'Zebra' putter, which Ray used for a few years before taking to a Ping. For some time he used a golden Ping, though he hastily hung it on the wall when he learned that it was, in fact, made of gold. He could have afforded to lose it. In March 1981 he made no less than $317,000 in a mere eight days when he took the Doral Eastern Open and followed up with the Tournament Players Championship. The fact that these wins were consecutive brought him a $200,000 bonus, which must have given him an extremely comfortable feeling so early in the year. For the remainder of the 1981 season, the characteristic Floyd lurching sway was much in evidence: on the US Tour, he did not once fail to make the cut and won once more. In recent years,

Ray Floyd

Floyd has been very much an international player. He has won the Brazilian Open, the Costa Rica Cup and the Canadian PGA and is a frequent visitor to Britain, where he has finished second and third in the Open (1978 and 1981). He has also played in the Ryder Cup four times. His best season yet was 1982, producing US money winnings of $386,809, behind only Craig Stadler, while he added the US PGA to his major championship record. This he won by 3 strokes with rounds of 63, 69, 68, 72 to add to two previous Tour wins in the season. At the end of the year he won the Sun City $1 Million Challenge in Bophuthatswana, golf's richest tournament, beating Craig Stadler in the play-off on the 4th extra hole for a first prize of $185,185. He could thus claim to be the best golfer of the year.

US wins 18 (1963–82)
US money $2,178,796 (1963–82) (4th all-time)
Europe money £75,445 (47th all-time)
World money $2,853,581 (1963–82) (5th all-time)

FORD, Douglas USA
b. West Haven, Connecticut 1922

Joining the US Tour in 1950, Doug Ford had his peak years from 1951 to 1960. In that period, he was never worse than tenth in the US money lists. Three more good years followed and Doug then faded from the tournament scene. His successes were gained in spite of a short, awkward swing and in some degree were due to his excellent short game. One of his most famous victories, the 1957 US Masters, illustrates this particularly well. Doug holed a bunker shot for a birdie on the last for a 66, easily the lowest round of those in contention, and beat Sam Snead by 3. He won one other major championship, the 1955 US PGA, and in that year was also named Player of the Year and came third in the money list to add to his second-place finishes in 1953 and 1957. He also twice won the Canadian Open, an event that ranks only a litle below major championship status, but he never came particularly close to taking his own national Open: fifth and sixth in 1959 and 1961 were his best finishes. Doug did not miss a Ryder Cup between 1955 and 1961 and now although near 60, is effective on the Senior Tour, coming seventh in 1981 and making $70,444.

US wins 19 (1952–63)
US money $414,663 (1950–82) (108th all-time)

FOUGHT, John Allen USA
b. Portland, Oregon 1954

After victories in the Pacific Coast Amateur and Pacific Northwest Open, John Fought represented the USA in 1976 in the World Amateur Team event. The following year he was in the Walker Cup team and his amateur career peaked when he took the US Amateur Championship. He soon turned professional, but all did not immediately go well for he twice failed the Tour qualifying school; but he was co-medallist at the end of 1978. In his first year on Tour John won money in only 14 of the 32 events he entered and finished in the top 10 of a tournament just twice. But this was enough to take his money winnings to $108,427, the third highest won by anyone in their first full competitive season, and also gained him the 'Rookie of the Year' award. For John had won two tournaments in succession, the Buick-Goodwrench Open and the Anheuser-Busch Classic. For his first win, his playing of the par-4 18th hole at Warwick Hills was intriguing. At the first two attempts he double-bogeyed it each time and improved little at the third try with a bogey. When he stood on the tee for the last time he was 1 behind the lead and this time hit a vast drive, knocked an 8-iron some 3 yards from the flag and holed the putt. He then won the play-off on the first extra hole. The next week he

won the Anheuser-Busch; again a birdie on the last secured a win, this time without previous traumas. Fought seemed set for future glories. But not so: from 32nd in the 1979 money list he sank to 65th in 1980, 124th in 1981 and 125th in 1982.

US wins 2 (1979)
US money $220,106 (1979–82) (178th all-time)

FRASER, Alexa: see Stirling

FUNSETH, Rod USA
b. Spokane, Washington 1933

The name of Funseth is one that seems to have been around for years. He is one of those journeymen US Tour professionals who seldom win but have inexorably built up a very respectable bank balance. He turned professional in 1956 and joined the Tour in 1961. Since then he has won three times, his victories being well spaced out: in 1965, 1973 and 1978. There is little doubt that his greatest moments came in the 1978 Masters. After an opening 73, his 66 in the second round put him in the eyes of the TV cameras and succeeding rounds of 70 and 69 kept him there until the final shots had been played. Funseth, like Tom Watson and Hubert Green, had a putt to tie the score of 277 that Gary Player had set with his record-equalling final 64. He missed and so did they, and together they finished equal second. Statistically his rounds of 65, 67, 68 and 64 in the Greater Hartford Open the same year look more impressive, but the Weathersfield course in Connecticut is one of the easiest on Tour and in that year's event you would have to go down to nearly 40th place in the results before coming across the first unfortunate golfer not to average under 70 a round. Nevertheless, Funseth won by 4 strokes, an unusually large margin on a low-scoring course. This was a surprising win, because Funseth is very much a golfer expected to par most of the holes but to make relatively few birdies – steady rather than spectacular – and more apt to be among the leaders on tight courses where avoiding bogeys is the target. In 1972, however, he set the Pebble Beach record at 64, and that is arguably the toughest course in the USA. Between 1963 and 1978 Funseth was always in the top 100; his years in the Top 60 were 1965–7, 1969–73, 1975 and 1978, the latter being his best year, at 28th.

US wins 3 (1965–78)
US money $644,381 (1961–82) (72nd all-time)

FURGOL, Edward   USA
b. *New York Mills, New York 1917*

Immediately after World War II Ed Furgol turned professional and joined the Tour in 1945. He came to it with one of the most severe physical handicaps that has been seen in a major golfer. His left arm is shorter than the right, withered, crooked and stiff at the elbow joint. And this is the arm that majority opinion would argue is the more important of the two for the golf swing. In fact, watching Furgol swing a club gave one a very distinct impression that he was hitting almost solely with the right hand and arm, the left being merely positioned at the top of the grip. He is variously credited with between five and seven US Tour wins (it is clear enough today which are official, recognized events, but the lines were drawn more indistinctly until recent times). There is no doubt at all, however, about one achievement: he won the 1954 US Open at Baltusrol, with Gene Littler in second place. Ed Furgol was in the Top 60 from 1945 to 1948 and 1950 to 1957, with a highest placing of seventh in 1957. He was also given the Player of the Year award in 1954, and in 1955 was individual winner of the Canada (now World) Cup. As defending champion, in the 1955 US Open he had an unusual experience. When Jack Fleck tied with Ben Hogan, the shock struck Fleck dumb. At a press gathering, Furgol held him up and did all the talking. It was Furgol's turn to be struck dumb when he played in the 1955 British Open at St Andrews. He complained to an aged retainer about the lack of showers, and was told: 'Their Lordships are accustomed to repair to their castles to bathe after a round of golf.'

US wins 7 (1947–57)
US money $124,137 (228th all-time)

FURGOL, Marty   USA
b. *New York Mills, New York 1918*

A good putter but a short hitter, Marty was a golfer of the 1950s. He turned professional before World War II and joined the Tour in 1947, his first wins coming in 1951 with the Houston and Western Opens. He won again in 1954 and twice in the last year of the decade, and was a Ryder Cup player in 1955. He is not related to Ed, although born in the same town.

US wins 5 (1951–9)
US money $135,684 (1947–59) (221st all-time)

GARBACZ, Lori   USA
b. *South Bend, Indiana 1958*

Winner of the Indiana Amateur in 1978, the same year Lori lost the final of the Trans-National to Nancy Lopez. In 1978 she won the Mexican Amateur. In 1979, her first year on Tour, she was second to Beth Daniels for Rookie of the Year honours and was 34th on the money list, improving to 16th and winning $61,120 the following year. She fell away to 58th in 1981. Lori Garbacz has yet to win a US LPGA tournament but has finished second. She won an event in Japan late in the 1982 season.

US money $145,849 (1979–82)

GARDNER, Robert A.   USA
b. *Hinsdale, Illinois 1890*

A very considerable all-round athlete, Bob Gardner was US Racquets Champion at doubles in 1926 and had earlier set the world pole-vault record, being the first man past the magic 13-foot mark. As a golfer, he was a name to conjure with for 15 years and more. In 1909 he took the US Amateur Championship for the first time at the age of 19 years 3 months, and he repeated the victory in 1915. He again reached the final the following year when in the third round he put out the young prodigy, Bobby Jones, who was making his first appearance on the national scene. He reached the final only once more, in 1921. He also reached the final of the British Amateur in 1920 when he was beaten by Cyril Tolley, who holed a long putt to do it, on the 37th green. He was four times a Walker Cup choice between 1922 and 1926, in the latter year as captain.

GARDNER, Robert W.   USA
b. *Hollywood, California 1921*

In a brief top amateur career, Bob Gardner was twice a Walker Cup player, in 1961 and 1963; he also played in the World Amateur Team Championship in 1960 and the Americas Cup the following year. He also once reached the final of the French Amateur and was twice a quarter-finalist in the British. In 1960 he was beaten by Deane Beman in the final of the US Amateur. As a professional he won the San Diego Open and the California Open twice, while in the minor Metropolitan Open he won five times consecutively between 1960 and 1964.

GEIBERGER, Allen Lee   USA
b. Red Bluff, California 1937

Al Geiberger immortalized himself by one round of golf, a 59 in the second round of the 1977 Memphis Classic, and that over a course measuring 7,249 yards at the Colonial Country Club. It was, of course, a record and has led to Geiberger now being popularly known as 'Mr 59'. The score has been done before – indeed lower ones have been recorded – but not on a course of full length in a fully recognized US Tour event. Geiberger's figures make interesting reading and his other rounds indicate the playing qualities of the Memphis Country Club: 72, 59, 72, 70. As is not unusual, Geiberger began on the 10th and completed the half in 30. The other took him 29. He had 6 pars, 11 birdies and an eagle, and on the last hole played had to hole an 8-foot putt for a birdie to break 60. Perhaps it may stand for some time as the greatest round of golf ever played, though not on a particularly great occasion. His 23 putts were by no means a record, but it was a miserly enough ration. Geiberger turned professional in 1959 and joined the Tour in 1960 after taking the National Jaycees in 1954. He was immediately in the Top 60 and remained there until 1969, returning again from 1973 to 1977 and in 1979. He has five times finished in the top 10 and his peak years came late – in 1975 and 1976, when he won $175,000 and $194,000, finishing sixth and fifth respectively. It is probable that his career is nearly over for he has long been plagued by both ill-health and injury. His slump from 1969 to 1972 was caused by a 'nervous stomach' disorder which allowed him to play the Tour only spasmodically. It was during this phase that he became known for his custom of taking peanut-butter sandwiches out on the course to quell his uneasy stomach. There were those who thought that it was the intense stress of professional golf that was Geiberger's undoing, but time has shown that there was more to it than that. In 1978, intestinal surgery became necessary and then late the following year there was a knee operation also. In 1980 his colon was removed and there were two further operations, one of which was said to involve removing a growth 'the size of a football'. Geiberger has taken one major championship, the 1966 US PGA, and has twice been second in the US Open – in 1969 and 1976. In 1975 he took the near majors of the Tournament Players Championship and the Tournament of Champions. He has twice played in the Ryder Cup team, 1967 and 1975. His win in the 1962 Caracas Open is his only one outside the US.

US wins 11 (1962–79)
US money $1,214,051 (1960–82) (23rd all-time)
World money $1,460,338 (1960–82) (26th all-time)

GERMAIN, Dorothy (formerly Porter)   USA
b. Atlantic, Iowa 1947

As an amateur, Dot Germain won the 1967 Broadmoor Invitational and the Arkansas state championship three times between 1968 and 1972. She turned professional in 1973 and has played the US Tour since 1974. Most unusually, between 1974 and 1981, her statistics show progress each year: from 97th down to 18th on the money list, while her stroke average has lowered from 77.40 in 1974 to 73.03 in 1981. She has won one Tour event, the 1980 S & H Golf Classic; she almost retained it the following year, losing a play-off to JoAnne Carner, who is famed for her abilities in this essentially matchplay situation. Dot Germain's mother is a teaching professional, and an aunt won the US Seniors in 1977, 1980 and 1981.

US wins 1 (1980)
US money $275,080 (1974–82) (35th all-time)

Al Geiberger

Vic Ghezzi

GHEZZI, Victor   USA
b. *Rumson, New Jersey 1912; d. 1976*

A tall, handsome figure, Vic Ghezzi won several US events, beginning with the Los Angeles Open in 1935. He reached Ryder Cup status in 1939, and in 1941 beat no less than Byron Nelson on the 38th green to take the US PGA. Later he featured in a memorable play-off for the US Open in 1946. After he had tied with Lloyd Mangrum and Byron Nelson, the trio all recorded 72s in the 18-hole play-off and they had to go out again. This time Nelson and Ghezzi had 73s and Mangrum, with 72, was champion. Vic Ghezzi was elected to the Golf Hall of Fame in 1965.

US wins 13

GIBSON, Althea (later Darben)   USA
b. *Silver, South Carolina 1927*

Winner of both US and Wimbledon singles at tennis in 1957 and 1958, Althea Gibson turned to golf the following year, having previously played only occasionally. She was winning competitions and was a club champion by 1962 and turned

professional in 1963, becoming the first black member of the US LPGA the following year. She competed regularly from 1964 to 1969 on the US Tour and was in the top 50 from 1964 to 1971, her best years being 1967 when she was 23rd on the money list, and 1970 when she came her closest to winning an LPGA event, the Immke Buick Open. She tied for first place and lost the play-off. In 1975 she was appointed Athletic Commissioner for the State of New Jersey.

US money $25,000 approx. (1964–75)

GILBERT, C.L., Jnr   USA
b. *Chattanooga, Tennessee 1941*

Nicknames have all manner of causes but Gilbert's is a new one. He was christened 'C.L.'. Someone had to call him something, and 'Gibby' it became. His surname too has grown on the golfing public, through the occasional win or outstanding performance. In the 1971 Westchester Classic, for instance, he birdied no fewer than six holes in a row, and the following year in Pinehurst Number 2 shattered the course record by 3 strokes with a 62. He turned professional in 1964 and first played on the Tour in 1968, having little success for his first two and a half seasons before winning the Houston Champions in 1970. Between that year and 1980 he was nine times in the Top 60 and tied for second place in the 1980 Masters. Because of his consistency – and today's inflated prize money – he reached the top 50 of all-time money-winners.

US wins 3 (1970–77)
US money $841,911 (1968–82) (50th all-time)

GILDER, Robert Bryan   USA
b. *Corvallis, Oregon 1950*

After turning professional in 1973 Bob Gilder three times failed to win his Tour card but filled in some of the time competing overseas, a phase during which he took the 1974 New Zealand Open after a play-off with Bob Charles and Jack Newton. When he did qualify for the Tour he immediately made an impact, becoming only the fourth player to top $100,000 during a first year. He won the Phoenix Open (the second event he played in) and came 24th in the money list. He has three times more exceeded $100,000. His best years were 1980, when he finished 19th and topped $150,000, helped by victory in the Canadian Open, and 1982, with no less than $308,648 for sixth place in the money list. He won three events and was chosen to represent the USA in the World Cup. Able to bend the ball both ways, Bob has had only one poor year, 1977, when he lost the ability to draw his shots, and found that his always excellent putting alone was not enough. Among his later achievements was a round of 62 in the 1979 New Orleans Open and a fourth-place finish in the 1981 US PGA, but 1982 brought him into the superstar limelight. Winning three events in a year is now quite a rare accomplishment, and most tournament players would be quite happy with one. His victories in the Byron Nelson, Westchester and Bank of Boston Classics obviously make him a good prospect for 1983.

US wins 5 (1976–82)
US money $881,955 (1976–82) (45th all-time)

GILES, Marvin, III   USA
b. Lynchburg, Virginia 1943

One of the very few amateurs to win both the US and British national amateur Opens, Vinny Giles had to wait some time for this kind of success, being runner-up in the US Amateur three years in a row – 1967–9 – before beating Ben Crenshaw and Mark Hayes by three strokes in 1972. Three years later he took the British title at Hoylake when he slaughtered Mark James – soon to be highly successful as a professional – by 8 and 7 in the final. Earlier in his career, Giles four times represented the US, from 1969 to 1975, in the Walker Cup and was in the US winning team in the Eisenhower Trophy three times, from 1968 to 1972. He was also top amateur in the 1968 US Masters and the 1973 US Open, when he completed his second round in 2, 3, 3, 3 – against a par of 4, 3, 4, 4. In 1971 he played what ought to become one of the most famous shots in golf history. In the Walker Cup at St Andrews he holed from the road at the 17th against Michael Bonallack, a feat which enabled him to win by 1 up. He now manages professional athletes.

GLUTTING, Charlotte   USA
b. Newark, New Jersey 1910

A Curtis Cup player from 1934 to 1938 and also selected in 1940, Charlotte Glutting won all her singles, beating amongst others Pam Barton, champion of both Britain and the USA. She won the Eastern and her own state championship three times, but never got past the semi-finals of the US Amateur.

GOALBY, Robert   USA
b. Belleville, Illinois 1929

Walter Hagen once declared that no one ever remembered who came second. In Bob Goalby's case there was an odd reversal. He won the 1968 Masters, after a final round of 66, yet this is a feat little remembered. Far more memorable, indeed a part of legend, is that Roberto de Vicenzo birdied the 71st hole but his partner, Tommy Aaron, marked it down as a par. Roberto signed his card as correct and, instead of playing off with Goalby over 18 holes for the championship, found himself second. Disaster for Roberto, but a different kind of disaster for Bob Goalby. He was treated as if he had not 'really' won and instead of making the normal fortune out of being Masters Champion, his achievement was, and is, largely ignored. No contracts flowed in. Oddly enough Goalby was much opposed to foreigners playing on the US Tour, and no doubt his experience with the Argentinian did little to change his mind! Goalby began as something of an all-round sportsman, rejecting offers to play major league baseball and then going to college on a football scholarship. He abandoned this to join the golf circuit in 1957. In 1958 he broke into the Top 60 and was named Rookie of the Year. He remained in the Top 60 until 1963 and was there again from 1965 to 1973. However, after his first few years, he found success hard to come by because his strong inside-to-out swing began and continued to produce an uncontrollable hook. Goalby is said to have spent some 200 hours of tuition with Johnny Revolta before, in 1967, he finally got the thing out of his system, began winning again, and finished tenth on the money list, his best placing since finishing fifth in 1963. Goalby was once a Ryder Cup player, in 1963, and though the 1968 Masters was his one championship victory he had earlier come very close, finishing second in the 1961 US Open and also in the following year's US PGA. He still, though now with Fuzzy Zoeller, holds the record for the most consecutive birdies recorded on the US Tour. He had eight in a row in the 1961 St Petersburg Open during his fourth round, having shot a 62 in his second round. Goalby was an extremely determined player, always able to make the best of a streak of good form and also quite noted for an unsunny temper. On one occasion he threw himself into a water hazard, on another stamped through puddles up a fairway after he had hooked, and in the 1968 Los Angeles Open, disgusted with the slow play of his playing partners, he left them and finished alone. In the first full year of the US Senior Tour he finished third in the official money list and in all senior events was second, winning $110,677, more than he ever won on the main circuit in one year.

US wins 11 (1958–71)
US money $645,013 (1957–82) (71st all-time)

GOLDEN, Johnny   USA
b. Austro-Hungary 1896; d. 1936

A partner Walter Hagen always wanted because of his straightness off the tee, Golden was twice a Ryder Cup player, in 1927 and 1929, and had a 100% record. Playing in the days before the US Tour was established, and when it was mainly a matter of winter events so that the professional could be away from a club job, he was a name player from the mid 1920s to the early 1930s, winning the Texas Open in 1924 and several other events. In the 1932 US PGA he beat Hagen on the 43rd green, then a record for length of match.

GOLDSMITH, Brenda   USA
b. San Antonio, Texas 1955

Winner of the Southern in 1976 and 1979 and the Trans-National also in the latter year, Brenda Goldsmith played on the 1978 and 1980 Curtis Cup Teams. She qualified for the US Tour in 1981, but has been plagued by injury and has achieved little or nothing to date. Hers, however, is the kind of amateur record that normally leads to professional success in the USA.

US money $6,887 (1981–2)

GOODMAN, John   USA
b. Omaha, Nebraska 1910; d. 1970

Such is the dominance of professionals in Open championships that we have to look back to 1933 and Johnny Goodman for the last amateur to take the US Open, and to 1930 and Bobby Jones for the last to take the British. Goodman shot a 66 in his third round, and Walter Hagen and Ralph Guldahl were unable to catch him in the last. Once a victor over Jones in the US Amateur, Goodman lost the final of the 1932 event to Ross Sommerville but came through to win five years later, thus becoming one of only five amateur golfers to have won both

the US National Opens. Chick Evans, Francis Ouimet, Jerome Travers and, of course, Jones, were the others. He three times played in the Walker Cup, winning all but one of his matches.

GRAHAM, Catherine: see Sherk

GRAHAM, Louis Krebs   USA
b. Nashville, Tennessee 1938

Lou Graham became a professional in 1962 and joined the US Tour in 1964, so his career has covered much the same span as that of Jack Nicklaus. There the similarity ends, for Lou has been a steady, unglamorous figure throughout, unchanged even by winning the 1975 US Open. He began with a 74, to be 7 behind the leader, and his second-round 72 left him 11 behind Tom Watson, who had set a 36-hole record for the US Open. But Lou continued on his way, probably hoping for no more than a moderate cheque at the end of the week, and had a 68 in the fourth round which pulled him up to 4 behind. Then, as most of the field fell away, he had a 73, which tied him for an 18-hole play-off with John Mahaffey. Lou got home by 71 to 73. The straight hitter who keeps fit and goes to bed at the right time had this time plodded into history. In fact Lou has performed very steadily in the US Open, benefiting from courses which always reward straight, consistent hitting. The

Lou Graham

previous year he was equal third and in 1977 was second. Three times in the US Ryder Cup team from 1973 to 1977, Graham had by 1979 not won since the US Open and then won three times in the space of eight weeks: the Philadelphia Classic, the Pleasant Valley Classic and the Texas Open. This gave him his best money year at $190,827, while he had topped $100,000 the previous three years. He was the 21st player to reach $1 million on the US Tour and he had done so with the fewest wins – six. From 1967 to 1979 Graham was only once out of the Top 60 and 11th in 1977 was his best placing.

US wins 6 (1967–81)
US money $1,279,890 (1964–82) (21st all-time)
World money $1,388,882 (1964–82) (28th all-time)

GRAY, A. Downing   USA
b. Pensacola, Florida 1938

A prominent amateur during the 1960s, Downing Gray was runner-up in the US Amateur in 1962, losing by 1 down to Labron Harris, and four years later was third, 1 stroke behind Gary Cowan and Deane Beman. The next year he was fourth. He played in the Walker Cup team in the three matches between 1963 and 1967, in the Americas Cup team in 1965 and 1967 and in the World Team Championship in 1966. He was low amateur in the Masters in both 1965 and 1966.

GREEN, Hubert Myatt, II   USA
b. Birmingham, Alabama 1946

A highly idiosyncratic player, Hubert Green has never been out of the Top 60 since his first full year on the US Tour in 1971. He has also won at least one tournament a year, except for 1980 and 1982. In 1980 he fell short of $100,000 for the first time since 1972. Three times he has passed $200,000 – in 1974, 1976 and 1978 – when he was each time in the top 5. In 1974 he won four times, a fairly rare achievement and enough to take him to his best placing on the money list, third. In 1976 he was one of only ten players in US Tour history to win three tournaments in a row. On two occasions he has faced tense situations of the kind much relished by golf tabloid writers. In 1977 he led the US Open throughout and, with a few holes left in his final round, an anonymous telephone caller threatened to kill him. Green was asked if he would like a suspension of play; he opted for continuing. There were no bullets and Hubert took the Open. The

following year there was a less happy ending. After an opening 72 in that year's Masters, he improved with a 69, followed by a 65, giving him a lead of 3 over Tom Watson and Rod Funseth. But this was the year of Gary Player's greatest of last rounds in the Masters. Player, many strokes behind, gave those following him home a 64 to think about, and Green played an up-and-down round, finishing by hitting a superb iron shot under extreme pressure to the last hole. It left him with a 2½-foot putt to tie. With the eyes of the nation, if not the world, upon him, he missed – by a large margin. In fact, Green is recognized as one of the best putters on the Tour and possibly the best chipper. He uses a putter made in 1930, with his hands spread well apart and right forefinger down the shaft. Unlike a clear majority of good putters he feels that the stroke is made with the left hand, as does Lee Trevino. For the full swing, he bends down to the ball, takes the club back on the outside and loops it to an inside position. He hits the ball relatively low and is not particularly long. Striving for more length in 1980 led to a relatively poor year from him on the US Tour. In general, it seems that Nicklaus was right: a golfer should strive for maximum length in youth and build on control as he matures. Hubert has competed frequently overseas, winning the 1975 Dunlop Phoenix in Japan and the 1977 Irish Open. He finished fourth in the 1974 British Open and third behind the unmatchable golf of Watson and Nicklaus at Turnberry in 1977. As he passes his mid 30s, it is likely that his best years are in the past. He may well go down in golf history as a very nearly great player.

US wins 17 (1971–81)
US money $1,597,101 (1970–82) (12th all-time)
Overseas wins 2
World money $1,949,478 (1970–82) (14th all-time)

GROUT, Jack   USA
b. Oklahoma City, Oklahoma 1910

At one time Stewart Maiden came to be known to the public because of his guidance of the young Bobby Jones. Jack Grout is in the same mould, though where Maiden merely gave Jones the odd word of advice, Grout is the man who taught the young Nicklaus and to whom he has returned ever since. Most of this teaching was done at Scioto Country Club. Grout turned professional in 1928 and played on the US Tour until shortly after World War II, winning one event.

GUILFORD, Jesse C.   USA
b. *Manchester, New Hampshire 1895; d. 1962*

Known as 'the Great Excavator' and 'the Boston Siege Gun' because of his power and ability to extract a golf ball from unlikely places, Guilford reached the semi-final of the US Amateur in 1916 and in 1921 won it, beating four past or future champions to do so. He was a Walker Cup player from 1922 to 1926.

GULDAHL, Ralph   USA
b. *Dallas, Texas 1912*

Perhaps Guldahl did not remain at the top quite long enough to be fully recognized as a great player. Instead he is sometimes referred to as a player who woke up one morning and found that his swing had gone in the night. Guldahl himself denies all this. He said it was not his swing that he lost but his interest in the game. Having, for those times, made his fortune, he preferred a club job and time with his family. He first came to the fore in 1933 when with Walter Hagen he chased amateur Johnny Goodman home in the US Open. Only a missed 4-foot putt on the last preventing him from tying. Little was then heard of Guldahl for a few years, mainly because he did not play on what Tour there then was between 1934 and mid 1936. He won $8,600 to leader Horton Smith's $9,000 in that short season of 1936, and won the Radix Trophy for the year's low stroke average at 71.65. Then came the year that Guldahl 'arrived'. In the spring of 1937, he finished second in the Masters. In that year's US Open he found that he had to par his way in to tie Sam Snead's 283. Guldahl promptly eagled a hole with a long putt and the only alarm came when he found his ball resting against a cigar butt in a bunker on the 15th. He got it out to 6 feet and holed the putt. His eventual total of 281 beat the Open record. In the following year's US Open Guldahl was 4 behind Dick Metz and Emory Zimmerman with one round to go, but Guldahl put in a 69 final round which gained him many strokes on the leaders and he won comfortably. In the 1939 Masters Guldahl's ability to put in a strong finish showed itself once more. Again Snead was the victim, and by now no doubt beginning to wonder what it would take to win a major championship. Guldahl beat him by 1 stroke, having completed the second nine at Augusta National in 33. And that was almost the end of Ralph Guldahl. He featured strongly in the 1940 US Open, finishing only 3

behind Little and Sarazen, and then disappeared. Guldahl is unofficially credited with 11 US Tour wins – including the oldest US tournament, the Western Open, three years in a row, 1936, 1937 and 1938 – and was a Ryder Cup player in 1937, when he competed in the British Open for the only time and was 11th, 10 strokes behind Henry Cotton.

US wins 11 (1936–9)
US money $50,000 approx.

GUNDERSON, JoAnne: see Carner

GUNN, Watts   USA
b. *Macon, Georgia 1905*

A Walker Cup player in 1926 and 1928, Watts Gunn won all his matches and also took the Southern Amateur and the National Intercollegiate. He was a contemporary of Bobby Jones and also belonged to the same East Lake Golf Club. When the two met in the final of the 1925 US Amateur this was the first and still the only time that members of the same club have met in the final. Things did not go well for Gunn: Jones beat him 8 and 7.

HAAS, Frederick   USA
b. *Portland, Arkansas 1916*

A Walker Cup player in 1938 and a Ryder Cup player in 1953, Fred Haas was the first man to play for the USA both as an amateur and as a professional against Great Britain. Of course those were days when professional golf did not offer the fortunes in prize money and endorsements that it does nowadays, so professional golf was less of a temptation to the amateur. Haas had won the 1937 NCAA to earn Walker Cup selection and when he won the Memphis Open as an amateur in 1945 he must have decided that it was a pity he could not accept the prize money. The event was significant for yet another reason: Haas had ended Byron Nelson's incredible run of 11 consecutive wins. As a pro Haas seldom made the headlines but he always made money – for 32 consecutive years in fact. He was in the Top 60 from 1950 to 1958 and again in 1960. He was both US and World Senior Champion in 1966. His best finish in the money lists was ninth in 1955. An unusual feature of his play was that he putted cross-handed. Well into his 60s, Fred still plays on the US Senior Tour.

US wins 5 (1948–54)
US money $150,999 (1946–77) (213th all-time)

HAAS, Jay Dean   USA
b. St Louis, Missouri 1953

A nephew of Bob Goalby, who has been his main teacher, Jay Haas was low amateur in the 1974 US Open and won the NCAA the following year, when he was also selected for the Walker Cup in which he won three matches. He was an All-American choice that year, and also in the following year when he won the Missouri Open. Turning professional in 1976 he joined the Tour in 1977 and finished fifth in the US Open that year and overall 77th on the money list. In 1978 he won his first tournament, the San Diego Open, and moved up to 31st on the money list, a position he approximately maintained the next two seasons, though by now passing $100,000 in both years. In 1981 he made further progress to becoming a star, for he moved up to 15th place and won twice. In 1982 he won the Spalding Invitational over five rounds by 4 from Bobby Clampett with the third-place man another 6 strokes away. Late in the season he won two tournaments in a row, the Hall of Fame and Texas Open, to end the year 13th on the money list with almost $230,000, his fourth consecutive year over $100,000 and best to date.

US wins 5 (1978–82)
US money $737,759 (1977–82) (60th all-time)

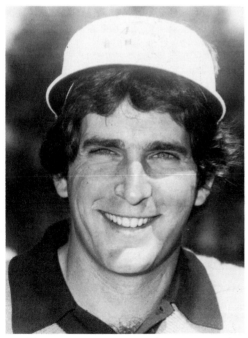

Jay Haas

HAGEN, Walter Charles   USA
b. Rochester, New York 1892; d. 1969

British Open Champion: 1922, 1924, 1928, 1929
US Open Champion: 1914, 1919
US PGA Champion: 1921, 1924, 1925, 1926, 1927

One of the great golfers of all time, Walter Hagen through his achievements in the US PGA has a very strong claim indeed to be considered the best matchplayer ever. In this event he won in 1921, did not enter again until 1924 and then won four titles in a row. This meant that he won a sequence of 22 matches. Extend the sequence a little, and you have Hagen winning 32 out of 34 matches and the championship five times in seven entries. No one else has won a major championship four times consecutively. Hagen's ability as a competitor in matches stemmed particularly from recovery shots. Always liable to hit an occasional wild wooden club or long iron, he was equally likely to disappear into the woods, bushes or deep rough, put his ball on the green and then hole the putt. If his opponent had driven down the fairway, sent his next to the green and two-putted comfortably, he of course felt aggrieved. He was also less likely to have his mind fully on the job in hand for the next hole or so. Hagen's strokeplay was scarcely less spectacular. In a sequence of ten entries in the British Open, for instance, he had four wins and a second and third. Even more typical of Hagen was that in his first Open at Deal in 1920 he finished last but one. Hagen's attitude was that no one remembered who came second and on this occasion he may well have felt that the publicity would be better if he finished dramatically badly. After this blow to his ego, if such it was, Hagen went off to France and took the French Open two weeks later. In 1922 he did win the British Open, at Royal St George's, but he found much to criticize on the British scene. Professionals were not allowed to change in the clubhouse or eat there: this was countered in typical Hagen fashion: he hired an Austro-Daimler limousine for changing his shoes and eating in – and parked it right in front of the clubhouse. Then, when he saw the size of the cheque for first prize, he handed it to his caddie. A year later Hagen .was runner-up to Arthur Havers and this time was invited into the clubhouse to attend the presentation. He refused and, having invited the crowd along for a drink at a local pub, left the presentation somewhat sparsely attended. Hagen's competitive golf career began in 1912, when he entered the Canadian Open. When he returned he was asked how he had done. Replied Hagen, 'I lost.' This typified Hagen's competitive attitude. In fact, for a first tournament, he had done quite well to finish 11th. His next entry came in the 1913 US Open and again he 'lost'. He missed the immortal play-off between Vardon, Ray and Francis Ouimet by a single shot and came fourth. This performance perhaps convinced him that golf rather than baseball was his métier. Although little attention has focused on the Hagen of the 1913 Open, he has been heard to tell a good story about it. After a run of 6, 5, 7 he recalled that he had been watching Vardon swing. He decided to give that swing a try and then had a sequence of 2, 3, 3, 3 and was well back in the running. His first victory was not to be long delayed. In 1914 he opened up with a 68, which beat the Open record, and held on reasonably comfortably though amateur Chick Evans, who finished strongly, was only a shot behind at the end. His next win came in 1919 when, on the 72nd hole, he had an 8-foot putt to tie Mike Brady and earn a play-off. This was the source of possibly the first famous Hagen story, many of which were apocryphal. He ordered that Brady be summoned to watch the putt go down, presumably in order to soften him up for the next day. The play-off nevertheless was close, with Hagen eventually taking it by 77 to 78. On the 17th Hagen's ball became embedded in mud and he asked for a ruling as to whether or not he could pick and drop. When the ruling went against him Hagen said that he would have to 'identify' his ball. After he had done that the ball lay considerably more favourably. Strangely, this was Hagen's last US Open win, even though this was the one event he seldom missed. Hardly ever again did he threaten to win, once being second, once third, and fourth on four occasions. One reason was that this was now the Bobby Jones era, and neither Hagen nor anyone else had much hope of success if Jones was in the field. Walter did, however, have one spectacular triumph against the prodigy from Atlanta, Georgia. By 1926 Hagen and Jones were firmly established as the greatest golfers of the day and eventually a match over 72 holes was arranged – with Walter getting all the gate money. Hagen won by the formidable margin of 11 and 10 and seemed to have settled the question of who was the dominant golfer of the era. Not so, as Jones completed his Grand Slam four years later. Money matches were of course much more a feature of golf

Walter Hagen

in the Hagen era than they have since become, and the superstar could expect to make a fair proportion of both his income and reputation from them. Two years after the match against Jones, Hagen played in another that has gone down in golf folklore. Just off a transatlantic liner, he arrived at Moor Park to confront Archie Compston, just about the best British golfer at that time. Hagen was, of course, very much out of practice, Compston not. The latter produced rounds of 66, 67, 70 and was then no doubt thanking Walter for a most pleasant game. He had won by 18 and 17. Yet shortly after Hagen took the Open at Sandwich. He had dieted, kept off champagne and apparently not consulted his 'little black book' in which he recorded likely names for après-golf. Similarly, the next year George Duncan in the Ryder Cup beat Hagen by 10 and 8 over 36 holes. Hagen duly appeared at Muirfield for the Open, and gave arguably his finest performance. Until this Open no one had broken 70 at Muirfield, but my father Percy returned a 69 in the first round. Walter improved on this in the second with a 67, the best round that had been played in any Open and one that Hagen was to consider his lifetime best. Nevertheless Leo Diegel was 2 strokes ahead. As Hagen enjoyed a convivial evening before the final day's 36 holes it was pointed out to him that his rival was long in bed. Replied Hagen: 'Yeah, but he ain't sleeping.' Diegel duly collapsed to an 82 in gale-force winds. Walter, using an exceptionally deep-faced driver, twice went round in 75, good enough to give him victory by 6 strokes. Hagen's swing was admired by few. He took perhaps too wide a stance, held the club in a light grip and seemed to drag it back – apparently leaving the clubhead behind. On the downswing there was a pronounced sway which some have seen as the reason for the fair number of erratic shots. Others claim that the sway came immediately after impact when it could do little harm. Often in trouble, he was not disturbed to be in remote places and his recovery shots were legendary. Yet it was on and near the green that he shone. Before the days of the sand-iron, none excelled Hagen's ability to flick a shot clean off sand, and his putting, quick and apparently casual, was only equalled by Jones's. But it was not merely his golfing abilities that brought Hagen such success. It was his mental attitude. For instance he claimed that he expected to hit about seven bad shots a round and was therefore unperturbed by them, where others would throw clubs and lose their temper. Similarly, he was little bothered by bad luck and held that such things levelled themselves out in the end. The well-known saying of his: 'Never hurry, never worry and be sure to smell the flowers along the way,' typifies his attitude to golf and life. Indeed it is probably true to say that Hagen was not even a keen golfer. He chose the game because it seemed to offer the chance of a reasonable living for an ex-caddie, and when he saw that there were opportunities for more than this he made the most of them. In this he changed the face of professional golf. Gene Sarazen said: 'All the pros who have a chance for the big money today should say a silent prayer to "the Haig". He made it all possible.' Hagen himself said: 'I never wanted to be a millionaire; I just wanted to live like one' – and that he did. That 1929 Open was perhaps Hagen's swansong and he never won another major title, though he continued to be a threat until the mid 1930s. He stands, with 11 wins, third in the all-time list of major championship winners, his total exceeded only by Jones and Nicklaus and, unlike Nicklaus, neither had the Masters to compete in during their best years. It is difficult to arrive at figures for Hagen's tournament victories and equally difficult to establish their status – a reason why major wins are so important in golf history. Nevertheless, Hagen is variously credited with between 60 and 83 wins, and that too puts him well up the list. Above all, however, he was the most colourful figure that golf has yet produced; and no rival in sight.

US wins 27 (1914–36) (13th all-time)
Total wins 54 (1914–36)

HAGGE, Marlene (née Bauer) USA

b. Eureka, South Dakota 1934

Marlene Hagge can boast one of the most consistent records in women's professional golf in a career that began at the age of 16 in 1950, when she became a founder and charter member of the US LPGA. More than 30 years later, she still plays the US Tour to a stroke average that has not worsened with the passing of the years. The young Marlene Bauer first attracted attention by winning the 1944 Long Beach *Boys'* Junior, then the Western and National Junior Championships in 1949. As a professional at the age of 18 she was soon a winner, the youngest to win an LPGA tournament, and in 1956 she was leading money-winner, her $20,235 setting a record at the time. She won eight times that year, including the US LPGA after a play-off with Patty Berg. Since then 'the Gremlin', as she is known, has not again been so dominant, but she had five wins in 1965 to be second on the money

Marlene Hagge

list. Since that time she has won only twice, in 1969 and 1971, but she has continued to win substantial sums of money and finish well up the field in tournaments. She has, in fact, a remarkable appetite for golf and each year averages not much fewer than 30 tournaments, stamina that might have earned her the nickname 'Iron Lady' to parallel the 'Iron Man' accorded to Bruce Crampton in the 1960s and 1970s. Marlene Hagge, whose sister Alice played the Tour for some years, is just 5 feet 2 inches tall. She uses a distinctly strong grip, a feature of the play of not a few top women players and a method that might suit many of the men players who are coached out of it.

US wins 25 (1952–71) (12th all-time)
US money $423,001 (1950–82) (19th all-time)

HAHN, Paul   USA
b. 1918; d. 1976

As a player on the US Tour after World War II Paul Hahn had little success, but then, like Joe Kirkwood, found that he was far more successful as a showman. His demonstrations of trick golf shots with a bewildering variety of strange clubs steadily won him both a following and a high income until he became the biggest name in a limited field. The US Golf Association museum at Far Hills, New Jersey, maintains a showcase of the more bizarre clubs he used in his act.

Paul Hahn

HALLBERG, Gary George   USA
b. Berwyn, Illinois 1958

A Walker Cup choice in 1979, Gary Hallberg is the only man in history to have been four times an All-American choice. During his college golf career he took 14 tournaments, the North–South Amateur in both 1978 and 1979 and the Illinois Open in 1977. He was NCAA Champion in 1979. In 1980 he turned professional and became the first man to qualify for his US Tour card without passing through the qualifying school. He did this by exceeding the minimum winnings of $8000, which he achieved by finishing equal third in the Quad Cities Open, only his second entry as a professional. By the end of the season, which for him had begun in July, he had won $64,244 and was named Rookie of the Year. His next season failed to consolidate on early success and he fell back to 91st place in the money list, from 63rd in only 11 entries the previous year. He was 111th in 1982, with some $36,000, but won the Chunichi Crowns tournament in Japan, his most important success as a professional, even better perhaps than his 1982 Argentine Open win.

US money $146,228 (1980–82) (217th all-time)
Overseas wins 2 (1982)

HALLDORSON, Daniel Albert   Canada
b. Winnipeg, Manitoba 1952

After turning professional in 1971; Dan Halldorson has twice qualified for the US Tour, in 1974 and 1978. For a long time he had little success, though he has gathered five Canadian provincial titles. In 1980, however, he won the Pensacola Open and was thus the first Canadian since George Knudson in 1972 to win on the US Tour. He was in the Canadian World Cup team in 1980 and 1982.

US wins 1 (1980)
US money $321,243 (1975–82) (140th all-time)

HAMILTON, Robert   USA
b. Evansville, Indiana 1916

Winner of the US PGA in 1944 by 1 up over no less than Byron Nelson, Bob Hamilton was later impeded in his career by burnt hands sustained in a light plane crash. He took three other tournaments in his career and was third in the 1946 Masters. Much later in life he became the youngest player to 'shoot his age' when he had a 59 at that age in 1975.

US wins 4 (1944–8)

HAMLIN, Shelley   USA
b. San Mateo, California 1949

One of the leading amateurs in the US for some years, Shelley Hamlin reached the final of the 1969 US Amateur, where she lost 3 and 2 to the great Catherine Lacoste. She won the California title four times and the National Collegiate in 1971, and represented the US in the 1966 and 1968 World Amateur Team Championship and the 1968 and 1970 Curtis Cups. She turned professional in 1972 and has been a good money-winner every year since then, more because of consistency than through tournament wins. She took the unofficial 1975 Japan Classic and the 1978 Patty Berg Classic. Shelley does some television work for ABC.

US wins 1 (1978)
US money $299,717 (1972–82) (29th all-time)

HANCOCK, Philip Ransom   USA
b. Greenville, Alabama 1953

As an amateur, Phil Hancock won the 1975 and 1976 Southeast Conference titles and, in the same years, the American Amateur Classic, and was selected an All-American. He turned professional and won his Tour card in 1977, the same year in which he won the Colombia Open. On Tour he finished 95th in his first season and improved to 44th, winning $66,460, the following year. His best season was 1980, when he topped $100,000, came 43rd on the money list and won the Hall of Fame tournament. He had a poor season in 1981, falling away to 136th and was 112th in 1982.

US wins 1 (1980)
US money $289,395 (1977–82) (153rd all-time)

HANSON, Beverly (later Sfingi)   USA
b. Fargo, North Dakota 1924

Beverly Hanson won the US Amateur in 1950 and played in that year's Curtis Cup, winning in both singles and foursomes. She then went on the US Tour the following year and was one of the best players for the next decade, winning 15 events, three in 1959 being the most in a season. In 1958 she was leading money-winner with $12,639 and two wins, and in 1955 she took the US LPGA. That first year of the championship, the format was that the leaders after 54 holes of strokeplay played 18 holes of matchplay. Beverly led on 220, followed by Louise Suggs on 223 and went on to win the

match by 4 and 3. This was the only time that the title was not decided by four strokeplay rounds.

US wins 15 (1951–60)

HARB, Helen: see Hicks

HARBERT, Melvin R.   USA
b. Dayton, Ohio 1915

As an amateur Chick Harbert won the 1939 Trans-Mississippi, and he turned professional the following year. He played on Tour from 1941 and was particularly known for his long hitting, winning dozens of long-driving contests. His career highlight was winning a major championship, the 1954 US PGA, an event in which he finished second in 1947 and 1952. In the same event he also holds the record, with Eddie Burke, for the longest match. Harbert won in the second round on the eighth extra hole. He captained the Ryder Cup team in 1955 and also played in 1949. He became a member of the PGA Hall of Fame in 1968.

US wins 10 (1941–58)
US money $78,752

HARBOTTLE, Patricia: see Lesser

HARDY, Carol: see Mann

HARLEY, Katherine: see Jackson

HARMON, Claude   USA
b. Savannah, Georgia 1916; d. 1976

Harmon was not a US Tour regular when he competed in the 1948 Masters. His invitation came because he had finished 20th in the previous year's US Open. He recorded 70, 70, 69, 70 and won over Middlecoff by 5 strokes, having led from the second round. His total equalled Ralph Guldahl's 1939 previous record, and his margin was a new record. A feature of his win was that in the last round he covered the 6th, 7th and 8th holes in 2, 3, 3 against a par of 3, 4, 5. After this success, despite a very shut-faced method, Harmon competed more regularly on the US Tour and had several successes. In 1959 he came third in the US Open, only 2 behind champion Billy Casper. He later became respected as an excellent teacher of the game.

US wins 5

HARNEY, Paul — USA
b. Worcester, Massachusetts 1929

Harney has recently been heard of when losing a play-off for the 1980 PGA Seniors to no less than Arnold Palmer. He had nearly had a similar experience in the 1963 US Open, when he finished fourth but just 1 stroke behind the trio of Jackie Cupit, Julius Boros and again Palmer, who played off for the championship. Harney turned professional in 1954 and joined the Tour the same year, though he was by no means always a Tour regular. He often competed only on the winter circuit and concentrated on his club job in the summer months. Despite this, he featured in the Top 60 from 1956 to 1965 and again in 1970 and 1972. In 1957 he won twice and came sixth in the money list, while his best money year was 1972 when, as prize money rose, he took home $51,507 in 48th place. Possibly his most memorable achievement was to win the Los Angeles Open in the successive years 1964 and 1965, for this event, held annually at the Riviera Country Club, is played on one of America's most testing courses.

US wins 7 (1957–72)
US money $361,884 (1955–74)

HARPER, Chandler — USA
b. Portsmouth, Virginia 1914

Inducted into the US PGA Hall of Fame in 1969, Chandler Harper had perhaps the least impressive record of anyone so honoured. The choice was perhaps too much a consequence of his having won the 1968 US PGA Seniors and then having won the World Seniors by defeating Britain's Max Faulkner, then still a considerable golfer with the prestige of having been British Open Champion. However, he was certainly a substantial golfer and has been credited with as many as 20 wins in the USA, though official figures are far lower, a fact which reflects the difficulty of deciding today which were substantial tournaments in the past and which were not. Once a Ryder Cup player, in 1955, Harper had his most important victories in the Canadian Open in 1949 and the US PGA the following year. At Brackenridge Park, San Antonio, in the 1954 Texas Open, he shot consecutive rounds of 70, 63, 63, 63. His last two rounds equal the US Tour 36-hole record while his last three, totalling 189, are the record. However, this was the course on which Mike Souchak set the 72-hole record that stood for many years, and low scoring on it was frequent.

Despite this, his 259 total was the second lowest ever recorded and at 25 under par was the third best. Harper has one other notable scoring feat in his record, a 58 on a course measuring over 6,100 yards. His best year was 1953, when he was fourth on the money list, and he had a consistently good short game.

US wins 7 (1942–55)
US money $69,070

HARRIS, Labron, Jnr — USA
b. Stillwater, Oklahoma 1941

Winner of the US Amateur in 1962, when he beat Downing Gray in the final, he also played in the World Cup team that year and the Americas and Walker Cups the following year. He turned professional in 1964. His first three years caused no stir, but he reached the Top 60 in between 1970 and 1972 and again in 1974. He then faded away during the later 1970s and does not now play on Tour. Harris was 33rd on the money list in 1970 and 36th in 1972; he won the 1971 Robinson Falls tournament.

US wins 1 (1971)
US money $296,036 (1964–76)

HARRISON, Ernest Joseph — USA
b. Conway, Arkansas 1910; d. 1982

'Dutch' Harrison turned professional in 1936 and went on Tour from 1937, soon becoming one of the best, and best liked, players on the circuit. One of his great qualities was durability: he won tournaments between 1937 and 1958. Three times a Ryder Cup player, he once, in 1949, opened up at Ganton against Max Faulkner with five 3s in a row, and not surprisingly went out winner by 8 and 7. Never to win a major championship, he did take the 1949 Canadian Open, was fourth in the US Open in 1950 and equal third in 1960 at the age of 50. In 1953 he was sixth in the US money list and won the Vardon Trophy for the lowest tournament stroke average the next year. Once he reached the age of 50 he won the National Seniors five times between 1961 and 1966. It is a comment on the lack of success of left-handers in golf that Dutch began, like Hogan, as a left-sided player. The only 'quality' left-hander, on the other hand – Bob Charles – is right-handed in everything except golf. 'Dutch' had a laconic sense of humour. When a minor player called Bud Holscher lashed an approach shot well through the

Dutch Harrison

green, a spectator was heard to voice the opinion that it was a courageous shot. Harrison looked at the ball – it was out of bounds – and said: 'Yeah, I sure liked playing against those courageous players.'

US wins 21 (1937–58)

HATALSKY, Morris   USA
b. San Diego, California 1951

The US Tour is notoriously tough. It is extremely difficult even to qualify to attempt to be one of the players who qualify for particular tournaments on Monday mornings. Morris turned professional in 1973 and had five attempts at qualifying school before he eventually struggled through in 1976. He then proceeded to win $249 for the season and finish 288th on the money list. There was improvement the next year and he managed a second-place finish, but he slumped again in 1978. At this point he realized that his game was almost wholly based on chipping and putting excellence and went

to Ken Venturi, 1964 US Open Champion, who put some method into his long game. Since then, Hatalsky has been a consistent money-winner, though he has yet to make the Top 60, reaching 65th in 1982. His highest achievement has been to win the 1981 Hall of Fame Classic. His short game has improved along with his long game: he registered as the second best bunker player and fourth in putting in the US Tour statistics for 1981.

US wins 1 (1981)
US money $247,167 (1976–82) (151st all-time)

HAWKINS, Frederick   USA
b. Antioch, Illinois 1923

In the 1957 Ryder Cup it was said that Fred 'couldn't play', and was bound to lose. But he played very tidily indeed and came out the only American winner on that tumultuous day when all exept he and Dick Mayer fell apart. Hawkins turned professional in 1947, went on the Tour and made money unspectacularly for some 20 years, twice finishing sixth in the US Open. He now competes on the Senior Tour.

US wins 2 (1956–8)
US money $196,371

HAYES, Mark Stephen   USA
b. Stillwater, Oklahoma 1949

After eagling the par-5 17th at Turnberry during the 1977 British Open, Mark Hayes dropped his first stroke of the round on the last. While trying out a reversed-hands putting grip he had broken the British Open record with a 63: 32 out and 31 back. It was 13 strokes better than his first round, and he eventually finished equal ninth. If this is the highpoint of his career, the low must be the 1979 Crosby. After a 66 at the fearsome Pebble Beach course in the third round, Hayes reached the 15th green in the final round 3 ahead of the field and only some 7 feet from the hole. Would he hole the putt and become unassailable? Far from it: Mark took four putts and then another three on the 16th! He finished tied with Lon Hinkle and Andy Bean and lost the play-off to Hinkle. Hayes had a similar putting experience in the 1982 US Masters, in which he eventually finished 6 behind winner Craig Stadler. In the second round he hit his approach to the last hole to 8 feet. He missed the birdie putt on a very fast green and the ball carried nearly off the putting surface. He ended up by taking four putts. Hayes had an excellent amateur career, being an All-American in 1970 and 1971, playing the 1972 World Amateur Team Championship and also, with Ben Crenshaw, finishing joint runner-up to Vinny Giles in the US Amateur. The following year he turned professional. After a period of adjustment, he has been a consistent money-winner, being in the Top 60 each year from 1975 to 1981 except 1980. From 1976 to 1978 he was in the top 20, 1976 being his best year when he finished 11th in the money list. Four times he has earned over $100,000. Now into his 30s with his results apparently declining, it is unlikely that he will prove to be more than a very good player who enjoyed several years of steady success on the US Tour. His peak of achievement may come to be seen as the winning of a near major, the 1977 Tournament Players Championship. He was a Ryder Cup player in 1979.

US wins 3 (1976–7)
US money $847,568 (1973–82) (49th all-time)

HAYES, Patricia   USA
b. Hoboken, New Jersey 1955

After some success in Florida golf, Patty Hayes failed to earn her US Tour card in 1973 and played for some while in Australia before qualifying for

Sandra Haynie

the Tour in 1974. She enjoyed negligible success for three seasons; but then in 1977 she lowered her stroke average more than 2 per round and has been successful ever since, winning nearly $60,000 in both 1980 and 1981 and being 18th and 19th on the money list in those years. She won her first event, the Sun City Classic, in 1981, but had a disappointing season in 1982.

US wins 1 (1981)
US money $179,636 (1974–82)

HAYNIE, Sandra   USA
b. Fort Worth, Texas 1943

As an amateur, Sandra Haynie won her Texas state title in 1959 and 1960 and the Trans-Mississippi in 1960. In 1961 she went on the US Tour and finished 21st in the rankings at the age of 18. The following year she achieved her first victory and thereafter had no winless year until 1976. From 1963 to 1975 she was never worse than ninth in the season's money list and was in the top 3 six times. By 1975 she was second on the all-time money list. From 1964 to 1976 her stroke average never rose to 74, and in her best years she kept in the 72 to 73 band. She had four wins in 1966 and 1975 and six in 1974. From 1977 she played only occasionally, partly as a result of business interests and partly through injury; but in 1981 she returned to the Tour, seeing the rise in prize money, and she took her first tournament since 1975 and in a remarkable come-back was 13th in the rankings. This was no last gasp of a player approaching her 40s: in 1982 she had one of her best years ever, finishing repeatedly in the top group and winning two more tournaments, at one time seeming likely to head the money list and ending with well over $200,000 in money winnings. In the three major championships she has a good record, winning the US LPGA in 1965 and 1974 while in the latter year she accomplished the rare feat of also winning the US Open in the same year. In 1982 she achieved the slam of adding the Peter Jackson Classic, and the US Open was one of her several second place finishes. In these championships perhaps her most dramatic feat came in the 1974 US Open, when she birdied the last two holes and won by a single stroke. Sandra Haynie, with 42 career wins by 1982, stands fifth on the list of all-time winners, only Kathy Whitworth, Mickey Wright, Betsy Rawls and Louise Suggs above her. Of her contemporaries, only JoAnne Carner is fairly close behind.

The prime strengths of her game are driving and putting.

US wins 42 (1962–82) (5th all-time)
US money $847,657 (1961–82) (10th all-time)

HEAFNER, Clayton   USA
b. Charlotte, North Carolina 1914; d. 1960

Twice a Ryder Cup player, in 1949 and 1951, Heafner was famed for his temper. On more than one occasion he is said to have walked out of tournaments. One day he stood on the first tee waiting to play his first shot of the competition and an announcer referred to a shot Heafner had had to play out of a tree the previous year. Heafner was not amused and, remarking that he was not going to give himself the chance of doing that again, he marched off to his car, threw in his clubs and drove off to the next week's tournament venue. He won the 1947 Jacksonville Open and the 1948 Colonial Invitational, and lost the valuable 1942 Tam o' Shanter only after a play-off. Twice he was near to the US Open Championship. In 1949 at Medinah Country Club he finished tied with Sam Snead 1 stroke behind champion Cary Middlecoff. Two years later, he went into the last round at Oakland Hills level with Ben Hogan. Heafner then proceeded to play one of the only two rounds under 70 in the championship and came in with a 69. Alas, Hogan stormed home with a 67. Afterwards Hogan remarked that he had brought the 'monster' (Oakland Hills) 'to its knees'.

HEAFNER, Clayton Vance   USA
b. Charlotte, North Carolina 1954

Son of a famous father, Vance Heafner is regarded as one of those most likely to succeed. He had a good amateur record, winning the Eastern Amateur twice, the Porter Cup in 1978, was three times an All-American and a Walker Cup player in 1977. He turned professional in 1978 but had difficulty in winning his Tour card, twice failing by 1 stroke. Eventually he qualified in the spring of 1980 and had a moderate first half-year. In 1981 he played in 37 of the possible 41 tournaments – formidable dedication – and was rewarded by making the Top 60 in last place with a stroke average of 71.52. During the season he recorded 388 birdies and in that department was number one. Relieved to make the Top 60, he then immediately went on to win the Disney World Team Championship, his pairing

finishing a record 42 under par. Early in 1982 he came near to his first individual victory, being equal second in the Tucson Open, the season's first event, and he topped $100,000 for the year in 33rd place in the money list.

US wins 1 (1981)
US money $198,359 (1980–82) (187th all-time)

HEARD, Jerry Michael   USA
b. Visalia, California 1947

Jerry Heard is one of the few golfers to be hit by lightning and continue to compete. It happened in the 1975 Western Open when he, Lee Trevino and Bobby Nichols were all struck, in the second round. Heard had begun with a 69, and despite a visit to hospital, finished 74, 72, 73. However, he had to endure a bad back for some time afterwards and his golf suffered. After he had joined the Tour in 1969 Jerry's first win came in 1971 and was followed by two more the following year. He had no ambition to be a real golf star, saying that his aim was to make $100,000 a year. This he did three times: in 1971, 1972 and 1974, when he was seventh, fifth and eighth on the money list. He was six times in the top 30 between 1971 and 1978. Perhaps his most bewildering experience was to finish 10 under par in the 1975 Phoenix Open and be second – no less than 14 strokes behind the comet of Johnny Miller. In 1974, on a rare trip abroad, he won the Spanish Open.

US wins 5 (1971–8)
US money $776,555 (1969–82) (58th all-time)
Overseas wins 1

HEBERT, Jay   USA
b. St Martinville, Louisiana 1923

One of the only pair of brothers both to take national championships, Jay's was the 1960 US PGA. He became a professional in 1949 and was in the Top 60 from 1953 to 1966. In his best season, 1961, he was fifth in the money list, yet his earnings were only $35,583. The same placing in 1981 would have earned over $300,000. An elegant player of French descent (his name is pronounced 'Aybear'), he captained the 1971 Ryder Cup team, having played in the event in 1959 and 1961.

US wins 7 (1957–61)
US money $289,155 (154th all-time)

HEBERT, Lionel USA
b. *Lafayette, Louisiana 1928*

By five years the younger of the two PGA-winning brothers, Lionel took his championship in 1957, his first year on Tour, when he beat Dow Finsterwald in the final. He was in the Top 60 from that year until 1966. He remained in the top 100 until 1971. Also a Ryder Cup player – in 1957 – Lionel still plays a lot and may have some impact on the new Senior Tour. He lists one of his main interests as music, and is a good jazz trumpeter.

US wins 5 (1955–66)
US money $408,455 (109th all-time)

HERRON, S. Davidson USA
b. *Pittsburgh, Pennsylvania 1897; d. 1956*

Davy Herron won a small piece of immortality via Bobby Jones, who wrote vividly of their encounter in the final of the 1919 US Amateur. Herron, facing the 17-year-old Jones, beat him 5 and 4 and was well under par to do so. He was little heard of again, though he did twice take the Pennsylvania title, in 1920 and 1929. His performance in the 1919 Amateur was perhaps the result of one of those brief inspirational visitations in which a golfer reaches a standard he is never again to achieve.

HICKS, Elizabeth (later Newell) USA
b. *Long Beach, California, 1920*

Betty Hicks Newell won the US Amateur in 1941 and, because of World War II, retained the title until 1946. However, by then she had been long a professional and in 1944, with Hope Seignious and Ellen Griffin, had incorporated the Women's Professional Golf Association. The three of them were the sole stockholders and, on the toss of a coin, Betty Hicks Newell was president. The organization was later superseded. Betty's best golf achievements were a second place in the 1954 US Open and a third in 1957. She later became women's golf coach at San José State College.

HICKS, Helen B. (later Harb) USA
b. *Cedarhurst, New York 1911; d. 1974*

Helen Hicks won the Canadian Ladies' Open in 1929 and was runner-up the following year. In 1931 in the US Amateur she disposed of the 1921 champion, Marion Hollins, and the 1931 British title-holder Enid Wilson, before reaching the final, where she faced Glenna Collett. Helen Hicks won by 2 and 1. She reached the final again in 1933, meeting the current champion Virginia van Wie, and lost by 4 and 3. The following year she signed with Wilson Sporting Goods, and by that act was the first woman player of stature to turn professional. Helen Hicks also won the Metropolitan twice (1931 and 1933) and was a member of the 1932 Curtis Cup team.

HIGGINS, Pamela Sue USA
b. *Columbus, Ohio 1945*

As an amateur Pam Higgins was successful in Ohio golf, taking her state title in 1968. In 1969 she joined the US Tour and broke through in 1971 with a win in the Lincoln-Mercury Open. She has won twice since then, the 1977 American Cancer Society Classic and the 1980 Lady Michelob, but has been noted more for consistency than for winning. She was in the top 60 from 1969 to 1978 and in 1980; her best years were 1977 when she was 19th, and 1971 when she was 15th. She is the only member of the US Tour to have run a certified marathon, which she completed in under 4 hours.

US wins 3 (1971–80)
US money $248,014 (1969–82) (41st all-time)

HILL, Carolyn USA
b. *Santa Monica, California 1959*

After many successes in California Carolyn Hill made the 1978 Curtis Cup team and in 1979 beat Patty Sheehan in the final of the US Amateur. Turning professional shortly thereafter, she was promising in her first two years on the US Tour, 1980 and 1981. She won $35,000 in 1980 with a second-place finish, and in 1981 this rose to $51,607 and she was second in the Dinah Shore. At the end of the season she was 21st on the money list.

US money $101,529 (1980–82)

HILL, Cynthia USA
b. *South Haven, Michigan 1948*

Cindy Hill had a long career in amateur golf before eventually turning professional. In 1970 she reached the final of the US Amateur but lost 3 and 2 to Martha Wilkinson. She was there again two years later, losing this time to Mary Anne Budke.

Two years later came her third appearance, and this time she made no mistake, defeating the holder, Carol Semple, by 5 and 4. Other important victories in her amateur career included the 1973 Broadmoor Invitational and, in 1975, the Doherty Cup, the North and South and the South Atlantic. She played in the 1970 and 1974 World Team Championships, in which her 307 total was the lowest score in 1974, and played four times in the Curtis Cup. She turned professional in time for the mid 1979 season and was 54th on the 1980 money list and 34th the following year, during which she was in a five-way play-off for the Florida Lady Citrus, eventually coming in tied for second place.

US money $109,213 (1979–82)

HILL, James David   USA

b. Jackson, Michigan 1937

To Dave Hill, golf was an obsession. Throughout his 20s he claims to have played golf every day and often to have practised up to eight hours a day. This is dedication of the Ben Hogan variety and indeed, like Hogan, he aimed for perfection for its own sake, something quite apart from the fame and fortune that can be won in tournament and championship golf. Said Hill, speaking of the lonely delights of the practice ground: 'You paint pictures out there and each good shot is a deft stroke.' Not surprisingly, Hill became one of the most gifted shotmakers on the US Tour. He remained, however, a perfectionist. After a first-round 64 in the Monsanto Open of 1972 he was dissatisfied, feeling

Dave Hill

that putting had played too big a part. Said Hill: 'It should have been a 76.' In 1975 he won the Sahara Invitational with four rather convincing rounds of 68, 66, 67, 69. Hill's comment was: 'My game is embarrassing. I haven't hit four good shots all week.' Yet this was not insincere. Hill knew what he could do in the way of pure striking. The result had been exemplary, the manner not. And there was another factor. By the mid 1970s he felt that his swing had gone; that the joy of shaping trajectory and curve was lost to him; that now he could hope only to fight his way round a golf course with a succession of shots that were not crooked enough to damn his round but which gave no satisfaction to the inner man. After 1976 Dave Hill dropped well out of the Top 60, grew to hate tournament golf and continued only because there were endorsement contracts to be fulfilled that required him to continue playing the Tour. With some relief in 1981 he felt able to announce that no longer would he be a Tour regular. Hill had joined the Tour in 1959 and, after two lean years, won his first tournament and began to play consistently. From 1960 to 1976 he was not once out of the Top 60, and was in the top 30 in 11 of those years. His best finishes were second in 1969, tenth in 1970 and 11th in 1974. There were three other money listings in the top 20. As a tournament-winner, he came first home four times between 1961 and 1968 and won every year but one in the period 1969–76. In 1969 he won three times in June and July and topped $150,000 for the season. (He had three more years at over $100,000). It was in keeping with his highly strung and dogmatic personality that Hill sometimes said too much. He finished a clear second in the 1970 US Open at Hazeltine National, a course that had been restyled by Robert Trent Jones – a result that seemed to indicate that Hill had been well able to cope with the architect's notions of how a championship golfer should be tested. But Hill called Jones 'an idiot', said that 'a monkey could play this course as well as a man', and further incensed those club members proud of their rolling landscape by saying : 'All the course lacks is 80 acres of corn and four cows.' And, as a variant, that the sheep were being 'robbed of good grazing'. Although members mooed at him as he made his way along the fairways, and the USGA fined him $150 for insulting its hosts, there was some justice in Hill's remarks. Too many bunkers were out of sight from the tee, there were 11 holes involving 'blind' shots to the green, and the flags were likewise positioned wholly or partly out of sight. Dave Hill was three times a Ryder Cup choice, and his first appearance in 1969 at Royal Birkdale produced more strong language. Britain's captain Eric Brown's instruction to his team not to look for US balls in the rough had made tempers rise, and there was ill feeling in the match between Brian Huggett and Bernard Gallacher and Ken Still and Dave Hill. Hill vowed at the end of the encounter: 'The only way I'd ever come to Britain again was if I died and someone shipped my coffin by mistake.' But Hill was chosen for the 1977 match at Royal Lytham and St Annes, the vow was broken, and Hill said that it was the greatest honour of his career.

US wins 13 (1961–76)
US money $1,126,341 (1959–82) (30th all-time)
World money $1,267,279 (1959–82) (38th all-time)

HILL, Michael   USA
b. Jackson, Michigan 1939

Less gifted than his brother Dave, Mike Hill nevertheless enjoyed some good years on the US Tour, winning three times and finishing in the Top 60 six times in his 1968–81 tournament career, which is now probably over. He felt that some of his success was due to his brother because: 'I have a great golfer to set me straight when things go wrong.' Mike Hill's best year was 1974, when he finished 28th in the money list for some $76,000, but by 1981 he was making 16 tournament entries for the rather low return of $627, having been in the money just once. He had made the top 100 in the period 1968–77 but thereafter began to slip away.

US wins 3 (1970–77)
US money $565,643 (1968–82) (79th all-time)

HILL, Opal   USA
b. Newport, Nebraska 1892

Opal Hill had an outstanding amateur record, despite the fact that she did not take up golf until her early 30s. She won the Western no less than five times and the Trans-Mississippi four times. In the US Amateur she three times reached the semi-finals in the years 1929–36, but never progressed further. She was a Curtis Cup member in 1932–6, and was past her 40th year on even the first occasion. After the death of her husband she turned professional in 1942, one of the first women players to do so.

HINKLE, Lon Currey   USA
b. Flint, Michigan 1949

Lon Hinkle had a dominant year in 1979, when he finished third in the US money list with over $247,000. Since then he has been many people's tip as a future major championship winner and great player, but as he begins to move through his 30s, time is perhaps getting short. Hinkle joined the US Tour in 1972 and it was not until his sixth season that he began to make any impact at all, when he just found a place in the Top 60. In the meantime he had played overseas a little, being runner-up in both the 1975 German Open and the Japanese Sanpo Classic. These, he felt, were interludes away from the 'real world' of the US Tour. In 1978 he made a further move forward, winning his first tournament, the New Orleans Open. In that event he opened with a 74, improved to 67, which meant that he had safely made the cut – though only by 2 strokes – and was 8 behind the leaders. His finish of 64, 66 was then enough for victory. Lon had the opposite experience later that year. In a low-scoring tournament he began 68, 67, which left him no fewer than 7 strokes behind Ben Crenshaw's 65, 63. Hinkle then improved to 67, 64, which put him 1 shot ahead of Crenshaw at the finish. But in the meantime an outsider, Ron Streck, had busied himself over the last two rounds by setting a final 36-hole record of 135 (63, 62). Hinkle was equal second. Despite that disappointment Hinkle won some $138,000, which easily exceeded his totals for the previous six seasons. The next year, he nearly doubled it, up to almost a quarter of a million dollars, and suddenly found himself third in the money list. Early in the season he won the Crosby and, later on, the World Series, worth $100,000. Both had confused finishes. In the Crosby he led by 5 after three rounds and was then caught by Mark Hayes, who promptly four-putted to let him back in. After the eventual tie Hinkle took the play-off. The World Series he won when Larry Nelson had a double bogey on the 17th in the final round. Despite these victories Hinkle won far more fame in an event in 1979 in which he finished equal 53rd. Professional golf is a pretty dour affair. While public and press alike appreciate excellence, a bit of a laugh, especially if the joke is on authority, does no harm at all. It was Hinkle who first spotted in the 1979 US Open at Inverness that the way to play the 8th hole was to hit your tee shot down the 17th fairway. If your drive found the clear gap in the tree barrier, the 8th was shortened by some 75 yards. Hinkle played the hole accordingly. Others followed. Authority was not amused and bought itself a 30-foot Black Hills spruce and manoeuvred it into the gap. Hinkle realized that 30 feet is really not particularly high, and drove over it to the 17th fairway again. The story ought to end in a US Open victory – but the rest of Hinkle's play did not reach this standard of inspiration, and he took 8 on one hole. Another example of imaginative play was to be seen in the World Series later that year. When his shot to the 16th flag was blocked by trees, Hinkle (he claims deliberately) struck an iron that skipped over a pond as the only way of getting in close. The following year, Hinkle made strong assaults on two of the major championships. At Baltusrol in the US Open he began with a 66, good enough to lead most years. This time, he was faced with not one but two men tying the US Open record with 63s–Jack Nicklaus and Tom Weiskopf. Thereafter the latter faded down to 36th place. Nicklaus did not, but going into the final round Hinkle had made up 2 strokes and lay just 1 behind. He finished equal third. In the PGA Championship, Hinkle and Nicklaus were level after two rounds. Hinkle's 69 was then bettered by a Nicklaus 66 and Hinkle's final 75 left him 9 behind – but still good enough for another equal third place. And so to Europe and an event struggling, without great success so far, to elevate itself to major championship status, the European Open at Walton Heath. Hinkle began 69, 65 and opened up a lead of 4 over Tom Kite, which was reduced to 1 after the third round. The next day Kite came to the last needing two putts to be sure of winning – and took three. A little later Lon Hinkle arrived needing two putts to tie Kite's total. He too three-putted and was equal second. In 1980 and 1981 Hinkle earned well over $100,000 each year and began the 1981 season by being runner-up in two of the first three events. He remained in the top 30 both years, and in the 1981 US Tour statistics was second for eagles and sixth in driving distance, averaging 272.5 yards. He also became the first Tour regular to win the Long-Driving Championship with a mighty blow of 338 yards 6 inches.

US wins 3 (1978–9)
US money $812,258 (1972–82) (53rd all-time)
World money $957,484 (1972–81)

Lon Hinkle

HINSON, Larry   USA
b. Gastonia, North Carolina 1944

Although golf demands both physical and mental fitness, the list is long of those who have been able to overcome bodily problems. Larry Hinson suffered polio and was left with a withered left arm. In 1970 he was given the Ben Hogan award, presented to a player considered to have set an example of succeeding despite infirmity. Larry Hinson won the 1968 NCAA Championship and then turned pro, becoming a US Tour player the following year. He won the New Orleans Open during his first season and made the Top 60. The following year he finished in eighth place on the money list with $120,897. Although he remained in the Top 60 in the 1969–74 period, he did not again feature strongly, and his best performance was in the 1975 Texas Open when he lost a play-off to Don January. He is no longer a Tour player.

US wins 1 (1969)
US money $382,321 (1968–81)

85

HISKEY, Bryant   USA

b. *Burley, Idaho 1938*

'Babe' Hiskey first went on the US Tour in 1963; his career was one that well illustrates the long grind of failure that is normal for most players, in Hiskey's case relieved by moments of success. For his first five years he found a sponsor – which he needed. He won $395 his first year and paltry sums in 1964, 1965, 1968 and 1969, but in this period he won a Tour event, the 1965 Cajun Classic. The next two years were a little better and he took the 1970 Sahara Invitational, but all in all it was fortunate that Hiskey had the consolations of religion as a member of the Tour Bible-study group. It was appropriate that his partner in the 1972 National Team Championship (a fourball event) was the devout Kermit Zarley. After they won it, Zarley commented: 'The preachers got 'em.' The win gave Hiskey easily his best season with nearly $50,000 and 51st place in the money list. He has faded again and now makes very few tournament entries.

US wins 3 (1965–72)
US money $200,521 (1963–81)

HOCH, Scott Mabon   USA

b. *Raleigh, North Carolina 1955*

As an amateur, Scott Hoch was an All-American choice in 1977 and 1978 and won the ACC Championship at that time. He was also twice Atlantic Coast Conference winner, took the 1977 Northeast Amateur and the 1978 Rice Planters Amateur; but perhaps his outstanding achievement before turning professional was a runner-up finish in the 1978 US Amateur. This and other performances won him both a Walker Cup and a World Team Championship place. He turned professional in 1979 and finished high in the Tour qualifying school event late that year. Since that time Scott Hoch has been serving his apprenticeship on the US Tour by playing the most possible events. He has won approaching $50,000 in each of his first two seasons (1980 and 1981). He secured his first Tour victory in 1980 with the Quad Cities Open and also took the New Orleans Open in 1982, easily his best season at 16th on the money list with almost $200,000, for he then went on to take the Pacific Masters in Japan.

US wins 2 (1980–82)
US money $289,068 (1980–82) (155th all-time)
Overseas wins 1 (1982)

HOGAN, Benjamin William   USA

b. *Dublin, Texas 1912*

British Open Champion: 1953
US Masters Champion: 1951, 1953
US Open Champion: 1948, 1950, 1951, 1953
US PGA Champion: 1946, 1948

Whenever talk turns to the greatest players in golf history perhaps just three names are omitted by no one: Nicklaus, Jones and Hogan. Perhaps Ben Hogan is the most revered golfer of any, because of the way he overcame a near-fatal accident which crippled him for nearly a year and left him in pain ever after. Hogan began in golf as an 11-year-old caddie at a Texas golf club, where his future rival as the greatest player of an era, Byron Nelson, also worked. A few months older, Nelson won the early matches between the two and in the later professional game was to become a major player well before Hogan, who was a comparatively late developer. Hogan turned professional in 1931 and shortly afterwards began to play on the then rather limited US Tour, with little success. For several years after this attempt Ben Hogan stayed at home, doing a variety of jobs, mostly outside golf, and practising in all his spare moments. In 1937 he felt ready to try again and with his wife followed the Tour, getting nowhere as his very close contemporaries Sam Snead and Nelson began to make headline news. (Both were Ryder Cup players in 1937. Snead had five tournament wins; Nelson

Scott Hoch

four, including the Masters.) The months went by, Hogan at times not far from starvation, with such good play as he managed to produce being negated by a snap hook. One morning the wheels of his car were stolen; he nearly gave up and went back to Texas. He was saved, temporarily at least, by a 1938 win in the Hershey Four-ball. No further successes came his way either that season or the next. Then suddenly, in 1940, he was leading money-winner with five wins and $10,655. He repeated the story in the following year and in 1942 also, though this time with six victories. In 1942 he had his best performance in a major championship up to that time, a runner-up finish to Byron Nelson when he lost a US Masters play-off. Then came World War II and Hogan was out of golf until 1945. In the meantime Byron Nelson, exempted from military service because of haemophilia, had been winning almost everything he entered in 1944 and 1945 and had earned the accolade of the nickname 'Mr Golf'. Hogan thought he knew who was the better player and was not amused. With the war over, Hogan won five times in the short 1945 season. In 1946 he demonstrated his superiority beyond doubt: he won 13 times. Nelson was by then out of the race, having retired earlier that year, worn out by competitive play. It was also in 1946 that Hogan won his first major championship, the US PGA. Of course, he was leading money-winner – for the fourth time, with $42,556. The next year he won eight times, his play partly overshadowed by the remarkable successes of Bobby Locke and Jimmy Demaret, who was leading money-winner. In 1948 Hogan reached a peak perhaps not bettered in his more famous days during the early 1950s. He won 11 events, this time including the 1948 Open at Riviera Country Club and the US PGA. He was leading money-winner for the fifth time and took the Vardon Trophy for the lowest stroke average for the third time. At 69.30 his scoring is the second lowest to Snead's 1950 mark of 69.23. Hogan had discovered his 'secret'. There were some who said later that this secret lay quite simply in finally learning how to conquer the hook; that he made changes in swing, grip and set-up that enabled him to hit flat out and be sure that the worst to result would be a slight fade towards the end of the ball's flight. He had lost a little of the length he once got from a low, boring flight with draw that often saw his ball pitch yards short of other players and then roll yards past theirs; instead, he came into the ball with the face of his club slightly open with a

resultant left-to-right movement at the end of flight. His woods held the fairway more readily, and the higher flight gave his irons into the greens more bite. Probably no one before or since has equalled the low drive through the hitting area with his right hand that was a hallmark of the Hogan swing. He had reached perhaps the nearest any golfer has yet come to mastery over the ball. Watchers felt that Hogan, particularly from the tee, was placing his shots exactly where he wanted. Yet Hogan himself still felt that he hit only two or three shots per round exactly right. The secret was that he hit few that were far wrong. From the opening of the 1949 season Hogan finished 11th at Los Angeles, won the Crosby and then the Long Beach Open and lost at Phoenix in a play-off to Jimmy Demaret. He captained the Ryder Cup team, inspiring them to win from 1–3 down in the foursomes. He decided that a rest was in order and set off back to Texas. He was seldom to play ordinary tournament golf again. On the morning of 2 February 1949 a Greyhound bus came at Hogan out of the mist on the wrong side of the road. He spent some time at the side of the road, given up for dead, while people tended to his less injured wife. He had suffered numerous fractures but began to make good progress in hospital until a clot began to form and a principal vein had to be tied off. There were doubts as to whether Hogan would walk again; golf was considered out of the question. In May he mailed his entry for the US Open, so determined was he to get back into competitive golf, though at the time he had got no further in the way of exercise than walking around a table. He did return, but not until the Los Angeles Open in January 1950. Hogan was caught only by a strong Snead finish and then lost the play-off. By this time his record in major championships stood at one US Open and two PGAs. Thereafter, the PGA, involving more play through a succession of matchplay encounters, was beyond his strength. He now set his sights almost exclusively on the US Masters and Open. Any other tournament entry was made solely for competitive practice: he won only five run-of-the-mill tournaments in the rest of his career. In the 1950 US Open at Merion Hogan opened 72, 69, 72 and stood 2 behind Lloyd Mangrum, the 1946 champion and 4 ahead of George Fazio. He tired over the final nine holes and in the end these three tied on 287. Few gave the limping, exhausted Hogan a chance in the next day's 18-hole play-off; but in the end he dominated, beating Mangrum by 4 and

George Fazio by 6, the scores being, 69, 73, 75. Hogan was back. The following year he took his first Masters, playing four consistent rounds. He went into the last round one behind Skee Riegel and played boldly in the early stages, then cautiously once he was in the lead. It was said at the time that Hogan did not make a single bad shot, or an error of judgement, in his final 68. And so to Oakland Hills for the US Open, and a course that had been revamped to test the best. Hogan disliked it and a first-round 76 did nothing to improve his opinions. Yet he had lost little ground to the majority of the field. When he followed up with a 73 his position improved, only Bobby Locke having a substantial lead of 5. Hogan then produced a 71, had nearly caught Locke, and was poised for one last effort. His final 67 is regarded as the best round he ever played. Said the new champion: 'I vowed to bring this monster to its knees.' His 67 was one of only two rounds below 70 in the championship. The other was the 69 of Clayton Heafner, which brought him home two behind Hogan. In 1952 Hogan won only the Colonial Invitational. He did not feature in the top half dozen in the Masters and after a 69, 69 start in the Open faded to third place, 5 behind Julius Boros. In 1953 he won the Colonial Invitational again and the Pan-American Open. In fact, Hogan played just five times in this, his greatest major championship year, and won them all. First it was Augusta and the US Masters. Hogan played what he judged to be the best golf over four rounds of his career: 70, 69, 66, 69. He had set a Masters record that stood for 12 years until Nicklaus broke it; he was first by 5 strokes. The US Open was held at Oakland Hills that year. It is one of Hogan's least remembered victories because he made it all seem rather easy. Opening with a 67, he followed with 72, 73, 71 and won by 5, the first champion to lead throughout for 42 years. After these two majors, he was urged that a win in the British Open was needed; that the career of no great golfer was complete without proof that he could win on a British links course, possibly in cold and wind. Hogan was persuaded and sent in his entry for Carnoustie. He arrived well before the qualifying rounds and, with an intensity rare at the time, set himself to learn the course; how to play the small 1.62-inch British ball; and whether the ball should be struck differently from links turf. He was delighted by the extra length he got from the small ball and altered his striking with irons so that he grazed the turf rather than taking divots. Carnous-

tie's greens he found deplorably slow and offered to send for a lawnmower to cut them to championship length, always shorter in the US than in Britain. He qualified easily, and in the championship proper opened with a 73 and then the progressively lower rounds of 71, 70, 68. Watchers of his final round felt that had a 66 been required Hogan would have readily produced it. He had become the only player to win these three majors in a single season, a feat paralleled only by Jones's wins of the Amateur and Open Championships of both countries in one year, 1930. In each case, they had entered all the majors for which they were eligible. (Jones, as an amateur, could not play in the US PGA and at this time there was no such thing as the Masters; Hogan could not play in both the US PGA and British Open, because of a clash of dates.) Hogan now stood at the second pinnacle of his career. To many it seemed impossible that he would not continue to collect major championships for several years to come, yet that spurt between 1948 and 1953 saw his whole collection of five Opens and two Masters assembled. He had two more second-place finishes to come in the US Open, once losing a play-off to Jack Fleck in 1955, while he three-putted the last green the following year and failed to tie Middlecoff. Finally in 1960 came his last chance to break the US Open record with a fifth win. He played a bold shot on the 71st hole, spun back into water, and that was that. In the Masters of 1954 he tied Snead and narrowly lost the play-off over 18 holes by 71 to 70; he finished second again the following year. Little more was heard from him in this event until 1967. By then he had become part of golf history, his last win being the 1959 Colonial Invitational. Hogan began the Masters with a respectable 74, 73 – but caused no stir. On the practice grounds the spectators continued to watch newer heroes; only in Britain would Hogan have had a following who would sooner watch a great player of the past than the newest flash in the pan – but Hogan had played only once more on that side of the Atlantic, when he won the individual title in the 1956 Canada (World) Cup at Wentworth. But after his third-round 66 at the age of 54, there was some speculation that he could win again. In fact, another 66 would have done just that for him, but Hogan faded into final twilight with a 77 and equal tenth place. In his 66 there had been an outward half in 30 which equalled the Augusta record. The prime cause of Hogan's decline was his putting. Before his car crash he was reckoned one of the best putters on the US Tour; thereafter his putter was rarely a saver. He won because he hit fairways and greens. By 1956 he was to be seen on the 72nd green in that year's US Open trying a variety of putting strokes before he three-putted. Hogan afterwards said he had been trying to find any kind of stroke that gave him a feeling that there was an outside chance he would get the ball into the hole. True, there were rounds when he putted well, like Palmer in later years, but the confidence and nerve had gone. At the end of his career Hogan had won nine major championships, placing him behind only Jones and Nicklaus. Fifteen times he was either first or second. In the Masters he was never worse than seventh between 1941 and 1956, and from 1940 to 1960 he was always in the top 10 of the US Open. He won every Ryder Cup match in which he played. With 62 wins he is third in the all-time list of US Tour winners, despite the fact that he ignored the Tour in most of his best years. How much of Hogan's success was the result of practice it is difficult to say. Perhaps more important is that the innumerable hours spent in this way

illustrate his drive towards perfection. For example, his friend Jimmy Demaret once reasoned with him on the practice ground after Hogan had just shot a round with some half-dozen birdies. Said Demaret: 'For Christ's sake Ben, nobody ever played better than you did today. You can't birdie every hole.' Hogan: 'Why not?' Or a dream Hogan once related: he had been playing a round in which he had 17 holes in one. Hogan said 'I woke up mad about the one I missed.' On another occasion, he was seen hitting 3-woods for hour after hour, all perfect or near-perfect shots. It was remarked that you could not improve on perfection, so what good was Hogan doing himself? He replied: 'I want to know how I hit them when I'm tired.' Hogan was thought of as the hardest, toughest, most relentless competitor ever, and his nicknames reflect this. To the Scots after his 1953 Open win he became 'The Wee Ice Mon'. (At 5 feet 9 inches he was no dwarf, but most of his contemporaries were taller.) In the USA he was simply 'the Hawk'. Hogan had saved his money during his peak playing years and had set up a golf equipment manufacturing company. He later sold it for a good sum, but he continued to manage it. His urge towards perfection continued here, and he is said not infrequently to have had whole runs of clubs destroyed if they fell short of his high standards. He was always conscious of the charisma of the Hogan name. Once Gary Player rang him up from South America about his current swing problem. Hogan listened patiently then asked: 'Gary, whose clubs are you playing?' 'Spalding.' 'Ask Mr Spalding, then,' said Hogan – and put the phone down. He was indeed adept at the 'putdown', as Dai Rees once discovered. At the flag-raising ceremony before the 1967 Ryder Cup match, Rees, as British captain, had to introduce his team, and did so listing each player's tournament successes. Hogan, when his turn came, said only: 'Ladies and gentlemen, the finest golfers in the world.' Similarly he dealt severely with Arnold Palmer, then beyond dispute the finest player in the world, during the 1967 Ryder Cup. Palmer was discussing what he was going to do in a forthcoming match. Hogan: 'Who told you you were going to be picked?' Now long retired from tournament play, even from his beloved Colonial Invitational at Fort Worth, he still goes to the Shady Oaks club and continues the search for the perfect swing.

Ben Hogan

US wins 62 (1938–59) (3rd all-time)
US money $207,779 (181st all-time)

HOLLINS, Marion USA
b. *East Islip, New York 1892; d. 1944*

Nicknamed 'the Golden Girl', Marion Hollins reached the final of the US Amateur in 1913, where she was defeated 2 up by the English player Gladys Ravenscroft, who had won the British title the previous year. Marion reached the final again in 1921 and put a stop to the reign of Alexa Stirling, who had held the championship since 1916. She also won the Metropolitan in 1913, 1919 and 1924. Later she became involved in the building of the Women's National Course on Long Island and Cypress Point.

HOLTGRIEVE, James USA
b. *Des Peres, Missouri 1948*

A Walker Cup choice in 1979 and 1981, Jim Holtgrieve also played in the 1980 World Amateur Team Championship, and in that year reached the semi-finals of the US Amateur before being beaten by the eventual champion, Hal Sutton. He was second low amateur in the 1978 US Open and the 1980 Masters. He won the 1978 Missouri Amateur and the 1981 Mid-Amateur, designed by the USGA for golfers over 25, the first time it was played. The event is intended to combat the dominance of college golfers, who are virtually full-time players, in the US Amateur.

van HOOSE, Myra USA
b. *Fort Walton, Florida 1955*

As an amateur Myra van Hoose won the Kentucky High School title four years in a row and the Junior from 1969 to 1971; she followed with the Women's in 1975 and 1976. She turned professional in 1978 but it took her four attempts to qualify for the US Tour. Meanwhile she was learning her trade in mini-Tour events. A Tour player from 1980, she had a close contest with Carolyn Hill for Rookie of the Year honours but secured them with $41,396 and 33rd place on the money list and came from behind with a 67 to take second place in the Corning Classic. In 1981 she won $7,000 more and was down to 26th place; she had another satisfactory year in 1982 finishing 33rd in the money list with a total of $44,747.

US money $134,457 (1980–82)

HORTON, Donna: see White

HOYT, Beatrix USA
b. *Westchester County, New York 1880; d. 1963*

At 16 years 3 months, Beatrix Hoyt remained the youngest US Amateur Champion until the advent of Laura Baugh in 1971. Beatrix played in the second championship of all in 1896 and won, repeating the performance in both 1897 and 1898. She is therefore one of a select group with Glenna Collett, Virginia van Wie and Juli Inkster to have won three consecutively. Beatrix won the qualifying medal from 1896 to 1900 and retired from championship play after reaching the 1900 semi-finals.

HUNTER, William Irvine Scotland & USA
b. *Forest Row, England 1892; d. 1968*

Son of the professional at Deal in Kent, Willie Hunter finished leading amateur in the 1920 British Open and in 1921 took the British Amateur by the near record margin of 12 and 11 over Allan Graham at Hoylake. Later that year he had a memorable match in the US Amateur against Bobby Jones, which he won when Jones had a rare lapse in concentration. Hunter reached the semi-final stage, as he did in Britain the following year. He turned professional later and, though hampered by lack of power, won numerous titles in California.

HURD, Dorothy: see Campbell

HUTCHISON, Jock Scotland & USA
b. *St Andrews 1884*

Jock Hutchison was a familiar face to Americans until the end of his life, a result of his being honorary starter, with Fred McLeod, of the US Masters. The two would play nine holes and then disappear from the course. At his best from just before World War I to the mid 1920s, Hutchison first made some mark by finishing fifth in the 1911 US Open and in 1916 was second, behind amateur Chick Evans. In 1919 and 1923 he was third, and was joint second in 1920. In the first US PGA of all, in 1916, he was beaten in the final by Jim Barnes but won in 1920 when he defeated the comet of the day, J. Douglas Edgar. His greatest moments came in the first post-war British Open at St Andrews. Here he finished tied with amateur Roger Wethered after 72 holes but won easily in the 36-hole play-off. So superlative was his play to the flag that his

Jock Hutchison

clubs were examined and some controversy ensued as to whether or not the roughly punched faces of his irons complied with the spirit of the game, some feeling that he was gaining excessive backspin from their use. In 1922 he threatened to win again but finished fourth, 2 behind Walter Hagen. In America he is considered to have won eight important tournaments, including the North and South and the Western. He later twice won the PGA Seniors – in 1937 and 1947 – and was elected to the PGA Hall of Fame in 1959.

HYNDMAN, William, III   USA
b. Glenside, Pennsylvania 1915

One of the best amateurs of his day, Bill Hyndman was a late developer, not reaching a national final until he was 39 and first playing in the Walker Cup at the age of 42. He was finalist in the 1955 US Amateur, being beaten 9 and 8 by the great Harvie Ward, and in 1959 first reached the final of the British Amateur, going down to Deane Beman. Hyndman again reached the final in 1969 and 1970, and each time found Michael Bonallack facing him. At Hoylake he lost by 3 and 2 and then at Newcastle, County Down, Bonallack completed three wins in a row by trouncing Hyndman 8 and 7.

He had been the oldest man to reach a final, at 54, since the Hon. Michael Scott in 1933. Hyndman played five Walker Cup matches – 1957 and 1959, 1961 and then again in 1969 and 1971, after his progress in the British Amateur had forced him into consideration once more. From 1957 to 1961 he won every match in which he played, and then in 1969 won his foursomes and halved his singles. On that rare occasion that the US lost a Walker Cup, 1971, he halved his singles with youthful Roddy Carr and then lost in his last Walker Cup game to Dr David Marsh. In other team events, Hyndman was three times in the Americas Cup team and played in the Eisenhower Trophy in 1958 and 1960, being captain on the latter occasion. In 1958 Bobby Jones was the captain, and in a desperately close finish to the event Hyndman came up the 17th needing to finish in par at St Andrews. After a good drive at the Road Hole he faced that unique and classic golf problem: shall I go for the top level of the green, skirting a bunker on the left and risking the road to the right and beyond? Hyndman saw Jones nod and took this to mean that boldness was in order. He hit a superb long-iron and the US tied with Australia, though losing the play-off. Another shot in Hyndman's career was less fortunate, but just as memorable. Playing the following year in the US Masters, he found himself with a putt of some dozen or more yards down to the pin, which was set close to the water fronting the 11th green. Again Hyndman was bold – and glided past the hole and into the water, earning from former US Open Champion Lloyd Mangrum the forthright comment: 'That was the dumbest putt I ever saw.' He won the 1973 USGA Seniors Championship.

INKSTER, Juli (née Simpson)   USA
b. Los Altos, California 1960

Until 1982, Virginia van Wie (1932–4), Glenna Collett (1928–30), Alexa Stirling (1916–20) and Beatrix Hoyt before the turn of the century had been the only women to carry off the American Ladies' Championship three years in a row. Juli Inkster accomplished the feat in 1980–82, defeating Patti Rizzo in 1980, the Australian Lindy Goggin in 1981 and Cathy Hanlon in 1982. In the Curtis Cup in 1982 she won her two matches playing top by 7 and 6. Later in the 1982 season she showed her quality internationally by taking the individual prize in the Women's World Amateur

Team Championship by 4 strokes with 290 from the Spanish champion of the British Open, Marta Figueras-Dotti. *Golf Digest* chose her as world number one woman amateur. If Juli Inkster had remained an amateur she obviously would have had a considerable chance of approaching Glenna Collett's total of six wins in the US Amateur but the lure of professional golf proved too strong.

INMAN, Joseph Cooper   USA
b. Indianapolis, Indiana 1947

Joe Inman is one of that talented group of players on the US Tour who make few headlines but are down there somewhere in the middle of the tournament finishers' list taking in a comfortable amount of money and, in his case, enjoying professional golf. He is, then, a player who earns $50,000 a year or so and has been on the Tour since 1974. As an amateur, he won the North–South Amateur in 1969 and was a Walker Cup team member the same year. He then chose to delay turning professional for a few years; but he suffered no growing pains on the US Tour when he eventually joined it, taking home over $46,000 in his first year. From 1975 to 1979 he was in the Top 60. He has fallen away a little since, though still winning money. His lowest score is a 62, produced in the 1978 Greater Hartford, and he won the 1976 Kemper Open. His best season was 1976, when he finished 38th on the money list, though his $69,000 owed much to $50,000 from the Kemper victory.

US wins 1 (1976)
US money $513,019 (1973–82) (91st all-time)

IRWIN, Hale S.   USA
b. Joplin, Missouri 1945

Hale Irwin is one of the most consistent of modern American golfers. After the 1975 Tucson Open, where he missed the 36-hole cut, he did not do so again until the 1979 Crosby – a sequence of 86 events, bettered in the history of the US Tour only by Byron Nelson and Jack Nicklaus. His seasonal money wins also illustrate this consistency. He joined the Tour in 1968, after winning the 1967 NCAA, but made little money in his first two years. He then broke into the Top 60 in 1970. From 1972 on he never failed to reach $100,000. Four times he has been past $200,000 – 1975, 1976, 1977 and 1981 – with his highest total, $276,499, coming in 1981. From 1971, he has only twice been out of the

Juli Inkster

top 13 and included are four seventh places, two fourths, and a third in 1976. Irwin's consistency best shows itself on more difficult courses. He first won in the Heritage Classic over the Harbour Town course, reckoned one of the most testing in the USA , and then repeated the victory two years later in 1973. He had no further victories until June 1974, when he was playing in the US Open at Winged Foot. Although he finished 7 over par, he won it by 2 strokes with scores of 73, 70, 71, 73. The course had proved exceptionally difficult and Irwin's virtues of straight driving and excellent long-iron play had helped very much to bring him through. 'I am no birdie machine,' Irwin says. To put it another way, he is not one of the best putters and depends on excellence through the green rather than saving strokes through wedgemanship and putting streaks. His win came not because he played a particularly strong last round. Rather, of those bunched at the top, he played the steadiest last round (third-round leader Tom Watson had a 79). It was in the 1979 US Open that Irwin played what came to be called the shot of the year. At Inverness Irwin had begun 74, 68. A little ahead of him, Tom Weiskopf was playing a great round and on the 11th, a hole of 523 yards, hit a 4-iron up to the flag and holed the putt for an eagle. Irwin, 225 yards out, selected a 2-iron, put the ball 3 feet away and also holed for an eagle. Weiskopf finished in 67 and so did Irwin, now leading Weiskopf by 3 into the final round. The next day Weiskopf did not repeat his form, and tailed off to a 76 and a fourth-place finish. Irwin, by the turn, had established a lead of 6 over his closest challengers, aided by good luck twice on the 8th hole. Here he had driven well off line into trees but rebounded back to the fairway. Inevitably short in two, he had then hit far too firm an approach but it clattered into the flag, stopped 8 feet away and Irwin grasped his chance and holed out. He had, he said, been 'choking from the first tee' and, after a birdie on the 12th, proceeded to hit shot after shot off line, especially tee-shots with woods. But his rivals were doing little, only Gary Player making any kind of move but that from the near hopeless position of starting his last round 9 behind Irwin. Nevertheless he finished in 68 and was the man to beat. As things turned out Player accomplished a 7-stroke swing on Irwin with that round, for Irwin came to the 17th with a 5-stroke lead and then finished double bogey, bogey – still good enough to win by 2 but doing little for the image of championship. Even Jones once wrote that his greatest regret in looking back on his career was that he did not feel that he had ever increasingly dominated a championship throughout but had tended to fall away if in too commanding a lead. Irwin finished in 75. About a month later things were to turn out differently. Seeking to be one of the few to win the British and US Opens in the same year, at Royal Lytham he began 68, 68 to lead and then fell off to a 75; but he still led into the final round, in which he was paired with Severiano Ballesteros. Here he was faced by his antithesis: Irwin finds fairways (he was eighth in driving accuracy in the 1980 US Tour statistics, for instance); Ballesteros does not, partly because of his greater length. But that day Ballesteros got his iron shots onto the greens, from unlikely places at times, and under this pressure Irwin lost his lead and in the end faded away to a 78 and sixth place. He once summed up the peculiar pressures of golf that ruined his game that day: 'On the football field you can blow off your emotion by belting someone. In golf, pressure just keeps building up within you and there is no outlet of relief.' David Graham had meted out similar treatment a few years previously. In the World Matchplay at Wentworth, Irwin had won in both 1974 and 1975, and again in 1976 he was in the final. Graham was never ahead and in the last few holes Irwin made no real error, while Graham certainly did. This time it was not recovery shots that did for Irwin but impossible putts. Of course, the mores of golf demand most strictly that you do not 'belt' anyone for holing a long putt. But after the

match, which went to Graham against the run of play, it is said that Irwin kicked his golf bag across the locker room. And who could blame him? Although Irwin mainly confines himself to the USA, he can be called an international player, having won in Britain, Japan (the 1981 Bridgestone Classic), Australia (1978 PGA) and South Africa (1979 PGA), a total of five wins outside his home circuit. In the USA he has won a tournament most years and even in 1978, when he did not, he set the record for the time of $191,666 for money winnings without a Tour victory. In one year, 1977, he won three times: the Hall of Fame Classic was particularly memorable. Irwin set out to play over Pinehurst Number 2 rather crossly: he had just learned that he had not earned a place to compete in that season's World Series. The response was 65, 62, 69, 68 for a total of 20 under par at 264, a win by 5 strokes and a place in the World Series, in which

Hale Irwin

he later finished second. Irwin's swing can best be described by the word 'neat'. He stands upright to the ball and his action is essentially hands and arms, with less leg drive than most and little hip slide. He normally plays with draw and his main fault is a push to the right when the draw does not 'take'. He is also good at inventing little shots from around the green. In 1982 Irwin won again, became the fifth man to reach $2 million on the US Tour, and at the end of 1982 stood sixth on the US all-time money-winners' list (the money list, of course, reflects the inflation of prize money that leaves Sam Snead in 76th place and Ben Hogan 181st!).

US wins 14 (1971–82)
US money $2,140,093 (1968–82) (6th all-time)
Overseas wins 6 (1974–82)
Europe money £69,688 (1975–82) (53rd all-time)
World money $2,462,929 (1968–82) (8th all-time)

JACKSON, Katherine (née Harley) USA
b. *Fall River, Massachusetts 1881; d. 1961*

Winner of the Eastern Amateur in 1914 and 1921, Mrs Jackson, as Katherine Harley, won the US Amateur in 1908; then again in 1914, this time under her married name.

JACOBS, K. Thomas USA
b. *Denver, Colorado 1935*

After reaching the semi-finals of the US Junior at the age of 15, Tommy Jacobs went on the US Tour in 1957 and quickly became a consistent and effective player. He was in the Top 60 from 1958 to 1964 and again in 1966, his best placing being 12th in 1964, the last year he won a US tournament. He twice came close to winning a major championship. Having been sixth in 1962, Jacobs was a leading performer in one of the great US Opens, that of 1964 at Congressional CC, Washington DC. He began 72, 64, 70 and at that point led eventual winner Ken Venturi by 2 strokes. While Venturi, suffering from heat exhaustion, looked at one time as if he would be unable to finish the event, Jacobs could only manage a 76 in the final round and was second. Two years later he tied for the Masters with Jack Nicklaus and Gay Brewer, and in the 18-hole play-off lost to Nicklaus by 2 strokes. He was a Ryder Cup choice in 1965 and won three of the four matches in which he was involved.

US wins 4 (1958–64)
US money $227,376 (1957–81) (175th all-time)

JACOBSEN, Peter Erling USA
b. *Portland, Oregon 1954*

As an amateur, Peter Jacobsen was a Collegiate All-American from 1974 to 1976, won the Pacific Eight Conference in 1974 and in 1976 took the Oregon and Northern California Opens. However, when he turned professional his experience had been regional rather than national. Nevertheless he qualified for the Tour at his first attempt and began playing in 1977, when he had little success – just $12,000. After improvement over the next two years on the Tour, and a win overseas – the 1979 Western Australian Open – he broke firmly into the Top 60 in 1980, with a 26th-place finish and winnings for the season of over $130,000. Towards the end of the season he took his first Tour event, the Buick Open, with improving scores of 70, 70, 69, 67 as the leaders, Rex Caldwell and Barney Thompson, fell away into the mid 70s. He gained 7 strokes on the third-round leader. The following week Jacobsen came second in the BC Open, having therefore earned more than $64,000 in a couple of weeks. Much troubled by various injuries (he even had to have an operation on his vocal cords) he fell away somewhat in 1981 to 50th place. He once again came close to a win in the Buick Open, but lost the play-off. He is considered one of the most promising younger players on the US Tour and was 25th in 1982, winning the Johnny Walker Invitational in Spain. If his golf fails he has another string to his bow, being much in demand for clinics and other exhibitions: as a good physical mimic he draws laughs for impersonations of the swings of other players.

US wins 1 (1980)
US money $466,252 (1977–82) (99th all-time)
Overseas wins 2 (1979–82)

JAECKEL, Barry USA
b. *Los Angeles, California 1949*

Son of Richard Jaeckel, a well-known film and TV character actor, Barry won the Southern California title as an amateur in 1968 and three years later was runner-up in the Pacific Coast and a semi-finalist in the Trans-Mississippi. Deciding to turn professional after these results, he did not qualify for the US Tour until early 1975 but was successful on the 'mini-tour' and overseas, taking the French Open in 1972 as the surprise winner of the season. His scores of 68, 67, 63, 67 at Biarritz tied him with Clive Clark, and he won the play-off. A couple of weeks later he walked out of the German Open after a ruling dispute. He showed some temperament again at the same event in 1974, and was censured for 'ungentlemanly conduct' when he walked off the last green and refused to mark José Cabo's card for the previous seven holes. On the US Tour from 1975 he has made money, except in his first season, placings of 37th in 1978 and 48th in 1981 being his best money-list finishes. Jaeckel has an unorthodox swing, a reason why he finds consistency difficult to achieve, but an excellent short game. This is illustrated in his only US Tour victory: the 1978 Tallahassee Open. In a last-round 65 he covered the homeward nine in 30, chipping in three times for a couple of birdies and an eagle. In 1981 he came close to winning the Tournament Players' Championship, only one rung below the four majors. He held a 3-stroke lead into the last round, but his 74 was overtaken by Ray Floyd's 68. Floyd won the championship in a three-way play-off with Jaeckel and Curtis Strange.

US wins 1 (1978)
US money $360,609 (1975–82) (129th all-time)
Overseas wins 1 (1972)

JAMESON, Elizabeth　　　　　USA
b. Norman, Oklahoma 1919

A youthful prodigy as a golfer, Betty Jameson won the Southern Amateur in 1934 at the age of 15, then in the following year the first of four consecutive Texas Amateur titles, and in the last of these years, 1938, the Texas Open also. Among major amateur titles, she took the Trans-Mississippi in 1937 and 1940 and the Western Amateur in 1940 and 1942, in the latter year also taking the Western Open. However, the crown of her amateur career was to win the US Amateur in both 1939 and 1940. She turned professional in 1945 and the following year reached the final of the US Open the only time it was a matchplay event, losing to Patty Berg. In 1947 she won it with a score of 295, the first woman to break 300 for a 72-hole tournament. By this time she was a leading figure on the fledgeling US Tour, winning the 1952 'World Championship' and having her best year in 1955, with four victories. In all, she took nine US LPGA events. In 1982 she donated the Vare Trophy for the best annual stroke average on the LPGA Tour.

US wins 9 (1948–55)
US money $91,740

JAMIESON, James　　　　　USA
b. Kalamazoo, Michigan 1943

Jim Jamieson went on the US Tour in 1969 and gradually pulled himself up the money list. In 1972 came his best season. He won the Western Open, the oldest US tournament (founded 1899) with rounds of 68, 67, 67, 69. After three rounds he was in a dominant position, leading by 8, and finished 6 ahead. That same season he tied for second place in the US PGA and represented the USA in the World Cup. The following season he lay one behind Jack Nicklaus after three rounds of the Masters, but fell away to equal third place after a closing 77. His 15th place in the money list in 1972 for $109,532 was by far his best performance. He was in the Top 60 from 1972 to 1974. He is now more or less retired from the Tour.

US wins 1 (1972)
US money $302,175 (1969–82) (145th all-time)

Betty Jameson

JANUARY, Don   USA
b. Plainview, Texas 1929

The career of Don January is hard, if not imposs-ible, to parallel on the US Tour. He joined it as far back as 1956 and remains a substantial money-winner to this day, though now concentrating principally on the Senior Tour. He has been in the Top 60 no fewer than 20 times; his best years were 1963 and 1976, when he was ninth. It is likely that in 1972 Don decided that there was not much successful golf left in him. He left the Tour and involved himself fully in golf-course construction in his home area, Dallas. After two and a half years, however, business was on the wane as a result of the recession, so back he came in 1975, to finish 30th on the money list at 45 and out of competitive practice – and competing is a knack hard to regain after a lapse of time. He also took the Texas Open. The next year he won $163,622, easily his highest, winning the Tournament of Champions for the second time. His form led to his inclusion in the 1977 Ryder Cup team at Royal Lytham (at nearly 48 the oldest US player ever chosen); he halved his foursome and lost in the singles. He had previously made the team in 1965. The secret of January's longevity in tournament golf may lie in two factors.

He never wore himself out by the grind of playing all the available tournaments, and once stated that he ended his season once he had won $60,000; certainly that figure crops up frequently in his annual winnings. He also likes to be slow in everything he does, especially for the duration of a tournament, and is similar to Bobby Locke in this. He became financially stable early in his career, winning twice in his first season, and was also no doubt helped by the $50,000 he picked up for a hole in one at Palm Springs in 1961. In 1981 he made only eight Tour entries – little strain – but still came away with over $50,000. He is now seen increasingly on the relatively new Senior Tour. He took the 1979 PGA Seniors from George Bayer by a clear 8 strokes, and he has also won the Australian Seniors. On that US Tour he topped the official money list in 1981 with $62,925, and with other Senior events nearly reached $100,000. Together with Arnold Palmer, Gene Littler, Miller Barber and Bob Goalby, he is among the best older players, and perhaps more than any of these is good enough to compete effectively on the full Tour. January has one major championship to his name, the 1967 US PGA , an event he also came close to winning in 1961 and 1976, in each year coming in second. In 1976 he had scores of 70, 69, 72 to be 1 behind Dave Stockton, while in 1961 he was thwarted by the finish of Jerry Barber who holed a sequence of long putts on the last four holes. January won the Vardon Trophy for low stroke average in 1976, the oldest winner ever. He has won five Senior events, including the 1982 PGA Seniors, and led the 1982 scoring averages.

US wins 11 (1956–76)
US money $1,138,609 (1956–82) (26th all-time)
World money $1,649,629 (1956–82) (22nd all-time)

JENKINS, Thomas Wayne   USA
b. Houston, Texas 1947

After being an All-American choice in 1970 and 1971 Tom Jenkins turned professional in 1971 and joined the Tour the next season. He was in the Top 60 in 1975, the only year he has recorded a victory, which was in the IVB -Philadelphia Classic. He was again in the Top 60 in 1981.

US wins 1 (1975)
US money $341,558 (1979–82) (133rd all-time)

Don January

JESSEN, Mary Ruth   USA
b. *Seattle, Washington 1936*

Ruth Jessen was Pacific Northwest champion in 1954 and 1955, Washington state champion in 1954 and runner-up in the 1956 Intercollegiate Championship. She turned professional that last year and had her first US Tour victory in 1959. Thereafter she won most years, reaching a peak in 1964 when she won five events and was second on the money list. Thereafter she suffered much from ill-health and injury, involving thyroid surgery, tendonitis and the removal of a rib. However, she continued to put in high finishes and it was really no great surprise when she won the Sears Classic in 1971, one of only five tournament appearances that year. It also won her the Ben Hogan Award, given for overcoming physical problems, as did that maestro after his 1949 car smash. The $10,000 she won for the Sears was then the highest on Tour.

US wins 11 (1959–71)
US money $145,017 (1958–76)

JOHNSON, Howie   USA
b. *St Paul, Minnesota 1925*

Howie Johnson went on Tour in 1956 and took two US events during his career – in 1958 and 1959. He also won the 1960 Mexican Open. He had a particularly consistent season in 1970, when he missed only one halfway cut and won over $60,000. He now plays over-50s golf and has won the 1980 Southern California Seniors and the 1981 US National Seniors Spring Championship.

US wins 2 (1958–9)
US money $280,897 (158th all-time)
Overseas wins 1 (1960)

JOHNSTON, Harrison R.   USA
b. *St Paul, Minnesota 1896; d. 1969*

In Bobby Jones's period of greatest dominance (1924–30) in the US Amateur, Jimmy Johnston picked up the 1929 championship, one of the two that Jones did not, and the following year led the US Open after two rounds. He also won the Western Amateur in 1924 and had a winning sequence of seven in a row from 1921 in the Minnesota State Amateur. He played four times for the USA in the Walker Cup (1923, 1924, 1928 and 1930), winning three out of four foursomes and the only two singles for which he was selected.

JOHNSTON, William   USA
b. *Donora, Pennsylvania 1925*

Bill Johnston is one of those players to find a new lease of life as a Senior, for he is certainly more of a name now than in his full Tour playing career. On the US Tour, which he joined in 1951, he won twice but apart from these successes his money winnings were low. He was second in the 1960 French Open and won 11 state Opens in Montana, Arizona, Colorado, Nevada and Utah. As a Senior he won the 1979 USGA Seniors and the 1980 USGA Seniors Spring Open. In 1979 he lost a play-off in the PGA Seniors to Jack Fleck.

JOHNSTONE, Ann Casey   USA
b. *Mason City, Iowa 1921*

A late developer, Mrs Johnstone did not reach her peak until her late 30s but then built a very good amateur record, playing on three Curtis Cup teams between 1958 and 1962 and winning four of the five matches in which she played. She did not manage a US Amateur win but twice came close, reaching the semi-finals in 1960 to be beaten by Jean Ashley, while she got as far as the final in 1957 to meet just about the most formidable opponent possible, JoAnne Gunderson. She lost by 8 and 6. Otherwise her best results were to win the Trans-Mississippi and North and South in 1959 and the Western the following year. She also took her state title half a dozen times.

JONES, Grier Stewart   USA
b. *Wichita, Kansas 1946*

Grier Jones won the 1967 and 1968 Big Eight Conference, was 1968 NCAA Champion and won the Broadmoor Invitational. He then turned professional and was medallist at the qualifying school event. In 1969 he was Rookie of the Year and in the Top 60, as he was again in 1970 before a decline in form in 1971. Then came his biggest year, 1972. In 35 tournament entries he won money in 30 and was in the first ten 13 times. There also came his first Tour victory, which was achieved in dramatic style. Going into the last round of the Hawaiian Open at Waialae Country Club 5 behind Bob Murphy, to his start of 65, 73, 72 he added a final 64 against Murphy's 69 and then won the play-off. Later in the year he also won the Robinson Fall Golf Classic and had two second places during the season. His placing of fourth on the money list proved to be easily the highest he would achieve, as were his money winnings of $140,177. He was in the Top 60 again in the years 1973–4 and 1976–9, and won again in 1977 in the World Team Championship with Gibby Gilbert. He also suffered one of the greatest late charges that Jack Nicklaus has ever made. In the 1978 Inverrary Classic Jack birdied each of the last five holes, holing two chips, for a 65. Jones was beaten into second place.

US wins 3 (1972–7)
US money $790,625 (1968–82) (57th all-time)

JONES, Robert Tyre, Jnr   USA
b. Atlanta, Georgia 1902; d. 1971

British Amateur Champion: 1930
British Open Champion: 1926, 1927, 1930
US Amateur Champion: 1924, 1925, 1927, 1928, 1930
US Open Champion: 1923, 1926, 1929, 1930

After Ben Hogan's victory in the 1953 British Open, which climaxed his greatest year, Bobby Jones met him at a dinner to honour the achievement. There had been some discussion in the press as to whether Jones or Hogan was the greatest player. Jones sought out Hogan to tell him that he wanted nothing to do with the dispute. Hogan replied that all a golfer could do was be the best of his time. If he could manage that, he had the skill and nerve to have triumphed in any era. When it comes to comparing the abilities of giants separated by time, that is probably as good a judgement as one can find. It is, however, possible to examine and contrast the careers of the three greatest golfers (with apologies to Hagen, Nelson, Snead and others) of the past 60 years: Nicklaus, Hogan and Jones. For a start, once they had reached their full powers, each dominated an era; each began as favourite in every event entered; each wanted to be, and was, the greatest player in the world. The careers of Hogan and Nicklaus are, of course, dealt with in their entries but, in brief, Nicklaus has won 19 major championships, two of them the US Amateur, and has nothing left to prove. He can only add a major or two to his 1982 total of 19, perhaps his most realizable ambition being to take a record-breaking fifth US Open or a sixth PGA. Hogan dominated from 1940 to about 1956 but his major championship wins, nine, were compressed into the period 1946 to 1953. Jones's period at the

top was relatively shorter: 1923 to 1930, and he achieved a final symmetry in 1930 when he won each of the majors that he was qualified to enter: the British Amateur and Open; the US Amateur and Open. Having done it all, and not being attracted by the professional golf of the day, he retired at the age of 28, the same age as Hogan was beginning to make a name for himself. Jones first played at about the age of five, tagging along behind his parents. A photograph of his position at the top of the backswing shows at least two of the characteristics of the mature Jones swing: it was long and there was none of the restricted hip turn introduced by Byron Nelson. Jones believed that everything in the swing should be free and rhythmic and his hip turn was through 90 degrees, nearly as much as Harry Vardon's. By the age of nine he was his club's junior champion and at 11 first broke 80. At 14 he was driving 250 yards (with hickory shafts, of course), was Georgia State Amateur Champion and won his first two matches in the US Amateur. At 15 he was winner of the Southern Amateur and on the threshold of being considered the best golfer in America: in 1919 he was runner-up in both the Canadian Open and the US Amateur, and a year later he tied for eighth in the US Open. At 20 he was runner-up in the US Open and, with his substantial record of achievement, was approaching the end of what his biographer O.B. Keeler was to call the 'lean years'. The 'fat years' began with the 1923 US Open, won in a play-off against Bobby Cruickshank. His brilliant long-iron from a bare lie and over water to the heart of the green at the last hole has gone down in golfing legend. In the years 1924–30, Jones then won the US Amateur five times in seven entries and was runner-up on one of the two remaining occasions. In 36-hole matches between 1923 and 1930 he was only once beaten over the distance, being a little more likely over the short 18-hole sprint to be caught by a player having a good streak. His record was no less impressive in the US Open, in which he was always facing the two greatest professionals – among others of great quality – Gene Sarazen and Walter Hagen. From 1922 to 1930 he had four wins, two seconds and lost two play-offs. Even in his worst year he never had anything below an 11th place. During this period if Jones did not win, it was headline news – as much as if Jack Nicklaus in his heyday were to fail to break 80. Perhaps his record in the British Open was even better – with one exception. He first played in it at the age of 19

Bobby Jones

and totalled 151 for 36 holes, only 4 behind the leader, but went out in 46 in the third round at St Andrews. Jones was then 2 over par on the next and, after bunker problems, took five to the 11th green. He then tore up his card. Jones was a highly temperamental player, said to lose pounds in weight in the strain of a tournament, but he always considered this act of his to be his greatest disgrace – far worse than the frequent club-throwing of his extreme youth. However, it does not compare too unfavourably with today's withdrawals through 'injury'. Jones decided from that moment on that his behaviour would have to be improved: no bad language, no club-throwing; anyway, there was never again any reason for tearing up a card. He became as near perfect in comportment as it is possible for a golfer to be; although he was seldom tested, as Jack Nicklaus was to be later, with having to accept defeat gracefully. His record in the British Open thereafter cannot be improved on. He did not make the Atlantic journey again until 1926, and

then also played in 1927 and 1930. Each time he won. This points up what was the most remarkable feature of all about Jones as a golfer. He was an amateur with a full-time career, variously academic or business. Normally he would play his three or four events a year, while the rest of his golf was confined to friendly four-balls and a little practice to get the feel of things at the start of the season. In the winter he usually did not play at all. In all Jones played in 52 tournaments and won 23. In the years 1928 and 1929, for instance, he made just five entries, won the US Open, lost a play-off and took the US Amateur. But in 1930 he did consciously, and certainly for the first time, decide to see if he could win 'everything'. That everything was the Amateur and Open Championships of Britain and America. (The Masters did not begin till 1934, and as an amateur he was barred from the US PGA.) The most formidable obstacle was the British Amateur, in which the 18-hole matches, except for the final, were faced by Jones with some trepidation, though he was better over 18 holes (and any other distance) than anyone else in the world. In the first round at St Andrews he faced Sid Roper, who began tidily indeed with five 4s while Jones was 5 under par and 3 up. That was just about the match; when it finished on the 16th Jones had recorded six birdies and an eagle. He brushed his second-round opponent aside and then faced Cyril Tolley, best British amateur. The wind howled without respite; both went round in about 75 and Jones won after a stymie on the 19th. After three more victories the next crisis came when Jones found himself 2 down with five to play in the semi-final against George Voigt. Voigt obliged by driving out of bounds on the 14th and was bunkered on the 16th. Both players birdied the Road Hole and Jones came through on the last with a par. In the final he just missed being the first man to play a round at St Andrews without a 5 on his card, but anyway was 4 up and won comfortably 7 and 6. Such a clear margin was not unusual for Jones: in his five US Amateurs, he took the finals by these scores: 9 and 8, 8 and 7, 8 and 7, 10 and 9 and 8 and 7. In his last three Walker Cup singles he beat Tolley 12 and 11 in 1926, Phil Perkins 13 and 12 in 1928 (the record) and Roger Wethered 9 and 8 in 1930. These were three golfers as good as Britain had to offer. He won all six of his Walker Cup singles and three of four foursomes. In the British Open that followed soon after, his form was poor, apparently partly because of a putter which did not suit him.

He opened with a 70 and followed with 72, 74 (in which he dropped eight shots in the first three holes to be 2 ahead of Leo Diegel and 1 behind Archie Compston, who had a 68 in the third round. In the last round, Jones played one of his most famous holes, the par-5 5th at Hoylake. Down a bank, just a little away from the green in two, he saw his third come back to his feet, and his fourth was not any too near, either. Three putts followed for a 7. Jones, undaunted by this horrible reverse, finished in 75. Others bettered this, of course, but no contenders did. Compston had an 82. Jones had had his luck, had survived, and returned to Interlachen for the US Open. Jones opened 71, 73, which had him well up the field, and then powered to a 5-shot lead with a 68. In his last round he had three double bogeys on par 3s but holed a nearly 20-yard putt on the last. His 75 was good enough to bring him in 2 ahead of Macdonald Smith and 5 ahead of the field. The final act of the drama remained. So intense was public interest that just a single US newspaper sent a team of 16 writers and photographers, while 50 US marines were assigned to protect Jones along the fairways of Merion. Jones equalled the record with 69, 73 in the qualifying medal rounds and won his matches by 5 and 4, 6 and 5, 10 and 8 and 8 and 7. They called it 'the Grand Slam' or 'the Impregnable Quadrilateral'. Space forbids an examination of the manner of Jones's other nine major championship wins, but they had certain factors in common: often a particular stroke that has gone into legend; often a distinct tendency to falter through lapses of concentration when in too commanding a lead; always superb driving with some draw, which, if not as long as today's, was long enough and done with hickory shafts and less resilient balls; always, too, excellent long-iron play; unmatched approach putting; and good holing out. Jones himself felt, however, that he was not a master of the pitch shot and he did not have the advantage of the modern sand-iron from bunkers. After his retirement from competition Jones remained in the eye of the golfing public. First he produced a series of instructional films and then, with Spaldings, designed the first matched set of flanged irons. They remained in production for some 40 years. Most, however, would agree that his greatest remaining contribution to golf lay in the design of Augusta National and the founding of the US Masters. From its start in 1934 Jones played every year, though he knew very soon that he had lost his competitive flair and

not infrequently had the 'yips' on the greens. In 1947, he withdrew after two rounds, complaining of a sore neck and shoulders. It was the last Masters in which he competed, though he struggled on with friendly golf for a few more years. By 1948 he suffered double vision; by 1964 his legs were paralysed and by 1968 his arms as well. After ill-advised operations it had been found that he had syringomyelia, a fluid-filled cavity in the spinal cord causing first pain, then loss of feeling and muscle wastage. He bore it all with the grace he had shown on the golf course.

JOYCE, Joan   USA
b. Waterbury, Connecticut 1940

Thought by many to be the greatest woman softball player ever, Joan Joyce, after a 20-year career as both amateur and professional in that sport, gave golf a try in 1975. Two years later she was good enough to win her player's card for the US Tour, remarkable progress. Age is likely to mean that she will never be an outstanding player; but she wins money at golf, has taken two mini-Tour events and was 74th on the 1982 money-list. In 1982, in the course of a final-round 67 in the Lady Michelob, she took only 17 putts, a record for the US LPGA Tour – and one better than the men's record, held by Sam Trahan.

US money $39,771 (1977–82)

KABLER, Carole: see Callison

KAZMIERSKI, Joyce   USA
b. Pontiac, Missouri 1945

As an amateur, Joyce Kazmierski did not win a major title but was Midwest college champion from 1965 to 1967, and National Collegiate runner-up in 1964 and winner in 1966. She was runner-up in the 1965 Trans-Mississippi and reached the semi-finals of the 1968 US Amateur, shortly afterwards turning professional. Since then she has never won a tournament but is a consistent money-winner, being within the top 30 from 1973 to 1979, and had been second eight times by the end of 1981. Her best season was 1973, when she was tenth in the rankings; her stroke average was below 75 from 1975 to 1980. She acts as an unofficial astrology consultant to the US Tour.

KEISER, Herman USA
b. *Springfield, Missouri 1914*

Herman Keiser turned professional in 1935 but was only on Tour from 1945 on. His big year was 1946, when he won three events, one of which was the Masters. He began 69, 68 to lead comfortably, held it with a third-round 71 to lead by 5, and then faltered a little with a closing 74. Ben Hogan picked up 6 strokes over these last two rounds, and, after Keiser had three-putted the last hole, had a chance of the tie – but three-putted himself. Keiser had played cautiously throughout, not attempting the par 5s with long seconds over water, and his victory was largely due to excellent chipping and putting. He and Hogan finished well clear of the rest of the field. Keiser played in the 1947 Ryder Cup, in which he was the only US player to lose his singles – to Sam King. He has also won four state Opens and now plays from time to time on the Senior Tour.

US wins 5 (1942–7)
US money $43,863

KERTZMAN, Karolyn USA
b. *Rapid City, South Dakota 1950*

A stalwart of the US Tour since turning professional in 1971, Karolyn had her best finish with third in the 1975 Wheeling Classic. She was in the Top 60 from 1972 to 1976 and maintains a stroke average in the 74-to-75 band.

US money $94,224 (1971–82)

KIMBALL, Judith Ann (later Simon) USA
b. *Sioux City, Iowa 1938*

As an amateur Judy Kimball reached the semi-finals of the 1959 Western and Trans-Mississippi; she has played on the US Tour since 1961. She won the American Open (not to be confused with the US Open) in her first year and then in 1962 took one of the major championships, the 1962 US LPGA. She did this with the then record score of 70, 69, 71, 72 for 282 and won by 4 strokes. She continued to be a leading player throughout the 1960s, being in the top 20 from 1961 to 1968 and then maintaining a Top 60 position until 1979. Her best placings were in 1966 and 1967, when she was eighth and seventh in the money lists.

US wins 4 (1961–71)
US money $181,106 (1961–82) (61st all-time)

KING, Elizabeth USA
b. *Reading, Pennsylvania 1955*

A member of the National Collegiate Championship-winning Furman University team in 1976, individually Betsy King was low amateur in the 1976 US Open, finishing in eighth position; earlier she had reached the semi-finals of the 1972 US Junior Championship. On turning professional she been a leading player since that time. However, she has not yet won a US Tour event, though she has been involved in a play-off. From 1978 to 1982 she has been in the top 50 and her highest money list placings were 20th and 19th in 1978 and 1979. In 1981 she won the Genjiyama Classic on the Japan Tour.

US money $232,075 (1977–82)

KIRBY, Dorothy USA
b. *West Point, Georgia 1920*

Four times a Curtis Cup player between 1948 and 1954, Dorothy Kirby was for many years a leading contender for the US Amateur. She reached the final in 1939 to be beaten by Betty Jameson, and again in 1947 when she went down to Louise Suggs. Finally in 1951 she won, having also reached the semi-finals in 1949 and the quarter-finals on three other occasions. Among her other achievements can be listed the Southern in 1937, the 1943 North and South and five Georgia titles.

KIRK, Margaret: see Bell

KIROUAC, Martha: see Wilkinson

KITE, Thomas O. USA
b. *Austin, Texas 1949*

Tom Kite is easily the best golfer in the world amongst those that hardly ever win a tournament. He may well also be the most consistent golfer currently on the scene. The season of 1981 illustrated these aspects most clearly. This time he did win, only for the third time on the US Tour, taking the Inverrary Classic, but more significant was his mass of high finishes. He was second three times, third three times, fourth once, fifth once and sixth five times. Overall, in 26 tournaments entered, he was in the top 10 21 times (compared to 10 in 1980 and 11 in 1979). In his last 18 entries he only once finished worse than eighth. Naturally he missed no cuts, and extended his personal sequence by the end of the year to 35. By the Crosby of 1982 he had played 26 consecutive rounds in par or better. He had won the Vardon Trophy for low stroke average, was leading money-winner with $379,699, the fourth highest ever, and had stopped Tom Watson winning for a fifth consecutive time. Kite himself emphasizes that prize money has inflated, and feels that his year did not compare with those of multiple victories by past heroes. Kite is 5 feet 8, and by current standards a short hitter. Superior wedge play is therefore vital to him for occasions when he cannot reach a par 5 or par 4 into wind in 2 strokes. To broaden his variety of shot from 50 yards in, he therefore added a third wedge, discarding his 2-iron and altering the loft on his 3-, 4- and 5-irons to fill the gap. He continued serenely on his way in 1982, tying for the Hope Classic with five rounds under 70 but losing the play-off to Ed Fiori. In a later play-off, for the Bay Hill Classic, Kite was more fortunate, beating Jack Nicklaus and Denis Watson on the first extra hole. Tom Kite had taken the conventional route towards professional golf: through college golf. As an amateur he was first heard of in 1970 as medallist in the Western Amateur, runner-up in the Southern Amateur and second to Lanny Wadkins in the US Amateur. He was chosen for the 1970 World Team Championship. The following year he earned Walker Cup honours and was one of only two in the US team to win their singles on the last day for this losing team. In 1972 he was, with Ben Crenshaw, co-Champion in the NCAA and, a rare first, won the All-American. He then turned professional. His first year on Tour was notable for consistency rather than sudden excellence. He missed only three cuts in 35 entries and won a second tour event, with fifth his best placing in a full event, when he finished 63, 65. At 56th place he broke into the Top 60 and was chosen Rookie of the Year. Every year thereafter Tom Kite has been in the top 26 and by 1976 was topping $100,000 each year; his best placing was 11th in 1978. He first won in 1976, the IVB-Philadelphia Classic and the BC Open followed in 1978. His money total was over $150,000 in the years 1978–80. In the last of these years he had his first and only win overseas, the European Open at Walton Heath, a course at which in 1981 he produced the most brilliant scoring of anyone in winning his Ryder Cup match against Sandy Lyle. Lyle was 7 under par and Kite beat him

Tom Kite

3 and 2. Overall, in two Ryder Cup matches he has taken 6½ points out of 8. In ten seasons to the end of 1982 Kite has taken more than $1½ million but only won five times. A look at the 1981 US Tour statistics may give some clues as to why Kite is a high finisher but seldom a winner. He had the lowest stroke average, the second most birdies, was fifth at hitting greens in the right number, 14th in putting, sixth at getting down in two from greenside bunkers, seventh most accurate driver; only in driving length is he nowhere, not in the first 50. However, these figures are the kind that one might expect of a man who has won half a dozen times in the season. The only answer at present will have to be that Kite does not produce inspirational surges. The par rounds keep flowing from his clubs but somewhere in each field there is a man or two who 'knows' this is his tournament, goes for every shot, takes the cheque and is then not heard from for a while. Kite has seldom featured strongly in the major championships, a weakness in his record. He has had three finishes in the top five of the Masters and tied for second, 2 behind Nicklaus in the 1978 British Open. His 1982 was again highly consistent. He was third on the US money list with some $340,000 and won the Vardon Trophy for the

lowest stroke average, followed closely by Calvin Peete, Curtis Strange and Tom Watson.

US wins 4 (1976–82)
US money $1,660,828 (1972–82) (11th all-time)
Overseas wins 1 (1980)
World money $1,926,953 (1972–82) (15th all-time)

KLASS, Beverly   USA
b. Tarzana, California 1956

Beverly Klass was the cause of the US LPGA instituting a minimum age limit of 18 for participating in the US Tour. At the age of eight she won the National Pee-Wee Championship by 65 strokes and her father was encouraged to have her turn professional the following year. By 1967 she was playing on the full Tour, though only 4 feet tall and weighing 88 lb, and only in a few events. Her stroke average of just over 90 was not bad for a girl of 10, and she actually won money, some $131. However, the exposure and publicity can hardly have been good for her, and she did in fact suffer mentally during her teens, by this time once more an amateur. At 19 she turned professional again and was in the top 60 in 1977 and 1979. In 1977 she won the Ram Long-Driving Contest, and the following year achieved a US LPGA record with 19 putts in a round during the 1978 Women's International at Moss Creek Plantation, Hilton Head (a record subsequently broken by Joan Joyce in 1982). She is now beginning to seem a substantial player.

US money $105,353 (1976–82)

KNIGHT, Nancy: see Lopez

KNUDSON, George   Canada
b. Winnipeg, Manitoba 1937

Ben Hogan is seldom eager to let words of praise pass his lips, so his judgement that Knudson had 'the best swing of the present generation' (the 1960s) should be given due weight. Blessed with such a swing, George Knudson's career, now over for some time as a winner of major tournaments, promised more than it achieved. Unlike Hogan himself, he lacked application and came to find that golf was work, not play, and preferred the bright lights and skiing. Nevertheless his golf successes were considerable. He turned professional in 1958 and after brief early visits to the US Tour became more or less a full-time com-

George Knudson

petitor from 1961, when he won his first event. From 1962 to 1972 he was always in the Top 60, but not thereafter. His best season was 1968, at 17th, and he won twice successively – the Phoenix and Tucson Opens – after which, feeling that enough is enough, he went back to Canada. His last US win came in 1972, and he also won four times on the Caribbean circuit. Canada's best player for some time, he won the Canadian PGA five times between 1964 and 1977 and the Ontario Open in 1978, which was his last important win. His nearest approach to a major championship was the 1969 Masters. Here he tied with Casper and Weiskopf for second, 1 behind George Archer. On a wider stage he won individual honours in the 1966 World Cup, and two years later helped Canada to victory.

US wins 8 (1961–72)
US money $532,157

KOCH, Gary Donald   USA
b. Baton Rouge, Louisiana 1952

Gary Koch won the Florida Open at the age of 16. A year later he won the US Junior Championship, and at that time once led the local qualifiers for the

103

Gary Koch

and 1958 (at the age of 45). In 1931 he beat the British Open Champion of that year, Tommy Armour, in a play-off for the Michigan Open, which he was to win on two further occasions; he took the amateur equivalent six times. In the remainder of the 1930s his achievements did not live up to so bright a beginning, the 1936 NCAA and runner-up in the Western Amateur the following year being his best results. He played on the losing American team in the 1938 Walker Cup, and again in 1949 when he won both his matches; a final appearance came in 1957 at the age of 44.

KRANTZ, Michael   USA
b. 1951

The career of Mike Krantz is illustrative of the toughness of the US Tour. He has failed to win his tournament players' card but has performed quite successfully elsewhere, particularly on the Asia Circuit. In 1978 he won $34,000 overseas, winning the Otago Charity Classic and the Indonesian Dunlop Matchplay. He had the curious experience in 1979 of winning the Thailand Open, despite being taken to hospital on account of dehydration. He has seldom competed in Europe, but was third in the 1979 Scandinavian Enterprises Open.

US Open by 11 strokes. His major success as an amateur was to win the 1973 Trans-Mississippi; he also reached the semi-finals of the 1974 US Amateur and twice won the South-East Conference. He was a Walker Cup choice in both 1973 and 1975, with a 50% success rate the first year and winning all his matches in 1975. First on Tour in 1976, he won the Tallahassee and the Florida Citrus in 1977, but without managing consistency overall. Since 1977 he has not won again, falling to 162nd on the money list in 1981, with winnings of only $12,000, and 98th in 1982, when he improved to some $43,000.

US wins 2 (1976–7)
US money $297,322 (146th all-time)

KOCSIS, Charles R.   USA
b. Newcastle, Pennsylvania 1913

Chuck Kocsis was both a youthful prodigy and a major amateur until well into his 40s. He first attracted attention in 1930 when he beat Francis Ouimet in the US Amateur and went on to reach the quarter-finals, something he also did in 1935

KRATZERT, William Augustus, III   USA
b. Quantico, Virginia 1952

Bill Kratzert, son of a club professional, won the Indiana Amateur at the age of 16 and the State Open the following year. He was an All-American choice in 1973 and 1974 and qualified for the US Tour for 1976. That first season he finished in 102nd place in the money list, but he shot to tenth place the following year, one of the most dramatic improvements on record. He had won in the World Team event at the end of his first season and took the Greater Hartford in 1977 by 3 with scores of 66, 66, 64, 69. In 1978, although winning no events, he was down to eighth place and approaching $200,000 in money winnings. He suffered from tendonitis in 1979 and fell off a little, though still topping $100,000; in 1980 he came back strongly to 12th place in the money lists with over $175,000 and won the Milwaukee Open. He had come close to winning Jack Nicklaus's prestige Memorial Tournament in 1978, pursuing Jim Simons to the end and losing only when Simons sank a 20-foot putt on the last green of all. His standard fell away

Bill Kratzert

during 1981 and 1982 (when he was 139th) and it remains to be seen whether Kratzert will consolidate his past achievements and become a major player or, like so many others, fade into obscurity. His hobby is collecting Arabian horses.

US wins 3 (1976–80)
US money $695,385 (1976–82) (65th all-time)

KROLL, Theodore   USA
b. New Hartford, New York 1919

After turning professional in 1937 Ted Kroll was called away by World War II, in which he won a Purple Heart. He rejoined the Tour in 1950. He first won in 1952 and had nine further victories on Tour, including the 1962 Canadian Open. He topped the money list in 1956, having three wins, and won $72,836. He had been sixth the previous year. His best finishes in the major championships were fourth in the 1956 US Open and third in 1960, while in 1954 he had a 60 at Brackenridge Park during the Texas Open, the equal second lowest round recorded on the US PGA Tour. Ted Kroll was three times a Ryder Cup choice: 1953,

1955 and 1957. He was crushed 9 and 7 by Fred Daly in the only singles he played in, but was far more successful in foursomes, being in the winning pair on each of the three occasions.

US wins 9 (1950–62)
US money $261,339 (167th all-time)

LAFFOON, Ky   USA
b. Zinc, Arkansas 1908

One of the true eccentrics of the US Tour in times past, Ky Laffoon had the nickname of 'the Chief', revealing the fact that he was part Red Indian. He had a love-hate relationship with his clubs: upset with the behaviour of his putter on one occasion, he attempted to strangle it. That proving indecisive, drowning was tried next. Laffoon then relented, deciding that mere punishment was perhaps enough: he attached it with string to his car and let it bruise itself severely as he drove on to the next tournament. With possibly another putter he once found himself in a minor North Carolina tournament 3 feet from the hole with two putts to win. Laffoon lipped out his first attempt – but to only 2 inches. Nevertheless the malevolent implement failed again. Laffoon then tried a less direct approach: he belted down on the top of the ball. It flew 2 feet up in the air and from there into the hole. Nothing against it in the rules. With the loving side of his distinctly ambivalent feelings towards the tools of his trade, Laffoon was much addicted to sharpening the leading edges of his irons on the road between tournaments. His method was to lean out of the door – preferably at high speed – and use the road surface as a grinder. As a youngster, he had made up a team with Titanic Thompson, the man who would bet on anything, particularly if it was a sure thing, and who found golf a good field for his talents. His stratagem using Laffoon's abilities was to contemptuously say to an opponent, 'Why, even my caddie could beat you!' The bet was then concluded and Laffoon would get his share of the resultant winnings. In 1934 Laffoon won the Radix Cup, forerunner of the Vardon Trophy, for low stroke average, and had four wins that year, which was his best. He won about four other tournaments which would today be recognized as of Tour status. Laffoon never came really close to a major championship, but finished fifth in the 1936 US Open, and in the Masters was sixth in 1936, fifth in 1937 and fourth in 1946. He played in the 1935 Ryder Cup team.

LAUER, Bonnie   USA
b. *Detroit, Michigan 1951*

Winner of the 1973 National Collegiate Championship, Bonnie Lauer that year also reached the semi-
finals of the US Amateur and played in the following year's Curtis Cup. A professional since
1975, she was in the top 60 from 1976 to 1982 and
has taken one tournament, the 1977 Patty Berg
Classic, a year she was 23rd in the money list, her
best placing.

US wins 1 (1977)
US money $192,508 (1975–82) (54th all-time)

LEMA, Anthony David   USA
b. *Oakland, California 1934; d. 1966*

It says much for the safety of air travel that, despite
the vast mileages that major and minor golfers
cover each year, very few have come to much harm.
A tragic exception was Tony Lema, killed in a
private plane with his wife when on his way to a
pro-am after the 1966 US PGA. His status as a
golfer therefore must remain unproven, for at 32 he
had reached the top but had not consolidated his
position. Lema was born the son of a labourer and
turned professional in 1955. His first win came in
1957 with the Imperial Valley Open, but there were
sparse pickings thereafter. In 1959 he earned just
$6,000, and only $3,000 the next year. Lema at this
stage was very much a party-goer and reckoned to
spend more on the Tour than he won. In 1961 he
did win the Hesperia Open, and the Mexican Open
both this and the following year, but 1962 was the
real turning-point for him – and earned him a
nickname. After three rounds he led the Orange
County California Open and promised the press
champagne if he won. He did and was 'Champagne'
Tony Lema to them thereafter. He won two other
events that year and in 1963 finished fourth on the
money list with some $67,000, though winning
once only. He also put up one of his best performances in a major championship. In the US Masters
he finished one behind Jack Nicklaus beaten only
because Nicklaus holed a long putt on the last
green. Nevertheless, his was the highest finish by a
first time player in the event since Sarazen won in
1935. The same year Lema was equal fifth in the US
Open. In 1964 Lema decided to enter the British
Open at St Andrews but, with a hectic schedule,
had no time to get to know the course. He decided
to rely on his caddie and hit the ball in the dir-

Tony Lema

ection he was told (many tee shots are blind at St
Andrews). All very well if you can hit it where you
want to: most are more concerned about where the
hazards are. Lema warmed up with a 73, and
followed with a 68 to lead. Even Jack Nicklaus did
not seem an ominous shadow. He lay 9 strokes
behind; but that was to change. On the last day,
Lema began 4, 5, 4, 5, 5, 4, and over that opening
stretch Nicklaus picked up 8 strokes on him.
However, Lema pulled himself together amazingly
well. He produced a sequence of five 3s, then three
4s and a finish of 3, 4, 4, 3. Nicklaus had a rousing
66 but gained little ground on Lema's 68 – a round
which was to win him the championship, for
Nicklaus, still 7 behind, had no real chance and
those others closest to Lema after the first two days
had lost ground the final morning. Although Nicklaus made up further ground in the afternoon with

a 68 and Vicenzo with a 67, Lema's calm 70 had him 5 ahead of Nicklaus at the finish and 6 on Vicenzo. He had done something previously thought impossible: won the British Open at his first attempt with no knowledge of linkland golf. On the US Tour that year, he had four wins and finished fourth on the money list with $74,000. He returned for the Open at Royal Birkdale the following year. Again, straight off the plane, he opened with a 68 and led and followed with a 72 to retain first place, now with Bruce Devlin. On the final day he was paired with Peter Thomson, who lay 2 strokes behind as they began the morning round, but had turned this into a 1-stroke lead by the afternoon. With five holes to go the position was the same but on the two closing par 5s Thomson had two 4s, while Lema fell away to a 5 and a 6, which dropped him to fifth place. There was an even more unpleasant experience to come for Tony on 15 October 1965, this time at the hands of a South African rather than an Australian, in the World Matchplay at Wentworth. There was some enmity felt by Player: Slazenger had just dropped his club-endorsing contract and signed up Lema, some indication that there were those who now thought that the 'Big Three' were Nicklaus, Palmer and Lema, with Player out in the cold. Over the first 18 of the semi-final, Lema established a 6-up lead, mainly a result of having birdies on five of the seven closing holes. He then went 7-up on the first hole in the afternoon – and lost, losing two of the last three holes and the first extra one: a classic collapse. He had a happier year in the USA. He won two tournaments and was second in the money list with over $101,000, a sum that only Nicklaus and Palmer had reached on the US Tour. Lema had a short but excellent Ryder Cup record. He was chosen in 1963 and 1965. In foursomes he took part in three wins and a half; in four-balls a win and a loss; and in singles he won three times and halved with me at Atlanta in 1963. In his final year he came fourth equal in the US Open and won the Oklahoma City Open by the widest margin on that year's Tour. At his death he was established as one of the top four players in the world. A feature of Lema's play was its fluidity and rhythm, possibly augmented by the fact that a distinct loop was discernible. He was a good putter, and his contemporaries regarded him as outstanding with the wedge and short irons.

US wins 13 (1957–66) (some not PGA-recognized today)
Overseas wins 3 (1961–4)

LENCZYK, Grace (later Cronin)   USA
b. Newington, Connecticut 1927

Grace Lenczyk had a short career at the top of amateur golf before an early retirement from competition. She reached the semi-finals of the 1947 US Amateur and won the following year, also taking the Canadian title in 1947 and 1948. In 1948 she was Intercollegiate Champion and played on the Curtis Cup team.

LEONARD, Stanley   Canada
b. Vancouver, British Columbia 1915

For a generation Stan Leonard was Canada's best golfer, which was shown in part at least by the fact that he took his national PGA eight times between 1940 and 1961. He was also chosen ten times to represent Canada in the World Cup, in which he was individual winner in 1954 and 1959, in the latter year in a play-off beating Peter Thomson, who made the very strange decision to take out a brand-new set of clubs. Leonard turned professional in 1939 but did not play the US Tour at all until 1948, and then infrequently until the mid 1950s. He was 42 when he won his first event, the Greater Greensboro', and followed with the Tournament of Champions the following year and the Western Open in 1960 at the age of 45. That his game lasted well can be seen by the fact that this excellent striker won the Canadian Seniors at the age of 60. It is estimated that he won 44 professional events during his career.

US wins 3 (1957–60)
US money $96,968 (246th all-time)

LESSER, Patricia Ann (later Harbottle)   USA
b. Fort Totten, New York 1933

Pat Lesser's first important achievement was to win the US Junior in 1950, and she did it by beating in the final Mickey Wright, who was later to become one of the greatest of all women golfers. She also won the Western Juniors' that year, and by 1952 she was Intercollegiate Champion. In 1953 she reached the quarter-finals of the US Amateur and was chosen for the following year's Curtis Cup. She then carried nearly all before her in 1955, winning the Doherty Cup, the Western and the US Amateur. She was again a Curtis Cup player in 1956, but eventually retired from serious competition to take up an equally demanding career as a wife and mother of five.

LEVI, Wayne John   USA

b. Little Falls, New York 1953

Wayne Levi turned professional in 1973 but twice failed to win his US Tour players' card. In the meantime he competed in minor events in Florida and New England, winning several. Eventually qualifying for the Tour, he had a miserable first season – $8,000 – and 1978 was little better, but at least it was punctuated by his first win, with Bob Mann in the World Team Championship. That exempted him from pre-qualifying the next season and he benefited to the tune of over $140,000, finishing 20th on the money list. He won the Houston Open, in which his first three rounds of 69, 65, 63 were the lowest that year. He won again in 1980, the Pleasant Valley Classic in which, after a moderate opening of 71, 71, he finished 65, 66. He was 32nd in money and took home over $120,000. By the end of 1981 he had lost his pre-qualifying exemption, having dropped to 69th, though still winning $62,000, but came back in 1982 by winning the Hawaiian Open (the first US tournament, incidentally, to be won with a coloured ball) and, late in the season, the LaJet Classic, to take his winnings over $200,000. He opened with a 64 and increased his lead every round. There is some problem about the pronunciation of his name, which seems to be 'Levee', but some have claimed that he was considering 'Leevi' in case a certain manufacturer of jeans might offer a clothing endorsement contract. Alas, this did not happen, so 'Levee' it remains. Since he won $280,681 during the season, it could have been of small importance.

US wins 5 (1978–82)
US money $637,790 (1977–82) (74th all-time)

LEWIS, Robert   USA

b. Warren, Ohio 1944

1n 1980 Bob Lewis was defeated in the final of the US Amateur by Hal Sutton. He was the second oldest to reach that stage since the event returned to matchplay in 1973. He is a reinstated amateur and played in the 1981 Walker Cup.

LIETZKE, Bruce Alan   USA

b. Kansas City, Kansas 1951

'For five weeks in 1977 I was in an absolute trance. I didn't think about the swing at all. I had no negative thoughts. I'd just stand over the ball and pull the trigger.' Thus Bruce Lietzke of a period

Bruce Lietzke

when he had 26 consecutive rounds in par or better, won the Tucson and Hawaiian Opens and was second in the Bob Hope Classic. It was also his first period of highly successful golf. He first played at the age of five, but as an amateur did not have a particularly glittering career: winning the 1971 Texas Amateur was its high spot. He turned professional in 1974 and, starting on the US Tour in 1975, never had a hard struggle to make money. By 1976 he was well into the Top 60, and then in 1977 came that inspired phase that was partly responsible for his finishing fifth on the money list and winning over $200,000. In 1978 he found that he could score well when not playing at such a peak. After opening the Canadian Open at Glen Abbey with a 76, he followed with two 67s which took him to a 2-stroke lead and eventual victory. Despite this his winnings fell to 'only' a little over $100,000, itself a figure which is becoming more and more commonplace. (It is not so long ago that Palmer was the first to break the six figure barrier to be followed later by Nicklaus, Lema and Casper.) Early in 1979 he again took the Tucson Open. He opened with a 63 and followed 66, 68, 68 to be 15 under par at the end, yet in the third round he pulled a stomach muscle and thought he would have to withdraw. Lietzke said he had had to just settle for 'bumping' it around the last day, which means that he played very much at half power; but as his power is considerable it made slight difference. He did not win again that year but was second twice and had ten finishes in the top 10, consistency that keeps the money flowing in. He was eighth on the money list. In 1980 he was 16th and the US Tour began keeping category performance statistics; they gave Lietzke a very useful piece of information. (If not carefully interpreted these statistics can be most misleading because, for instance, the player with the least putts per round is likely to be a man who misses many greens but ought to get his next shot near the hole and single-putt, or the leader in driving accuracy will inevitably be a short hitter.) What Lietzke learned was that he was the worst bunker player amongst the US Tour élite: he was listed 127th for getting down in two from sand. He practised and was down to a more acceptable 50th in 1981. Part of his reward was that by the end of 1981 only Watson, Trevino, Miller and Floyd had won more than he in a single season. Lietzke's total was $343,446, only fourth in the money list, yet only a little behind Kite, Floyd and Watson. He had won three times and been another seven times in the top five. In 24 entries he had 22 times won money and had 13 times been in the top 10. He had scored more eagles than anyone and broken par more frequently. He was third best at hitting greens in the right number and second in stroke average at 70.01. His driving showed a balance between length (average 266 yards, only about 14 yards behind the longest hitter) and accuracy, so that no one who was longer than he was as consistently on the fairway. In part this is probably due to the fact that Lietzke plays with fade, therefore holding fairways more readily, while it is also nearly always a more predictable shape of shot. (Nicklaus and Hogan would agree; Jones would not have.) Like Nicklaus also, he is one of relatively few players with an interlocking grip and one of even fewer who putt with left hand below the right. Lietzke makes the grip look extremely natural; for him it was not a method adopted merely to combat extreme difficulties with the putting stroke, and he has used it for years. At this stage in his career and despite his huge money-winning achievements, Lietzke does not seem likely to become accepted by history as a great, or near great, player. Relatively, he has failed in major championships, though he won the Canadian Open again in 1982; otherwise his best results are sixth in the 1979 US Masters, sixth in the 1981 British

Open and fourth in the 1981 US PGA. His name is pronounced Litski, which would be easier to spell, and he is married to a sister of Jerry Pate's wife. He declares he will not play competitive golf for many more years as he hates the pressure, and who can blame him? He won over $200,000 again in 1982 to be 14th on the year's money list.

US wins 9 (1977–82)
US money $1,339,286 (1975–82) (19th all-time)
World money $1,445,076 (1975–82) (27th all-time)

LINDSTROM, Murle: see Breer

LITTLE, Sally   **South Africa & USA**
b. Sea Point, Capetown, South Africa 1951

The best South African woman golfer ever, Sally Little built up a good amateur record in South African golf, winning the Western Province Matchplay three times, the Transvaal Strokeplay three times and then the South African Stroke and Match Championships in 1971. In 1970 she was low

Sally Little

individual, and the only woman to break 300, in the World Amateur Team Championship. In 1971 she qualified for the US Tour and, although she had time to play only seven events, she finished 51st on the money list and was named Rookie of the Year. Already she had one of the best swings in women's golf, and was in the top 50 for the next four years; but she admits that she couldn't handle the pressure of being in contention during this learning period. When her first victory came in the 1976 Women's International it almost took her unawares. Playing for a tie with Jan Stephenson, she holed a bunker shot on the last for a 1-stroke victory. That year she shot up the money list to 13th and $44,764. Thereafter, she has increased her money winnings each year, reaching $142,251 in 1981 and well over $200,000 in 1982, a year in which she headed the money list for some months before giving way to splendid late-season performances from JoAnne Carner. Sally won a tournament in 1978, three in 1979 and two in 1980, one of which was the US LPGA. Her victory was only the second time that a non-American player had won (Chako Higuchi had done it first). In 1981 she won three times, but bettered this in 1982 with four victories, including a spectacular 64 in the last round to win the Dinah Shore. She has been in the top 10 from 1977 to 1982, and was third in 1982, the season she topped the magic $200,000 mark.

US wins 14 (1976–82)
US money $866,641 (1971–82) (9th all-time)

LITTLE, William Lawson　　　　　　　USA
b. Newport, Rhode Island 1910; d. 1968

Although Lawson Little accomplished much as a professional his outstanding amateur feats are more remembered and approach comparison over a short period with those of Jones. Little won the Northern California Amateur in 1928 but first made news in 1929. Johnny Goodman had just made the national headline by knocking out the 'unbeatable' Bobby Jones – and was immediately knocked out by Lawson Little. His next important success was to take the Broadmoor Invitational in 1932 and to reach the semi-finals of the US Amateur in 1933. These achievements earned him a Walker Cup place in 1934. In the top foursomes match he and Goodman put Britain's top players, Wethered and Tolley, to the sword by 8 and 6; and much the same happened to Tolley in the singles – 7 and 5 to Little. No doubt in good heart, Little moved on

from St Andrews to Prestwick and in due course reached the final of the Amateur Championship, where he met the Scot, J. Wallace. Several of the latter's supporters took the afternoon off work but they arrived too late. Little had won by the record margin of 14 and 13. In doing so he had an estimated 66 in the morning and began the afternoon more tidily with four 3s and a 4. Some of the statistics are still impressive: 82 for 23 holes; an average per hole of 3.56; he had scored 12 3s; he was 10 under level 4s (the way of reckoning par at the time). It was perhaps the greatest stretch of golf ever played by an amateur. Back in the USA, Little took the Amateur Championship by 8 and 7 over D. Goldman, who may have been relieved that the margin was no greater. Little was of medium height – about 5 feet 9 inches – and nearly as broad. He had a reputation as an outstanding birdie putter, and the rest of his game was based on great length from the tee and a formidable pitching game. For this latter department of the game he carried between five and seven wedges and in the 1935 British Amateur was carrying 26 clubs in all. Officialdom thought that enough was enough, for there is actually no limit to the number of clubs that some players might choose to carry to meet different requirements in a round. Certainly today's players would follow Little in the pitching club range. So the maximum became 14. In 1935, Little met Dr William Tweddell at Royal Lytham in the British Amateur final and slaughter was anticipated, for Tweddell's golf was largely confined to holidays. He had an ugly swing and was vastly outgunned by Little from the tee. But the doctor defied the odds and the 1935 final was one of the closest-fought on record. Little won by 1 up. Back in America he took the Amateur by 4 and 2 in the final. No one doubted that Little could live with professionals. He had, for instance, finished sixth in the 1935 Masters. In 1936 he turned professional with a feat that paralleled Jones's 1930 Grand Slam or Hogan's three majors in 1953 behind him. In 1936 he took the Canadian Open, then two US tournaments the following year and an estimated seven in all. Yet he failed to be the tremendous player so many had expected. He finished well in the Masters in particular almost every year, and as late as 1951 was sixth, while his best placing was third in 1939. He also brought his total of major championships to five in 1940, when he won the US Open after a play-off with Gene Sarazen. There is no doubt, however, that his best time was 1934 and 1935 when he won 31 consecutive matches in the US and British Amateurs. He felt that the key to victory was that 'Winners hit their bad shots best.'

US wins 7 (1937–48)

LITTLER, Eugene Alex   USA
b. San Diego, California 1930

Some great players have wanted to be the best in the world – Jones, Hogan, Player and Nicklaus are obvious examples. Others have seemed content with lesser achievements, and undoubtedly Gene Littler is of this number. Always able to make a good living off the US Tour, a win or two or a sequence of high finishes often prompted him to go home to his family and his collection of vintage cars. Littler won the US Amateur in 1953, the year before Arnold Palmer, and entered the 1954 San Diego Open as an amateur. He won the trophy, and Dutch Harrison the money; Littler speedily turned professional. In that first season, he was 28th in the money list and in the period 1954–79 was only once not in the Top 60. That year was 1972 and the reason very simple – in April he had had an operation for cancer of the lymph glands under the left arm. The usually casual Gene worked hard at recovery and by October was finishing seventh in the Pacific Masters. Of the great golfers of today his career has lasted longer than anyone's, eclipsing his contemporary Arnold Palmer and rivalled only perhaps by Gary Player, several years his junior. On the US Tour he has twice been second in the money list (1959 and 1962) and ten times in the top 10; at the age of 45 he was fifth and had three wins. He was 47 at the time of his last success. At today's money values there would have been very few years that he would have failed to pass $100,000,

Gene Littler

though in real terms he accomplished the feat only four times, all since 1968. (Palmer was the first to top the figure in 1963.) On the US Tour he won 29 times, which puts him in 11th place. With winnings of over $1½ million he was also 11th at the end of 1981 but falling, of course, all the time from fifth in 1970. His being fifth for the year in 1975 at the age of 45 is one of the more remarkable achievements in Tour history. At the time he was asked if he was surprised to find himself still playing so well and replied: 'I'm surprised to be playing at all.' He had won three times on the US Tour and taken the Pacific Masters in Japan. Two years later Littler should have won another major championship, the 1977 US PGA, but dropped stroke after stroke over the last nine holes to allow Lanny Wadkins to catch him and then win on the third play-off hole. In fact Littler's major championship record for a golfer of such stature is not good. Apart from the 1953 US Amateur he won just one other, the US Open of 1961, by 1 stroke after a closing 68, from Bob Goalby and Doug Sanders. He came second as a new professional to Ed Furgol in the 1954 event, and fourth four years later. Otherwise his name does not feature in the top half dozen. The story is similar in the US Masters: fourth in 1962 and 1971, with his best performance a very steady 69, 70, 70, 70 in 1970 to tie Billy Casper. He then lost the play-off with 74 to 69. As suggested already, Littler perhaps lacked a little of the drive to be an all-time great player, one who must want to win major championships with special intensity, as Jack Nicklaus has now shown for a decade or so. The cheque for the Memphis Open or the Dunlop Masters is very nice indeed, but posterity demands major championships. This is not intended as a strong criticism of Gene Littler, but more as an observation that he marched to different music. Golf was important but by no means everything. Back at Rancho Santa Fe was his family, and also his classic cars. Littler has had a collection that includes three Rolls-Royces, two of them vintage, and many other cars. Although Littler has lasted so well, he considers that his best years were in the middle 1950s, when the ball always seemed to come to rest in the middle of the fairway. He was a natural swinger or, as Gene Sarazen said: 'Here's a kid with a perfect swing like Sam Snead's ... only better.' He suffered a slump in form from 1957 to 1958, and had to think about his technique for the first time. He had the clubface too shut at impact as a result of a strong grip. Paul Runyan got him to weaken the grip and not swing flat. Soon Littler was back on course (five wins in 1959) and earned the nickname 'Gene the Machine'. His strongest features are keeping the ball in play, excellence with the short irons, which he tries to play with left-side dominance, and very good putting. During 1980 Littler became eligible to play on the Senior Tour. He proceeded to win three of his first five entries and in 1981 won the Vintage Invitational by 9 strokes, finishing 65, 64, the two lowest rounds returned in the tournament. During 1981 he won the most money, $137,427. Littler, of course, had a very long Ryder Cup career, running from 1961 to 1975, only 1973, as a result of his operation, being missed. He won two-thirds of his matches.

US wins 29 (1954–77)
US money $1,569,320 (1954–82) (14th all-time)
Japan wins 2 (1974–5)
World money $2,257,602 (1954–82) (11th all-time)

LLOYD, Joseph   England & USA
b. 1870

Joe Lloyd won the third US Open on the last occasion it was played over 36 holes, at Chicago in 1897. He beat the far greater player, Willie Anderson, by 1 stroke with the aid of a 3 on the 466-yard last hole, no mean feat with a guttie. He featured high up only once again when he was fourth in 1898 at the Myopia Hunt Club in Massachusetts.

LOPEZ, Nancy (later Melton, Knight)   USA
b. Torrance, California 1957

Only reaching the age of 26 in 1983, Nancy Lopez has already proved a key figure in the history and commercial development of the US Women's Tour. Babe Zaharias was the first great player and crowd-puller, to be succeeded by Mickey Wright, who raised the scoring standards of the women's game dramatically, but who was too reserved in personality to stir the passions of the galleries. Nancy Lopez has a friendly, outgoing personality, and her deeds were phenomenal in the period 1978–9. She had an outstanding amateur career, but even this did not fully presage what was to come when she turned professional. At the age of 12 she won the New Mexico Amateur and followed by winning the US Junior twice, the Western Junior three times and, in 1975, the Mexican Amateur. That same year she tied for second in the US Open, behind Sandra Palmer. The next year she won the Trans-Missis-

sippi, the Western and the AIAW National Collegiate, and represented the US in both the Curtis Cup and the World Team Championship. In mid 1977 she turned professional: her first event was the Colgate European Open at Sunningdale, in which she was second. She played five more events that year to total $23,000 and be 31st on the money list with a stroke average of 73.24, a sign of what was to come. In 1978 she won nine Tour events, including the US LPGA by 6 strokes. Seven of the wins were in America and she also won in Japan and the European Open in England. What caused the uproar, however, and a tripling of Tour gates, was that five of her US wins were consecutive, a record and one much harder to achieve, with rising standards, than in earlier years. She ended the year as number one money-winner with $189,813 – a record – and won the Vare Trophy with her stroke average of 71.76, and was chosen Player of the Year. That she should also have been Rookie of the Year was automatic. No man had then equalled her total in his first year. At one point in 1979 she had

Nancy Lopez

entered just 50 tournaments and won 17 of them during her career as a professional, and had reached 11th on the list of all-time money-winners after about two seasons in golf. She ended that second season with eight wins, a new money record of $197,488, was again Player of the Year and set the Vare record at 71.2. Her money total was some $20,000 ahead of the next player, while she had been no less than $70,000 in front the previous year. In 1980 she began to experience some problems with her game. Nancy is a fairly unorthodox swinger. The process looks a little laborious, though powerful, and her clubface is shut at the top of the backswing. This is a position likely to produce a hook, and that is in fact the flaw that has appeared in her game from time to time. However, she still won three times and with $209,078 became the fourth woman to pass $200,000 in a year. She was fourth on the money list. Since that time, in the following two seasons, Nancy Lopez has added more victories; but she is by no means a dominant player, but rather one of a group of half a dozen or so leading figures: Beth Daniel, for instance, has a better record in the 1980–82 period. In her early peak years it was suggested that she had at least ten swing faults, perhaps some reason for her relative decline. Nancy Lopez drives some 240 yards, and a feature of her game is an excellent feel for distance. She is an excellent and bold putter – rated the best woman putter ever by some – seldom leaving her putts short. With ten birdies in the second round of the 1979 Mary Kay Classic, including seven on the first eight holes, she set the record for the most in a round on the US Tour, but now shares this record with Beth Daniel.

US wins 25 (1978–82) (13th all-time)
US money $951,673 (1977–82) (5th all-time)

LOTT, Clinton Lynwood, III   USA
b. Douglas, Georgia 1950

Lyn Lott's 1981 shows that a player has to average under 72 per round to make the top 100 on the US Tour. Lot averaged 71.91 to be 96th. He has, however, twice made the Top 60 – in 1976 and 1977 – with a best finish of 39th in the latter year. Although his achievements may seem meagre he has been steady enough to win money consistently and run up a good total in an eight-year career.

US money $293,336 (1974–82) (152nd all-time)

LOTZ, Richard   USA
b. Oakland, California 1942

Dick Lotz was an almost top US player for a couple of seasons. He joined the Tour in 1964 and reached the Top 60 five years later, also winning his first event. The following year, 1970, he won the Monsanto and Kemper Opens, took home $125,023 and was sixth on the Tour. Since then he has tailed away and no longer plays tournaments.

US wins 3 (1969–70)
US money $281,966

LOW, George   Scotland & USA
b. Carnoustie, Scotland 1874; d. 1950

One of the immigrant Scottish golfers in the 1890s, George Low was second behind Willie Smith in the 1899 US Open at Baltimore CC. He did not feature as prominently again but was sixth in 1900 and fifth in 1907, and won a few US tournaments. Famed as a putter, he originated the saying 'Golf is a humbling game.' He was professional at Baltusrol from 1903 to 1925 and taught golf to two US Presidents, William Howard Taft and Warren Harding. His son became a famous putting teacher, much consulted by professionals.

LUCKHURST, Terri: see Moody

LUNDQUIST, Dale: see Eggeling

LUNN, Robert   USA
b. San Francisco, California 1945

When Bob Lunn won the US Public Links Championship in 1963 he was the equal youngest to do so. He turned professional the following year and joined the US Tour in 1967. After a poor first season he won twice in a row in 1968, and then had victories in each of the next four seasons. He was in the top 24 from 1968 to 1971 and Top 60 from 1968 to 1972. Weighing some 225 lb, he decided in 1971 that he would be a better player if lighter but, as have other golfers, found this was not so, and allowed himself to become heavier again. By the end of 1972 he had won $100,000 twice, was one of the longest hitters on Tour, had six wins and a third place in the 1970 US Open. After this he fell right away, adding few dollars to his career total.

US wins 6 (1968–72)
US money $455,640 (1967–82) (101st all-time)

LYE, Mark Ryan   USA
b. Vallejo, California 1952

Mark Lye achieved some success overseas before concentrating on the US Tour. He won the 1976 Rolex Trophy in Switzerland, and in the same year the Champion of Champions in Australia, and headed that country's 1977 Order of Merit. He has not won on the US Tour but is reckoned as highly promising. In his first three years he progressed steadily and in 1980 topped $100,000 and was 39th in the money list. He remained in the Top 60 in 1981 and was 61st in 1982.

US money $339,825 (1977–82) (135th all-time)
Overseas wins 2 (1976)

LYON, George S.   Canada
b. 1878

George Lyon was an all-round sportsman who included in his record the Canadian highest innings at cricket: 238 not out. He is said to have first played golf at the age of 38. Two years later, in 1898, he won his first Canadian Amateur by 12 and 11, which remains the record, though shared with a later Lyon victory. Between 1898 and 1914 he took the title eight times, three in a row from 1905 to 1907, all his wins being by comfortable margins. He was also twice runner-up, reached the final of the 1906 US Amateur and won the golf gold medal at the 1904 Olympics.

McALLISTER, Susan   USA
b. New Orleans, Louisiana 1947

A US Tour player from 1971, Susie McAllister is one of the players who makes few headlines but a tidy living. She has been in the Top 60 from 1971 to 1977, in 1979, 1981 and 1982; in her best year, 1975, she finished 11th in the money list and won her only tournament, the Wheeling Classic. She lost a play-off for the same event in 1981. She was second to JoAnne Carner in the 1982 Rail Charity Classic.

US wins 1 (1975)
US money $244,949 (1971–82) (42nd all-time)

McCULLOUGH, Michael Earl   USA
b. Coshocton, Ohio 1945

Although a winner of two mini-Tour events, Mike McCullough found the going hard on the full Tour, not reaching the Top 60 until his sixth season in

1977, his best year, when he won $79,413 for 36th position. He was also in the Top 60 in 1978, but has been falling away since and was 99th in 1982.

US money $360,536 (1972–82) (130th all-time)

McCUMBER, Mark Randall   USA
b. Jacksonville, Florida 1951

Mark McCumber turned professional in 1974 but needed six attempts before he won his US Tour card; then he won only $7,000 his first season. He improved to the Top 60 the following year, though he owed most of his winnings to victory in the Doral-Eastern Open, an event for which he had to pre-qualify, having failed to qualify in two of six previous entries or missed the 36-hole cut in the four for which he did pre-qualify. His previous best Tour finish had been joint seventh. He did not hold his Top 60 position.

US wins 1 (1979)
US money $176,866 (1978–82) (201st all-time)

McDERMOTT, John J.   USA
b. Philadelphia, Pennsylvania 1891; d. 1971

Johnny McDermott tied for the US Open in 1910 at the age of 19, but lost the resultant play-off to Alex Smith. He was again in a play-off the following

Johnny McDermott

year, this time with Mike Brady and George Simpson; this time he became the first home-born American to take the US Open. He then did it again the following year with the very respectable scores for the time of 74, 75, 74, 71. In 1913 he further proved himself in the Shawnee Open by winning and leaving the touring Harry Vardon and Ted Ray 13 strokes behind. He also won the Western Open and the Philadelphia Open that year and, determined to prove he was as good as anyone, went to Britain for the Open. He finished joint fifth. In the US Open that year he came in ninth. It was his last entry. McDermott had got to the top very fast (he is still the youngest winner of a major championship) and he disappeared just as quickly. Some have claimed that he competed with such passionate determination that he burned himself out. This is unlikely to be true. His problem was a more general mental instability: he had a breakdown in 1915 and retired thereafter. McDermott was famed for his ability with medium-length approach shots.

MACDONALD, Charles Blair   USA
b. Niagara Falls, New York 1856; d. 1939

Macdonald learned his golf in Scotland while a student at St Andrews University, where he played with 'Young Tom' Morris and all the leading players of the time. In 1893 he built the first 18-hole course in the USA, Chicago GC. Two years later he won the first US Amateur by 12 and 11. His most important achievement was the National Golf Links of America at Southampton, Long Island. Macdonald used his experience of golf in Britain to copy in his design all the holes that he considered outstanding. The course was begun in 1901 and completed some years later. As an administrator in later years he struggled to unite the USGA and the R & A with considerable success. His account of his life in golf, Scotland's Gift – Golf, was published in 1928.

MACFARLANE, William   Scotland & USA
b. Aberdeen, Scotland 1890; d. 1961

Willie Macfarlane had one major championship success but it was an historic one. After a tie with Jones in the 1925 US Open at Worcester CC, Massachusetts, on 291, he then defeated him in the play-off. They both recorded 75 over the first 18 and with a hole to go were still level. Macfarlane then had a 4 to Jones's 5, giving a result of 72 to 73.

Macfarlane also won the 1925 and 1928 Shawnee Opens, the 1929 Westchester, the 1930 Metropolitan and the 1932 New England. There is no doubt however, that the 1925 Open was his peak: he never featured strongly in the event before or after.

McGEE, Jerry Lynn   USA
b. New Lexington, Ohio 1943

Jerry McGee, a smiling, witty man, went on Tour in 1967, and began to improve during his sixth season when he broke into the Top 60 for the first time. By 1979 he had repeated the achievement a further seven times, with best placings of 16th in 1975 and 1976 and 15th in 1977. He has topped $100,000 three times – 1976, 1977 and 1979, when he won over $160,000. His first win did not come until 1975, with the Pensacola Open, when he commented: 'At least they won't be able to say sudden success spoiled me.' He won again in 1977 and had two wins in 1979, the Kemper and Greater Hartford. In the former he had a tidy 61 to start, and in the latter his scores were 68, 67, 67, 65. These two victories came despite the fact that he had court appearances concerning his previous sponsorship hanging over him. Previous to these successes 1972 had been quite a good year. He had finished joint fifth on his first Masters entry, which he described as 'the biggest thrill I've had in golf', and won no fewer than four cars in closest-to-the-pin prizes during that single year. Tuition from 'Iron Man' Bruce Crampton helped improve his game. McGee himself is anything but an iron man, suffering from low blood sugar which causes his stamina to be suspect. He is now director of golf at a large country club, and is limiting his Tour appearances and has fallen well out of the top 100. He made his only Ryder Cup appearance in 1977 and his tournament career may now be considered over.

US wins 4 (1975–9)
US money $871,545 (1967–81) (47th all-time)
World money $950,000 approx. (1967–81)

McINTIRE, Barbara Joy   USA
b. Toledo, Ohio 1935

Having been twice runner-up in the US Juniors, in 1951 and 1952, Barbara McIntire progressed to being one of the best women amateurs of her day. She first played in the US Amateur at the age of 15 and (an oddity of golf history), beat Glenna Collett Vare in her first match. In 1959 at Congressional she won through in the final; the following year at Harlech she defeated Philomena Garvey 4 and 2 in the final of the British Amateur, thus becoming one of ten women who have won the amateur championships of both countries. In 1964, she reached the final of the US Amateur again and faced the greatest woman amateur of modern times, JoAnne Gunderson. Barbara crowned her career by winning 3 and 2. Barbara McIntire is one of the few amateurs to come close to winning the US Open. In 1956 she made up 8 strokes on Kathy Cornelius in the last round to tie, but in the 18-hole play-off lost by 82 to 75. She made no fewer than six appearances in the Curtis Cup: from 1958 to 1966 and then again in 1972. She also appeared in the 1964 World Team Championship where, in the first event of all, she dropped 3 strokes on the last two holes which let in the French team to a 1-stroke victory.

MACKENZIE, Ada   Canada
b. Toronto, Ontario 1891; d. 1973

Perhaps the best woman golfer in Canada between the wars, Ada Mackenzie was runner-up for her national Closed title in 1923 and 1925 and then won in 1926, 1927, 1929, 1931 and 1933. She won the Open title in 1919, 1925, 1926, 1933 and 1935, and in later years went on to take her country's senior title on eight occasions. She won the Ontario Ladies' eight times and had hosts of wins in other Canadian tournaments. She reached the semi-final of the US Amateur in 1927. Miss Mackenzie founded what is claimed to be the first women-only golf club at Toronto in the 1920s and managed it for some years, though males were later allowed in. She was the first woman chosen for the Canadian Golf Hall of Fame.

McLENDON, Benson Rayfield   USA
b. Atlanta, Georgia 1945

Mac McLendon went on Tour in 1968 and made the Top 60 his first season, also winning the Magnolia Classic, a non-Tour event. He was in the Top 60 in 1969 also and again from 1975 to 1978. His best season was 1978 when he finished 22nd on the money list with more than $100,000, and won twice. He had intended to give up the Tour towards the end of the 1974 season, but his win in the Disney National Team Championship with Hubert Green persuaded him to keep trying. He played a

full season in 1980 to little effect, made only two appearances in 1981 and won no money in 1982.

US wins 4 (1974–8)
US money $542,120 (1968–81) (83rd all-time)

McLEOD, Frederick Robertson
Scotland & USA
b. North Berwick, Scotland 1882; d. 1976

Freddie McLeod went over to the USA in 1903 and soon established an excellent record in the US Open. In 1907 he was joint fifth; then he tied with Willie Smith and won the play-off the following year. He is thought to be the smallest man to win a major championship, weighing just 108 lb at the time. Thereafter he was eight times a finisher in the top 10 in 20 US Opens and came close to winning on other occasions. He was fourth in both 1910 and 1911, and only 1 behind both years. He was equal third in 1914 and, with Hagen, second in 1920. He was runner-up in the US PGA in 1919 and won the PGA Seniors in 1938. He was seventh in the 1926 British Open when well past his best playing years, was elected to the PGA Hall of Fame in 1960, and had seven other wins. He was professional at Chevy Chase for about 50 years up to his retirement in 1965 at the age of 83. From 1963 he was honorary starter at the US Masters, beginning the occasion by playing nine holes with his former compatriot and rival, Jock Hutchison.

Fred McLeod

McMULLEN, Kathy   USA
b. Bradenton, Florida 1949

Having won the 1969 All-American Junior title, Kathy McMullen turned professional and, after a moderate start in 1972 and 1973 on the US Tour, has been a consistent money-winner since. She has been in the Top 60 from 1974 to 1981, with a best placing of eighth in 1975, when she won some $39,000. Kathy has not won a Tour event, but had second places in 1974, 1975 and 1977, and in 1980 she finished third in the US Open. With Sandra Haynie, she won the 1982 Portland Ring team event.

US money $250,022 (1972–82) (39th all-time)

McNAMARA, Tom   Scotland & USA

One of the best US professionals early this century, Tom McNamara was several times within range of victory in the US Open. From 1909 to 1919 he was five times among the top five and three times in second place.

McSPADEN, Harold   USA
b. Rosedale, Kansas 1908

'Jug' McSpaden made big news in 1944 and 1945, when he seemed to be the only golfer able to compete with Byron Nelson in his best two years. McSpaden finished second in the money in both those years, and won occasionally when Nelson let him. Together they were called 'the Gold Dust Twins', a reference to their money-winning exploits. Nelson retired soon after the Hogans and Mangrums returned from World War II and McSpaden followed him in 1947 (he too had been exempted from military service as an asthma sufferer). He won the Canadian Open in 1939, was runner-up in the US PGA in 1937 and won the 1934 National Matchplay Championship; altogether he took 17 official US PGA events. He retired to an interesting course: Dubs' Dread Golf Club, Piper, Kansas, with a standard scratch of 78 and a length of some 8,100 yards.

US wins 17

MAHAFFEY, John Drayton   USA
b. Kerrville, Texas 1948

An All-American choice in 1969 and 1970, Mahaffey was low amateur in the 1970 US Open and 1970 NCAA Champion. He qualified for the US Tour in 1971 and was always comfortably in the top 40 during his first four full seasons. Mahaffey is not at all the typical American young giant who belts the ball immense distances and then reaches for his wedge. He is about 5 feet 9 inches tall and a short hitter, relying on accuracy from the tee and good judgement of distance. During a career where only injury has kept him out of the Top 60 he has five times been 16th or better with 8th in 1975 his best placing. The US Open has twice been within his grasp, and twice it has eluded him. In 1975 at Medinah he tied with Lou Graham, and the two 'unknowns' played off over 18 holes. Mahaffey was unable to hole a putt of any distance and lost 73–71. In 1976 at Atlanta Athletic Club he began 70, 68, 69 to lead eventual winner Jerry Pate by 2 into the last round. At the 10th in the last round he missed a short putt that would have given him a lead of 6 strokes, and then began to slip; but was still not out of it even on the last. Here, Pate played one of the great decisive shots of championship golf – a 5-iron over water to 2 feet from the flag and victory, while Mahaffey, less well placed to attempt the carry, did not make it and finished joint fourth, 3 behind. In 1978 he took his first and only major championship, this time coming from behind. At Oakmont, Mahaffey began the US PGA with a 75 but followed with 67, 68. At this point Watson led on 203, Pate followed on 208, and then came Weiskopf and Inman at 209. Mahaffey was next, 7 behind Watson. Putting well, Mahaffey began to overhaul Watson, a turning-point being his 3 to Watson's 6 on the 10th hole. After 72 holes, Watson had compiled a final 73 to Mahaffey's 66 and Pate's 68, and they were all tied on 276. Mahaffey birdied the second play-off hole to be champion. It was only his second US win, and his first since 1973. The following week he took the Pleasant Valley Classic. Later in 1978 he had the lowest individual score in the World Cup. Mahaffey has continued to play consistently, remaining one of the most accurate drivers and with superb touch on the greens. He won again each year from 1979 to 1981, and by the end of 1981 had six times exceeded $100,000 in a season. The 1982 season was not one of his best, but he still won some $77,000.

US wins 6 (1973–81)
US money $1,118,026 (1972–82) (31st all-time)
World money $1,280,196 (1972–82) (36th all-time)

MALTBIE, Roger Lin   USA
b. Modesto, California 1951

After an amateur career that included two wins in the Northern California Amateur, Roger Maltbie qualified for the US Tour in 1974 and first played in 1975. Halfway through his first season he accomplished the rare feat of two wins in a row, and ended 23rd in the money list. In 1976 he won the Memorial, only a rung below a major championship; but then, with the world about to be at his feet, began to fall away. In 1977 he barely remained in the Top 60, and he became a complete also-ran in 1978 and 1979, finishing well out of the best 100. He improved a little in 1980 and substantially in 1981, clawing his way back into the Top 60 – but only just. By this time he had won again – the Magnolia Classic, which is played while the big boys fight out the Masters. In the 1982 season he hung on gamely to finish 55th in the money list.

US wins 3 (1975–6)
US money $463,438 (1975–82) (100th all-time)

MANERO, Tony   USA
b. New York 1905

Tony Manero got into the US Open of 1936 by winning a play-off amongst non-qualifiers. He was previously known mainly for having won the 1932 Westchester. Scoring was good that year at Baltusrol, 'Light-Horse' Harry Cooper in particular starting 71, 70, 70 to lead, and when he had completed his last round in 73 he had broken the previous US scoring record, set in 1916 by Chick Evans, by 2 strokes. Manero meanwhile had been largely unnoticed, and his rounds of 73, 69, 73 had left him 4 behind Cooper with a round to go. But that final afternoon Manero was in one of those blessed trances that sometimes come to golfers. He came in with a 67 and won by 2. Very little was heard of him again, perhaps because he was happy as a club professional and his various business ventures took up much of his time.

MANGRUM, Lloyd Eugene   USA
b. Trenton, Texas 1914; d. 1973

Usually to be seen with a cigarette in his mouth, with his hair parted in the middle, and a narrow moustache of the kind that in 1930s Hollywood movies used to decorate the upper lips of gamblers, Lloyd Mangrum did not entirely look the part of professional golfer. He had just, however, arrived at

Lloyd Mangrum

the top when World War II stole away some of his best years but he compensated by twice winning the Purple Heart while serving under General Patton, being twice wounded in the Battle of the Bulge. After this professional golf can have made little demand on his nerve. He began his career with little success during the 1930s, but began to emerge in 1940 when he won the Thomasville Open and started the 1940 US Masters with a 64, a round that has still not been beaten at Augusta. He did not sustain that pace, finishing second to Jimmy Demaret. A little later he was fifth in the US Open. In 1941 he was seventh on the money list and moved up again to fourth place in 1942, by which time he had won four more events. Then came the war. By chance sent to St Andrews to recover from his war wounds, Mangrum won a GI tournament there before rejoining the US Tour for the 1946 season. For the next nine years he was never out of the top 10 money winners. He opened his campaign by winning the US Open. After the four rounds Mangrum, Vic Ghezzi and Byron Nelson were tied on 284. All three then tied with 72s and went out again. This time Nelson and Ghezzi had 73s; Mangrum 72, in one of the few 36-hole play-offs in US Open history. Mangrum was not to win another major championship, but his consistent record in the US Open and Masters during this period illustrates his quality. By 1954 he had tied for the 1950 Open and this time lost a play-off, and had had three more finishes inside the top four. In the US Masters during the period 1948–56 he was just once out of the top 6, with one second and two thirds. He never reached the final of the US PGA, however, and very seldom competed in the British Open. He played the Ryder Cup from 1947 to 1953 and won three of four matches in both foursomes and singles, being captain on the last occasion. He topped the money list in 1951 (with $26,088!) and twice won the Vardon Trophy (1951 and 1953). His tournament career encompassed 46 wins, of which 34 were PGA-recognized US Tour events. He got into his stride in 1948, when he won eight events: only Nelson, Hogan and Snead have otherwise exceeded seven wins. In 1949, he won four, which included the longest play-off in US Tour history. In the Motor City Open, he and Middlecoff agreed to call it a tie with darkness coming after 11 extra holes. There were four more wins in 1950 and five the next year, which included the St Paul Open, during which he received a death threat. In 1952 he again won five, and four the following season. After this he became an infrequent winner, his career declining at much the same time and age as his contemporary Hogan. He had a reputation for being a hard man, but fair.

US wins 34 (1940–56) (8th all-time)

MANLEY, Norman   USA

This amateur's claim to fame is based solely on his ability to accomplish the overrated achievement of holing in one. However, Manley's record is prodigious: at the end of 1980 he had done it 47 times. He is also the only player known to have holed successive par-4s with his tee shot. This he did on 330-yard and 290-yard holes at Del Valley, Saugus, USA.

MANN, Carol (later Hardy)   USA
b. Buffalo, New York 1941

In a brief amateur career Carol Mann won the Western Junior in 1958 and the Chicago Amateur two years later. Since 1961 she has played the US Tour, and from 1961 to 1977 never ranked worse than 29th in the money list; her best placings were leading money-winner in 1969, second in 1968 and third in 1965, 1967 and 1975. In the period 1964–75 she missed a tournament win only in 1971. In 1968 she challenged the supremacy of Kathy Whitworth, who had taken over from Mickey Wright as leading tournament-winner, and they both had no fewer than ten wins each, the remaining Tour players sharing the other 12 events. Carol was number two on the money list, but set a Vare Trophy scoring-average record of 72.04 which lasted until Nancy Lopez broke it in 1978 with 71.76. The following year the result of the Whitworth–Mann duel was reversed, with Whitworth taking the Vare by 72.38 to 72.88 while Carol was leading money-winner, setting a new record with $49,152. She had eight victories and Whitworth seven. Whitworth re-established her supremacy in the next few seasons while Carol Mann continued to be one of the leading group of players until 1976. She had a particularly good year in 1975, her stroke average being 72.48 with four wins for third place in the money list. Carol has one major championship to her credit, the 1965 US Open; she was second the following year. In 1968 she had 23 rounds in the 60s, a record that stood until beaten narrowly by Amy Alcott in 1980. She shares the nine-hole scoring record with a 29 during the 1975 Borden Classic, and her seven consecutive birdies in the same event are a record. Her 200 for 54 holes in the 1968 Carling Open stood as a record until 198 from Jan Stephenson in 1981 beat it. Carol began to compete less frequently during 1978 and now works for NBC and in public relations, a field for which her lively personality well suits her. She was president of the US LPGA in 1974 and was elected a member of the Golf Hall of Fame in 1977. She is perhaps the tallest woman to compete highly successfully – at 6 feet 3 inches or, as she expresses it, 5 feet 15 inches. She is a natural left-hander who followed Ben Hogan's example and chose to play right-handed. Her other commitments prevented her from playing in any Tour events in 1982.

US wins 38 (1964–75) (7th all-time)
US money $506,666 (1961–81) (16th all-time)

MARR, David　　　　　　　　USA
b. *Houston, Texas 1933*

Dave Marr turned professional in 1953 but did not attempt the US Tour until 1960. He then jumped straight into the Top 60 and remained there until 1968. Thereafter he continued moderately successful for five more years and still makes occasional appearances, though he is now also a television commentator for ABC and a very readable journalist. His most successful years were the mid 1960s, when he was joint second in the 1964 US Masters and fourth in the 1966 US Open, and won the 1965 US PGA. In that year he also had his highest money placing, seventh, and was named PGA Player of the Year. He won four times on Tour between 1960 and 1965. He was a Ryder Cup player in 1965 and captain in 1981. In this he followed a family tradition, his cousin Jack Burke Jnr being US Ryder Cup captain in the years 1957 and 1973. Surprisingly for a man from a solid golfing background, Dave Marr was never quite powerful enough as a player, though his short game was excellent.

US wins 4 (1960–5)
US money $366,571 (1960–77) (125th all-time)

MARSTON, Maxwell R.　　　　USA
b. *Buffalo, New York 1892; d. 1949*

Max Marston's outstanding achievement came in the 1923 US Amateur when he beat Bobby Jones, Francis Ouimet and then the defending champion, Jess Sweetser, on the second extra hole in the final. He again reached the final, in 1933, but this time lost by a wide margin to George Dunlap. He played for the US against Britain in 1922, 1923, 1924 and 1934.

MARTI, Frederick　　　　　　USA
b. *Houston, Texas 1940*

Fred Marti was an All-American in 1962 and 1963, was 1962 NCAA Champion and named as best college player in 1963. He turned professional and went on Tour in 1964. Four times in the Top 60 between 1968 and 1972, he made 39th in 1971. Marti never won a tournament, but secured considerable amounts of money and had second-place finishes. In the 1972 Phoenix Open he had six birdies consecutively.

US money $404,643 (1964–80) (110th all-time)

MARTIN, Katherine　　　　　USA
b. *Berwyn, Illinois 1945*

On the US Tour from 1972, Kathy Martin has yet to win a US Tour event but has recorded second-place finishes. Her nearest approach to victory was in the 1976 Birmingham Classic where her start of 66, 65 is a 36-hole record shared with Silvia Bertolaccini. She finished second, caught by Jan Stephenson, who had a 68 to her 76 in the third and final round. Kathy has been in the top 60 in 1973 and 1974, from 1976 to 1978 and in 1980 and 1981, with 20th in 1976 her best season.

US money $170,336 (1972–82) (65th all-time)

MASSENGALE, Donald　　　　USA
b. *Jacksboro, Texas 1937*

Don Massengale turned professional in 1960 and was active mainly as a tournament player during that decade. He was in the Top 60 in 1962, 1966 and 1967 with a best placing of 26th in 1966, the year he won both the Crosby and the Canadian Open. In 1967 he tied with Don January for the US PGA but lost the play-off. He is the brother of Rik.

US wins 2 (1966)
US money $206,663

MASSENGALE, Richard Gregg　　USA
b. *Jacksboro, Texas 1947*

After amateur wins which included the Western and Southwest Conference, Rik Massengale joined the professional Tour in 1970. For a few years his success was limited as he lacked confidence in his swing, but he eventually made the Top 60 in 1975 and remained in it for two more years, twice winning over $120,000 and including three wins in the same period, with a top placing of 13th in 1977. He fell right away the following season and his best placing since has been 70th in 1980.

US wins 3 (1975–7)
US money $535,734 (1971–82) (87th all-time)

MASSEY, Deborah　　　　　　USA
b. *Grosse Point, Michigan 1950*

Debbie Massey had an excellent amateur career and postponed turning professional rather longer than has become the norm. Perhaps her highest achievement was to take the Canadian Amateur at strokeplay three years in a row, 1974–6. In the USA she

Debbie Massey

MAXWELL, Susan: see Berning

MAXWELL, William J.   USA
b. Abilene, Texas 1929

En route to his victory in the 1951 US Amateur Billy Maxwell defeated both Deane Beman and Harvie Ward. He was also runner-up in the Mexican Amateur in 1951 and won it in 1953. He went on the US Tour the following year and, thanks to an excellent short game, was soon successful, winning first in 1955 and taking three events in his best year, 1961. He was tenth in the money list that year and 12th in 1955, 1959 and 1962. Like many golfers, his career was curtailed by persistent back trouble. He played in the 1963 Ryder Cup and is one of few players to have a 100% record: he won all four of his matches. For many years he was a professional at Las Vegas.

US wins 8 (1955–62)
US money $375,598 (118th all-time)
Overseas wins 1 (1956)

MAYER, Alvin Richard   USA
b. Stamford, Connecticut 1924

After joining the US Tour in 1950 Dick Mayer reached the peak of success with his victory in the 1957 US Open. He had scores of 70, 68, 74, 70 and eventually beat Jimmy Demaret's 283 with an 18-foot putt, one of the longest to tie or win a major championship. However, Cary Middlecoff put in a great finish of 68, 68 to tie, himself holing a useful putt on the 72nd hole. In the resultant play-off Mayer was wary of Middlecoff's exceptionally slow play and therefore took out with him a camping stool on which he sat while Middlecoff pondered and then set himself up for the shot. Perhaps this unsettled his opponent, for Middlecoff soared to a 79 and Mayer's 72 won him the championship with some comfort. Mayer went on to win the so-called 'World Championship' that same year to be leading money-winner ($65,835) and to be named US PGA Player of the Year. Playing in the 1957 Ryder Cup at Lindrick for the only time, he and Tommy Bolt beat Christy O'Connor and Eric Brown by 7 and 5 in the foursomes, and in the singles Mayer was one of only two US players not to be beaten when he halved with Harry Bradshaw. Mayer did not maintain his form and virtually disappeared, emerging briefly in 1965 to take the New Orleans Open. Shortly afterwards he

won the 1972 and 1975 Western Amateur and the 1975 Eastern. She played in the Curtis Cup and World Amateur Team Championship twice each and was low amateur in the 1974 US Open. During this period she partly supported her golf by being a skiing instructress in the winter. On the US Tour since 1977, she has always been a leading player, with the consistency to produce a scoring average that has been around 73½ in the years 1977–81, while the least she has won is $46,000, in her first year, and the most $70,211 in 1978. In the five years she has been placed between 11th and 25th on the money list. She has won two Tour events, the Mizuno Japan Classic in her first year and the Wheeling Classic in 1979. She also achieved the considerable feat of winning the British Open in consecutive years, 1980 and 1981. In 1982, she finished fifth, 3 strokes behind Marta Figueras-Dotti. That year she suffered back problems, however, and dropped to 81st on the money list.

US wins 2 (1977–9)
US money $304,281 (1977–82) (26th all-time)

stopped playing the Tour. He had two other high finishes in major championships: third in the 1954 US Open and fourth in the 1959 Masters.

US wins 7 (1953–65)
US money $185,049 (198th all-time)

MEHLHORN, William E.   USA
b. Elgin, Illinois 1898

When Bobby Jones wrote of the horrors of putting when one's nerve has gone he described his own symptoms (after his retirement in the 1934 US Masters) and gave 'Wild Bill' Mehlhorn as an example of the result of twitching putts. He recalled seeing Mehlhorn, faced with a 3-footer, unleash one of the fiercest 'twitches' on record: the ball flew across the green and for his next putt Mehlhorn was faced with a bunker shot! However, it was not his putting that gave him his nickname: it was after Wild Bill Hickok, because of his liking for playing in cowboy hats, and possibly also for his keenness on cards. He was one of the best of his time through the green, but never a comparable putter until quite late in life – when it no longer mattered. He played for the USA against Great Britain in 1921, 1926 and 1927 and had a number of high finishes in the US Open during this period:

Bill Mehlhorn

fourth in 1922, 2 behind Gene Sarazen, third in 1924 and 1926, fifth in 1927 and fourth in 1931. In 1925 he was beaten by Walter Hagen in the final of the US PGA. He won about half a dozen tournaments, including the 1924 Western Open, and competed in the British Open but without ever threatening to win.

MELNYK, Steven Nicholas   USA
b. Brunswick, Georgia 1947

Steve Melnyk seemed set for great heights when he turned professional towards the end of 1971. He had been one of the few to win both the US and British Amateur Championships. An All-American from 1967 to 1969, he won the US Amateur in 1969; was top amateur in the 1970 British Open, 15 behind winner Nicklaus; was top amateur in the 1971 Masters; and then won the British Amateur. He had been also chosen US amateur golfer of the year in 1969. However, his professional record has been rather moderate. On the US Tour from 1972 he has almost always been successful as a money-winner, but not highly so, and second is his best tournament placing. He was in the top 100 in the years 1972–5, 1977–8 and 1981–2 and in the Top 60 in 1974, 1975 and 1982. His best placings were 46th in 1982 and 52nd in 1974, two of three years in which he has topped $50,000. He is recorded as taking only 99 putts in four rounds of the 1980 Sea Pines Heritage Classic, the second lowest in Tour history. Although the saying is that 'You drive for show and putt for dough', this did not hold good on this occasion. Melnyk finished tied for 56th, had an 80 amongst his rounds and won only $681 for his scintillating putting.

US money $446,414 (1971–82) (103rd all-time)

MELTON, Nancy: see Lopez

MENNE, Robert   USA
b. Gardner, Massachusetts 1942

Now retired from the US Tour, Bob Menne had his best year in 1974 when he won $61,682 and the Kemper Open, which accounted for almost all his winnings that year – $50,000. He was 40th in the money list, the only time he broke into the Top 60. In 1977 he set a record for the fewest putts in a tournament, though he is now in second place. At the 1977 Tournament Players Championship at Sawgrass he took 99 but he who has the fewest putts is often he who misses the most greens in the regulation number of shots. Menne hit only 23 greens as he should have, chipped in twice and had 41 single putts. Menne also tied for the 1970 National Airlines but lost the play-off to Lee Trevino. He missed a 4-foot putt.

US wins 1 (1974)
US money $163,980 (1970–80) (206th all-time)

METZ, Richard   USA
b. Arkansas City, Kansas 1908

Dick Metz was an occasional winner of tournaments in the years 1930–40 but continued a prominent golfer into the 1950s. He finished second in the 1938 US Open but 6 strokes in arrears of Ralph Guldahl, and was sixth in 1952 at the age of 44. His best year was 1939, when he won four tournaments and was fifth amongst the money-winners. In 1982, when he had been a member of the PGA for 53 years, he had won a total of 28 state and sectional PGA events, though relatively few of these were full PGA-recognized tournaments; he had also been picked for the 1939 Ryder Cup match, which did not take place because of World War II. Runner-up in the 1946 Canadian Open, he later won the 1960 PGA Seniors and followed by taking the World event also. He has recorded 16 holes in one and has produced two golf instructional books.

US wins 13 (1930–40)
US money $61,156

MEYERS, Patricia   USA
b. Beverly, Massachusetts 1954

Winner as an amateur of the Florida and South Atlantic titles in 1976, Pat Meyers turned professional that year and was in the top 30 of the US Tour from 1977 to 1980, with best placings of 20th in both 1977 and 1980. She won the 1979 Baltimore Classic and came close to the 1981 LPGA, in which she finished in joint second place, 1 stroke behind Donna Caponi. In the 1982 season she fell to 72nd place on the money list.

US wins 1 (1979)
US money $230,481 (1976–82) (45th all-time)

MIDDLECOFF, Cary   USA
b. Halls, Tennessee 1921

Nicknamed 'Doc' because he was a qualified dentist, Cary Middlecoff won the Tennessee Amateur

four times consecutively from 1940 to 1943. He turned professional in 1947 and was immediately successful, winning a tournament his first season and continuing to do so every year until 1961. By 1949 he was US Open Champion, winning by 1 at Medinah from Clayton Heafner and – as so often – Sam Snead. He did not come near doing so again during the years of Hogan dominance, but emerged again in 1956 to again win by 1 from Boros and Hogan at Oak Hill. He had very consistent rounds of 71, 70, 70, 70. In 1957 he holed a 10-foot putt on the last green to tie with Dick Mayer but lost the play-off 79–72. This was the occasion that Dick Mayer took out a camping stool with him because of Middlecoff's supposed slow play. Bobby Locke was accused of slowing golf down in Britain because of his walking speed and Middlecoff is also regarded as one of the progenitors of the four-hour, or longer, modern tournament round. In his case he took a great deal of time to set himself up for the stroke, so that even gentle Bobby Jones was moved to comment that the alignment process was an unlovely sight. Middlecoff also carried the notion of a barely perceptible pause at the top of the backswing to extremes: he came to a clearly visible stop. Beside his US Open victories he also won the 1955 Masters. He was runner-up in the 1955 US PGA and 1948 Masters. In the 1955 Masters he dominated the event after going out in 31 in the second round and finishing with a 65. He won by a then record 7 strokes over Ben Hogan, equalling or bettering Hogan's score in every round – no mean feat. During the event he is credited with the longest measured putt in a major tournament, one of 86 feet for an eagle on the 13th. (It is, however, highly unlikely that this is the true record. Both Bobby Jones and Jack Nicklaus, no doubt among others, have holed across the double greens of St Andrews, and the length of putts is very seldom measured.) Good as Middlecoff's record was in major events, he was possibly more successful as a US Tour player. His 37 wins put him in seventh place, behind only Snead, Nicklaus, Hogan, Palmer, Nelson and Casper. He was always within the top 10 money winners from 1949 to 1956, and was second in 1949, 1951, 1952 and 1955. He won the Vardon Trophy for stroke average in 1956. He had five wins in 1949, six in 1951 and five in 1955, before his career came to a premature end through a chronic twitch on short putts. Perhaps the longer you take to putt, the more tension builds up and the more likely becomes the twitch after the wear and tear on the nerves of prolonged competition. He took part in the longest play-off in US Tour history when darkness enforced an agreed halt after 11 holes in the 1949 Motor City Open with Lloyd Mangrum. Middlecoff was a Ryder Cup player in 1953, 1955 and 1959.

US wins 37 (1947–61) (7th all-time)
US money $295,168 (149th all-time)

MILLER, Allen   USA
b. San Diego, California 1948

Allen Miller is a steady money-winner each year, but not on a large scale. He was in the top 100 from 1973 to 1976 without breaking into the Top 60, 62nd in 1973 being his best placing. He has won one tournament, the 1974 Tallahassee, and still maintains a very full tournament schedule. His amateur career promised rather more, for he was twice a Walker Cup choice, in 1969 and 1971, played in the 1970 World Team event and took the 1970 Canadian Amateur by 10 strokes.

US wins 1 (1974)
US money $306,976 (1971–82) (143rd all-time)

MILLER, John Laurence   USA
b. San Francisco, California 1947

'I climbed to the top of my personal mountain and decided to sit back and relax... People were saying I was better than Nicklaus. I suppose I couldn't handle it. Maybe I backed off.' Or: 'I went away and worked on my ranch and ruined my golf muscles.' Or: in 1975 Johnny Miller signed a clothes endorsement contract said to be worth $1 million a year to him. All these can be seen as reasons why Miller plummeted down from being for a short while the most successful golfer in the world, winning 13 tournaments and well over $600,000 in the two seasons 1974 and 1975, to 111th place on the US Tour in 1978. By then he was even studying film of himself as a teenager to see why he was promising then and what swing differences had come about in the intervening years. Some were that he appeared more hurried and on occasion almost heaved at the ball; the necessary pull into the ball had sometimes become a push; he was aiming too much to the right; the ball was too far forward in his stance. But more than these things it was confidence that had gone. When Miller was at his peak he commented: 'Happiness is when you know that even your worst shots are going to be quite good.' As he stood over

Johnny Miller

the ball in 1978 his thoughts were more 'Where's this one going to go?' Perhaps initially the reason for his falling off was that Miller had achieved the American dream: he had become rich and a high income was guaranteed for years to come: his reputation stood as high as anyone's, Nicklaus included. His motivation was no longer strong, for Miller did not have that intense passion of a Nicklaus to be not merely the best, but the best who ever lived. Miller had first attracted attention in 1964 by winning the US Junior Championship. Then in 1966 he went to Olympic Country Club in San Francisco expecting to caddie in the US Open. Instead he qualified, and finished leading amateur and eighth overall. He turned professional in 1969 and by 1970 was 40th on the US Tour. In 1971 he won his first event, the Southern Open, and was 18th, achieving a similar result the following year. He had come close to winning a major championship, the 1971 Masters, in which he finished 68, 68, and errors over the closing holes let Charles Coody turn Miller's 2-shot lead with four holes to play into a 2-stroke deficit. Miller finished joint second with Nicklaus. It was in 1973 that Miller became truly a name to conjure with. At Oakmont in the 1973 US Open he began 71, 69 and then had a 76. He was 6 strokes behind Palmer, Boros, Schlee and

Heard. He began the final round with four birdies and suddenly was in with a chance. He continued to pepper the flag with his irons, hit all the fairways and made and missed some putts. He went over par on one hole but added five more birdies and was home with a 63 and 279, the lowest closing round in any major championship either then or since, and at that time a record for any US Open round. Schlee and Weiskopf closed with tidy 70s to be second and third. Miller was suddenly in the superstar category and enhanced that in the British Open at Troon shortly afterwards, when he was the only real contestant against Tom Weiskopf, but finished joint second. If 1973 had seen Miller go to the top, confirmation was certainly still needed. He began 1974 by winning the Crosby and immediately again at Phoenix with 69, 69, 66, 67. Then at Tucson, over a course measuring 7,305 yards he began with a 62 and held on to win. He did not win the next time out but extended a sequence of par or better rounds to 23. After eleven tournaments he had won five of them, adding the Heritage and Tournament of Champions. Miller has said that he is bored with golf by about the time of the Masters and has therefore to win early. These victories had all come by the end of April. Thereafter his appearances were spasmodic and at one point he had been off the Tour for two months. Then at Westchester he played a sequence of 69, 68, 65, 67 to win, while the 65 was one of the rounds of the season: he hit every green in one or two strokes and was only once not on the fairway. It put him past $¼ million for the year. In September he won a play-off for the World Open, including a 63 in the second round and at the end of the month won the Kaiser by 8 strokes. At the end of the year he played in the Dunlop Phoenix in Japan and again dominated, despite an enforced change of clubs between rounds, winning by 7. Back in the USA for a new season he began better even than in 1974. At Phoenix he scored 67, 61, 68, 64 for a total of 260, fourteen better than Jerry Heard's second place. It was the lowest total for 20 years and the margin of victory has been bettered only by Bobby Locke's 16 strokes in 1948. Then, on a longer course at Tucson, Miller had 66, 69, 67, 61 for 263, this time leaving John Mahaffey in second place 9 behind. In the 1975 Masters his final 65, 66 was the lowest final 36 holes ever in the event, and raised him from 10 strokes to only 1 stroke behind the winner, Nicklaus. He won twice more that year, and was third in the British Open. In 1976 he again won

twice early in the US Tour season but the high-point was his win at Royal Birkdale in the British Open. Trailing Ballesteros into the final round, Miller used a 1-iron off the tee until in control and then drove home to a 66 and a very comfortable winning margin of 6 strokes. Miller's reign as one of the modern greats had lasted from June 1973 to July 1976. Yet already he was slipping, as the US Tour money lists show. From his beginnings as a professional he had progressed through the order almost inexorably to ninth in his USA Open year, then first with record money winnings of $353,000 and second in 1975; but then he had slipped to 14th in 1976. The British Open was his last success for a long time. Down the money list he went to 48th, then the unimaginable 111th, with a slight improvement to 76th in 1979. However, hope returned at the end of that year. Miller won the Lancôme in Paris. Back in the USA for the new season he began to pick up some higher placings in events and then in early March won the Inverrary Classic, his first US win for four years. He was 30th that year, and the rehabilitation continued in 1981 when he won twice, was second in the Masters and his 12th place in the money lists was worth nearly $200,000. At the turn of the year he took first place in the $1 million Sun City event after a long play-off with Ballesteros. The fact remains, though, that for three years Miller was playing to a standard that has never clearly been bettered. Today he is merely a good player once more and in 1982 he was 20th on the US money list with $169,065. He is a Mormon; recently he moved his family of six to Utah to escape the 'drugs scene' of Napa, California.

US wins 21 (1971–82)
US money $1,700,119 (1969–82) (8th all-time)
Overseas wins 3 (1974–9)
World money $2,568,002 (1969–82) (6th all-time)

MILLER, Lindy Ray   USA
b. Fort Worth, Texas 1956

In 1977 Lindy Miller won the Southern and Pacific Coast Amateurs, was low amateur in the US Open and a Walker Cup choice. In 1978 he was low amateur in the US Masters and completed his third year as an All-American. He then turned professional. He had a promising first year, finishing with over $50,000 but has sagged since, being 184th in 1981 and 144th in 1982.

US money $120,711 (1979–82) (230th all-time)

MILLER, Sharon Kay   USA
b. Marshall, Michigan 1941

A winner of the West Michigan title four times and the Michigan state title twice, Sharon Miller attracted more national attention when she won the 1965 Trans-Mississippi. The following year she gave up a career as a teacher to turn professional, and was in the top 30 from 1967 to 1974 with a best placing of 12th in 1969; she was in the top 20 from 1968 to 1972. In the later 1970s she continued to win money, but was increasingly troubled by physical ailments. She won the 1973 Corpus Christi Open and the 1974 Columbus Open.

US wins 2 (1973–4)
US money $163,193 (1968–82)

MILLS, Mary   USA
b. Laurel, Mississippi 1940

Mary Mills first won the Mississippi Amateur in 1954 at the age of 14 and continued doing so until she turned professional – eight consecutive victories up to 1961. She also won the Gulf Coast Amateur twice. A professional from 1962, in that year she was the LPGA's first Rookie of the Year, coming 11th in the money list, and thereafter was only once out of the top 20 players until 1975. Her best placings were sixth in 1973, seventh in 1965 and ninth in 1964. Although she has not been a prolific tournament winner, she has done particularly well in major championships, taking the US Open in 1963 (her first win) and that year also finishing joint second in the US LPGA. This championship she took in both 1964 and 1973, in 1964 setting a record for the event with her 278 (68, 69, 72, 69).

US wins 9 (1963–73)
US money $341,192 (1962–81) (24th all-time)

MITCHELL, Jeffrey Keith   USA
b. Rockford, Illinois 1954

After joining the US Tour in 1977 Jeff Mitchell won the 1980 Phoenix Open by 4, with scores of 69, 67, 69, 67, the $54,000 cheque providing nearly half his year's winnings and enabling him to make the Top 60 in 37th place. Although he did not make the Top 60 the following year, he had four tournament placings in the top 10.

US wins 1 (1980)
US money $294,397 (1977–82) (150th all-time)

MITCHELL, Robert Wayne   USA
b. Chatham, Virginia 1943

In 1981 Bobby Mitchell earned just $638 from 22 tournament entries and has had little success since 1975. His best years were 1969, 1971 and 1972 when he was in the Top 60. The last year was easily his best, for he was 11th in the money list and won the Tournament of Champions.

US wins 2 (1971–2)
US money $416,866 (1966–82) (107th all-time)

MIZRAHIE, Barbara   Indonesia & USA
b. Surabaya, Indonesia 1951

One of the first women to play golf in her native country, Barbara Mizrahie won the Indonesian title from 1967 to 1970; and while this was probably no great feat, she proved her worth when she came to the USA in 1972 and in 1974 won the California Public Links title. She turned professional the following year but did not play regularly until she felt ready, in 1978. She was 53rd in the money list in 1980, 54th in 1981 but plummeted to a disappointing 102nd place in the 1982 season, when she won only $9,410.

US money $69,624 (1978–82)

MONTI, Eric   USA
b. Pekin, Illinois 1918

Eric Monti turned professional in 1943 and went on Tour in 1947. He was successful in California, winning ten state titles there, and on the US Tour he won three times between 1955 and 1961. His best year was 1955, when he was 36th in the money list. He is now professional at Hill Crest Golf Club, Los Angeles.

US wins 3 (1955–61)
US money $43,508

MOODY, Orville Cleve   USA
b. Chicasha, Oklahoma 1933

In 1967, as a staff sergeant with 14 years' service, Moody decided to try the professional Tour. He had won the 1958 All-Army Championship and the 1962 All-Service title, and the Korean Open three times. This part-Cherokee Indian had never had a lesson in his life, seldom or never practised but, in his mid 30s, he wanted to see how he measured up to the world's best golfers. In 1968 he was 103rd on the money list, which was none too rewarding – the Army paid better – but he had given himself two or three years to succeed. If not, he would rejoin the Army and resume work as a supervisor of Army golf courses. By the time of the 1969 US Open, he had been doing distinctly better, had won $36,000 for that season so far and was among the top 20 money-winners. He remained as unknown as before and had had to pre-qualify both by section and nationally for the event. He became the least-known winner in living memory, his rounds of 71, 70, 68, 72 leaving him 1 shot ahead of Al Geiberger, Bob Rosburg and Deane Beman. But Moody did not find, as most have done, that his victory was a passport to instant riches; indeed, so little money came to him that he became bitter. Oddly, this was to remain his only win in a PGA -recognized event. Later that same year, he won the World Series, and also was with Trevino in the US World Cup-winning team. In 1971, he won the Hong Kong Open and the Moroccan Grand Prix. His only other win was the 1977 International Caribbean Open. On the US Tour, Moody came 21st in his Open year, then slipped away, so that he was 126th in 1972. After this 1973 was his best year. He was 36th and came close to a second win when he led the Crosby by 4 going into the final round, but then he three-putted the last green and lost the play-off. In 1975 and 1976, he played little tournament golf but thereafter earned useful if hardly spectacular sums. By 1981 he was playing only occasionally.

US wins 1 (1969)
US money $383,008 (1968–81) (115th all-time)
Overseas wins 4 (1969–77)

MOODY, Terri (later Luckhurst)　　　USA
b. *Athens, Georgia 1959*

After winning the National Collegiate Champion-ship in 1981 and playing in the 1980 Curtis Cup, Terri Moody joined the US Tour for the 1982 season and came close to her first victory when she produced a run of 71, 71, 70, 70 for 282 in the Boston Five Classic, to finish second 1 stroke behind Sandra Palmer. Her brother Griff played on the US Walker Cup team: they are the only brother-and-sister combination to have represented the USA in Walker and Curtis Cups. She was low amateur in the 1979 US Open.

US money $30, 203 (1982)

MOREY, Dale　　　USA
b. *Martinsville, Indiana 1918*

Dale Morey is a golfer in whom both ability and desire to play survived into his 50s. He is still as outstanding a senior golfer, winning the USGA Seniors in 1974 and 1977, as he was a leading amateur international in the 1950s and 1960s. Morey is thought to have won about 250 amateur events of varying status, including the Southern in 1951 and 1964, the Western in 1953, the North and South in 1964 and the 1972 Mid-Atlantic. He was runner-up in the 1952 US Amateur, represented the US in the 1954 and 1965 Americas Cup and was twice in the Walker Cup side: 1955 and 1965. He lost both his singles and won and lost a foursomes. He was beaten finalist in the 1981 USGA Seniors Championship.

MORGAN, Gilmer Bryan　　　USA
b. *Wewoka, Oklahoma 1946*

Gil Morgan waited until he had secured his future with a doctorate in optometry before turning pro-fessional in 1972. He has been a full-time tourna-ment player since and, if not a frequent winner, is a highly consistent money-maker, having topped $100,000 in each of the years 1977–81. He has a simple, correct swing which makes him one of the more accurate Tour drivers and means that he tends to produce better placings on the tighter courses. From 1975 he has always been in the Top 60 and has been better than 29th every year since 1977. He first won in 1977, and his biggest year followed at once. In 1978, helped by a $100,000 cheque for first place in the World Series, he won some $267,000 and the Los Angeles Open, while in Europe he tied with Bernard Gallacher and Bobby Wadkins for the European Open and lost the play-off. In Japan he took the Pacific Masters. This apparent climax of a career that had been tending inexorably to superstar status has not since been fully realized: Morgan is an excellent player but he is unlikely now to become a major-championship winner. His best placing in a championship was third in the 1980 PGA, the event dominated by Jack Nicklaus. He played in the 1979 US Ryder Cup team.

US wins 4 (1977–79)
US money $1,064,196 (1973–82) (34th all-time)
Overseas wins 1 (1978)
World money $1,200,760 (1973–82)(40th all-time)

127

MORLEY, Michael E.   USA
b. Morris, Minnesota 1946

Mike Morley won the North Dakota Amateur in 1966 and 1967 and was an All-American in 1967 and 1968. After an unrewarding first year on the US Tour he began to win money from 1972 onwards and has never been worse than 95th in the years 1973–81, with 29th his best placing in 1976 and 31st the following year. For the rest of his career he has been out of the Top 60; but he has shown that even with the need to pre-qualify every Monday there is still money to be won – almost half a million in his case. Morley won the 1972 Magnolia Classic (most prestigious of the mini-Tour events), the 1978 North Dakota Open and one Tour event, the 1977 Quad Cities. In 1982 he began to suffer a lack of form and fell to 129th in the money list.

US wins 1 (1977)
US money $503,099 (1970–82) (94th all-time)

MORSE, Catherine   USA
b. Rochester, New York 1956

Twice winner of the New York state Amateur and runner-up for the 1972 US Junior, Cathy Morse joined the US Tour in 1978 and made money in each of her following seasons, having occasional high placings. In 1982 she won her first event, the Chrysler-Plymouth Classic, and her money winnings of $71,519 for the year were double what she had accumulated in any previous season.

US wins 1 (1982)
US money $165,200 (1978–82)

MOXNESS, Barbara   USA
b. Montevideo, Minnesota 1953

Barbara Moxness won the Minnesota Junior title in 1970 and thereafter did hospital work for some time before turning professional in 1978. Immediately paying her way, Barbara has also improved her stroke average each season and was 30th and 32nd in 1980 and 1981, winning more than $40,000 in each of these years. In 1982 she moved up a notch to be 18th in the money list with winnings of around $75,000. This as comfortably her best year, and though she did not win a tournament, her highest placing was a creditable joint second in the Lady Michelob Open.

US money $204,985 (1978–82) (56th all-time)

Jodie Mudd

MUDD, Joseph Martin   USA
b. Louisville, Kentucky 1962

Having scored a 67 in the 1982 Masters, Jodie Mudd was encouraged enough to turn professional immediately. He had an excellent amateur career behind him, having been US Public Links Champion in 1980 and 1981. He was an alternate choice for the 1980 World Amateur Team Championship, reached the quarter-finals of the 1980 US Amateur and was in the 1981 Walker Cup team. One of the newest US Tour players, he is regarded as one of those most likely to succeed. He was 114th on the 1982 money list, playing only part of the season.

US money $34,216 (1982)

MUNSON, Edith: see Cummings

MURPHY, Robert J.   USA
b. Brooklyn, New York 1943

Although he has a rather awkward long swing and lacks power Bob Murphy has never lacked consistency. Since joining the US Tour in 1968, only in 1979 and 1982 has he failed to make the Top 60. His arrival as a pro was dramatic. In 1968 in the space of three weeks he finished second once and then followed up with consecutive wins, ending the season in tenth money place, Rookie of the Year and with the then record money winnings for a first-year player of $105,595. Perhaps he has not quite lived up to this start, though he came ninth in the money in 1970 and 11th in 1975 and has three other placings in the top 30. Murphy took to golf at the University of Florida when he hurt his shoulder as a baseball pitcher. In 1965 he was US Amateur Champion, and NCAA Champion the following year. He was in the 1966 Eisenhower Trophy team and the 1967 Walker Cup team, his Ryder Cup place in 1975 making him one of about a dozen to represent the USA in both matches. The winner of four US Tour events, he must have felt cheated out of another, the 1973 Westchester Classic, for he tied and then lost the play-off after Bobby Nichols eagled the last hole. Murphy was fifth in the 1969 US Open and joint third in 1975, one behind the Graham-Mahaffey play-off; he was second in the 1970 US PGA Championship. The strengths of his game are that he seldom misses fairways, excels at getting down in two from sand and is a smooth putter.

US wins 4 (1968–75)
US money $1,174,425 (1968–82) (25th all-time)
Overseas wins 1 (1972)
World money $2,283,784 (1968–82) (35th all-time)

NELFORD, James Cameron   Canada
b. Vancouver, British Columbia 1955

Perhaps today's best Canadian player, Jim Nelford won the Canadian Amateur in 1975 and 1976 and the Western Amateur in 1977. He then turned professional and competes full-time on the US Tour; he lives in Utah. He represented Canada in the 1979 World Cup, his team finishing seventh; and then in 1980, with Dan Halldorson, when Canada came in first. This was very much a surprise result, for both are US Tour players of thin achievement. Nelford has topped $20,000 each of the four years to 1981 that he has played, but 87th on the 1978 money list is his best position, while he was 94th in 1982. Many putting methods have been tried and Nelford's answer to getting the ball into the hole is not unique, but certainly rare: he is a right-hander who putts left-handed.

US money $172,264 (1978–82) (204th all-time)

NELSON, John Byron   USA
b. Fort Worth, Texas 1912

Byron Nelson is a key figure in the evolution of the golf swing and, because of his unparalleled successes on the US Tour from 1944 to 1946, perhaps the most influential in modern times. (No one cares how a loser swings a club. What was effective in the Trevino swing was analysed only when he had shown he was consistently a major player.) Nelson took the club back in a 'one-piece' movement with no part of the body seeming to dominate, had a restricted hip turn but very full shoulder turn, a very straight left arm, tried to keep the clubface square and hit through the ball with considerable leg drive. On the downswing he led the stroke with his legs and the club was pulled into the ball rather than pushed. While Cotton and others were advocating hitting against a firm left side, Nelson's legs and knees were carrying on through the hitting area. This leg action keeps the clubhead low through the hitting area longer and therefore increases the chances of consistent striking. Nelson began in golf as a fellow caddie with Ben Hogan. His first success came in winning the 1930 Southwestern Amateur, and he turned professional two years later. His early efforts in tournament golf were highly unsuccessful: he won just $12.50 in his first year. In 1935 he won the New Jersey Open, and that brought in enough money for him to continue. He won once the following year, and then in 1937 became a major figure. In the US Masters, he began with a 66, despite single-putting only once, but then faded to 72, 75, which left him 4 behind Ralph Guldahl's 69, 72, 68. The championship then swung in a space of minutes on two holes. Nelson played the 12th and 13th in 2, 3 and Guldahl took 5, 6. Nelson came home 2 ahead. In 1939 there came a similarly sudden swing in a major championship, this time the US Open. After 72 holes, Nelson, Craig Wood and Densmore Shute had tied on 284. Wood and Nelson then tied with 68s, Shute being eliminated. In the second 18-hole play-off, after Nelson birdied the 3rd hole he holed a full 1-iron on the next for an eagle. That 3-stroke win saw Nelson Open Champion. At this time, the British Open was not an aim of US golfers, but Nelson did compete in the 1937 event as it was a Ryder Cup year; he finished 5th. The US PGA was his next target: he was to reach the final three years consecutively from 1939, and five times in the seven years to 1945. He lost to Henry Picard in 1939, beat Snead in 1940, lost to Vic Ghezzi in 1941 and to Bob Hamilton in 1944 and beat Sam Byrd in 1945. In 1946 he reached the quarter-finals and then announced his retirement from tournament golf. Perhaps the most dramatic match was against Mike Turnesa in 1945. Nelson found himself 1 down, with Turnesa 7 under par, but responded with a run of birdie, birdie, eagle which made him the winner. In the championship as a whole he was 37 under par for the 204 holes he played. By the time World War II put a stop to tournament golf in America Nelson had a formidable record. He had won the PGA, the Masters twice (beating Hogan in 1942 with a run of 6 under when Hogan was himself 1 under) and the US Open. He had also twice been second in the PGA and been third and second in the 1940 and 1941 Masters. He had 26 tournament victories to his name. I stress this because Nelson's phenomenal US Tour successes from 1944 to 1946 have been disparaged because it is said that all the best players were away at the war. Yet by the time of Pearl Harbor Nelson was already firmly established at the top of US golf. As a haemophiliac, he was exempt from military service. In 1944 tournament play was resumed. Nelson finished leading money-winner with seven victories and the remarkable stroke average of 69.67 for 85 rounds. The following year made him a legend and produced a flow of wins that has not been approached before or since. From 11 March to 4 August, Nelson won every event for which he entered, a total of 11 consecutively. For the whole

season he totalled 18 and averaged 68.33, almost a stroke better than the next best in history, for 120 rounds played. In the year he was never over par for 72 holes, was in the money every event and won 17.5% of the total prize money – again an all-time record, and may be compared with Watson's less than 4% in his over $1½ million in 1980. Of the Nelson of these years Tommy Armour said: 'The finest golfer I have seen.' Bobby Jones admitted: 'At my best, I never came close to the golf Nelson shoots.' By 1946 the leading US professionals were back from the war, particularly Ben Hogan, who began to better Byron Nelson's victory rate. Nelson kept on winning: five in 1946, and he tied with Lloyd Mangrum and Vic Ghezzi for the US Open before losing the play-off. Then came his retirement after the US PGA. Some have said that he was suffering from a nervous stomach; others that back trouble was the cause. Nelson himself has said that he was not happy at being so much the centre of attention, at having to shake so many hands, attend lunches and all the myriad demands on his patience and stamina. His Texas ranch beckoned and Nelson went, leaving behind no doubts about his greatness but some that grew with the passing of time as to his exact placing among the giants. If his appetite for victory had persisted there is little doubt that he would have increased his tally of five major championships. On the US Tour he had 54 wins in all, the fifth most, bettered by Snead, Nicklaus, Hogan and Palmer with 84, 68, 62 and 61. It seems likely that he could have gone on to second or third place. Nelson did occasionally reappear in events he particularly liked, the US Masters for instance, in which he continued to perform well for many years. He had rounds of 70, 74, 72, 74 as late as 1965, good enough for 15th place at the age of 53. His last US win was in the 1951 Crosby. In 1955 he made a sentimental journey to Europe, winning the French Open in fine style with a superb display of irons. He is now considered one of the best coaches in America: among his pupils have been Harvie Ward, Frank Stranahan, Tony Lema, Bobby Nichols, Ken Venturi and Tom Watson. Since the passing of Freddie McLeod and Jock Hutchison, he and Gene Sarazen now play the ceremonial opening nine holes of the US Masters.

US wins 54 (1935–51) (5th all-time)
US money $190,256 (192nd all-time)
Overseas wins 1 (1955)
Total wins 66 (1930–55)

Byron Nelson

Larry Nelson

NELSON, Larry Gene   USA
b. *Fort Payne, Alabama 1947*

On 20 September 1981 Larry Nelson defeated Mark James by 2 up in the Ryder Cup singles at Walton Heath. On this occasion it was his fourth winning match and, added to his five wins at the Greenbrier in 1979, extended his record to nine matches, nine wins – the best record in Ryder Cup history. Nelson had got into the US team on the second occasion only because a little over a month before he had won the US PGA in some comfort. His scores of 70, 66, 66, 71 left him 4 ahead of Fuzzy Zoeller and gave him his most important success, a major championship. Nelson is highly unusual as a golfer in one respect: he began late. Most current professionals seem to have begun to play at a very early age – five or six is not in the least uncommon – and most are quite good by their early teens. Nelson claims not to have swung a club until he

was 21 and happened to find himself at a driving range. He quite liked the game and two years later turned professional, qualifying for the US Tour in 1974. The four-round school event was only the second 72-hole competition he had played in. The other had given him second place in the Florida Open. He made money his first two seasons and in 1976 broke into the Top 60, remaining there comfortably in 1977 and 1978. His first Tour win came in 1979, the Inverrary Classic, and he also won the Western Open, was fourth in the US Open and equal second in the World Series. He had one other second place and was in all nine times in the top 10. He had risen from 45th on the money list in 1978 to second, behind Tom Watson. In the next two seasons Nelson came in 11th and 10th and added three more Tour victories. His win in the 1981 Greater Greensboro' was particularly dramatic. He led after three rounds with 69, 68, 69 but faded considerably in the last to 75. At the last hole, he was 2 to the bad on Mark Hayes who was on the edge of the green in two, while Nelson had so difficult a bunker shot he feared he might not get it on the green. He holed out, Hayes three-putted and Nelson won the play-off. Nelson has a simple rhythmic swing that leads to consistency and is not long off the tee. His strongest playing card is driving accuracy, shown by his finishing sixth for driving accuracy in US Tour statistics in 1980 and fifth in 1981. He was 21st on the 1982 money list with over $150,000.

US wins 5 (1979–81)
US money $1,110,982 (1974–82) (32nd all-time)
World money $1,271,039 (1974–82) (37th all-time)

NEWELL, Elizabeth: see Hicks

NICHOLS, Robert Herman   USA
b. *Louisville, Kentucky 1936*

An elegant long hitter, Nichols has had to endure two physical disasters. After 1952 he had to concentrate on golf and give up football and basketball. A car crash had left him with a broken pelvis, internal and back injuries, and concussion, and for a time he was paralysed from the waist down – a worse collection by at least a little than Hogan suffered in 1949. The second disaster may have finished him as a golfer. Nichols was one of those, with Trevino and Jerry Heard, who were struck by lightning during the 1975 Western Open. Since then, although still a quite regular competitor on the US Tour, Nichols, always in the Top 60 from 1960 to 1975, has not been better than 121st. In his long run among the leading money-winners Nichols made the top 20 eight times from 1962 to 1974, with 1964 his best year at fifth. Then he also won his single major championship, the US PGA, when he seemed to be hitting a flow of superb shots from all over the course and holing putts of inordinate length. He came in 3 ahead of Palmer and Nicklaus. He also won the Carling World Open that year but, after the PGA, his most important win was the 1974 Canadian Open. Perhaps his most dramatic victory was in the 1973 Westchester Classic. With a round to go Nichols lay 5 strokes behind and was not even in realistic contention playing the last hole. However, he eagled that to tie with Bob Murphy and then birdied the first play-off hole to win.

US wins 12 (1962–74)
US money $978,497 (1960–82) (39th all-time)
World money $1,128,951 (1960–82) (46th all-time)

NICKLAUS, Jack William   USA
b. *Columbus, Ohio 1940*

British Open Champion: 1966, 1970, 1978
US Amateur Champion: 1959, 1961
US Masters Champion: 1963, 1965, 1966, 1972, 1975
US Open Champion: 1962, 1967, 1972, 1980
US PGA Champion: 1963, 1971, 1973, 1975, 1980

From his late teens, Jack Nicklaus set his sights on being the greatest golfer who ever lived; he has always had an awareness of golf history. The route to immortality lies by way of wins in major championships and Nicklaus's closest rival in some golfing Valhalla is Bobby Jones, with 13 to the Nicklaus 19. No one except among present-day established golfers, other than perhaps Tom Watson, has any prospect of even approaching his major championship record, and even Watson cannot imagine he will do more than distantly approach the impossible target. Although Nicklaus has played on the US Tour less and less with the passing of time, mainly fulfilling obligations, playing in the ones he specially likes or using them for honing his competitive edge, his record of dominance is unparalleled. He turned professional in 1961 and first played the US Tour the following year, his first entry, in the Los Angeles Open, bringing in $33. From that year to 1977, he was always in the first three of money-winners, except

in 1970 when he was fourth, as he was again in 1978. Eight times between 1964 and 1976 he was number one. From 1963, when he became the second man to win $100,000 in a season, he has only missed 1979 as regards that target, and topped $200,000 in each of the years 1971–8 and 1982 and $300,000 in 1972 and 1973. He was the third man to reach $1 million in career money winnings, the first to reach $2 million and $3 million, and will be the first to reach $4 million. In world money, he will almost certainly reach $5 million. Despite the fact that Nicklaus centres his year on the major championships, he is a formidable winner of tournaments also, winning 18 times outside the US and 69 on the US Tour, the US Tour total bettered only by Sam Snead's 84. He has also won the Australian Open six times, one of the few events outside the USA, other than the British Open, in which he has competed frequently. Nicklaus first broke 80 at the age of 12; at 16 he won the Ohio Open. In 1957 he first qualified for the US Open but missed the halfway cut; however, he played all through the following year. In 1960, he came close to winning, leading with a few holes to go and finishing second at Cherry Hills with scores of 71, 71, 69, 71, still the best produced by an amateur. That same year he scored 269 around Merion in the Eisenhower Trophy, which was 18 strokes better, it was noted, than Ben Hogan's US Open winning score of 1950. In other amateur competition, among others he won the Western, the North and South, the Trans-Mississippi, was NCAA Champion in 1961, in 1959 beat Charles Coe in a closely contested US Amateur final and two years later crushed Dudley Wysong by 8 and 6 in the final. He played in two Walker Cup matches – 1959 and 1961 – and in both won his foursomes and singles. In his last three years as an amateur he lost only four of his competitive matches. The choice of whether or not to remain an amateur was a very difficult one. One suspects that with his sights set so high he would have liked to emulate Jones's amateur achievements, but Nicklaus eventually felt that the top competition was on the US Tour and that was where he had better be. He turned professional towards the end of 1961. Thereafter, there is not space to chronicle his achievements other than by taking major championship performance as the main yardstick. His two US Amateurs gave him a start and, in his first professional season, he took the US Open at Oakmont – a highly unpopular victory, for he had been tactless enough to tie the

Jack Nicklaus

most popular figure in golf, Arnold Palmer, and beat him 71–74 in the play-off. His next major came with the 1963 US Masters in rough weather, and that same year he added the US PGA. In 1965 he gave one of his best major championship performances, going round Augusta in 67, 71, 64, 69. His 64 tied the single-round record and his 271 broke Hogan's record of 274. His total has since been matched by Ray Floyd (1976), but his winning margin of 9 remains the record. Bobby Jones, who was there watching, said that Nicklaus should 'wind up shooting in the 50s' and called his win 'the greatest performance in golf history'. The British Open had still eluded his grasp, though he had been 1 away from the first-place tie in 1963 at Royal Lytham, and second with a finish of 66, 68 at St Andrews in 1964. In 1966 the venue was Muirfield, a course that Nicklaus came to regard as one of the fairest in the world. That year Nicklaus thought the rough looked like wheat swaying in the wind, and a special penalty had been imposed on the longer hitters, the fairways being narrowed to only some 25 yards about 250 yards from the tees. Nicklaus shared the lead after the first round with a 70, and followed with a 67 to lead outright. He had faced the challenge of deep rough and narrow fairways by relying on the accuracy of his iron play rather than woods for his tee shots. In the third round he was level par after 13 holes, but then leaked shots to finish in 75. Phil Rodgers, completing the second nine in 30 strokes, had gone into a 2-stroke lead, but a Nicklaus birdie to a Rodgers 5 on the par-4 1st hole squared them. After ten holes Nicklaus was 3 ahead of David Thomas and 4 ahead of Rodgers and Doug Sanders. He faced a putt of about 2 yards for a birdie on the next, missed it, and then again from about a foot. Thomas, with a birdie just ahead, had immediately drawn level. From the 15th on Nicklaus knew he needed level par to tie Thomas and Sanders. He won it on the 528-yard 17th. He hit a 3-iron from the tee and found the green with his 5-iron second shot, two-putting for his birdie. Even into wind on the last, 429 yards, he still was home with a couple of irons and was British Open Champion. He had now become one of a rare band who have taken the US and British Opens and the US Masters and PGA. Sarazen, Hogan and Player are the only other golfers to have done so. Nicklaus added his third US Masters that year after a play-off with Tommy

Jacobs and Gay Brewer, and the following year produced a stirring 65 in the last round to beat Palmer for the US Open. His deeds had induced respect and awe in the US, but not popularity. Now his career went into the doldrums – by his standards. In 1968 he won only twice on the US Tour, three times in 1969 and twice in 1970. At the time of the 1970 British Open he had added no more major championship victories and the target of Bobby Jones's 13 lay far distant, with Nicklaus two years past the age at which Jones had retired. Many think that his win at St Andrews refired his ambitions, and certainly it has become one of his most legendary. Not, however, because of the manner of his victory but of another man's loss: Sanders missed a short putt on the last and then in the play-off came to the same green 1 to the bad. Sanders birdied, while Nicklaus allowed himself the rather theatrical gesture of taking off his sweater before hitting a 3-wood through the green, getting down in two more to win. He now entered his most prolific period as a tournament and major championship winner. His game too began to change. In his 20s his play had not been subtle, neither had it needed to be. A sledgehammer blow from the tee overpowered many courses, leaving him little to do for the shot into the green on the par 4s and frequently only a short-iron on par 5s. Nicklaus began to change. He slimmed down for a start, and grew his hair. 'Ohio Fats' or 'the Fat Boy', as he was called by some Tour regulars, was suddenly no more. The jockey cap disappeared, and so did the baggy trousers. As a result of the weight change he lost a little length from the tee, but as late as the early 1980s he was still one of the longest drivers on the US Tour, averaging between 260 and 270 yards, only a few strides short of the longest. He won five US events in 1971, seven in 1972 and again in 1973, and five in 1975. Four of his Australian Open wins came between 1971 and 1978. In the major championships he took seven in the years 1970–75. His 1973 PGA was historically significant, for with it he overhauled Bobby Jones's 13. His status as world number one had been challenged by Palmer, Player and Weiskopf in 1973 and Miller from 1974 to 1975. All had been overcome and Nicklaus was approaching the age of 40 before most were prepared to concede that the crown had passed to Tom Watson. Three championships were particularly memorable. The 1975 Masters has been called the greatest of all time. Nicklaus dominated the first 36

holes with 68, 67, to lead Weiskopf by 6 and Miller by 11, but there was a large swing in the third round, in which Nicklaus fell away to 73, while Weiskopf had a 66 to lead Nicklaus by 1 and Miller pulled back 8 shots with his 65, having gone to the turn in a record 30 with six consecutive birdies. Nicklaus was out with Tom Watson in the last round, followed a hole behind by the Weiskopf and Miller pairing. Nicklaus took 35 to the turn, Weiskopf 34 (to lead by 2) and Miller 32, with five birdies. The 15th might have been the crucial hole, for it demands a very long drive so that a reasonably lofted second can be played into this par-5 green – otherwise the ball will run through. Nicklaus hit a 1-iron of about 230 yards' carry; Miller a 3-wood and Weiskopf was through with a 4-iron, saving his birdie with a good putt, while both Nicklaus and Miller got their birdies in some comfort. The 16th is about 190 yards and over water. Nicklaus did not strike his iron well this time. He pitched short of the flag and rolled further away back down the slope. Watson held matters up by putting two attempts into the water. Nicklaus then holed perhaps the most memorable putt of his career. It measured around 15 yards, was uphill and had a big swing on it. Miller parred; Weiskopf, from the front of the green, three-putted and Nicklaus was in the lead again, by 1 over Weiskopf and 2 over Miller, who birdied the next. Both Miller and Weiskopf had putts to tie on the last, and both came very close; but it was Nicklaus's fifth Masters victory. The 'Young Pretender', Tom Watson, again featured at Turnberry in 1977 in the lowest scoring major championship of all. He and Nicklaus began identically with 68, 70 and were paired the final two days. Both then had 65s and the rest of the field was out of sight, except for Ben Crenshaw, 3 to the bad. Nicklaus and Watson exchanged blow for blow until the par-5 17th, where Nicklaus was just short in two and then missed a shortish putt. He went to the last tee 1 behind, tried a big drive which was almost in a bush to the right while Watson played an iron down the middle and sent his approach almost dead. Nicklaus replied by putting his second on the green and holing a very long putt for a birdie, but Watson safely holed his putt to clinch the championship. Third man Hubert Green was 11 behind the winning score of 268, and the British Open record had been smashed by 8 strokes. From 1975 on Nicklaus won only one major championship, the 1978 British Open, again at St Andrews, and the following season had his worst year ever. For the first time he failed to win a tournament, plummeted down from always being in the top four on the US Tour to 71st place and had only one result that in Nicklaus terms could be called a success: he tied for second place in the British Open. With Watson leading money-winner for the third consecutive time and holder of the Vardon Trophy in the same sequence, there seemed no longer any question of who was the top player. Nicklaus worked exceptionally hard on his short game that winter, even learning some new shots. His stroke average came down almost 2 strokes a round and he dominated two of the major championships, beginning the US Open at Baltusrol with a 63 and holding on to beat Isao Aoki by 2. A couple of months later at Oak Hill he scored 70, 69, 66, 69 to win the US PGA by 7 from Andy Bean. He now held the record number of Masters wins with five, tied Walter Hagen with five for the US PGA and tied Jones, Anderson and Hogan with four US Opens. The record of five wins in the latter was to be snatched from him by Watson's 2, 4 finish against par of 3, 5 in the 1982 Pebble Beach Open. Yet in his final round Nicklaus had secured five successive birdies. What is it that has made Nicklaus so great a player? His main strengths are long and accurate driving; excellent long and medium irons; reliable approach putting. He does very little wrong in the rest: short approaches, chipping and short putting. He does, however, not rate in the top class in these, and Trevino has pointed out that Nicklaus's fellows are fortunate he was not 'born with a sand iron'. But shotmaking is only a part of successful golf and Nicklaus rates higher than any of his contemporaries for mental abilities. His concentration can seldom be faulted; his nerve has lasted; his thinking about how to play course and shot is incisive; his will to win has kept him going when those with less sense of history would have long sat back. Few have lasted as long as Nicklaus, and the time is obviously now not far off before he is no longer a major force in golf. Yet his appetite for major championships remains. He was 12th in money winnings on the 1982 US Tour, with some $232,000, some way short of his career best of $320,542 in the 1972 season.

US wins 69 (1962–82) (2nd all-time)
US money $3,992,071 (1962–82) (1st all-time)
Europe money £99,000 (36th all-time)
Overseas wins 18
World money $4,915,568 (1962–82) (1st all-time)

NIEPORTE, Tom   USA
b. Cincinatti, Ohio 1928

Tom Nieporte was 1951 NCAA Champion and also took the 1953 All-Army Championship. He joined the US Tour in 1955 and was in the Top 60 from 1957 to 1960, with 18th in 1959 being his best placing. He won events between 1959 and 1967, including the Bob Hope Desert Classic, and also eight Long Island titles. Since his Tour retirement he has gained a reputation as a golf teacher.

US wins 3 (1959–67)
US money $94,554

NORMAN, Moe   Canada
b. Kitchener, Ontario 1930

Moe Norman's principal successes are that he was Canadian Amateur Champion in 1955 and 1956 and won the Canadian PGA in 1966 and 1974, but he is far more known as one of the characters of modern golf than as a tournament-winner. Norman's sights seem never to have been set on tournament victories but much more on enjoying the game of golf, and often enjoying it unconventionally. As a prominent amateur in Canada, he attracted some disapproval by his preference for carrying his own bag for, as he said, 'It's not heavy', and picking the prize he wanted and then producing the necessary score. If a sixth-place prize tempted him, why try to come first? In one event, he is said to have put his ball on the last green, needing to get down in three more to win. Not very interesting, thought Moe Norman, and, to stimulate himself a little, deliberately putted into a bunker and got down from there in two strokes. His main aim has been to make a living by playing money matches, in Ontario in the Canadian summer months and then down to the resort golf of the American south. While there he is more likely to sleep in the back of his car than in a hotel. He also likes to collect course records, and is said to hold about 30 in the US and Canada. He is one of very few indeed to have dropped out of the US Masters when in contention. The story goes that Norman was so taken by a tip that Byron Nelson gave him that he hit hundreds of shots to try out the new thought and woke up the next day too stiff and swollen to swing a club. On another occasion, in the Los Angeles Open, he drove off with a Coca-Cola bottle. In tournaments he often makes side bets with spectators on the results of certain shots. He now appears on the US Seniors Tour.

NORRIS, Timothy Garrett   USA
b. Fresno, California 1957

Dixie Amateur and California Open champion in 1980, Tim Norris was also an All-American that year. He then turned professional and qualified for the 1981 season. He finished his first year at 106th on the money list with $32,424 and ranked ninth in driving accuracy, quite a rare placing for a young player. Still an unknown in 1982, he came to the fore suddenly with a win in the Greater Hartford Open. The Wethersfield course almost always produces low scoring, but Norris's 259 was only the fourth time 260 has been broken in US Tour history (Mike Souchak's 257, referred to in more detail elsewhere, is still the record). Norris began with a 63 and followed with 64, 66, 66 to beat Hubert Green and Ray Floyd by 6 strokes. There was a winner's cheque for $54,000 to be added to the $3,500 he had won so far that season.

US wins 1 (1982)
US money $98,067 (1981–2)

NORTH, Andrew Stewart   USA
b. Thorp, Wisconsin 1950

The theory is that it takes a great player to win a major championship. Andy North may be the exception that proves the rule. When he won the US Open of 1978 he was little known, having at that point taken one US tournament; and he has not added another since. At Cherry Hills, Denver, he scored 70, 70, 71, 74. He led by 2 strokes after the second round, and by 1 going into the final round. He made his position more secure by establishing a 4-stroke lead with five holes to play, but then he dropped 1 on the 14th and 2 on the 15th. He faced the 480-yard last hole needing a 1-over-par 5 to win. With water on the left and rough on the right he did not go for the green in two, but played safely short so that he was left with a simple pitch over a bunker and two putts for the championship. North then lobbed his next into the bunker and was left with the less attractive prospect of having to get down in two to win. He splashed to 4 feet, after which he was by no means eager with the putt, backing away twice in the hope that his nerves would come under control. He holed it, and commented 'Thank heavens it's over.' North had come on to the US Tour in 1973 with a good amateur record. He had three times been an All-American choice, had won the 1969 Wisconsin Amateur and the 1971 Western Amateur, and been

runner-up in the 1976 US Junior. He immediately made a good living on Tour and was in the Top 60 from 1974 to 1977. In the last of these years he won the Westchester Classic by 2 strokes with 66, 70, 65, 71. After the US Open his game fell away, perhaps because the new demands on him reduced his time for the practice his 6-foot 4-inch frame needs to maintain co-ordination and timing. From 14th on the money list in 1978, his best placing, he fell to 54th, then 69th; but he was back to 30th in 1981, and 49th in 1982.

US wins 2 (1977–8)
US money $809,964 (1973–82) (54th all-time)

O'BRIEN, Kyle   USA
b. Indianapolis, Indiana 1958

The 1979 AIAW Collegiate Champion, Kyle O'Brien was by common consent the college golfer of the year in 1979. She was an All-American choice in 1979 and 1980. She qualified for the US Tour in 1981 and came close to a win, finishing second in the Rail Charity Classic, her scores of 70, 67, 70 leaving her 2 behind JoAnne Carner. She was second to Patty Sheehan as LPGA Rookie of the Year, while *Golf Digest* made her their choice. She finished 28th in the money list. Kyle O'Brien is regarded as one of those most likely to succeed in the 1980s, though she did not make the expected advance in 1982 because of a back injury.

US money $59,735 (1981–2)

OLIVER, Ed   USA
b. Wilmington, Delaware 1916; d. 1961

It must be mortifying to tie for the US Open and then be disqualified. In the 1940 event 'Porky' Oliver and his playing companions set out at Canterbury, Ohio, a little in advance of their start time, hoping to miss an approaching storm. Oliver's score would have tied him with Lawson Little and Gene Sarazen, but he was disqualified. It would not have happened in more formal days: now you are disqualified for arriving late and you are unlikely to be allowed to set off early. That was the nearest he came to a major championship victory, but he was third in the 1947 US Open and second in 1952; in the US PGA he was runner-up in 1946, and in the 1953 Masters he was second a long way behind Ben Hogan. Nevertheless Oliver was an outstanding striker, despite the overweight that gave him his

Ed 'Porky' Oliver

nickname, and he won eight US tournaments in a career that included Ryder Cup places in 1947 – when he was fourth in the year's money list – 1951 and 1953. In the 1947 match he and Lew Worsham overwhelmed Henry Cotton and Arthur Lees by 10 and 9 in the foursomes and he beat Charlie Ward in the singles. Lees was later to have his revenge in both foursomes and singles in 1951. Oliver was chosen as non-playing captain for the 1961 match, but was prevented from taking up the role by his fatal illness. On the 223-yard 16th at Cypress Point, when in contention for the 1954 Crosby, he met the fate most fear when faced with the tee shot across the Pacific Ocean: he put four or five balls into it and ended up scoring in the mid teens.

US wins 8

O'MEARA, Mark Francis   USA
b. Goldsboro, North Carolina 1957

Mark O'Meara won the US Amateur in 1979, beating John Cook, the previous year's champion, in the final. In the same year he won the California title and also the Mexican Amateur, beating Gary

Hallberg. He then turned professional. By the middle of his first season on the US Tour he had made sure of a Top 60 place and in mid August was in 22nd position and had tied for the Tallahassee Open, losing the play-off. His game fell away a little in the remainder of the season but he was still 55th and was later selected Rookie of the Year. In 1982 he was only 118th. O'Meara makes putting look a very natural activity. He likes to draw his wood shots for extra length, but fade irons for accuracy.

US money $107,773 (1981–2) (235th all-time)

ORCUTT, Maureen   USA
b. New York 1907

Maureen Orcutt had a brilliant amateur career between the wars which began with the 1922 Metropolitan Junior, an event she was to win at adult level ten times in her career. In major US events she took the North and South three times and the Eastern seven times but never the US Amateur, being beaten in the 1927 and 1936 finals, by Pam Barton on the latter occasion. However, she took the Canadian title in 1930 and 1931 and the US Seniors in 1962 and 1966; here she was runner-up in 1963. She became a golf writer in the 1920s and eventually wrote for the *New York Times*. She is estimated to have won more than 60 championship events.

OUIMET, Francis de Sales   USA
b. Brookline, Massachusetts 1893; d. 1967

It is hard to believe now that there was a time when British players so dominated what there was of world golf that even the US Open was usually won by a British player of less than the highest class who had emigrated to the USA for the better living to be had there. In 1913 at Brookline there was assembled a formidable field. Even *The Times* had sent its golf correspondent, Bernard Darwin, from London, mainly to report on whether the current British Open Champion, Ted Ray, or Harry Vardon won. At the time Francis Ouimet had failed to qualify for the US Amateur three years in a row and, when he succeeded in doing so in 1913, he was beaten by Jerry Travers in the second round. Ouimet entered the Open only because it was being held in his home town. He was in poor form, barely being able to break 90. After two rounds Vardon led Ouimet by 4 strokes but Ouimet levelled in the third with a 74 to a 78; at that point Ray was also on

225. By early in his final round Ouimet knew that both Englishmen had finished in 79 and that he was in with a good chance. However, he then went to the turn in 43 and took a 5 on the par-3 10th. All hope seemed gone, except for the faint chance that he could tie if he played the last six holes in 2 under par, something not at all to be expected with the equipment and course conditions of that era. But Ouimet did it. In the play-off all reached the turn on the water-logged course in 38 but Ouimet took the lead on the 10th, when the others three-putted, and retained it to the end. Nevertheless Vardon was only 1 behind on the 17th tee. On this par 4 Vardon attempted to carry the angle of a dogleg, was bunkered and took 5. Ouimet was on in 2 and knew the Open was his if he could get down in 2 more. He got down in 1. The final scores were Ouimet 72, Vardon 77, Ray 78. His win began the first boom in US golf. An American professional had won before, but not against Harry Vardon; furthermore, Ouimet came from a comparatively poor background: he was a 20-year-old shop assistant with the Massachusetts Amateur his best achievement. If he could do it golf must be a game for all. Ouimet did not go on to pile success on success, but he did finish fifth in defence of his title the following year and in 1925 was joint third, 1 stroke away from the play-off between Jones and Macfarlane. His sights were, however, set more on the US Amateur which he won in 1914, beating Jerry Travers 6 and 5 in the final. The same year he went to test himself in Europe and came home with the French Amateur title. In the post-war years Ouimet ran up against the dominance of Bobby Jones and, after losing the 1920 US Amateur final to Chick Evans, could manage no better than five semi-final appearances. By 1931 Jones had retired and Ouimet reached and won the final. The following year he again reached the semi-final and won the Massachusetts Open, his final fling in major golf. Among his other successes at amateur level were six Massachusetts Amateur Championships, the North and South and the Western Amateurs. He represented the USA versus Britain and Ireland in every match from 1921 to 1949, first as player and then as non-playing captain. In 1951 he was elected captain of the Royal and Ancient, the first non-Briton to be so honoured; he also served with the USGA for many years. In 1963 the US Open was again held on the Brookline course to commemorate the 50th anniversary of Ouimet's historic victory.

Francis Ouimet

PAGE, Estelle Lawson USA
b. East Orange, New Jersey 1907

Estelle Page reached the finals of the US Amateur in both 1937 and 1938, meeting the same opponent, Patty Berg, on each occasion. In 1937 she beat her by 7 and 6 but in the following year lost by 6 and 5. She reached two other semi-finals. Otherwise her most successful competition was the North and South, which she won on no less than eight occasions in the period 1933–49 and was a finalist two other times. Mrs Page played in the 1938 and 1948 Curtis Cup teams.

PALMER, Arnold Daniel USA
b. Latrobe, Pennsylvania 1929

British Open Champion: 1961, 1962
US Amateur Champion: 1954
US Masters Champion: 1958, 1960, 1962, 1964
US Open Champion: 1960

In 1981 Tom Kite became the possessor of the first Arnold Palmer award. It had been decided to award a trophy to each year's top US Tour money-winner and to name it after Palmer. The choice of name was appropriate, for Palmer is in large measure responsible for the huge expansion in interest in

US tournament golf and the great increases in prize money that followed once he had become the man who always seemed to be ramming the putts home, driving with violent abandon and sending small bushes flying with recoveries from wild country. There was, too, the feeling that he was a great man for making a charge from behind, typified by his 65 last round to win in the 1960 US Open and a similar effort (which brought him only to runner-up) in the British Open the same year. The effect of all this on US Tour purses was dramatic. From 1945 to 1954, they had climbed from $400,000 annually to about $600,000, but as Palmer peaked during the early 1960s they climbed to $1 million by 1958, $2 million by 1963, $5 million by 1968 and nearly $9 million in 1973, Palmer's last good year. Although $14 million had been reached by 1981 this increase was because of inflation. Golf itself had become no more popular as a spectator sport, either live or on television. If Palmer's magnetism increased public interest in golf, and therefore professional earnings, there were increasing spin-offs for the successful player, and these too originated from Palmer and his agent, Mark McCormack. Whereas a player's earnings outside tournament and club golf had been mainly confined to giving clinics and exhibitions and endorsing golf equipment, McCormack perceived that a name could be used to sell goods in other fields. So it came about that there were tie-ins with insurance, dry cleaning, power tools, lawn mowers, clothes, deodorants, cigarettes and even catering by your own Arnold Palmer-chosen maid! Soon Palmer was making far more money than anyone else in the field from advertising endorsements alone, and where Palmer had led others were to follow. For Palmer himself there was a substantial business empire, which was eventually sold to RCA for several million dollars in the mid 1960s. Such was the man's fame and popularity that some urged him to go into politics, get himself the governorship of Pennsylvania or perhaps a Senate seat: a little later the Presidency itself might not be out of reach. But Arnold Palmer was not strongly interested in either business or politics. Unlike so many top players he remained passionately interested in playing and winning at golf. The business he left to McCormack and others. Still, well into his 50s, he cherishes the hope that there is another major championship in him, or at least a tournament, and his standard of performance is still good – he led the British Open for a while as

late as 1982 and finished in the top 30, not bad for a man of nearly 53. Palmer's first success came in 1947 with the Western Pennsylvania Amateur, and in 1953 he won the Ohio Amateur. But it was in 1954, after three years' service in the US Coastguard and a golf scholarship at Wake Forest, that he began to make his name. He won the US Amateur, defeating such well-known names as Frank Stranahan, Frank Strafaci, Don Cherry and Robert Sweeny to do so. He then turned professional and next year won the Canadian Open with rounds of 64, 67, 64, 70. He was to win at least one US tournament every year until 1973. For a while his progress was steady, and by the 1958 season he had accumulated seven wins. Then came his first major victory, the US Masters, and he was also leading money-winner, a position worth only $42,000 at the time. In 1960 he reached the heights of achievement. First he won the Masters again, this time having birdies on the last two holes to pass Ken Venturi. A couple of months later he lay 6 strokes behind the leader at the opening of the last round of the US Open at Cherry Hills. Now he did what he had been attempting all week: he drove the green. Then he went on to be out in a record 30 and, coming back more circumspectly in 35, won by 2 strokes. Next followed his historic entry in the British Open, which few Americans had been interested in entering since World War II. Although Kel Nagle gave the performance of his lifetime and held Palmer off by 1 stroke, it was Palmer's presence and performance that aroused the most interest. He had also come as near as anyone since Hogan to a modern version of Jones's Grand Slam of winning the British and US Opens, the Masters and the US PGA. On the US Tour it was his most dominant year. Beside his two majors he took six other tournaments, a total since equalled only by Miller in 1974. He followed with five 1961 Tour events and a win by 1 stroke over Dai Rees in the Royal Birkdale British Open. After it a rare honour was conveyed by the club, which set up a plaque on the 16th hole to commemorate a shot from some heavy overhanging rough near the foot of a bank which he managed to land on the green. Only Jones's long-iron from sand on the 17th at Royal Lytham in 1926 has been similarly commemorated. In 1962 Palmer was again leading money-winner, for the third time, and took seven US events, including the Masters again for a record-equalling third time. He dominated it for three rounds with 70, 66, 69 before falling away to a 75 which allowed Dow Finsterwald and Gary Player to overhaul him. In the 18-hole play-off Player led by 3 after nine holes, but Palmer then came home in 31 for a 3-stroke victory. The legend of the charge was still bright. It was during this season that he gave perhaps his greatest performance in the British Open at Troon. Palmer's game had been limited up to 1962 in its shot-making, and was based on low punched irons and drives struck with the clubhead still descending. With the latter he got more run on the ball and his irons held receptive greens. The flaw was that the long-running drives could run into rough and bunker; the irons did not hold greens as well as more lofted strokes. He modified his technique to produce a higher trajectory, which served him well at bone-hard Troon that year. Palmer scored 71, 69, 67, 69 to beat Nagle by 6 with the third-place man no less than 13 behind. Palmer broke 70 three times, and in the top 20 finishers only three other rounds under that mark were recorded. By now Jack Nicklaus was on the scene, had indeed already beaten Palmer in a play-off for the 1962 US Open. In 1963 Palmer again lost the play-off, this time to Julius Boros after he had finished weakly in 77, 74. Nevertheless, he was again leading money-winner, the first to top $100,000, and had seven wins. In 1964 Nicklaus took over as leading money-winner, though by a mere $82, and Palmer only won twice; but one of these was a record fourth win in the US Masters, when with scores of 69, 68, 69, 70 he left his rival and Dave Marr 6 strokes behind. Strangely, that was Palmer's last major championship victory, all seven as a professional having been crammed into the space of the years 1958–64. Yet at the time a spent force was the last thing he seemed. The question remained for some time whether he or Nicklaus was the world number one. Palmer stayed in the top 10 of US money-winners until 1972 but was never again first, though he had one second place and two thirds in this period. It seems that what happened was that Palmer lost his boldness. In some people's view his play had technically improved, for he certainly became less prone to wildness off the tee. Perhaps he lost the confidence to bang his putts at the back of the hole, knowing that if he missed he was sure to get the returns in. His wedge play, always the weakest feature of his game, came under more strain for, as his putting grew unsure, he felt he had to get his short-irons closer. The last-round charge happened less frequently, and came more often to be replaced by a strong start and weaker finish. Despite this

Arnold Palmer

Palmer remained highly successful, for instance winning four events in each of 1966, 1967 and 1971, by this time past 40. He continued a major figure in the US Open in particular, leading after two rounds in 1964 before fading to fifth; he had it in his pocket in 1966 with a 7-stroke lead with nine holes to go but threw it away to Casper after a play-off which he early dominated; he was second in 1967; sixth in 1969; third in 1972; fourth in 1973 and fifth in 1974. In none of these did he play as good a last round as the winner. In team events Arnold Palmer was seven times in the US World Cup pairing and six times in the winning team, taking the individual title in 1967. He was in the Ryder Cup team from 1961 to 1973, missing only the 1969 match, and had a 68.75% winning record. Palmer remained an effective competitor until 1975, a year when he won the Spanish Open and British PGA. He is still eager to play competitive golf, and at other times is happiest in his home workshop, where he has a collection of some 4,000 clubs that he likes to work on, perhaps hoping that the perfect instruments will make him a winner again. He has not won on the US Tour since 1973, but did take the Canadian PGA as recently as 1980. The US Senior Tour is eager to have him compete regularly but Palmer was not at first very enthusiastic, feeling that he may yet pull off one more victory on a more important stage. However, he took the

1980 PGA Seniors and the 1981 USGA Seniors. He was US Ryder Cup captain in 1963 and 1975.

US wins 61 (1955–73) (4th all-time)
US money $1,868,367 (1955–82) (7th all-time)
Overseas wins 19
World money $2,454,431 (1955–82) (9th all-time)

PALMER, John　　　　　　　　　　USA
b. Eldorado, North Carolina 1918

A short hitter, Johnny Palmer was an effective US Tour performer in the ten years following World War II. Joining the Tour in 1946, he featured in the top 15 money-winners in 1949, 1950, 1952 and 1954. His most important victories came in the 1947 Western Open and the 1952 Canadian, while he also won the 1954 Mexican Open. In major championships he was sixth in the 1947 US Open and fourth in the US Masters in 1949, the year in which he won the Tam o'Shanter, or 'World Championship' – as George S. May, the promoter, liked to call it – and lost to Sam Snead 3 and 2 in the final of the US PGA. He won eight Carolinas PGAs or Opens, and his last 36 holes of 62, 64 in the 1948 Tucson Open is still the equal second-best finish in a US tournament. He lost both his matches in the 1949 Ryder Cup at Ganton.

US wins 5 (1946–54)
US money $132,145
Overseas wins 3

PALMER, Sandra Jean　　　　　　　USA
b. Fort Worth, Texas 1941

In 1982, in the Boston Five Classic, Sandra Palmer took her victory total on the US Tour to 20 in a professional career that began in 1964. As an amateur she had been runner-up for the National Collegiate in 1961, won the West Texas four times and her state title in 1963. As a professional she enjoyed only moderate success until 1968, but since that time she has been a major figure, her best years being from 1968 to 1977, a period during which she was never worse than ninth in the money list. She was leading money-winner; US Open holder and Player of the Year in 1975. She won five events in 1973, was 23 times in the top 10, and came third in the money. In 1970 she won the Japan Women's Open. Sandra Palmer is an aggres-

sive, brisk player; her grip features the strong left-hand position favoured by many top women players.

US wins 20 (1971–82)
US money $807,209 (1964–82) (11th all-time)

PARKS, Louise (née Bruce)　　　　Canada
b. Toronto, Ontario 1953

Of good golfing pedigree, for her grandmother was Scottish champion in 1924, Louise Parks showed great early promise by taking the Junior World title in 1968 and 1970, and was also a leading golfer in California. Turning professional for the 1972 US Tour, she has been a steady rather than spectacular performer and in the Top 60 in 1974, 1975, 1978 and 1980. Her best placing was 36th in 1975.

US money $108,313 (1972–82)

PARKS, Samuel McLaughlin, Jnr　　USA
b. Hopedale, Ohio 1909

Sam Parks turned professional in 1933 and was a surprise winner of the 1935 US Open. It was probably as much a surprise to Sam as anyone else, for he had entered only because Oakmont was

Sandra Palmer

conveniently near – he was professional at South Hills in Pennsylvania. His score of 299 is the highest of modern times, but everyone else was over 300. He later left professional golf and became a member of the club where he had won the Open.

PATE, Jerome Kendrick USA

b. Macon, Georgia 1953

Judges as diverse as Tom Weiskopf and Lee Trevino have named Jerry Pate as having the best swing in modern golf – best in the sense that it seems free and rhythmic but is without looseness. Pate had a brilliant career as an amateur. He won the 1973 Intercollegiate title, was runner-up for the 1975 NCAA and in 1974 won the US Amateur. The same year he tied for the individual in the World Amateur Team Championship. He ended his amateur career in the 1975 Walker Cup – but he lost every match in which he played. He was also knocked out in the first round of the British Amateur. He went home and was medallist at the autumn 1975 US Tour school. His first year as a professional was watched with interest, and quite a year it was. He finished tenth on the money list, set a record in first-year prize winnings and was chosen Rookie of the Year. More important, he was US Open Champion. At Atlanta Athletic Club, he scored 71, 69, 68, 68 to win from Tom Weiskopf and Al Geiberger by 2. He also hit the shot of the year: on the final hole, he was faced with a 5-iron shot from the rough over water to a tightly positioned flag. He sent it in to 2 feet. A little later he was even more startling in the Canadian Open, finishing with a 63 to beat Jack Nicklaus by 4 strokes. Obviously a star of the first magnitude had arrived, and Pate went off to Royal Birkdale to see if he could equal Trevino's capture of all three titles of 1971. Alas, again the British air did not agree with him. He produced the highest score of the championship, an 87 in the third round in which he had an 8 and three 7s during the second nine. However, on a later overseas trip, to Japan, he won the Taiheiyo Pacific Masters. Harsh critics might say that Pate has not fully capitalized on that early promise. He has only once again come close to a major championship, the 1978 US PGA, which he threw away when he three-putted the final green to tie Watson and Mahaffey and lost the play-off. Nor is he a particularly frequent winner, having taken only six US Tour events in the following half dozen seasons. He is, however, formidably consis-

Jerry Pate

tent. Although he did not win between the 1978 Southern Open and the 1981 Memphis Classic, he accumulated eight second-place finishes in the meantime. He celebrated his win by diving into the lake by the 18th green. At 27 he became the youngest player to reach $1 million in career money winnings. In 1981 he did not once miss a cut. He also won the Brazil Open. Since his debut Pate has only once failed to earn $100,000, has three times topped $150,000 and in the three years 1980–82 has gone well over $200,000, with $280,000 in 1981 and 1982 being his highest. After that US season he went to the Colombian Open and produced the remarkable figures of 64, 67, 66, 65 to be 26 under par and the winner by 21 strokes, probably a world-record margin for a national Open or any important event. Despite Pate's exemplary swing, putting is perhaps his outstanding strength. In 1980 he was first in that category; but he was only 107th at hitting greens in regulation. He was third in 1980 scoring averages and fourth in 1981. He finished sixth in the money list in both 1980 and 1981 and in 1982 was ninth. At the end of the year he featured strongly in early play in the $1 Million Challenge in Bophuthatswana, but then faded to a last-round 80, the worst card of any of the ten competitors. To refute the charge of being prone to 'blowing up' under pressure, however, Pate can cite his performance in the 1982 Tournament Players' Championship. On the last round he birdied the 17th and 18th for a 67 and victory by two strokes.

US wins 8 (1976–82)
US money $1,404,955 (1975–82) (15th all-time)
Overseas wins 3
World money $1,815,247 (1975–82) (17th all-time)

PATTON, William Joseph   USA

b. 1922

In his first invitation to the US Masters in 1954 'Billy Joe' Patton led after two rounds, dropped to 5 behind after a 75 and went into the lead again after 12 holes in the final round, partly a result of a hole in one on the 6th; but then he fell foul of the second-half par 5s. Going for the green over water, he had a 7 on the 13th and a 6 on the 15th. Nevertheless he finished in 71 to Hogan's 75 and Snead's 72, after which he missed their play-off by 1 stroke. Commiserated with afterwards, he uttered the immortal words that put golf in its place: 'Hell, it ain't like losing a leg!' As consolation he took home a cup and medal for having been best amateur (with Charlie Coe in 1961 the nearest to winning); a vase for his hole in one, and another one for having had the lowest first round; he had had already won the long-driving contest preceding the event. Patton was indeed a long hitter, and wild with it, so that his spectacular recoveries were much relished by onlookers. His lightning-fast swing was reckoned one of the quickest in golf. Oddly, he never reached the final of either a US or British Amateur, but he won the North and South three times and was in the US teams for the Americas Cup from 1954 to 1958 and in 1963; the World Amateur in 1958 and 1962; and the Walker Cup from 1955 to 1959 and in 1963 and 1965. In 1955, 1957 and 1963 he won in both foursomes and singles, and won two other foursomes and lost a single. He was leading amateur in the US Opens from 1952 to 1954, the first to achieve this three times consecutively.

PAVIN, Corey   USA

b. Oxnard, California 1960

Currently one of the top US Amateurs, Pavin was a 1981 US Walker Cup choice, having won the South Western Amateur with a record score of 276 and also having taken the final of the North and South by 11 and 10. He won the golf event in the 1981 Maccabean Games in Israel.

PECK, Michael   USA

b. Kansas City, Missouri 1956

A US Walker Cup choice in 1979, Peck had reached the semi-finals of the 1978 US Amateur, won the 1976 Intercollegiate Championship and the 1977 and 1978 Pacific Eight titles. He played the US Tour with little success in 1980 and 1981.

US money $15,337 (1980–81)

PEETE, Calvin   USA

b. Detroit, Michigan 1943

The value of the US Tour statistics kept in nine categories has often been doubted, but they did bring the name of Calvin Peete into more public view. In 1980 he rated second in driving accuracy and third for hitting greens in regulation strokes. By 1981 he was topping both categories. Statistically, accuracy in driving is as much the result of short hitting as anything else, but accuracy into the greens should be a fair measure of a golfer's form. Peete ought to have been doing better than his 42nd and 43rd money-list placings and one US Tour victory in 1979. In 1982, perhaps conscious of what he ought to be doing, Calvin Peete began to come much more strongly to notice. With rounds of 69, 70, 68, 69 he came joint third in the US PGA but, like everyone else, was effectively knocked out by Ray Floyd's opening 63. He had earlier performed well in the US Open, finishing 6 strokes behind Tom Watson. He had a very good July, first winning the Greater Milwaukee Open, then leading the Quad Cities Open after three rounds with 67, 67, 69 (though falling away in the last round) and ending the month with victory and $63,000 in the Anheuser-Busch Classic. From the three tournaments he had earned $111,100 and jumped to tenth place on the US money list. Another $27,500 from the US PGA just around the corner took him well past $200,000 for the year. Later, he won again, taking the BC Open by an emphatic 7 strokes with 69, 63, 64, 69, and the Pensacola Open with 65, 66, 72, 65, again by 7. I am sure Peete would lead US Tour statistics in another category – if such records were kept. He comes from a family of 19. He also came to golf extremely late, at the age of 23, having thought it a game only for the rich, but he noted that a certain Jack Nicklaus seemed to be making goodly sums of money at it. Although it was a silly game involving chasing a little ball around under a hot sun, it might be worth the inconvenience. Besides the late start, Peete brought a considerable disability to the game. As a child he fell out of a tree and the resultant damage meant that he cannot straighten his left arm, though there have been others – Ed Furgol is a prime example – who like him have overcome a similar condition.

Peete has a considerable loop in his swing but maintains good balance through the ball, something he considers the main reason for his accuracy on full shots. As a young man he sold jewellery to migrant workers, and a legacy of this phase was that he had diamonds (now removed) set into his front teeth. After he took up golf he played as an amateur for some years and failed in two attempts to secure his US Tour player's card. He eventually joined the Tour in 1976 and averaged about $20,000 his first three seasons. One breakthrough came in 1979, when he won the Greater Milwaukee with rounds of 69, 67, 68, 65 to win by 5 strokes and set the tournament record. That took him well into the Top 60 for the season, at 27th, and he won more than $100,000 both that year and in 1980 while by 1982 he was beyond doubt the best black golfer on the scene. He was chosen for the US World Cup pair, but was unable to play. In 1982 he came near to doubling his US Tour money winnings with $318,470 and fourth money-list place and then, after four US victories, took the Dunlop Phoenix in Japan. For the US Tour he had topped the statistics for driving accuracy and hitting greens in regulation. He was second in the scoring averages. Peete had added good putting to an otherwise consistent game.

US wins 5 (1979–82)
US money $703,860 (1976–82) (63rd all-time)
Overseas wins 1 (1982)

Calvin Peete

PENNA, Antonio   USA
b. Naples, Italy 1906

Tony Penna turned professional at the age of 16. He first tried tournament golf in 1932 and enjoyed a modestly successful career, being in the top 20 money-winners in 1938, 1944, 1945, 1947 and 1949 and winning a tournament from time to time. He was interested in golf club design and eventually set up a golf-equipment company. Fashions come and go in this field: glass fibre, titanium and carbon fibre shafts, investment casting, metal 'woods', deep-faced irons. Penna's woods have been much prized in recent years. He has done 14 holes in one, unhindered by his modest stature of 5 feet 6 inches.

US wins 4 (1933–47)
US money $40,465

PFEIL, Mark Glenn   USA
b. Chicago Heights, Illinois 1951

Mark Pfeil played in the 1973 Walker Cup match, in which he won and halved in foursomes and in singles lost to Willie Milne and beat Howard Clark. He turned professional and qualified for the 1976 US Tour, but he won just $439 that year and had to re-qualify. After the 1977 season he barely held his place, finishing 149th in the money list; but since then he has improved a little. His best years were 1980, when he was 72nd and earned exemption from pre-qualifying by winning the Tallahassee Open, and 1982, when he was 71st.

US wins 1 (1980)
US money $187,556 (1976–82) (196th all-time)

PICARD, Henry G.   USA
b. Plymouth, Massachusetts 1907

Henry Picard played in the first Masters of all in 1934. He should perhaps have won the second year, for he began 67, 68, to open up a lead of 4 on Sarazen, the eventual winner, and Ray Mangrum. However, he then fell away to 76, 75 and came in fourth. But then in 1938 he produced the extremely steady scoring of 71, 72, 72, 70 and took the championship by 2 shots from 'Light-Horse' Harry Cooper and Ralph Guldahl. Picard took another major, the US PGA, the following year, when he beat Byron Nelson by 1 up in the final. He was even more successful as a tournament player in the second half of the 1930s, his first important victory coming in the 1934 North and South. Thereafter until World War II he was a consistent tournament

Henry Picard

winner, his total of 27 leaving him in joint 13th place, just behind Tom Watson and level with Walter Hagen. He is claimed to be the only player to have beaten Hagen in a play-off. He had four wins in both 1936 and 1937 and in the latter year was second money-winner. In 1939 he won six times and was leading money-winner with $10,303. At this time he was something of a par machine and once had a run of 54 tournaments during which he broke or equalled par 50 times, figures as good as those being achieved on Tour today. He played in the 1935 and 1937 Ryder Cup teams and won both his singles, while losing and winning in foursomes. He was chosen again for 1939, though the match was not played. Picard was considered to have an exemplary swing. His influence in golf continued even after he became an infrequent competitor through ill health from about 1940: he gave Sam Snead the driver he used for so many years to such effect.

US wins 34 (1934–45)

PLATT, J. Wood   USA
b. Philadelphia, Pennsylvania 1899; d. 1959

There have been thousands of rounds of golf that have broken par by 6 strokes but I cannot think of another round of golf in which a player reached that position after four holes. 'Woody' Platt once did this at Pine Valley, a course where the members used to bet low-handicap visitors that they wouldn't break 90 first time out – and usually won. Platt birdied the first hole and then holed his iron shot to eagle the next. Encouraged, he then holed out in one on the 3rd and birdied the 4th. The story of how he continued will never be told. Platt retired to the clubhouse for a quick bracer and did not re-emerge, so a round of 46 or so never materialized. Among his more conventional achievements were seven wins in the Philadelphia Amateur, a US appearance against Britain in 1921 and the USGA Seniors Championship in 1955.

POHL, Danny Joe   USA
b. Mount Pleasant, Michigan 1955

Dan Pohl is just about the longest driver on the US Tour, and possibly, among tournament players, in the world. Greg Norman's 281-yard average in 1982 might seem to put him marginally ahead, but more of his statistics have come from courses in Europe where greater run after pitching can be expected than on the more lush fairway grass of US courses. Pohl rated first in the US in 1980 with 274.3 yards and improved to 280.1 in 1981. He is followed, no more than 5 yards behind, by Fred Couples, Tom Purtzer and Fuzzy Zoeller. The measurements are made on the par 4s and 5s but, of course, they do not take into account the fact that players frequently take an iron for safety off tees where the fairway is tight, or trees, deep rough, water and out of bounds threaten. Pohl has had one drive measured at 359 yards. He has done well to be also a successful golfer, for spectators crowding to see him hit a golf ball farther than it ought to go are scarcely a help towards consistency. Pohl won the Michigan State Amateur twice before turning professional, and then qualified for the US Tour in mid 1978. In the rest of the season he won just $1,047, and had to re-qualify in June the following year. This time he seemed to have made his place secure when he led the Western Open with three holes to play. In this position, the adrenalin flows and the golfer finds himself hitting the ball farther. This was no help at all to Dan Pohl, for on the last three holes he hit all his approach shots through the greens and dropped a shot on each to finish in third place. In 1980 he had second place in the Crosby, a closing 67 leaving him only 1 behind the winner, George Burns; he also had four other top-10 finishes. He passed $100,000 for the season and was 44th in the money list. In the following season he featured strongly in the 1981 US PGA, his scores of 69, 67, 73, 69 giving him third place behind Zoeller and winner Larry Nelson, and he had six other top-10 finishes to win $94,000 and be 42nd on the money list. Although still hitting as far as ever, he was swinging more easily and had learned to move the ball either way. In 1982 he came very close to winning a major championship. He began the Masters with two 75s, and when he followed with a 67 he was still well off the lead. His score was made by a spell of eagle, eagle, birdie, birdie from the 13th to the 16th. Stadler began the final round with a lead of 3 and after 11 holes had increased it to 5. Pohl finished in another 67 and found himself in a tie as Stadler dropped shots on the 14th, 16th and 18th, but he lost the play-off to a par on the first extra hole. A couple of months later, he finished tied with Clampett and Bill Rogers for third place in the US Open, behind Nicklaus and Watson, the champion. Pohl has still to win a tournament but his record of three near misses in major championships makes him a coming man. He was 39th on the US money list in 1982 with nearly $100,000. He had lost his 'longest driver' position but became a better player.

US money $335,963 (1978–82) (137th all-time)

POOLEY, Sheldon George, Jnr USA
b. *Phoenix, Arizona 1951*

Don Pooley played the mini-Tours for a while after leaving college. Only on his third try did he qualify for the US Tour, and at the end of his first season, 1976, he was back again, having won only $2,139. He then won a little over $24,000 in 1977 and over $30,000 the following year before a disastrous 1979 brought in less than $7,000, partly the result of injuries. In 1980 he made the biggest improvement of anyone that year, going up to over $150,000 and 18th place on the money list and winning his first event, the BC Open. He maintained his Top 60 placing in 1981 and 1982.

US wins 1 (1980)
US money $387,189 (1976–82) (114th all-time)

PORTER, Dorothy: see Germain

PORTER, Mary Bea (later Cheney) USA
b. *Everett, Washington 1949*

Qualifying for the US Tour in 1973, Mary Bea Porter won the Golf Inns of America in 1975; in the Lady Keystone Open in 1977 she had a round of 63, one above Mickey Wright's Tour record 62. She was in the Top 60 in 1975 and 1977, 37th place in the money list in the former year being her best season. She now competes in tournaments only occasionally.

US wins 1 (1975)
US money $44,153 (1978–82)

POST, Sandra Canada
b. *Oakville, Ontario 1948*

As an amateur Sandra Post won the junior championships of both her state and Canada three times each, and the US South Atlantic. As a professional playing the US Tour from 1968 she made a remarkable start, winning a major championship, the LPGA, her first year after a play-off with the formidable Kathy Whitworth. She ended the season Rookie of the Year and in 13th money list position. Since that time she has always been in the Top 60; but the going was not smooth, for she suffered the back trouble professional golfers are so

Sandra Post

prone to. In the 1970–72 period her stroke average drifted upwards, but thereafter she has scored consistently well. In 1974 she took the Colgate Far East, an unofficial event; but a US Tour event eluded her until 1978, when she won twice, including the rich Dinah Shore. In the 1974–81 period she was not worse than 15th in the money list and won each year from 1978 to 1981. Her big year was 1979 when she won three times, including the Dinah Shore, and was second in the money list with $178,750 at a stroke average of 72.43. In 1980 she again topped $100,000. Her 1979 performance won her two Canadian awards as Female Athlete of the Year and Outstanding Athlete of the Year.

US wins 8 (1968–81)
US money $721,988 (1968–82) (13th all-time)

POSTLEWAIT, Kathy　　　　　USA
b. Norfolk, Virginia 1949

Winner of the Southern Junior in 1966, Kathy Postlewait has played the US Tour since 1974 and has been in the Top 60 from 1975 to 1982. A Tour victory has eluded her, though she has had a number of second-place finishes. In 1981 she lost a play-off to Hollis Stacy in the West Virginia Classic, and in 1982 to Patty Sheehan in the Agri-Fol. However, in the period 1977–82 she has been very consistent, not finishing worse than 36th in the money list. Her best years have been 1978 when she was 17th, and 1982, her most profitable year with around $80,000 in 15th place.

US money $300,161 (1974–82)

POTT, John　　　　　USA
b. Cape Girardeau, Missouri 1935

Johnny Pott won five US Tour events in the 1960s and lost four more in play-offs, one of these being particularly unfortunate. In the 1958 Crosby he, Bruce Devlin and Billy Casper played off for the event, Casper winning when he missed the green but chipped in to win. He was in the Top 60 on the US money lists from 1958 to 1967, with a best placing of 14th in 1965. In this period he made the Ryder Cup team in 1963 and 1967, in the latter year having a particularly good record of two wins in foursomes, one in four-balls and one in singles. He played little after the early 1970s.

US wins 5 (1960–68)
US money $371,397 (120th all-time)

POWELL, Renee　　　　　USA
b. Canton, Ohio 1946

One of the best black women golfers, Renee Powell was outstanding as a junior, winning the UGA national title from 1959 to 1961 and the Midwest from 1959 to 1961 and in 1963. In 1964 she took the UGA National Women's. She was eight times her club champion. In 1967 she turned professional; at this time she and Althea Gibson were the only black LPGA Tour players. She was in the Top 60 from 1967 to 1973 and an effective player for some years after. She went to live in England.

US money $34,438 (1967–76)

PRENTICE, JoAnn　　　　　USA
b. Birmingham, Alabama 1933

Alabama champion in 1954 and runner-up on three occasions, JoAnn Prentice also reached the quarter-finals of the US Amateur in 1954 and turned professional towards the end of 1956. In 1958 she lost a play-off; but she had already established herself as a Tour player by that time. From 1957 to 1975 she was always in the top 30 of money winners, and in the top 21 from 1958 to 1974. Her best years were highly consistent in the latter period, by far the best coming in 1974 when she won $67,227, was fourth in the money list and won three tournaments, including the Dinah Shore. She also won one tournament in each of the years 1965, 1967, 1972 and 1973. She competes little now and owns a country club in Alabama.

US wins 6 (1965–74)
US money $367,568 (1957–82) (22nd all-time)

PRESSLER, Leona:　see Cheney

PREUSS, Phyllis　　　　　USA
b. Detroit, Michigan 1939

'Tish' Preuss holds one record that she will not wish to remember too clearly. She reached the final of the 1961 US Amateur, where she faced Anne Quast. At the welcome break for lunch she was 12 down; eventually she lost by 14 and 13. Not surprisingly this is the record margin for the US Women's Amateur. Phyllis Preuss, however, won the North and South, the Southern and the Eastern and was twice low amateur in the US Open, in 1963 and 1968. She played on all the US Curtis Cup teams from 1960 to 1970.

PUNG, Jacqueline   USA
b. *Honolulu, Hawaii 1921*

Winner as an amateur of the Hawaiian Women's four times between 1938 and 1947, Jackie Pung won the US Amateur in 1952 and turned professional the following year. In her first season she won more than $7,000 (a good sum at the time), and tied with Betsy Rawls for the US Open but lost the play-off 77–70. Four years later the US Open and Betsy Rawls were again to feature – but far more dramatically – in her career. Jackie Pung handed in a final-round card of 72 which initially gave her victory over Betsy Rawls. However, when her card was checked it was noted that, while the 72 total was correct, a 6 she had scored on the 4th hole was down as a 5. She was disqualified, a disaster for Jackie as severe as Roberto de Vicenzo's in the 1968 Masters. The members of Winged Foot, where the championship was played, collected a consolation 'prize' of $3,000. The amount was ironic, for first place in the championship at that time was worth $1,800. Jackie Pung remained an effective Tour player until 1964, and thereafter played little. She attempted a come-back in 1976 when in her mid 50s, losing 100 lb in weight to do so.

US wins 5 (1953–8)
US money $60,093 (1953–64)

PURTZER, Thomas Warren   USA
b. *Des Moines, Iowa 1951*

As an amateur Tom Purtzer won the Southwest Open in 1972 and the Broadmoor Invitational the following year. On turning professional he twice failed to win his US Tour card and played on the US mini-Tours and also abroad, winning the Thailand Open in 1975. In that year he qualified for the US Tour but won very little money. Since 1977, however, he has been in the Top 60. He is one of the longest US drivers, averaging only about five yards less than the longest hitter. From 1979 to 1982 he won over $100,000 annually. He has only one Tour victory, the 1977 Los Angeles Open, but was medallist in the USA versus Japan team matches in 1979 and in 1981 won the Jerry Ford Invitational, a non-Tour event. He has also produced some good results in Open Championships, coming fourth in the 1977 US Open. In the 1979 event he led with Larry Nelson after a 70, 69 start and began his last round by having birdies on three of the first four holes before a 7 effectively put him out of the running. He also came in joint fourth in

the 1982 British Open with scores of 76, 66, 75, 69, only 2 strokes behind Tom Watson's winning score.

US wins 1 (1977)
US money $621,115 (1975–82) (75th all-time)

PYNE, Julie Stanger   USA
b. *Escondido, California 1956*

Julie Pyne was Arizona state champion in 1976 and 1968 and was second in the 1978 AIAW Championship. She then was medallist at the summer LPGA qualifying school. Since then she has looked to be one of the more promising young players, being in the top 40 in 1980 and 1981, with over $40,000 each of those years and a second-place finish in 1981. Her performance in 1982 was not up to expectations, with a final position in the money list of 64th. Outside of golf, her hobbies include jogging, skiing and tennis.

US money $118,618 (1978–82)

QUAST, Anne (later Decker, Welts and Sander)   USA
b. *Everett, Washington 1937*

One of relatively few top US amateurs not to turn professional in the past 20 years, Anne Quast must be the only player to win the national Open titles of Britain and America under four different names. She first competed in the US Amateur at the age of 14 and won for the first time in 1958, just before her 21st birthday. In the final which she won against Barbara Romack by 3 and 2 it is claimed she used only 55 putts in the 34 holes played. In 1961 she won again, under the name of Decker. Against Phyllis Preuss she was no less than 12 up at lunch (a record) and shortly thereafter completed a 14 and 13 victory (also a record). Her last victory in the US Amateur, this time as Welts, came in 1963 when she beat Peggy Conley. She also reached the final in 1965, 1968 and, as Sander, in 1973. Anne Quast is one of ten women also to win the British Amateur, which she did in 1980, beating Liv Wollin of Sweden by 3 and 1. She was a Curtis Cup regular from 1958 to 1980, her six appearances equalling the US record; won the Western Amateur in 1956 and 1961; was twice low amateur in the US Open; and finished in fourth place in this event in 1973. By that year she had reached the quarter-final stage of the US Amateur 14 times in 19 entries.

RAGAN, David William   USA

b. Daytona Beach, Florida 1935

Dave Ragan played in the 1963 Ryder Cup at Atlanta, where he and Billy Casper beat Christy O'Connor and me in foursomes, and lost and halved the fourballs in which he partnered Bob Goalby. Earlier, he had become the first American player to win a British tournament since Joe Turnesa in 1929. In 1963 he finished runner-up to Jack Nicklaus in the US PGA and was eighth in the 1962 money list with $37,327. He won a total of five tournaments in his career.

US wins 5 (1959–62)

RANKIN, Judy (née Torluemke)   USA

b. St Louis, Missouri 1945

A child prodigy at golf, Judy Torluemke won the Missouri State title at the age of 14; more significantly she was leading amateur in the US Open the following year. She won the Missouri title again in 1961 and was twice a semi-finalist in the US Junior in 1960 and 1961. She turned professional in 1962, playing her first Tour season at the age of 17. She finished 41st in the money list, subsequently getting a better placing than that every year to 1981. By the age of 19 she was a fully effective Tour

Judy Rankin

player and was 13th, 9th and 7th in the money list in the next three years. Her form then fell away for a couple of seasons, though she took her first tournament in 1968. In the period 1969–79, 15th was her worst money list placing and she was in the top 9 every year from 1970 to 1977. In 1973 she was second, but her most successful year came in 1976 when she won six events and was leading money-winner. That year she became the first woman ever to win $100,000, in fact totalling $150,734. Again in 1977 she led the money list, winning five events for $122,890. By this time she had established a very high reputation. In 1978 she again topped $100,000 though, money apart, her other best season was 1973, when she won four tournaments and had 25 finishes in the top 10 in 33 tournament entries, was declared Player of the Year and won the Vare Trophy with 73.08. Until 1979 she never missed a cut in an LPGA tournament. Her record in the three women's major championships is, surprisingly, not strong. She has taken only one, the 1977 Peter Jackson Classic in Canada, but added a near major, the Dinah Shore, in 1976. In the Peter Jackson she was second in 1973 and 1976, in the US Open joint second in 1972, and in the US LPGA was second in 1976 and joint second the following year. At the end of the 1979 season she was second on the all-time money-winners list, though the inflation of prize money had dropped her down to fifth by the beginning of the 1982 season. It seems strange that such a player should have what has been described as 'the worst left-hand grip in golf'. Judy has an exceptionally 'strong' position on the shaft with this hand, but that is in common with many top women players. It may, however, in part account for the back trouble she has experienced since 1977. Judy Rankin is a very fierce competitor indeed and, in particular, seldom relinquishes a lead during a final round. Hitting a low drawn ball, she has often performed well in wind and is very highly rated with fairway woods.

US wins 26 (1968–79) (11th all-time)
US money $878,962 (1962–82) (8th all-time)

RANSOM, Henry   USA

b. Houston, Texas 1911

Henry Ransom was a leading American player in the years immediately following World War II, though he had been a professional since 1932. To win the 1948 Illinois PGA, he birdied no less than eight of the last 11 holes. He also won three other state titles. On the US Tour he took six tournaments between 1946 and 1955 when he retired, in part because of hay fever. His best year was 1950, when he won four times, including George S. May's so-called World Championship, and finished fourth in the money list. He was in the Ryder Cup team the following year at Pinehurst, losing with 'Porky' Oliver in foursomes to Charlie Ward and Arthur Lees. His best performance in a major championship was to finish joint fifth in the US Open. One of many to come to grief on the 16th at Cypress Point during their career, Ransom once tried to hit a wedge from the Pacific Beach to the green. The ball rebounded and hit him in the stomach. Said Ransom: 'That's it! When a hole starts hitting back, I quit.'

US wins 5 (1946–55)

RASSETT, Joseph   USA
b. Turlock, California 1958

A Walker Cup choice in 1981, Joe Rassett had not won any major amateur titles but had been low amateur in the 1981 US Open after starting with two 70s and joint second lowest in 1979, the year he reached the semi-finals of the US Amateur and was medallist in the Western Amateur. He was an alternate for the 1980 World Amateur Team Championship and second in the 1981 Northeast Amateur. As a professional he played on the European Tour in 1982, finishing 73rd, and then qualified for the 1983 US Tour.

Europe money £6,192 (1982)

RAWLINS, Horace   England & USA
b. Isle of Wight, England 1874; d. 1940

Horace Rawlins emigrated to the USA in order to be assistant professional at Newport CC, Rhode Island. As the first US Open in 1895 was played on the course, he entered (it was only his third competition) and won with scores of 91 and 82 to beat a field of ten professionals and one amateur and take the first prize of $150. He came in second the next year, but little was heard of him after that.

RAWLS, Elizabeth Earle   USA
b. Spartanburg, South Carolina 1928

Although not starting golf till the relatively late age of 17, by 1949 Betsy Rawls was holder of the Trans-

Mississippi and Texas titles and the following year, while still an amateur, finished second in the US Open and won the Texas Amateur and the Broadmoor Invitational. In 1951 she turned professional and in a few months was US Open Champion, a feat she repeated in 1953, 1957 and 1960; she shares her record of four wins with Mickey Wright. Her victory in 1957 created some sensation, for her score of 299 was 1 higher than that returned by Jackie Pung, who was disqualified because of a scoring error on her card for the last round. It was an irony that she had also lost to Betsy in 1953, this time after an 18-hole play-off. Betsy Rawls brought her total of major championship victories to six with wins in the US LPGA in 1959 and 1969. On the US Tour she was very successful, taking at least one tournament a year from 1951 to 1965 and winning her last event in 1972. Her total of 55 wins is third in all-time rankings. Her best years lasted until the mid 1960s and she was twice leading money-winner, in 1952 and 1959. The latter was undoubtedly her most successful season, for during it she won no fewer than ten tournaments a feat in one year bettered only by Mickey Wright (twice). She won the Vare Trophy for stroke average that year with 74.03 and was elected to the LPGA Hall of Fame the following year. In 1975 she retired from tournament golf and, having twice acted as president of the LPGA, was appointed tournament director, a position she held until retiring in September 1981; she now acts as director of an individual tournament. In 1980 she became the first woman to serve on the rules committee for the US Open (men's). Betsy Rawls was not a long hitter but was recognized as an excellent shotmaker; she had the best short game of her time.

US wins 55 (1951–72) (3rd all-time)
US money $302,664 (28th all-time)

REID, Michael Daniel   USA
b. Bainbridge, Maryland 1954

Mike Reid was low amateur in the 1976 US Open, having led by 3 strokes after an opening 67. The same year he took the Pacific Coast Amateur and was Western Athletic Conference champion. He then turned professional and made $26,000 his first year on the US Tour. He first made the Top 60 in 1980 and was there again in 1981. By far his best year was 1980. He finished ninth on the money list, having finished in the first three on four occasions, with four more top-5 placings. Without a win, he took $206,097 and was chosen for the World Cup pair. On the US Tour that year he was rated the most accurate driver and was second for hitting greens in regulation. In 28 entries he missed just one 36-hole cut. Reid is a short hitter and, having to use fairway woods a lot, is rated as one of the best practitioners of these in America. His lack of power means he will win money but not tournaments.

US money $507,080 (1977–82) (92nd all-time)

REINHARDT, Alexandra　　　　USA
b. *Albuquerque, New Mexico 1953*

Alex Reinhardt won the New Mexico state title as an amateur and was a college All-American in 1973. On the US Tour from 1974 she was highly unsuccessful and lost her card at the end of 1975, returning in 1977. She was in the Top 60 that year and 1978, when she was 24th and won $37,831; but she tailed away in the next three years. She then had a good year in 1982, winning over $60,000.

US money $151,504 (1974–82)

RENNER, Jack　　　　USA
b. *Palm Springs, California 1956*

Jack Renner comes from a golfing family, his brother Jim also being a professional and his sister Jane an LPGA Tour player. Jack had a remarkable junior career, being runner-up in the World Junior in 1971 and 1973 and winning in 1972. He was also US Junior Champion in 1973. Later he kept largely out of collegiate golf, believing, most unusually, that he could progress better by working on his game rather than playing college events. He joined the US Tour in 1977 and made useful money, breaking into the Top 60 the following year in 33rd place. In 1979 he was 14th, winning $182,000; he won his first tournament, the Westchester Classic, immediately after a second place the previous week. He fell away to 45th the following year, but in 1981 rose again to 11th and won the Pleasant Valley Classic, was second in the Memorial and had seven other top-10 placings. He was 41st in 1982. Renner plays Hogan clubs and wears a Hogan-type hat but is a different style of player, relying on an excellent short game. Thin and lightweight, he is not a long hitter, but is highly accurate. He is a tireless practiser, particularly keen to achieve more length.

US wins 2 (1979–81)
US money $656,023 (1977–82) (69th all-time)

RENNER, Jane　　　　USA
b. *Evanston, Illinois 1953*

A sister of Jack Renner, a leading player on the men's Tour, like him Jane won the World Junior, in 1969, the California Junior the following year and the Mexican Amateur in 1972. Also like her brother, she is not a long hitter and depends in part on an excellent short game. She played the US Tour from 1975 to 1980 but did not make the Top 60, though she had five years in the top 100.

US money $33,034 (1975–80)

REVOLTA, Johnny　　　　USA
b. *St Louis, Missouri 1911*

One of the all-time masters of the short game, Revolta was noted for his waggle on short shots, which varied according to the kind of stroke he was about to play. He was leading money-winner in 1935, with $9,543 out of the then total purse of $135,000, and second in 1938. His best year was 1935: during it he won the Western Open and the US PGA, here beating Walter Hagen in the first round and going on to defeat Gene Sarazen in the final. He played in the Ryder Cup for the only time that year, and won in both foursomes and singles. Revolta won four times in 1934. His last important victory came in the 1944 Texas Open. He has since become a most respected coach.

US wins 19

Johnny Revolta

151

REYNOLDS, Catherine (later Derouaux) USA
b. Kansas City, Missouri 1957

In a good amateur career, Cathy Reynolds won the Missouri Junior three times and the full state title in 1976. The following year, she took the Mexican Amateur and the Trans-National. On the US Tour from 1978 her best year was 1981, when she won the Golden Lights and was 20th in the money list. Her looks cause as much stir as her golf.

US wins 1 (1981)
US money $110,655 (1978–82)

RIDLEY, Fred USA
b. Lakeland, Florida 1952

Fred Ridley won the US Amateur in 1975, beating the present US Tour player Keith Fergus by 2 up. Ridley decided to remain an amateur, and played in the 1977 Walker Cup. He lost in the foursomes but beat Sandy Lyle twice in singles.

RIEGEL, Robert Henry USA
b. New Bloomfield, Pennsylvania 1914

'Skee' Riegel had an excellent amateur career in the years immediately following World War II. He took the Trans-Mississippi in 1946 and 1949, the Western Amateur in 1948 and the US Amateur in 1947. He played in the 1947 and 1949 Walker Cups, winning every match, and was low amateur in the 1949 US Open. He turned professional in 1950, by which time he was almost 36. In 1951 he finished eighth in the money list and was second, 2 behind Ben Hogan, in the US Masters that year.

RILEY, Polly Ann USA
b. San Antonio, Texas 1926

One of the best US amateurs from the end of World War II to the early 1960s, Polly Riley never managed to capture the US Amateur, her closest approach being losing finalist to Mary Lena Faulk in 1953. However, she is estimated to have won over 100 amateur events, amongst which are the Southern Amateur six times between 1948 and 1961, the Western in 1950 and 1952 and the Trans-Mississippi in 1947, 1948 and 1955. She had a remarkable run in the Curtis Cup, playing every match from 1948 to 1958 and being non-playing captain in 1962. She took part in two famous matches, both against Frances Stephens. In 1956 Polly lost to her on the last hole, and with that result went the

Cathy Reynolds

Curtis Cup; in 1958, she lost on the last green, leading to a tied Cup. Prior to the 1956 defeat she had never lost in her series of matches. Her 1954 defeat of Elizabeth Price by 9 and 8 shares the record margin.

RITZMAN, Alice USA
b. Kalispell, Montana 1952

Winner of the Montana Juniors three times and the Women's twice, Alice Ritzman has been on the US Tour since 1978. In 1979 during a round of the Colgate European Open, she set an LPGA record by having three eagles. Needless to say, she is a very long hitter. She was 47th on the 1979 money list, 38th in 1980 and 33rd in 1981. She had a second place in 1979; in 1981 she lost two play-offs, one to Kathy Whitworth and the other to Hollis Stacy.

US money $141,246 (1978–82)

RIZZO, Patricia USA
b. Hollywood, Florida 1961

Runner-up to Juli Inkster in the 1980 US Amateur, Patti played in the winning 1980 US World Team Championship side. She also won the World Amateur, Trans National, Eastern and Mexican titles in 1980. She was runner-up in the 1980 and 1981

AIAW Championships and ranked as the top US amateur in 1980 and the top collegiate player in 1981. Also in 1981, still as an amateur, she took part in a five-way play-off for the Florida Lady Citrus. She had got there by means of a closing-round 66, a record for an amateur in an LPGA Tour event. She made a good start in 1982 to her professional career, at 31st in the money list, and was the LPGA's Rookie of the Year. She looks a bright prospect for the future.

US money $46,441 (1982)

ROBBINS, Hillman   USA
b. *Memphis, Tennessee 1934*

Hillman Robbins won the NCAA Championship in 1954, and in 1956 the North and South and Air Force titles. In 1957 he won the All-Services event. In 1955 he reached the semi-finals of the US Amateur and in 1957 was champion. He played in the 1957 Walker Cup, halving in foursomes and losing in singles to Guy Wolstenholme. He represented the US in the Americas Cup in 1956 and 1958, after which he turned professional. After enjoying little tournament success he became primarily a club professional.

ROBERTS, Susan   USA
b. *Oak Park, Illinois 1948*

A US Tour player from 1969, Sue Roberts was in the Top 60 from 1969 to 1976. Although she won little in her first five seasons, she became a tournament-winner in 1974 and was 19th in the money list that year and 18th in 1975. She had her last tournament win in 1976 and competed little after 1979.

US wins 4 (1974–6)
US money $121,045 (1969–80)

RODGERS, Philamon Webster   USA
b. *San Diego, California 1938*

As an amateur, Phil Rodgers was NCAA Champion in 1958. He joined the US Tour in 1961, breaking into the Top 60 and remaining there till 1967, then returning in 1971 and 1972. His best Tour years were 1962 and 1966, when he was 11th and 6th and won twice each year. At one time he looked an inevitable major championship winner, finishing third in the 1962 US Open, despite an 8 during his first round, and sixth in 1966. He tied for the

British Open with Bob Charles in the 1963 British Open, but in the 36-hole play-off was beaten by the New Zealander's putter. In 1962 he had tied for third; he was sixth in 1966, having led with a round to go. Rodgers still makes occasional appearances on the US Tour, but he has now earned a high reputation as a teacher, being very knowledgeable always about the golf swing and a short-game specialist. In the latter role he worked with Jack Nicklaus after his poor 1979 season – with results the world knows. Later Australian millionaire Kerry Packer hired him for two weeks' tuition for a reputed $50,000, on Nicklaus's recommendation.

US wins 5 (1962–6)
US money $482,771 (1961–81) (97th all-time)

RODRIGUEZ, Juan   Puerto Rico
b. *Bayamon 1935*

'Chi Chi' Rodriguez's career has been a rags-to-riches story. He began playing golf – of a sort – at nine when he made a club out of a branch of a guava tree and hit cans around. Later, Ed Dudley coached him, gave him a job as a shoe-shine boy and then made him caddie master. At 17, he led the Puerto Rico Open by 6 strokes, although eventually he finished 1 behind the winner. He joined the US Army, going to bed at 7.30 in order to save money. In 1960, he joined the US Tour but had little success his first three seasons; then in 1963 he made the Top 60 and won his first tournament. After that, he was out of the Top 60 only three times up to 1978; since then he has continued making well over $30,000 each year, and $65,000 as recently as 1981. His best money-list placings came in 1964 when he was ninth, and 1972 when he was 12th and topped $100,000 for the only time. On Tour he strove to be an entertainer and came to be known as 'the Clown Prince of the Tour'. Fellow competitors were less enthusiastic and another nickname, 'the Four-Stroke Penalty' was used of him, meaning that his antics caused loss of concentration and therefore dropped shots. Both Arnold Palmer and Jack Nicklaus are said to have suggested that he tone down his wisecracking and dancing about greens when he holed putts. Rodriguez modified his behaviour. Between 1973 and 1979 he did not win on Tour, but then bought a used set of clubs and scored 66, 69, 67, 67 over a 7,124 yard course to win and break the Tallahassee tournament record by 4 strokes. That same year he followed Lon Hinkle's example by driving over a tree that the USGA had had planted overnight to prevent players driving up the wrong fairway, but he added a touch of his own by teeing up on a pencil. Rodriguez is 5 feet 7 inches tall and at the time of his first tournament win weighed only 107 lb, though he later put on some weight when he stopped smoking. He is, however, a driver who can sometimes reach 300 yards, mainly the result of his hitting a low ball. He is highly talented at improvising shots and an excellent bunker player. He has a bent-knee swing and dips and sways away from the ball and then lunges back into the shot. As late as 1981 he had a second place on the US Tour and came joint sixth in the US Open. He was a Ryder Cup choice in 1973 and has represented Puerto Rico in 12 World Cups.

US wins 8 (1963–79)
US money $942,825 (1960–82) (40th all-time)
World money $1,057,953 (1960–82) (50th all-time)

ROGERS, William Charles   USA
b. Waco, Texas 1951

Bill Rogers took the 'normal' college route to the US Tour and on the way won the 1972 Southern Amateur and the 1973 All-American Collegiate event; he was a Walker Cup choice that year, but not regarded as a key player in the team, playing only two of a possible four matches. He then turned professional and, with $30,000, did well enough his first Tour year. By 1977 he was 29th in the money list and won the Pacific Masters in Japan. The next season he won his first US tournament, the Bob Hope Desert Classic, while still an unknown. In 1978 he passed the $100,000 milestone for the first time and in 1979 set a record of an unglamorous kind: his $230,500 was the most won on the US Tour by a player without a victory. It took him to sixth in the money list. He did, however, come fourth in the US Open, and won outside the USA when he beat Isao Aoki in the final of the World Matchplay at Wentworth, a shoot-out between two of the world's best putters. In the semi-final and final he averaged only just over 67 a round. His 1980 was again consistent rather than dramatic. He had two second-place finishes in the USA and again won in Japan, this time the Suntory Open. The then new US Tour statistics pointed up one aspect of his consistency: he was third in driving accuracy and one of 11 players with a scoring average under 71. In 1981 he lost that consistency early on, when after beginning

Bill Rogers

with two high finishes he then missed five cuts out of six. However, with the Sea Pines Heritage Classic at the end of March he suddenly won his first US event for three years and was on a high plateau that was to last for the remainder of the season. In June he gave easily his best performance to that date in a major championship. Round Merion Cricket Club in the US Open he scored 70, 68, 69, 69. After three rounds he was still outside George Burns's record US Open three-round score of 203 and was also 1 behind David Graham. Rogers caught Burns, but one of the great last rounds in major championship history, a 67 from David Graham, left Rogers joint second. The performance gave Rogers confidence. He now felt that he could be a major-championship winner as well as a big earner. His close friend, Ben Crenshaw, persuaded him to enter the British Open. At Royal St Georges he was almost disqualified before he had teed a ball. After he had misread a starting sheet, a newspaperman told him on the practice green that he was due on the first tee. Rogers began with a 72, but his second-round 66 gave him a lead of 1 stroke over Nick Job and Ben Crenshaw, while the 67 he followed with had him 5 ahead of Mark James and Bernhard Langer. The championship was his, Rogers was confident, if he could play just a steady last round. Rogers began with four pars, a bogey, a par and then two bogeys in a row. This was the crisis point, his lead cut to 1 stroke. Rogers then birdied three of the next four holes and cruised home to a 4-stroke victory, his progress checked only by a policeman who stopped him among stampeding spectators near the final green. Rogers explained where he was going and was soon the 1981 Open Champion. Not long after, he took the World Series, the Suntory and Texas Opens, reached the semi-finals of the World Matchplay but lost to Crenshaw, and then in Australia took both the Open and the New South Wales Open – five wins in six tournament entries. The US PGA named him Player of the Year. Rogers's achievements in six months or so had now established him as an international winner and a superstar – if he could stay on the plateau. During 1982 this did not seem to be so, for although he took well over $100,000 he did not win again. There was, however, a strong performance in the US Open, which he led after three rounds of 70, 73, 69 at Pebble Beach before his putting became insecure in the final round and he finished joint third behind Watson and Nicklaus. Rogers plays from a closed stance and reaches the fully shut position at the top of the backswing so frowned on by stylists. His left-hand grip is weak, with no knuckles showing, and there appears to be little right-hand hit into the ball. His putting style is very similar to Ben Crenshaw's, mostly an arm movement. He is unusual in not wearing a glove. One explanation for his relatively poor 1982 may be that he lost his edge competing in British and Australian tournaments during the US closed season.

US wins 4 (1978–81)
US money $1,078,992 (1975–82) (33rd all-time)
Overseas wins 7 (1977–81)
World money $1,551,587 (1975–82) (23rd all-time)

ROMACK, Barbara Gaile   USA
b. Sacramento, California 1932

'Barbie', or 'Li'l Tiger' as she was often known, took the US Amateur in 1954, beating the great Mickey Wright to do so; in 1958 she was runner-up to Anne Quast. She also reached the final of the 1955 British Amateur, where she lost heavily to Jessie Valentine. Other key achievements of her amateur career were wins in the 1952 North and South and the 1953 Canadian Amateur, and a place in the Curtis Cup teams from 1954 to 1956. She turned professional in 1958 and played the US Tour into the mid 1970s with some success, winning the 1963 Rock City Open. In 1968 she was a passenger on the first plane hijacked to Cuba.

US wins 1 (1963)
US money $62,922 (1959–76)

ROSBURG, Robert   USA
b. San Francisco, California 1926

All kinds can be tournament winners. Bob Rosburg had one of the ugliest swings ever to be seen on the US or any other golf circuit and was not a great striker, but the other side of the coin was that he was one of the best putters ever, employing a wristy rap at the ball. He once needed only 19 putts in a tournament round during the 1959 Pensacola Open, the second lowest total recorded on the US Tour. Rosburg first tried the US Tour in 1953, and from 1954 to 1963 was never lower than 40th in the money list. He faded almost completely from sight for several years, and then reappeared in 1969 to be almost US Open Champion. He finished joint second behind Orville Moody, having missed a short putt on the last to tie, and having incurred a penalty by playing the wrong ball. The following year, encouraged further by winning the club professionals' tournament, he first finished joint third in the 1971 US Open and then, next year, took the Bob Hope Desert Classic, his first win for 11 years. Perhaps satisfied, he then returned to his business interests. Previously he had won his first tournament in 1954. A climax in his career was the 1959 US PGA, which he won from 6 strokes behind at the start of the last round. That year he also had his highest money-list placing at seventh, one of two times he was in the top 10. The other was in 1958, when he was ninth and also won the Vardon Trophy with a stroke average of 70.11. As well as his US Tour wins he also took the 1957 Mexican Open and was in the 1959 Ryder Cup team, winning both in foursomes and singles. He had to play golf in spectacles, and is one of the few to use a baseball grip. He now works for ABC TV as a golf commentator.

US wins 7 (1954–72)
US money $436,446 (105th all-time)

ROSS, Alexander   USA
b. Dornoch, Scotland 1881; d. 1952

The son of a Dornoch stonemason, Alex Ross was something of a Pinehurst specialist, winning the North and South Open there five times between 1904 and 1915. He also won the US Open at Philadelphia Cricket Club in 1907 and was altogether six times in the first ten, but never again very near winning. Among other achievements he won the Massachusetts state title six times in a row and took the Swiss Open three times from 1923 to

1926. His brother Donald established a very high reputation as a golf architect, designing an estimated 500 courses, including Seminole, Pinehurst, Oak Hill, Brae Burn, Scioto, Inverness and Interlachen. He is said to have arrived in America with $2 in his pocket in 1898.

ROTH, Nancy: see Syms

RUDOLPH, Mason   USA
b. Clarksville, Tennessee 1934

At one time Mason Rudolph was one of the few players to have represented the USA in both Walker and Ryder Cup matches, though this has become not a rare achievement now that so many of the best amateurs turn professional. Rudolph was 1950 US Junior Champion, having been runner-up the previous year, reached the semi-finals of the 1957 US Amateur and was in the Walker Cup team that year, halving in foursomes and beating Philip Scrutton in singles. After representing the USA in the Americas Cup he turned professional. He was Rookie of the Year in 1959, won a tournament and finished 30th in the money list. He remained in the Top 60 until he dropped to 65th in 1968, but returned again in 1970 and 1973. His best years were 1963 and 1964 when he was seventh and eighth in the money list, while from 1963 to 1965 he had 54 consecutive entries that brought in money. When past his best he was chosen for the 1971 Ryder Cup team, and halved in foursomes, won in the four-ball and lost to Brian Barnes in the singles. His nearest approach to a major championship came in 1973 in the US PGA. He was tied for the lead after two rounds but was 2 over par on the last hole to fall from second place to joint third. Rudolph is now off the US Tour.

US wins 6 (1959–70)
US money $557,820 (1959–81) (81st all-time)

RUNYAN, Paul Scott   USA
b. Hot Springs, Arkansas 1908

Paul Runyan stood 5 feet 7½ inches and was a superb putter, two reasons for his gaining the nickname 'Little Poison'. He was at his best from the early 1930s to early 1940s and was leading money-winner in both 1933 and 1934. He is estimated to have won some 50 tournaments in his career, 15 of which are now recognized as of full Tour status. He won the US PGA twice, in 1934 beating Craig Wood on the 38th hole, and in 1938

dismissing the young Sam Snead by a record 8 and 7. In other major championships, he was fifth in the 1941 US Open and as late as 1951 was sixth, after being 1 ahead of Ben Hogan after three rounds at Oakland Hills. He had four finishes in the first four of the US Masters in between 1934 and 1942 and was equal third in the first one of all, won by Horton Smith. Runyan won the Radix Trophy, precursor of the Vardon, in 1933, and played in the Ryder Cup both that year and in 1935. He lost to Percy Alliss in the first, but won in both foursomes and singles two years later. When his main career was over, Runyan was runner-up in the US PGA Seniors in 1959 and went on to win it in 1961 and 1962, in both these years going on to beat Sam King for the World title. He became renowned as a teacher, specializing in putting problems.

US wins 15

SANDER, Anne: see Quast

SANDER, William Knox   USA
b. Seattle, Washington 1956

US Amateur Champion in 1976, Bill Sander was in the 1977 Walker Cup team at Shinnecock Hills, where he had some unfortunate experiences against Allan Brodie who beat him twice in singles and, in foursomes with Steve Martin, again won against Sander paired with Dick Siderowf. Turning professional in 1977, Sander has found the transition to the US Tour hard to make. In five seasons he has never been higher than 144th in the money list, with $13,644 in 1980 his highest money winnings. He is one of the longest drivers on the Tour, averaging 266.3 yards in 1980 and 273 in 1981, behind only Pohl, Couples, Purtzer and Zoeller.

US money $45,663 (1977–82)

SANDERS, Gary   USA
b. Lynwood, California 1949; d. 1975

US Junior Champion in 1966, Gary Sanders went on to win such major amateur titles as the 1969 Pacific Eight, in 1971 the Southwestern, the Guadalajara and Mexican and in 1972 the Western Amateur. He played on the US Tour in 1973 and 1974, winning the Amelia Open in 1974, a mini-Tour event. He died of a stroke early in 1975.

US money $26,055

Doug Sanders

SANDERS, George Douglas   USA

b. Cedartown, Georgia 1933

Walter Hagen said that no one remembers who finishes second – but there are exceptions and Doug Sanders is one of them. In the 1970 British Open, having slipped far down on the US Tour and being required to pre-qualify for the event, Sanders seemed to have it won when he had played one of the most difficult sand shots in golf: to splash *just* out of the bunker at the Road Hole at St Andrews to a pin set close to it. Sanders got his 4 and now was faced with one of the easiest par 4s in golf: the 18th at St Andrews, with a broad fairway and a second shot that demands relatively little of the player as long as he is neither too short nor too long. Sanders drove long and straight, and then made his fatal error. All week he had been playing stabbed pitch-and-run shots but, needing to get down in three more for the Open, he elected to pitch full to the green. It seemed to observers that he struck the ball a little low on the club – but his ball was on the green, if well to the back. Sanders putted up to about 4 feet and missed the next. Irony followed the next day. Sanders played a perfect running shot to the 18th and duly birdied it, but Nicklaus in the play-off had reached the 18th tee with a 1-stroke

lead and retained it with a birdie of his own. Nevertheless Sanders's missed putt has remained the most famous in modern golf history and earned him more sympathetic friends than the championship would have. Although this was Doug Sanders's nearest approach to the British Open he had two other strong performances, coming in joint second 1 stroke behind Jack Nicklaus again at Muirfield in 1966; at the same course he was fourth in 1972. He had come similarly close to the US Open in 1961 at Oakland Hills, when he came in tied for second with Bob Goalby, 1 behind Gene Littler, whom he had led by 3 strokes going into the final round. In the US PGA he had tied for second place in 1959 and had been equal third twice. Sanders had burst into professional golf when he won the 1956 Canadian Open, the only amateur ever to do so. A US Tour player from 1957, he remained better than 23rd in the money list between 1958 and 1967, and continued to earn good money until 1974. Thereafter he has competed only in selected tournaments, or not at all some years. His best years on Tour were 1961, 1962 and from 1965 to 1967 when he was in the top seven of money-winners. In 1961 he was third and won five tournaments; he won three in 1966, a year in which he had the galling experience of beginning 63, 67 in the Pensacola Open and then being disqualified for not signing his card. By the end of 1972 he stood 11th among all-time money-winners, though that position has since been much eroded by prize-money inflation: he only twice topped $100,000 in a season, whereas at today's values he would have had several $200,000 and even $300,000 years. Sanders was always a distinctive figure on the golf course. One reason was that he was a vivid dresser, apt to appear in nicely varied hues of mauve; the other that he had the shortest swing ever seen in a major golfer, barely passing shoulder height. He said he had developed it as a youth in order to stay on the fairway and thus not lose balls, which he could then ill afford. Short or not, he hit the ball very firmly indeed and was an excellent improviser of shots, one reason why he was so good a performer on links courses. He was also a good performer in other ways, as revealed in his biography *Come Swing with Me*. He received much publicity from being struck on the head by a misdirected shot from Vice-President Spiro Agnew in the 1970 Hope Classic. Doug Sanders suffered much from injury during his career, a minor example of this being that he often had a split between the first two fingers of his right hand, a consequence of the amount of right hand he put into his iron play. He has recently done much work for junior golf.

US wins 20 (1956–72)
US money $772,334 (1957–81) (59th all-time)

SARAZEN, Eugene   USA
b. Harrison, New York 1902

US Open Champion: 1922, 1932
US PGA Champion: 1922, 1923, 1933
US Masters Champion: 1935
British Open Champion: 1932

Gene Sarazen's career fell into at least three phases. He came to the top as the youngest major championship winner of all, and was dominant for a short time. He then experienced problems of technique and for several years won no championships – though plenty of tournaments. Finally he earned almost as much applause and press coverage for competing into his 70s as he had done in his peak years. He arrived, an unknown aged 20 years 4 months, at the 1922 US Open at Skokie, Illinois. With a round to go he lay behind such players as Hagen, Jones and Mehlhorn but he came through to win in the last round with a 68, then the record

Gene Sarazen

closing round by a champion. Later the same year he also won the US PGA at Oakmont, and then challenged Walter Hagen to a 72-hole match for 'the world championship', and beat the greatest matchplayer ever. He did it again the following year in the final of the US PGA. Sarazen at 5 feet 5 inches was the shortest golfer among major champions, and he also had one of the strangest grips. That of his left hand, was extremely 'strong'. he showed four knuckles: his theory was that having the side of the left hand and wrist leading into the ball was ideal. It had something of the power of a karate chop. Having small hands, he interlocked for full shots but, strangely, allowed his left thumb to dangle in space. For shorter shots, he switched to the more standard overlapping grip. In his first flush of youthful confidence it usually all worked very well – though his entry for the 1923 Troon British Open went sadly awry. Playing a qualifying round in foul weather, Sarazen took 85 and was out of the championship proper when the weather changed and allowed later starters to profit. He won the North of England Professional on that trip, however, and, like General MacArthur in the Pacific campaign, vowed he would return – even if he had to swim. After two or three years of poor results, mainly caused by a tendency to hook – a likely result of his grip – he returned to form in 1927 and thereafter began to win several tournaments a year. However, the majors eluded him. He managed third in the US Open in 1926, 1927 and 1929, fifth in 1925, sixth in 1928 and fourth in 1931. He also figured strongly in the 1928 British Open at Prince's, Sandwich, where a 7 dropped him to second place behind Walter Hagen, and later at Carnoustie in 1931 where he was 2 behind Tommy Armour in joint third place with Percy Alliss. He came close also to the US PGA when Tommy Armour beat him 1 up in the 1930 final. In US tournaments, he was probably the leading money-winner in this period, though records are thin; for instance the Agua Caliente Open, which he won in 1929, carried a then record £2,000 in prize money. In 1932 he played possibly the finest golf of his career. At Prince's, Sandwich, he outdistanced the field with 70, 69, 70 to lead Arthur Havers by 4 strokes and the remainder by more. He slipped a little in his last round to a 74 but that was good enough for a 5-stroke win. His 283 was a record, unbeaten until Locke's 279 in 1950. A fortnight later he was at Fresh Meadow for the US Open. He began 74, 76 and started his third round none too well either. He then proceeded to play the last 28 holes in 100 strokes. This gave him 70 in the third round and a final 66 in a 3-stroke victory from Bobby Cruickshank and the Englishman Phil Perkins. Sarazen's 66 broke his 1922 winner's closing-round record of 68; it was not to be beaten in the US Open until Palmer's 65 in 1960. Sarazen had two more major championships to come. In 1933 he won the US PGA, and in 1935 played in the Masters for the first time. He began strongly in 68, 71 but was behind Henry Picard's 67, 68 while after three rounds his 73 put him behind Craig Wood's 69, 72, 68. The position remained basically unchanged when Sarazen came to the par-5 15th. After a good drive he hit what is still the most famous golf shot ever in a major championship. Sarazen was doubtful of carrying over water to the green but he had strokes to make up on Craig Wood so, in his words, 'I rode into the shot with everything I had', using a 4-wood. He holed out for a double eagle and had caught the leader. When they played off Sarazen won comfortably, the first man to win all four majors. That was his last major win, though he was a contender at least until World War II and tied for the US Open in 1940, losing the play-off to Lawson Little. After the war, he retained his interest in golf and progressed from having been a very young US Open winner to being the oldest major championship competitor. He still had a few shots left in his locker and was good enough to reach the last eight of the US PGA in 1947; he particularly liked to be at the US Masters, where he was likely to regale one and all with the tale of his double eagle in 1935. In 1950, his final rounds were 70, 72, 72, which might have been good enough to win but for a first-round 80. He was 10th that year and 12th in 1951. Sarazen also liked to see old friends again at the British Open, and played in it well into his 50s; he was 17th in 1954 and 16th in 1958. A lasting memory came much later at Troon, where he punched a little 5-iron in for a hole in one on the Postage Stamp and followed that the next day by being bunkered from the tee and splashing his next shot in. Bunker play had indeed been specially significant to Sarazen, and he credited a major part of his 1932 successes to his development of a sand iron. He had wanted a clubhead that floated through sand rather than digging in and experimented by soldering lead to the leading edge to achieve the right effect. Whether or not he was the inventor of the modern sand iron is subject to rival claims, but he is certainly the man most

usually credited. The impression that his golf left on many observers was that he made it look a simple game. As one writer said: 'Gene Sarazen was the simplest golfer I ever saw. He stood with both feet rooted to the ground, grasped the club firmly in both hands with a couple of inches of shaft showing at the top and gave the ball a tremendous elementary thump.' His putting was equally simple. There was a quick stride to the ball, a glance at the hole and a firm tap with the aim of hitting the back. Sarazen won the US PGA Seniors in 1954 and 1958 and was a Ryder Cup player for every match between 1927 and 1937, losing only once in singles. He later became known to an even wider public for his commentaries in the *Shell World of Golf* series. Today, with Byron Nelson, he begins the US Masters with a ritual nine holes.

US wins 18 (1922–41)
Total wins 36

SARGENT, George USA
b. Dorking, England 1880; d. 1962

Before emigrating to the USA Sargent was an assistant to Harry Vardon. He put what he learned to good use. He won the US Open in 1909 with a last round of 71 to win by 4 strokes. In 1914, he was joint third, and in the meantime had won the 1912 Canadian Open, an event in which he had been runner-up in 1908. He was president of the US PGA from 1921 to 1926, and is thought to have been the first man to use film for golf instruction.

SCHLEE, John USA
b. Kremling, Colorado 1939

A keen student of astrology, Schlee believed that 'When your signs are right, you can do anything.' Schlee's signs were favourable for the 1973 US Open week: after three rounds he was tied for the lead with Arnold Palmer, Julius Boros and Jerry Heard. In the last round his 70 beat them all, but he still finished second. Someone with better signs, Johnny Miller, had come home in 63. Earlier in the year he had scored 70, 68, 67, 68 to win the Hawaiian Open. On that occasion he faced Tom Watson the final day with a 4-stroke lead after 68, 65, 68. Tom Watson had not learned how to win at that time, and finished in 75. Schlee has not won since. In 1965, Schlee had been medallist at the Tour qualifying school and was Rookie of the Year for his 1966 season, when he finished 47th. He was also in the Top 60 from 1971 to 1975, tenth in 1973 for $118,017 being easily his best year. In 1974 he came second in the Canadian Open, holing a 16-foot putt to do so, and led the US PGA after two rounds.

US wins 1 (1973)
US money $475,354 (1966–78)

SCHLEEH, Gerda: see Boykin

SCHROEDER, John Lawrence USA
b. Great Barrington, Massachusetts 1945

If one's father is a champion at a sport it may be more sensible to choose a different one. John's father was Ted Schroeder, US Open Champion in 1942 and Wimbledon Champion in 1949; but John is the better golfer, his father having a handicap of six. John Schroeder went on the US Tour in 1969 and has made money every year, being in the Top 60 in 1973, when he won the short-lived US Matchplay event, and from 1977 to 1979. He also lost a play-off for the 1979 Bay Hill Classic, tied for fourth place in the 1981 US Open and won the 1977 Bogota Invitational. Schroeder has some reputation for slow play. When the US PGA allowed certain players to be 'wired for sound' it was his pace of play that attracted strong language from Tom Kite. The idea was abandoned, and Kite and Schroeder are friends again.

US wins 1 (1973)
US money $540,753 (1969–82) (84th all-time)

SEMPLE, Carole Keister USA
b. Sewickley, Pennsylvania 1948

A Curtis Cup team member in the 1974–82 period, Carole Semple was on the winning US team in the 1975 World Team Championship and in 1973 took the US Amateur, beating Anne Quast 1 up in the final. The following year she reached the same stage, but this time was defeated by Cynthia Hill. Carole Semple is one of the relatively few also to win the British title, which she did in 1974, beating Angela Bonallack by 2 and 1. She reached the semi-finals in 1980. She is the daughter of Harton Semple, former president of the USGA.

SFINGI, Beverly: see Hanson

SHAW, Tom USA
b. Wichita, Kansas 1942

The recent career of Tom Shaw well illustrates what a difference one stroke a round in average can make. Roughly speaking, 72 will probably be worth $50,000 to $60,000 while 70 might bring you around $400,000, but what of 73, Tom Shaw's performance in 1981? He entered 24 tournaments, won money four times to total $3,082, and was 206th on the money list. In the last six seasons he has totalled only around $60,000, yet ten years or so ago he was a top player on the US Tour, finishing 16th in 1969 and 15th in 1971, with two wins in each of these years.

US wins 4 (1969–71)
US money $394,548 (1963–82) (113th all-time)

SHEEHAN, Patricia Leslie USA
b. Middlebury, Vermont 1956

Patty Sheehan had a notable amateur career, winning the Montana state title from 1975 to 1978 and the California in 1978 and 1979. She reached the quarter-finals of the 1976 US Amateur and was a finalist in 1979, losing to Carolyn Hill. The fol-

Patty Sheehan

lowing year she played in the Curtis Cup, taking all four of her matches, won the National Collegiate and turned professional, coming 63rd in the money list with a stroke average of 72.86 in just six events. The professional future looked more than promising; and so it proved. In 1981 she won $118,463 to be 11th on the money list, lost a play-off for the Florida Lady Citrus but won the Mazda Japan Classic at the end of the season. She was Rookie of the Year. In 1982 she began fast, being second in the S & H Golf Classic in February and then in April to May having a spell in which she finished second, first, second to be fourth on the money list. At the end of May she won again to go to third place. She had other high places during the season and two more wins to go past $225,000 at fourth on the money list. She was named the most improved player of the year and seems certain to continue for some time as one of the dominant women golfers on the US Tour.

US wins 4 (1981–2)
US money $360,624 (1980–2) (23rd all-time)

SHEPARD, Alan B.　　　　　USA

b. East Derry, New Hampshire, 1923

A 6-iron shot struck by Alan Shepard was seen by more people than any championship-winning stroke by Watson, Nicklaus, or any name you care to think of. Shepard's was hit on the Moon during the Apollo 14 expedition in 1971, the first extraterrestrial golf shot.

SHERK, Catherine (née Graham)　　Canada

b. Bancroft, Ontario 1950

Cathy Sherk won the Canadian Amateur in 1977 and was runner-up to Beth Daniel for the US title. The next year she did better, again taking the Canadian and this time adding the US Amateur. That year she was ranked the world number one woman, won the North and South and Ontario titles, and was low scorer in the US World Team Championship. Turning professional, she played full-time on the US Tour in 1979 for 39th money list place but played only about two-thirds of the events in 1980 and 1981. Nevertheless she was in the Top 60 and won $38,177 in the latter year for 42nd place, with a good stroke average of 73.66. Her programme is restricted because she is married and has a young son.

US money $102,849 (1979–82)

SHUTE, Herman Densmore　　　　USA

b. Cleveland, Ohio 1904; d. 1974

Shute turned professional in 1928 and finished sixth in the US Open that year, and joint third the following year. He became a US tournament-winner in 1930, when he took the Los Angeles and the Texas Opens. Perhaps his best performance came in the 1933 British Open at St Andrews; it followed closely on a disaster. At Southport and Ainsdale, he had just crashed in the Ryder Cup by three-putting the last green to lose to Syd Easterbrook by 1 hole. At St Andrews, in conditions especially difficult for Americans as the course was very fast running, he had rounds of 73, 73, 73, 73 to tie with Craig Wood, leaving Syd Easterbrook 1 stroke behind in third place. Shute then won the play-off. He was also a major-championship winner in the USA, taking the PGA in 1936 and 1937, the last to win two years in a row, and beating Jimmy Thomson and Harold 'Jug' McSpaden in the finals. He played on three Ryder Cup teams, his first results being the most remarkable. In the 1931 foursomes he and Walter Hagen beat George Duncan and Arthur Havers by 10 and 9, and Shute then went on to win his singles almost as decisively, beating Bert Hodson 8 and 6. In 1933 he lost both matches, and in 1937 halved in both singles and foursomes. The Open followed shortly after this and, following Henry Cotton's victory at Carnoustie, an unofficial 'world title' challenge match over 72 holes took place at Walton Heath, which Cotton won by 6 and 5. In the US Open Shute came fourth in 1935; he tied with Craig Wood and Byron Nelson in 1939 but was eliminated after 18 holes of the play-off. In 1941 he finished second, behind Wood. Shute had not been a regular competitor on the embryo US Tour of the 1930s, devoting much of his time to his club job. He played little after World War II. He was elected to the PGA Hall of Fame in 1957 and is estimated to have won about ten events that would today be of recognized US Tour status.

SIDEROWF, Richard L.　　　　USA

b. New Britain, Connecticut 1937

Four times a Walker Cup player between 1969 and 1977, Dick Siderowf was non-playing captain in 1979. As a player, he compiled a foursomes record of 2½ points out of 8 and in singles 2½ of a possible 6. Apart from numerous US amateur tournaments, his best performances have come in the British Amateur, which he won in both 1973 and 1976, beating Peter Moody 5 and 3 on the first occasion and in 1976 reaching the first extra hole against John Davies, at which point he won by holing a putt of about 5 feet, after which Davies missed for the half from closer. Siderowf represented the US in the Eisenhower Trophy in 1968, a year in which he was low amateur in the US Open; and he was also in the Trophy in 1976. He is a stockbroker.

SIECKMANN, Tom   USA
b. 1955

Unable to earn his US Tour player's card despite being a mini-Tour winner, Tom Sieckmann has done well elsewhere. In South America he has twice won the Brazil Open and was second on the 1980 money list. In Asia he won the 1981 Philippine and Thai Opens, coming fourth in the Asian Circuit Order of Merit. He tied for the 1982 Cathay Pacific Open in Hong Kong but lost the play-off. He played in Europe in both 1981 and 1982 and made the Top 60 in both years.

Europe money £14,587 (1981–2)

SIFFORD, Charles   USA
b. Charlotte, North Carolina 1923

The first black golfer to win real success on the US Tour, Charlie Sifford turned professional in 1944 and made occasional appearances on the Tour from 1947, though he did not appear on the money list until he earned just $281 in 1954. For part of this period he was personal golf pro to the singer Billy Eckstein. In 1967 he became the first black winner of a Tour event, the Hartford Open, and that year came 25th on the money list, winning $472,025. He won again in 1969, taking the Los Angeles Open at the age of 46 and was in the Top 60 from 1960 to 1969. His other successes include wins in the 1963 Puerto Rico Open, the 1956 Long Beach Open, the 1971 Sea Pines, the latter a mini-Tour event, and the Negro National Open five times. As a Senior he was the first black winner of the PGA Seniors, in 1975, but was beaten by Kel Nagle for the world title. He won the 1980 Suntree Classic. Earlier in his career he had been banned on grounds of his colour from playing in some events in the Deep South.

US wins 2 (1967–9)
US money $339,960 (134th all-time)

SIGEL, Jay   USA
b. Berwyn, Pennsylvania 1945

Jay Sigel is one of a vanishing breed in US amateur golf, a top player who has not turned professional. He has won the Pennsylvania Amateur nine times and three top amateur tournaments, but his greatest achievements have been to take the 1979 British Amateur and the 1982 US Amateur, the latter a rare success for an older player. He has also done well in major championships, being top amateur in the 1980 British Open and in the US Masters in 1980 and 1981. He reached the semi-finals of the 1977 US Amateur and has been a Walker Cup player three times from 1977 to 1981. He was runner-up in the 1961 US Junior.

SIKES, Dan   USA
b. Jacksonville, Florida 1930

As an amateur Sikes was 1955 Army Champion, and Public Links Champion in 1957. He joined the US Tour in 1961 and was a Top 60 player from 1962 to 1971 and in 1973. He had passed his bar exams, but remarked: 'I can't make this much money this fast in law.' In 1967 he came close to a major championship, the US PGA, in which with Jack Nicklaus he finished in third place, 1 stroke behind the Don Massengale-Don January play-off. Sikes had needed to finish par, par to tie after his 69, 70, 70 had given him a lead of 4 over January and 6 over Massengale, but his 73 last round did not match their 68, 66. This was his best year on Tour, for he had two wins and was fifth in the money list, winning some $111,000. Sikes favoured low, drawn shots and was both a long and a consistent player, having a pause at the top of the backswing. He was much involved, as a lawyer, in the dispute towards the end of the 1960s between US tournament players and their PGA.

US wins 6 (1963–8)
US money $819,601 (51st all-time)
World money $965,163 (1961–80)

SIKES, Richard H.   USA
b. Paris, Arkansas 1940

Dick Sikes had an outstanding amateur career, being US Public Links Champion in 1961 and 1962 and, in 1963, runner-up in the US Amateur and NCAA Champion. That year he appeared in the Walker Cup, and in singles was beaten at Turnberry 7 and 5 by Joe Carr. In foursomes he won and lost

Jesse and Sam Snead

real run at a major championship 14 years earlier than Snead (1960 as opposed to 1974). They were very nearly the same age. Through the green Snead's game had no weak link. Perhaps, with his natural draw, he was likely to hit the occasional drive into the woods, but infrequently, and both his long and short irons were equally good. He was one of the best wedge players from fairway or bunker. On the green he was an excellent long putter, that is, at distances when the putting stroke is at least a small imitation of the golf swing; but at close quarters he was more uncertain. Snead himself has written that he suffered from twitching in different phases of his career and that his first decline in 1947 and 1948 was caused by this. He was able to effect a temporary cure when he found a putter that gave him confidence. Later, in 1966, he changed to putting between his legs croquet style and then, when that was unkindly and unnecessarily banned, adopted a similar stroke, chest-on to the hole but having the ball to the side of his right foot. It may have looked a strange solution for so gifted an athlete to settle on, but it beat the twitch. That is something, with the rule being 'Once you've had 'em, you've got 'em.' As a Senior no one has approached Snead's feats. He is the oldest US Tour event winner, at nearly 53; winner of the US PGA Seniors in 1964, 1965, 1967, 1970, 1972 and 1973; and he went on to win the world final every time except once. In 1979 he became the first player to equal and beat his age in a full US Tour event when he had a 67 and a 66 in the Quad Cities at the age of 67. Earlier, in 1978, he had a 64 in a non-PGA tournament. In 1979 also he scored 73, 71, 71, 73 over Oakland Hills in the PGA Championship. He was by no means in contention but did better than, for example, Fuzzy Zoeller, Lanny Wadkins, Raymond Floyd and even Jack Nicklaus. However, by this time it had at last to be admitted that his swing was on the wane: there was extra shoulder movement and a suggestion of groping for the ball, and the rhythm was partly gone. The US Seniors Tour had arrived too late even for Snead, though this was partly disproved when as late as 1982, in partnership with Don January, he won a tournament by 12 strokes! The deeds in major championships and age omitted, it may be that Snead will most be remembered as a tournament winner. There are various estimates as to his worldwide victory total. Some go into the high 160s, but 135 is the total that most agree on. His only rivals in this area are Gary Player and Roberto de Vicenzo, with

win it twice again, by 3 and 2 over Johnny Palmer in 1949, and in 1951 when he trounced Walter Burkemo, who was making his first of three final appearances in four years, by 7 and 6. He was also twice the beaten finalist, in 1938 and 1940, and remained prominent when the event switched to strokeplay from 1958. He was third that year and in 1960 and joint fourth at the age of 60 in 1972; two years later he scored 69, 71, 71, 68 to be joint third, 3 behind winner Lee Trevino. Merely recounting Snead's achievements in the major championships begins to make clear the unparalleled length of time he remained a championship-level player: 37 years. When others are retired from a sedentary job, Sam Snead was still breaking 70 round a golf course as often as not. There is little doubt that the reason for that longevity was his swing. He had the power to be the first 275-yard driver who was also a great player, and the whole process was accomplished with apparent ease; a slow coiling-up and then rhythmic and unstressed acceleration into the ball. He began as a prodigious hitter and, although he became shorter as the years passed, he was still long enough into his 60s. More obviously powerful players such as Palmer and Nicklaus are unlikely to last as long, while his great rival, Ben Hogan, won his last major a year before Snead and made his last

Player having won fewer and Vicenzo some 165, with more of his total being out of the top class of tournaments. There is, however, no rival in sight of Sam Snead as a winner on the US Tour. In his first 15 seasons, apart from his twitching spell in 1947 and 1948, he was never out of the top seven players. He was leading money-winner in 1938, 1949 and 1950, second twice and third three times. By the end of 1952 he had won 65 US PGA-recognized events. He added another 19 in his less dominant years up to his last win in the 1965 Greensboro' Open. In that second phase he was in the Top 60 every year but one. From that time on he has twice again made that group, in 1968 and 1974 when, at 62 he was 49th and, with $55,562 actually won his highest total in a year. At present values it is estimated that he would have won over $8 million. In total, to 1981 he had played 44 years on the US Tour and won money every year except 1980 and 1981. His total victories are 84, 15 ahead of Jack Nicklaus. He has four times won the Vardon Trophy for low stroke average: 1938, 1949, 1950 and 1955; and he was a Ryder Cup choice every year, except 1957, from 1937 to 1959. In that he won six singles and lost one, and in foursomes was in the winning pairing four times out of six, with one halved.

US wins 84 (1936–65) (1st all-time)
US money $620,126 (1937–79) (76th all-time)
Total wins 135
World money $827,000 (1937–80)

SNEED, Edgar Morris   USA
b. Roanoke, Virginia 1944

One defeat of Ed Sneed's will be remembered when some famous victories have been forgotten. In the first two rounds of the 1979 US Masters Sneed did not once go over par and scored 68, 67. He dropped a shot on the 5th in his third round and finished in 69. At that point he held a 5-stroke lead on Tom Watson and 6 over Fuzzy Zoeller. On the final day he went to the turn in 38, not good but probably good enough, though his lead had by then been cut to 2 strokes. However, he then birdied the par-5 13th and 15th, and level par over the last three holes would have seen him with the Masters green jacket and a 3-stroke win. Alas for Ed Sneed, he three-putted both the 16th and 17th and was just short of the green in two on the last hole, now needing a par to win, his ball near the edge of a bunker. He chipped up to about 6 feet, narrowly

missing the putt and was in a play-off with Zoeller, who had been playing for second or third place, and Tom Watson. Zoeller birdied the second play-off hole: Sneed and Watson didn't. If it was all most discouraging, Sneed had faced this problem before. He had turned professional in 1967 and played a little on Tour in 1969 and 1970, before competing full-time in 1971 and 1972. In none of these years did he finish better than 118th in the money list, but a trip to Australia in 1973 improved matters. He won the New South Wales Open, flew back to pre-qualify for the Kemper Open, and won that too. He was in the Top 60 and remained there, except in 1977 and 1981. One of his closest friends was Tom Weiskopf, renowned for his swing; Tom thought that Sneed's was even better and there was therefore no reason why he should not be a successful player. Sneed has also won the Milwaukee Open in 1974, the Tallahassee Open in 1977 and the Houston Open in 1982. In Morocco, he took the 1980 Grand Prix. He is considered an expert backgammon player and is also good at chess, billiards and bridge. He played in the US Ryder Cup team in 1977.

US wins 5 (1973–82)
US money $799,547 (1969–82) (55th all-time)
Overseas wins 2 (1973–80)

SOLOMON, Elizabeth   USA
b. Middletown, Indiana 1952

Winner of the 1970 Indiana state championship, Beth Solomon has played the US Tour since 1975, her best year being 1980 when she was 22nd on the money list. She has been in the Top 60 from 1977 to 1981, and has one Tour victory: in the 1981 Birmingham Classic, she overcame Jane Blalock in a play-off.

US wins 1 (1981)
US money $176,811 (1975–82)

SOMERVILLE, Charles Ross   Canada
b. London, Ontario 1903

Sandy Somerville was the dominant force in Canadian amateur golf from the late 1920s to late 1930s. He won the Canadian Amateur six times between 1926 and 1937, was also runner-up four times and won five province titles. On the last leg of Bobby Jones's Grand Slam in 1930 Somerville gave Jones a good run in their match, and in 1932 he became the first Canadian to win the US Amateur, also reaching the semi-finals of the British Amateur in 1938. He was an excellent iron-player and bold putter. In the 1960s he twice won the Canadian Seniors and was twice joint winner, and was president of the Royal Canadian Golf Association in 1957. In those less specialized days Somerville was an all-round sportsman, reaching a high standard also at ice hockey, cricket and football.

SORENSON, Carol (later Flenniken)　　USA
b. Janesville, Wisconsin 1942

Winner of both Western and National Junior Championships in 1960, Carol Sorenson also took the National Collegiate the same year. In 1962 she added the Western Women's, and in 1964 the Trans-Mississippi. However, the best achievement of her career was victory in the 1964 British Ladies' at Prince's, Sandwich, where she beat Bridget Jackson on the first extra hole of the final. Carol Sorenson played on both the 1964 and 1966 Curtis Cup teams, and in 1964 also in the World Team Championship.

SOUCHAK, Michael　　USA
b. Berwick, Pennsylvania 1927

World records in golf scoring are sometimes recorded in freak conditions. Peter Tupling's 255 for four rounds is such an example. It broke Souchak's 257 at Brackenridge Park, San Antonio in the 1955 Texas Open with rounds of 60, 68, 64, 65, which was established in a rather open course with rubber tee mats, where low scoring was extremely frequent. Nevertheless no one else matched Souchak's feat in the years when some tournament organizers wanted the publicity that exceptionally low scoring attracts and allowed fairway teeing up or placing and forward tee markers (even the ladies' tees being used at times). Souchak's 60 contained the remarkable inward half of 27. He needed no more than a wedge to the green for his second shot five times and his scoring was 2, 4, 4, 3, 3, 3, 3, 3, 2. It still equals the world tournament nine-hole record, while his total is the lowest achieved on the US Tour and at 27 under par is equal best. His first three rounds are the lowest ever in the USA, while his first-round 60 has only been bettered by Al Geiberger's 59. Souchak became one of the leading Tour players that year, finishing in the top 10 money-winners for the first time as he did also in 1956, 1959, 1960 and 1964. He never won a major

championship but had a remarkable run in the US Open from 1959 to 1961 finishing third each time. In 1960 perhaps he ought to have won. After a start of 68, 67 he had opened up a lead of several strokes and a third-round 73 cost him little ground. However, Palmer produced a last-round 65 to Souchak's 75. Souchak was a very powerful player with a barrel chest who had been a top-class college footballer. He was one of the longest hitters in his best years. He was in the US Ryder Cup team in 1959 and 1961, winning both foursomes and singles in 1959 while in 1961 he won and lost in foursomes and took both his singles. He is an expert on wine.

US wins 16 (1955–64) (30th all-time)
US money $286,876 (156th all-time)

SPEER, Roberta:　　see Albers

SPUZICH, Sandra Ann　　USA
b. Indianapolis, Indiana 1937

As an amateur Sandra Spuzich was three times runner-up for her state title and the Western and also a champion bowler (at the age of 17 she had a 289 game). She has played the US Tour since 1963 and in a full tournament year has never been placed worse than 40th. She won the Corning Classic in 1982, after a play-off with Patty Sheehan, at the age of 45, a record. Later she bettered that with a win in the Mary Kay Classic. Her best years were 1968 and 1969 when she was placed fifth and sixth respectively in the money list, and she has six other times been in the top 20. She is a steady money-winner, in the last ten years or so making the 20s and 30s of the annual list. Sandra Spuzich first won in 1966, defeating Carol Mann by 1 stroke in the US Open. After that she has added victories in 1969, 1974, 1977, 1980, 1981 and 1982. In 1982 she won well over $80,000, more than she had ever done before.

US wins 7 (1966–82)
US money $436,258 (1962–82) (18th all-time)

STACY, Hollis　　USA
b. Savannah, Georgia 1954

Hollis Stacy set a record, which will be very difficult to beat, at the beginning of her national golf career. She is the only girl to have won the Junior Championship three times, and in her last victory in 1971 was 4 under par when she defeated Amy Alcott on the first extra hole. As an amateur her other important success was the 1970 North and South. She played in the 1972 Curtis Cup. She has been on the US Tour since 1974 and has been one of the top players since 1977, a year in which she won two tournaments and the US Open. That can be considered her best year, for she also achieved her best money-list position – fifth. However, she was sixth in 1978 and again won the US Open, one of four players to win consecutively. In 1981, with $138,908, she topped $100,000 in a year for the first time; she was in even better form in 1982, going well past $150,000, winning three events and extending her sequence of winning years to six. Still under 30 in 1983, she should have many more top years before her, and has not been worse than 11th in the years 1977–82. However, despite this evidence of consistency, Hollis Stacy feels she is a 'fits and starts' player liable to both brilliance and a lower standard. In 1977, with scores of 68, 65, 69, 69 for 271, she set an LPGA record for a 72-hole tournament while her 36- and 54-hole totals also set or equalled records for 72-hole tournaments. The same year she won the Mixed Team Championship in partnership with Jerry Pate.

US wins 12 (1977–82)
US money $710,746 (1974–82) (14th all-time)

STADLER, Craig Robert   USA
b. San Diego, California 1953

Craig Stadler was first noticed in 1971 when he won the World Junior Championship. In 1973 he found himself in top form for the US Amateur the year it returned to matchplay at Inverness. He knocked out the defending champion Vinny Giles in the semi-finals and went on to win the final by 6 and 5. During his amateur career he won no other important titles, but was an All-American choice in 1974 and 1975, and in the latter year was chosen for the Walker Cup at St Andrews. There he had an unblemished record, winning in his two foursomes matches and his only singles. The transition to the US Tour was not a particularly easy one. He failed on his first attempt to get his player's card and, qualifying for the second half of the 1976 season, played badly, as he himself said, to win only $2,702. Then and for some years after Stadler had difficulty in controlling his temper. There was a certain amount of club-throwing and in Britain his caddie was once abused enough to throw Stadler's golf bag to the ground and walk off. Yet such a temperament is not all disadvantage. It can arise because a golfer is confident of his abilities and correspondingly disgusted when he fails to live up to them. The player who, for instance, shrugs to himself when he misses a putt or drives out of bounds because he knew it was very likely anyway

Hollis Stacy

Tom Watson and Craig Stadler

170

is equally unlikely to be a winner, while the stress of restraining emotions can also destroy. Perhaps Snead's advice that a player should try to be 'cool mad' is the answer. After that introduction to the US Tour Stadler made his way steadily and un-dramatically to the ranks of major players. In 1977 he did not make the Top 60, but at 66th he was close. The following two years he did so comfortably but his highest placings were no better than fourth; he did win the 1978 Magnolia Classic, a mini-Tour event played while the stars are at the Masters. In 1980 and 1981 he became a name player, winning the Hope Classic and Greater Greensboro' the first of these years and the Kemper in 1981, when he was also twice second and three times third. In both years he came eighth in the money list with over $200,000. However, he was still not consistent, producing a proportion of poor finishes. The following year he had a fast start by winning the Tucson Open, first event of the year, and a month later should have won the Crosby but had a couple of 6s in his final round and came in second behind Jim Simons. In the US Masters he began with a 75, followed with a 69 and then took a 3-stroke lead into the last round after a 67, in which he birdied the last three holes. After 11 holes that lead was stretched to 5 but thereafter he seemed likely to repeat the experience that in 1979 had overtaken Ed Sneed; in fact Stadler had played with him during that collapse. He dropped shots on the 12th, 14th and 16th and needed a par for outright victory on the last but three-putted. Dan Pohl, with a last-round 67 to Stadler's 73, had caught him. However, Stadler parred the first play-off hole and was Masters Champion, and one of the potentially hottest properties in US golf, the golfer whose signature all the money men suddenly wanted at the foot of a contract. Stadler, unconventional in both character and appearance, refused and went away to finish second in the Tournament Players' Championship, after a last-round 64. By June he had reached $300,000 for the season and was nearly $100,000 ahead of Watson in second place. He had also added the Kemper Open to his record and later the World Series; he became only the second man to earn over $400,000 on the US Tour in a year, and had passed $1 million in his career. Stadler is 5 feet 10 inches tall and weighs over 200 lb. He has unkindly been called 'Super-slob', 'the Walrus' – because of both girth and moustache – and even 'the Waddling Walrus'. Certainly he does not look an athlete as he pads the fairways, but once he deals with a golf ball the impression changes, for he hits with savagery. He is not the longest hitter on Tour but is within 10 yards or so of the leading men; while with a putter he showed himself well able to deal with the fastest greens seen at Augusta for a good many years. His $446,462 for the US 1982 season was the second most won in a season to Watson's 1980 $530,808 and was $60,000 ahead of the second-place man, Ray Floyd.

US wins 7 (1980–2)
US money $1,054,111 (1976–82) (35th all-time)
World money $1,366,692 (1976–82) (31st all-time)

STEWART, Marlene (later Streit)   Canada
b. Cereal, Alberta 1934

The greatest of Canadian women golfers, Marlene Stewart took her national Closed championship consecutively from 1951 to 1957, at which point it was not held for two years. She won again in 1963 and 1968, the last year it was held. She won the Canadian Open Amateur in 1951, 1954–6, 1958–9, 1963, 1968–9 and 1972–3. Her totals of nine and 11 wins respectively for the two championships are easily records. She was also runner-up in the Open event in 1953. Most of her wins were by comfortable margins: three times she faced Miss M. Gay in the final and beat her by 9 and 8, 11 and 9, and 8

Marlene Stewart

and 6. In the United States she won the North and South in 1956 and beat JoAnne Gunderson by 2 and 1 in the final of the US Ladies' the same year. She reached the final again in 1966, this time losing to the same opponent on the 41st hole, the longest final. Among other achievements she won the Australian Open title in 1963, the World Amateur in 1966 and the British title in 1953, beating Philomena Garvey by 7 and 6 in the final. She was runner-up in the 1982 Canadian Open Amateur. She is one of only two players, with Dorothy Campbell, to have won Canadian, British and US titles, and the only player to have also won the Australian title. Ten players have taken both US and British events.

STEWART, William Payne   USA
b. Springfield, Missouri 1957

Payne Stewart was Southwest Conference co-Champion in 1979 and turned professional late that year. He played the Asia Circuit and finished third in its Order of Merit with wins in the 1981 Indian and Indonesian Opens. He played part of the 1981 US Tour season and in 1982 won the Magnolia Classic, only a mini-Tour event but perhaps the highest ranking of them, and a month or so later the Quad Cities Open after a closing 63. He made the Top 60 comfortably at 38th and also won an event in Australia.

US wins 1 (1982)
US money $112,086 (1981–2)
Australia wins 1 (1982)
Asia wins 2 (1981)

STILL, Kenneth Allan   USA
b. Tacoma, Washington 1935

Ken Still turned professional in 1953 but did not qualify for the US Tour until 1960. Thereafter he experienced lean years from 1961 to 1965, totalling only $17,000 or so in money winnings. In 1966 he broke into the Top 60 and remained there until the 1974 season. He won twice in 1969, the Florida Citrus and Greater Milwaukee, and took the Kaiser in 1970. His best money position was 25th in 1969. That year he was chosen for the Ryder Cup team at Royal Birkdale and, partnered with Dave Hill in a four-ball against Brian Huggett and Bernard Gallacher, was involved in a match that showed considerable ill feeling. On the 7th hole Huggett claimed that Hill had putted out of turn and the USA conceded the hole when the putt could

actually have been retaken. To stir the fires further, Gallacher conceded a fairly long putt of Still's on the next hole to prevent Hill learning anything about his line of putt. The US pair won that match by 2 and 1. Still was an extrovert, intelligent, eccentric, with a gift for self-deprecation. He described himself as 'the hotdog pro', meaning that when he came in sight the galleries felt it a good time to go and buy one.

US wins 3 (1969–70)
US money $504,551 (93rd all-time)

STIRLING, Alexa (later Fraser)   USA
b. Atlanta, Georgia 1897

With the same town of birth as Bobby Jones, Alexa Stirling also had the same teacher, Stewart Maiden. Jones and she were childhood friends and played golf together on occasion. Her first important success was her victory in the 1915 Southern Amateur, a success she repeated in 1916 and 1919. In 1916 she won the US title for the first time and, with the 1917–18 events cancelled owing to World War I, her wins in 1919 and 1920 make her one of five to have won three consecutively. She also reached the final in 1921, 1923 and 1925, losing to Glenna Collett on the last of these three occasions. She was medallist in 1919, 1923 and 1925, her 77 in the last of these years setting a record not beaten until 1933, by Enid Wilson. Alexa Stirling also won the Metropolitan once and, after she married and moved to Ottawa, Canada, the national championship in 1920 and 1934, being runner-up in 1922 and 1925.

STOCKTON, David   USA
b. San Bernardino, California 1941

At 14, Dave Stockton broke his back. Throughout his career this has meant that he is unable to practise for long periods and has also affected his hitting power. Of this Stockton himself says that he has none and merely guides the club through the ball with little or no snap. How then has he managed to become a very successful golfer with two major championships in his record? Stockton believes that golf ability is 90% mental and gives the credit for his success to sensible thinking and good nerve when in a contending position. Undoubtedly he is an excellent putter, once playing a stretch of ten rounds without using more than 28 strokes on the greens. He turned professional in

1964 and broke through on the US Tour in 1967, when he had two wins. From that year he was in the Top 60 until the 1979 season, 1974 being his best year with three victories, $155,105 and sixth place in the money list. He was in the top 20 in 1967, 1968, 1970, 1971 and 1973. Stockton's first major championship came in 1970 at Southern Hills when he beat Arnold Palmer and Bob Murphy into second place in the PGA Championship. He won again in 1976 at Congressional, holing a putt of several yards on the last green to beat Ray Floyd and Don January by a single stroke. He has been close to two other majors. He was joint second with Jesse Snead for the 1978 US Open, and joint second with Tom Weiskopf behind Gary Player for the 1974 Masters on a course that hardly suits shorter hitters. He is now past his best, having finished out of the top 100 since 1979. He was a Ryder Cup player in 1971 and 1977.

US wins 11 (1967–76)
US money $1,138,477 (1964–82) (27th all-time)
World money $1,367,571 (1964–82) (30th all-time)

STONE, Elizabeth   USA
b. Harlinger, Texas 1940

Growing up in Oklahoma, Beth Stone won the state junior title in 1957 and the women's in 1960 and was runner-up for the 1957 US Girls'. On the professional Tour since 1961 she has never managed a victory but has five times been second, two of those placings coming in the 1967 and 1974 Opens, 2 behind Catherine Lacoste and 1 behind Sandra Haynie. On the US Tour from 1961 to 1978 she was always well within the top 50, her best money list placings coming in 1964 (18th), 1967 (17th) and 1973 (18th).

US money $195,827 (1961–82) (53rd all-time)

STRANAHAN, Frank R.   USA
b. Toledo, Ohio 1922

Frank 'Muscles' Stranahan was a man who made golfers aware that physical fitness was more important than had once been thought. This was particularly so in Britain, where he was perhaps at his most formidable and usually arrived with his weight-lifting kit. For several years after World War II, financed by his millionaire father, he was just about the best amateur in the world. In Britain he won the Amateur in both 1948 and 1950, beating Charlie Stowe and Dick Chapman by handsome

Frank 'Muscles' Stranahan

margins, and was runner-up to Harvie Ward in 1952. In the Open Championship he was perhaps even more impressive, though he did not win. He was five times top amateur, tied second in 1947, despite a round of 79, was ninth in 1950, 12th in 1951 and tied for second again in 1953, Hogan's year. He was unpopular with certain British caddies used to having their advice heeded. The story is told that one, on being sent ahead to give Stranahan the line for a blind shot to the green, instead gave him a line to thick gorse. When Stranahan then came in sight the caddie showed him his ball and said: 'Well, sir, if you think you know so much about it, let's see you get out of that,' and departed the course. In the USA Stranahan won a host of major amateur titles including the North and South three times, the Western four times, the Tam o' Shanter World Amateur consecutively from 1948 to 1953 and the Canadian Amateur in 1947 and 1948. He was also joint second in the 1947 US Masters, a performance as good as any put up by an amateur in that major championship. The title that eluded him was the US Amateur, his closest approach coming in 1950 when he was beaten on the 39th hole of the final by Sam Urzetta. Perhaps his most dominant year was 1948, when he won the national titles of Canada, Britain, Brazil and Mexico (which he repeated in 1951), the North and South, Tam o' Shanter and three state opens. In 1952 he set a US Tour record with his 61 in the Tucson Open. He turned professional in 1954 when a year or two past his best. Although he is considered not to have been a success he won the 1955 Eastern Open and the 1958 Los Angeles Open.

US wins 2 (1955–8)

STRANGE, Curtis Northrup   USA
b. *Norfolk, Virginia 1955*

Curtis had a short, brilliant career as an amateur, winning the Southeastern Amateur at 18, while in 1974 he was NCAA Champion and won the Western Amateur. In 1975 he won the Eastern Amateur, which his father had won in 1957, and the North and South; he was in the Walker Cup team, taking 3½ points of a possible 4. In 1976 he again won the North and South and turned professional. Strange considers that it took him three years to adjust to the US Tour to the point when he felt he was playing as well as in his amateur days, but in fact he won useful sums in both 1977 and 1978 before breaking into the Top 60 in 21st place in 1979. Thereafter he became a very big money-winner, and also highly consistent. He won his first tournament in 1979, the Pensacola Open with a 62 in the third round, and won the Houston Open and the Westchester Classic the following year when, with $271,888, he was third in money winnings. He did not win in 1981 or 1982 but topped $200,000 both years and lost a play-off for the 1981 Tournament Players' Championship. In 1982 he set a new high in income for a non-winner with $263,378 and was third in stroke average. Only 27 in 1983, he is one of those most likely to become a major championship winner and a more frequent tournament winner.

US wins 3 (1979–80)
US money $932,638 (1977–82) (41st all-time)
World money $1,148,622 (1977–82) (44th all-time)

STRECK, Ron   USA
b. *Tulsa, Oklahoma 1954*

In mid-September 1978 in the Texas Open, Ron Streck needed a par 3 to close his second round in order to make the 36-hole cut. He put his tee shot into a bunker, splashed out and single-putted. At that point he had won $6,933 on the US Tour, was

Curtis Strange

156th and needed either to earn $10,000 or be in the top 160 to retain his player's card. In the third round he went out in 29, followed with an eagle and a bogey and then parred the rest for a 63. The next day he birdied five of the opening eight holes and later added three more for a 62. He had won the Texas Open and set a US Tour 36-hole scoring record. He had had one bogey, 19 pars and 16 birdies in the two rounds. He was 68th on the money list that year, winning $46,933, $40,000 of which came from the Texas Open. A 62 was once again to feature prominently in his career. In 1981 he had one in the third round of the Houston Open to lead by 2 strokes. It rained heavily for the next two days and Streck was declared the winner. That contributed a little less than half the winnings which took him into the Top 60 for the first time, in 29th place. In 1982 he suffered a fairly unusual penalty in the Tournament Players' Championship. He was seen to 'adjust' a branch that was in his face after a wayward tee shot and was given a 2-stroke penalty which dropped him down from clear second place behind winner Lanny Wadkins to joint third. He was 60th on the money list for the year.

US wins 2 (1978–81)
US money $331,017 (1978–82) (138th all-time)

STREIT, Marlene: see Stewart

SUGGS, Louise   USA
b. *Atlanta, Georgia 1923*

As an amateur, Louise Suggs won just about everything that was on offer, including such major amateur events as the North and South and Western Amateurs, three times each, and also the Southern. In 1947 she took the US Amateur and followed up with the British equivalent the next year, one of only ten players to have won both championships. Shortly afterwards she turned professional. Her success in professional golf was immediate, for she won the US Open her first season by a record 14 strokes from Babe Zaharias, and took two other events. Thereafter she was a very consistent winner after a blank year in 1950. She described the early contests between herself, Babe Zaharias and Patty Berg as being like 'watching three cats fighting over a plate of fish'. In the early Tour they were the star figures, shortly being joined by Betsy Rawls, Betty Jameson, Marilynn Smith, Beverly Hanson and, in the late 1950s,

Hal Sutton

Mickey Wright. Louise piled up event after event, taking another Open in 1952 (she was second four times) and the US LPGA in 1957. Her best years were in the mid 1950s, while in 1952 she took six tournaments and in 1953 eight; she won the Vare Trophy for low stroke average at 74.64 in 1957. She was leading money-winner in 1953 and 1960, though both years were worth less than $20,000. From 1951 to 1962 she won each year, but never again. After 1961 she had begun to restrict her tournament appearances to under a dozen a year and usually far fewer, but she continued to make the occasional appearance up to 1980. Only Kathy Whitworth, Mickey Wright and Betsy Rawls have more Tour wins to their credit.

US wins 50 (1949–62) (4th all-time)
US money $190,475 (57th all-time)

SULLIVAN, Michael James   USA
b. *Gary, Indiana 1955*

Mike Sullivan turned professional in 1975 and won four mini-Tour events before qualifying for the main Tour in 1976. In 1978 he lost a play-off to Jack Newton for the Buick Open, and in 1980 won the Southern Open by 5 strokes and took second place in the Bob Hope Classic. In 1981, he produced a final-round 64 in the Southern Open, which earned him a play-off with J.C. Snead, but this he lost. Sullivan was in the Top 60 in both 1980 and 1981, his best being the former year when, with $147,759, he was 22nd in the money list.

US wins 1 (1980)
US money $371,510 (1977–82) (119th all-time)

SUTTON, Hal   USA
b. *Shreveport, Louisiana 1958*

When Hal Sutton joined the US Tour for the 1982 US season he was nearly everyone's tip for the first-year player most likely to make a big impression. He did, making the Top 60 in great comfort, winning over $237,000 and taking the season's last event, the Disney Classic, to finish 11th on the money list. He produced strong performances in the Tallahassee, where he came joint second and had a spell in which he was successively joint third in the Anheuser-Busch Classic and second, 2 strokes behind Bruce Lietzke, in the Canadian Open. He may prove to be one of the stars of the 1980s. Sutton's first important win as an amateur was in the 1976 Cotton States Invitational. In 1978 he was second in the North and South and won the Dixie Amateur, which he again won the following year. Also in 1979 he won the Western and Rice Planters' and was in the US Walker Cup team. He had a host of successes in 1980, losing the NCAA Championship after a play-off but winning the North and South, Northeastern, Western and US Amateurs. Perhaps he proved himself the best amateur in the world when he won the World Amateur team championship individual by 9 strokes at Pinehurst. His 12-under-par 276 was a record. In 1981 he was top amateur in the British Open and again a Walker Cup player.

US wins 1 (1982)
US money $237,434 (1982) (171st all-time)

SWEENY, Robert, DFC   USA
b. Pasadena, California 1911

Robert Sweeny is a kind of mid-Atlantic figure who has divided his time between Britain and the US. In Britain he reached the semi-finals of the Amateur Championship in 1935 and in 1937 got to the final, beating Lionel Munn at Sandwich by 3 and 2. In the pre-war period he also won the *Golf Illustrated* Gold Vase in 1937 and the Gleneagles Silver Tassie on two occasions. When war came he joined the Eagle Squadron, which was made up of Americans either resident in Europe or who came over to get into the war in the early days: hence his British decoration. He reached the first post-war final of the British Amateur, where he lost to James Bruen. The following year he was a reserve for the US Walker Cup team, and in 1954 reached the final of the US Amateur where his route to the rare feat of winning both championships was barred by Arnold Palmer, who beat him by only 1 hole.

SWEETSER, Jess W.   USA
b. St Louis, Missouri 1902

In 1920 Jess Sweetser won the Intercollegiate title; he was second the following year. He was in dominant form in the US Amateur of 1922, when he knocked out the defending champion, Jess Guilford, the previous year's British champion, Willie Hunter, and then met Bobby Jones in the semi-final. If Jones had yet to reach his peak he had nevertheless tied for second in the US Open earlier that year. Sweetser beat him by 8 and 7, the worst defeat Jones ever suffered in the US or British Amateurs. In the final Sweetser beat Chick Evans,

another champion. The following year he again reached the final but this time was beaten by Max Marston. In 1926 he became the first American-born player to win the British Amateur (Walter Travis was Australian by birth) and only the third player to win both championships. He did so despite knee and wrist trouble and an illness, diagnosed as 'flu, which was severe enough for him to be carried off the liner on his return to the USA. He was unable to play tournament golf again for some time. Sweetser was a Walker Cup team member six times between 1922 and 1932 and later, in 1967 and 1973, was non-playing captain. A powerful player, he had also been a very good quarter-miler at Yale University.

SYMS, Nancy (née Roth)   USA
b. Elkhart, Indiana 1939

At her best in the early 1960s, Nancy Syms won the North and South in 1963 and 1966, the Eastern from 1963 to 1965, the Southern in 1964 and 1966,

Jess Sweetser

the Doherty Cup in 1963, 1964 and 1966 and the Broadmoor Invitational in 1972 and 1975. The latter year was an Indian summer for her, for she was medallist in the US Amateur with a 71, only a stroke above the record, and won the British Ladies', beating the youth prodigy Suzanne Cadden by 3 and 2 in the final. Nancy Syms played in the 1964, 1966 and 1976 Curtis Cup teams.

TABOR, Vicki USA
b. Oakland, California 1955

Once a Pinkertons detective but with no considerable record in amateur golf, Vicki Tabor did some of her learning in mini-Tour golf in California, and on the full Tour has made much ground after a most unpromising beginning. In 1978 she earned nothing at all and only $2,500 the following year; but she began to make headway in 1980. In 1981 she was 41st on the money list and approached $40,000 in money winnings. In 1982 she repeated her pattern of improvement every season and won well over $50,000. At 5 feet 1 inch she is one of the shortest women golfers now playing on the US Tour.

US money $106,908 (1978–82)

TAPIE, Alan Francis USA
b. Lynwood, California 1949

As an amateur Alan Tapie won the 1970 Pacific Eight Conference and qualified for the US Tour in 1974. Since 1975 he has twice been in the Top 60, in 1978 and 1979, the latter his best year when he was 42nd, winning over $88,000. In 1981 he showed that the US Tour statistics can be misleading: he rated best for putting at 28.70 per round but was 152nd on the money list. (He must have missed a lot of greens, then pitched or chipped close.) He gave a good performance for three rounds in the 1975 British Open with 70, 72, 67 to be in contention before falling right away to a 79 and 16th place.

US money $271,389 (1975–82) (162nd all-time)

TAYLOR, Frank M. USA
b. 1926

Dr Frank Taylor was runner-up to Hillman Robbins in the 1957 US Amateur at Brookline. He played on three Walker Cup teams from 1957 to 1961, played four matches and won them all.

TEWELL, Douglas Fred USA
b. Baton Rouge, Louisiana 1949

Doug Tewell joined the US Tour in 1975 and first made real money in 1977. He was in the Top 60 in 1979 and 1980, with the latter being easily his best year. His $161,684 almost equalled his total winnings from 1975 to 1981, and he finished in 17th place with wins in both the Sea Pines Heritage Classic and the IVB-Philadelphia Classic. In 1982 he was 52nd.

US wins 2 (1980)
US money $421,737 (1975–82) (106th all-time)

THOMPSON, Leonard Stephen USA
b. Laurinburg, North Carolina 1947

Leonard Thompson has been on the US Tour since 1971 and since 1973 has been in the Top 60, except in 1976 and 1978. He has topped $100,000 in 1974, 1977 and 1980, and was 15th on the money list in both 1973 and 1974. He has two records to his credit, a 62 in the second round of the 1981 Canadian Open at Glen Abbey and a 29 at Pinehurst in 1977.

US wins 2 (1974-7)
US money $868,263 (1971–82) (48th all-time)

THOMSON, James USA
b. North Berwick, Scotland 1908

Jimmy Thomson emigrated to the USA as a boy of 12. He was for long much in demand for exhibitions on account of his remarkable driving. He once won a long-driving competition with a hit of 386 yards and in competition was the equivalent of the current longest drivers on the US Tour, averaging 270–280 yards. He gave two fine performances in major championships, coming second to Sam Parks in the 1935 US Open at Oakmont after leading at 36 holes, and was also runner-up to Densmore Shute in the 1936 US PGA. He came second in the Canadian Open that year. His best victory was in the 1938 Los Angeles Open.

THORPE, James Lee USA
b. Roxboro, North Carolina 1949

On 18 June 1981, Jim Thorpe became the first black man to lead the US Open when he birdied the last two holes at Merion for a 66. In the succeeding days he held his game together so that his following

177

scores of 73, 70, 72 brought him home tied for 11th. The prize money of $5,500 neared the amount he had won in the season up to that time. Jim Thorpe qualified for the US Tour for 1976 but the $2,000 he won was not enough for him to retain his player's card. He returned in 1979 and made the top 100 in the four following seasons, but never the Top 60.

US money $194,047 (1976–82) (190th all-time)

TORLUEMKE, Judy: see Rankin

TOSKI, Bob   USA
b. *Haydenville, Massachusetts 1927*

Standing only 5 feet 7 inches and lightly built, Bob Toski not surprisingly came to be known as the 'Mighty Mite'. He turned professional in 1945 and joined the US Tour three years later, first winning in 1953. The following season was easily his best, for he won four times, including the Tam o' Shanter 'World Championship', then worth $50,000 to the winner, and a series of exhibitions worth about the same amount. He was leading money-winner that year. In 1957 he stopped playing the Tour full-time to concentrate on teaching golf, at which he has built up a very high reputation, being much sought out by professionals. He has published *The Touch System to Better Golf*. He lost a play-off to Casper for the US Seniors.

US wins 7 (1953–8)
US money $101,253

TOUSHIN, Gail (née Denenberg)   USA
b. *New York 1947*

On the US Tour from 1969 Gail Toushin was in the Top 60 from 1970 to 1975, in 1978 and in 1979. Easily her best season was 1974 when she was 13th on the money list and won her only tournament, the Sears Classic. In 1981 she had her best round, a 65 in the Dinah Shore.

US wins 1 (1974)
US money $134,180 (1969–81)

TRAHAN, Sam   USA
b. *Franklin, Louisiana 1955*

Sam Trahan won the 1977 Southeastern Conference title and turned professional in 1978, qualifying in last place for the 1979 US Tour. In the IVB-

Philadelphia Classic that year he set the Tour record for the least putts used at 18. Alas, he did not score in the late 50s or even early 60s. Sam had a 70 only, having missed 14 greens, while his putt total had been assisted by three chip-ins. The 70 came in the final round, when he was already assured of $485, and the magic putter earned him only another $10. He finished the year in 217th money list place with $2,038, and does not now play on the US Tour. During the 18-putt round Trahan also set a nine-hole putting record with only eight on the last nine.

TRAVERS, Jerome Dunstan   USA
b. *New York 1887; d. 1951*

Jerry Travers was one of the outstanding US amateurs in the years leading up to World War I, battling in particular with Walter Travis for almost a decade for supremacy. He is the only man other than Bobby Jones to win four US Amateur Championships. He is also one of five amateurs to have won the US Open. His Open victory, which came in 1915 at Baltusrol, was particularly remarkable in that Travers had been considered good only at matchplay because erratic driving was apt to cost him too many strokes. Even more remarkable, perhaps, was that Travers did not defend his title the following year, and indeed never played in it again! The son of a rich man, Jerry Travers first competed in the US Amateur at the age of 15, and two years later began to make a reputation by beating Walter Travis in the final of the Nassau Invitational. His first US Amateur win followed in 1907, and he repeated it in 1908. Perhaps oddly, he did not enter the following two years, either through a waning of interest or because he had become a playboy and heavy drinker. He did, however, go to Britain in 1909, when he was knocked out in the first round of the Amateur Championship. He was back in the US Amateur in 1911, to be beaten by the eventual winner, the Englishman Harold Hilton. In 1912 he was champion again, beating the great Chick Evans in the final; he repeated his victory in 1913. He made a further effort to add the British title in 1914 but was again knocked out in the first round, not surprising as he had gone round the 18 holes in an estimated 90 strokes. However, he reached his fifth US Amateur final, being beaten by Francis Ouimet. In 1915 Travers announced his retirement for the first time, declaring that it was not possible to earn a

Walter Travis

fessional in 1927. Little was heard of him, however, and he spent the last ten years of his life as an aircraft-engine inspector at Pratt and Whitney.

TRAVIS, Walter J.   USA
b. Maldon, Australia 1867; d. 1927

Walter Travis did not try his hand at golf until he was in his mid 30s and then, within a couple of years, he was a championship contender. He won his first US Amateur at the age of 38 in 1900, won again the next year and also in 1903. He then decided to see what he could do to the British, and went over for the 1904 Amateur at Sandwich. At this time Travis was renowned mainly for his putting, though he was also a very straight, but short, hitter. In practice before the championship began he discovered that his putting had deserted him and in the end turned to a centre-shafted putter with a mallet type of head, called the Schenectady. He was himself again. He cruised through round after round of the championship, and in the last stage he, as one of the world's best putters, met Edward Blackwell, famed for his long driving. Travis was consistently outdriven by 50 yards and more but, by 4 and 3, he became the first overseas player to win the British Amateur. It was not a popular success: silence greeted his win. The British found him cold, and Travis thought them unfriendly and even hostile. A little later the R & A banned centre-shafted putters and Travis felt this was another example of enmity, with the irony that it was largely through chance that he had used a Schenectady to win the title. Travis reached the semi-finals of the US Amateur in 1898, 1899, 1906, 1908 and 1914 and was second in the 1902 US Open. In 1905 he founded *The American Golfer* and continued to edit the magazine for many years while he went on playing tournament golf (he won his last event at the age of 54, the Metropolitan Amateur) and took up course designing. He was declared to have forfeited his amateur status in 1910 because of these activities, but it was later restored.

TREVINO, Lee Buck   USA
b. Dallas, Texas 1939

Lee Trevino turned professional in 1960, but for several years confined himself to local competition and money matches. In 1966 he qualified for the US Open and won $600, so he decided to give it a try again the following year. This time he finished a

living and play championship-standard golf as well; but it is more likely that he had lost the desire to compete, which was so central to his success. Travers, in fact, has sometimes been judged as one of the most supreme competitors of all. He is surely the only golfer of comparable stature who as often as not used an iron off the tee because of unreliable wooden club play. He was at his best near the green, and one of the relatively few early players to devote far more time to the short game than the long. His reward was that he became one of the greatest putters ever. After trying a great variety of methods in order to see what the results of each were, he decided that the cardinal rules for him were that the stance should be upright, the body must be kept still and that the putterhead must follow through on line. Among other achievements Travers won the New Jersey Amateur three times and the Metropolitan Amateur five times. He played in some war-time exhibitions, but when peace returned he had lost the desire or nerve to win championships. With the Depression, he lost what remained of his money and turned pro-

scarcely noticed fifth. Continuing to play the US Tour that year, he totalled over $26,000. He realized that he must be rather better than he had thought, and that there was real money to be made in this game of golf. He became a name to be reckoned with during the 1968 US Open at Oak Hill. For two rounds, Bert Yancey played superbly for 67, 68 – but Trevino, with 69, 68 was not far behind. With 70 to Trevino's 69, Yancey still led into the final round, but then began to miss putts and finished in 76 for third place. Nicklaus from well back made a last-round charge for a 67, which was good for second place but still 4 strokes worse than Trevino's total after a closing 69. His 275 equalled the Open record, and he was the first to break 70 in every round. A major new figure had arrived, though this was by no means clear to all at the time. One eminent British golf writer described the Trevino swing as 'agricultural'. Although that judgement proved very wide of the mark, Trevino himself did not realize at the time that he was a major player, and did not rate his swing highly. It has been written about Hogan that his method was made up of 'compensations', but this has never been more so than with Trevino. He is a hooker who fades the ball. His grip is too strong with the left and the clubface is almost fully closed at the top of the backswing: together these should mean that he hits every shot sharply left. That is where the compensations come in. In his set-up Trevino plays from just about the most open stance ever seen, lifts the club at the beginning of the back-swing, and on the downswing leads emphatically with the legs and pulls the club into the ball with a left-side dominant action, both of which help to keep the face open. The particular features that have helped his great consistency are that his swing is flat at the bottom of its arc, both before and after the strike point. The clubface is therefore at, and along the target line far longer than it is with most players, which at worst helps to ensure that bad shots are not very bad. His shape of shot is based on the thought that 'You can talk to a fade but a hook doesn't want to listen.' Trevino carries this method through to his short game also, still believing that every shot is a kind of left-handed backhand, where a majority argue that the chip is best seen as a bowling action with the right hand and that in putting the left hand controls the club while the right provides the hit. However, it was not his golf that so quickly made Trevino a big name but his personality. Both press and galleries warmed to

a man who made golf seem a good deal less grim, who liked to crack a joke and chat away between shots. There was also the 'rags to riches' element. Trevino had grown up on the wrong side of the track, had left school early, and his first job was as handyman on a pitch-and-putt course. After some four years in the US Marines he worked in El Paso in the unglamorous role of assistant. Although he was able to develop his golf, a main part of his job was to polish shoes and clubs, fit grips and shafts, generally help out in the pro shop, and teach. He was paid $30 a week. Trevino ended his 1968 season at sixth in the money list, adding a win in the Hawaiian Open. Over in Britain to play in the Alcan Golfer of the Year, he attracted much publicity, both favourable and the opposite by turning up in top hat and tails. It was his response to the suggestion that his standard of dress was not high. The 1969 Alcan at Portland, Oregon, also provided Trevino with some memorable moments. He eagled the 15th in his final round to establish a 6-stroke lead on Billy Casper, and it was little matter that he dropped a shot on the next. However, on the 17th, a par 3, he underclubbed, buried his ball in a bunker lip, took two to get out – and then three-putted. On the last, he narrowly missed a 5-yard putt for a birdie. His finish therefore was 5, 6, 4. Casper's was 3, 2, 3 and thank you very much for the cheque. Trevino won a tournament that year, however, and was seventh on the money list. He also won the World Cup individual title, but otherwise it was a year of little progress. In 1970 his trademark of consistency was first fully apparent. He won the first of his five Vardon stroke-average trophies (the first of three in succession) and was leading money-winner. He also made his first real impact in Europe by finishing joint third in the British Open, a final-round 77 dropping him out of the lead. The following year he became fully recognized as a great player, in four weeks winning the US, Canadian and British Opens. In the US Open he tied with Nicklaus at Merion and then won the play-off 68–71. The British Open was really a three-way battle between Trevino, Lu Liang-Huan and Tony Jacklin, with Trevino coming home by 1 stroke, after taking a 7 on the 71st hole. He had already won the Tallahassee and the Memphis Classic, which amounted to five wins in 11 weeks. Victories in both US and British Opens had been achieved before only by Jones in 1930, Sarazen in 1932 and Hogan in 1953. Since then Tom Watson has followed in 1982. Trevino won the British Open again

Lee Trevino

US Masters. Trevino believes that to play Augusta it is necessary to draw the ball and hit high shots. But his shape of shot is low and faded. Consequently he has sometimes declined to play, but when he has, his best finishes have been 10th in 1975 and 14th in 1978. Usually he does not at all feature on the leader board. This may reveal a flaw in his competitive make-up: he is not a battler against odds in the Gary Player or Jack Nicklaus mould. If Trevino is not playing well, he tends to fall well down the field, particularly in the major championships. On the US Tour it is more often a different story: he has had his share of wins coming from behind and his overall record is highly consistent. From 1968 to 1975 he was never worse than ninth on the money list and from 1970 to 1974 constantly in the top four. The seasons of 1976 and 1977 were a little below standard, mainly the result of back trouble that necessitated an operation, but he came back into the top six each year from 1978 to 1980. The last of these years was particularly remarkable. He was second in the money list with $385,814 (then the third most ever), won three events, was second three times, in the top ten 13 times and in 21 US entries won money every time. His Vardon-winning stroke average of 69.73 was the lowest since Sam Snead's 69.23 in 1950. Inevitable decline may at last have set in, unless a 1982 back operation has cured the damage caused to the lower spine by Trevino's idiosyncratic swing. However, another victory in 1981 extended his sequence of winning years to 14, which was broken in 1982 though he was third in the Sun City Challenge after a last-round 67. Trevino played in every Ryder Cup side from 1969 to 1979 save 1977, and compiled a singles record of 5½ points out of 7, and in foursomes and four-balls 10 points out of 17. He was in the US World Cup pair five times.

US wins 26 (1968–81)
US money $2,643,085 (1966–82) (3rd all-time)
Overseas wins 9 (1971–82)
Europe money £94,250 (1970–82) (40th all-time)
World money $3,499,470 (1966–82) (2nd all-time)

the following year, in one of the most memorable tournaments ever. Paired with Jacklin over the final two rounds, he had luck running his way, first with a thinned bunker shot that hit the flag and fell in, followed by long putts and chip-ins, the climax of which was a chip that went down on the 71st hole when the championship seemed to be in Jacklin's grasp. One more major championship was to follow, the 1974 US PGA when, after an opening 73, he caught and passed many players with 66, 68, 69 to beat Nicklaus by 1 stroke. Since that time he has not often been a contender in major championships. He was fourth in the 1977 British Open at Turnberry, but never really within reach of the kind of golf that Watson and Nicklaus were playing that week. He came second in the same event in 1980. That year Trevino was the in-form player and after two rounds led Watson, eventual winner, by 3 strokes with his 68, 67 start at Muirfield; but Watson then produced a 64 and that, more or less, was that. So far no mention has been made of the

TURNESA, James USA
b. Elmsford, New York 1912; d. 1971

The sixth son of Vitale Turnesa, a greenkeeper, Jim, like all but one of his brothers, turned professional in 1931. In the 1952 US PGA he beat Chick Harbert in the final. In 1942 he had also reached the final but on that occasion had presented Sam Snead with his first major championship victory, though Turnesa had held the lead at one point. He was also third in the 1948 US Open and fourth the following year, and was fourth in the 1949 US Masters. He played in the 1953 Ryder Cup, winning his singles.

TURNESA, Joseph   USA
b. Elmsford, New York 1901

Joe Turnesa's best years came at the end of the 1920s. In 1926 he came close to the US Open title, losing by 1 stroke to Jones after he had finished in 77 to Jones's 73. He finished sixth in 1928. In between, he reached the final of the 1927 US PGA, where he met Walter Hagen and lost by 1 down. Hagen was 30 minutes late for the start of the match. After conceding three longish putts he said: 'That makes up for me being late. Now we'll play!' Turnesa played in the US Ryder Cup team in 1927 and 1929. In the first match he won in foursomes and lost to George Duncan in singles, and on the second occasion halved in foursomes and lost his singles to Aubrey Boomer.

TURNESA, William P.   USA
b. Elmsford, New York 1914

The youngest of the Turnesa brothers and the only one of seven not to turn professional, 'Willie the Wedge' was a leading US amateur in the years before and after World War II. In 1938 he won the US Amateur, beating his opponent 8 and 7 in the final, during which he is said to have got down in two strokes from off the green in about half the holes played, largely the result of his old rusty-headed wedge. He won again in 1948, this time beating Ray Billows. He was almost as successful in Britain, taking the Amateur title in 1947 with a win over Dick Chapman in the final. He reached that stage again in 1949 but was this time defeated by Irishman Max McCready. It was reported that in the semi-final that year he missed the fairway with just about every tee shot but was still round in an approximate 71. Turnesa also won the Metropolitan Amateur and the North and South. He was in the Walker Cup team from 1947 to 1951, and captain in his final year. He won both his matches in 1947 but in 1949 came up against Ronnie White at the peak of his form, losing when they met in the foursomes and also losing to him by 4 and 3 in the top singles. In his last appearance he won in foursomes but lost to Alex Kyle in singles.

Howard Twitty

TWITTY, Howard Allen   USA
b. Phoenix, Arizona 1949

As an amateur, 6-foot 5-inch Howard Twitty was an All-American in 1970 and 1972, and in the NCAA Championship the latter year finished immediately behind Tom Kite and Ben Crenshaw. In 1973 he turned professional but could not win his Tour place for a while. He filled in time overseas and won the 1975 Thailand Open. He has been on the US Tour since 1975 and was in the Top 60 from 1976 to 1980. In the last of these years he had a remarkable spell for three and a half weeks when he was 57 under par for a 14-round sequence. Thirteen of those rounds were in the 60s and included a 63, a 64 and five 66s. They allowed him, among other high placings, to win the Greater Hartford Open. The previous year he had won the BC Open. In 1981 his placing in the US money list qualified him for a Ryder Cup place as long as an outsider did not win the PGA Championship. He lost his place when Larry Nelson won it.

US wins 2 (1979–80)
US money $670,649 (1975–82) (67th all-time)

UPDEGRAFF, Dr Edgar R.   USA
b. Boone, Iowa 1922

Winner of the Western Amateur in 1957 and 1959, the Southwestern three times and the Sunnehanna and Pacific Coast once each, Ed Updegraff also reached the semi-final stage of the 1963 British Amateur. He was a Walker Cup team member in 1963, 1965 and 1969. He halved and won in foursomes the first year and beat Joe Carr 4 and 3 in singles. In 1965 he played in only a singles and lost to Michael Lunt, and in 1969 he won and lost in singles and lost a foursome. He was non-playing captain of the 1975 Walker Cup team, and won the 1982 US Seniors. By profession he is a urologist.

URZETTA, Sam   USA
b. Rochester, New York 1926

Sam Urzetta has two very considerable achievements to his name. He won the 1950 US Amateur against the great Frank Stranahan on the 39th hole, and played in the 1951 and 1953 US Walker Cup teams where he had the unblemished record of four matches, four wins. He turned professional in 1955 and won regional events.

VALENTINE, Thomas Ervin   USA
b. Atlanta, Georgia 1949

As an amateur, Tommy Valentine won the 1970 South East Conference title and was an All-American from 1970 to 1971. He turned professional in 1974 and qualified for the US Tour in 1977, having to requalify in 1978. In 1981 he finished 39th in the money list, was third in the LaJet Classic and tied with Tom Watson for the Atlanta Classic, losing the play-off. He has won twice in Canada and won the Johnny Miller Invitational, a non-Tour event, in 1980. He is, at an average of 270 yards, one of the US Tour's longest hitters.

US money $225,043 (1977–82) (177th all-time)

VARE, Glenna: see Collett

VENTURI, Kenneth   USA
b. San Francisco, California 1931

Ken Venturi was runner-up for the 1948 US Junior Championship, the first, and was a Walker Cup player in 1953, with Sam Urzetta beating Joe Carr and Ronnie White in foursomes and winning his singles by 9 and 8. Three years later he was a leading participant in one of the most dramatic of US Masters. Still an amateur, Venturi began 66, 69 to lead and, as the weather worsened, his third-round 75 did him little harm. In the final round

there were only two scores as good as 71, but one of them came from Jack Burke and it carried him to a 1-stroke victory over Ken Venturi, who had an 80. With two holes to go, he was still leading but had a 5 on the 17th to Burke's birdie 3. Shortly after that he turned professional. In 1960 he had his second daunting experience in the US Masters. After three rounds he lay 1 behind Arnold Palmer but with two holes to go on the final day had changed this to a 1-stroke advantage. Palmer then birdied the last two to win by 1 stroke. At this stage in his career Venturi was noted as a superb iron player and had become a frequent winner on the US Tour. In his first year, 1957, he was tenth in the money list and followed with third, tenth, second. From 1957 to 1960 he had ten Tour wins, four of them in 1958. At about this time he decided that he needed more length from the tee, and worked on drawing the ball for extra run. He lost consistency and then found he could not change back to his old method. Additionally he began to suffer difficulties with his hands, and for a period was also partially paralysed down the right side of his body. In 1962 he won $6,951 for 66th place and the following year just $3,848 for 94th. It was a shift of fortune as catastrophic as Johnny Miller's in the late 1970s. In 1964 his iron play began to come back: he had a third place in a US Tour event and qualified for the Open at Congressional for the first time in four years. He began 72, 70, which put him 6 behind Tommy Jacobs, who had had a 64, and 5 behind Arnold Palmer, who had begun 68, 69. Two rounds were still to be played on the final day. Venturi went to the turn in 30, coming home in 66 which put him 4 ahead of Palmer, 7 ahead of Bob Charles but still 2 behind Tommy Jacobs. Heat and humidity had been high and Venturi seemed to be the worst affected of anyone. There was considerable doubt that he would be able to carry on, and he was accompanied by a doctor throughout the last round. His energy revived towards the close as the championship neared his grasp. His final 70 far outscored both Palmer and Jacobs, whom he beat by 4. Venturi added two more wins that season to be sixth on the money list, but his health collapsed again the following year, when he won just $295 though he played in that year's Ryder Cup, losing his singles. He won again in 1966 but, apart from a moderate 1967 season, that was the end of his career. He is now a commentator for CBS.

US wins 14 (1957–66)

US money $268,293 (1957–75) (163rd all-time)

VINES, Ellsworth   USA
b. *Pasadena, California 1911*

Winner of the British Open in 1932 and the US
Open in 1931 and 1932, Ellsworth Vines performed
these feats at Wimbledon and Forest Hills rather
than St Andrews and Baltusrol. Although his
golfing feats did not match his tennis performances, Vines did become a top-class golfer, turning
professional in 1942. He won several tournaments,
was runner-up in the 1946 All-American Open and
reached the semi-finals of the 1951 US PGA.
Perhaps only Babe Zaharias has switched from
other sports to golf with more success – though
some readers may have their own candidates, for
example Lottie Dod.

VOIGT, George   USA
b. *Buffalo, New York 1894*

A prominent name in amateur golf during the
1920s and 1930s, Voigt had the prevention of the
Jones Grand Slam in his hands when he was 2 up
with 5 to play in the 1930 British Amateur. He
promptly drove out of bounds and Jones was
eventually able to win on the last hole. Voigt
played in the Walker Cup from 1926 to 1930 and
had an excellent record: of his six matches he won
five, losing only in a foursome in 1930 to Cyril
Tolley and Roger Wethered. He compensated the
following day by annihilating Sir Ernest Holderness by 10 and 8. Voigt won the North and South
three times in a row from 1927 to 1929, and
reached the semi-finals of the US Amateur in 1935,
where he lost to Lawson Little, the eventual champion.

WADKINS, Jerry Lanston   USA
b. *Richmond, Virginia 1949*

Lanny Wadkins had a brilliant career as an amateur. At the age of only 16 he finished well up the
field in the US Amateur, 9 strokes behind the
winner. In 1968 he won the Southern Amateur,
followed by the Eastern Amateur the following
year. In 1970 he had the best record of anyone,
winning the Southern again, the Western and the
US Amateur Championships. He was in the 1969
and 1971 Walker Cup teams and in the latter year,
playing number one against Michael Bonallack,
was one of only two US singles winners on the
final day. He turned professional towards the end
of that year and went on the US Tour, having

already finished runner-up in one Tour event, the
1970 Heritage Classic. In his first full year, 1972, he
won the Sahara Invitational, took in $116,616 and
was tenth on the money list, one of the best
performances by a first-year player. It won him the
Rookie of the Year award and set a record in money
winnings at the time. The following year he took
two tournaments, topped $200,000 and was fifth in
the money list. At the time, he seemed set to be one
of the greatest stars of the Tour. Since then there
has by no means been steady progress: he has had
brilliant years and relatively poor ones, the overall
results reflecting the fact that in individual tournaments he is either very, very good or distinctly
poor. He fell away to 54th place in 1974, impeded
by gall-bladder problems; he came back, in his
opinion, too soon so that his 1975 and 1976 results
kept him out of the Top 60 both years. However, he
then followed with arguably his best year in 1977.
In the US PGA he had the steady scoring of 69, 71,
72, 70 – very good for Pebble Beach – and tied with
Gene Littler who had had the championship in his
grasp with nine holes to go after his first three
rounds of 67, 69, 70. He collapsed in the closing
stages and Wadkins and Littler played off, with the
US PGA becoming Wadkins's second major championship (after the US Amateur) on the third play-
off hole. His achievement attracted less attention

Lanny Wadkins

than it otherwise might have done because Littler's narrow failure at the age of 47 made better copy. Wadkins went on to win the World Series of Golf later in the year, and was third in the US money list with some $244,000. On the Tour in 1978 his form fell away considerably and he just failed to make the Top 60, but he won twice outside the USA, in the Canadian PGA – by 12 strokes – and the Garden State PGA in Australia. The following year he was back to form again, giving one of his career-finest performances in the Tournament Players' Championship. He began 67, 68 to lead George Burns by 3 strokes and still held a 3-stroke lead after a third-round 76, mostly caused by strong winds. On the final day conditions worsened, with gale-force gusts, but Wadkins played a superb 72 to win by 5 strokes. His scoring in the last two rounds can be compared to Burns's finish of 76, 83 or, more strikingly, to that of Dan Halldorson. The Canadian had been well placed after a start of 69, 70 but finished 81, 89! Wadkins also won the Los Angeles Open and the Bridgestone Open in Japan. His performances in the next two years were again poor by his standards – 58th and 81st in the money list – but there was an upswing again in 1982 when he won the Tournament of Champions and two other titles. Early in the year he scored 65, 70, 63, 65 to win the Phoenix Open by 6 strokes, and he defeated the new US Masters Champion by 3 strokes in the Tournament of Champions. He finished seventh in the money list for the year with over $300,000. Lanny Wadkins was in the US Ryder Cup team in 1977 and 1979, and had an almost 90% success rate in his matches. A main reason for his variation in form is that Wadkins is no journeyman professional, but plays a fast attacking game. He always tries to rip his iron shots in at the flag in a cavalier style. When things go well they go brilliantly; but then there are spells when his bold play is punished rather than rewarded.

US wins 10 (1972–82)
US money $1,359,173 (1971–82) (18th all-time)
World money $1,791,454 (1971–82) (18th all-time)

WADKINS, Robert Edwin   USA
b. Richmond, Virginia 1951

The younger brother of Lanny, Bobby Wadkins once shared the Richmond junior title with him for six consecutive years. He had a less successful amateur career than his brother but won the Virginia Amateur and was an All-American choice in 1972 and 1973. He has been on the US Tour since 1975. He first attracted attention in 1977 when he led the Memorial after one round with a 67 which included a second nine in 29 strokes. In 1978 he made the Top 60 and was second in the Tucson Open, but his best result was to win the European Open at Walton Heath after a play-off with Bernard Gallacher and Gil Morgan in a very strong international field that included at least 20 top players from the US Tour. In 1979 his position improved to 28th on the US Tour and he tied for the IVB-Philadelphia Classic, losing the play-off to Lou Graham. He also won the Dunlop Phoenix in Japan. In 1980 and 1981 he won over $50,000 each year, but was still out of the Top 60.

US money $443,980 (1975–82) (104th all-time)
Overseas wins 2 (1978–9)

WALKER, Cyril   USA
b. Manchester, England 1892; d. 1948

Ten years after emigrating to the USA in 1914, Cyril Walker became one of the most surprising winners of the US Open at Oakland Hills. With rounds of 74, 74, 74, 75, he finished 3 strokes ahead of Bobby Jones, the previous year's champion. Walker was a short hitter with an excellent short game, but little was heard of him after his Open success.

WALL, Arthur J.   USA
b. Honesdale, Pennsylvania 1923

Always an outstanding putter, Art Wall had an exceptionally long playing career on the US Tour and, approaching 60, was still one of the most effective players on the US Senior Tour, winning the 1978 US National Senior Open and the Legends of Golf with Tommy Bolt in 1980. He first played the Tour in 1949 and by 1952 was in the Top 60, where he was to remain until 1965, to return again from 1966 to 1968, and in 1971 and 1975. One of his more remarkable feats was to win the Greater Mikwaukee Open in 1975, one of the oldest ever to take a Tour event at the age of 51. He had not won since 1966 and, oddly, had played 35 tournament rounds before Milwaukee without once breaking 70. There he began 67, 67, 67, and a closing 70 gave him a 1-stroke victory. Art Wall first won in 1953 and the following year took the Tournament of Champions. In 1957 and 1958 he was seventh and fifth on the money list, but 1959 was his greatest year. He won four Tour events including the

Crosby and the US Masters. In the latter he began 73, 74, 71 and went into the last round 6 strokes behind Arnold Palmer and Canadian Stan Leonard. In his last-round 66 Wall had eight birdies, but even more unusual was his finish of 5 under par for the last six holes, ending with a 12-foot putt on the last hole. He beat Cary Middlecoff by 1 stroke. The same year he was leading money-winner with $53,167 and US PGA Player of the Year, and won the Vardon Trophy for lowest stroke average. Beside his 14 US Tour wins, which include the 1960 Canadian Open, Art Wall won ten events on the Caribbean circuit and was a Ryder Cup player from 1957 to 1961. Holes in one are one of the mysteries of golf. Harry Vardon, for instance, had only one in his playing life. Art Wall held the record, which he has probably increased by now, of an astonishing 41.

US wins 14 (1953–75)
US money $638,816 (1950–81) (73rd all-time)

Harvie Ward

WARD, E. Harvie USA
b. Tarboro, North Carolina 1925

The 1952 British Amateur was Harvie Ward's first taste of international competition and he won it defeating the formidable Frank Stranahan 6 and 5 in the final. He reached the final again the following year, but this time was bested in a close-fought match by Joe Carr, the best British amateur at the time. Ward made a tremendous impression in Britain and many judges thought him the best amateur seen since Bobby Jones and a superb swinger of the club, perhaps the best in golf at the time. In the USA, however, he did not have a comparable reputation, although he had won the 1948 National Collegiate and the North and South. He then won the Canadian Amateur in 1954 and won the US Amateur in both 1955 and 1956, beating Bill Hyndman in the first of these finals by 9 and 8 and then Charles Kocsis 5 and 4. It was discovered in 1957 that he had received expenses from his employer while playing in competition, and his amateur status was withdrawn for about a year. If the employer had merely paid him a higher salary, there would have been no difficulty. Thereafter Ward's feelings towards amateur golf were perhaps soured and he was never again quite as good a player, though he continued to represent the USA for a short time. He was in the US Americas Cup team from 1952 to 1958 and played in the Walker Cup in 1953, 1955 and 1959. He won all six of his matches, in singles defeating Joe Carr by 4 and 3, Ronnie White 6 and 5 and Guy Wolstenholme 9 and 8. He was twice low amateur in the US Open and three times in the Masters, fourth in the 1957 US Masters being his best finish.

WARD, Marvin Harvey USA
b. Olympia, Washington 1913; d. 1968

Bud Ward was twice a winner of the US Amateur in 1939 and 1941. In 1939 he came fourth in the US Open, only 1 stroke behind the three-way play-off for the championship. He was fifth in 1947. He also won the Northwest Open five times in his home area and the Western Amateur three times. He played in two Walker Cup matches, 1938 and 1947, losing in foursomes both years; but he had a dramatic record in singles. On the losing 1938 US team he demolished Frank Pennick by 12 and 11, and in 1947 won the top singles 5 and 3 against Leonard Crawley. He later became a club professional.

Jo Ann Washam

WASHAM, Jo Ann   USA
b. Auburn, Washington 1950

One of the longest hitters amongst American women, Jo Ann Washam nevertheless did not have a strong amateur record behind her when she turned professional in 1973. By 1975 she was a leading player, having two tournament wins that season and finishing 12th in the money list. She was in the top 16 in 1979 and 1980, and won another Tour event in 1979. However, perhaps her best season, though she did not win, was 1980. That year she had her lowest stroke average at 73.01 and won $107,063 for the year. She also had a second place during 1982. Jo Ann has two unofficial events to her credit: the 1976 Mixed Team Championship with Juan Rodriguez, and the 1979 Portland Ping Team event with Nancy Lopez. She is the only US Tour player to have twice holed in one during a tournament round, performing the feat during the 1979 Kemper Open.

US wins 3 (1975–9)
US money $414,596 (1973–82)

WATROUS, Andrew Albert   USA
b. Yonkers, New York 1899

Al Watrous turned professional in 1920, and in 1922 came perhaps his most prestigious victory, the Canadian Open. Among many other wins he took the 1926 Western Open. Perhaps most remembered, however, is his second place at Royal Lytham in the 1926 Open – because of another

man's master shot. After a third-round 69 Watrous led Jones by 2 strokes and had maintained exactly that lead with five holes to play. However, Jones was level on the 17th tee. Watrous drove well and put his second on the green, while Jones was in sand away to the left. His famous 170-yard shot carrying much rough country to the green then followed, while Watrous, shaken by seeing the championship slipping from his grasp, three-putted. He played three times for the USA against Great Britain and Ireland, losing both his matches in 1926, winning both in 1927 and losing his singles to Henry Cotton in 1929. As a club professional Al Watrous became part of the fixtures at Oakland Hills, and while there won the Michigan Open six times and the PGA on nine occasions. He also proved a formidable senior golfer, winning the PGA Seniors in 1950, 1951 and 1957, the year he also won the International Seniors.

Al Watrous

WATSON, Thomas Sturges   USA

b. Kansas City, Missouri 1949

British Open Champion: 1975, 1977, 1980, 1982
US Masters Champion: 1977, 1981
US Open Champion: 1982

Two months in the summer of 1982 have elevated
Tom Watson from the ranks of great moderns to
those of the great players of all eras. A third-round
68, after a pair of 72s at Pebble Beach in the US
Open, moved Tom Watson into a tie for the lead
with Bill Rogers, with Jack Nicklaus 3 strokes
behind. It seemed that another duel between Nicklaus and Watson was in prospect, with both highly
motivated. Nicklaus is aware that his time as a
major championship winner is limited and seeks to
be the only man in history to win the US Open five
times; Watson carried the burden of having won
five major championships while his record still
lacked the essential US Open title. There was, of
course, the third man, Bill Rogers, who had come
close the year before and gone on to win the British
Open; and for a while a fourth appeared, David
Graham, US Open holder. It was Nicklaus who first
stirred the senses. After beginning with a dropped
shot he birdied five holes in a row from the 3rd to
make up his deficit. The 10th and 11th were the
first crisis points. On the 10th Watson holed from
about 20 feet to save his par while ahead Nicklaus
putted past the hole and missed the return. Nicklaus, Graham and Rogers were 1 behind Watson. By
the 13th Rogers, who had begun missing short
putts, and Graham, who put his approach in the
collar of rough around the green and dropped two
strokes on the hole, were out of it. The contest was
a match between Nicklaus and Watson, the advantage moving from man to man. Nicklaus put in a
fine enough finish. He birdied the 15th to share the
lead and had chances on each of the final holes, but
succeeded only with his final putt. Playing about
two holes behind, Watson holed an unlikely downhill putt of more than 15 yards to lead again but
was then bunkered badly on the next and had to
play out sideways. His third shot at this 403-yard
16th was a touch too strong and he was well to the
back of the green, three putts more than a possibility; but he got the approach putt close. With two
to play Watson had to finish in par to earn a play-
off. On the 209-yard 17th he hit a 2-iron about level
with the flag and only 4 to 5 yards away, but though
so near, it was in grass about 5 inches deep. Watson
then played a stroke of which he is a master: a firm,

high pop into the air with a sand iron – and in it
went. Needing only a par now on the 548-yard last
hole, but with the Pacific uninviting on the left, he
played a 3-wood from the tee, followed by a
cautious move up the fairway with an iron and
then a 7-iron to about 5 yards for a safe par. It was
by then almost an irrelevance that he holed it for a
2-stroke victory. And so to Troon and the British
Open. He began competently with 69, 71, good

Tom Watson

enough most years to be near or in the lead, but not with Clampett producing one of the greatest starts ever in a major championship with 67, 66. Watson's 74 in the third round should have gained him no ground at all, but it was an oddity of the third day's play that no one made a move, while Clampett with a 78 gave all his pursuers cause for hope. Watson did not then produce a dazzling last round; he merely did nothing very much wrong with a single key shot, a 3-iron on the par-5 11th to 4 feet for an eagle. His 70 was good enough to overhaul the leaders and to keep those behind him at bay. Watson himself felt that he had fairly won the 1982 US Open, but that its British equivalent had been handed to him. In this he did himself less than justice: his nerve was strongest. It was not always so. He came to the US Tour in 1971 with a moderate record in amateur golf – four wins in the Missouri Amateur – and played a few events. In 1972 he won some $30,000 and came close to a tournament win, finishing 1 stroke behind Deane Beman in the Quad Cities Open. In 1973 he began to be known, but more for losing tournaments than for winning them. In the Hawaiian Open he began 68, 65, 68 to lead by 3 strokes, but collapsed to a 75 to allow John Schlee to win his only tournament. There was a similar story in the mammoth World Open, played for a $100,000 first prize over ten rounds at Pinehurst. In the fifth round Watson found himself 6 ahead of the field after a 62 but then had a pair of 76s and a 77 to be fourth. He had, however, become an established player, at 35th in the US money list. In 1974 he first contended for a major championship. At Winged Foot in the US Open he had a 1-stroke lead after three rounds but, as he said, 'blew it' with a final 79. The same month he at last became a winner, taking the Western Open from 6 strokes behind with a last-round 69. By the end of 1975 he was more fully accepted as a new major player, with 12 top-10 finishes and seventh place in the US money list. But there were disasters too. A couple of tee shots into water during the Masters dropped him down the field, and his experience in the US Open at Medinah must have left scars. He led after a first-round 67 and, with a following 68, had tied the US Open record for 36 holes. How good this scoring over Medinah was is emphasized by the fact that his horrid final rounds of 78, 77 still had him only 3 strokes behind Lou Graham, the winner. But perhaps the learning process was continuing. Watson went off to Carnoustie in Scotland to see

what the British Open was like. Throughout he captured little attention – the TV cameras ignored him almost totally – but he entered the final day 2 strokes behind Jack Newton, with whom he was to play off, and 3 behind Bobby Cole, who had had a pair of 66s. Many were still in contention but Watson produced the steadiest golf of any of them; yet oddly his finish was technically not good. On the long par-3 16th he thinned a tee shot right and was 30 yards from the green and dropped a shot; on the next he cut his iron shot to the green but got down in two more; but then on the last he holed a putt of at least 5 yards for a birdie. The last hole was again kind to him the next day: he parred and Newton did not in the 18-hole play-off and Watson had his major championship, one of the few (Hogan, Lema and Rogers are others) to win the British Open at first sight of linksland golf. Later in the year he won the World Series; but the following year he did not make the move to the top that many had expected, finishing 12th in the US money list without a win. However, 1977 was his first great year. He won four US Tour events, one of which was the US Masters. With scores of 70, 69, 70, 67 he beat Jack Nicklaus by 2 strokes. Although they were not playing together in the final round it was their first real confrontation in a major championship, the result in balance until near the end. They were level until Watson holed a 6-yard putt on the 17th to lead and Nicklaus, ahead, dropped a shot on the last. Three months later the two were at Turnberry for the British Open. Here both Watson and Nicklaus began 68, 70 and were paired for the third round. Both with 65s, they outdistanced the remainder of the field, except for Ben Crenshaw, who was 3 strokes behind but was not long to remain a factor in the last round. This was almost a repeat of round three. Nicklaus established a lead but was first caught and then passed by Watson, who birdied the par-5 17th while Nicklaus did not, missing a short putt. On the last Watson banged an iron down the middle, while Nicklaus, having to birdie, went for length and pushed his drive well right, nearly into bushes. Watson then sent his short-iron in to a couple of feet and it was all over. Or was it? The drama was not quite over. Nicklaus managed to find the green and then holed a putt right across the green; but the nerve of perhaps the world's best short putter held. Watson finished just 1 ahead of Nicklaus but 11 strokes ahead of Hubert Green in third place, his 268 total having smashed the Open record by 8 strokes. It has not since been approached – except by Watson himself. At the end of the US Tour season Watson was leading money-winner, Vardon Trophy holder with a stroke average of 70.32 and Player of the Year. In some respects 1978 saw a repeat performance. Watson won five US events, his money winnings rose some $42,000 to $362,429, a new record; he had reached $1 million quicker than anyone; and he was again Player of the Year and Vardon Trophy winner with 70.16, the lowest for ten years. He did not add to his major championships. In the Masters he was joint second, 1 stroke behind Gary Player; was sixth in the US Open; challenged for the British Open but faded to 14th; and led the US PGA after each of the first three rounds but was caught in the last round and lost the play-off. In 1979 he increased the US Tour money record to $462,636, won the Vardon Trophy with 70.27 and was again Player of the Year. No one else had accomplished these three feats twice in a row, let alone three. He won five events, including the prestige Tournament of Champions, by 6 strokes, and the Memorial. In the major championships he lost a play-off for the Masters to Zoeller; missed the cut in the US Open; had a surprising 81 in the last round of the British Open; and was 12th in the US PGA, though he had led after the first round. Still Watson's best season lay ahead. In the 1980 US Tour he was in 22 events, won money in every one of them and was in the top 10 for 16 of those entries. More important than this consistency, however, he won six tournaments. All of that was worth $530,808. Between 20 April and 25 May he produced a sequence of first, first, first, joint fourth, second, which was worth $198,600. In the three US major championships, he was joint 12th at Augusta, joint third in the US Open and joint tenth in the US PGA. In the British Open he began 68, 70 at Muirfield, which left him 3 behind Lee Trevino, who was also having a good year. Watson then put in a 64 to lead by 4 strokes, and in the final round no one bettered his 69. He was British Open Champion for the third time. Late in the year he won the Dunlop Phoenix in Japan. His stroke average in the US was down to 69.95. Of his performance in 1981 Watson said: 'I fought myself and my swing.' This is the kind of remark normally made by a player who has scored badly all year. However, he still won three times in the US, including his second Masters, though he finished well down the field in the US and British Opens and PGA. Nevertheless he was third in the money list. He topped $300,000 for the fifth time, and in

1982 made that six times. Only Tom Kite and Ray Floyd have done it twice. Why has Tom Watson become so dominant a player? I think we might rate nerve as highly as anything: the quality which the early Watson seemed to lack but which is now fully present in a close-fought finale, whether he is coming from behind or in the equally testing position of having to conquer the fear of surrendering a commanding lead. As to his technique, it is becoming increasingly recognized that he is one of the best putters to appear in the history of golf. On this topic, the US Tour statistics for the 1980 and 1981 seasons are particularly revealing. He averaged 28.93 per round in 1980 and 28.71 in 1981, in each case being second in the rankings. Mere numbers apart, Watson is conspicuously the man who seems almost always to coast his long putts dead to the hole and hit the short ones firmly home. 'Firm' indeed is a word that has much to do with his putting grip. Most great putters of the past have stressed that the putter should be held gently (Locke declared so tenderly that the club should almost fall out of the hands) but Watson does not agree, perhaps feeling that too loose a grip tends to allow the clubhead to waver from being square to the line. Equally important, there is no weak feature to his game. Of Nicklaus, for instance, it has been said that he 'has no sand iron'; of Palmer that he was a poor wedge player; others have been too short from the tee or too wild. Apart from Watson's strength in putting he rates highly as a bunker player, and in driving length is only a dozen yards or so shorter than the longest hitters.

US wins 28 (1974–82)
US money $2,866,384 (1971–82) (2nd all-time)
Overseas wins 5 (1975–82)
Europe money £97,283 (1975–82) (39th all-time)
World money $3,352,489 (1971–82) (3rd all-time)

WEAVER, DeWitt   USA
b. *Danville, Kentucky 1939*

DeWitt Weaver first tried the US Tour in 1964 but decided that his game was not good enough and so disappeared to a club job. He returned in 1967. He was an exceptionally long hitter but lacked control. His greatest success came in 1971 when he won the short-lived US Matchplay Championship, beating the formidable array of George Archer, Doug Sanders, Julius Boros, Lou Graham, Bruce Crampton and Phil Rodgers to do so. He still plays frequently on the US Tour and has had one other victory, the 1972 Southern Open.

US wins 2 (1971–2)
US money $262,950 (1967–82) (164th all-time)

WEIBRING, Donald Albert   USA
b. Quincy, Illinois 1953

D.A. Weibring is always referred to in that way to distinguish him from his father, also called Donald Albert. He played his first full season on the US Tour in 1978, finishing 75th on the money list that year. He has improved every year since then, entering the Top 60 in 1979, moving to 45th in 1981, and after a slightly better year in 1982, finishing in 31st place with $117,941. He has had one victory, the 1979 Quad Cities Open.

US wins 1 (1979)
US money $402,993 (1977–82) (111th all-time)

WEISKOPF, Thomas Daniel   USA
b. Massillon, Ohio 1942

Tom Weiskopf has often been credited with the most majestic swing amongst present-day golfers, though he himself disagrees. He is perhaps the greatest golfer of today who has failed to win a good share of major championships. Although some-times described as inconsistent, Weiskopf has one of the best records of the past 20 years on the US Tour. He first played in 1964 and from 1966 to 1982 has never fallen below 48th in the money list placings, that being his worst finish in 1979. He has three times been third in the list, in 1968, 1973 and 1975; and twice sixth, in 1972 and 1977. He has won over $100,000 eleven times and passed $150,000 six times: $219,000 in 1975 and $245,000 in 1973 were his best years. In 1981 he became the fourth man in the history of the US Tour to reach $2 million, and has added to that during a success-ful international career during which he has won the 1972 World Matchplay, the 1973 British Open and South African PGA, the 1979 Argentine Open and the 1981 Benson and Hedges. Although Weis-kopf did not become the winner of many major championships that so many felt he would, he has often been in contention. In the US Open, for instance, he was five times in the top 4 between 1973 and 1979, with second in 1976 his best finish. In 1980 he equalled the Open record, set by Johnny Miller in 1973, with a 63 in the first round, though on that occasion he tailed away thereafter. In the

Masters he was second in 1969, 1972, 1974 and 1975; but he attracted as much attention in the first round of the 1980 Masters by taking a 13 on the short 12th in the first round, and improving that only to 7 the next day. This was probably the result of Tom getting cross with himself rather than not being able to hit a 7- or 6-iron onto the green; such recurrences have been not infrequent in his career, for he is a perfectionist. He first played golf at the age of 15; such was his natural talent that he was scoring in the mid 70s in a matter of months. He turned professional in 1964 after winning the Western Amateur, but his early results on the US Tour were disappointing and he nearly gave up. He began to improve in 1966, but then suffered a duodenal ulcer, probably a result of tension. In the Canadian Open that year he stood 5 under par on the 15th tee and then hit a bad drive, put off by camera noise. Weiskopf then dropped five shots over the closing holes and backhanded the ball

Tom Weiskopf

down the last fairway before withdrawing. He hit top form for the first time in 1968. His first win came with the San Diego Open. By the time the US Masters came round he had set what was then a US Tour record of $70,000 at that stage of the season: from that time it was clear that he was a leading player. The next big advance came with his win in the 1972 World Matchplay at Wentworth. Up to that time he had won five US tournaments, but this one carried the prestige of being nearly of major championship status. Then came his best year, his golf not bettered by anyone. In May he began to play really well, taking the Colonial Invitational and a fortnight later finished second to Jack Nicklaus in the Atlanta Golf Classic, which he followed at the turn of the month by winning the Kemper Open and the following week the IVB-Philadelphia Classic. The US Open followed: Weiskopf came third, one of those dismissed by Johnny Miller's last-round 63. Between 13 May and 17 June he won $130,000, still a healthy sum even in terms of the higher prize money of the 1980s. In July he was at Troon for the British Open. He allowed himself plenty of time to learn the course and to adjust to the British 1.62-inch ball, being used for the last time in the Open. He began with a 68 to lead and improved to a 67 the second day, to lead Yancey and Miller by 3 and Nicklaus by 4. In the third round Miller went to the turn in 32 to Weiskopf's 37 and held the championship lead for a while; but, despite being bunkered three times later, Weiskopf got back in 34 to Miller's 37 and at the 'end was again the leader, with Miller close on his heels. Nicklaus and Yancey had both faded considerably, the former with a 76. Although Coles finished the final round with a 66 to set a target of 279, and Nicklaus had one of his frequent fine last rounds, a 65, the championship still lay between Weiskopf and Miller, providing that neither of them strayed much above par. Weiskopf increased his lead to 3 strokes on the 1st and at the turn was 4 ahead. Only on the 13th did Miller manage to get a shot back, and Tom Weiskopf came in with a 70 and a 3-stroke victory, his 276 equalling what was at that time the Open record, set by Palmer, also at Troon, in 1962. Later that same July Tom added the Canadian Open, which meant he had won five of his last eight entries, and after that the World Series. Worldwide he won about $350,000 that year and, nearly three years younger than Jack Nicklaus, was being spoken of as a rival to his crown. But it was a much younger man, Tom Watson, little known at

the time, who was to emerge as the best player in the world; while Weiskopf, though he has much money and other wins to his credit, did not again manage to reach the peaks of his 1973 season. Perhaps he lacked some of the necessary will. Tom himself has said: 'Desire to win is the most necessary thing', and he certainly had it at Troon in 1973. He has also said: 'The US Tour provides me with the means to do what I like to do in the fall.' And that is to hunt. A third remark: 'It's tough to stay motivated.' The last two statements reveal that, very sensibly, Tom does not have the attitude to golf that Jones, Hogan and Nicklaus have shown. Of course, he wanted to win other major championships and was again to come close, but he lacked the single-mindedness that was necessary. Apart from desire Weiskopf had just about all the shot-making equipment. At the age of 40 in 1982, he was still one of the longest drivers on the US Tour, able to average about 270 yards. He has always been a sound putter: at Troon he did not three-putt once. He believes that fairway woods, wedge play and chipping are his weakest areas. The first of these he seldom needs. Tall, powerful swingers have frequently been less at home with wedge and sand iron. Chipping at one time he paid little attention to, having the attitude that golf is a matter of getting off the tee well and then hitting, not missing, the green. Later he was to spend more time on his short game. Although he is apt to hit the ocasional wild shot, usually a result of rolling the clubface open, that is to be expected from any long hitter. Probably on the decline now, he still won the 1982 Western Open and some $150,000 in the year.

US wins 15 (1968–82)
US money $2,158,632 (1964–82) (5th all-time)
Overseas wins 6 (1972–81)
World money $2,550,514 (1964–82) (7th all-time)

WELTS, Anne: see Quast

WESLOCK, Nick   Canada
b. Winnipeg, Manitoba 1917

Perhaps the best Canadian amateur of the 1960s, Nick Weslock won his national Amateur in 1957, 1963, 1964 and 1966, and was runner-up in 1950. He was low amateur in the Canadian Open no fewer than 11 times. He also won the Ontario Open five times. The strongest features of his game were putting and short irons, the latter so much so that he was sometimes called 'Nick the Wedge'.

WESTLAND, Alfred John USA
b. Everett, Washington 1904

Jack Westland's amateur career was remarkable in that it came in two sections. In 1929 he was French Amateur champion, and in 1931 he reached the final of the US Amateur, where he was defeated 6 and 5 by Francis Ouimet. He played in the US Walker Cup teams in 1932 and 1934, halving both the singles in which he played and winning in foursomes. He was then successful mainly in his home area, winning the Pacific Northwest title four times and the Washington State three times. In 1952 his second 'life' began. He was again a finalist in the US Amateur and this time the winner, at 47

Kathy Whitworth

the oldest on record. He won his title in Seattle while a Republican nominee for Congress, and the following year he was elected and served until 1965. He also played in the 1953 Walker Cup team, winning both his matches comfortably, to preserve his unbeaten Walker Cup record; he was non-playing captain in 1961. His last major achievement was to win the US Seniors title in 1962.

WHALEN, Gerda: see Boykin

WHIGHAM, Henry James USA
b. Tarbolton, Scotland 1869; d. 1954

H.J. Whigham won the fourth and fifth US Amateurs, in each case very comfortably: by 8 and 7 in 1896, and 8 and 6 in 1897. Oddly, there was some parallel between him and Bernard Darwin. The latter covered many British Amateur Championships in which he played for *The Times*, while Whigham was covering the US event for the *Chicago Tribune*. He had earlier captained the Oxford University golf team. Later he went on to be a war correspondent in the Boer War, the Spanish-American War, the Boxer Rising in China and the Russo-Japanese War.

WHITE, Donna (née Horton) USA
b. Kinston, North Carolina 1954

Donna Horton reached the final of the 1975 US Amateur, where she lost to Beth Daniel but came back the following year to win. She played in the 1976 Curtis Cup and won both her matches by wide margins. She joined the US Tour in mid 1977 and in only five entries managed a joint second place and 71st place on the money list. She was 33rd the following year, then 14th and in 1980 13th. With two victories in 1980, she had established herself as a major player. She did not play in 1981 because she was having a baby, but was in good form again in 1982 with some $75,000.

US wins 2 (1980)
US money $254,619 (1977–82)

WHITWORTH, Kathrynne Ann USA
b. Monahans, Texas 1939

During her more than 20 years' career on the US Tour, Kathy Whitworth has assembled the most impressive statistical record of any woman professional golfer, and it is worth immediately setting out some of these achievements:

US wins: 83 (1962–82) (record)
US money: $1,041,791 (1959–81)
Leading money-winner: 1965–8, 1970–73 (record)
Vare Trophy: 1965–7, 1968–72 (record)
All-time leading money-winner: 1969–81
Player of the Year: 1966–9, 1971–3 (record)
First to total $1 million: 1981
Major championships: 1967, 1971 and 1975 US LPGA; second in 1971 US Open
Stroke average: under 73 1965–72, 1975, 1977, 1981, 1982
LPGA Hall of Fame: 1975

Although there are 'lies, damned lies and statistics', at the least the above amply shows that Kathy Whitworth is one of the greatest players of modern times. With her career by no means over her ultimate place must be left to history. She began her career by taking the New Mexico Amateur twice and went on the US Tour in 1959 at the age of 19, when Mickey Wright was coming to be the leading player. By 1962, she had become one of the key players and won twice that year, and in the following two years was second and third in the money list. At this point Mickey Wright ceased competing full-time. The astonishing achievement of Kathy Whitworth in terms of tournament wins over an 11-year period is also worth detailing:
1963: 8; 1964: 1; 1965: 8; 1966: 9; 1967: 8; 1968: 10; 1969: 7; 1970: 2; 1971: 5; 1972: 5; 1973: 7. During this peak period she had 70 tournament victories, figures only exceeded by Mickey Wright and unlikely to be bettered by future players in times when there is a much greater number of players with the ability to win. Her money-winning achievements will soon pale under the onslaught of such players as JoAnne Carner who, with vastly increased prize money, became in 1982 the first player to win more than $300,000. Yet Kathy Whitworth began on the Tour as so many before and since: she won no money at all in her first six months and her first cheque was for $30. At the end of the season her stroke average was an unimpressive 80.30. From 1974 she was no longer the dominant force which she had been for so many years, but remained a leading player. In 1979 and 1980 she did not win and began an apparently final decline down the money list to 30th and 24th place, but there were ambitions remaining: she wanted to be the first to reach $1 million and to

beat Mickey Wright's record total of 82 Tour wins. Both seemed beyond her, but in 1981 she showed greatly revived form to achieve the first target and draw to 1 behind Wright's total. The revival was maintained in 1982. She equalled the record with a win by 9 strokes in the CPC International, later lost a play-off and then broke the record the following week with victory in the Lady Michelob. She moved to second in the money list at that stage of the season. Kathy Whitworth has an uneasy, flat swing. She considers that a prime reason for her success is that she 'keeps the ball in play' and avoids destructive shots. She is also one of the best putters in the modern game, good enough to have ranked top in seven Tour seasons.

US wins 83 (1962–82) (1st all-time)
US money $1,178,489 (1959–82) (2nd all-time)

van WIE, Virginia   USA
b. Chicago, Illinois 1909

Five times a finalist in the US Amateur, Virginia van Wie had something of a running battle with her great, and slightly younger, contemporary, Glenna Collett. She was beaten by the then record 13 and 12 in the 1928 final, and by 6 and 5 in 1930. In 1932 she turned the tables with a 10 and 8 victory, at that time the second highest margin achieved and no doubt balm to past wounds. Virginia went on to win the title the following two years, the last time three successive wins were to be achieved until Juli Inkster completed a run of three in 1982. Feeling perhaps that there was nothing more to conquer, Virginia 'did a Jones' and retired in 1934. She played on the 1932 and 1934 Curtis Cup teams.

WILKINSON, Martha (née Kirouac)   USA
b. Los Angeles, California 1948

US Amateur Champion in 1970, defeating Cynthia Hill in the final, Martha Wilkinson was on the winning US World Team Championship team in 1970 and played in the Curtis Cup that year, winning in both foursomes and one singles, losing the other.

WILLING, Dr Oscar F.   USA
b. 1889

Particularly active in the Northwest of the USA, Dr Willing won the Oregon Amateur four times and the Northwest Amateur in 1924 and 1928, in the latter year also taking the North West Open. He played in the Walker Cup in 1923, 1924 and 1930. In 1929 he reached the final of the US Amateur, where he lost to Jimmy Johnstone.

WILSON, Margaret Joyce   USA
b. Meridian, Mississippi 1934

It was a dream that caused Peggy Wilson to take up golf. At the age of 15 she saw herself playing the game in front of a large crowd, and took the hint. By 1962 she was on the US Tour, having twice been runner-up for the Mississippi state title. She was in the top 50 from 1964 to 1972 and had her best seasons in 1966, when she was 18th in the money list, and 1969 for 13th and $16,000. In the latter year she finished second in the US Open, 1 stroke behind Donna Young.

US wins 1 (1968)
US money $83,218 (1962–76)

WININGER, Francis G.   USA
b. Chico, California 1922; d. 1967

'Bo' Wininger turned professional in 1952 and won three events before giving up the US Tour between 1960 and 1961. He returned in 1962 and won the Carling Open and the New Orleans Open the following year.

US wins 5 (1952–63)

WOOD, Craig Ralph   USA
b. Lake Placid, New York 1901; d. 1968

A formidable player in the 1930s and early 1940s, Craig Wood established quite a reputation for just failing to win major championships. In 1933, for instance, he was third in the US Open, and at St Andrews tied Denny Shute for the British Open, although he had begun with a 77. Shute took the play-off. During this championship Wood drove into the Swilcan Burn on the 1st, about 350 yards; and on the 5th hit one of the longest drives recorded in major golf. It found a bunker 430 yards out. 1934 saw the first US Masters tournament and Wood was second again, beaten by 1 stroke by Horton Smith's birdie, par finish. Worse was to follow: he lost the final of the US PGA that year on the 38th hole to Paul Runyan, a case of massive hitter coming off second best to a short-game expert. The gods had not yet finished their sport

with Craig Wood, for 1935 saw one of the most outrageous finishes to a major championship. In the US Masters Wood began 69, 72, 68 to lead Gene Sarazen by 3 strokes. In the final round he faltered badly but pulled himself together finely to play the last eight holes in 4 under par, having a birdie on the last from several yards. The press photographed and congratulated the surprised winner, and the committee prepared the cheque. Alas for Craig, he was the man who suffered from Sarazen's 4-wood shot on the 15th that gave him a double eagle. Sarazen had needed to play the last four holes in 3 under to tie, and had done so with one master, and lucky, shot. What Craig felt about it, and what his mental attitude to the play-off was, is not recorded; but he lost it by 5 strokes over 36 holes. Fate had one more unpleasant experience in store for him. In the 1939 US Open Shute, Wood and Nelson were tied on 284. In the play-off over 18 holes, Craig had a 68, good enough to win – but it did not. Shute was eliminated with a 76, but Byron Nelson added

Craig Wood

another 68 to the one that had enabled him to overhaul the leaders in the final round. Out the pair went again and Wood lost again, a nearly conclusive blow having been struck early on in the 18-hole second play-off when Nelson holed a full 1-iron shot. Wood opened the 1941 Masters with a 66 and followed with a pair of 71s to lead Byron Nelson by 5. It was all going to happen again, he must have thought, as Nelson went to the turn in the last round in 33 to Craig's 38. But he did not lose heart, and came back in 34 to Nelson's 37. At last a major championship was his, by 3 strokes. Perhaps the best of the year was still to come. The US Open at Colonial saw Craig Wood in the first round 3 over par, wearing a back brace and in a ditch. To complete the picture a storm was in progress. He thought the wisest course would be to go home. Tommy Armour persuaded him to continue, and Wood completed his first round in 73, following with 71, 70, 70 to take the Open by 3 strokes from Denny Shute. He is one of just four players to take both these championships in a single year. Wood was a Ryder Cup player from 1931 to 1935, then had the professional's job at Winged Foot for many years and later went to Grand Bahama Islands.

US wins 17 (1928–44)

WORSHAM, Lewis Elmer   USA
b. *Alta Vista, Virginia 1917*

If Gene Sarazen's 4-wood to the 15th for a double eagle to win the 1935 US Masters is the most renowned shot ever hit in golf, Lew Worsham hit two during his career that cannot be too far behind. In the 1953 'World Championship' – more often known as the Tam o' Shanter – Lew Worsham needed to get down in two from a little over 100 yards out on the last hole to tie Chandler Harper. He holed the wedge shot, which was worth a first prize of $25,000 plus a very lucrative exhibitions contract. Lew Worsham's other 'career' shot was far less spectacular but equally important, for it made him US Open Champion. At St Louis, Missouri, in 1947 he tied Sam Snead on 282 after 72 holes and the pair were still level after 17 holes of the play-off and both some 2½ feet from the hole. Snead was just the further away and settling to putt when Worsham queried if it was his putt. After measurement, it was decided that it was indeed Snead to putt. He did so and missed; Worsham holed his. He

Lew Worsham

played in the Ryder Cup that year and had a 100% record, with Ed Oliver beating Henry Cotton and Arthur Lees in the first post-war Ryder Cup foursomes by 10 and 9, and going on the following day to beat Jimmy Adams in singles. A successful US Tour competitor for some years, Lew Worsham was leading money-winner in 1953, with $34,002. Later he earned a high reputation as a teacher from his Oakmont base.

WRIGHT, Mary Kathryn   USA
b. *San Diego, California 1935*

One of the names always to the fore when the question of the great women players of all time is raised is that of Mickey Wright; few would deny that she is the best woman player in the history of American professional golf. She began to play at the age of 11, encouraged by her father, who had wanted a boy and had already introduced her to baseball at the age of four. In 1950 she reached the final of the US Junior Championship. In 1952 she won it and was on her way. In 1954 she played her only full year in top amateur golf, winning the

World and All-American Amateurs, reaching the final of the US Amateur and finishing fourth in the US Open and leading amateur. She then turned professional, securing her first win in 1956. With three wins in 1957 she was beginning to be one of the leading names, together with Patty Berg, Betsy Rawls and Louise Suggs. The position did not remain static for long. In 1958 Mickey Wright moved right to the front with five Tour victories, which included her first US Open and US LPGA. The following year she won the US Open again, and three other events. It was not, however, until 1960 that she became fully the supreme player, winning six times, including the LPGA again – and from there the pace quickened to 10 wins in 1961; another 10 in 1962; 13 in 1963, 11 in 1964. At this point she had won 63 US tournaments, including both the US Open and US LPGA four times each. She was, and still is, the only player twice to take both the major events in the same year: 1958 and 1961. Her 13 victories in 1963 is the US LPGA record, and her 11 in 1964 is second best. She was also leading money-winner in the years 1961–4; six times won the most tournaments in a season; and won the Vare Trophy for stroke average every year from 1960 to 1964. For the Vare, she had set new standards that are worth detailing. The Trophy was first awarded in 1953, when 75.00 was good enough to win. For the years up to 1959, the average of the winner began to come down, but was still in the 74-plus range until Mickey Wright brought it down to 73.25 and 72.46 in her best year, 1964. It was then not until 1978 that the 72 barrier was broken, by Nancy Lopez. So, at a time when competition was not as stiff as it was later to become, Mickey Wright set a scoring standard not bettered for many years. In 1965 she played relatively little, for she was on a course of studies at a college and was also having trouble with an arthritic wrist. Thereafter she played relatively full-time again up to the end of 1969, winning often but not being absolutely dominant. From 1970 she played far fewer tournaments and had her last win in the 1973 Dinah Shore. However, as late as 1979 she tied for the Coca-Cola Classic, losing the play-off to Nancy Lopez. Beside the handicap of a bad wrist and foot trouble that meant she had to play in soft shoes, Mickey Wright had probably become bored with winning, and had other interests outside golf. Mickey Wright did not, as did Joyce Wethered and Babe Zaharias, add a new dimension to women's golf but she was as long a hitter as the

Mickey Wright

latter – some say longer – averaging about 230 yards from the tee. She has been described as the best long-iron player of them all, aided by a hand action as crisp as the best men players. According to her great contemporary Betsy Rawls, she was the only woman professional with a perfect swing that had no idiosyncrasies. Three players have caused a great surge in women's golf: Babe Zaharias, Mickey Wright, and Nancy Lopez. Mickey Wright achieved this almost solely by the magnificence of her play, for she was shy and retiring and withdrew from press and public gaze as much as possible but, as Judy Rankin put it: 'Mickey got the outside world to take a second hard look at women's golf and when they looked they discovered the rest of us.' Among Mickey Wright's other records her 62 at Hogan Park, Midland, Texas, is still the lowest; she is the only player twice to win four events consecutively; and her 82 tournament wins remained the record for many years, eventually being overhauled by Kathy Whitworth in 1982 after a much longer full-time playing career.

US wins 82 (1956–73) (2nd all-time)
US money $368,770 (1955–80) (21st all-time)
Major championships 8 (1958–64)

Bob Wynn

WYNN, Bob   USA
b. *Lancaster, Kentucky 1940*

Bob Wynn turned professional in 1959 but did not become a Tour player until 1971. He made the Top 60 in both 1975 and 1976, and in 1975 won the Magnolia Classic, a mini-Tour event run in parallel with the US Masters. In 1976 he took the BC Open and was 34th in the money list. He won no money in 1982.

US wins 1 (1976)
US money $262,060 (1971–81) (166th all-time)

WYSONG, Dudley   USA
b. *McKinney, Texas 1939*

Dudley Wysong came close to two major championships in his career. In 1961 he defeated Irishman Joe Carr in the semi-finals of the US Amateur but fared less well at the final hurdle, being beaten by Jack Nicklaus 8 and 6. After turning professional he came second in the 1966 US PGA, 4 strokes behind Al Geiberger. However, Wysong did have two US Tour successes, winning the 1966 Phoenix Open and the 1967 Hawaiian Open.

US wins 2 (1966–7)
US money $143,610 (218th all-time)

YANCEY, Albert Winsborough   USA
b. *Chipley, Florida 1938*

Bert Yancey has a strong sense of golf history, a reason why he was specially passionate about winning major championships and on occasion he came quite close. Perhaps he felt most intensely about the US Masters, to the extent that he built models of the Augusta National greens so that he could better study the undulations. In his first attempt at this championship in 1967 he began with a 67 and eventually finished third; he repeated the placing the following year, mainly the result of a final-round 65; and in 1970 he was fourth. In 1968 he began 67, 68 to lead the US Open and had opened up a 5-stroke lead with 27 holes to play. Still leader into the last round, though only by 1 stroke, he fell away to a 76 which brought him third place behind Lee Trevino. He was again third in 1974. He entered less frequently for the British Open, but in 1973 at Troon he began 69, 69 before eventually finishing fifth. Yancey had been a West Point cadet, and while there was diagnosed as having suffered a nervous breakdown, yet he was to

Bert Yancey

do formidably well when he joined the US Tour a few years later in 1964. He made the Top 60 his first season and continued to do so in the 1964–74 period. In 1966 he won three tournaments and the following year achieved his best money-list placing, at 13th. In 1975 he again began to suffer health problems and dropped out of the Tour thereafter, mainly because the drugs he had to take for physiological imbalance caused his hands to shake, a condition that obviously makes putting well-nigh impossible. Bert Yancey for some years was thought to have one of the best swings in the game and was capable of inspired scoring spells. For example, in 1972 he once had seven consecutive birdies, and in 1973 his nine holes in 28 was the best on the US Tour that year. At Indian Wells in 1974 he had a round of 61, the lowest on Tour for four years – and that included a missed 3-foot putt. Recently, improved diagnosis and treatment of his health problems has allowed him to come back into golf as a teacher. He is an authority on the golf swing, and has numbered Tony Jacklin among his pupils, in the latter's early days on the US Tour. Yancey considers that the hook is the most destructive shot in golf, to the extent that he once said: 'I don't even want to drive a car that turns left.'

US wins 7 (1966–72)
US money $688,125 (1964–75) (66th all-time)
World money $882,562

YATES, Charles Richardson   USA

b. Atlanta, Georgia 1913

Charlie Yates won the 1934 Intercollegiate title and the Western Amateur the following year. He then appeared in the 1936 Walker Cup team, halving in the foursomes and winning his singles by 8 and 7. In the 1938 match he was on one of the few losing US teams, at St Andrews; but no blame for the defeat could be laid at his door, for he won in both foursomes and singles, in the latter defeating the British star, James Bruen, in the top singles. After the match he endeared himself to the crowds by singing Scottish songs. That year he also won the British Amateur, beating Cecil Ewing in the final. A notable achievement of his was to be three times leading amateur in the US Masters, twice finishing in the top 20. He has since become much involved in the organization of this tournament.

YOUNG, Donna: see Caponi

ZAHARIAS, Mildred Ella (née Didrikson)   USA

b. Port Arthur, Texas 1914; d. 1956

As adults, few have been able to take up golf after excelling at other sports and then reach great heights. Babe Zaharias did so – but she could do anything, perhaps the most deserving of the title 'Athlete of the Century'. The nickname 'Babe' derived from Babe Ruth the baseball player, for the young Mildred Ella Didrikson developed a habit of hitting home runs in her school days. In fact basketball was the first game at which she excelled nationally, being an All-American from 1930 to 1932. At this time she also took up athletics, and in her first season set the US record for javelin and followed by taking national titles in long jump and hurdles. In the 1932 US AAU Championships she

Babe Zaharias

entered no fewer than eight events in 2½ hours and won six of them, breaking four world records while she was about it. The Los Angeles Olympics followed shortly after. She won the javelin and 80 metre hurdles and led the high jump, from which she was disqualified for using the Western Roll technique. She had set three world records. The Babe had already tried golf casually and during the Olympics was persuaded to play a round by the sports writer Grantland Rice. She scored quite well but it was her remarkable hitting that most raised eyebrows. This was to become legendary, and today it is hard to separate fact from legend. Byron Nelson, for example, declared that there were only some half dozen or so men that were longer off the tee, but this was just about certainly an exaggeration. However, a drive of 246 yards was once measured. On a 540-yard hole at Gullane Number 1 in the 1947 British Ladies', she hit through the green with a 4-iron second shot. The truth of the matter is that, while she may occasionally have hit a ball around the 300-yard mark, her normal good drives travelled about 250 yards. The Babe did not concentrate on golf for some time, but played professionally at baseball and basketball, taking golf lessons and playing when there was the opportunity. She is thought to have played her first competition in 1934; in 1935 she won the Texas Amateur. She was then banned from amateur golf by the USGA on the grounds that while not a professional at golf she was at other sports. Shortly after she went barnstorming with Horton Smith, Gene Sarazen and Joyce Wethered. Here there was the contrast between the woman whom Bobby Jones had called the greatest golfer, male or female, he had ever seen and the Babe. Wethered drove about the length of a Didrikson long iron but had a far superior all-round game, for at this time the Babe was mainly interested in hitting flat out and had yet to develop touch and short-game skills. In 1938 she married George Zaharias and gave tennis a try, but was banned from amateur competition by the USLTA. As George had a good income from wrestling, fighting under the banner 'the Weeping Greek from Cripple Creek', she was eventually able to apply to the USGA for reinstatement as an amateur. In 1940 she won both the professional events, the Western and Texas Opens, refusing the prize money and by 1943 was again an amateur. Between the summers of 1946 and 1947 she claimed to have won 17 tournaments – consecutively! They included the 1946 US Amateur which

she dominated throughout, winning the final 11 and 9. In 1947 she set sail for Britain to attempt to be the first American to win the British title. By the time she had reached the final she had played six matches, beaten such players as Frances Stephens and Jean Donald and had lost only four holes in doing so. Against Jean Donald in the semi-final she was 5 under 4s when the match ended. In the final she met Jacqueline Gordon, who put up such a resistance that she was 2 up after 11 holes, but at lunch the match was all square. Thereafter, the Babe cruised away to win by 5 and 4. Not much later that year she again turned professional and began an exhibition tour managed by Fred Corcoran. Soon, with Patty Berg, they organized a fledgeling US Women's Tour. In 1948 she won three of the eight events including the Open, and two of seven the next year. In 1950 she was more dominant, taking six of the nine, which again included the US Open. In 1951 she won seven times out of an expanded Tour of 14. In each of the four seasons she had been leading money-winner, though her total prize money was under $40,000. Of course she was the main drawing card and, in the early phase of US women's professional golf, only Patty Berg, Betty Jameson, Beverly Hanson, Betsy Rawls and Louise Suggs also won events. By 1952 she was not quite the leading player, both Louise Suggs and Betsy Rawls winning six times to her four, and the next year she had a major operation for cancer. She was back again on Tour in a matter of months and in 1954 won five events, which included the US Open by a margin of no fewer than 12 strokes! It was her last appearance in the Open. In 1955 she won twice, but from early that year until her death in 1956 was in and out of hospital for further operations. The Babe was a revolutionary figure in women's golf for she had shown that a golf ball could be hit by women rather than swept away with a long, rather flat stroke. Her swing was long – past the horizontal – but as upright as Jack Nicklaus's, and she had in full measure the snap as the right elbow is straightened; that is given to very few women, but after all, she was a champion javelin thrower. Other women have followed who have perhaps been longer – a little – off the tee, but she was the first to show that a woman can hit a golf ball as far as all but the longest hitters in the men's game.

US wins 31 (1948–55) (9th all-time)
US money $66,237 (1948–55)

Kermit Zarley

ZARLEY, Kermit Millard　　　　USA

b. Seattle, Washington 1941

On account of his, to say the least, unusual name, Zarley has been dubbed 'the pro from Outer Space', which really derives from a Bob Hope remark: 'It sounds as if he's the pro from the Moon.' As an amateur Zarley won his state and the Northwestern Amateur titles, and also the NCAA Championship in 1962. He went on the US Tour in 1963, and from 1966 to 1973 was in the Top 60 each year except 1969, 21st in 1968 being his best finish. He has made at least one strong attempt at a major championship. This came at Pebble Beach in 1972 when he was only 1 stroke behind Jack Nicklaus with one round to go; but he fell away to a 79 and sixth place in high winds. His most prestigious success was to take the 1970 Canadian Open. He is now virtually retired from the US Tour. Kermit Zarley is reputed to be a very serious fellow, his interest outside golf being Bible study. The story is told that Tom Weiskopf, during a Hawaiian Open, told him that eating the pineapple tee markers was allowed. Zarley tried one, but was not aware that you ought to remove the skin!

US wins　3 (1968–72)
US money　$698,068 (1963–82) (64th all-time)

ZIEGLER, Lawrence Edward　　　　USA

b. St Louis, Missouri 1939

One of the longest hitters on the US Tour, still averaging over 270 yards when past 40, Larry Ziegler had the unusual experience of winning a US Tour event – his first at that – the 1969 Michigan Classic, and then being informed that there was no cheque because the tournament had gone bankrupt. The US PGA eventually paid him. Ziegler was in the Top 60 in 1969, 1970 and from 1973 to 1976, 27th in 1974 being his highest money list placing. Besides his US Tour victories, he also won the 1974 Moroccan Grand Prix and the 1978 Central and South American Open in Costa Rica.

US wins　3 (1969–72)
US money　$647,214 (1963–82) (70th all-time)
Overseas wins　2 (1974–8)

Larry Ziegler

ZOELLER, Frank Urban   USA
b. New Albany, Indiana 1952

Although the nickname derives from the 'FUZ' of his initials, 'Fuzzy' Zoeller early in his professional career sported a big, frizzy hairstyle and sweeping moustache, so the name was appropriate. Extremely popular with fellow players and spectators alike, he is regarded as one of the current hopes of the US Tour in that he has the crowd and TV appeal in a relatively drab age when all are well turned out and behaved but none have either the bravura of Arnold Palmer in his heyday or the majesty of Nicklaus. His outstanding achievement to date is undoubtedly his victory in the 1979 US Masters, achieved despite his never having held the lead in the tournament. After Ed Sneed had birdied the 15th at Augusta he seemed an assured winner, but he dropped strokes at each of the last three holes and found himself tied with Zoeller, a man he had led by 6 after the third round. He had also lost 5 strokes to Tom Watson, and these were the three who went into the play-off. All parred the first play-off hole. On the next Zoeller stood by as Sneed narrowly failed to hole his third shot from a greenside bunker and then Watson failed with his putt. Zoeller holed his and shortly thereafter was wearing the traditional green jacket presented to every Masters champion. Although at the time of this victory he stood third on the 1979 money list few had rated his chances. He had turned professional in 1973 and qualified for the US Tour in 1975 but this was the first year he had qualified for the Masters, and in the history of the event only two others had won on their first appearance: Horton Smith in 1934 (anyway the first time the Masters was held) and Gene Sarazen the following year. Zoeller first attracted national attention in 1976 when he recorded a 63 in the Quad Cities Open at Oakwood Country Club, Coal Valley, Pennsylvania. Although 63s are rare enough it was not this that aroused press attention. He had birdied each of the last eight holes and, with Bob Goalby, shares the record for consecutive birdies on the US Tour. His progress to the top of US golf was by no means immediate. In his first year on Tour Zoeller earned just $7,300, and claimed he had nevertheless enjoyed himself spending some $35,000. He first passed the magic $100,000 in a year in 1978 and his first victory (which qualified him for the Masters) followed in the 1979 San Diego Open. In all he has won just three times on the US Tour, also taking the Colonial National Invitational in 1981. He has been in the Top 60 since 1976, with 1979 being his best year when he finished ninth, with over $196,000. Zoeller is a prodigious hitter, finishing third in the 1980 US Tour driving statistics at 271.5 yards, and fourth in 1981 at 274.9. This power derives from a highly unorthodox style. Zoeller crouches low over the ball, addresses the ball with the heel of the club and his hands near his knees; but he has proved that just about any method of hitting a golf ball will do, provided that the player is 'right' in the hitting area.

US wins 3 (1979–81)
US money $815,912 (1975–82) (52nd all-time)

ZOKOL, Richard   Canada
b. Kitemat, British Columbia 1958

Zokol was the 1981 Canadian Amateur Champion and played in the national World Cup team. In the same year he won the International Amateur Championship in Morocco and turned professional, securing his US Tour player's card the same year. In his first year on the US Tour, 1982, Zokol found an odd, if temporary, solution to the problem of maintaining concentration during a tournament round: he plugged a radio earpiece into his ear. In the Greater Milwaukee Open he began 65, 69, 70 to lead after each round. A final 75 might mean that the trick wore off; he finished in fifth place. He was 156th in the 1982 money list.

US money $15,111 (1982) (302nd all-time)

Fuzzy Zoeller

GREAT BRITAIN & IRELAND

ADAMS, James — Scotland
b. Troon 1910

A Ryder Cup player four times between 1947 and 1953 (and also chosen for the unplayed 1939 matches), Jimmy Adams won both his matches in the 1949 series, having been a professional since ~~...~~ for the length of his swing,

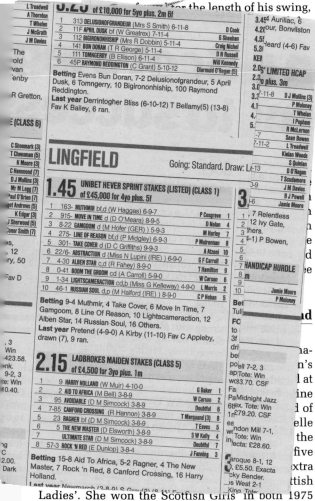

Ladies'. She won the Scottish Girls' in both 1975 and 1977 and in the latter year also took the British title. She has won the West of Scotland in 1978 and 1981 and that regional girls' title three times, was second in the British Ladies' Strokeplay in 1978 and won the 1982 Avia Foursomes. A Scottish international from 1978 to 1982 she was also in the 1982 Curtis Cup team and played in the 1979 and 1981 European Team Championship.

ALLAN, Dr A.J.T. — Scotland
b. Dorset, England 1875; d. 1898

Jack Allan did not try the game of golf until 1891 but six years later became the then youngest

Wilma Aitken

winner of the British Amateur. Allan cycled to Muirfield for each of his matches, plucked off his cycle clips and played in his ordinary shoes. He died the following year of a lung disease.

ALLISS, Percy   England
b. Sheffield 1897; d. 1975

Percy Alliss, my father, was in the top handful of British golfers from the late 1920s and through the 1930s and one of the best players who failed to win a British Open. His swing was balanced and rhythmic, his long-iron play recognized as superb, but the main chink in his armour was a none too efficient putting stroke. This is known to have let him down in the British Open on occasion. In the 1932 Open, for instance, he finished fourth, 9 strokes behind Gene Sarazen, but felt he might have been as many ahead had he managed a target of two putts per green. The previous year he had faced the last two holes at Carnoustie looking certain of winning, or at least tying, but had gone out of bounds and finished behind Tommy Armour and José Jurado in third place. In other Opens he came fourth in 1928 and 1929 and was fifth in 1936. He was something of a travelling man, starting as a professional at Royal Porthcawl in Wales, during which period he won the Assistants' title and the Welsh Championship twice before moving to the east of England and winning the Essex Open a couple of times. He then did something that was remarkable for a British professional of that time: took a job in Europe, at the Wannsee club in Berlin, and there he remained from 1926 to 1932, accumulating five German Open wins in those years. He also found time to travel and competed in the 1931 Canadian Open, where he lost a play-off to Walter Hagen after 37 holes. Walter was most impressed with his game and tried to persuade him to settle in the USA, but perhaps settling down in England had come to seem more attractive. Not long after he took a job at Temple Newsam, Leeds, an area to which I followed him some 35 years later. In 1938 he went to Ferndown Golf Club and remained there until he retired. Percy, from his Berlin base, competed fairly frequently in Europe and twice won the Italian Open, in one of these victories setting a four-round total of 262 which was the record in a national champion-

ship until equalled by Lu Liang Huan in 1971. Perhaps his best wins, however, were in the British Professional Matchplay in 1933 and 1937. He was selected for the British Ryder Cup team four times: in 1929, 1933, 1935 and 1937.

Europe wins 16 (1926–38)

ALLISS, Peter   England
b. Berlin, Germany 1931

Putting is, I believe, a main reason that, for instance, I never won a British Open (three eighth-place finishes were the best I managed) and did not dominate British golf from the mid 1950s to the late 1960s to the extent I might have done. I was considered to have one of the best swings of the time. Nevertheless, over the years I built up a creditable record. In the Ryder Cup I represented Great Britain and Ireland from 1953 to 1969, with 1955 the only interruption, though it all began badly with my losing a vital singles which I should have won to Jim Turnesa at Wentworth in 1953. After that, however, my record bore comparison with anyone's, and I took the scalps of many

Percy and Peter Alliss

leading Americans, including Palmer in his peak years. During the same period, I represented England ten times in the World Cup. I turned professional in 1946, shortly after having been a boy international, and played in my first Open in 1947 at the age of 16. Two years later, the leading judge of the game, Leonard Crawley, was recommending I be given a place in the Ryder Cup team as by far the most promising new talent. By this time I was in the RAF and did not play in the Open again until 1951. I won the British Assistants' in 1952 and my first major victory came in 1954 with the Daks tournament. In the rest of my career I won 20 major tournaments and the West of England Open four times, the Sunningdale Foursomes with Jean Donald twice and the Wentworth Pro-Am with Guy Wolstenholme. I once recorded 127 over 36 holes in the Irish Hospitals tournament of 1961, and this is still the second lowest total for the European circuit. I became the holder of five national Opens in Europe and one of my best spells of sustained golf was to take three of these in sequence in 1958: the Italian, Spanish and Portuguese. But my best golf ever was played in the Esso Golden Round Robin tournament in 1964 when I beat all but one of my opponents easily. Golf seemed such a simple game. I also won the Vardon Trophy in 1964 and 1966. Towards the end of the 1960s I began to twitch on the short putts and announced my retirement from international matches at the end of the 1969 Ryder Cup. I had intended to remain a frequent tournament player, but other work prevented me. Since that time I have been much involved in golf-course construction and as a broadcaster, where some of my programme series have been *Around with Alliss*, *The World of Golf*, *Play Golf* and a long-running pro-celebrity series. I am a frequent commentator on tournament golf in Britain for the BBC and for ABC in the USA. The best features of my game were the long shots. I had the ability to hit the ball a long way, if not as far as some of today's titans, with a controlled fade, and was especially good with the 1- to 3-irons.

Europe wins 20 (1954–69)
Europe money £28,000 approx.

ANDERSON, James   Scotland
b. St Andrews 1842; d. 1912

The son of a caddie who later sold on-course refreshments at St Andrews, Jamie was the second man to take three British Opens in a row, from 1877 to 1879. The 1878 win was particularly memorable in that Jamie knew he had to complete the last four holes in 17 shots in order to beat J.O.F. Morris – and did so with the help of a hole in one, the first in championship golf. Not a dashing player, his strengths were steadiness and accuracy and he was an exceptionally fine putter. After his playing career was over he gained a great reputation as a clubmaker. It is a comment on the status of golfers at that time that he died in Dysart Combination Poor House in Perth.

ANDERSON, Jean: see Donald

ANDERSON, Jessica: see Valentine

ANSTEY, Veronica: see Beharrell

ASHBY, Harold   England
b. Consett 1946

An England international in 1972–4, Harry Ashby achieved the rare feat of winning the English Amateur for two years in a row, 1972–3. In 1974 he gave up his teaching job and sought fame and fortune on the professional circuit but achieved little. He was a master wedge player but perhaps rather underpowered. He sought reinstatement as an amateur in 1981.

ATTENBOROUGH, Michael F.   England
b. 1939

After captaining the Oxford University golf team, Attenborough was four years an English international in 1964 and from 1966 to 1968. He was Club Champion of Champions in 1964 and a Walker Cup player in 1967. He has twice won the President's Putter, a competition for Oxford and Cambridge University golfers.

AUCHTERLONIE, Laurence   Scotland
b. St Andrews 1904

Son of Willie, who was the professional at St Andrews for nearly 30 years, Laurence took over from his father in 1964. He is mainly known as a superb clubmaker and is a collector of 19th-century wooden clubs.

AUCHTERLONIE, Laurie: see North America

AUCHTERLONIE, William — Scotland
b. St Andrews 1872; d. 1963

Willie first played in the Open at the age of 16 and was later to become the last Scots-born resident to win it. This he did in 1893, winning by two from amateur Johnny Laidlay, with Sandy Herd third. He was 21 and did it with clubs he had made himself. In the winner's photograph he is shown with all seven of them! In fact he only found a use for five. He did not feature strongly in the event again though he finished fifth in 1900, 17 behind the winner, J.H. Taylor. Instead he concentrated on building up a famous clubmaking business and in 1935 was appointed professional to the Royal and Ancient in succession to 'Old Tom' Morris and Andrew Kirkaldy. He was elected an honorary member of the R & A in 1950.

BAILEY, Diane: see Frearson

BALFOUR-MELVILLE, Leslie — Scotland
b. Edinburgh 1854; d. 1937

In those more spacious Victorian days a man had the time to excel at a variety of sports. Balfour-Melville was Scottish Champion of tennis, billiards and long jump and represented his country at both rugby and cricket. In the time that he found to play golf he won medals at St Andrews over the very long spell 1874–1908 and played for Scotland in the first international in 1902. He was captain of the Honourable Company of Edinburgh Golfers (Muirfield) from 1902 to 1903 and of the Royal and Ancient in 1906. In the British Amateur Championship he was a finalist in 1889 and in 1895 he won, beating no less a golfer than John Ball. He won each of his last three matches at the first extra hole when, in each case, his opponent struck his shot to the green into the Swilcan Burn, now a rare event amongst good golfers but not so in those days when a long hit with a gutta-percha ball was required for the second shot.

BALL, John, Snr — England
b. Hoylake

Father of the great John Ball, his fame was soon eclipsed by that of his son. He did, however, reach the semi-finals of both the 1886 and 1887 Amateur Championships.

BALL, John, Jnr — England
b. Hoylake 1861; d. 1940

One of the greatest and most enduring British amateurs, he was the only man other than Bobby Jones to win both the British Amateur and Open in the same year (1890). He first competed in the Open at the age of 17 in 1878 and finished in fourth place. For John Ball, the Amateur Championship did not start quite soon enough; otherwise he would doubtless have been champion more often. When it began in 1885, Ball soon became the most prolific winner there has ever been, triumphing in 1888, 1890 – when he also won the Open – 1892, 1894, 1899, 1907, 1910 and 1912. His eight victories are a record; so too is the span of 24 years between his first and last victories. Even after World War I, Ball was not ready to call it a day; he played his last event in 1921 at the age of 60. He reached the sixth round. Credit is usually given to J.H. Taylor for being the first man to be able to impart considerable backspin and to be accurate with iron shots to the flag. However, it was probably John Ball who originally set the pace. Surprisingly, he had a strong dislike for the lofted iron, believing that the golfer should adjust the set of the clubhead to get whatever result was required. Thus he was considered, with a shut face, to be supreme at keeping

John Ball Jnr

his ball low into wind, and for lofted approaches he opened the face and cut the ball. The implement intended for the job, the niblick (the modern equivalent would be an 8-iron) he used to describe as 'just another bloody spade'. Of his swing as a whole, Bernard Darwin, who saw everyone between about 1900 and 1950, said: 'Personally, I should get more aesthetic ecstasy out of watching him than from Bobby Jones and Harry Vardon put together.' Praise indeed. In the Amateur he had many famous encounters. In the 1899 event, for instance, he found himself 5 down to Freddy Tait after 14 holes but won on the 37th. (Both were soon to serve in the South African War, in which Tait was killed.) Then in his last winning year, 1912, he was 5 down with only 7 to play in the fifth round and fought back to win.

BALL, Thomas   England
b. Hoylake 1882; d. 1919

Four times a professional international early this century, Tom Ball was good enough in the days of the all-conquering Great Triumvirate of Vardon, Taylor and Braid to finish second in the Opens of 1908 and 1909. He won the Matchplay Championship in 1909 and the Belgian Open in 1913. His method was hardly orthodox: he had a generous loop in his swing, moved his left foot forward as he came into the ball and performed a kind of pirouette at the end.

BANNERMAN, Harry   Scotland
b. Aberdeen 1942

In the European Top 60 between 1971 and 1973, Harry faded out in the late 1970s and has now not played on tour for a few years. Easily his best year was 1971, when he played extremely consistently and, although not winning, was placed high several times, which accounts for his coming sixth in the Order of Merit that year. Previously he had confined his play mainly to Scotland, for which he played in the 1967 World Cup and then again in 1972. Chosen for the Ryder Cup in 1971, in his singles matches he beat Gardner Dickinson and halved with Arnold Palmer after being 2 down with three to go. In the four-ball series against Nicklaus and Palmer, he and Townsend reached the turn in 29 but lost by 1 down. He was a boy international, won the Scottish Professional title twice and the Northern Open three times.

BARBER, Sally (née Bonallack)   England
b. Chigwell 1938

A sister of Michael Bonallack, Sally made a habit of playing Dinah Oxley in the final of the English Ladies'. In 1968 she beat her at Hunstanton by 5 and 4 but fared less well in both 1970 and 1971, when she was beaten at Rye and Hoylake by 3 and 2 and 5 and 4. She also took the German Ladies' in 1958, the Astor Salver in 1972 and the Avia Foursomes in 1976 and was ten times (six consecutive) Essex champion between 1958 and 1971. She played on the 1962 Curtis Cup team. She turned professional in 1979 but later applied for reinstatement as an amateur.

BARNES, Brian   Scotland
b. Addington, England 1945

After winning the 1964 Youths' Championship, Barnes turned professional and by 1967 was 11th in the Order of Merit. Since then, 26th in 1982 has been his worst finish and he has three times been fourth and twice fifth. Overall, from 1968 to 1980 he had 11 finishes in the top eight or better. In much the same period, he was in the Ryder Cup team on every occasion between 1969 and 1979 and there were many who thought that one of Britain's premier matchplayers should not have been omitted from the 1981 series. He has frequently won tournaments in Africa and Europe, and has taken the Australian Masters. Yet there remains the feeling that Barnes is a failure, a man who has made an excellent living out of golf but has not achieved the heights that his talents should have commanded. It might all have been different had he taken the 1968 Open at Carnoustie. There he finished 6 strokes behind Gary Player in equal sixth place, beaten by an 80 in the third round opposed to Gary's 71. Later, at Muirfield in 1972, he performed more consistently and came fifth, 5 behind Trevino, but never threatened to win. One of a crop of new players who appeared at the end of the 1960s, Barnes most certainly did not, like some, fade away. He also did not rise to the heights of a Jacklin, yet in European money winnings he is one place ahead of him – in all-time third place, behind only Ballesteros and Coles. Coles he will catch but will himself be caught in a couple of years or so by Faldo, Lyle, Norman, James and Langer – if the German's superb iron play is not defeated by obviously severe putting yips. He is a player whom many have thought well suited to American conditions, and in 1970 he won the US qualifying school competition by 5 strokes. On the US Tour that year he won $14,000 in 13 events but made little further effort, and a third place in the Doral Open in Florida remains his best result in the US. Since that time, his overseas forays have mainly been confined to Africa and the Far East. Barnes's greatest day has the stuff of legend in it. On 21 September 1975 he had the good fortune to be twice drawn in one day to oppose Jack Nicklaus in the Ryder Cup. 'Good fortune', because without this luck of the draw he would not have had the opportunity to win twice. Other high spots are five wins in continental Opens, the 1976 Matchplay Championship and the 1970 Australian Wills Masters. More recently, in the 1981 Tournament Players' Championship he came from 6 strokes behind Brian Waites to tie and win the play-off after four extra holes. He had done so with a superlative finish – a round of 62 (third lowest in European Tour history), with a last nine in 28 (second-lowest nine holes). This included hitting a driver shot to just over a foot from the flag at the 309-yard 17th hole at Dalmahoy. Barnes's play is extremely powerful, with a slow, short backswing followed by a controlled lunge at the ball. His putting is reliable – despite the fact that he once took 12 putts on a green during the 1968 French Open, the result of a tantrum. He has always seemed something of an eccentric, perhaps influenced a little by his father-in-law and coach, Max Faulkner. A pipe is often in his mouth during play, shorts are in evidence in hot weather and his clothing has often been highly colourful. He has also been outspoken: in 1979, he declared that the Brabazon course at the Belfry golf complex was unfit for tournament play. He was fined £500 and bookings for visitors fell by 30%! However, the 1981 Ryder Cup venue was transferred to Walton Heath.... Barnes probably began his career with hopes of being a truly major golfer, but as time has passed he has settled just for being a very good one. He makes a good living and has time to enjoy family life and his other major passion, fishing. His 1982 results showed what may be the start of a slow decline. Although he won more than £20,000 for the fifth consecutive year, he was 26th, his worst placing since 1966.

Europe wins 11 (1969–81)
Europe money £251,943 (1965–82) (4th all-time)
Africa wins 4 (1967–81)
Australia wins 1 (1970)

Pam Barton

BARTON, Pamela   England
b. London 1917; d. 1943

With Dorothy Campbell and Catherine Lacoste, Pam Barton was one of three players to have held the US and British Amateur titles in the same year. She did it in 1936, when 19. Her first major achievement was to take the French Championship at the age of 17 in 1934, and in this event she was to be runner-up in 1936 and 1938. In 1934 she also came through to the final of the British Amateur; she reached the same stage again in 1935 before her victory the following year. She won once again, in 1939. Of sturdy build, she had a free swing and hit few bad shots, Henry Cotton judging that she would have continued to be a fine golfer for many years. She was a Flight-Officer in the WAAF during World War II, and was killed on take-off in a light aircraft crash at Manston RAF base in Kent. Her sister Mervyn was an England player and prominent in Surrey golf under her married name, Sutherland-Pilch. Pam Barton was one of many natural left-handers who have been persuaded to play right-handed.

BECK, Dorothy (née Pim)   Ireland
b. Cabinteely 1901

Wife of John Beck, Dorothy won the Irish Ladies' in 1938 and was runner-up in 1949. At the age of 60 she reached the semi-finals of the British Ladies' in 1961 and four times won the Veteran Ladies' title. She was a Curtis Cup choice in 1954, played for Ireland for more than 20 years and was also an international at hockey.

BECK, John Beaumont, MC   England
b. Luton 1899; d. 1981

Winner of some half dozen important amateur events, John Beck was a Walker Cup player in 1928 and non-playing captain in 1938 – the first team to beat the Americans – 1947 and 1949. He was captain of the R & A 1957–8, and later a 'character' at Royal St George's, Sandwich.

BEDDOWS, Charlotte (née Watson) Scotland
b. Edinburgh 1887

Charlotte Beddows had an enormously long competitive career, first representing her county in 1909 and making her last appearance for East Lothian in 1966, when aged 78, surely a record. She also had a very long career at a higher level, winning the Scottish Ladies' in 1920, 1921, 1922 and 1929 and finishing runner-up in 1923 and again in 1950, when well into her 60s. With few years omitted, she represented Scotland between 1913 and 1951, making 21 appearances in the home internationals – and of how many players can it be said that their achievements were affected by *two* world wars? Charlotte Beddows made one Curtis Cup appearance, in 1932, and won the Scottish Veteran Ladies' in 1947 and from 1949 to 1951. She was also a hockey international.

BEHARRELL, John Charles   England
b. 1938

Charles Lawrie, Ian Caldwell, Gene Andrews, Frank Deighton, Reid Jack and Leslie Taylor – six· internationals, three of whom were Walker Cup players – all fell to John Beharrell at Troon in the 1956 British Amateur when, at 18 years and one month he became the youngest winner of the championship. He had kept the ball in play and putted and pitched very well. Apart from a win in the Antlers at Royal Mid Surrey and the Central

England Mixed Foursomes, the rest has been silence; but Beharrell works hard within the game, serving on R & A committees.

BEHARRELL, Veronica (née Anstey) England
b. 1935

A very natural player, Veronica Anstey was a girl international little more than a year after first taking up golf, and her highest achievements came young. During a tour of British juniors in 1955 she won the Australian Ladies' by 10 and 9 in the final and was the youngest winner. On the same tour she took the Victoria state title and the New Zealand Open. In 1957 she reached the semi-finals of the British Ladies' and played in the 1956 Curtis Cup team. She married John Beharrell, winner of the British Amateur in 1956, and restricted her competitive appearances. She won the Warwickshire Ladies' successively from 1955 to 1958, and had several other victories in later years. With her husband she reached the final of the Worplesdon Mixed Foursomes in 1960.

BEMBRIDGE, Maurice   England
b. Worksop 1945

No one has pursued golfing success worldwide more diligently than Bembridge: Britain, Europe, the US, Australia, the Far East – all have seen him. Besides Europe, he has won in New Zealand and Zambia, and the Kenya Open three times. These are perhaps thin rewards for all his travels. Bembridge was one of a group of British golfers, including Jacklin, Gregson and Townsend, who appeared towards the end of the 1960s, and some of whom remain prominent to the present. He first competed in 1965 and from 1966 to 1981 was only once out of the Top 60 in Europe. His best years were from 1968 to 1975 and during that period he was three times in the top 5 with second in 1973 being his best result. After first winning the Kenya Open in 1968, he took the Matchplay Championship the following year and also made the first of four Ryder Cup appearances. In 1971 he won the Dunlop Masters and the PGA three years later. In the Open, he equalled the record for a qualifying round with a 63 in 1967, and the following year he was the highest placed Briton in fifth place. He also achieved a remarkable scoring feat in the 1974 US Masters. After rounds of 73, 74, 72 he played the first nine in 34 and then took only ten putts over the back nine. This resulted in 30 for the nine and a total of 64. The first equalled Ben Hogan's 1967 record and the 64 has only been equalled by Lloyd Mangrum, Gary Player and Jack Nicklaus. Alas, it made him no better than equal ninth. Bembridge has always been better with his irons than he is with his woods, where he lacks both power and consistency. He uses shafts half an inch or so longer than standard to give himself a wider swing arc. Recently, he was second in the 1982 Carrolls Irish Open, a late revival of form. Bembridge maintains his jet-setting image by being attached to the Le Touquet club in France, while residing in the USA.

Europe wins 9 (1969–81)
Europe money £127,132 (1965–82) (29th all-time)
Africa wins 4 (1968–79)
New Zealand wins 1 (1970)

de BENDERN, Count John   England
b. 1907

As John de Forest, he was runner-up in the 1931 British Amateur Championship and then won it the following year, also representing Great Britain in the Walker Cup. Later successes included the Czechoslovakian and Austrian Championships. He was a somewhat eccentric player, an extreme oddity of his play being the condition known as 'choking', in which the afflicted player cannot take the club away from the ball but waggles the clubhead to and fro for an eternity or remains rigidly immobile. Invited to play in the US Masters, he one year found water at the 13th hole but could reach the ball if he put one foot in the water. John therefore removed one shoe and accompanying sock and advanced on his ball into the water hazard. Alas, he had miscalculated: it was the shod foot that found itself in the water.

BENKA, Peter   England
b. 1946

This player sparkled briefly in British amateur golf and then faded from sight. He was British Youths' Champion in 1967 and 1968 and was top amateur in the 1967 British Open. He won the 1968 County Champion of Champions title, and the following year was victor in the Sunningdale Foursomes and played in the Walker Cup. His other principal achievements have been to win the 1972 Dutch Amateur Championship and represent England between 1967 and 1970.

BENTLEY, Arnold Lewis   England
b. Southport 1911

Having been runner-up in the 1938 French Amateur Championship, Arnold Bentley took the English equivalent the following year. He was an amateur international and is the brother of Harry Bentley.

BENTLEY, Harold Geoffrey   England
b. 1907

Harry Bentley had a prolonged career in top amateur golf which falls into two distinct phases: the 1930s and then again in the early 1950s. For instance, he won the French title in 1931 and 1932 and was runner-up in 1953, a year in which he was chairman of selectors for the Walker Cup. The English title he took in 1936 and was runner-up in 1954, when he also won the Italian Amateur Championship. He was an international from 1931 to 1938 and again in 1947. Other major achievements were to win the German Amateur in 1933 and twice to be a Walker Cup team member, in 1936 and 1938, the latter occasion the first that Britain won. He became a man of some wealth; but it is said that the more upper-class the company, the more broad became Harry's Lancashire accent!

BISGOOD, Jeanne Mary   England
b. Richmond, Surrey 1923

A top English player during the 1950s, Jeanne Bisgood is daughter of a former president of the English Golf Union. She took the English Ladies' three times: 1951, 1953 and 1957, winning the last of these finals by 10 and 8. In this same period she won the national titles of Sweden, Germany, Italy, Portugal and Norway and was an England international from 1949 to 1958. Jeanne Bisgood played for the Curtis Cup team from 1950 to 1956 and was non-playing captain in 1970. In other tournaments she won both the Astor Salver and the Roehampton Gold Cup in 1951, 1952 and 1953, and the *Daily Graphic* in 1945 and 1951. Later she became a JP and was Veteran Champion in both 1979 and 1980.

BLACKWELL, Edward B.H.   Scotland
b. St Andrews 1866

Ted Blackwell played in one of the legendary matches of amateur golf. It was the final of the 1904 British Amateur and his opponent was the dour

American Walter Travis. Travis was renowned as a putter, but as the event approached he found that his skill had deserted him. He then borrowed a Schenectady centre-shafted putter and they all began to drop. Blackwell consistently outdrove Travis by 50 yards and more, but Travis was remorseless on the greens and won. The R & A riposted a few years later by banning centre-shafted putters. To reach this final was perhaps Blackwell's finest achievement, for he never won a major title, his nearest approach being the 1922 Scottish Championship, when he was runner-up at the age of 56. He did, however, win a host of medals at St Andrews and holds what is thought to be the record drive with gutties, a hardly credible 366 yards.

BLAIR, Major David Arthur, MBE, MC
Scotland

b. Nairn 1917

David Blair won the Scots Boys Championship in 1935 and became a key figure in British amateur golf after World War II, though never able to give as much time to the game as he might have wished. He was a superb striker of a golf ball, able to play well immediately after long lay-offs. Possibly this was proved in 1978, when he drove himself in as captain of the R & A: it is said he hit the best drive anyone could remember of a new captain. His putting through his career was less reliable and, like Joe Carr on occasion, David Blair often resorted to a 3-iron for the job. He was a Scottish international from 1949 to 1957; won the British Army Championship in 1948; was runner-up in the Scots Amateur in 1950, before winning three years later; and holds the record of 139 for the George Glennie Medal, which is awarded for the best aggregate for the R & A Spring and Autumn Medals. A Walker Cup selection in 1955, he was one of two to win their singles, which he did again in 1961. He was low amateur in the 1950 Open and finished in the first ten in 1960.

BONALLACK, Angela (née Ward)   **England**
b. Birchington 1937

Wife of the great amateur Michael Bonallack, Angela has an excellent record herself in amateur golf and is even now probably good enough to merit a Curtis Cup place. She played in this event from 1956 to 1966 and was again selected in 1974,

though she had on that occasion to decline. In foursomes she was in the losing pair only once of five occasions but was less successful in singles, mainly because she seemed often to be drawn to play against JoAnne Gunderson! She was runner-up for the British Girls' in 1953 and then won the title in 1955; she also won the national titles of Germany, Scandinavia, Portugal and Sweden between 1955 and 1957. She first won the English Ladies' in 1958, beating Bridget Jackson in the final, and won again against Elizabeth Chadwick in 1963. She was runner-up three times, the last occasion coming in 1972. In the British Amateur she was runner-up in 1962 and 1974 to Marley Spearman and Carol Semple respectively. Angela Bonallack has won five other major titles, the Kent championship three times and the Essex six times. She was an England international between 1956 and 1972 and was leading amateur in the European Opens of 1975 and 1976.

David Blair

BONALLACK, Michael Francis, OBE

England

b. Chigwell 1934

It is difficult to see what more Michael Bonallack could have accomplished in amateur golf, given his impressive achievements. But, for instance, he failed to beat John Ball's record of eight wins in the British Amateur Championship and he also failed to be the first amateur since Bobby Jones to win the British Open. He also never broke 60 in competition, though at Ganton in the 1968 English Amateur he came close, for he went out in the final in 32 and came back in 29. Bonallack went to Haileybury School, where he made a name for himself at cricket, and this game might have claimed the lion's share of his attention but for the fact that he beat Alec Shepperson in the final of the 1952 Boys' Championship. This success against another brilliantly gifted youngster seems to have persuaded him to give golf his full attention. However, it then took him some time to get into his stride, and Bonallack himself has said that he did not turn professional because he was not good enough until he was 'too old'. In fact he was a Walker Cup player at the age of 22 and Essex Amateur Champion at 21, but he did not fully begin to dominate championships until past his mid twenties. Thereafter, through the 1960s and into the 1970s, he carried all before him. If he did not beat Ball's record in the British Amateur, no one in an era of high-quality fields has approached his five wins, and even Ball himself did not come near Bonallack's three in a row between 1968 and 1970. Besides these three wins, he also took the championship in 1961 and 1965. The English Amateur he also won five times, a record, and he also won it twice successively, again a record. His four wins in the English Strokeplay are, almost inevitably, another record. Perhaps surprisingly, despite this unparalleled sequence of successes, Bonallack had by no means a perfect swing. He himself once described it as 'more suited to shovelling coal', and he spent much time in the winter of 1967–8 at the Leslie King Golf School seeking to improve it. King considered he had managed to give Bonallack a new swing and had got rid of a 'Mae West' movement in it. That achieved, Bonallack entered what was to be his best year. During the ensuing season he won both British and Amateur Championships and the English Strokeplay, was leading amateur in the British Open (he led the eventual winner, Gary Player, by 4 after one round and was thought a credible conten-

der), and won some half dozen other important amateur competitions. New swing or not, Bonallack was always able to compete effectively with whatever he brought with him on the day. If the drives were not going very far or in the wrong direction, Bonallack did not appear to fret. He knew his mastery of the short game was equal to a few missed greens. Indeed, even in his Ganton 61 he missed four greens and, playing against Alan Thirlwell in the 36-hole final of the English Amateur, he was down in 2 no less than 22 times from off the putting surface. All in all, he probably had the best short game of any British player of this – or any other – era. His putting method was fairly simple. He spread the legs wide, crouched over the ball, held the club low on the grip and then 'willed' it into the hole. Perhaps he was the most daunting as a matchplay opponent when he was not playing well. It is surely worse for an adversary to find himself playing superior golf through the green and to be holes down as chip after chip nestles close and all the putts seem to drop. Even as late as 1981

Michael Bonallack

he was still good enough to win the Prince of Wales and St George's Champion Grand Challenge Cup. As a team member, he was a Walker Cup player without interruption from 1959 to 1973. Oddly his record was not a good one. In the singles, he won only three times, halved twice and lost eight times. One of the halves was remarkable. Against Bruce Fleisher he stood 5 up after nine, then it all crumbled away on the route home. Of course, there was often the burden of playing number one and of so much being expected of him. He played in the Eisenhower Trophy between 1960 and 1972, in 1968 being the equal first individual, and for Great Britain versus Europe from 1958 to 1972. In 1971 he became only the second man to captain a winning British Walker Cup team. As he became less active as a competitive golfer, Bonallack moved into administration with equal distinction. He was chairman of the R & A selection committee in 1975, chairman of the PGA from 1976 until he became president of the English Golf Union in 1982, and has now been appointed secretary of the R & A. His brother Tony, though overshadowed by Michael's fame, distinguished himself as a county player.

BONALLACK, Sally: see Barber

BOOBYER, Frederick   England
b. *Failand 1928*

Speaking with a West Country burr, Fred Boobyer was a straight hitter and an excellent putter who had a career-best 61 in the Middlesex Championship. His major successes were to win the 1965 Ramstein International in Germany and the 1966 Bowmaker. In 1967 he was 12th in the Order of Merit and third in the Dunlop Masters. In 1968 he finished equal fourth in the Alcan International. He now owns his own golf course.

BOOMER, Aubrey B.   England
b. *Grouville, Jersey 1897*

One of the early British golfers to confine himself mainly to continental Europe, Boomer was professional at St Cloud and the Royal Golf Club of Belgium. He won the French Open five times between 1921 and 1931 and was second four times. He also won 11 national titles in all in Europe. Playing infrequently in Britain, he won the 1926

Daily Mail tournament and was equal second, 6 strokes behind Bobby Jones, in the 1927 British Open at St Andrews. He was a Ryder Cup player in 1927 and 1929 and also played against the US in 1926. He also toured in South America with Henry Cotton, and Canada and the USA with Percy Alliss in 1931, and once recorded a 61 at St Cloud.

BOUSFIELD, Kenneth   England
b. *Marston Moor 1919*

Ken Bousfield was always underpowered, which left him with the formidable disadvantage in tournament play of having great difficulty in reaching the par 5s in 2 strokes. He made up a great deal, however, for this deficit in length by being an excellent putter and, using an unusually long backswing, one of the best pitchers on the British scene during his quite long tournament career. After a wartime career as a Marine colour sergeant he was a Ryder Cup player six times between 1949 and 1961. Bousfield held his own against his usually longer-hitting US opponents and established a 50% success average in his matches, considerably better than the norm for British players. Consistency was the key to his game, and this quiet man was competitively tough. He won six European Opens between 1955 and 1961, as well as eight major tournaments in England. As late as 1974 he won the Southern England Professional title at the age of 54, two years after he had won the Seniors. Possibly his outstanding achievement was to take the 1955 PGA Matchplay, while he was a World Cup player in the period 1956–7.

Europe wins 14 (1951–61)

BOYLE, Hugh   Ireland
b. *Omeath 1936*

A considerable player on the British scene from the mid 1960s to early 1970s, Boyle was the first British player to win in Japan when he took the 1966 Yomiuri Open. The following year, he was both a Ryder and World Cup player and took the Blaxnit Tournament in Britain, which followed his first success, the 1966 Daks. He made the record books in 1965 by playing the Dalmahoy East course in 61, the second lowest 18-hole score on the British circuit. He was tenth in the Order of Merit in 1971 and thereafter gradually faded from sight. He was a dedicated practiser, but his game was sometimes marred by a fiery temperament.

BRADSHAW, Harry   Ireland

b. Delgany 1913

Harry Bradshaw introduced his own variation on the Vardon grip: instead of conventionally overlapping the little finger, he overlapped three digits, leaving only the forefinger of his right hand on the shaft. A dominant golfer on the Irish scene, he won the Irish Professional title ten times between 1941 and 1957, took the Irish Dunlop in 1950 and the Irish Open in both 1947 and 1949. He is also one of the very few British golfers since World War I who have come close to winning a British Open. At Royal St George's in 1949 Bradshaw played rounds of 68, 68 and 70 but his second round was a 77, partly due to an incident that has gone down in golfing lore, though not always any too accurately retold. Bradshaw is usually said to have hit his ball out of a beer bottle and thereby lost the Open. In fact, playing the 5th hole, he found his ball against a piece of broken bottle with more of the same around. In these days, most players seem to ask for rulings far more often than is strictly necessary. Bradshaw suspected he was entitled to a free drop but was not sure so played the ball 'traditionally' – as it lay. His ball went 15 yards and a piece of glass struck his eye, but did no harm. Eventually a 6 went down on the card instead of a probable 4. Bradshaw went on to tie for first place with Bobby Locke and in the 36-hole play-off that followed he was massacred by 12 strokes. It was Locke's first Open win; Harry never again came close. In Britain he won four major tournaments, with his greatest achievements being to win the Dunlop Masters twice, in 1953 and 1955. He played for Ireland in the World Cup from 1954 to 1959 and in 1958 was in the only winning British team to date. Bradshaw was second in the individual competition despite being affected by severe nose-bleeds because of the altitude in Mexico City.

GB wins 4 (1953–8)

BRAID, James   Scotland

b. Earls-Ferry 1870; d. 1950

For 45 years professional at Walton Heath Golf Club, James Braid recorded a 74 on his 78th birthday. Beating his age, though a rare feat, was something he did most regularly, and especially on his birthday. This kind of achievement is well worth bearing in mind when the question arises as to whether or not golfers of bygone years were as

Harry Bradshaw

good as their successors. Braid's record in the PGA Matchplay Championship in 'old' age is equally worthy of note. In 1927, at the age of 57, he reached the final but was beaten by Archie Compston, perhaps at that time the best British player. As a younger man, Braid had won the first event in 1903 and had won three out of the first five by 1907. He won once again, in 1911. His record compares most favourably with his companions and rivals in the Great Triumvirate: J.H. Taylor and Harry Vardon. Taylor won twice; Vardon once. Braid's four wins remained unchallenged for many years until equalled in 1950 and 1967 by Dai Rees and Peter Thomson. However, it is as a performer in the British Open that James Braid is best remembered. During his long career he was no less than 15 times in the first five, was third twice, second four times and won it five times, an achievement equalled only by J.H. Taylor and Peter Thomson and excelled by Harry Vardon's six victories. Braid first played in the Open in 1894 as an amateur and apprentice joiner, a clubmaker at the Army and Navy Stores in London. In 1895, after local successes, he became nationally known when he halved an exhibition match with the Open Champion, J.H.

Taylor. Shortly after, he became professional at Romford Golf Club, where he remained until moving to Walton Heath in 1904. In 1897 he had his first real run at the Open. He led into the final round but faltered a little and in the event needed to hole a putt on the last green to tie amateur Harold Hilton. The following year he finished well up the field and then was fifth in 1899 and third in 1900, a long way behind the winner, J.H. Taylor. It is a commonplace of golfing lore that Braid awoke one morning and found himself a long hitter. What seems to have happened is that James suddenly found a driver that suited him, possibly one with a flatter lie or perhaps one with which he could produce more clubhead speed. The first stage in his metamorphosis to major golfer was achieved. But he still could not putt. In the 1900 Open, using, as many did, a cleek (a shallow-faced iron roughly the equal of a modern 1- or 2-iron), he had three-putted repeatedly. Shortly afterwards he changed to an aluminium-headed club and, again according to legend, became a good putter overnight. Two clubs, driver and putter, had changed his life. Braid then proceeded to dominate both Open and Matchplay Championships as neither Vardon nor Taylor did. Only the Thomson of the 1950s and 'Young' Tom Morris can stand comparison with Braid's achievements between 1901 and 1912. In this period he was never worse than sixth and won five times. At Muirfield in 1901 he began in unlikely fashion by hooking his first shot out of bounds and then going to the turn in 43, but he salvaged the round by returning in 36. A good third round saw him 5 ahead of Vardon and he won fairly comfortably by 3 strokes. The following year he finished second with Vardon, both beaten by Sandy Herd, the first man to use a rubber-wound ball in the Open. In 1904 he began 77, 80 and in the third round became the first man to break 70 in an Open and was one ahead of the eventual winner, Jack White. However, in the final round White duplicated the feat and finished on 296, one ahead of Braid and Taylor, the latter of whom had beaten the new record with a 68. All three had beaten the previous 300 record. The following two years at St Andrews and Muirfield, Braid beat Taylor by 5 strokes one year and by 4 the next. At Hoylake in 1907 an 85 in the second round effectively put Braid out of it, but he salvaged some pride at least by having the best two final rounds on the last day and pulled up to within 6 of the winner, Arnaud Massy of France. At this stage Taylor and Braid had both won three Opens

and Harry Vardon was ahead with four. Then at Prestwick, first home of the Open, Braid played perhaps his most accomplished Open, dominating throughout, after initial rounds of 70, 72 which left Vardon, for example, no fewer than 15 strokes in arrears. Although Braid ran up an 8 in the third round he lost little ground and came home in extreme comfort with another 72 in the final round. His 291 total gave him the margin of 8 over Tom Ball in second place, and set an Open record which stood until Jones equalled it at Royal Lytham in 1926 and beat it with an unprecedented 285 at St Andrews the following year. In 1910 Braid became the first man to break 300 in a St Andrews Open and won by four. He was also the first of the Triumvirate to win five Opens and his short-term record was that he had won four of the last six played. Shortly thereafter he is said to have suffered increasing eye trouble, perhaps the result of damage from lime in his youth, when apprenticed to a plasterer. He finished well up in both 1911 and 1912 and then, unlike the other members of the Triumvirate, was no longer a major force after World War I. It is interesting to speculate how

James Braid

much better Braid's record would have looked, as regards major championship wins, had more existed in his time. Only the US Open existed, however, and no British player considered it worth while making the Atlantic crossing for that reason alone. In fact Vardon competed in it at least three times when he was engaged in sales promotions in the USA, but Braid never did. Nevertheless his record of four wins in the Matchplay Championship deserve to be counted as majors, which would bring his tally to nine, though this event has in the last 20 years much declined in status.

BRAND, Gordon, Snr — England
b. Baildon 1955

An England international as an amateur, he joined the European Tour in 1977 and first attracted attention in the 1979 PGA at St Andrews when he was strongly in contention throughout, fading, as did many others in foul weather, to a 78 and equal fourth place in the final round. Brand has not won in Britain but did take the 1981 Ivory Coast Open and won the Tooting Bec Cup for the lowest round by a British golfer for his 65 in the 1981 British Open. His best European performance is an equal second in the Madrid Open of 1979. He made the Top 60 from 1979 to 1981, with 30th in 1979 being his best placing. He is no relation to his younger namesake, the Scottish Gordon Brand.

Africa wins 1 (1981)
Europe money £54,998 (1977–82)

BRAND, Gordon, Jnr — Scotland
b. 1958

A Walker Cup player in 1979 after winning the British Youths', Brand played for Great Britain in the 1978 and 1980 Eisenhower Trophy and the St Andrews Trophy the same years. His first successes had been the 1977 Gloucestershire Amateur and the South-Western title followed by the English Amateur Strokeplay in 1978 and Scottish Strokeplay in 1980. In 1981 he took the Portuguese Amateur and turned professional, winning the ETPD qualifying school tournament in Portugal by 3 strokes from another recent top amateur, Roger Chapman. Like Peter Oosterhuis before him, Brand started his professional career in South Africa and early on produced rounds of 72, 68, 67, 68 in the South African PGA and finished equal second in a strong international field behind Gary Player. A

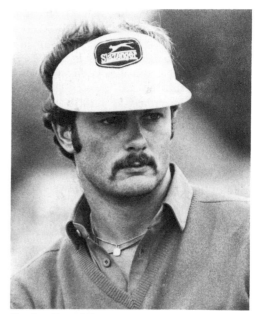

Gordon Brand Jnr

little later, he achieved an almost identical result in the Lexington PGA. In the next event, the Sharp's Classic, he had a 63 but finished some way down in the field. He had already established himself as the most promising, by some distance, of the new professionals, and this promise seemed fulfilled when he won the 1982 Coral Welsh Classic by 4 strokes from Greg Norman. (He was the first since Ronnie Shade to win as a rookie.) Later in the year he produced rounds of 65, 73, 65, 69 to win the Bob Hope British Classic at Moor Park. His first season in professional golf had brought him almost unprecedented success and seventh money-list place. As long as he can continue to control a naturally hot temper, his future seems assured, for he has a simple rhythmic swing, no particular weakness and good nerve.

Europe wins 2 (1982)
Europe money £38,842 (1982)

BRIGGS, Audrey (née Brown) — Wales
b. Kent, England 1945

Audrey Briggs was a member of the Welsh international team from 1969 to 1981, eventually as captain. She won the Welsh Ladies' in 1970, 1971, 1973 and 1974 and was runner-up as recently as 1981. She has also taken the Sussex, Cheshire and North of England titles.

BRODIE, Allan   Scotland
b. 1947

After being second in the Scots Amateur in 1973, Brodie won in 1977 and was chosen for the Walker Cup team, an invitation repeated in 1979. He was an amateur international from 1970 to 1980, and further achievements may still lie ahead.

BROOKS, Andrew   Scotland
b. Lanark 1946

A boy international in 1964, Brooks followed up with youth caps from 1965 to 1968 and was a senior international in 1968 and 1969. In the last of these years he played in the European Team Championships and the Walker Cup. Here he was unbeaten and won his singles convincingly. He then turned professional and his first entry, in the Algarve Open, brought him second place behind Brian Huggett; he also won a minor tournament in Scotland, the Cameron Corbet Vase. He finished the year 26th in the Order of Merit. For the next few years he maintained that level of performance and twice played for Scotland in internationals. But then, to achieve greater success, he attempted to change his style, and he quickly faded away. He does not now play on the circuit.

BROWN, Audrey: see Briggs

BROWN, David   Scotland
b. Musselburgh 1860

David Brown won the British Open in 1886; but this was at a time when the event was attracting little attention, between the Morris achievements and the Open's increase in importance in the 1890s. Later, in 1903, he tied for first place in the US Open, but lost the play-off to Willie Anderson.

BROWN, Eric Chalmers   Scotland
b. Edinburgh 1925

Eric Brown's proudest achievement is to have four times played in the Great Britain Ryder Cup team and each time emerged victorious in his singles. In the 1953 match he disposed of Lloyd Mangrum by 2 up; Jerry Barber by 3 and 2 in 1955; Tommy Bolt 4 and 3 in 1957; and finally Cary Middlecoff by 4 and 3 in 1959. The most important of these wins came in 1957. Brown played number one that year and his early dominance of Bolt perhaps set a mood that led to exhilaration throughout the whole team. The British team's six wins were all by crushing margins. Later, in 1969 and 1971, Brown went on to captain the team, and produced the creditable results of a tie in 1969 at Royal Birkdale, followed by the best British performance in the US, a loss at St Louis by 13½ to 18½. He was at his best as a matchplayer, thriving on the greater element of personal combat in that form of golf. Three times he reached the final of the PGA Matchplay Championship, winning in 1960 and 1962, when he was a little past his best days. Eric Brown won the Scottish Amateur in 1946 and turned professional. It is some comment on the restrictions of those days that he was not allowed to win money until he had served a five-year apprenticeship (what would Ballesteros think of that?). His first major success came in 1951, with the Swiss Open, and he had taken three more national Opens by the end of 1953. In Britain he won seven major tournaments, including the Dunlop Masters of 1957, the year in which he also took the Vardon Trophy for the lowest stroke average. Brown was for some time a leading British hope in the Open and six times finished ninth or better. His best year was in 1957, when, after a third-round 65, Brown was one of several players who came to the last hole of all with a chance of winning or tying. Two, Thomson and Thomas, parred the last; Brown was amongst those who were bunkered from the tee and thus, with Christy O'Connor, he finished 1 behind in third place. With John Panton, he dominated Scottish and northern golf for many years. He won the Northern Open five times, the Scots Professional eight times, and seven Scots regional titles. He was a Scotland World Cup player 13 times from 1954 to 1968. Eric Brown had a hooker's left-hand grip and played with laid-off woods to alleviate his problems off the tee. For most of his career he was one of the best pitchers of the ball in the British game and a courageous putter. He was most unfortunate in that all his best years came well before the dramatic rises in prize money.

Europe national Opens 4 (1951–3)
GB wins 7 (1952–62)

BROWN, Kenneth   Scotland
b. Harpenden, England 1957

Ken Brown's name rapidly became one of the best known in British golf, this despite a thin record of achievement. In golf, as other sports, individualism

Ken Brown

can attract more attention than quality of play. Brown's stick-like figure earned him the nickname of 'the walking 1-iron', his superb putting stroke, usually with a rusty, hickory-shafted veteran club, was eminently newsworthy, as was his golfing attire. Against the norm of spick-and-span – if not downright dazzling – Brown used to be seen in baggy trousers and sagging cardigan, though his appearance has since become thoroughly conventional. Most newsworthy of all, however, was the fact that Ken was – and is – supposed to be the slowest player in Britain, if not the world. This is long likely to continue, for he considers that he plays at the pace which suits him and that disaster occurs if he attempts to speed up. He has also attracted notice for not speaking to his partners in pro-ams or in the foursomes of the 1979 Ryder Cup, when his partner was Des Smyth. In this event he considered that the team blazer smacked of regimentation, and said so. All this added up to a fine of £1,000 and suspension from any international

event for one year. In 1981 Brown wryly claimed that he was leading the money list for slow-play fines. This slow play was seen at its most extreme in the 1980 Open at Muirfield. Brown had begun 70, 68, 68, which put him in joint second place but 4 behind leader Tom Watson. In the final round they were paired. Watson is an exceptionally quick player so the blame was easy enough to attach when they finished some three holes behind the field. Undoubtedly this championship was Ken Brown's finest achievement, for it is increasingly rare for a last round to begin with a British player still in with a chance. Ken Brown was a boy international in 1974 and won the Carris Trophy the same year. The following year he won the Hertfordshire Open and turned professional, being given special permission to play in four events, winning money in three. In his first full season he finished 47th on the money list. In 1977 he placed 21st and was chosen for the Ryder Cup and Scottish World Cup teams, selections repeated in the following two years. In 1978 he went to fourth place and with four rounds under par at Portmarnock won the Irish Open against a very strong international field, so far his only tournament success though he has threatened to win the PGA and was three times second in 1980. A final criticism that has been levelled at Ken Brown is that he practises *too much*, the implication being that he is burned out for actual tournament play – an odd accusation in Britain, where it is common belief that American players are good because each and every one spends all his waking hours either competing or on the practice ground. Whatever the truth of these and other matters, Ken Brown is not the sort to settle for being a run-of-the-mill tournament player. Presently he is at a crossroads, and who can tell if he will become a major player, an Open Champion, or will gradually fade from view?

Europe wins 1 (1978)
Europe money £149,265 (1975–82) (19th all-time)

BROWN, Stuart   England
b. Sheffield 1946

After turning professional in 1965, Stuart Brown won the 1966 Assistants Championship and topped the qualifiers for the Open from 1969 to 1971. In 1970, he went on Tour full time and finished 36th in his first season, winning Henry Cotton's Rookie of the Year award. In 1971, he had his first win in the Lusaka Dunlop tournament and came 17th in the European Order of Merit. He had two second-place finishes and was equal third in the Dunlop Masters. With the future looking exceptionally bright, he failed to make the Top 60 the following year and after continuing lack of success dropped out of tournament golf. However, he returned in 1982, to no real effect.

BRUEN, James   Ireland
b. Belfast 1920; d. 1972

James Bruen is given much of the credit for a British victory in the 1938 Walker Cup at St Andrews, and this despite the fact that he lost his singles against Charlie Yates. The reason is that his form during practice gave impetus to the British side. Bruen repeatedly broke 70 around St Andrews, and the team felt that they possessed the best player on either side. Bruen's talent was both phenomenal and unorthodox, and he was one of the most exciting golfers of his, or any other, time. He took the club back almost directly away from his body and whirled it around before a whiplash attack on the ball. Using this unlikely method he hit the ball vast distances and quite frequently into unusual parts of the course, where his power enabled him to treat deep rough with little respect. He was also an excellent approach putter. In 1936 he won the Boys' Championship and the following year won the Irish Closed Amateur, a win he

James Bruen

repeated in 1938 together with the Open event. There followed his first Walker Cup appearance and in 1939 he was top amateur in the Open Championship, after leading over the two qualifying rounds. After World War II he was no longer quite the same force, though he made the Walker Cup team in 1949 and 1951. A wrist injury was probably the main reason for his decline. When he last played in the British Amateur in 1960, it caused his withdrawal.

BURKE, John   Ireland
b. Lahinch 1900; d. 1972

John Burke was a prolific winner of Irish amateur titles. Between 1930 and 1947 he eight times took the Irish Closed title, and won the Amateur Open in 1947, when he beat Joe Carr in the final. He also won the West of Ireland six times and the South of Ireland eleven times between 1928 and 1946. He was a Walker Cup choice in 1932 and an international every year from 1929 to 1949.

BURTON, Richard   England
b. Darwen 1907; d. 1974

Dick Burton had the misfortune to win little money from his greatest achievement. He won the 1939 British Open by 2 strokes at St Andrews from Johnny Bulla. The war came, and with it no chance of the endorsement contracts that would have otherwise flowed in. He finished his win in some style, driving boldly down the line of the fence at the last hole and then lofting in a 9-iron before sinking his birdie putt. Burton had been equal fourth in 1938 at Sandwich and was fifth at Hoylake in 1947. He had the longest reign of any Open Champion: seven years. In 1949 he set what was then a scoring record for a British tournament with 266 (68, 66, 64, 68). His brother, John Burton, a very good long-iron player, was professional at Hillside and was also in tournament golf. Dick Burton himself was professional at Coombe Hill for many years.

BUSSELL, Alan Francis   Scotland
b. Glasgow 1937

One of the most promising amateurs to appear since World War II, Alan Bussell had a rather short golfing career. He won the British Boys' Championship in 1954 and followed that with the Youths' two years later. He was a Walker Cup player in

1957 and one of only two on the British team to win his singles. He represented Scotland four times, and played for Great Britain against Europe in 1956 and 1962 and won two important amateur events. From the age of 25 he mainly confined himself to local events, being Nottinghamshire Amateur champion seven times between 1959 and 1969, and Matchplay champion in 1960 and 1962. In addition, he won the Nottinghamshire Open twice, also in 1960 and 1962.

BUSSON, John Joseph England
b. *Hinckley 1910*

Winner of the 1934 Matchplay Championship, Busson was selected for the Ryder Cup in 1935. In the 1938 British Open he held the lead after 36 holes and finished equal fourth. His brother Harry earned a reputation as a superb clubmaker, was also a good player, and took over at Walton Heath from James Braid.

BUTLER, Peter England
b. *Birmingham 1932*

Butler turned professional in 1948, went on Tour in 1958 and from then to the end of the 1978 season he was never out of the Top 60. Seven times in the period 1964–72 he was seventh or better, with second in 1968 being his best performance. He was perhaps the best British player at that time, the most reliable at keeping the ball in play, fading the ball into the fairway. He was barred from higher achievements only by lack of length. Despite this shortness from the tee, Peter produced two of the rare good British performances in the US Masters on a course where length is considered essential. In 1964 he finished 13th, at that time the highest placing achieved by a Briton, and two years later he held the lead after 36 holes, before again finishing 13th. He was also the first Briton to qualify to play in six successive US Masters. He has several low-scoring feats in his record, the most notable being the second lowest score achieved in Britain, a 61 on Sunningdale Old in the 1967 Bowmaker Tournament; the second longest run of birdies, seven, in the 1974 PGA; and in 1968 he had 24 consecutive rounds in par or better. He played in the Ryder Cup four times: 1965, 1969, 1971 and 1973, in 1969 winning both his singles on that final day which ended in a dramatic tie. He also has three World Cup appearances in his record: 1969, 1970 and

1973. Butler was a particularly good putter and had the necessary nerve for tournament success.

GB wins 12 (1959–74)
Overseas wins 3 (1963–75)
Europe money £103,099 (1958–82) (34th all-time)

CADDEN, Suzanne (later McMahon) Scotland
b. *Old Kilpatrick 1957*

Suzanne Cadden had an outstanding spell as a junior, winning the 1973 World Championship, the Scottish Girls' in 1974 and 1976, the British in 1975 and the Scottish Girls' Strokeplay in 1976 and 1977. She was a girl international for five years from 1972 to 1976, and a full international from 1974 to 1979. Suzanne had a remarkable year in 1975, for in addition to the distinctions listed she was runner-up to Nancy Syms of the USA in the British Ladies' and also second in the British Strokeplay. She was the Daks Woman Golfer of the Year before the age of 18. She also won the Scottish Ladies' Foursomes in 1972 and the Dumbartonshire titles in 1976, 1977 and 1979, and she played in the 1976 Curtis Cup, being defeated by Nancy Lopez and Donna Horton in singles. Her sister Gladys is good enough to have won the Scottish Girls' title in 1972 and the Scottish Open Strokeplay in 1975.

CALDWELL, Ian England
b. *Streatham 1930*

Son of a clergyman, Ian Caldwell was an international between 1950 and 1957 and again in 1961. This was the year of his greatest achievement, victory in the English Amateur, when he holed a putt of some 15 feet at Sunningdale to take the championship. It made a fitting ending to his golf career. He was also a Walker Cup choice in 1951 and 1957, and is now a Harley Street dentist.

CAMPBELL, Dorothy: see North America

CAMPBELL, William Scotland
b. *Musselburgh 1862; d. 1900*

One of a host of good Victorian golfers hailing from Musselburgh, Willie Campbell was primarily known as a fine matchplayer. However, perhaps his best moment came in the 1887 Open Championship. With a few holes to go he looked a sure winner but then took 8 on a par 4 to finish 3 strokes in arrears of Willie Park Jnr. Campbell was third. Four years later he emigrated to the USA.

CAMPBELL, William Thomas   Ireland

In 1964 at Dun Laoghaire in Eire, Tommie Campbell set the level-ground drive record of 392 yards. He is also known as an entrepreneur and for his concern with Irish civil rights.

CARR, Joseph Benedict   Ireland
b. Dublin 1922

Joe Carr first took an important title with the 1941 East of Ireland Amateur and he did not fall out of contention until the 1970s. His career had been one of the most sustained among British amateurs, and he can claim to have been the best British amateur from the end of World War II until Michael Bonallack became a dominant force. During this long career Carr won well over 30 important titles, and these included the British Amateur on three occasions: 1953, 1958 and 1960. In the first of these he ended an American run of success by defeating the great Harvie Ward, and his later victims were Alan Thirlwell and the USA's Bob Cochran. He reached the semi-final stages on three other occasions – all during the 1950s – and was a finalist in 1968 at the age of 46. His most dominant performance came in the 1960 final, when he stood 10 up after 28 holes and eventually won by 8 and 7. In Ireland he was of course a living legend, and for a long time the outstanding figure – amateur or professional. Besides regional titles he took the Irish Closed Amateur six times and won the Irish Open Amateur in 1946, 1950, 1954 and 1956. Joe Carr was an extremely long hitter, employing – until he modified it – a swaying slash of a swing with a pronounced lean into the shot and the right hand quite well under the shaft. The method, not surprisingly, got him into wild country, and frequent experience there made his recovery shots excellent. He was also an outstandingly good sand player. His only weakness was on the greens, and it was by no means unknown for him to resort to using a long iron when all putters had failed him. As a team member, he was a Walker Cup choice on every occasion between 1947 and 1965, in the last year as captain and two years later as non-playing captain. He holds the record for the number of appearances for a player of either side. He also

Joe Carr

represented Britain three times in the World Team Championship. Carr competed infrequently in the USA, but reached the semi-finals of the 1961 US Amateur and was only the second Briton to be elected a member of Augusta National. He sometimes competed in professional events. In 1956 and 1958 he was leading amateur in the Open, and in 1960 a third round of 67 at St Andrews put him two behind the leader Kel Nagle. After a closing 73 he finished eighth. He was even closer to success in the 1959 Dunlop Masters at Portmarnock but had to rest content with second place after a rousing finish from Christy O'Connor. As an amateur golfer, Carr thrived from the base of a securely prosperous business. He had a house overlooking Sutton Golf Club near Dublin, and he was allowed to erect floodlights on a section of the course to practise chipping and putting in the evenings. His regular regime was a morning run, half an hour's practice and then away to the office. In the evening, he usually managed a further couple of hours. Two of his sons have made some impact on the game, with John reaching the semi-finals of the 1981 British Amateur.

CARR, Roderick J.   Ireland
b. Sutton, Dublin 1950

The second son of Joe Carr, Roddy at one time seemed set to emulate the deeds of his father. He won four important amateur titles and played a major role in the British win in the 1971 Walker Cup (the first since 1938) in which he took 3½ points out of a possible 4. He was a long hitter and a good putter. Much was expected of him when he turned professional, but he failed to break into the top 100 in his first two seasons, though improving to 48th position on the European Tour in 1974. He then faded gradually from the scene. He is now employed in administration by the Mark McCormack organization in the USA and is most successful.

CARRICK, Angela: see Uzielli

CAYGILL, Gordon Alexander   England
b. Appleby 1940

After he turned professional in 1962, it was not long before Alex Caygill came to be recognized as a leading hope of British golf. In 1963, he had his first victory in the Rediffusion Tournament, which seemed to fulfil the promise of two wins in the British Youths' Championship. He then went into a decline, said to be at least in part caused by ulcers; but he surfaced again in 1969 when he won the Penfold and was equal first in the Martini International. These achievements won him a Ryder Cup place though he played only once, in the four-ball, when he halved with Brian Huggett against Ray Floyd and Miller Barber. Thereafter Caygill again declined, his temperament increasingly thought to be the main cause. In 1981 he was fined £500 for discourtesy and using bad language in the 1980 Wansbeck Classic at Bedlington near Newcastle, and in 1982 he was reported to be working as a fish porter in Bradford Market.

Europe wins 3 (1963–9)

CHADWICK, Elizabeth (later Pook)   England
b. Inverness, Scotland 1943

Elizabeth Chadwick packed all her serious competitive career into a short period, her achievements taking off in 1963 and ending with her retirement from serious competitive golf in 1968. She was runner-up in the English Amateur in 1963, losing to Angela Bonallack. Her peak years were

1966–7, when she performed the rare feat of winning the British title in consecutive years, beating Vivien Saunders and Mary Everard in the respective finals. She played on the 1966 Curtis Cup side, won the Central England Mixed Foursomes and North of England Ladies' three times each and the Cheshire Ladies' every year from 1963 to 1967.

CHAMBERS, Doris Elaine, OBE   England
b. Liverpool

An England international between 1904 and 1924, Doris Chambers won the British title in 1923, almost an interloper in the dominant years of Cecil Leitch and Joyce Wethered. She was also twice non-playing captain of the Curtis Cup team, in 1936 and 1948, and captained British touring teams in the 1930s. She was 1937 Veterans' Champion.

CHAPMAN, Roger   England
b. 1959

Chapman's first important success was to win the 1977 Kent Open Championship, followed by victory in the 1979 English Amateur. In 1981, he won the Lytham Trophy, finished 68th in the Open, while including the drama of a hole in one, and in the 1981 Walker Cup won three times (including a victory over Hal Sutton, a US Tour winner in 1982) and lost once and then by one hole only. With George Will, he also won the 1979 Sunningdale Open Foursomes. Chapman turned professional at the end of the 1981 season and finished second in the European Tour qualifying competition. Recognized as one of the most promising British golfers, he began his professional career with a sequence of sound performances culminating in a second place in the Spanish Open. He made the Top 60 for the season.

Europe money £8,804 (1982)

CHRISTMAS, Martin J.   England
b. 1939

Martin Christmas is one of many golfers whose amateur career was cut short by the demands of business. In 1960 he was second in the English Open Amateur Strokeplay and in the same year reached the final of the English Amateur. There he met Doug Sewell, who defeated him in a match that went to the 41st hole. The following year he went to the semi-finals of the British Amateur and repeated this both three and four years later. A Walker Cup player in 1961 and 1963, he was the only member of the team to win his singles but went down to Billy Joe Patton in 1963. During this period, Christmas was an automatic England choice and played for Great Britain versus Europe three times. In 1962 he was chosen for the Eisenhower Trophy. Noted for attacking iron shots, Martin Christmas did not build a formidable record in tournament golf, his best achievements being to win the 1961 Gleneagles Pro-Am, the 1962 Wentworth Pro-Am Foursomes and then, much later on, the 1976 Belgian Amateur.

CLARK, Clive Anthony   England
b. Winchester 1945

In 1965, Clive Clark had one of the best (but also most disappointing) years experienced by a British amateur in modern times. He won three important amateur tournaments, but in the championships the prizes were plucked away. Against Michael Bonallack in the British Amateur, he was a commanding 6 up after 13 holes but eventually lost by 2

Clive Clark

and 1. He faced Bonallack again in the English final, this time going down by 3 and 2. In the English Open Amateur Strokeplay he finally came in first, but tied with two others. In retrospect, his finest moments may have come in that year's Walker Cup. Here he took 3½ points of a possible 4. At the end of the first day, Great Britain and Ireland stood an unlikely 8–3 in the lead but on the last afternoon the USA put their opponents to the sword in the singles. Only Gordon Cosh won; Clark stood 1 down with two to play, was unfortunate, with his opponent in trees, not to win the 35th but then holed a putt of more than 30 feet on the last. It halved both Clark's match and that year's Walker Cup. At the end of the year Clive turned professional, and in his first season won the Danish Open. His finest performance as a professional came the following year in the British Open. Although it was de Vicenzo's year, Clark returned 70, 73, 69, 72, finishing equal third with Gary Player. He ended the year third in the Order of Merit. In 1968 Clark secured his US Tour playing card but after little success decided that his future lay in Europe. There, he won the 1968 Agfa tournament, the 1970 John Player Trophy and the 1974 Sumrie Better-Ball. He also lost the 1972 French Open in a play-off, and became only the fourth player to represent Great Britain as amateur and professional when he was chosen for the 1973 Ryder Cup. He gradually withdrew from tournament play during the mid 1970s and now has one of the best addresses in Britain as professional at Sunningdale. He is a golf commentator for both the BBC and CBS.

CLARK, Gordon James   England
b. Newcastle upon Tyne 1933

Winner of four Northumberland county titles, Gordon Clark had his best years in the 1960s. In 1964 he beat Michael Lunt on the 39th to take the British Amateur, compensation for his runner-up placing in the 1961 English Amateur, when Ian Caldwell won on the first extra hole. When his best years seemed past, Gordon Clark had a revival of form to tie for the Scots Strokeplay title in 1973 and then won the Portuguese Amateur the following year. Clark played as a boy international in 1950, and seven times for England between 1961 and 1971. When into his forties, this very steady golfer turned professional and now has a club job in Durham.

CLARK, Howard K.   England
b. Leeds 1954

Howard Clark was for three years a boy international, taking the British Boys' Championship in 1971, and was then a youth international for three further years. Chosen for the 1973 Walker Cup team, he performed well at Brookline and shortly afterwards turned professional, going under Henry Cotton's wing at Penina for some 13 weeks to learn to manoeuvre the ball. His ability at hitting the ball low is some reflection of this experience. Clark made a slow start to his professional career, coming in 53rd in the 1974 Order of Merit and only 73rd the following year, though he was encouraged by winning the Manchester Open, a non-Tour event. Then came improvement to 22nd and 16th, the latter earning him a Ryder Cup place. Clark played only once at Royal Lytham, where he looked extremely nervous while being beaten 4 and 3 by Lanny Wadkins. Then came a remarkable start to 1978. The first event was at Penina, the Portuguese Open, and under Henry Cotton's eye. In a high-scoring tournament, Clark was the only player to break par, and won his first important event. On to El Prat for the Spanish Open in which Clark began with a pair of 67s to lead. A third-round 74 lost him ground but he retained the lead. His final 70 should have seen him home but Brian Barnes returned a 64 to win by 2 with Clark second. The next event was the Madrid Open at Puerta de Hierro. Clark's scores were 70, 70, 72, 70. He won by 2 strokes to complete the remarkable 1–2–1 sequence. The next month he took third place in the British PGA and later had a sequence of six consecutive tournaments in the top 8. He finished the season fifth in the Order of Merit and then helped England to third place in the World Cup. To date that season has been Clark's best and he has not won again, though he remains a consistent money-winner, being 22nd, 26th and 14th in the Order of Merit. He regained his Ryder Cup place in 1981 and turned in one of the best European performances in demolishing Tom Watson by 4 and 3, with six birdies and an eagle on his card. This was one of the rare occasions on which he did full justice to his considerable talent. He was a disappointing 28th in the 1982 money list (this being his worst result since 1975) and seldom featured among the ranks of the tournament leaders.

Europe wins 2 (1978)
Europe money £142,878 (1974–82) (25th all-time)

COLES, Neil, MBE   England
b. London 1934

Neil Coles turned professional at the age of 16 in 1950, rather optimistically, for at the time he had a handicap of 14! His confidence was well placed, however, for he has since established the most consistent record of any British golfer of modern times. Winning his first cheque in 1955, Coles was a major figure on the European scene by 1961. In that year, he finished fifth in the Order of Merit and has never been worse than 16th since that time. Every year from 1961 to 1976 he was in the top 10 and in 1963 and 1970 he topped the order and also took the Vardon Trophy. In all he has 12 times been in the top 6. He topped the money list in 1964 and 1966 and was the first European player to reach the £200,000 mark in career money winnings. His present career total is still exceeded only by Severiano Ballesteros; many will overhaul him in the next few seasons as prize money rises, but few will equal his 27 career wins. Coles first won anything of significance in 1955, with the Hertfordshire Open, and the next year took the Assistants Championship. In later years he would not have qualified, for he was to become Britain's first tournament professional, and except in his earliest years has sought to avoid the constraints of a club professional's job. His first major victory was delayed until 1961, in part the result of a fiery temperament which in later years he has kept well under control, and partly through a certain looseness in the backswing. Coles also had, and still has, a hooker's grip, but he has come to earn a reputation for straightness. From that 1961 Ballentines, when he produced a 65 in the last round, he won every year up to 1966 and then started another sequence in 1970, which continued until a winless 1975. He played 68 tournaments between 1973 and 1979 without missing a cut. All this has been achieved in spite of his grip, which seemingly should allow him to play well only in fits and starts. At address the clubface is hooded and is also shut at the top of the backswing. He is also a no more than competent putter, but his chipping is superb. One event Coles has missed out on is the Open Championship. He has never threatened to win, despite finishing well up on occasion. In 1961 he was equal third, four behind Palmer. In 1973, he finished equal second with Johnny Miller after a last-round 66 which made up 4 strokes on the winner, Tom Weiskopf, when he had started 7 in arrears. Perhaps his best chance was 1973, when he opened 72, 69, 67 and at

Neil Coles

the first event in 1964, despatching Tony Lema by 4 and 3 and Bruce Devlin by 2 and 1. In the final he met Arnold Palmer, still at his best, and lost a close match 2 and 1. He has also performed well in the other European matchplay event, the PGA, winning it three times; 1964, 1965 and 1973. Otherwise, he has taken two national Opens, the German in 1971 and the Spanish two years later. He also won the 1966 Dunlop Masters, the British tournament with most prestige after the Open Championship, unless his 1976 PGA can rival that. In his mature years, Coles has come to be seen as a highly idiosyncratic player. The petulant club-banging of his youth has given way to an almost totally impassive mask. Did the long putt drop? Is the tee shot over there in a bush? In a bunker? Almost impossible to tell from Coles's face. He has also rejected flamboyant golf attire. Where others may be sporting close relatives of pyjama trousers, two-tone shoes and vivid colours, Coles is more likely to be seen in black shoes, grey trousers and a sweater of subdued colour. Partly bald for most of his career, he has made up for this by growing a pair of bushy side whiskers, and these and the tufts of hair on the side of his head, wafting in the breeze, give him the look of a benign archdeacon. He is an artist of golf, for the young to watch and learn from. He won the Sanyo Open in Spain late in 1982, his first important win for five years, and came a highly creditable 16th on the year's money list. He is Chairman of the PGA European Tour.

Europe wins 27 (1961–82)
Europe money £294,350 (1955–82) (2nd all-time)

COMPSTON, Archibald Edward Wones
England

b. Wolverhampton 1893; d. 1962

Archie Compston was one of the leading British golfers in the period from 1925 to the early 1930s, and also something of a legend in his own lifetime. Part of that legend came from his outrageous defeat of Walter Hagen by 18 and 17 in a challenge match at Moor Park in 1928. Compston played superlative golf over what should have been 72 holes and Hagen, just off a transatlantic liner, was shaking hands in concession of defeat with almost a full round to go. Shortly afterwards they met in another kind of competition, the 1928 Open at Sandwich. Hagen buckled down to his task, having practised diligently (most unusual for him) and came in 3 ahead of Compston. Nevertheless, Compston's

this stage was one of a dozen players with a chance to win at Carnoustie. A 70 would have seen Coles home, but his actual 74 left him equal seventh. He has, however, three times won the Tooting Bec Cup, awarded to the British player with the lowest round, and the Braid Taylor Memorial Medal twice for the best-placed British player. Perhaps Coles would have improved on these performances had he been fonder of playing links golf. He has a much stronger aversion to another activity: flying, after a frightening experience on a London to Scotland flight. It is doubtful if Coles would have chosen to play the US Tour, but he would certainly have been far more international a player had the circuits of Japan, the Far East and Africa been open to him. As it is, he has long thought only of events he can get to by land and sea – and that means Europe only. What then, have been his outstanding achievements? The Ryder Cup perhaps should have pride of place. He was chosen or qualified for each match from 1961 to 1977, winning seven points out of a possible 15. His total of 40 matches played is the highest on either side. He has three times qualified for the World Matchplay at Wentworth and, until Sandy Lyle did it in 1980, was the only Briton to reach the final. This he achieved in

third place was one of his best performances in the championship. He had also been in sight of victory in 1925 at Prestwick, finishing tied for second place with Ted Ray, and with Jim Barnes the winner, a stroke better. Hoylake in 1930 saw the second leg of Bobby Jones's Grand Slam achieved – but it was not easily done. Jones was below his best but led Compston by 5 after two rounds. Jones had a 74 in the morning, and as he prepared to play his final round in the afternoon, Archie was completing his third round. Jones wrote later: 'I had the feeling that spectators, tee boxes, benches even, might be swirled up in his wake.... As he made his beaming way to the club-house... he was about as happy a figure as I have ever seen.' Compston had done a 68, after beginning the homeward nine 3, 3, 3, 2, and had gained 6 strokes on Jones to hold a 1-stroke lead. In the afternoon, Jones had troubles but played manfully over the closing holes to come in with a 75, his worst round in this championship. For Compston, the morning 3s turned to 5s in the afternoon. It is said after his 82 he was never a considerable player again. His most notable tournament wins were to take the PGA Matchplay twice, in 1925 and 1927, and the French Open in 1929. He was also said to make considerable sums of money from betting on his own matches with wealthy amateurs. The Inland Revenue attempted to tax him, the case went to court and, to applause throughout the nation, Compston won. Compston played for Britain in Ryder Cup matches, or their earlier equivalent, four times between 1926 and 1931. Later he coached the Prince of Wales (the future Edward VIII), once accompanying him on a Mediterranean cruise during which 3,000 balls were struck into the sea. He is also given much credit for the successes of Pam Barton. He spent the later part of his life at the Mid-Ocean Country Club in Bermuda. A reputation for gruffness, and even rudeness and arrogance, was undeserved; those who knew him better found him very kindly and generous.

CONNACHAN, Jane McGrath Scotland
b. Haddington 1964

There is a strong tendency for women golfers to mature sooner than their male counterparts, but Jane Connachan is an exceptional case, sweeping the field in girls' events and formidable in adult competition also, while not reaching her 20th birthday until early 1984. At 12 she was a girl

international and at 14 winner of the East Lothian championship, in an area that is a hotbed of golf, housing such courses as Muirfield, Gullane, North Berwick, Longniddry and a host of others. At 14 she was Scottish Girls' Champion and won again in 1979 and 1980, in the latter year, at 16, becoming British Girls' Champion and holding the title the following year. She has also won the Scottish Girls' Open Strokeplay, in 1978 and 1980; was second in the 1981 British Ladies' Amateur Strokeplay, winning it by 5 strokes in 1982; and Scottish Champion in 1982, representing Great Britain in the World Team Championship. At 15 she made the full Scotland team and at 16 became the youngest ever to play in a Curtis Cup match; she was again in the 1982 team. Late in 1982 she was in the winning British pair for the World Junior Team Championship and also won the Australian Junior. If she remains an amateur she could beat the record for Curtis Cup appearances by the time she is 30.

COOK, John H. England
b. Wembley 1949

John Cook was first a boy and then a youth international between 1965 and 1969, and won both the British Youths' and English Amateur that year, in the latter defeating Peter Dawson by 6 and 5 in the final. He then turned professional and began his career in fine style by almost immediately taking the Nigerian Open, nearly repeating this feat the following year when he came second. Although he took the Southern Professional in 1972 he had little more success. In 1973 he was 70th on the money list and 98th a year later. After spending a year or two in Sun City, South Africa, he now runs a pub in Cornwall.

Africa wins 1 (1970)

COOK, Nancy: see Wright

COOPER, Harry: see North America

COSH, Gordon B. Scotland
b. Glasgow 1939

Gordon Cosh began a successful amateur career as a youth international and went on to represent Scotland in the period 1964–9, and also Great Britain. He was once a Walker Cup choice, in 1965, and won both his singles at Baltimore, beating D. Allen on both occasions. With Michael Lunt he also won the top foursomes match, but he went down to Ed Tutwiler and Billy Joe Patton in the four-ball. His 3 points out of 4 were a major factor in the Great Britain side earning a tie in the match as a whole. Four times a winner of Scottish regional titles, Cosh was runner-up for the Scots Amateur in 1965 and won three years later, when he was also second in the Strokeplay Open. He played in the Eisenhower Trophy in 1966 and 1968. He is now a prominent executive with a construction company.

COTTON, Thomas Henry, MBE   England
b. Holmes Chapel 1907

Now well into his 70s, and long-established as a guru of the game of golf, Henry Cotton can look back on a playing career which has established him in the eyes of history as the best British golfer since World War I. Had he been born in an earlier age he would have ranked as an equal with the Great Triumvirate; if in a later, the ease of world travel would have seen him a great player on the world stage. As it was, Cotton played mainly in Britain and, far more than most of his contemporaries, in Europe. Otherwise his trips to other continents were very few, though he played in South America and the USA, the latter first as a young man in

Henry Cotton

1928–9 to gain experience, and later in 1948 to restore his health by a change of climate. On his first visit he covered his expenses and learned from Tommy Armour how to draw the ball for added length; on the second he performed creditably in the US Masters and won the Greenbriar Invitational at White Sulphur Springs. And that was just about that for US competition. In Britain Cotton was unique among the competitive golfers of the time: he was the first great practiser, so much so that when still a young man he walked with a most pronounced list to starboard, the result of so many hours in golfing stance with right shoulder set well below the left. He even had to do correctional exercises. Educated at a public school – Alleyn's in Dulwich – he was probably the first 'gentleman professional', one who did not come to the game either from the caddies' ranks or because his father was a club professional. This background helped to give Cotton wider horizons when he moved in the 1930s to improve his own income from golf and his status, a move that was also to benefit his fellow professionals. The same had already happened in the USA thanks to Walter Hagen. Cotton even did one thing that had not occurred to Walter, the prime showman: he topped the bill at London's Coliseum, giving a clinic and exhibition. But before all this there was first a reputation to be established. By the end of the 1930s, Cotton was recognized as the coming man. He won the Kent Open from 1926 to 1930, but this was a minor event. He played in the 1929 Ryder Cup, won the Mar del Plata Open in Argentina, together with the Belgian Open, his first national championship, was twice runner-up in the PGA Matchplay by 1930 and took the Dunlop Southport in consecutive years – 1931 and 1932. But Cotton wanted a British Open to set the seal on his excellence, and that proved beyond him for some time. At times, he was in contention and then dropped away. Cotton later declared that this was because he paid too much attention to what others might be doing on the course. His experience in 1933 was not untypical. Going into the final round he was tied for the lead after scores of 73, 72, 71, but fell right back with a last-round 79 and seventh place, leaving Americans Craig Wood and Densmore Shute to play off for the championship. In 1934 he practised at Royal St George's, Sandwich, and found himself in terrible form. In the end he abandoned practice in despair. Yet in the first qualifying round at Deal he shot a 66, a round that he felt just about the best of his life. Rejuvenated, he launched into the championship proper with scores of 67 and 65 (the round that gave a name to a golf ball, the 'Dunlop 65') and took an unparalleled lead of 9 strokes. A steady morning round of 72 on the final day and he stood 12 ahead of his closest pursuer. In the afternoon the crowds gathering to cheer him home caused some delay and Cotton began by playing thoroughly bad golf. Despite putting well he was out in 40 on the nine that included three short holes. He began home with three 5s, the Open now slipping from his grasp. Then came a birdie and thereafter Cotton was himself again. He had staved off what would have been the most abject collapse in championship golf, and came home a winner by 5 strokes. The Open continued to be the focus of his year, and on the next eight occasions he was only once worse than seventh place, with five placings in the top four. At Carnoustie in 1937, as it was a Ryder Cup year, he faced the whole of the US team, which included such players as Snead, Byron Nelson, Horton Smith, Hagen, Sarazen and Ralph Guldahl, the latter enjoying his short spell at the very top of US golf. The last two rounds were played in foul weather, there being considerable doubt if the greens would remain playable. Cotton's driving was long and straight, his iron play less sure but his short game was excellent. On that last day he needed just 52 putts in the two rounds and in his closing 71 he was nine times down in 2 strokes from off the green. Only one player, Charles Lacey, matched his final-day scoring, but he had been too far behind. This win of Cotton's set him at the pinnacle of world golf despite his ignoring the American scene (but so did all his contemporaries). In other events during the 1930s Cotton took two PGA Matchplays and five other British events (tournaments were few at this time). Based for some of the time in Belgium, by the time World War II came he had taken a total of nine continental European national Opens, including the German three times in a row. Several of his best years were then lost to Hitler, and Cotton also suffered poor health – he was invalided out of the RAF with ulcers and a burst appendix. Despite these problems Cotton renewed his number one position in British golf after the war. He won the French Open in 1946 and 1947, took one of the few 1945 tournaments and finished fourth in the first post-war Open after a final round of 79 to Snead's winning 75. At Muirfield for the 1948 Open he was his dominant best again, including a second-round

66 with King George VI in his gallery. Cotton claims to have hit 56 drives in that championship and to have missed just four fairways. His consistent use of the driver (as opposed, for example, to Nicklaus's 1966 victory in which his seldom left the bag) points to one of Cotton's greatest strengths: straight hitting. Indeed, with Byron Nelson, he is possibly the only great player who has tried and succeeded in hitting the ball straight; the rest have taken the easier and safer course of using fade or draw. Not as long as his successors, Cotton would today have made up for this by the excellence of his fairway woods. Putting was thought to be his weakness, and certainly Cotton frequently changed styles. Perhaps the inevitability of his play through the greens made his putting seem worse in contrast. After Muirfield Cotton felt that enough was enough. He became an infrequent tournament player and did not enter another Open until 1952, when he finished fourth, while he was sixth at the age of 49 in 1956, ninth the following year and eighth in 1958 at 51. He won his last tournament of note at the age of 47, the 1954 Penfold. Cotton has written much about golf, including several books, *This Game of Golf* being a minor classic. Since the late 1960s he has been golf director at the Penina Golf Hotel in Portugal, where many young hopefuls have been under instruction with him. During the 1975 revolution in Portugal he was locked out as 'a capitalist who works too hard' – perhaps aptly for the first man to practise between tournaments and between tournament rounds. Cotton, at 76, still likes to play every day, and one story about him emphasizes that he still likes to play well. He presented his 1948 Open-winning set of clubs to the PGA, but on a visit many years later was reminded by his wife how good he had been with the putter. He took it back.

Europe wins 30
Overseas wins 2

COX, Simon   Wales
b. Cardiff 1952

A Welsh international from 1970 to 1974, Cox won both the Duncan Putter and Welsh Amateur in 1974 and turned professional at the end of that season. He had some immediate success, winning the South Wales title in 1975 and 1976 and the Welsh Professional in 1976. He was a World Cup choice in 1975 and played in the Double Diamond in 1977.

Leonard Crawley and Roger Wethered

COX, William James, OBE   England
b. Chalfont St Giles 1910

A leading tournament player of the 1930s, Bill Cox won no events in the rather sparse competitions of the day. In 1938 he shared the 36-hole lead in the Open but then fell away badly. After World War II, he took the *Daily Telegraph* Foursomes in 1951, but thereafter gradually left tournament golf in favour of teaching. Based at Fulford, he became well-known for the 'Cox method'. Later on he was one of the early TV commentators, known for his confiding style and sense of humour. In voice and content he contrasted usefully with Henry Longhurst.

CRADDOCK, Thomas   Ireland
b. Malahide 1931

The best of four golfing brothers, Tom Craddock was thought to have rather an agricultural swing, but he was nevertheless a player of quality. He first played for Ireland in 1955, when he marked his debut by winning all his three singles; afterwards he represented his country many times: 1955–60, 1965–7 and 1969. Most of the first gap was accounted for by his dropping out of top golf for a few years. He also represented Ireland four times in the European Team Championship and Great Britain in the 1967 and 1969 Walker Cups. He won the East of Ireland Amateur three times, the Irish Closed title in 1959, when he beat Joe Carr on the 38th, and the Irish Open Amateur in 1958.

CRAWLEY, Leonard George   England
b. Nacton 1903; d. 1981

Leonard Crawley excelled at three sports: golf, racquets and cricket. At the latter he played for two counties, Worcestershire and Essex, and toured the West Indies with the MCC in 1936. He did not turn his full attention to golf until the early 1930s, but then he began to pile up a total of 26 important amateur tournaments. For England he played fairly consistently between 1931 and 1955, playing 97 international matches in all. His only major title was the 1931 English Amateur, an event in which he was runner-up in 1934 and 1937. He won the Irish Open Strokeplay in 1934 and just missed the French Open in 1937, finishing second. He was a Walker Cup player four times: 1932, 1934, 1938 and 1947. After World War II he became golf correspondent for the *Daily Telegraph*, and continued this into the 1970s. During this phase, he once led a team of British amateurs against the US Curtis Cup team, headed by the formidable Babe Zaharias. There was some doubt as to what terms the match should be played under. Crawley offered the ladies' tees. Said the Babe: 'No, Len, the men's tees will do for me.'

CRITCHLEY, Bruce   England
b. 1942

Son of a champion, Diana Fishwick, and of Brigadier Critchley, also a good golfer, Bruce, scarcely surprisingly, took to the game himself. He three times represented England between 1962 and 1970 and was a Walker Cup choice in 1969, when he halved three of the matches in which he was involved and lost a singles to Allen Miller by 1 down. Known as a particularly good 1-iron player, he took four important amateur competitions but no major titles. He is now a part-time commentator for the BBC and an executive in industry.

CRITCHLEY, Diana: see Fishwick

CRUICKSHANK, Robert: see North America

CULLEN, Gary: see Africa

CUNNINGHAM, Gordon   Scotland
b. Ardrossan 1934

A quiet, stocky player from the west of Scotland, Cunningham turned professional in 1955 and from 1961 spent five years in Barbados. He first played the European circuit in 1967 and from 1970 to 1972 was comfortably inside the top 50 with a best Order of Merit placing of 31st in 1972. By that time he had won twice: the 1969 Scottish Professional Championship and the 1972 Scottish Uniroyal, the latter a minor event. He also represented Scotland in the 1971 Double Diamond. After 1972 his performance declined. He was for some years at Mount Irvine Bay in Tobago, but has since returned to Scotland and is now professional at Troon Municipal.

Europe wins 1 (1969)

CURTIS, Donald Allen   England
b. Broadstone 1904

Once renowned as the longest professional hitter, Donald Curtis won a long driving competition in 1923 with 278 yards, 2 feet, 6 inches. Small beer by today's standards – but he was using hickory shafts, almost impossible to hit full out with. He reached the semi-final of the 1937 *News of the World* Matchplay and won the 1936 *News Chronicle* and the 1938 Dunlop Southport. He was runner-up for the 1939 *Daily Mail* tournament, and in that year represented Britain against the Argentine.

DABSON, Kim   Wales
b. Cardiff 1952

After being second in the 1968 British Boys' Championship and winning the 1969 Welsh Boys', Dabson turned professional. His first three years on the European tour were quite promising, with Order of Merit finishes from 1970 of 63rd, 37th and 47th. He had also won second place in the 1971 Classic International. However, he did not live up to the early promise and later gave up competitive play and went to live in South Africa.

DALGLEISH, Colin   Scotland
b. Helensburgh 1961

One of the pick of the current crop of young Scottish amateurs, he took his national amateur title in 1981 and was chosen for the 1981 Walker Cup match at Cypress Point later the same year.

DALY, Frederick   Ireland
b. Portrush 1911

Fred Daly had a highly successful career, though it spread over relatively few years – mainly as a result of his having lost much of his golfing prime to World War II. He first made some impact by winning the Irish Native Professional Championship in 1940, a success he was twice to repeat, in 1946 and 1952. In his Ulster stamping-grounds, he took the region's Closed title 11 times in all. After World War II Daly soon established himself as a key figure on the British scene, winning the Irish Open in 1946, as tournament play restarted. He also finished 8th in the Open that year. He was, in fact, on the threshold of a remarkable record for several years in the latter event. At Hoylake in 1947 he began with 73 and 70 in difficult conditions to lead comfortably but, on the morning of the final day, sagged to a 78. In better weather, he then returned a 72 to set a target of 293. The weather then worsened and none of the later starters could match his score. Reg Horne and the great American amateur, Frank Stranahan, finished 1 stroke back. At Muirfield the following year Daly returned the steady rounds of 72, 71, 73, 73, but Henry Cotton had re-entered his kingdom with a 66 on the second day and Daly was clear second but 5 strokes behind. At Troon in 1950, Bobby Locke set a new Open record of 279, while Daly had begun with a 75 but improved thereafter with 72, 69, 66. He gained 3 strokes on Locke that last day but still finished 3 behind for equal third place. The next Open was played at Fred Daly's birthplace, Portrush (this was the only occasion the British Open has not been played in either England or Scotland). Daly played well but could not match the golf of Max Faulkner, playing in the trance of knowing that he could hole all the short ones. Daly came in tied for fourth. Back in England at Royal Lytham, Daly began in high form to lead with 67, 69. A couple of steady rounds the last day would have seen him home. But all the leading contenders made up ground on him, Locke gaining 6 strokes, and Daly finished third after his closing 77, 76. This was his last clear chance of winning an Open, for he began to suffer ill health and was not a major force in British golf after the early 1950s, when into his 40s. He remains one of just four British golfers to win the Open since World War II, Faulkner, Cotton and Jacklin being the others. Fred Daly was an excellent matchplayer. Three times he took the Professional Matchplay Championship: in 1947, 1948 and again in 1952. His 1947 win was the first occasion a British golfer had taken this and the Open in the same year since James Braid did it in 1905. In 1952 his third-round match against Alan 'Tiger' Poulton went to the 30th hole, a record for the event, before the Irishman came through. His Ryder Cup record was also good. In all he played in each of the four matches between 1947 and 1953. In this last year at Wentworth he and Harry Bradshaw beat Walter Burkemo and Cary Middlecoff, and were the sole foursome winners, but Daly began to set things alight on the second day when he annihilated Ted Kroll by 9 and 7. With this inspiration, Great Britain and Ireland came within an ace of winning. Daly was a short man and had to strive for length. His swing had some unorthodox features. For a start, his clubs were about 2 inches longer than standard and he used a driver that weighed 17½ ounces. He made a wide arc away from the ball, combined with a pronounced sway to a backswing position well past the horizontal. Nevertheless, he was a superb straight hitter. On the greens he appeared uneasy, but in reality he

had a wonderful feel for pace and for several years had few equals in this area. He was also known for his habit of glancing sideways at the hole – as many as nine or ten times – when addressing the ball on greens, and of whistling between his teeth while he did so.

GB wins 9 (1946–52)

DARCY, Eamonn   Ireland
b. Delgany 1952

The club is picked up, the backswing fast, the right elbow flies high, the left elbow is bent and there is a dip at the top but the position into the ball is exemplary. All in all, Eamonn Darcy has one of the oddest swings on the European circuit yet, when he is on his game, it is highly effective and adds strength to the case of those who argue that any swing is a good one if it works. Darcy is also a good putter and has arguably the best touch on the European Tour for chipping and little pitch shots. He turned professional in 1969 and first won money on the tour in 1973. He broke into the Top 60 in 1974 but remained relatively unknown. The year 1975 saw him shoot to the top, with a best performance of finishing second to Arnold Palmer in the British PGA. Suddenly he had come up from 38th in the Order of Merit to third. In 1976 he did better, winning over £25,000 for second place and winning twice: the Sumrie Better-Ball and the Cacharel World Under-25s Championship in France. Again he was second in the PGA, this time reaching a play-off with Gary Player and Neil Coles, with the Englishman coming through on the third extra hole. The next year he fell away to a respectable 14th place but won the Greater Manchester Open. Then followed three lean years, though he remained in the top 50, before returning to ninth place in 1981 and 21st in 1982. Over the years, Darcy has proved that he can compete outside Europe and has had successes in Australia, New Zealand and Africa, with the 1982 Kenya Open being his most recent tournament win. He has been a Ryder Cup choice in 1975, 1977 and 1981 but has a poorer record than might have been expected: defeats in each of his singles matches and only a couple of halves in the foursome and four-balls.

Europe wins 5 (1976–82)
Europe money £144,906 (1973–82) (23rd all-time)
Africa wins 2 (1981–2)
Australasia wins 2 (1981–2)

Fred Daly

DARWIN, Bernard, CBE   England

b. Kent 1876; d. 1961

A grandson of the great author of *The Origin of Species*, Bernard Darwin became famed as a writer in far different fields. He was an authority on the novels of Charles Dickens, and the best of golf essayists. The first regular golf correspondent for *The Times*, he combined this with contributions to *Country Life* for almost half a century, from 1907 to his retirement in 1953. Although he was by no means the first golf writer, Darwin was really the first man to write about the game with expertise in a newspaper, because before his time the tendency had been to ask someone on the staff to go to the Open Championship and send in reports; often lack of knowledge of the game was blatantly displayed. Darwin's writing on golf (he also wrote many books from the 1920s to 1950s) reached the level of at least minor art and was influential in causing some of his contemporaries and successors to strive to write divertingly rather than be content with mere blow-by-blow reportage. Strangely, to a modern reader, he was not over-concerned to report the whole of an event and the progress of the victor to triumph. Rather he wrote about what he actually saw. If such events were not in the end of great significance to the result of a tournament, Darwin was unworried: the writing was the thing. As well as being the leading authority on the game for many years, Bernard Darwin was also fanatically enthusiastic and no mean player. He reached the sixth round of the 1908 British Amateur and the semi-finals in both 1909 and 1921. In 1922, he went to the USA to report on the Walker Cup for *The Times* and was called upon to play when one of the team fell ill. Darwin did all that could have been asked of him, beating the US captain, Bill Fownes. Between 1902 and 1924 he played for England fairly regularly, eight times in all, while his main successes in tournaments were to win the 1919 *Golf Illustrated* Gold Vase and the President's Putter in 1924. When 57, he partnered Joyce Wethered to a win in the Worplesdon Foursomes. He was captain of the R & A from 1934 to 1935.

DAVIES, E.N.   Wales

b. Tonyrefail 1936

E.N. Davies represented Wales in every international from 1954 to 1974 and was a choice in the European Team Championship four times between 1965 and 1973. He won the North Wales Amateur five times and the Welsh Amateur in 1970 and 1972, and in the latter was three times runner-up. Davies also took six county titles, the Duncan Putter in 1962 and the Harlech Gold Cross in 1972.

DAVIES, John C.   England

b. London 1948

One of the best British amateurs of the 1970s, John Davies primarily has a fine record at coming second in major amateur championships, the most galling of these coming in the 1976 British Amateur. Here, on the first extra hole, Dick Siderowf holed from 5 feet, while Davies followed by missing from 3 feet – and away the title went across the Atlantic. Davies was also runner-up that year in the English Amateur, after being 4 up on Peter Deeble after 11 holes, and also ended up in that position in 1971. The run of second-place finishes was completed by the English Strokeplay of 1977 and the South African in 1974. Davies has often enough been runner-up in

Bernard Darwin

other major amateur competitions but he has also won a very fair share, some 20 in all, with six successive wins in the Royal St George's Challenge Cup being an outstanding achievement. Davies has been a keen gambler on his own matches and it is said there was a substantial side bet on the result of his 1975 Walker Cup match with George Burns. Davies took the money. He was in fact four times a Walker Cup choice and compiled a good record between 1973 and 1979, particularly in the first two years. First he beat both Gary Koch and Dick Siderowf in his singles, then in 1975 halved with Curtis Strange and beat George Burns.

DAVIES, William Henry   England
b. Hoylake 1892

With such a birthplace, it ought to have been no surprise that Davies became a leading professional. He played on two Ryder Cup teams – 1931 and 1933 – and his most important win was in the 1933 Dunlop Southport tournament. He also won the Leeds Cup (of which Harry Vardon was the first winner in 1902) in 1931 and 1939 and the Northern Championship in 1931 and 1935.

DAWSON, Peter   England
b. Doncaster 1950

Blessed with a slow and measured swing, Peter Dawson at one time seemed the first left-hander to be a significant figure on the European or even World scene since Bob Charles won the 1963 British Open. (Why left-handers make such negligible impact when they, for example, often dominate world tennis is a mystery. The only viable theory – and that none too convincing – is that golf courses are designed from a right-hander's perspective. A left-hander therefore often has the feeling that the course would look 'right' if only someone would move all the par-3 greens to the left and all the fairways in the same direction.) Peter Dawson was a boy, youth and full England international before he became a professional in 1970, having reached the final of the 1969 English Amateur. He went on the European circuit in 1973 and from 1974 to 1976 was comfortably within the Top 60. In 1977 he had a number of high finishes, and at the end of the season in the Tournament Players Championship would have won but for taking 7 on the last hole of all. He still came second, to that date his best achievement though he had taken the

individual title in the two-round Double Diamond International. He played then for England in the World Cup and the match versus Europe. A Ryder Cup selection as a result of his seventh-place finish in the Order of Merit, he beat Don January in his singles by 5 and 4. The following year Dawson slipped in the rankings to 38th – but far worse was to come. By 1980 he was 112th, in 1981 182nd, with a stroke average of 78.50, and 135th in 1982. Still in his very early 30s, it is possible he may yet come back.

Europe money £50,000 approx. (1973–82)

DEEBLE, Peter George   England
b. Alnwick 1954

The winner of some half-dozen regional titles in the north-east of England, and of other open events such as the Royal Mid-Surrey Antlers, the Lytham Trophy and the 1982 County Champion of Champions, Deeble has twice won the English Amateur, in 1976 and 1980. On the first occasion he met John Davies in the final and came through by 3 and 1 despite having been 4 down after the first 11 holes. Several times an England international, he was a Walker Cup choice in 1977 and 1981. Peter compiled this record despite suffering a disease at one time thought incurable.

DeFOY, Craig Bryan   Wales
b. Pennsylvania, USA 1947

Many times an international for Wales as a professional, Craig fell a little short of what was expected of him and has now largely settled for the life of a club professional. In 1971 he finished fourth in the British Open after a strong finish of 68, 69 and his best years ran from the beginning to the middle of the 1970s. Oddly, he was far more an outstanding success in Zambia than anywhere else. There, he first won in 1970 and followed up by winning the Mufulira Open in 1971 and 1972 and the Zambian Open in 1972 and 1973. Craig DeFoy himself has said that he expected to win in Zambia – and that he did is some illustration of the power of positive thinking. It is likely that Tom Watson has similar feelings after four wins in eight years (all in Scotland) in the British Open or that Arnold Palmer did after his great run in the US Masters from 1958 to 1964. On the European Tour, DeFoy was comfortably in the Top 60 in the period 1968–

76 and was four times in the top 30 with a best placing of 19th in 1974. In the late 1960s he won both the Under 23 and Under 24 titles and the Junior Matchplay, but as a more senior player won only in Zambia. Apart from the 1971 Open, when he came home 3 behind Lee Trevino, DeFoy's best performances were to finish third in the 1970 Wills Tournament and as runner-up in the 1976 PGA Matchplay.

Europe money £40,000 approx. (1966–82)

DEIGHTON, Dr Frank William Gordon
Scotland
b. Glasgow 1927

A Walker Cup choice in 1951 and 1957, Frank Deighton was unfortunate not to get a game in 1951 and then to lose both his matches on the next occasion. He was also chosen for the Commonwealth event twice, and many times for Scotland. His championship successes were to take the Scottish Amateur twice, in 1956 and 1959, while he also won five other important titles. Deighton was particularly a St Andrews specialist, and his record of 20 R & A medals in the period 1953–79 is unparalleled in modern times, and beaten only by Leslie Balfour-Melville generations ago.

DOBELL, Gladys: see Ravenscroft

DOD, Charlotte   England
b. 1871; d. 1960

One of the greatest of all-round sportswomen, Lottie Dod took the Wimbledon singles title at tennis five times between 1887 and 1893, and at 15 years 8 months remains the youngest winner, despite the modern tendency for women tennis players to be precocious. At golf, she reached the semi-finals of the British Ladies' in 1898 and 1899, and then beat one of the Hezlet sisters, May, in 1904. Lottie was also good at billiards, a champion skater, international hockey player, won the silver medal at Olympic archery and was a keen alpinist.

DODD, Muriel   England
b. Crosby 1891

Winner of the 1913 British Ladies' by 8 and 6 in the first 36-hole final, Muriel also won the Canadian title that year, reached the semi-finals of the British in 1914 and was defeated at that stage in the semi-finals of the English Ladies' in 1923. She was an England international from 1913 to 1926.

DONALD, Jean Macalister (later Anderson)
Scotland
b. North Berwick 1921

A key British player in the immediate post-war period, Jean Donald reached the final of the 1948 British Ladies', where she met Louise Suggs. Level with four to play, they were both level on the last green with Suggs looking likely to hole her first putt. She didn't, but Jean Donald sent her first well past and missed the return to lose. The previous year she won the French title from Francis Stephens and the Scottish, a victory she repeated in 1949 and 1952, being runner-up in 1953. She four times reached the semi-finals of the British Ladies'. She was in the Curtis Cup teams from 1948 to 1952, and won the Sunningdale Foursomes on four occasions, the first two with Tom Haliburton and the other two partnering me. She turned professional in 1953 and won the 1954 Spalding event, the Kayser-Bondor Foursomes in both 1959 and 1962 and the professional prize in the 1976 Newmark. Jean Donald was a powerful player with both woods and long irons.

Jean Donald

234

DOUGLAS, Findlay S.: see North America

DOWNES, Paul   **England**
b. 1960

The only Englishman to have represented his country at boys', youths' and full international level, Paul Downes completed this feat in 1976, the year he won the Midlands Open Amateur, then being held for the first time. He played for England in the European Team Championship the following year, won the English Amateur in 1978 and the English Amateur Open Strokeplay in 1982. He was a boy international 1974–7, and both youth and full 1976–81.

DREW, Norman Vico   **Ireland**
b. Belfast 1932

Norman Drew was one of a formerly very small group who represented Great Britain and Ireland as both amateur and professional. Such a distinction is now less rare as amateur achievement has become an important stepping-stone on the route to a professional career. As an amateur Drew won three regional Irish titles and took the Open Amateur in both 1952 and 1953. In the latter year he was a Walker Cup choice, losing by the daunting total of 9 and 7 in his singles. He turned professional in 1958 and the following year won his only major event on the British circuit, the *Yorkshire Evening News*, while in Ireland he took the Irish Professional and the Irish Dunlop. These achievements secured him a Ryder Cup place that year, when he halved his singles with Doug Ford. His only later successes were to twice win the Ulster title and represent Ireland twice in the World Cup. Drew was lacking in power but had a good short game. His strong left-hand grip may have contributed to his game not lasting long.

DUNCAN, Colonel Anthony Arthur, OBE
           Wales
b. Cardiff 1914

Tony Duncan was a Welsh international almost every year from 1933 to 1959 and won the Welsh Amateur four times: 1938, 1948, 1952 and 1954. He was once runner-up, a position he also reached in the 1939 British Amateur. He won the President's Putter twice and the Army Championship six times. Non-playing captain for the 1953 Walker Cup match, he coined a phrase that deserves immortality. A US player found that he was carrying 15 clubs, which meant a loss-of-match penalty. Said Duncan: 'Britannia waives the rules.' The less severe loss of two holes was agreed. Although this situation had been solved with great tact by Duncan, he was later involved in another controversy less easily settled. During the World Matchplay in 1970 on the 9th hole at Wentworth, Jack Nicklaus, in a horrid lie, claimed relief on the line-of-sight rule because of an advertising hoarding. Duncan refused, feeling that it was the lie rather than the obstruction to sight that Nicklaus wished to escape. Hot words followed and Duncan withdrew, his referee tasks taken over by Gerald Micklem. A present judgement might be that Duncan was following the spirit of the rules; Nicklaus the letter. Tony Duncan was particularly an excellent putter and it is appropriate that he founded the Duncan Putter competition. Played at Southerndown in Wales, it was designed to give Welsh golfers more experience of 72-hole competition. He still plays a lot of golf, despite failing eyesight.

DUNCAN, George   **Scotland**
b. Methlick 1883; d. 1964

In 1920, George Duncan began his British Open at Deal with a round of 80. In those days so high a round was not an ultimate disaster, for scoring was higher. But Duncan's second-day score was again an 80 and at that point he lay 13 strokes behind the leader, his friend and rival Abe Mitchell. Duncan wandered into the exhibition tent and a driver caught his eye. After a few experimental swishes with it, he paid the few shillings asked. On the final day he then went round Deal in 71 in the morning and 72 in the afternoon. Mitchell had meanwhile slumped to 84, 76 for fourth place and Duncan was Open Champion by 2 strokes over Sandy Herd. It was the greatest turnaround ever achieved in Open history. The next year Duncan had to settle for a quiet fifth place, then in 1922, the Open returned to the Kent coast again – Royal St George's at Sandwich. Walter Hagen was there, determined to make amends for his 53rd-place finish in 1920. After two rounds, Duncan lay 2 behind Hagen and then soared again into the 80s, with an 81. Hagen faltered also, to a 79. Jock Hutchison, 1921 champion, led Hagen by 2, J.H. Taylor by 1 and Jim Barnes and Charles Whitcombe were level. Hagen then played one of the best rounds of the championship and was home in 72. Soon it was apparent that he would be champion as the other contenders played steadily but were unable to match Hagen's score. Congratulations were being offered when the news came in that Duncan was playing a round that was altogether extraordinary. He came to the last needing a par 4 for 68 and a tie with Hagen. His spoon approach missed the green, his quick short pitch was by no means dead and then, after a glance at the line, Duncan missed the putt. Such speed of play in a crisis was by no means caused by nerves. Duncan was one of the speediest players the game has known, a reflection of his mercurial, explosive temperament – he even wrote a book entitled *Golf at the Gallop*. Duncan had first become a nationally known figure in 1910 when he beat both James Braid and J.H. Taylor in the PGA Matchplay before going down to Sandy Herd in the final. In 1913 he again reached the final, in which he beat James Braid. His other main achievements before golf was interrupted by World War I were to finish third in the 1910 Open and fourth in 1912. He had also won the 1912 Belgian Open and the 1913 French. After World War I the Vardon, Taylor, Braid Triumvirate were overcome by age and

Mitchell and Duncan were heirs apparent, though they had lost some of their prime years to the war. Duncan's style was modelled on Vardon's, he considered, but his quick temperament and liking for golf theory caused him to make changes almost from day to day. He always retained his putting method, however: putter in front of the ball, then behind and the stroke followed, executed with a cutting action because he thought that sidespin, especially on short putts, helped to hold the ball on line. Some of Duncan's greatest moments came in the Ryder Cup and its predecessor, the international matches between Great Britain and the USA. The first was held in 1921: Duncan halved his foursome and beat British Open Champion Jock Hutchison in the singles. In 1926 he beat Hagen in the singles by 6 and 5 and then followed the next day's foursomes with a 9 and 8 win over Hagen, partnered by Jim Barnes. In 1927 the tide turned towards America, but Duncan was Britain's only singles winner. In 1929 came his most extravagant achievement: he demolished Walter Hagen by 10 and 8 in singles, still the record margin in Ryder Cup play. His final match came in 1931 in the foursomes. Shute, partnered by a Hagen intent on revenge, crushed Arthur Havers and Duncan by 10 and 9. Among other Duncan successes were the 1927 French and Irish Opens, the *Daily Mail* in 1920 and 1922 and the 1920 and 1924 Gleneagles. Together with Abe Mitchell, George Duncan was the best British player of the era that linked the Great Triumvirate with the Age of Cotton. But Duncan won the Open Championship; Mitchell didn't. His son Ian is a club professional at Alwoodley in Yorkshire.

DUNN, Thomas   Scotland
b. Musselburgh 1849; d. 1902

Son of 'Old Willie' Dunn, Tom was one of the early golf architects and belonged to the penal school: he was addicted to cross bunkers both for the tee and second shots, reinforced by a ditch if possible. He was professional at Wimbledon until 1881 and then returned to Scotland and North Berwick – at which popular Victorian golfing resort he numbered A.J. Balfour and W.E. Gladstone among his pupils. He then returned south to Bournemouth in 1894 and spent his remaining years doing what he loved most – designing golf courses. It is estimated that in eight years he managed a staggering total of 137!

George Duncan

DUNN, William, Snr   Scotland
b. Musselburgh 1821; d. 1880

One of the finest matchplayers of his time, 'Old Willie' went south to historic Blackheath and was professional and custodian of the course for some 20 years before returning successively to Leith Links and North Berwick, where he died. With his brother Jamie, he played a famous foursomes against 'Old Tom' Morris and Allan Robertson in 1849, definitely the two best players of their overlapping eras. In 1843, he played Robertson, at his best at the time, over 20 rounds and lost by 2 and 1 (rounds). Dunn was thought to have a particularly graceful style, and was also the longest driver of his time. His son Willie was also a good player and successful professional.

DUNN, William, Jnr   Scotland & USA
b. Musselburgh, Scotland 1865; d. 1952

One of the first travelling golf professionals, Willie Dunn stayed at Westward Ho! from 1886 to 1888 before going to Biarritz for six years. There he met W.E. Vanderbilt, who persuaded him to go to America. In 1892 he began constructing Shinnecock Bay, Long Island, which has the first substantial clubhouse in the USA. It was in keeping with the course's name that 150 Red Indians helped in the course construction. In 1894 he first played in a US Open and won it, though this one is not regarded as official. In the first US Open proper, 1895, he was second; two years later he was third. A friend of such figures as J.D. Rockefeller, John L. Sullivan and Buffalo Bill Cody, Willie inaugurated such changes as less penal bunkering and the first indoor golf school in the USA (on Fifth Avenue, New York); and he experimented with golf equipment. In this last field he tried hollow aluminium heads, wooden and paper tee pegs and steel shafts. The latter were steel rods inserted into cane or lancewood.

EDGAR, John Douglas   England
b. Newcastle-upon-Tyne 1884; d.1921

Little remembered today, but one of the most fascinating figures in golf history, J. Douglas Edgar merits far more attention than he has received, and even his death is still a matter for speculation. As professional at the Northumberland Golf Club in Newcastle, he leapt to at least temporary fame by leading the 1914 French Open throughout and, averaging 72s, left Harry Vardon 6 strokes in his wake. Then came war. He emigrated to the USA in 1918 and the following year saw his most remarkable achievement. In the Canadian Open he opened with 72, 71, and then demolished the field with closing rounds of 69, 66. He had won by 16 strokes against the usual high-class field assembled for the event. The following year, he was less dominant and had to play off against Tommy Armour and Charles Murray, but won again. He also came close to taking the US PGA, losing only because he three-putted the final green to give Jock Hutchison the title. In the US Open he was less successful in his brief flicker of greatness. In 1919 he began as favourite but finished 19 strokes behind Walter Hagen, who was recording his second and, oddly, last success. The next year Douglas finished no better than 20th, 12 strokes behind Ted Ray, the last Englishman to win the US Open until Tony Jacklin in 1970. Armour is a key figure in any assessment of Douglas Edgar. He had lost a play-off to Edgar in the 1920 Canadian Open, and Armour is beyond dispute still one of the best thinkers about golf who has appeared in print. Armour said that Edgar was 'the best golfer I ever saw'. And Armour saw all the great players from the Triumvirate and Jones, Hagen and Sarazen, through Nelson, Snead and Hogan to the moderns. In fact, Tommy Armour believed that his considerable successes were the result of Edgar's teaching. He said: 'I spent six months with Douglas Edgar and changed from being a bad golfer to my present state of mediocrity.' Mediocre Armour may have called himself, but he won his British and US Opens and PGAs and is still said to be one of the greatest of iron players. If Armour's opinion is not of sufficient stature, what about that of Harry Vardon? He said: 'This is the man who one day will be the greatest of us all.' But these are thoughts and opinions from long, long ago. Douglas Edgar's writings go some considerable way to showing that he was the first of the moderns. After his Canadian Open victory, he produced an instruction book entitled *Through the Gate*, and it is the first to emphasize hitting 'from the inside out'. He also stressed left-side dominance, saying that golf was essentially a matter of 'left eye, left side, left hand'. He also anticipated Bobby Jones, who was later to write that the club should 'freewheel' through the ball, in saying that 'The ball is only an incident that lies in the way of the swing.' Photo sequences of the Edgar swing still exist, and they illustrate that he did not fan the clubface open on the backswing as was usual at the time, had a strong left-hand grip (long considered fatal to good golf but a feature of the grips of no less than Sarazen and Trevino and a high proportion of the best US women pro golfers – Nancy Lopez especially) and kept his right elbow close to his side. But perhaps these are incidentals. Where J. Douglas Edgar is remarkable in the extreme is that he was the first major golfer to play with a very full shoulder turn and a restricted hip turn. In his day, there were the two great players, Vardon and then Jones, who both particularly exemplified the full shoulder movement, but accompanied it with a particularly free hip movement that has long been out of favour after the influence of Byron Nelson from the mid 1940s onwards. Yet Douglas Edgar was using the modern method 20 years earlier, when the accepted norm was to swing just about everything freely away from the ball. Edgar, then, by many years anticipated the modern theory of retaining the tension between free shoulder movement and restricted hip turn. He also seems to have led the downswing with leg drive towards the ball. Edgar's triumphs in the USA came when he was in his late 30s. There must be some doubt as to whether he would have continued much longer as a major figure. In 1921, however, in Bobby Jones's town of Atlanta, Georgia, where he was a club professional, he was found dead. At first the local police declared that he had been hit by a car that had failed to stop. The truth of the matter is more likely to be that he was 'mugged' while walking home late at night. The cause of death was a narrow deep cut on the inner left thigh – a form of injury seldom inflicted by automobiles. He bled to death; no one heard his calls for help.

ELSON, Philip   England
b. Kenilworth 1954

It is perhaps too late for Elson to fulfil the early hopes that were expressed for him. He opened his career with caps for England at both Boys' and Youths' level, also captaining the teams. In 1971 he was Youth Champion; he turned professional the following year. Henry Cotton considered him a considerable prospect and both coached him and gave him his 'Rookie of the Year' award after the 1973 European season. Elson had immediately broken into the Top 60 that first year and seemed to have taken to professional golf with some confidence. He had, for instance, completed all four

rounds of the first seven tournaments he entered and followed with the same achievement in that year's British Open. Although only once out of the Top 60 since that first year his progress has otherwise been disappointing. His best position was 38th in the Order of Merit in 1977, and he has seldom looked likely to win a tournament. After the 1982 season, he took a club job at Stratford.

Europe money £62,949 (1973–82) (59th all-time)

EVANS, A.D.   Wales
b. 1911

Welsh Amateur Champion in 1949, Evans repeated the feat 12 years later at the age of 50. He also captured no less than 17 county titles during his long career and represented his country in the home internationals most years between 1931 and 1956. He reappeared in 1961 and was later captain.

EVANS, Duncan   Wales
b. Leek 1962

In 1980 Duncan Evans became the first Welshman to take the British Amateur Championship, and the following year he took the Welsh Strokeplay and was selected for the Walker Cup team. He performed ingloriously in the 1981 US Masters, having the second worst score of all entries at the halfway stage. Although he has a good short game, this 6-foot 5-inch player seems unlikely to succeed and his first professional year earned him just £50, last but one on the PGA official money list.

EVERARD, Mary (later Laupheimer) England
b. Sheffield 1942

Mary Everard lost to Marley Spearman in the final of the 1964 English Ladies' but returned to win in 1972, beating Angela Bonallack in the final. She was runner-up in the British Ladies' in 1967 to Elizabeth Chadwick, and she won the British Open Strokeplay in 1970, was second in 1971 and 1973, and was runner-up in the 1977 British Open. Mary was a Curtis Cup player from 1970 to 1974 and again in 1978, her best performance coming in 1970, when she took 2½ points out of a possible 3. She also played in the 1968 and 1972 World Team Championship, was six years an England international and took the Yorkshire title five times. She is now married and resident in the USA.

EWING, Reginald Cecil — Ireland

b. Rosses Point 1910; d. 1973

The longevity of Cecil Ewing's international amateur career is testament to a simple method. He stood with feet close together and pivoted only slightly in a three-quarter backswing. The secret was in the powerful forearms that gave him some mastery of long, low iron shots. First selected for the Walker Cup in 1936, he was still there for his sixth appearance in 1955 at the age of 45, during which perhaps his best performance was to beat Ray Billows in the 1938 series, one of Great Britain and Ireland's rare victories. During the same year came his best result in the British Amateur in which he was a finalist at Troon before going down 3 and 2 to Charlie Yates, the American number one. In the home internationals Cecil represented Ireland between 1934 and 1958 and was then non-playing captain from 1960 to 1969, a period during which he also served as a Walker Cup selector. In Ireland Ewing twice won the Irish Closed Amateur and was a finalist at the age of 48. He also took the Irish Open Amateur twice. His dominance in the West of Ireland was such that he took that title no less than ten times.

FALDO, Nicholas Alexander — England

b. Welwyn Garden City 1957

For several years now Nick Faldo has shared with Sandy Lyle the reputation of being the best British prospect. With three Ryder Cup caps behind him he has a considerable record in European golf and is currently easily the most successful British player on the US Tour. As an amateur Faldo had a brief but glittering career. After being a youth international in 1974, he swept much before him the following year, winning the Berkshire Trophy, the Scrutton Jug, Hertfordshire Amateur and the County Champion of Champions. More importantly, he took the English Amateur at a record age of 18 years 8 days. He played for both England and the Great Britain team, and then in April 1976 did the inevitable – turned professional. Although he did not achieve anything spectacular that first season he was recognized as a coming player, and 1977 saw his first push towards the top of British and European golf. He improved his Order of Merit placing from 58th to eighth and took his first tournament, the Skol Lager Individual. The following year, he improved to third and won what is classed by many the second most prestigious title

Nick Faldo

on the British circuit, the PGA Championship, a victory he was to repeat in both 1980 and 1981, equalling my own record. In 1979 also he looked a very likely winner after scorching round St Andrews in 65 and following with a 70 to establish a 4-stroke lead. Alas for Nick, in worsening weather he declined to 78, 79 and came in tenth, well behind Vicente Fernandez. He had done well at St Andrews the previous year in the Open, being under par in each round and finishing seventh. Although Faldo is not the longest hitter on the current European Tour, he is not far behind Ballesteros, Norman and Lyle, and it is all done with a deceptively slow rhythm that puts me in mind of a man having a casual practice swish. However, he has won the British Long-Driving Championship. It is really his excellent leg drive leading the downswing that causes the whole production to seem effortless. As a putter, I know Dai Rees thinks him one of the best he has seen. His short putting is particularly decisive: he does not coast the ball at the hole but rather bangs it at the middle. It can hardly be said that any British golfer has been a consistent success in the USA since Vardon and Taylor in 1900, though there have been occasional triumphs such as Ted Ray's and Tony Jacklin's US Open wins in 1920 and 1970. Peter Oosterhuis has given some steady performances over the years, culminating with the 1981 Canadian Open; but of the current youth of British golf, Faldo has easily the best record. He led the 1981 Hawaiian Open at the halfway point with a second-round 62 and finished third in the Greater Greensboro' Open. In seven entries that year he won $23,320 and came 119th on the US money list, good enough to suggest that he would make the Top 60 if he played the full schedule of 43 tournaments. Returning to Europe, he ended the season in second place in the Order of Merit, the fourth time in the past five years that he has been in the top eight.

Europe wins 6 (1977–82)
Europe money £248,322 (1976–82) (5th all-time)
Overseas wins 1 (1979)
US money $79,987 (1981–2) (254th all-time)

FALLON, John   Scotland
b. Lanark 1913

Something of a specialist at St Andrews, where he finished equal third in the 1939 Open, 4 strokes behind winner Dick Burton, and second in 1955, 2 behind Peter Thomson, Johnny Fallon never won a major tournament. His nearest approaches were to tie for the 1956 Stuart Goodwin 5,000 Guineas and to be the defeated finalist in the 1954 PGA Match-play. Once a Ryder Cup player, in 1955, when incidentally he was preferred over me, he has the perfect record of played 1, won 1. Playing with John Jacobs in the foursomes at the Thunderbird Country Club, Palm Springs, he had to hole a 14-foot putt with about 18 inches of borrow to win their match, and did so. Johnny was non-playing Ryder Cup captain in 1963 and his minor tournament wins included the Leeds Challenge Cup twice and the Northern England Professional three times.

FAULKNER, Max   England
b. Bexhill 1916

In my opinion the most talented British player of his era, Max was also the most eccentric, and seemed to make everything difficult. He never possessed a halfway respectable set of golf clubs, for instance. They were always being influenced by some new theory that Max was toying with, so you would find him with a mix of stiff and whippy shafts, perhaps three 1-irons of assorted lengths ... and goodness knows what putter he might turn up with on the day. He is reputed to have made no less than 300 of them, the most renowned being one with a driftwood head and a shaft made out of a

Max Faulkner

billiard cue. Putting was a major factor at Portrush in 1951 when he became one of just four British golfers to win the Open since World War II. After two rounds, Max was signing autograph books with his name followed by 'Open Champion 1951' and was so enthused about his putting that he frequently declared he would never again miss a short putt. This was indeed tempting the gods, but the spell at least lasted for the Open and he finished 2 strokes ahead of Antonio Cerda, helped, he said, by a 'mystery guiding light'. On that occasion he did not play well through the greens but putted superbly – yet he was usually at his best with woods and long irons and at manoeuvring the ball – I have yet to see his equal at 'bending' shots with lofted irons. Five times in the Ryder Cup team between 1947 and 1957, Max had the daunting experience in the 1949 singles against Dutch Harrison at Ganton of facing five 3s in a row. Playing number one he lost by 8 and 7, and indeed never won a Ryder Cup singles. Besides eight major UK tournaments, Max won the Spanish Open three times and, at the age of 52, the Portuguese Open. He certainly relished the sun, perhaps because it suited the colourful clothes he favoured on the golf course.

Europe wins 16 (1946–68)
GB Seniors 1968, 1970

FERGUSON, Marjory (née Fowler)   Scotland
b. North Berwick 1937

A Scottish international in 1959 and from 1962 to 1970, Marjory Ferguson was runner-up in the 1966 and 1971 Scottish Ladies' and took the 1970 Portuguese Championship. She also took the East Lothian title (in that hotbed of golf) from 1957 to 1964 and on four later occasions. She played in the 1966 Curtis Cup team and three times in the European Team Championship.

FERGUSON, Robert   Scotland
b. Musselburgh 1848; d. 1915

With Peter Thomson, Jamie Anderson and 'Young Tom' Morris, Bob Ferguson is in the select band who have won the British Open three times in a row. He achieved this between 1880 and 1882, and followed by tying with Willie Fernie and then losing the play-off. Earlier he had achieved the feat of beating 'Old Tom' Morris six times in matchplay in the late 1860s. The status of professional golf and of Open winners at the time is illustrated by Bob's later life. He contracted typhoid and his golf game fell away. He was to end his days as a greenkeeper and caddie back in Musselburgh.

FERNIE, William   Scotland
b. St Andrews 1851; d. 1924

Willie set up a formidable record for second-place finishes in the British Open: 1882, 1884, 1890 and 1891. In 1883 he did better, tying with Bob Ferguson and thus preventing him winning four in a row. In the play-off, he defeated Ferguson, partly as a result of holing one monstrous putt from the edge of a green. Later he was the first professional at one of the early English clubs, Aldeburgh, before returning to his native Scotland, where from 1887 he was professional at Royal Troon Golf Club until his death.

FISHER, Elizabeth: see Price

FISHWICK, Diana Lesley (later Critchley)   England
b. London 1911

After winning the British Girls' title in both 1927 and 1928, Diana Fishwick progressed to the final of the English Championship in 1929, but was beaten by Molly Gourlay. The following year, with Joyce Wethered not playing, she was somewhat surprised to find herself in the final of the British Ladies', facing the great Glenna Collett. 'What a lark,' she said, a flippant but perhaps commendable approach to a championship final, and went out and won by 4 and 3. Diana had another good year in 1932, when she won the English Ladies' and beat Molly Gourlay in the final of the French Ladies'. Thereafter she was particularly effective in European golf, taking the championships of Germany twice and also the Dutch and Belgian. In 1946 she reached the final of the French again but was this time beaten by Maureen Ruttle with the phenomenal score of 13 and 11. Diana Fishwick played in the Curtis Cup teams of 1932 and 1934 and was selected non-playing captain for the 1950 match. This had one remarkable result. She entered the English Ladies' in 1949 mainly to be on the scene to see at close hand the abilities of leading players – and won. Diana Fishwick played for England in the period 1930–36 and again in 1947. She married Brigadier A.C. Critchley, who himself was capable of carrying off Continental championships, and their son Bruce played in the 1969 Walker Cup team.

de FOREST, John: see de Bendern

FOSTER, Martin   England
b. Bradford 1952

This giant 6-foot 4-inch Yorkshireman shot dramatically through the European Order of Merit from 90th in 1974 through 28th the next year to a dazzling seventh in 1976, a year in which he twice secured tournament second-place finishes. He was the coming man. But this former Boys' Champion and amateur international lost both form and confidence and, having been a World Cup player, suddenly found difficulty in making the Top 60 on the European circuit. He was 121st on the 1982 money list.

FOSTER, Rodney   England
b. Yorkshire 1941

This insurance broker was at the peak of his amateur playing career from the mid 1960s to the early 1970s, with five consecutive Walker Cup appearances between 1965 and 1973. Later he was non-playing captain in 1979 and 1981. He was also nine times an England international, twice played in the Eisenhower Trophy for Britain and six times appeared in the European Team Championship. Foster was one of that increasingly rare breed: a top amateur who did not turn professional. In individual competition, he was five times Yorkshire champion and won four major amateur titles. He was runner-up in the English Amateur in 1964 and the English Open Strokeplay the following year. In the same event he was then equal first in 1969 and outright winner in 1970.

FOULIS, James   Scotland
b. St Andrews, 1868; d. 1925

Golf grew in popularity in the USA very rapidly during the 1890s and many Scotsmen, from Carnoustie and St Andrews in particular, emigrated to teach the game and to take advantage of the higher incomes offered across the Atlantic. One such émigré was Jim Foulis, who won the second of all US Opens in 1896. In doing so he recorded a 74, which was to remain a record for the next seven years. He had been third in 1895, and was again third in 1897.

FOWLER, Marjory: see Ferguson

FREARSON, Diane Jane (née Robb, later Bailey)   England
b. Wolverhampton 1943

As Diane Robb, a girl international from 1957 to 1961, she took the British Girls' title in 1961 and also reached the final of the British Ladies', being defeated by Marley Spearman. She also that year won the Scottish Girls' Open Strokeplay, a title she had also taken in 1959. She was an England international in 1961, 1962 and 1971, played in the 1968 World Team Championship and the 1962 and 1972 Curtis Cups, in the former year being the only singles winner. She won the Worplesdon Mixed Foursomes in 1971 with A. Smith and the Avia Foursomes with Belle Robertson the following year.

GADD, Herbert   England
b. Malvern 1909

French Open champion in 1933, Bert Gadd won another national title, the Irish, in 1937 and was an England international from 1933 to 1938, but never won a Ryder Cup place. He was third in the 1938 Dunlop Metropolitan and second in the Penfold events of 1938 and 1939. After the war he settled in the north-east of England and was successively professional at Brancepeth, Beamish Park and Bishop Auckland golf clubs. While there he won a host of open events, including the Northumberland and Durham Open four times.

GALLACHER, Bernard   Scotland
b. Bathgate 1949

This Scotsman is a man who has consistently made the most of his talents, who seldom if ever gives up in tournament play and is possibly at his best when he faces an American on the tee in Ryder Cup matches. As Lee Trevino says, 'You gotta dance with what you brung' and if Gallacher finds that he is in a phase of not hitting the ball far because he is cutting every shot, or that the ball is going rather further but a duck hook is likely to intrude, then he still keeps on trying and allows for the way he is playing that day, that week. He was a winner right from the beginning of his career, one of the first of the 'new names' at the close of the 1960s, despite

Bernard Gallacher

having a left-hand grip that should have doomed him to failure. The grip was soon modified and he has been consistent enough to be chosen for, or to qualify for, the British Ryder Cup team every year from 1969 to 1981, beginning as the youngest player to have represented Great Britain and Ireland. In these matches he defeated Trevino by 4 and 3 on the final day of that tied match in 1969, was undefeated in 1971, halved with both Geiberger and Trevino in 1975 and had his finest match in 1979 when he won 4 out of 5 possible points. Bernard began as a boy international in both 1965 and 1966 and in his brief amateur career took the Scottish Open Strokeplay the following year before turning professional. In his first full season he showed promise, coming 2 strokes behind Peter Townsend in the Young Professionals tournament, despite the still unmodified strong grip and a loop in the backswing. Already, he was excellent from between 20 and 50 yards of the flag and was, and is, one of the most effective putters on the European circuit. He finished 32nd in the Order of Merit. British professionals were by this time far more adventurous overseas in the British winter and early in 1969 Bernard secured his first wins – in Africa, where he took two tournaments in Zambia. Yet many British professionals have won on the African circuit fairly consistently but have failed to repeat that form anywhere else. Not so Bernard Gallacher: the year 1969 made him a name in the relatively small pond of the British circuit, at the highly precocious age of 20. He won the Schweppes at Ashburnham to be the youngest player to win a British tournament, and later also took the Wills Open. During the season Gary Player had told him he had little chance of becoming a consistent winner and, though Bernard finished first in the Order of Merit, he knew that his left-hand position was far too strong and he set to work to modify it. Possibly this was the reason he was far less successful in 1970. He was now showing just two knuckles, but such changes take time to adjust to. In 1970, he fell to 22nd, one of his poorest placings ever. He has always ranked in the top 30 and has seven times been in the top 10, though he has only once approached his 1969 placing, with third in 1974. Bernard has picked up a tournament most years and one of his most outstanding achievements has been to take the Dunlop Masters in successive years – 1974 and 1975 – the first man to have done so. Another was to tie for first in the 1978 European Open, though losing to Bobby Wadkins in the sudden-death play-off. He has also twice won the Martini International: in 1971, after an unpromising start of 80, he followed with 67, 68, 67, and again in 1982.

Europe wins 12 (1969–82)
Europe money £219,991 (1968–82) (8th all-time)
Overseas wins 3

GARNER, John R. England
b. Preston 1947

Professional golf is full of stories similar to the rise and fall of John Garner. A dedicated practiser, he had a slow climb to the top during the late 1960s and in 1969 was 13th in the Order of Merit, having taken second place in the Algarve Open and the British PGA. In 1971 he was 12th. His best achievement came the following year when he took the PGA Matchplay, climaxed by the highly unlikely success of defeating none other than Neil Coles by 7 and 6 in the final. His successes had been based on steady play through the green and an excellent short game; but disaster came when he decided to try for more length, and thereafter he rapidly faded from view. He was twice a Ryder Cup player but suffered the indignity of being asked to play only once in 1971 and not at all in 1973.

GARVEY, Philomena Ireland
b. Drogheda 1927

In the top half dozen of British players for a decade and more, Philomena Garvey almost totally dominated the Irish scene for many years. She won the Irish Ladies' every year from 1946 to 1963 with only four exceptions, and brought her total to 15 in 1970. She won every final that she reached. On the British scene she five times reached the Ladies' final between 1946 and 1963, losing to Jean Hetherington in 1946, Marlene Stewart in 1953, Barbara McIntyre in 1960 and Brigitte Varangot in 1963. The 1960 final was particularly memorable in that when 8 down she played six holes in 20 strokes and won back five holes. Miss Garvey, however, did not always lose: in 1957 at Gleneagles she beat Jessie Valentine. She represented Ireland most years from 1947 to 1963 and played six times in the Curtis Cup team: from 1948 to 1956 and again in 1960. An Irish nationalist, she once refused to wear the team badge unless 'and Ireland' was added to 'Great Britain'. She turned professional in 1964 but was reinstated as an amateur in 1968.

GOURLAY, Mary Perceval, OBE   England
b. Basingstoke 1898

When Molly Gourlay decided the time had come to give up golf she was 73 yet was still playing to a handicap of 4. She had been at her best in the mid 1920s to mid 1930s, being an England international during that period. She won the French Ladies' in 1923, 1928 and 1929, and was runner-up in 1932, took the Swedish title three times and won the Belgian in 1925 and 1926. She won the English Ladies' in 1926 and 1929, beating Diana Fishwick the latter year; but herself was beaten by Wanda Morgan in the 1932 final. She also reached the semi-finals several times. Surrey champion seven times, Molly Gourlay also won the Worplesdon Mixed Foursomes in 1929, 1930 and 1934 and played in the 1932 and 1934 Curtis Cup teams. Later she was Veteran Ladies' Champion in 1962 and served as England captain and chairman and president of, respectively, the ELGU and the ELGA. As a rules expert her services were much in demand at tournaments.

GRAHAM, John   England
b. Liverpool 1877; d. 1915

Although he four times reached the semi-final stage, Jack Graham was thought by many to be the best player to fail to win the British Amateur Championship. He was ten times an amateur international and lost only two matches. Perhaps he was unable to sustain his form over a long championship week. He also performed very effectively in the Open, five times being top amateur between 1904 and 1913. An all-round sportsman, John Graham reached a high standard also at cricket, rugby, racquets and billiards. He was killed in action in World War I.

GREEN, Charles Wilson   Scotland
b. 1932

In 1981 Charlie Green announced his retirement from competitive golf at the highest level at a time when he was captain of the Scots team. He had had a long career at the top of amateur golf, though the supreme prizes eluded him. A Walker Cup player in 1963 and again from 1969 to 1975, Charlie represented Scotland between 1961 and 1965, and then again from 1967 to the end of the next decade. He was also in the British Eisenhower Trophy team in 1970 and 1972. He won the Scots Amateur in 1970 and was runner-up the following year. He was second in the Scots Open Amateur Strokeplay in 1967 and won in 1975. He was appointed 1983 Walker Cup captain and won the 1982 Scottish Amateur, aged 50.

GREENHALGH, Julia   England
b. Bolton 1941

A girl international from 1957 to 1959 and runner-up of the British Girls' in 1959, Julia Greenhalgh took the Scottish Girls' Open Strokeplay in 1960, won the Northern Ladies' in 1961 and 1962 and began her haul of nine Lancashire titles in 1961. She was an England international from 1960 to 1977, and in 1979, and was first chosen for the Curtis Cup in 1964, again in 1966 when she had to withdraw, and in 1970, 1974, 1976 and 1978. Of national titles, she won the New Zealand in 1963, the English in 1966 and 1979, the Welsh Open Strokeplay in 1977, and the British Open Strokeplay in 1974 and 1975; here she was runner-up in 1978.

GREGSON, Malcolm   England
b. Leicester 1943

In 1967 it seemed that Malcolm would become a star on the world stage, and indeed he was one of a small group of players at that time who had the ambition and were prepared to go where the competition was: the USA, Africa and the Far East. He won a US Tour card in 1968 and played most of the following season there. Malcolm was a boy international in 1959 and 1960 and a finalist in the French Boys' Championship, and after turning professional in 1961 had his first success three years later with the Assistants' event. At that time he played with a high fade and was already an excellent putter. In 1967 he reached the peak of his career, finishing top of the British Order of Merit and winning the Vardon Trophy. He took three of that year's tournaments. The following year he again took the Daks and, except for a four-ball and a Zambian tournament, has not won since. His later best placings in the Order of Merit have been a couple of 17ths. He remained in the Top 60 until 1980 but faded out of the top 100 thereafter. Gregson was a Ryder and World Cup player in his best year, 1967.

Europe wins 5 (1967–72)
Europe money £86,284 (1963–82) (44th all-time)

HALIBURTON, Thomas Bruce   Scotland

b. 1915; d. 1975

Once a World Cup player for Scotland and twice a Ryder Cup player – in 1961 and 1963 – Tom Haliburton turned professional in 1937. He was a well-known name in British golf from the end of World War II until the mid 1960s, but his elegant swing lacked power. Perhaps he also lacked the nerve to win tournaments, though he did take the *Yorkshire Evening News* in 1963 and was runner-up in the 1952 Spanish Open. His 61 at Worthing in the 1952 Spalding tournament is still the second lowest round recorded on the European circuit. He followed that opening round with a 65 to hold the record for the lowest 36-hole total. Another magnificent achievement came in the 1963 Open at Lytham and St Annes when he covered the first nine in 29 strokes. After his tournament career was over, Tom Haliburton was professional at Wentworth for many years and was PGA captain in 1969.

HARRIS, Marley: see Spearman

HARRIS, Robert   Scotland

b. Dundee 1882

Harris twice reached the finals of the British Amateur Championship – in 1913 and 1923 – before winning. This he did in 1925 by the massive margin of 13 and 12. He was three times Walker Cup captain: 1922, 1923 and 1926.

HAVERS, Arthur Gladstone   England

b. Norwich 1898; d. 1981

When Arthur Havers won the British Open in 1923 it was still quite commonplace for a British player to do so. Yet American dominance lay just ahead and Cotton in 1934 was the next British player to win. Havers had first qualified for the Open at the age of 16 in 1914, and in 1921 came fourth. Again in 1932 he looked a very possible winner but Gene Sarazen came through. He belonged to an era of challenge matches. One of his feats was to go over to the USA as British Open Champion and take on Jones and Sarazen. He accounted for Jones by 2 and 1 and Sarazen 5 and 4. Henry Cotton has commented that he could at times look a very inferior player. He had a four-knuckle left-hand grip and made little use of his right. The swing was a lunging one with the hands too far in front of the

Tom Haliburton

clubhead. At times, the result was one shank after another. Havers, whose aureole hairstyle gave him a clerical appearance, always appeared unmoved, as if these monstrosities were no concern of his. He played against the USA five times between 1921 and 1933.

HEATHCOAT-AMORY, Joyce: see Wethered

HEDGES, Peter J.   England

b. 1947

One of the few substantial amateur British golfers in recent years who has not turned professional, Hedges was consistently an England international during the 1970s. His only championship win has been the 1976 English Open Amateur Strokeplay Championship but he has also won nine major tournaments and the Kent Open twice. He played in the European Team Championship between 1973 and 1977, in the Eisenhower Trophy in 1974 and was a Walker Cup player in both 1973 and 1975.

HEDGES, Susan (née Whitlock) England
b. *Beckenham 1947*

Sue Hedges won the Welsh Open Strokeplay in 1978 and was second in the English Ladies' in 1979, in which year she was third overall and leading amateur in the British Open. She has taken the national titles of Belgium (1974), Luxembourg (1976–7), and – an unusual one – Zaïre (1980), and won the Central England Mixed Foursomes in 1977 and the Kent title in 1976 and 1979.

HENSON, Dinah: see Oxley

HERD, Alexander Scotland
b. *St Andrews 1868; d. 1944*

The career of Sandy Herd is considerable evidence that players of the 1890s were the equal of those at least 30 years later. Sandy accomplished what is perhaps still the outstanding feat by an 'old' man by taking the 1926 *News of the World* PGA Match-play at the age of 58, the oldest winner of a major tournament. He had also won it in 1906 and been a finalist in 1909. Sandy played for several years as an amateur while he was first apprenticed to a baker for four years and then to a plasterer for a further five. Eventually, at the age of 23, he took the plunge and went as a professional to Huddersfield in 1892. This was the year that he began to establish a formidable record of endurance in the British Open. In the 1892 event he tied for second place (in the same year he also won three tournaments and beat Harry Vardon over 72 holes). In the years before 1902 he had five more finishes in the top five, one of these being a second place in 1895. Before the 1902 Open he was persuaded to have a hit at the new Haskell rubber-wound ball by John Ball. Reluctantly, Sandy did so – and hit the longest drive of his life. An instant convert, he was the only player not to use a gutty in the event and won from Harry Vardon and James Braid by a single shot. This was to be his only Open win, yet in 1910 at St Andrews he was again second and equal third the following year, one stroke behind the Vardon and Massy play-off. Then came World War I. At the end of it, the Triumvirate of Vardon, Braid and Taylor featured little in championship golf, though Taylor had a sixth- and a fifth-place finish. Herd, some 35 years after his first entry and at the age of 52 in 1920, came close to winning again. After two rounds he was 7 strokes ahead of the eventual winner, George Duncan, but in the end

came second by a couple of strokes. He had been joint leader after three rounds and was to repeat that level of performance the following year. Sandy continued to compete in the Open and had eventually established a 54-year span when he played for the last time in 1939. A feature of Sandy's game was the speed of his play, despite the fact that each shot was preluded by a rapid shifting of the feet and a prolonged but quick-action waggle. Indeed, he made waggling famous and helped to convince the golfing world that to-and-fro movements of the club before hitting prepare and loosen the muscles for the action to come.

HERD, Frederick Scotland
b. *St Andrews 1874; d. 1954*

A brother of Sandy, Fred never featured in the top half dozen of a British Open but he did compete in the US Open the first time it was played over 72 holes in 1898, when the nine-hole Myopia Hunt Club course was played eight times. What is more, he won by 7 strokes over Alex Smith, who was to feature strongly in the event for many years and twice be a champion. Fred had gone out as a professional to the South Shore Country Club in Chicago, but he returned to Knebworth in England in 1900. His brothers Jim and John remained in Chicago until they retired.

HETHERINGTON, Jean Clara (née McClure, later Holmes) England
b. *Wanstead 1923*

As Mrs Hetherington, she took the most prestigious of her titles, the British Ladies', at Hunstanton in 1946 while on her honeymoon. As Mrs Holmes, she reached the final of the 1966 English Ladies', but was defeated at Hayling Island by Julia Greenhalgh. She has totalled five wins in the Essex and Nottinghamshire championships and was twice an England international, being non-playing captain in 1967.

HEZLET, May Ireland
b. *1882*

The three Hezlet sisters, through a friendship with the Curtis sisters, were influential in setting up the Curtis Cup. Having first entered at the age of 13, May Hezlet had just reached the age of 17 when she won the British Ladies' in 1899. She repeated the performance in 1902 and 1907, this time beating her sister Florence by 2 and 1 in the final at Newcastle, County Down. May Hezlet was also runner-up to Lottie Dod in 1904. In Ireland, she won the national championship in 1899 (having been runner-up the previous year), from 1904 to 1906 and in 1908. Her sister Florence was also runner-up in the British Ladies' in 1909 and five times for the Irish title. Another sister, Violet, was beaten by Dorothy Campbell for the British Ladies' in 1911 and was three times runner-up for the Irish title. It is doubtful whether any other three sisters can rival their achievements. The last survivor of the three, Violet, died in 1982 at the age of 99.

HILTON, Harold Horsfall England
b. West Kirkby 1869; d. 1942

Amateur Harold Hilton enjoyed a very long career in championship golf. He lasted as a top player from the beginning of the 1890s until World War I, a span of close to a quarter of a century. Fairly short, at 5 feet 7 inches, Hilton swung fast and furiously, coming up on his toes in the impact area, and often losing the cap he habitually wore. Despite this violence Hilton was an extremely accurate player, especially to the flag with woods. Only three amateurs have won the British Open: John Ball, Bobby Jones and Hilton himself. He was the

Harold Hilton

second amateur to win and did so the first time it was played over 72 holes – at Muirfield in 1892. Hilton had rounds of 78, 81 and the very fine closing ones, for the time, of 72, 74. He won by 3 strokes. Five years later at Hoylake he did it again, winning by 1 shot from James Braid and leaving the previous year's champion, Harry Vardon, 6 in arrears. This was the last win by an amateur until Jones's first victory in 1926. Hilton again finished close on two later occasions: in 1898 he came third, 2 strokes behind Harry Vardon; and in 1911, in a period of revived form, he finished 1 behind the Vardon-Massy play-off. The latter year was Hilton's *annus mirabilis*. He won the British Amateur for the third time and then went to America and won the US Amateur as well, the first of a very few to achieve this major feat. In the US Hilton had been 7 up in the final against Fred Herreshoff, a 42-year-old matched against a 23-year-old, but they ended the 36 holes all square. On the first extra hole Hilton hit a bad tee shot and a bad approach but Herreshoff played the hole even worse and the deed was done – never yet repeated by a British player. Hilton's first victory in the British Amateur was long delayed. He finished runner-up in 1891, 1892 and 1896, then took it successively in 1900 and 1901. There followed a barren patch until the 1911 victory, and then a final championship in 1913. Being based at Hoylake, Hilton found Ireland convenient for championship golf and won the Irish Open Amateur in 1897, 1900 and 1902. By the end of his career he had established one of the greatest records achieved by an amateur, with four British Amateurs, two British Opens and one US Amateur. Only the greatest have exceeded that total of seven and even then, except for Nicklaus and Jones, not by much. Harold Hilton was the first editor of *Golf Monthly* and was also editor of *Golf Illustrated*. He was a designer of many golf courses.

HITCHCOCK, James England
b. Bromley 1930

After long years of struggling towards success, Jimmy Hitchcock reached his peak with victory in the 1960 Dunlop Masters. Despite a short, flailing backswing, he remained a considerable player for some years. He had a good season again in 1965 when he took the Agfa-Gevaert tournament and the Honda Foursomes. Hitchcock was chosen for the 1965 Ryder Cup at Royal Birkdale but lost his three matches. He now lives in South Africa.

HOAD, Paul   England
b. 1958

Paul Hoad was runner-up in the 1978 English Amateur and a Walker Cup reserve the following year. He then turned professional and went on the European Tour in 1980. He finished 71st that first season and was considered sufficiently promising to be given the Rookie of the Year award by Henry Cotton. In 1981 he moved up the money list to 46th and came to be regarded as one of the most promising young British players, an opinion he partly justified in 1982 by finishing equal second in the Car Care Plan International at Moor Allerton and rising to 36th on the money list.

Europe money £29,178 (1979–82)

HOLDERNESS, Sir Ernest William Elsmie
England
b. Lahore, India (now Pakistan) 1890; d. 1968

Sir Ernest Holderness was a good all-round sportsman but after two appendix operations settled on golf. With a house near Royal Dornoch far up in north-east Scotland he honed a game that made him one of the best British amateurs during the early post-World War I era. A steady rather than brilliant player, he won the British Amateur in both 1922 and 1924. He played for Great Britain in the international matches against the USA that eventually became the Walker Cup, in 1921, 1923, 1926 and 1930. He also established a near monopoly of the President's Putter, a competition held at Rye each winter for former Oxford and Cambridge men. From its beginnings in 1920, Holderness won the first four and then once again. In all he played 47 matches and lost six, the record matchplay rate of success for the event of 87.23%. Holderness pursued a career in the Civil Service, and played relatively little competitive golf after his marriage in 1926.

HOLMES, Jean: see Hetherington

HOMER, Trevor Walter Brian   England
b. Bloxwich 1943

After becoming Amateur Champion for a second time Trevor Homer in July 1974 decided to test himself against the professionals. In the seasons 1975 and 1976 together he won less than £1,000, and he reckoned the experience had cost him

£20,000 in expenses. He also found that his action was suspect: he hit too much with arms and hands and made little use of body and legs. The big ball also found him out, and he finished respectively 118th and 133rd in the 1975 and 1976 European Order of Merit. His pattern of play, using a fade, had served him well as an amateur and he had been long enough off the tee. As a professional he was neither long enough nor a sufficiently consistent striker. He was reinstated as an amateur in 1978. Trevor Homer had taken the 1972 Amateur by beating Alan Thirlwell by 4 and 3 and repeated his win in 1974 against the American Jim Gabrielson, despite the fact that on the last hole he drove into a bunker and failed to get out at the first attempt. He played in the 1972 Eisenhower Trophy and the 1973 Walker Cup.

HOOD, Vincent   Ireland
b. Belfast 1942

After turning professional in 1960 Vince Hood had his first success of note in 1966 with the Assistants' Championship – the year after Tony Jacklin had won it. He had Order of Merit placings of 33rd in 1967, 25th in 1968, then fell out of the top 50 for two years before coming back quite strongly in 1971 to 23rd place. 1972 was his best season, at 21st, and he also gave his best tournament performance in finishing equal second in the John Player Trophy, while he represented Ireland in the Double Diamond International for the second time. Thereafter, despite his excellent putting, his game fell away, perhaps in part the result of being overweight, and he increasingly concentrated on club professional duties. He was involved in a very serious car accident in Portugal in 1980, which he was lucky to survive.

HORNE, Reginald W.   England
b. London 1908

An excellent striker of the ball, Reg Horne was thought by his contemporaries to be a far better player in practice-rounds than in tournaments. However, he had notable successes: the PGA Matchplay in 1945, beating Percy Alliss, the 1948 *News Chronicle* and the 1952 Silver King. He also won the 1949 *Daily Telegraph* Pro-Am and, a final success, the 1970 Seniors. Despite these achievements, his most outstanding performance was probably in the 1947 British Open at Hoylake. After an opening 77 Horne had rounds of 74, 72, 71. He accomplished the quite rare feat of lowering his score in each round, but the opening 77 was too heavy a burden. He came in joint second with US amateur Frank Stranahan, 1 behind Fred Daly.

GB wins 3 (1945–52)

HORTON, Thomas   England
b. St Helens 1941

Since beginning his tournament career in 1964, Tommy Horton has never been lower than 48th in the Order of Merit and only four times has he been out of the top 30. He has seven finishes in the top 10, was once second, in 1967, and three times fifth – 1968, 1970 and 1976. Despite his consistency it was not until 1975 that he gained a Ryder Cup place, when at Laurel Valley he lost the three partner matches in which he was involved but halved his singles against Hale Irwin and beat Lou Graham. Picked again in 1977, he lost all his matches. Perhaps one reason for his delayed selection was that many considered him underpowered and a suspect putter, but his long game is rated particularly highly. A very straight driver, he found he gained much length from the use of a carbon shaft, and he is one of the best long-iron players in Britain. With Brian Barnes, Horton was in Ernest Butten's training scheme to produce a British major golfer – a surprising choice because power, which Barnes has, was thought to be a prime requirement,

Tommy Horton

while Horton is 5 feet 8½ and weighs about 140 lb. Coached by Max Faulkner, they may neither have become great players but are nevertheless great successes. Horton has since put something back into the game by his work with young golfers. With this grounding, Tommy Horton was soon successful, winning the Carroll's Irish tournament in 1965 and 1967 (not ranked as a PGA event). Together with a string of high finishes, that pushed him to second in the Order of Merit for 1967, but not to a Ryder Cup place. In 1968, he took the RTV International as his first fully recognized victory and won again the following year. In 1970 came one of his most prized successes, the South African Open against a strong international field, disturbing Gary Player's near monopoly of the championship. He also won the PGA Matchplay Championship the same year. During the 1970s, Horton notched up wins most years, including two national Opens, the Nigerian and Zambian; but his most prestigious victory was in the 1978 Dunlop Masters, which he won with a 8-foot putt on the last green in the year of his PGA captaincy. Horton has put up some good performances in the British Open, though he has never looked a winner. He opened with a 66 at St Andrews in 1970 before eventually coming seventh, managed equal fifth at Royal Birkdale in 1976 and, at ninth, was the highest-placed British competitor in 1977 at Turnberry, when he included a third-round 65, second lowest round of the championship. He has once had a 63 in tournament play, but rates his best round as the 69 he had in a virtual hurricane during the 1973 John Player Classic.

Europe wins 8 (1968–78)
Europe money £168,118 (1964–82) (15th all-time)
Overseas wins 3 (1970–77)

HOWELL, Henry Rupert   Wales
b. Penarth 1899

The esteem in which Howell is held in Wales is shown by his honorary membership of 11 clubs. He was Welsh Amateur Champion eight times between 1920 and 1932, once winning three times consecutively and four in a row up to 1932. In this last year, in the home internationals, he beat all three national champions. He represented Wales most years from 1923 to 1947. He once played a round in 63 strokes and 68 minutes, probably the lowest score ever recorded for a round played so fast.

HUDSON, John   England

Never very successful as a tournament golfer, John Hudson has one achievement to his name that is difficult to match. Playing in the Martini International at Royal Norwich in 1971, he holed in one at the 195-yard 11th hole; then on the 12th, a 311-yard hole, he did it again. This is the only time the feat of successive holes in one has been accomplished in a major tournament and is even more remarkable because his second ace was on a par 4. Despite being no less than 5 under par on those two holes, Hudson finished in a conventional 72. In the tournament as a whole he was joint ninth, finishing 5 behind Bernard Gallacher, who was a surprise winner after an opening round of 80.

HUGGETT, Brian George Charles, MBE
Wales

b. Porthcawl 1936

The best Welsh golfer since Dai Rees, Brian Huggett had made the most of his talents by the time he retired from tournament golf at the end of the 1980 season. He took one of the prime jobs in Britain, club professional at St Pierre Golf and Country Club, but has now left there to work as an organizer in business golf events. He joined the tournament

Brian Huggett

circuit in 1961 and immediately finished a credible 22nd; thereafter 52nd in his final season was his lowest placing. Once, in 1968, he was leading money-winner and he was four times third: 1963, 1969, 1970 and 1972. He had three further finishes within the top 10. He also won the Vardon Trophy in 1968, a year in which he had three wins, a feat he also managed in 1967 and 1970. Huggett's most important wins were three national Opens (the German, Dutch and Portuguese), the 1968 PGA Matchplay and the 1970 Dunlop Masters. In that last event he finished with a 65. His qualities of toughness and pugnacity earned the 5-foot 6-inch Huggett the nickname of 'the Welsh Toy Bulldog'. He represented Wales many times in both the World Cup and the Double Diamond team events. He played six times in the Ryder Cup, having a win rate of 45.83%, above average for British team members. Two years were particularly memorable. In 1969 he holed a 5-foot putt to halve his match with Billy Casper and broke down in tears – he thought his result had won the Ryder Cup for Great Britain, though the match eventually ended in a tie. Later, in 1973, he had even better results, taking 3½ points out of 4, the best play on either side. Perhaps because of his reputation for aggressiveness, he was given the captaincy for the 1977 match, and made the controversial decision to drop Tony Jacklin from the singles line-up because he felt he had been playing badly. Huggett once came close to winning the Open. In 1965 he was 2 shots behind Peter Thomson in joint second place with Christy O'Connor. After a 73, 68 start, he had fallen away to a 76 before his final-round 70, a better score than any of the leading contenders. He finished equal third and leading British player in 1962 at Troon, but was 13 strokes behind the winner, Arnold Palmer.

Europe wins 17 (1962–78)
Europe money £111,737 (1961–82) (32nd all-time)
Overseas wins 1 (1962)

HUISH, David   Scotland
b. Edinburgh 1944

Never a full-time tournament player, David Huish (pronounced 'Hush') had his finest hour at Carnoustie in 1975. He began 69, 67 and led the field, a far rarer achievement for a minor golfer than to jump into a first-round lead. Thereafter David fell away to a 76, and in the fourth round to an 80 and 32nd place. He won the 1971 Scottish Uniroyal tournament (not a full Tour event) and came second in the Scottish Skol the same year. Perhaps his best tournament performance was to be second behind Peter Oosterhuis in the 1971 Agfa-Gevaert. Huish's best placing in the Order of Merit was 36th in 1971. He won the Northern Open in 1973, the year he represented Scotland in the World Cup. He is professional at the historic North Berwick course and a well-known teacher.

HUKE, Beverly Joan Mary   England
b. Great Yarmouth 1951

Beverly Huke reached the final of the 1971 British Ladies' but was there beaten by Michelle Walker, then at a peak of her game. She compensated in 1975 by winning the English Championship. Amongst other amateur achievements, she was a girl international from 1966 to 1968, a full international from 1971 to 1977, and won the Scottish Open Girls' Strokeplay in both 1970 and 1971. She won the Roehampton Gold Cup in 1971, as well as three other major events, and played in the 1972 Curtis Cup. Turning professional in 1978, she took three tournaments between 1978 and 1981 and in 1982 was, with Jenny Lee Smith, the only British player to be qualified to play the US Tour.

HUMPHREYS, Warren   England
b. Kingston 1952

Humphreys first made news when at the age of 16, in partnership with John Davies, he won the Sunningdale Foursomes, beating Brian Barnes and Max Faulkner 6 and 4. The following year he won the Antlers, a major amateur foursomes, again with Davies. A boy international from 1967 to 1969, Humphreys was also a youth England player from 1969 to 1971 and in the full team in 1970 and 1971. In the last of these years he won two major amateur events, the Duncan Putter and the Lytham Trophy, trounced John Davies 6 and 4 in the final of the English Amateur and, although only 19, was an automatic Walker Cup choice. He partnered Michael Bonallack in the top foursomes and won, but was beaten in the singles by Jim Gabrielson. In the vital last-day singles he contributed to the 6–2 advantage Great Britain gained by beating Steve Melnyk. He then turned professional and the glory days abruptly departed. A gifted young amateur such as Humphreys is likely to do better on the professional circuits than a lad who turns professional on leaving school at 16: he has almost

certainly had more and better teaching, and more and tougher competition, for local professional events cannot compare with the trial by fire of national championships and the Walker Cup. In recent years top US amateurs such as O'Meara, Cook and Clampett or British players such as James, Faldo and Gordon Brand Jnr have made the transition fairly painlessly. Humphreys began in 1972 by reaching 33rd place in the Order of Merit and being declared Rookie of the Year by Henry Cotton. The following year he was up to 20th and finished equal third in the Dunlop Masters. That was just about the end of Warren Humphreys as far as the 1970s are concerned. He had decided that the swing he brought into professional golf was not good enough and tried to make it a perfect mechanical action, spending years with a British guru of golf, Leslie King. Year after year he had to prequalify for tournaments, and in 1978 had also to requalify to play the circuit. Not until 1980 did he begin to make progress again, and in 1981 he was 39th in the Order of Merit before a successful 1981–2 winter in South Africa where he was eighth in the money list and tied with Gary Player and John Bland for the South African Open, after opening and closing 65s, before losing the play-off. In 1982 he was 43rd on the European money list.

Europe money £43,272 (1972–82)

HUNT, Bernard John, MBE   England
b. Atherstone 1930

One of the best British professionals in 20 years from 1953 to 1973, Hunt was renowned for his short backswing. A man of well over 6 foot, he had begun with a long swing and plenty of body movement and was consequently a wild driver. He decided that control must be aimed for and emerged as a tournament-winner in 1953 with a flat three-quarter swing, though his hands remained high. Hunt never became a great driver but he was a great practiser, his strengths becoming excellent medium- and short-iron play and good putting. If 1953 was the year he became nationally known, winning six events, it was not the year he got rich. It is a comment on the different level of rewards at that time that Hunt took home only a little over £3,000. A man could make a comfortable living out of golf; riches were the other side of the Atlantic, and it was not until the late 1960s that players such as Jacklin and Townsend made determined efforts on the US Tour. Meanwhile the years passed.

Bernard Hunt

Geoffrey Hunt

Bernard Hunt never had a bad year and his wins mounted up. On the way he had some remarkable scoring feats. In the 1953 Spalding, which he won, he had a 28 for the first nine in the second round, still the second lowest nine-hole total ever. In the Daks in 1958 he birdied seven holes consecutively, also second in the record book. In the 1966 Piccadilly Strokeplay over Wentworth East he had rounds of 66, 63, 66, 67, and his 54-hole total of 195 is equal second lowest. By the end of his career he had 37 wins in important events, not all of which were PGA-recognized. For a long time considered a likely winner of the Open, Hunt four times finished in the top 5. He was third in the 1960 Centenary Open, 4 behind Kel Nagle, after a 66 in the last round at St Andrews. Four years later he was again leading British player in fourth place, but 8 behind Tony Lema's winning 279. Hunt's overseas play was mainly confined to the Ryder Cup, and entries in US tournaments while there. He did, however, have two wins outside Europe, in the 1956 Egyptian Open and the 1962 Brazilian. In the Ryder Cup he was chosen eight times, missing only 1955 in the years 1953–69. In his first match, his foursomes was lost but in his singles he came to the last needing to get down in two putts to beat Dave Douglas so that the Ryder Cup would be tied. However, Hunt three-putted. In the years that followed, Hunt collected some notable scalps: Doug Ford by 6 and 5 in 1957, Jerry Barber by 5 and 4 in 1961, Dow Finsterwald in 1963, Gene Littler in

1965, and in 1967 he halved with both Julius Boros and Bobby Nichols. Of ten singles, he won four and halved three. He was Ryder Cup captain in 1973 and 1975. Hunt won the Vardon Trophy for low stroke average in 1958, 1960 and 1965 and perhaps his most important victories were two Dunlop Masters titles, in 1963 and 1965. His last exceptional year was 1970, when he won the first three tournaments and finished sixth in the Order of Merit. Thereafter he began to slip down the lists and also competed less, but remained in the top 50 until 1975. For many years, he has been professional at Foxhills.

Europe wins 24 (1953–73)
Europe money £68,167 (56th all-time)
Overseas wins 2 (1956–62)

HUNT, Geoffrey Michael   England
b. Atherstone 1935

Brother of the far more successful Bernard, Geoffrey Hunt was a short hitter and, self-confessedly, not a good competitor. He won the Assistants' Championship twice, in 1953 and 1963 (the gap in years well illustrates how long an apprenticeship had to be served) and was also a Ryder Cup choice in 1963. This was the first time brothers had represented Great Britain since the Whitcombes before World War II. He lost by 5 and 3 to Tony Lema. Hunt withdrew from tournament golf towards the end of the 1960s, partly as a result of calculating his

252

money winnings. He found that in the period 1961–6 he had averaged only a little over £500 annually, and in his best year, 1963, he had totalled £742 16s 3d – and that was good enough to earn his Ryder Cup place. He took over at Hartsbourne GC when his father retired.

HUNT, Guy L.　　　　　　　　England
b. *Bishops Stortford 1947*

Guy Hunt turned professional in 1963 and won the Under 23 Championship in 1968 and the Southern England Professional. Only 5 feet 6 inches tall, he had his best season in 1972, when he came second in the Order of Merit. He did not win that year but had two seconds, three thirds and a fourth. He totalled 11 finishes in the top 10. All this was a startling improvement on his previous best performance in a major tournament of third in the 1970 Penfold. Hunt fell away the following season to 43rd, but in 1974 he missed not a single cut and was back to 16th place. This performance, coupled with 17th the following year, won Hunt a place in the 1975 Ryder Cup side. In 1976 his form fell away again, and he had still to win a major tournament. However, that came in 1977 in a prestige event, the Dunlop Masters, when he beat Brian Barnes in a play-off. Thereafter, Hunt's form slipped again and he is now off the European Tour.

Europe wins 1 (1977)
Europe money £67,000 approx. (1968–80)

HUNT, Noel　　　　　　　　England
b. *Manchester 1948*

Noel Hunt turned professional in 1969 and joined the European Tour in 1971. He was in the Top 60 in 1972 and 1973, lost his form but returned in 1980 and 1981. His best result was to finish third in the South African PGA in the 1973–4 season.

HUNTER, William: see North America

HURD, Dorothy: see Campbell, North America

HUTCHEON, Ian C.　　　　　　　Scotland
b. *Monifieth 1942*

Ian Hutcheon has been one of Britain's best amateurs from the beginning of the 1970s to the present day. He has been a Scotland international throughout that period (1971–81) and has played in the Walker Cup team from 1975 to 1981, when he was the oldest team member. In the 1975 match he beat Jerry Pate, and managed a half against Bill Campbell, thus becoming the first British player not to lose to him in Walker Cup matches. Winner of numerous regional Scottish titles, he helped Great Britain to victory in the 1976 Eisenhower Trophy with Steve Martin, Mike Kelley and John Davies. Hutcheon was the man on whom eventually all depended, and he played the last eight holes in 4 under at Penina over a nine measuring 3,665 yards. With a total of 293, Hutcheon tied for the individual title with T.M. Chen of Taiwan. He won the Scottish Amateur in 1973 and the Scots Open Amateur Strokeplay in 1971, 1974 and 1979.

HUTCHINSON, Horatio Gordon　　　England
b. *London 1859; d. 1932*

Horace Hutchinson lost the final of the first British Amateur to A.F. MacFie in 1885 but triumphed in the next two, beating the redoubtable John Ball in the second final. He reached one more final and was also a semi-finalist three times – 1896, 1901 and 1904. He believed in loose-wristed putting and photographs of him show that the high-flying right elbow was not introduced by Jack Nicklaus. After his active career in golf, which lasted over 20 years, he became the first Englishman to captain the R & A (in 1908) and was well known as an excellent writer on golf, cricket and other outdoor sports.

HUTCHISON, Jock: see North America

INGHAM, Michael B.　　　　　　　England
b. *Bradford 1943*

In Ernest Butten's attempt to build a major British player, which embraced figures such as Brian Barnes and Tommy Horton, Mike Ingham was a 'Butten Boy' for three years. More even than Barnes, he had the power seen as a first essential (most British golfers at the time were shorter hitters than their American counterparts). Barnes and Horton did not become major-championship winners but came to make excellent livings from the game; Ingham did not, although his hitting aroused awe. For some years he was the longest driver on the European circuit, regularly carrying 230 yards and more. Perhaps his progress was hindered by the knot of spectators who usually followed him to see a golf ball projected further than they had previously considered feasible. It is this aspect of top golf that is most beyond the ken of the club golfer: they have all played a deft chip, floated one to the flag from sand and holed putts from all distances, but know they are never going to experience the sight of one of their drives leaving the clubhead low and bullet-like, before lifting up into the wild blue yonder. Alas, the rest of Ingham's game was not so awesome. In 1968, for instance, he confessed to having completed all four rounds of a tournament only three times, despite the fact that he had managed one of his best finishes, an equal fifth in the Wills. But Mike went on plugging away, often suffering back problems, and in 1970 achieved a little more consistency to finish 39th in the Order of Merit. After slipping to 81st the following year he was back in the Top 60 in 1972 with a 46th-place finish. Then in 1974 he went right down to 141st, the pattern of his seasons thereafter. He had rather more success overseas, winning the Zambian Cock o'the North in 1971 and 1973. He then began to compete irregularly, which allowed him to join the PGA Cup team against the USA in 1976 and 1978. After 1979 he dropped off the Tour and concentrated on his club job at Cleckheaton and District. He made the sometimes difficult transition to club professional with ease, and is well respected as a teacher of the game.

Overseas wins 2 (1971–3)

INGRAM, David   Scotland
b. Huntly 1945

First playing on the European Tour in 1965, David Ingram was at his most successful in the 1970s. He was five times in the Top 60 despite the fact that he was more a club professional than a tournament golfer, perhaps the reason for his giving up a secure club billet at Dalmahoy near Edinburgh to try his luck as a full-time player. Ingram's best placing in the Order of Merit was 42nd in 1973, and he hovered between 52nd and 55th place from 1976 to 1979. He won the Scottish Uniroyal in 1973, played for Scotland in the 1971 Double Diamond matches and in the 1973 World Cup. He then took up the professional's job at Kingswood golf club in Surrey.

Europe money £30,121 (1970–81)

IRVIN, Ann Lesley   England
b. 1943

One of the best English players for a long period, Ann Irvin reached the final of the 1960 British Girls', but went one better by taking the French title three years later. By that time she was a Curtis Cup player (1962) and was to be selected again in 1968, 1970, 1974 and 1976. Her first national title came in 1967 when she took the English Ladies', which she repeated in 1974. She also took the British Ladies' Strokeplay (now the Open) in 1969 with the good score of 295 and the same year reached the final of the British Amateur, where she lost a tense struggle with Catherine Lacoste by 1 hole, a fine performance in the Frenchwoman's all-conquering year. In 1973 Ann Irvin won, defeating Mickey Walker, who had taken the title the previous two years. Ann Irvin was an England international from 1962 to 1975; among her other achievements were five wins in the Roehampton Gold Cup, three in the Hovis Ladies', one in the Avia Foursomes, two in the Northern Ladies' and six Lancashire titles. In the 1968 Curtis Cup she won 3½ points out of 4 playing top.

Ann Irvin

JACK, Robert Reid   Scotland
b. *Cumbernauld 1924*

Reid Jack was a late developer, not winning any important amateur competition until he was 25. Major honours eluded him until he was into his 30s. He is particularly remembered for two Walker Cup matches, with Billy Joe Patton his opponent on both occasions. In 1957 at lunchtime in the singles matches at Minikahdu, Great Britain seemed finally to have a chance of winning again on US soil, and that after having been massacred 10-2 at St Andrews two years previously. Jack looked a banker to win, standing 5 up on Billy Joe, but in the afternoon Billy Joe produced inspired golf, sometimes from unlikely parts of the course. Jack eventually lost by 1 hole and, with this being the top match, the US team seemed inspired and ran out very easy winners. In his second and last Walker Cup appearance Jack turned the tables at Muirfield in 1959 and took one of only 3 British points from the whole match when he defeated Patton by 5 and 3. Reid Jack won the Scots Amateur in 1955 and reached the semifinals of the 1956 British Amateur before securing his Walker Cup place in 1957 by winning it,

Reid Jack

defeating a US Army sergeant, Harold Ridgley, in the final by 2 and 1. In his career he played nine times for Scotland and was in the Commonwealth and Eisenhower Trophy teams. He also had two strong performances in the Open. In 1959 at Muirfield he was 2 strokes ahead of eventual winner Gary Player with a round to go, and eventually finished top amateur and equal fifth. The following year at the Centenary Open at St Andrews he was 10 behind in 16th place.

JACKLIN, Anthony, OBE   England
b. *Scunthorpe 1944*

The career of Tony Jacklin demonstrates the importance of the major championships to a golfer seeking fame and fortune. His story can almost be summed up by what happened in two weeks in 1969 and 1970. First Royal Lytham and St Annes in July 1969 and the British Open, with Jacklin a fancied player but by no means the favourite (of course Jack Nicklaus was that). His best placing hitherto had been fifth at Hoylake in 1967, 7 behind Roberto de Vicenzo. At Lytham Jacklin, fresh from the US Tour where he had been performing well and had won the Jacksonville Open the previous year, began with a 68. This was one of the leading scores, 2 behind Bob Charles but the vital 7 ahead of Jack Nicklaus, who had been playing his customary cautious opening round. He followed with a 70, which lost him 1 stroke on Bob Charles and left him level with George Caygill, another British prospect at the time, and 2 behind Christy O'Connor, who had begun 71, 65. Jacklin's third-round 70 was vital. It lost him ground only to those who were comfortably behind. Caygill, with a 79, was gone; Nicklaus was still 5 behind; Thomson 3; O'Connor 2; and, most important, Bob Charles had shot 75. Tony Jacklin headed the field by 2 shots. That is how it remained at the end. No one in contention had made up ground on him and as he stood on the last tee it looked as if a bogey would see him home. But Jacklin finished in style; he split the fairway with the longest drive seen there all week, found the green with a 7-iron and hit his approach putt close. He was the first British Open Champion since Max Faulkner in 1951 and, equally, the first world-class British golfer since Henry Cotton and the Braid, Taylor, Vardon Triumvirate. And so to Chaska, Minnesota, and Hazeltine National, a course of 7,151 yards and after heavy rain playing its full length and more. Also, that 18 June

Tony Jacklin

1970 there was a 40 mph north-westerly. While others complained Jacklin began 3, 5, 5, 2, 3, 3 to be 3 under par, and completed his round in 71. He led Julius Boros by 2 and the rest by 4 strokes. The most fancied players – Palmer, Player and Nicklaus – were almost out of it with 79, 80 and 81 respectively. After the second day Jacklin's 70 had him 3 in the lead over Dave Hill. The third day he faltered a little but made up for errors with a good wedge or putt. A moment of crisis came on the 344-yard 17th, when his 2-iron from the tee finished behind trees. He had the problem of whether to play safely back to the fairway or attempt to carry over them – for which he would need an 8-iron – while also needing 160 yards in distance. Boldness was rewarded on this occasion: Jacklin reached the green and soon after had another 70 and a lead of 4 over Dave Hill. Gay Brewer came next, 7 in arrears. In the final round he was once threatened. He dropped shots on both the 7th and 8th, then was in the rough on the 9th; he reached the green with his second but a long way from the hole. His approach putt was much too strong but he had the luck most champions need: it hit the back of the hole, jumped in the air – and fell back in. He faced the last hole with a lead of 6, found the green in regulation and

holed a long putt for another 70 and a win by 7. To put his achievement in perspective: before him the only overseas players to have won the US Open had been Vardon, Ray and Player; only Hagen, Barnes and Hogan had led a US Open throughout; he was the first Briton to win since Ted Ray in 1920; only Jones, Sarazen, Hogan and Nicklaus had held both British and US Opens at the same time (later to be joined by Trevino and Watson); his was the highest winning margin (and remains so) since Jim Barnes's 49 years earlier. Jacklin returned to Britain a national hero and at St Andrews in the Open went to the turn in 29, fading over the final few holes the following morning after a storm had washed out play for the day. He remained in contention and came in leading British player but 3 behind the Nicklaus-Sanders play-off. In 1971 he was there throughout once more, this time finishing third behind Trevino and Lu Liang-Huan. There are those that think what happened to Jacklin at Muirfield in the 1972 Open finished him as a major golfer. Be that as it may, it is certainly true that he has never contended in any major championship since. After two rounds Jacklin's 69, 72 had him level with Trevino's 71, 70 and in the third round, partnered with Trevino, he played better than the American for a 67. But Trevino finished his round as follows: 14th, a birdie from a 7-yard putt; 15th, another birdie from a longish putt; 16th, missed green, thinned bunker shot, hit flag and holed for another birdie; 17th, huge drive, on the green of the 542-yard par-5 in two and another birdie; 18th, through the green in two and holed chip of 10 yards. Trevino was back in 30 for a 66 after these five consecutive birdies, with a lead of one on Tony. When they reached the 17th tee in the last round the pair were level with two to play and had to par in to beat Nicklaus, who had produced a stirring 66. Jacklin drove long and straight; Trevino pulled his into a bunker and had hit three more and was through the green before Jacklin struck his short pitch third shot about 15 feet short of the hole. Said Trevino: 'I've had it.' He pulled out a club, gave a quick glance towards the hole and ran it in. Jacklin now needed to hole his putt to go ahead. Instead he hit a little strongly and missed the 3-foot return. Game, set and Open to Trevino, with Jacklin still the unluckiest loser in most people's memory and not even in second place after a 5 on the last. Destroyed or not, it was not immediately apparent, for he was second in the Swiss Open later the same month and won the

British PGA in August. Jacklin had been an apprentice fitter at Appleby Frodingham in Scunthorpe before he turned professional in 1962. The following year he was declared Rookie of the Year and won the Assistants' Championship in 1965. After wins in South Africa and New Zealand, he took his first British event in 1967 and won the Dunlop Masters the same year, having a hole in one on the 16th. In the US Masters he had come in 16th after being with the leaders after each of the first three rounds. He first played on the US Tour in 1967, and in 1968 came 29th in the money list and won the Greater Jacksonville Open, the first British-based player to have won a fully recognized US tournament since Ted Ray's 1920 US Open. By the end of his US career, which tapered off during the 1970s, he had won once more and had four times been in the Top 60 with a best placing of 20th. No British-based player has remotely approached that standard. As late as 1977 he came second in the Crosby. In 1974 Jacklin began to fade, though he won in South America and produced a dazzling performance in the Scandinavia Enterprises Open to win by 11. From then until victories in the Venezuela and German Opens of 1979, Jacklin won only once, in Ireland. He later won the 1981 Jersey Open and in 1982 took the British PGA, finding that a new blade putter gave him confidence and solved some problems on the greens. He was helped by the fact that Bernhard Langer four-putted the 16th in the final round, but when they played off (after Jacklin had himself three-putted the 18th) Jacklin produced a masterstroke by hitting a short iron on the first extra hole to no more than 2 feet. At his best Jacklin was one of the longest straight drivers in the world and perhaps the best striker in Europe. Putting came to be the weakness he continually blamed for his misfortunes, but he also came to be more apt to hit other loose shots. Perhaps even at his best he was not quite as good a player as the British press and public, starved of a golf hero for 20 years, hoped and came to believe for a while. Certainly, though, he was a major force between 1968 and 1974, and for 12 months or so as good as anyone in the world. He is now likely to become increasingly involved in television work.

Europe wins 13 (1967–82)
Europe money £213,953 (1963–82) (10th all-time)
US wins 3 (1968–72)
US money $280,000 approx. (1967–81)
Overseas wins 7 (1966–79)
World money $836,000 (1963–81)

JACKSON, Barbara Amy Bridget   England
b. Birmingham 1936

Winner of the British Girls' in 1954, Bridget Jackson went on to take the English Ladies' in 1956 and was runner-up two years later. In 1964 she reached the final of the British Ladies' and was beaten only at the 37th hole by the American Carole Sorenson. The premier achievement of her career was perhaps her victory in the 1967 Canadian Championship. She won the German title in 1956 and was a Curtis Cup choice in 1958, 1964 and 1968. She took the Staffordshire title twelve times from 1954 onwards.

JACKSON, Hugh   Ireland
b. Newtonards 1940

Hugh Jackson turned professional in 1962 and earned some reputation as a straight hitter and a very good putter. He won the Ulster Professional title in 1963 and repeated this five times up to 1971. On the British circuit his only win was in the 1968 Piccadilly Four-ball, but he did well in the 1970 Open, finishing eighth but only 5 strokes behind winner Jack Nicklaus. He also won the Irish Professional title that year to add to his Irish Dunlop title of 1968. His consistent play in 1970 took him to eighth place in the Order of Merit and an Irish World Cup team place. In 1971 he was 16th, in 1972 26th and in 1973 19th. He played for Ireland in the Double Diamond International from 1971 to 1973. After the early 1970s his form began to fade and eventually he dropped out of tournament golf. A friend of Tony Jacklin, he went to work at Holme Hall Golf Club in Jacklin's home town of Scunthorpe, but eventually returned to Ireland.

JACOBS, John Robert Maurice   England
b. Lindrick 1925

John Jacobs turned professional in 1947 and spent some considerable time at the Gezira Club in Egypt at the beginning of his career. As a tournament player he enjoyed moderate success, winning the South African Matchplay and the Dutch Open in 1957. He was also runner-up in the 1954 Italian Open, after losing a play-off to Ugo Grappasonni. Eventually Jacobs decided that he was unlikely to achieve further significant success, and gave up tournament play so that he could be a more effective teacher. It seems that the decision was a

John Jacobs

feat is downgraded a little because play was on 'browns' – greens which are anything but green, being made from sand bound by oil with the surface swept after the passage of each set of players. They are easy to read and the ball runs true. Jagger is one of a quite substantial group of British players who blossom in Africa, return home in the spring covered with a fair measure of glory and then wilt in the harsher competitive climate of the European Tour. He has five victories in Africa: the 1974 Kenya Open, the Nigerian three times in 1975, 1977 and 1982, and the 1982 Kalahari. He topped the 1982 Safari money lists with his two wins plus a second in the Kenya Open and a third in the Ivory Coast Open. In Europe he has won two minor events, the 1973 Northern Open and the 1980 Club Professionals' Championship, and recently has not been a tournament regular. He has, however made the Top 60 in several years: 1971, 1973–6 and 1980, with a best placing of 26th in 1976. He spent some time at Mount Irvine Bay, Tobago, and is now professional at Selby. He played in the 1976 Hennessy Cup matches for England.

Europe money £54,315 (1966–82)
Africa wins 5 (1974–82)

wise one, for Jacobs blossomed in several fields. He became one of the highest-paid coaches and remains much sought after by professionals with problems. As a writer, his instructional books sell very well. As a businessman, he is best known for the driving ranges, sometimes with attached courses, that bear his name. As an administrator, he was appointed Tournament Director of the PGA in October 1971 and set out to raise prize money and devise an integrated European Tour, as distinct from the separate British and continental European scenes that existed when he took over. He succeeded admirably with both aims. It is for that achievement that he is most likely to be remembered. He returned to the Ryder Cup in 1979 as non-playing captain and was chosen again for the 1981 match. He had been chosen as a player once only, in 1955, and had won both his matches. He commentates on British independent television and has very successful golf schools in the USA.

JAGGER, David   England
b. Sheffield 1949

David Jagger is one of that select band who have broken 60. He did this in the pro-am before the 1973 Nigerian Open with nines of 29 and 30. The

JAMES, Mark H.   England
b. Manchester 1953

Mark James is one of the few players who has made the transition from amateur to professional without apparent pain, jumping immediately to 15th place in the European Order of Merit in his first season, 1976, and coming joint fifth in that year's British Open. As an amateur Mark James was an international at all age levels between 1971 and 1975, being a full international while still a youth. He won the English Amateur at the age of 20 in 1974 and reached the final of the British the following year, when he was beaten 8 and 7 by Vinny Giles at Hoylake. In the same year he was a Walker Cup player and had the good record at St Andrews of winning in both his foursomes and defeating Jerry Pate in the top singles before finally going under to Gary Koch by 5 and 4 on the last afternoon. He had won 3 of Great Britain's 8½ points total. James then turned professional at the end of the year. In addition to that high Open finish, in which he came in with a final-round 66, at the tail-end of the season he put together a 69, 66, 70, 69 sequence in the Benson and Hedges International to finish in

Mark James

second place, 2 behind Graham Marsh. Although his standard fell away in 1977 he had earned a Ryder Cup place, thus representing Great Britain at both amateur and professional levels in the space of two years. Only Sandy Lyle has made the transition as quickly. He lost the three matches in which he was involved, however. Again chosen in 1979 he was injured while in the USA and played little part in the matches. He did, however, win a fine of £1,500, the highest ever imposed by the European Tournament Players' Division, for undisciplined behaviour. Some magnanimity was therefore shown in 1981 when he was one of two players chosen who had not qualified for automatic selection. Paired with Sandy Lyle, James won two and lost two partner matches, and was defeated by Larry Nelson in the singles. James's first tournament victory came in Africa with the 1977 Lusaka Open; but he did not have long to wait for his first success on the more important soil of Europe, when he took the prestige Matchplay Championship. He also took five other places in the top five at tournaments to be seventh in the Order of Merit, and at the end of the season was given a World Cup place. With Howard Clark, England took third place in Hawaii. James had shown one of his flights of eccentricity during the Italian Open. He played

the last five holes of a round, because of a hand injury, with one hand only, and proved to be none too good at it, finishing in 111. There was further improvement from James in 1979. He was fourth in the Open and finished the season in third place in the Order of Merit, having secured two wins, in the Welsh Classic after a play-off and in the Irish Open. In the latter event he was 8 behind after two rounds but finished 69, 65 to beat Ed Sneed into second place. He again represented England in the World Cup in 1979; but in 1980 he declined the honour. Said James: 'You can't live on pride and honour. There's no money in it.' James made no real progress in the 1980 and 1981 seasons, falling away a little to sixth and 15th in the Order of Merit, though he won the Irish Open again in 1980 and the São Paulo Open in 1981. The Italian Open early in 1982 and, later in the season, the individual title in the Hennessy Cup matches at Ferndown, where he finished with two birdies, also fell to him. He produced another best British performance in the 1981 Open, being joint second going into the final round and paired with Bill Rogers but 5 strokes behind him. Early on some good putts failed to drop for James, when the American was faltering, and at the end of it all he finished in tied third place. Putting had become a problem for him. In 1980, for instance, he reckoned his average was 33 per round, and that he had broken 30 on just seven occasions while he had twice soared to 42 and 45. In play through the green James is a perfectionist, wanting to strike every shot exactly right. This perhaps accounts for his demeanour on course. Throughout, he looks as if the news he has just received in the morning post has been of death, damnation and ultimate tragedy. As each shot curves away, he observes the flight of the ball with disgust, then the shoulders slump and he plods drearily after it, no hope lighting his features. Perhaps a small, world-weary smile may just be detected if he holes a putt from the edge of the green – but even then he has the look of a man who knows that disaster still lies ahead. Some judges would rate James in the top three of British golfers with Faldo and Lyle. His swing is too short for elegance, but effective and powerful. He excels with what many players would judge the most difficult club in the bag, the 1-iron. He was 12th on the 1982 money list with over £35,000.

Europe wins 6 (1978–82)
Europe money £191,380 (1976–82) (13th all-time)
Overseas wins 2 (1977–81)

JAMIESON, Andrew — Scotland
b. Glasgow 1905

The fame of Andrew Jamieson rests on one feat: he beat Bobby Jones, something scarcely anyone did in matchplay once he had reached the peak of his powers. The victory came in the British Amateur Championship of 1926. Jamieson was in the 1926 Walker Cup team, won the Scots Amateur in 1927 and was runner-up in 1931. He represented Scotland seven times between 1927 and 1937.

JOB, Nicholas — England
b. Surrey 1949

Nick Job is one of many players who can produce glittering spells of scoring but finds it far more difficult to put a tournament-winning sequence of rounds together. One instance is the PGA Championship at Wentworth in 1973. There he broke the course record by 2 strokes with a 63, which was then no fewer than 11 under par. Alas, this score followed on a 79 in the first round, but the 16-stroke swing must be one of the highest ever recorded in tournament play. After two steady final rounds he came in fourth equal. Nick Job is reputed to 'choke' under the pressure of leading or heading for a good placing and has taken tranquillizers to steady himself down. He has been a tournament player since 1968, and during that time has never been worse than 76th on the money list and has been in the Top 60 ten times, with the 1978–81 seasons being his most consistent and 26th in 1981 his best placing. Early in his career he took the 1969 Under-24s tournament and in 1970 the Rising Star event. He has won the Victoria Falls Classic, but has not succeeded in a European tournament. Two of the best performances here were to start 65, 65 in the 1980 Benson and Hedges, where he came in fourth, and at Hoylake in 1981 when he put together rounds of 71, 70, 69, 69 in the European Open for third place. He also lost a play-off for the 1978 Greater Manchester Open. He was chosen for the 1980 Hennessy Cup match for Great Britain. His brother is also a professional. Nick, at the end of the 1982 season, was considering leaving tournament golf, having won only £1,700 or so, at 120th place on the money list. This would be a pity, for he is a good putter, and if he could improve his slightly wayward long game he could become a consistent tournament winner, and an asset to the Tour.

Europe money £87,344 (1968–82) (43rd all-time)
Africa wins 1 (1976)

JONES, Ernest — England
b. 1887; d. 1966

Having showed promise as a professional and won the Kent Open, Ernest Jones had his career abruptly ended when he lost a leg in World War I. Thereafter, while still a good player, he became far more known as a teacher and especially as a theorist. In 1920 he published *The Golf Swing*, which emphasized that the golf stroke must be a swing, not a hit. He was fond of demonstrating his ideas by using a penknife tied to the end of a pocket handkerchief, the point being that any jerk in the swinging action ruined everything. Many tried to adopt his principles both in Britain and the USA, where he went in 1923 to open one of the first indoor golf schools.

JOWLE, Frank — England
b. Sheffield 1912

Having a short, fast swing, Frank Jowle was inclined to be inconsistent, but he had a tough Yorkshire competitiveness. He reached one of the peaks of his form during the 1955 Open. There he had a 63 in the qualifying rounds, which equals the Open record, and went on to play a strong championship. One behind Peter Thomson after three rounds, he went on to finish in third place, 3 strokes adrift. He was runner-up in the 1950 PGA Matchplay and won three major tournaments during the late 1950s. He was unlucky not to be chosen for the Ryder Cup, since, in my opinion, he deserved to be in the team for at least two matches during the 1950s.

GB wins 3 (1957-8)

KELLEY, Michael John — England
b. Scarborough 1945

One of the best British amateurs of recent years, Kelley is perhaps worthy of an Amateur Championship. His highest achievement has been to be a member of the winning Great Britain side in the 1976 Eisenhower Trophy. He has also won a number of important regional and national amateur competitions. A boy international since 1962, then at youth level and since 1974 at full level, Kelly has also been a Walker Cup choice on two occasions, in 1977 and 1979, and in the former year beat Dick Siderowf in the singles. In 1981 he won the County Champion of Champions title.

KIDD, Tom   Scotland
b. St Andrews

The British Open began at Prestwick in 1860 and was played there for 12 years before the decision was taken to vary the venue with St Andrews and Musselburgh, which became the routine until 1892, when Muirfield was added (after the Honourable Company of Edinburgh Golfers moved from Musselburgh), and, a little later, Sandwich, Hoylake and Deal. The first St Andrews Open was held in 1873, and Tom Kidd won it with a score for 36 holes of 179 in good weather. This was the highest total to win an Open until the event began to be played over 72 holes from 1892.

KING, Michael   England
b. 1950

Michael King would make a fortune if he could tauten his game a notch or two. He might then be counted among the top half dozen British tournament players. He has the looks, the friendly, outgoing personality, and something of the image of fast cars and faster living that might well bring the money pouring in for endorsements, company days, exhibitions and the like. King has in fact done it, but for one season only – 1979. Then he was in the top half dozen, in fifth place, did not miss a cut, was sixth or better eight times, made the Ryder Cup team and won his first – and only – tournament. The latter was the Tournament Players Championship at the end of the season at Moor Park, which he won with a good display of steady golf. As an

Sam King

amateur he won four major competitions and seven regional titles and made the Walker Cup team at 19, though he lost all his matches. He was chosen again in 1973 and this time got 1½ points out of 4. He then tried stockbroking for a while, an activity that once would have combined admirably with being a well-to-do top-class amateur. However, he turned professional in time for the 1975 season and after a poor first year has been in the Top 60 in Europe ever since, though in the 30s and 40s rather than the single figures that really cause the money to flow. In 1978 he lost a play-off to Sandy Lyle for the Nigerian Open and in the Ryder Cup match the following year was asked to play only one singles, which he lost to Andy Bean. Michael King is an excellent striker of the ball but may not fully have the competitive nerve to progress much further. Aside from golf, he is an excellent player of backgammon and bridge.

Europe wins 1 (1979)
Europe money £93,769 (1975–82) (41st all-time)

KING, Samuel Leonard   England
b. Sevenoaks 1911

Sam King was one of the pre-war generation that continued to feature strongly in the late 1940s. He made Ryder Cup appearances in 1937, 1947 and 1949. In 1937 he halved his singles with Densmore Shute and the 1947 match at Portland, Oregon, went as follows: Foursomes: USA 4, Great Britain 0; Singles: USA 7, Great Britain 1. Playing last, it was Sam's defeat of Herman Keiser in the last match of all that saved a little face for Britain. In 1949 he lost in both foursomes and singles, when, as a short hitter, he was matched against Chick Harbert, one of the longest in the world at the time. Sam King produced some strong performances in the Open. In 1939 he came in third, 4 behind Dick Burton; in 1947 he was sixth, again 4 behind; fourth in 1949, 3 behind; and fifth in 1952. At the age of 48, he produced a final effort at Muirfield in 1959, the scene of Gary Player's first major championship win. After three rounds, he led Player by 4, but of those in contention, it was Player who produced the good last round, having a 68 to King's 76, which left him in fifth place. Later, in 1961 and 1962, he won the British Seniors and on each occasion went on to be beaten by Paul Runyan in the World Seniors. King was a very straight hitter but lacked length. He had been one of the best pre-war putters, though he lost much of this ability in later years. He was excellent in the 5-iron-to-wedge range. He first came to notice with a win in the 1932 Assistants' Championship and, beside his three full tournament wins, he took the Kent Open a record 12 times from 1932 to 1937 and 1946 to 1951. He spent just about all his golf career at Knowle Park, but has retired to Lincolnshire, where he enjoys shooting and observing wildlife.

KINSELLA, James J.   Ireland
b. Skerries 1939

The best way to describe Jimmy Kinsella's swing briefly is to say that it was both shorter and faster than that of Doug Sanders, and the most extreme in these respects yet seen on a golf course in a player of some class. He turned professional at the age of 15 and began to play competitive golf from 1954, reaching his finest achievement in 1972 when he was a surprise winner of the Madrid Open, holing an 8-foot putt on the last green after middle rounds of 69, 67. He had played most consistently in 1970 to be tenth in the Order of Merit, his best position and worth £2,116 (it is interesting to reflect that this placing would now be worth over £30,000). Kinsella once had a 62 in the Irish Championship, and most of his successes were on the local Irish scale. Here he won the Irish Dunlop in 1961 and 1971, the Irish Professional in 1972 and 1973, the Southern Ireland twice and the Carrolls No. 1 in 1967. If his swing was individualistic so too were some of his theories on golf and he played for some time with a driver with two shafts, basically one stuffed inside another. He spoke quickly in a broad accent and had a variety of rather Irish hobbies which included racing, cycling and the keeping of racing donkeys.

KIRKALDY, Andrew   Scotland
b. Denhead 1860; d. 1934

The origin of a wealth of stories (he once called Muirfield 'nothing but an old water meadow'), Andra' Kirkaldy succeeded 'Old Tom' Morris as professional to the R & A, a post he took up in 1910 and held until his death. Perhaps the best golfer of his day not to win the Open Championship, he was second in 1879 and 1881, went off to fight in the battle of Tell-el-Kebir in 1882, and in 1889 tied for the title with Willie Park Jnr, losing the play-off. He was second in 1891, fourth in 1890 and 1893 and third in 1894, 1895 and 1899, his career thus forming a link with the Great Triumvirate, in whose company he was not outclassed. On one famous occasion he missed a 1-inch putt in the Open – but for that, he would almost certainly have won.

KIRKALDY, Hugh   Scotland
b. Denhead 1865; d. 1894

Brother of the more famous Andrew, Hugh was more successful finally in the Open. He won it the last time it was played over 36 holes in 1891, his brother being 2 behind in joint second place. He was also joint fourth, with his brother, in 1893. He was the original owner of the President's Putter, competed for by past and present Oxford and Cambridge players at Rye each winter.

KYLE, Alexander Thomson   Scotland
b. Hawick 1907

British Amateur Champion in 1939, Alex Kyle was later to come second in both the 1946 Irish Open Amateur and the 1952 English Open Amateur Strokeplay; he also won four regional titles in a long career which extended to his appearance in the British Seniors at the age of 68. He was a Walker Cup player in 1938, 1947 and 1951, winning the only two singles in which he played but losing all three foursomes. He was seven times capped for Scotland, though he spent most of his life in Yorkshire.

LACEY, Arthur J.   England
b. Burnham Beeches 1904; d. 1979

Arthur Lacey was perhaps the longest hitter on the British scene during the 1930s. This derived from a slashing swing rather than ponderous power. Dai Rees recalls having seen him drive over the last green at St Andrews, as did Ted Blackwell with a guttie and Jack Nicklaus with a 3-wood in 1970. Nevertheless it is a rare feat, and with a guttie, one would think nigh on impossible. He played in the 1933 and 1937 Ryder Cup teams and was non-playing captain in 1951. He was beaten by Hagen and Henry Picard in singles, and also lost his only foursome. He won the Belgian Open in 1931 and 1932, the French Open in 1932 and a Cannes tournament in 1936. In Britain he won the *Leeds Evening News* twice and in 1937 the Dunlop Metropolitan. From 1949 to 1951 he was chairman of the PGA.

LAIDLAY, John E.   Scotland
b. Seacliff, 1860

The 'Vardon grip' of course takes its name from Harry Vardon, and many have assumed that it was Vardon who first employed it. Not so. Vardon was the great player whose methods many tried to follow, and who happened to be one of many who overlapped the little finger of his right hand. Before him most had used an all-fingers-on-the-shaft arrangement, with the grip tending to the palm rather than in the fingers. Johnny Laidlay is usually reckoned the first influential golfer to use this grip, a good many years before Vardon and his contemporaries. He is said to have learned much of his golf while at Loretto School. Against the rules, Laidlay would abscond on moonlit nights to Musselburgh links to play and take lessons from Bob Ferguson, Open Champion from 1880 to 1882. Laidlay was at his peak from the late 1880s to the early 1890s, and only once from 1888 to 1893 was he not a finalist in the British Amateur, though all the great players of the day – Ball, Hutchinson and Hilton – were there. Ball twice beat Laidlay in the final, in 1888 and 1890, and Laidlay also lost to Peter Anderson in his last appearance in 1893; but he came through in 1889 and 1891, in the latter year against Harold Hilton, the year before he won the Open. Laidlay was also runner-up once in the British Open, when he finished 2 behind Willie Auchterlonie in 1893. He was also a dominant player at St Andrews, winning 15 important events there, while it is said that during his career he totalled 131 medal victories. Beside the 'Vardon grip' Laidlay may have had another first to his credit. He is thought to be the first man to bring golf to Egypt (where it has since made comparatively little progress) and put down a nine-hole course near the Pyramids at Giza. Laidlay played with an excessively closed stance, the left foot near the ball and the right much withdrawn. He addressed the ball with the heel of the club and gripped low. Before an important match he usually bought a new brassie. The main feature of his game was excellence in approach play and putting.

LANGLEY, John D.A.   England
b. Northwood 1918

John Langley was a youth prodigy. He played for England Boys from the age of 14 for four years and won the British Boys' at 17. A year later he became one of the youngest of Walker Cup players and was again chosen in 1951 and 1953, though he lost all his matches. He was runner-up in the English Amateur in 1936 and won it in 1950.

LARGE, William   England
b. Liverpool 1937

Bill Large holds the record for the fewest putts in a PGA event, 22, when qualifying for the Benson and Hedges matchplay in 1972. (This record is a suspect one. Stan Taggart, professional at Westwood Ho!, is thought to have taken just 18 in an Open of 50 years ago, but such statistics are not formally kept in Europe.) His best year was 1968, when he finished 12th in the Order of Merit. He tied with me in the 1966 Martini, scoring a birdie on the last hole. In 1968 he also tied for the Alcan International and was second in the Wills Open. He also won the Honda Foursomes in 1965. He is now professional at Dyrham Park, in Hertfordshire.

LASSEN, E.A.   England
b. Bradford 1876

Lassen won the British Amateur in 1908 and was second three years later. He was three times an England international and played for the Amateurs versus the Professionals in 1911. He was second in the 1913 French Amateur, and Yorkshire champion five times.

LAUPHEIMER, Mary: see Everard

LEES, Arthur   England
b. Sheffield 1908

Despite two cancer operations, Arthur Lees still plays golf and beats his age most times he plays. For many years professional at Sunningdale, he showed there that he might be better when playing with his own cash than when competing for prize money. A dour but very human Yorkshireman, he once produced one of golf's *bon mots* by telling an opponent: 'If you mark your ball again it'll be a bloody gimme.' Lees was at his best as a matchplayer, and was chosen for the Ryder Cup four times – 1947, 1949, 1951 and 1955. In his eight matches, he had a 50% success record, good for British players against Americans. He won in both foursomes and singles in 1951, the only singles winner for Great Britain in a 9½–2½ defeat, and also won his singles in 1955. Before World War II he was runner-

263

up in the Czech Open twice and the German Open once, and won the 1939 Irish Open. After the war his major victories were in the 1947 Dunlop Masters and the Penfold in 1951 and 1953. He won the British Seniors in 1959.

GB wins 3 (1947–53)

LEE SMITH, Jennifer Constance   England
b. *Newcastle upon Tyne 1948*

The best British woman professional since she left the amateur ranks in 1977, Jenny Lee Smith had her greatest success in winning the British Ladies' Open Strokeplay in 1976. The same year she also took the Newmark tournament, and won the Wills Matchplay in 1974. She won the Northumberland title from 1972 to 1974, and in team events was in the 1974 and 1976 Curtis Cup sides, an England international from 1973 to 1976, and played in the 1976 World Team Championship. After turning professional she qualified to play the US Tour the following month but her main successes have been in Britain, where she was leading money-winner in both 1981 and 1982 – when her prize money was double that of the next player – on the new WPGA Tour. She won one tournament in 1979, five in 1980 and added two more in 1981 and 1982. Easily the most consistent WPGA player in the 1982 season, she was placed joint second in the British Women's Open.

LEITCH, Charlotte Cecilia Pitcairn   England
b. *Silloth 1891; d. 1977*

Cecil Leitch was a strong attacking player with a male approach to the game – for, gifted with strong hands and arms, she could produce punching shots. She reached the semi-finals of the British Championship in 1908 and won the French title in 1912 for the first time. In 1910 she played a 72-hole match against Harold Hilton and won, though she was being given a stroke on alternate holes; later she repeated the feat against John Ball. She reached her peak by 1914, in that year winning the national championships of Britain, France and England; she did just the same after World War I, when the events were next held. In 1920 she was a strong favourite to take the English title again, but met and was beaten by the then unknown Joyce Wethered in the final. There was little doubt that Joyce was the better player, but there were a number of close-fought matches between the two and Cecil Leitch sometimes came out on top. In 1921 she beat her in the finals of the British and French Championships, though that was the last time she was to do so; and she completed her record fourth win in the British in 1926, when Wethered was not playing. In 1925 she had lost one of the greatest finals in the history of the event to Joyce Wethered on the 37th hole. Indeed for the first half of the 1920s the story of British women's golf can almost be told in terms of the supremacy of these two players. It ended with Cecil having a record six appearances in the final and sharing a record four wins with Joyce Wethered, who did not compete as often. Her most overwhelming victory came in the final of the 1921 Canadian Championship. At lunch she stood no fewer than 14 up and completed her victory by winning the first three afternoon holes. This is probably a record margin for the final of a major national championship. Cecil Leitch's championship record is remarkable:
British: 1914, 1920, 1921, 1926
French: 1912, 1914, 1920, 1921, 1924
English: 1914, 1919
Canadian: 1921

Cathy Panton and Cecil Leitch

LLEWELLYN, David J. Wales
b. *Dover, England* 1951

One of few good Welsh professionals, Llewellyn represented his country in the World Cup and frequently in the Double Diamond internationals. A better matchplayer than a strokeplay competitor, he had his only major win in the 1972 Kenya Open, having been chosen Rookie of the Year in 1971. He was 39th in the 1974 Order of Merit.

LLOYD, Joseph: see North America

LONGHURST, Henry Carpenter England
b. *Bedford* 1909; d. 1978

A runner-up in both the Swiss and French Amateurs, Longhurst won the German title in 1936. Earlier he had captained Cambridge University. Brought up on a course that encouraged the slice (all the trouble and out of bounds were on the left), he did not make further progress. He did, however, become the finest British golf writer of his time. From 1947 onwards he always had a piece in the centre of the back page of the *Sunday Times*, and many non-golfing readers of the newspaper turned to it first to relish his urbanity and wit. Indeed his writing had that artless quality that conceals art, giving the reader the feeling that he was being spoken to at a club bar – a place where Henry Longhurst indeed often held forth. The author of many books, some of which were collections of his journalism; his most popular was *My Life and Soft Times*, which appealed to non-golfers and golfers alike. After his death an anthology of his writings, *The Best of Henry Longhurst*, was a bestseller. He was also the first commentator on golf for BBC television, and his fruity voice became nationally known. He also worked in the USA, the 16th at the Masters being 'his' hole. He was an enthusiast for big-engined American cars.

LONGMUIR, William Scotland
b. 1953

Bill Longmuir's finest hours came on the first day of the 1979 British Open at Royal Lytham. Here he went out in 29, which equals the championship nine-hole record, and held himself together very well to finish in 65. He had birdied the 3rd to the 7th and the 9th for his 29, and then birdied the 10th and 12th before dropping a couple on the route

home. He won the Tooting Bec Cup for the lowest round by a British player and came in 29th. In 1976 he won twice overseas, the Nigerian Open and the New Zealand Southland Classic. Since then he has had high finishes in Africa, including the 1980 Nigerian Open again. He fared well in the event again in 1981, when he had two 62s, together with a 69 and a 68, good enough normally to win by a street. But Peter Tupling was busy setting a new world record of 255, and Bill was 6 behind that. (The importance of length and green surface was illustrated in this event. Iyoki GC at Lagos measures only 6,024 yards and the greens are 'browns' made of sand bound with oil, which are very true.) Longmuir finished fifth on the 1981 Safari money list, and was second in 1980. However, he is one of that band who have been unable to produce African form in the tougher European competition. It took him four years to make the Top 60, with 40th in 1979 his best placing until his 24th in 1982, when he twice nearly won. He was 50th in 1980 and 52nd in 1981.

Europe money £52,068 (1976–82)
Africa wins 2 (1976–80)
Other overseas wins 1 (1976)

LOW, George: see North America

LUCAS, Percy Belgrave, CBE, DSO, DFC England
b. 1915

With a father who had won the first Norfolk Amateur in 1894 and was later co-founder of Prince's Sandwich, 'Laddie' Lucas had the advantage of being brought up on a premier course which has hosted the British Open. He used his local knowledge to considerable effect during the Battle of Britain as a fighter pilot when he needed to make a forced landing quickly. He went down on one of the fairways. The course itself was used for bombing practice by the RAF, which prompted the comment from Lord Brabazon: 'My God, it's like throwing darts at a Rembrandt!' Lucas won the Boys' Championship in 1933 and was a boy international for four years, and a full international three times in the period 1936–49. A Walker Cup choice in 1936, he was found on arrival at Pine Valley to be suffering from too much wildness from the tee to play in a match. After one such soared away into the trees Lucas called out: 'Watch it! Watch it!' Said the caddie: 'You don't have to watch 'em. You gotta listen for 'em.' He might as well have played: Great Britain lost all but one singles. In 1947 at St Andrews he won his foursomes but was beaten by Dick Chapman in his singles. Laddie Lucas had a good spell from 1947 to 1949, when he won four important amateur events and also the President's Putter, in which he was also three times runner-up. Later he was very prominent in golf administration, the Greyhound Racing Association and, with John Jacobs, in the driving-range business. He has written three books, *The Sport of Princes*, *Five-Up* and *Flying Colours: The Epic Story of Douglas Bader*.

LUNT, Michael Stanley Randle   England
b. Birmingham 1935

Michael Lunt won the English Amateur in 1966. His father had won it in 1934. They are the only father and son combination to have done so. Michael had already been runner-up in 1962. He played in four successive Walker Cup teams from 1959 to 1965, but in the first three gained only one half from seven matches. In 1965, however, he won two and lost two. He did better against American opposition in the 1963 British Amateur, for all the US Walker team took part, none reaching the final, which Michael Lunt won against John Blackwell. He reached the final again the following year and did not go down to Gordon Clark until the 39th hole. Michael Lunt was nine times an England international between 1956 and 1966, and was for four years non-playing captain in the early 1970s. He represented Great Britain in the 1964 Eisenhower Trophy and the 1963 Commonwealth event. He was an excellent striker of the ball and a long hitter, if sometimes wild with woods. His amateur status was threatened at one time because he worked for a sporting goods firm, which was prohibited on the grounds that his prowess at golf could be useful to the firm.

LYLE, Alexander Walter Barr   Scotland
b. Shrewsbury, England 1958

Although only 25 in 1983 Sandy Lyle had already been recognized as a major prospect since as early as 1972, when he was first chosen as a boy international. Three years later he was an international at boy, youth and full level and won the Carris Trophy. By 1977 he was winning the important amateur competitions and had taken the Eng-

lish Strokeplay twice, as well as the British Youths', had been three years an England international, and had played for the Great Britain Commonwealth team and in the Walker Cup side. At 17 years 3 months he had been youngest to win the English title. It had long been inevitable that he would turn professional, and he duly did so in time to play in the European Tour qualifying school. He won that too. Early the next year he went off to Nigeria and took the Nigerian Open, after beginning 61, 63. Back in Europe he was learning his trade in professional golf, and had an unspectacular season but with four tournament finishes in the top 20. He was 49th in the Order of Merit and was chosen Rookie of the Year. In Africa again, he won money in each of the five Safari events. Never lower then seventh, he was third in the Lusaka Open and second in the Zambian. He finished third in Safari money winnings. This consistency provided a springboard for the 1979 European season, in which Lyle became the first British player to top the Order of Merit since Peter Oosterhuis in 1974. His first European win came in Jersey at La Moye, then a few weeks later he faced Ballesteros over the final two rounds of the Scandinavian Open, his closing 65, 69 outscoring the Spaniard by 3. After this, he took the Scottish Professional title and then

Sandy Lyle

went on to Turnberry for the European Open, which saw his finest performance of the year. Going into the final round with a lead, he began with seven 3s, finished in 65 and won by 7 strokes. Suddenly he was number one in Europe. At the end of the season he tied for second in the small but high-quality Lancôme field at St-Nom-la-Bretèche, and also finished second in the individual standings of the World Cup. In 1980 Lyle won only one tournament, the Welsh Classic, but he added consistency to his performance. He had seven finishes in the top 3, was never out of the top 20 and 13 times in the top 10. He was closely pursued by Greg Norman; these two enormous hitters were separated by only £277 at the end of the season, but with Lyle retaining his number one position. He then became the first British player to reach the final of the World Matchplay since Neil Coles in 1964, and matched Norman shot for shot before losing on the last hole. He finished first in the World Cup. The salient features of Lyle's game had now become apparent. He is one of the longest hitters in world golf, and when playing a long iron for safety, still longer than most touring professionals with their drivers. Therefore, he makes many par 5s into a drive and a medium iron, and 400-yard par 4s into a drive and a little pitch. As a putter he appears to be without nerves; often indeed uninterested, and this may point to a flaw in the Lyle golfing make-up. He was born with immense talents (Gary Player has called him the best striker he has ever seen in Britain) so that he was already a player of class when scarcely into his teens, while, as we have seen, he did not have to struggle on turning professional. Even the number one position seemed to come while no one was looking. There is, then, considerable danger that Lyle may not make the best of his ability and certainly he throws away more strokes as a result of error than anyone of comparable stature. Questions about his motivation still remain to be answered. Nicklaus and Jones had enormous talent when young and responded by wanting to be not only the best in the world but the best ever. That latter ambition has probably already passed Lyle by. In 1981 Lyle added the French Open at St-Germain, by 4 strokes, and the Lawrence Batley International, and had five top 3 finishes but fell to third in the Order of Merit and was outgolfed by Greg Norman and Bernhard Langer in the season as a whole. In 1982 he showed increasing signs of inconsistency. He should, for instance, have walked home in the

French Open after beginning 72, 64 and ending 67, but his third round was 79 and Lyle finished 4 behind Ballesteros. For the first time he had a smell of the British Open after a second-round 66, and a couple of 72s would have seen him home. He shot 73, 74 to be three behind Tom Watson in 8th place. In the 1982 World Matchplay at Wentworth he took part in one of the most remarkable matches ever. After 18 holes he was 6 down but played the first nine in the afternoon in 31 and was all square with seven to play, and 2 in the lead after the 15th. His opponent, Nick Faldo, then holed a bunker shot to win the next; Lyle followed immediately by holing from off the green to win by 2 and 1. Faldo was only 1 over par for his second round; Lyle had played 59 shots for the 17 holes. Lyle then went on to face Raymond Floyd, number two on the US money list, and won 3 and 1; next he dismissed Tom Kite by 8 and 7. In the final against Severiano Ballesteros he was 3 down with six to play, but with inspired putting pulled back to all square with two to play. He lost on the first extra hole, but only because the Spaniard holed a putt of 10 yards. To inspire him, Lyle needs a major title and a large crowd spurring him on. At present both Lyle and the spectators seem to lack passion; yet he has the nerve and ability of a truly great player. To steel this nerve and hone this ability he needs to play more outside Europe.

Europe wins 7 (1979–82)
Europe money £258,231 (1977–82) (3rd all-time)
Africa wins 1 (1978)

McCLELLAND, Douglas W.　　　　England
b. *South Shields* 1949

At 19, Doug McClelland was an England international at boy and youth level and also a Great Britain choice. He then turned professional and was 85th in the Order of Merit his first season, a position he steadily improved to 30th, 22nd and 14th in successive seasons. In 1973 he reached the final of the British Matchplay Championship, going down to Neil Coles, and took his first tournament, the Dutch Open. On the brink of becoming a major player, McClelland began to make changes to his swing, with adverse results. He remained in the Top 60 for three more years, however. In later years his best achievements were a second-place finish in the 1976 New Zealand Open and a win in the 1982 Southern Professional.

Europe wins 1 (1973)

McCLURE, Jean: see Hetherington

McCORKINDALE, Isabella: see Robertson

McCREADY, Samuel Maxwell Ireland
b. *Belfast 1918; d. 1981*

A former squadron-leader in the RAF, Max McCready had a short career at the top of amateur golf but a good one, including the British Amateur of 1949 at a time when Americans were dominant in the championship. McCready beat Willie Turnesa in that year's final. He played two Walker Cups in 1949 and 1951, but lost all his matches. He lived for a while in South Africa. After his return to Britain he was mostly content with regional golf, winning three county championships – but also the 1948 Jamaica Amateur; and he was four times an Ireland international between 1947 and 1952.

McEVOY, Peter England
b. *London 1953*

In 1982 Peter McEvoy was the only amateur rated as high as plus 2 by the English Golf Union; but later that year he appeared to be approaching the end of really active competitive golf. He had a particularly impressive record as an England international. He played 28 individual matches and won 25, halved four and lost only once, to Ronan Rafferty. He tied for the 1980 English Strokeplay and was second in 1978. He was runner-up in the 1980 English Amateur. He won eight major amateur tournaments between 1976 and 1980, as well as a dozen regional titles. He was three times a Walker Cup choice, from 1977 to 1981; was leading amateur in the Open in 1978 and 1979; and in 1978 was the first British amateur to complete a US Masters. Perhaps his outstanding achievement was to take the Amateur Championship in the successive years 1977 and 1978, only the fifth to do so. He is now in sports management.

MACFARLANE, William: see North America

MacFIE, Allan F. Scotland

Allan MacFie is credited with being the first winner of the Amateur Championship in 1885. The event was recognized retrospectively, for it was billed as 'a tournament open to all amateur golfers'.

On his way to the final MacFie had to replay his match against H.W. de Zoete twice, there being no sudden-death system in operation. In the final he defeated Horace Hutchinson conclusively 7 and 6. Hutchinson was to remain a power in amateur golf for many years, but little was heard of MacFie again. It is indicative of the different distances that modern clubs compel the modern ball to travel that MacFie never cleared the burn before the first green at St Andrews in two strokes.

McKENNA, Mary Ireland
b. *Dublin 1949*

The best Irish woman player for a decade and more, Mary McKenna has a shared record seven Curtis Cup appearances and has played the most matches, 27. She has reached the Irish Ladies' final ten times in the years 1968–82 and won seven times: 1969,

Mary McKenna

1972, 1974, 1977, 1979, 1981 and 1982. In the same period she has represented Ireland in all international competition, with no omissions. Mary has tried top-class competition in the USA, her best results being semi-final placings in the 1972 Western and Broadmoor and, in 1980, the same stage of the US Amateur. She is probably the best current player to fail to take the British Ladies'; but she went on from second in the British Ladies' Amateur Strokeplay in 1976 to win in 1979. Among other events Mary McKenna won the Players No. 6 Cup three times, the Avia Foursomes in 1972 (with Diane Frearson) and in 1977 (with Tegwen Perkins), the Dorothy Grey Strokeplay three times, was top amateur in the 1977 and 1979 European Opens and Daks Woman Golfer of the Year in 1979.

McKINLAY, Samuel Livingstone   Scotland
b. *Glasgow 1907*

Sam McKinlay won six important amateur competitions and made the Walker Cup team in 1934. He was nine times a Scottish international between 1929 and 1947. For many years he has been a Scottish golf journalist, and is regarded as the doyen of his trade. He is an excellent after-dinner speaker.

M'LEAN, Jack   Scotland
b. *1911; d. 1961*

Winner of the Scots Amateur in 1932 and 1934, M'Lean was also runner-up in 1935. In the same period he twice won the Irish Amateur and once was runner-up. He played in the 1934 and 1936 Walker Cup sides, but his greatest achievement was to be one of the rare British players to reach the final of the US Amateur, which he achieved in 1936. Towards the end, he looked like a winner but was overhauled by the American, John Fischer, who avoided being 2 down with two to play by laying M'Lean a dead stymie at the 34th. M'Lean shortly after turned professional. For many years he had a post at Gleneagles.

McLEOD, Frederick: see North America

McMAHON, Suzanne: see Cadden

McNAMARA, Tom: see North America

MADILL, Maureen Elizabeth Jane   Ireland
b. *Coleraine 1958*

A girl international from the age of 14, Maureen Madill has been a full international since 1978 and a rival of Mary McKenna for supremacy in Irish golf. Unlike Mary McKenna, however, she has achieved the feat of winning the British Amateur, which she did by defeating Jane Lock of Australia in the 1979 final. She won the British Ladies' Open Strokeplay in 1980, and was joint third the following year. She also won the 1980 Avia Foursomes; reached the final of the 1982 Irish Ladies', where she was beaten by Mary McKenna; and appeared in the 1980 Curtis Cup match.

MARCHBANK, Brian   Scotland
b. *1958*

After winning the Boys' (1975), Scottish Boys' (1976), British Youths' (1978) and two major amateur titles and a Walker Cup cap in 1979 Marchbank turned professional and joined the European Tour in 1980, where he found the going hard. He won just over £2,000 his first year, but got into the Top 60 in 1981, with a best finish of eighth. In 1982 he had won less than £1,000 during the season at the time of the State Express Classic at the Belfry. In contention for the first time in his career, Marchbank came home in 32 in the last round, with birdies on the last two holes, that on the last achieved after a superb long-iron and 5-yard putt. His second-place cheque for £8,890 came close to equalling his entire career winnings. He finished the year in 38th place with what must have been a welcome total of £13,416.

Europe money £23,076 (1980–82)

MARKS, Geoffrey C.   England
b. *Stoke-on-Trent 1938*

Geoff Marks was twice runner-up in the English Strokeplay (1973 and 1975) and a semi-finalist in the British Amateur in 1968 and 1975; he also won six important amateur tournaments and was a county champion eight times. A long hitter, he was eight times an England international between 1963 and 1975, and both English and British captain, having already been chosen earlier at both boy and youth level. He was a Walker Cup player in 1969 and 1971, and had some success, managing to beat Lanny Wadkins in the 1969 singles and Ed Updegraff in the following match.

MARSH, Dr David Max — England
b. *Southport 1934*

David Marsh was 13 times an England international between 1956 and 1972, four years as captain, a position he also held with the 1973 and 1975 Walker Cup teams. He twice won the English Amateur (1964 and 1970) and three important tournaments. He did not get a game in the 1959 Walker Cup match, but in 1971 he won and lost a foursomes and played one of the vital winning singles on the last afternoon. An excellent long-iron to the 17th at St Andrews in his match against Bill Hyndman much contributed to both his own win and that of the Great Britain team. He now has a medical practice in Southport.

MARTIN, James — Ireland
b. *1924*

Jimmy Martin once had a record eleven birdies and an eagle in a round of the 1961 Swallow-Penfold at Stoneham. He should therefore have done even better than his eventual 63. He did, however, win the 1964 Piccadilly Medal, the 1965 Silentnight and the 1968 Carrolls on the British circuit, and also three important Irish tournaments. Above all, he was an excellent putter. Martin was chosen for the 1965 Ryder Cup but played only one match and lost it. He was a World Cup choice for Ireland five times between 1962 and 1970.

GB wins 3 (1964–8)

MARTIN, Robert — Scotland
b. *1848*

Bob Martin was winner of one of the more unusual Open Championships. In 1876 he tied with Davie Strath, who refused to play off, and he walked the course to win. He won again in 1885 and was runner-up in both 1875 and 1887.

MARTIN, Stephen W. — Scotland
b. *Dundee 1955*

Once nicknamed 'Night Fever', because of a liking for night clubs while touring, Steve Martin has nevertheless made good progress in his beginnings as a professional. As an amateur Martin was both boy and youth international (the latter for four years) and won the Scottish Open Amateur Strokeplay in 1976, beside other regional events. In that year he played on the winning Great Britain Eisenhower Trophy team and in 1977 was a Walker Cup choice, losing one and winning one foursomes, and in the singles beating Gary Hallberg and narrowly losing to Lindy Miller. His first two seasons saw little success as a professional, though he had the 1979 season's lowest round, a 62 in the Greater Manchester. In 1980 he moved up to 29th in the Order of Merit and was second in the Avis-Jersey Open. In 1981 he was 19th, his best finish being second in the Spanish Open. Playing with Sandy Lyle, he helped the Scottish team to second place in the 1980 World Cup. Martin could progress to being one of the leading young British professionals, though he had a poor 1982 – 67th in the money list.

Europe money £47,028 (1977–82)

MARTIN-SMITH, Eric — England
b. *1909; d. 1951*

There was considerable extra press interest in the 1931 British Amateur at Westward Ho! because Douglas Fairbanks Snr had entered. However, by the end of the week attention was concentrated on the unknown Eric Martin-Smith. Even his best friends were amazed at his progress, and on the morning of the final he received an unflattering telegram which read: 'Quite ridiculous but keep at it.' He did, beating John de Forest (later Count John de Bendern) by one hole. As a golfer little was heard of him after his hour of glory, but he later became Conservative MP for Grantham, then died suddenly.

MARVIN, Vanessa Price — England
b. *Cosford 1954*

In 1977 Vanessa Marvin was runner-up to Angela Uzielli for the British Ladies' and won the English Ladies' that year, beating Mary Everard in the final; she repeated the victory the following year, defeating Ruth Porter. In her amateur career she won the Roehampton Gold Cup in 1976, the Hampshire Rose in 1975 and the North of England Ladies' in 1975. She was an England international and in 1978 was top amateur in the European Open, a Curtis Cup choice and Daks Golfer of the Year. She then turned professional.

MASON, Carl — England
b. *1953*

Carl Mason won three important amateur tournaments in 1973 and reached the final of the English

Amateur. He was Youths' Champion the same year. He then turned professional and in his first European entry, the Portuguese Open, needed two closing pars to finish in third place. He did not manage it and came in joint 17th. Nevertheless it had been an auspicious beginning, for his first three rounds had been 70, 66, 70. At the end of that season he lay 67th in the Order of Merit and was chosen as Rookie of the Year. The following year he won his first event, the Lusaka Open, and moved up to 38th place in the Order of Merit, then 26th the following season. However, this rate of progress has not since been maintained, his best moments coming in the 1980 British Open. Here Carl had rounds of 72, 69, 70, 69 to be top British player and joint fourth with Jack Nicklaus. He later played for England in the World Cup. His swing is stilted, but he plays with determination. He finished 31st in the 1982 money list.

Africa wins 1 (1975)
Europe money £98,042 (1974–82) (38th all-time)

MAXWELL, Robert   Scotland
b. *Edinburgh 1876*

Maxwell reached the semi-finals of the British Amateur in 1902 and then won his final against Horace Hutchinson the following year at Muirfield by 7 and 5. A finalist at Muirfield again in 1909, he beat C.K. Hutchison by 1 hole. He was leading amateur in the British Open in 1902, when he finished fourth overall but only 2 strokes behind the winner, Sandy Herd, and again the following year. He was second amateur in 1906 and 1909. His introduction to championship golf was dramatic in the extreme, for on the first day of the 1897 Amateur he beat the two greatest players: Harold Hilton and John Ball. His record might have been even better, but he disliked playing in front of crowds – the downfall of many players, both amateur and professional. He believed that the left arm should be kept very straight during the swing, and this may have helped him towards consistency. Robert Maxwell was eight times a Scotland international and, as a member of the Honourable Company of Edinburgh Golfers at Muirfield, was influential in administration. In 1919 he called on the clubs to hand over the organization of the Amateur Championship to the Royal and Ancient Golf Club of St Andrews (R & A).

MELVILLE, Janet Kay   England
b. *Barrow-in-Furness 1958*

Janet Melville had an outstanding 1978, winning the British Amateur Strokeplay and the British Open. She has won four other important tournaments and was an England international in 1978, 1979 and 1981.

MICKLEM, Gerald Hugh   England
b. *Burgh Heath 1911*

Gerald Micklem was something of a late developer, not emerging as a prominent amateur until past his mid 30s. Then he took the English Amateur in both 1947 and 1953 and began his Walker Cup career, in which he played from 1947 to 1955, except in 1951. In six matches he was in the winning pair in one foursomes. Micklem was second in the 1948 English Strokeplay, and at the end of 1976 had set the record of playing in 36 consecutive President's Putter events. During these he won 76 of 111 matches and 12 times reached the semi-final stage, though he won only the 1953 final. An England international from 1947 to 1955, Gerald Micklem later became an important figure in golf administration. At various times he has been chairman of the R & A Rules of Golf Committee, Selection Committee and Championship Committee; president of the English Golf Union; president of the European Golf Association; and captain of the R & A. He received the Bobby Jones award for services to golf in 1969.

MILLENSTED, Dudley   England
b. *New Malden 1942*

Dudley Millensted won three important amateur events and also tied for first in the 1965 English Strokeplay and was runner-up in the 1966 English Amateur. Chosen for the 1967 Walker Cup team, he lost his singles to Ed Tutwiler but won a foursomes with Rodney Foster. The great strength of his game was chipping and putting, which earned him the not too original nickname of 'Deadly Dudley'. He turned professional and now works at a West of England club.

MILLS, Ralph Peter   England
b. *Virginia Water 1931*

Peter Mills still has the second lowest nine holes in European golf. He had 28 at Sunningdale during the 1958 Bowmaker tournament in which he was joint first. The same year he won the Wentworth Pro-Am Foursomes on the course where he was brought up, his mother and father being stewardess and steward. However, perhaps his best performance came in the Ryder Cup. In 1957 he beat the US captain Jack Burke at Lindrick by 5 and 3 and Great Britain and Ireland went on to win. He later gave up professional golf and opened a wine export-import business and a wine bar in Jersey, applying for reinstatement as an amateur.

GB wins 2 (1958)

MILNE, William T.G.   Scotland
b. Perth 1951

Willie Milne is probably the largest player on the European circuit at 6 foot 3 inches and around 240 lb. He would probably be a better player if quite a few of the pounds were shed, for he has a powerful long game but has not capitalized on the promise he showed as both amateur and. young professional. He was a youth and full international, and was a Walker Cup team member in 1973, when he lost in both foursomes but, more important perhaps, took both his singles. When he turned professional at the end of the year he was quickly successful in Africa, winning the Lusaka Open; then he took the Northern Scottish Open in both 1974 and 1975. Since then he has achieved little, second place in the 1979 French Open being his best performance, during which he holed in one for a Mercedes (though there was some considerable difficulty in actually getting hold of it). This was the only year he made the Top 60, in 46th place. He played only once during the 1981 season, finishing 7 behind the winner; but he may be considered to have given up tournament golf. In 1982 he played in the PGA Cup match against the USA.

Africa wins 1 (1974)
Europe money £18,127

MILTON, Moira: see Paterson

MITCHELL, Abraham   England
b. East Grinstead 1887; d. 1947

With Archie Compston and George Duncan, Abe Mitchell was probably the best British player of the 1920s and has been called by J.H. Taylor 'the finest player who never won an Open Championship'. Mitchell was in the first six five times, and in the first post-World War I Open in 1920 at Deal led the eventual winner, George Duncan, by 13 strokes after two rounds. Duncan then had a 71 (though Mitchell thought it was a 69) and Abe began his third round by three-putting the first three greens and later having a 7 on his card for an eventual 84. Perhaps this experience marked his confidence for life, for he seldom looked likely to take the Open again, either starting or finishing badly. His last chance came in the 1933 at St Andrews. He was right up with the leaders after three rounds and then fell away to a 79. His failure to win an Open was doubly unfortunate in that he won the 1919 'Victory' tournament, which was the Open Championship in all but name. Mitchell first made his name as a prominent amateur at a time when the route to professional golf was through being a caddie or working as an assistant to a professional. Mitchell was indeed the first artisan to play for England. (An artisan was a player who either could not afford to be or would not be acceptable, probably because of working-class origins, as a full member of a golf club. Many British clubs allowed a limited form of membership with, perhaps, restricted playing times.) As an artisan he reached the semi-finals of the 1910 Amateur and the final in 1912, going down only on the 38th hole at Westward Ho! to John Ball. During this period he was also an amateur international. After turning professional he quickly showed his mettle by a fourth-place finish in the last pre-war Open, a position he was never to better in the Open. Mitchell was thought to be a worrier and essentially unsuited either to strokeplay golf or to playing in front of an audience. Indeed some have said that he won tournaments only because he was so outstandingly good a player. In Matchplay he was a vastly different proposition. He won the Matchplay Championship three times – 1919, 1920 and 1929 – and as a Ryder Cup player halved with Hagen in 1921 and also halved his foursomes; then in 1926 he beat Jim Barnes 8 and 7 and, with Duncan, annihilated Hagen and Barnes by 9 and 8 in the foursomes. In 1929 he and Fred Robson beat Gene Sarazen and Ed Dudley, though Mitchell lost his singles to Leo Diegel very heavily – 9 and 8. His last appearance came in 1933. He and Arthur Havers beat Densmore Shute and Olin Dutra, and Mitchell followed up by defeating Dutra by 9 and 8. Seven points of a possible 10 was his overall record, his last match played at the age of 46. Abe Mitchell was a long hitter, playing in the modern style with a slight fade. His swing would give spectators the immediate impression of massive power in wrists and forearms.

MOFFITT, Ralph Lawson   England
b. Ryton-on-Tyne 1932

Beginning tournament play in the mid 1950s, Ralph Moffitt was a coming man in the early 1960s and a Ryder Cup player in 1961. In that same year he played six consecutive rounds in 67. Four of them were at Woodbrook in the course of coming second in the Irish Hospitals event. He then went off to Longniddry, one of the toughest par 68s around, and did two more before finishing 72, 66 for third place. That year he also reached the final of the Matchplay before losing to Peter Thomson. Moffitt had tied in the 1960 Dunlop tournament and had a remarkable run in the Dunlop Masters: from 1962 to 1964 he was second, once losing a play-off. In 1962 also, he once had a run of being five times in the first four. In 1964, however, his game began to decline, and during a 1965 tournament he felt unable to strike another shot. Moffitt had caught one of golf's most dread diseases, a driving twitch, so that he was unable to take the club away from the ball because of the nervous fear about what might eventually happen to it. The complaint is more common among club golfers than professionals – but equally fatal. He was an excellent putter.

MOODY, Peter Henry   England
b. Clitheroe 1948

Peter Moody had a brief period of success in amateur golf, and then little more was heard of him. He won the President's Putter twice in 1969 and 1972 and the British Universities Championship in 1970; he had been both boy and youth international and had full England status in 1971 and 1972. He won the English Strokeplay in 1972 and reached the final of the British Amateur in 1973, losing 5 and 3 to Dick Siderowf at Royal Porthcawl.

Ralph Moffitt

MORGAN, John   England
b. 1943

A youth international in 1964, John Morgan became a tournament player in 1970 and since then has been in the news from time to time. In 1968, for instance, playing in the Carnoustie Open, en route to a 92, he had the fairly rare experience of being bitten by a rat; in another Open, the 1974 at Royal Lytham, he shared the first-round lead and went on to finish 13th equal. Professional for much of his career at Royal Liverpool (Hoylake), Morgan did not follow the European Tour full-time, allowing him to be three times in the British PGA Cup team. Eventually he made the brave decision to give up his plum club job in favour of full-time play, but he has not produced results to justify that choice fully. He has four times been in the Top 60: 1974, 1977, 1978 and 1979, with 28th in 1974 and 1978 being his best placings. In Europe he has twice featured strongly in the Martini, being third in 1978 and

joint second, battling it out with Greg Norman, in 1979. Perhaps Morgan, like not a few others, produces his best form in Africa, where he has won the 1979 Lusaka and Nigerian Opens and the Ivory Coast in 1982, finishing fourth that year on the Safari money list.

MORGAN, John Llewelleyn   Wales
b. *Llandrindod Wells 1918*

A Welsh international between 1948 and 1967, with the exception of just two seasons, Morgan was a reinstated professional. He was three times a Walker Cup player from 1951 to 1955. He lost both foursomes and singles in 1951 and 1955 and won both at Merion in 1953. He won the Welsh Amateur in 1950 and 1951 and was runner-up the following year; he took the Berkshire Trophy in 1953, and the Duncan Putter in 1968 at the age of 50. He took the Seniors title in 1974.

MORGAN, Wanda   England
b. *Lymm 1910*

Wanda Morgan won the British Ladies' in 1935, beating Pam Barton in the final to do so. In the English Championship she had three victories: 1931, 1936 and 1937. In this period she had three Curtis Cup places and was runner-up for the British title to Enid Wilson in 1931. She won the *Daily Graphic* tournament in 1941 and 1942, and three major foursomes competitions. She took the Kent title seven times and was an England international from 1931 to 1937 and again in 1953. At one time she was a member of no fewer than twelve golf clubs, most of them in her home county of Kent.

MORRIS, J.O.F.   Scotland
b. *St Andrews 1852; d. 1906*

The second son of 'Old Tom' Morris: it is hardly surprising that his deeds remain unknown, compared with those of his great brother. He was, however, good enough to come in fourth in the 1876 Open and third in 1878. After 'Young Tom's' death, he frequently partnered his father in challenge matches.

MORRIS, Thomas, Snr   Scotland
b. *St Andrews 1821; d.1908*

Son of a handloom weaver, Tom Morris (later to be 'Old Tom') was apprenticed as a feathery-maker to Allan Robertson at the age of 18 and in due course became one of the premier players of his day. How good he was is difficult to estimate, as his abilities as a player are obscured by the achievements of his son, 'Young Tom'. But it is worth remembering that 'Old Tom' was already 39 at the time of the first Open Championship and yet managed to win it four times, remaining the oldest winner at 46 years 99 days for his 1867 win. He played in every Open from 1860 till 1896, when he was 75. Apart from his four wins 'Old Tom' was second on three other occasions, fourth three times and fifth in 1881 at the age of 60. 'Old Tom' only left Allan Robertson in 1851, having annoyed the Scottish Champion by using a gutta-percha ball, a development in golf equipment that seemed to threaten the livelihood of the feathery-makers. At that point he departed for Prestwick; then, in 1853, beat Robertson in a challenge match, after which it is said that Robertson would never again play against him in singles, though they partnered each other in challenge matches. 'Old Tom' narrowly missed the distinc-

Old Tom Morris

tion of being the first Open Champion when in 1860 he came in second behind Willie Park of Musselburgh, but he was to win in three of the ensuing four years. In 1864 he returned to St Andrews as the first professional there, and also greenkeeper. He and his long beard became part of the fixtures. He died there as a result of falling down the clubhouse stairs.

MORRIS, Thomas, Jnr   Scotland
b. St Andrews 1851; d. 1875

'Young Tom' was the first golfer to be solely a tournament player, something that did not occur again in British golf for the best part of a century, with Ken Bousfield and then Neil Coles. Perhaps this gives at least some indication of how 'Young Tom' dominated his contemporaries, whose status at the time was only a little above that of caddies, tolerated to partner their amateur betters in money matches or for practice games, but regarded more as greenkeepers and clubmakers and repairers. This attitude did not disappear until the arrival of the Great Triumvirate of Taylor, Braid and Vardon – and even then not wholly so. 'Young Tom' won a tournament against leading professionals at the age of 13, but attracted more attention when he tied for a Carnoustie tournament with Willie Park and Bob Anderson and then won the play-off. At 17, in 1868, he was Open Champion at Prestwick and repeated this the following year, his father being second on this occasion. Young Tom's dominance was seen most clearly in his third successive win, which was by 12 strokes. He covered Prestwick's 12 holes three times in 149 strokes, scoring not approached in the remaining years of the championship played over 36 holes. Although this represents scoring in the mid 70s, it must be remembered that golf of the time was a cross-country game, played through gorse, hillocks, and sand where nature put it; and when, after such ordeals had been left behind, the greens were reached, a lofted putter was used to get your ball hopping over the scythed area. There was no championship in 1871, for 'Young Tom' had won the winner's belt outright. When it resumed in 1872 'Young Tom's' was the first name on the now so familiar silver claret jug. It is thought that his health declined thereafter. Second was his best placing in the next three years. In 1875 his wife died in childbirth, and some say 'Young Tom' suffered from depression and took to heavy drink-

ing. He died on Christmas Day 1875, some say of a broken heart, others of a burst artery in the lung. Little is known of how 'Young Tom' played the game. It is said, however, that he used to break the shafts of his clubs with the fury of his hitting, and even on his waggle. Perhaps he was the first man to favour iron-shot approaches, appreciating the greater accuracy of the increased backspin. He is also thought to have popularized the lofted approaching-iron (niblick). In 1872 he set the record for St Andrews at 77, beating Allan Robertson's mark by 2 strokes; in 1874 he bet that he would beat 83 per round over the course for a week – and did so. It is not possible to compare 'Young Tom' with the great players who have followed him. He was certainly the greatest of his day, all a player can be, and no one stood as high in general esteem until the Great Triumvirate arrived a generation later.

MORRISON, John Stanton Fleming   England
b. Newcastle upon Tyne, 1892; d. 1962

An all-round sportsman of a kind no longer seen in these days of specialization, Morrison was captain of cricket at Cambridge University and later played county cricket for Somerset. He was even more formidable as a soccer player, representing Sunderland and also Corinthians in their great days. As a golfer he was an England international in 1930, having won the Worplesdon Mixed Foursomes in 1928 and the Belgian Amateur in 1929. He later practised as a golf architect, at Prince's Sandwich and Wentworth in particular, and had a house delectably placed by the first green at Turnberry. In his later years he competed regularly in the Halford-Hewitt Foursomes, partnered by Henry Longhurst. His dilapidated clubs aroused much interest.

MOSEY, Ian   England
b. 1951

An England international at boy, youth and full level, Ian Mosey has been playing tournament golf for about ten years and has made the Top 60 of the European Tour in 1976, 1980, 1981 and 1982, the latter his best year with 34th place. He has won the 1980 Merseyside International and in the same year the South African Kalahari Classic. He also came very close to winning the South African Open. He needed a par 4 on the last hole to win but took 6, which included a missed putt of about a yard for the tie. He also won the 1981 Holiday Inns tournament in South Africa. In 1982 he lost a play-off for the Sharp's Classic and finished second in the Italian Open. Ian Mosey is a quality player, one of that group which has more often produced best performances in Africa than Europe. His father, Don, is a BBC cricket commentator.

Europe wins 1 (1980)
Europe money £54,417 (1973–82)
Africa wins 2 (1980–81)

MURRAY, Ewen — Scotland
b. 1954

In recent years, Ewen Murray has sometimes attracted attention for using a putter with an extra long shaft, the idea being to lock the left wrist as he braces the butt against his left elbow. Having been a Scottish amateur international and World Junior Champion, he turned professional in 1971; but he made little progress thereafter for a good many years. It was 1979 before he made the Top 60, and this year included one of his best performances, third in the Tournament Players' Championship at the end of the season. Ewen Murray remained in the Top 60 the following two years, 33rd in 1981, when he was third in the Bob Hope Classic, being his best Order of Merit placing. He won the 1980 Zambian Open, his only important victory.

Europe money £62,605 (1972–82) (60th all-time)
Overseas wins 1 (1980)

MURRAY, Gordon H. — Scotland
b. Paisley 1936

A Scottish international for several years, Gordon Murray made the 1977 Walker Cup team at Shinnecock Hills, in which he lost his singles to Scott Simpson by 7 and 6 but came through in his foursomes. He won the Scottish Amateur in 1974 and 1976 and was runner-up in 1975. He has been the holder of four regional Scottish titles.

MURRAY, Stuart W.T. — Scotland
b. Paisley 1933

Stuart Murray was a Scottish international between 1959 and 1963, the year he played in the Walker Cup match, beginning on the first day by partnering Michael Bonallack to victory against Billy Joe Patton and R.H. Sikes and then beating Deane Beman in singles. The following day the foursomes

result was reversed and he lost to Billy Joe Patton in the singles. Murray was runner-up in the 1961 Scottish Amateur but won the following year, and also won seven major Scottish competitions. He turned professional in 1963 and won the Midland Open three times and the Middlesex once. He would probably have preferred to remain an amateur, but his job with a sports firm infringed the rules of amateur status.

MUSCROFT, Hedley — England
b. Leeds 1938

One day in 1970 on the practice ground before the Classic International, Hedley Muscroft found that he could draw and fade the ball with equal ease and even manage the far more difficult trick of hitting it straight. More simply he had hit that kind of form that makes the golfer believe that he can make the ball obey his every whim. Hedley said that he could win the tournament and, confidence being half or more of competitive success, he proceeded to do so, beating Christy O'Connor on the fourth play-off hole. He had begun with a pair of 67s, followed with a 72 and came to the last needing a par 4 to win outright. He reminded himself to hit flat out from the last tee as the surest recipe for straightness, but then he three-putted to tie and go into the play-off. He finished 19th in the Order of Merit that year, following his best placing of 11th in 1968, when he won the Evian Open in France. Muscroft remained in the Top 60 until the mid 1970s, having a revival of form in 1973 when he finished 13th; he had tried driving with graphite and found himself a much longer hitter. Muscroft was always in the top 40 from 1964 to 1971. His other successes included reaching the semi-finals of the 1964 Matchplay and being second in the 1966 Agfa-Gevaert tournament. Overall, however, he should have achieved more than he did as a tournament player, his brash confidence on the Yorkshire scene being less in evidence on a wider stage. He was, however, with his friend Lionel Platts, a raconteur and humorist *par excellence* in the north of England, where they were famed for their talent in local money matches. He has remained in his beloved Leeds and is now professional at the Roundhay municipal club. He is married with several children, one of whom, Duncan, shows promise at the game and may choose to follow in his father's footsteps.

Europe wins 2 (1968–70)

NEW, Beverly Jayne   England

b. Bristol 1960

Winner of the English Championship in 1980, Beverly New was second in the Welsh Open Strokeplay in 1979 and was an Under 22 international from 1979 to 1981 and at full level in 1980 and 1981. She has won two other major tournaments, took the South-West Under 21 title in 1980, and was runner-up for the Roehampton Gold Cup in 1981 and 1982. She is one of the most promising young English players, winning at Worplesdon in 1982 and also taking a professional event.

NICHOL, Margaret: see Pickard

O'CONNOR, Christy, Snr   Ireland

b. Galway 1924

In 1982, at the age of 57, O'Connor won the Seniors for a record fifth time and, perhaps even more significant, came joint third in the Carrolls Irish Open. I think that one supreme test of a golfer is how long his skill and nerve lasts and, in this

Christy O'Connor

sense, Christy O'Connor is in the same class as Roberto de Vicenzo, Sandy Herd, Sam Snead and Fidel de Luca. He was a late developer, not winning his first major tournament until the Swallow-Penfold in 1955. Thereafter he was a consistent tournament winner into the 1970s; in 1970 he won the record first prize of £25,000 in the John Player Classic at Hollinwell. In 1955 he had also been the first man to win a prize of £1,000 in a British tournament. Despite these much lower winnings of his peak years, O'Connor still ranked 19th in all-time European money winnings at the beginning of the 1982 season. He is one of the best players not to have won the British Open but has a good record, having been in the top 6 seven times from 1958 to 1969. His best chance of winning came in 1958. That year he began 67, 68, the best start since Cotton's 67, 65 in 1934; but then faded to 73 in the third round because of indifferent putting. He came to the last hole at Lytham needing a par to tie. He did not manage it, and David Thomas and Peter Thomson played off for the title with O'Connor joint third. He was again equal third in 1961 and joint second in 1965. When in his mid 40s, in 1969, he finished fifth and included a 65 among his rounds; he was seventh in 1973, when approaching 50. O'Connor has an extremely relaxed swing, so much so that he has said he fears to practise before a tournament round as the normal process of loosening up makes him too loose and therefore apt to lack tautness in his swing. He has been thought in the genius class as a striker of the ball despite relaxing his left-hand fingers at the top of the backswing, and is an extremely straight hitter. O'Connor has all the shots except one, the putt. Here his extremely wristy method has led to inconsistency, and this more than anything has prevented him from becoming a world-beater. Often he looks extremely nervous and hesitant yet manages to hole a good share. As a Ryder Cup player O'Connor was chosen every time from 1955 to 1973, ten consecutive, the most on either team. He played 36 individual matches, also a record. He did not shine in the singles, losing ten matches and winning two, but had far better results in the partner foursomes and four-balls. In 1973 he became the second oldest to play in the matches. He also represented Ireland 15 times in the World Cup and, in 1958 in Mexico City, he and Harry Bradshaw became the only British pairing to win the World Cup. He won the World Seniors in 1976 and 1977. As a tournament player he won the

Vardon Trophy for stroke average in 1961 and 1962 and was in the top 10 of the Order of Merit from 1955 to 1970. Tenth was in fact his worst placing during this period; otherwise he was always better than eighth. The 1960s were his dominant period, when he was second no less than seven times: in 1961–2, 1965–6 and 1969–70. Second place during those years was likely to be worth about £4,000, a far cry from the £65,000 such a finish brought in 1981. An extremely popular golfer, O'Connor was particularly so in Ireland. If Palmer had his 'Army' he had his 'Black Pack', the name given to the priests that urged him on to victory. His highest achievements, perhaps, were to take the 1957 PGA Matchplay and the Dunlop Masters in 1956 and 1959, on the last occasion finishing with a 66. In another win, the 1966 Carrolls, he produced a finish of eagle, birdie, eagle over Royal Dublin, his home course.

Europe wins 24 (1955–72)
Europe money £135,311 (1954–82) (27th all-time)
Ireland wins 18 (1953–76)

O'CONNOR, Christy, Jnr   Ireland
b. Galway 1948

It is seldom that a man hits an air shot and leads the British Open, yet this nephew of Christy O'Connor did just that at the 13th in the first round of the 1976 Open at Royal Birkdale, and eventually took an 8 on that hole. However, he pulled back to 69 for the round and finished equal first for the day; he went on to finish joint fifth and equal best British player. This was at a time when Christy Jnr was playing his best golf and had finished seventh in the 1975 Order of Merit, winning the Irish Open and the Martini and being chosen for the Ryder Cup. He has not since repeated that form, though he has been three times a World Cup choice for Ireland, in 1974, 1975 and 1978. He had an improved 1982, proving himself the most accurate driver on the European Tour, and was 40th on the money list.

Europe wins 4 (1975–8)
Europe money £73,221 (1970–82) (48th all-time)
Africa wins 1 (1974)

O'LEARY, John   Ireland
b. Dublin 1949

When John O'Leary won the 1982 Carrolls Irish Open it was a return to the limelight of a man who had promised great things early on, begun to

achieve them, and then stayed in the middle ranks of tournament players. He began playing for Ireland as an amateur international in 1969 and 1970 and was Irish Youths' Champion in the latter year, at which time he turned professional and by 1972 was in the Top 60. He has since remained there, his worst finish being 45th in 1977 while, until 1982, his best placings were 18th, 20th and 16th in the years 1974–6. In 1982 he was 18th. His best early performance was in the 1972 South African Dunlop Masters, in which he began 67, 67, 64 but was beaten by Gary Player when he took a 6 on the last hole. He again did well in this event in 1979, coming in second. He had his first win in 1975, the Holiday Inns tournament in South Africa, and then won the Sumrie with his friend Jack Newton. Chosen for the Ryder Cup team, he lost the four matches in which he was involved. During his early years O'Leary was highly visible on the course, mainly a result of his liking for bright clothing and his great bushy mop of hair; but he became less flamboyant as touches of grey began to streak his hair.

Europe wins 3 (1975–82)
Europe money £126,093 (1971–82) (30th all-time)
Africa wins 1 (1975)

OOSTERHUIS, Peter A.   England
b. London 1948

The career of Peter Oosterhuis well illustrates how tough the US Tour is. He has enjoyed moderate success in the USA since he began to compete full-time in 1975; but he had led the European Order of Merit in the four previous seasons and on his rare appearances in Britain usually does well. He is still perhaps the most likely British player to take the Open Championship, having finished equal second as recently as 1982, and he was also in very strong contention in 1978. But Oosterhuis decided that the USA must be the place to learn to be a major golfer and he has stuck to his guns, even though in the 1980s the European Tour is probably more profitable for a player just below major rank. Peter Oosterhuis achieved his first handicap at the age of 14 in a rather unusual way: he entered the Surrey Junior without one, had rounds of 79, 71 to win and came out of it a 5-handicap player. En route to becoming a top British amateur he won it twice more, and also the South-Eastern Counties in 1965 and 1966. In the latter year, he took his first important senior event, the Berkshire Trophy,

Peter Oosterhuis

during which he had seven successive 3s, and also won the British Youths'. By this time he was an England international and in 1967 was in the Walker Cup team, halving and winning foursomes but losing both singles. He represented Britain the next year in the Eisenhower Trophy, and then turned professional. He began his career in South Africa and almost immediately showed that he might be successful as a professional by coming close to winning his second tournament entry and eventually finishing 16th in the Order of Merit. On the European scene, Oosterhuis began to become a top player in the 1970 season, when he won the Young Professionals' title and finished seventh in the Order of Merit. For the next four years he was to carry all before him, leading the Order of Merit and taking the Vardon stroke-average trophy for four consecutive seasons, winning frequently and being extremely consistently high placed. In 1972, for instance, he came in the top ten 17 times in 19 entries and in 1974 was only twice out of the top three in 11 consecutive tournaments between May and September. By this time he had probably replaced Tony Jacklin as the most effective British player, though most felt that Jacklin was the more

talented. The prime features of Oosterhuis's game were now established, the excellence of one department highlighting his deficiencies in another. Many tall players – and at 6 feet 5 inches he is one of the tallest of all – seem to have an excellent short game but suffer co-ordination problems on full shots. Oosterhuis had become a determined and consistent putter, but probably excelled even more as a chipper and at the general ability to get the ball near the hole from around the green. For full shots he always appeared more uneasy, his setting up for the stroke being accompanied with a great deal of foot shuffling at times resembling a dance. In later years Bert Yancey advised him that he had to have a clear idea what he wanted to do before each shot, and develop a consistent routine. The dance went and Oosterhuis now sets up much more quickly, initiating the stroke by getting the feel of the first couple of feet of the backswing. He has never been amongst the top players as a striker: a main fault is that on occasion he will carve a tee shot out to the right. Oosterhuis's sights were soon set on America, and this was accentuated by his performance in the 1973 US Masters. He began 73, 70, 73 and at that point led the field by 3 strokes. A last round of 74 then dropped him down to joint third place, but this remains the best finish yet achieved by a British player. The following year he came close to his first win in a US tournament. He seemed to have the Monsanto Open at Pensacola won with scores of 70, 63, 72, 69, but Lee Elder birdied three of the last four holes to tie. In the play-off, Oosterhuis twice missed short putts to win and was beaten by an Elder birdie on the 4th hole. From 1975 he was a full-time US Tour player. He left the UK with the record of having played in 200 professional tournaments, won 20, been second 26 times, third on 17 occasions and placed in the top 10 116 times. His stroke average was 71.45. Oosterhuis liked to keep his own statistics and reckoned that at that point he had played 62,301 rounds of golf as a professional for an average of 71.45. In 1975, he came 34th on the US money list and had one second-place finish. He was dissatisfied, yet this was to be his best placing until 1981 for in only one other year, 1977, did he make the Top 60. However, he did average over $40,000 annually, except in 1980, when he dropped to 105th in the money order. He had some high finishes, including a second in the 1977 Canadian Open and second in the 1975 New Orleans Open. In that latter year he also worked his way into strong contention for the

GREAT BRITAIN & IRELAND

US Open at Medinah, eventually finishing a couple of strokes out of the Mahaffey-Graham play-off. In 1981 Jack Nicklaus said to him: 'I'm very happy for you, Peter. You've been very patient waiting for this win.' Replied Peter: 'I think I was just stubborn.' The win was the Canadian Open Championship, the next best thing to a major. Oosterhuis had rounds of 69, 69, 72, 70 to beat Bruce Lietzke, Andy North and Jack Nicklaus by 1 stroke. The $76,500 he won was more than he had made in any one year on the US Tour, and he finished the year in 28th money-list place. Again in 1982 he easily made the Top 60. In the major championship he most wants to win, the British Open, he has made several strong efforts. At the age of 22, he came in joint sixth, his closing rounds of 69, 69, 76 being the best of anyone in the field. In 1974, a Gary Player year, he was second and in 1975 he was best British player, 3 behind Tom Watson. In 1978 he shared the lead with nine holes to go but was too bold with a putt on the 17th and finished 3 behind Jack Nicklaus. In 1982, though never in a winning position, he birdied the last hole and found himself joint second with Nick Price but 1 behind Tom Watson. As an amateur Oosterhuis considered himself weak from 50 yards into the flag and as a matchplayer. Both have since become strengths, his Ryder Cup record being particularly good. There he established the best record in singles of a British player with the following record. 1971: beat Gene Littler and Arnold Palmer. 1973: beat Palmer, halved Lee Trevino. 1975: beat Johnny Miller and Jesse Snead. 1977: beat Jerry McGee. In the next two matches he then lost narrowly to Hubert Green and Ray Floyd.

Europe wins 10 (1970–74)
Europe money £142,971 (1969–82) (24th all-time)
Africa wins 6 (1970–73)
US wins 1 (1981)
US money $535,822 (1973–82) (86th all-time)
Other overseas wins 3 (1973–4)

OXLEY, Dinah (later Henson)   England
b. Dorking 1948

Dinah Oxley first came to the fore in the mid 1960s, winning the British Girls' in 1963, the English in 1965 and the French in 1969. It was not long before she had established herself as a leading English player, finishing runner-up to Sally Barber in the 1968 English Championship and then reversing the position by beating the same opponent in the 1970

and 1971 finals. She was second in the 1969 British Ladies' Strokeplay and in 1970 took the British Amateur, finally beating Belle Robertson by one hole. Four times a Curtis Cup choice between 1968 and 1976, she was also an England international from 1967 to 1970 and 1975 to 1978 and, among other successes, twice won the Wills, the Newmark International and the Worplesdon Mixed Foursomes. A long hitter, she was also leading amateur in the 1974 European Open. Eventually she married a man whose car window she had sliced a drive through, an unusual introduction.

PADGHAM, Alfred Harry   England
b. Caterham 1906; d. 1966

Two good judges thought very highly of Alf Padgham. Dai Rees considers his swing, with Snead's, the best he has seen, and Harry Vardon declared it perfect. What had impressed them was the ease of the operation. Padgham gave a lazy waggle, drew the club back three-quarter distance and then let the club flow into the ball. For a long time he was by no means a good putter; but he was an excellent chipper and eventually decided to try to putt with the same action, the arms and ball well away from the body. It worked, and for a while Padgham was a world-beater. In the Open Championship he was particularly consistent: from 1933 to 1937 he was always seventh or better, and from 1934 to 1936 he had a sequence of third, second, first. To win his Open he had to commit a kind of theft. When Padgham turned up at Hoylake at 8 am ready to begin the final day's 36 holes, he found his clubs were still locked away in the professional's shop. He had to put a brick through the window before he went out to join the immortals with two 71s and a 1-stroke victory over Jimmy Adams and Henry Cotton. He was seventh the next year, and was one of those who faced the fearsome Sandwich gales in 1938. With the wind behind him at one hole he drove a 382-yard green for a 2 and at another, into the wind, was still short of the green with four driver shots! In tournaments he set a record of four consecutive wins from 1935 to 1936 and won three national Opens, the 1932 Irish, the 1934 German and the 1938 Dutch. In Britain he took the *News of the World* PGA Matchplay in 1931 and 1935 and was beaten finalist in 1940. In the same period he played three Ryder Cup matches from 1933 to 1937 but lost each time. His day was largely done after World War II, but he did make the limelight once more in 1948 when in Cotton's Muirfield Open he was only 2 behind after three rounds, but he faded to a 77 and seventh place. He was captain of the PGA in 1936. Other successes were the Silver King in 1936, 1939 and 1947, the *News Chronicle* in 1939 and the *Daily Mail* in 1936 and 1946.

PANTON, Catherine Rita   Scotland
b. Bridge of Allan 1955

Cathy Panton is the daughter of former Ryder Cup player John Panton and won the Scottish Girls' Championship as early as 1969. From 1972 she appeared in the Scottish team and reached her amateur peak in 1976, when she was voted Scottish Sportswoman of the Year, mainly a result of her winning the British Ladies', beating Alison Sheard of South Africa by one hole in the final at Silloth. That year she played in the World Team Championship. Turning professional, she became a leading player on the WPGA Tour and was leader of the Order of Merit in 1979, winning an event in 1982. She qualified to play on the 1983 US Tour.

PANTON, John, MBE   Scotland
b. Pitlochry 1916

Glenbervie is almost a part of John Panton's name, for he has been professional at that Scottish club since World War II and a dominant figure in Scottish tournament golf into the late 1960s. He won the Scottish Professional title from 1948 to 1951, in 1954, 1955 and 1959; the Northern Open seven times from 1948 to 1962, the West of Scotland strokeplay seven times and the matchplay on four occasions. Although not a major figure until into his 30s, he remained one for a long time, finishing runner-up in the British Matchplay in 1968 when approaching 54. He had previously won this important title in 1956. In his best years Panton had as high a reputation as anyone for long and medium irons and might have been an Open winner had he been more secure with his woods. As it was his best performance came in 1956, when he came in fifth and was leading British player. He had six wins in major British tournaments, one of these being the 1952 North British-Harrogate in which he played one nine-hole stretch in 28, still the second lowest score for half a round. His consistency in 1951 won him the Vardon Trophy for the season's lowest stroke average. He was three times in the Ryder Cup team, in 1951, 1953 and 1961; but he lost each match in which he participated. Nevertheless he was a very good team man and represented Scotland in the Canada (World) Cup 13 times from 1955 to 1968, by which time he was 53 and renowned in senior golf. Here he won the British Seniors in 1967 and 1969, going on to beat Sam Snead 3 and 2 in the 1967 World final and losing on the 38th to Tommy Bolt two years later.

GB wins 6 (1950–56)
Overseas wins 3 (1958–60)

PARK, Mungo, Snr   Scotland
b. Musselburgh 1839; d. 1904

A brother of Willie Park Snr, Mungo was a seafarer for much of his early life but won the Open Championship in 1874, beating none other than 'Young Tom' Morris into second place by 2 strokes. He was third the following year and fourth in 1876. He was an early pioneer of golf across the border when he went to Ryton-on-Tyne in 1879.

John Panton

281

PARK, Mungo, Jnr   Scotland
b. Musselburgh 1877; d. 1960

Brother of the far more successful golfer, Willie Park Jnr, he was a pioneer of golf in the US and settled for a while in New York. Later he went to the Argentine, where he designed the San Andres course.

PARK, William, Snr   Scotland
b. Musselburgh 1834; d.1903

Winner of the first Open Championship in 1860, Park had a remarkable record of consistency in the event. Between 1860 and 1868, he was never out of the first four, winning three times and coming second four times. His form declined for several years; then he came back to win in 1875, and was third in 1876; his last entry was 1878 for sixth place. His great rival was 'Old Tom' Morris, and his career also crossed the path of 'Young Tom'. Park was regarded as the best putter of his day and was the originator of the remark: 'A man who can putt is a match for anyone.' He also stressed the importance of not leaving putts short.

PARK, William, Jnr   Scotland
b. Musselburgh 1864; d. 1925

One of the first professionals to take to golf-course design, Willie Park Jnr won from golf historian Sir Guy Campbell the judgement: 'It was only when Willie Park entered the lists that the foundation stone of golf architecture was laid.' Sunningdale was one of his courses. Park was also a leader in other fields. As a maker and designer of golf clubs, he sold 17,000 of his 'lofter' at 7s 6d apiece, and popularized the 'bulger', a driver with a shorter head and convex face, the latter intended to decrease the tendency of a ball hit off the toe of the club to hook and slice from the heel. His famous wry-necked putter design was patented in 1891 and remained popular for many years. His 1896 book, *The Game of Golf*, was the first produced by a professional. He followed it in 1920 with *The Art of Golf*. He brought in the diamond-mesh pattern for golf balls in 1890. As a player he was fifth in the 1881 Open at the age of 17, fourth three years later and then won in both 1887 and 1889. He continued a top player for another decade, being in the top six four times between 1890 and 1900, in 1898 finishing second, 1 stroke behind Harry Vardon's second Open-winning score. This latter result seems to show that he was almost the equal of the Great Triumvirate, while the professional's status and expected behaviour in his day is indicated by the following commendation: 'He is held in high esteem for his exemplary conduct and for his rigid adherence to those temperance principles, the neglect of which has brought so many of his brother professionals to grief.'

PATERSON, Moira (later Milton)   Scotland
b. 1923

In a short career at the top of British Women's golf Moira Paterson's greatest achievement was to take the 1952 British Ladies', beating Frances Stephens (later Smith) in the final at Troon on the 39th hole. In 1949 she was runner-up to the same player for the French title, and in 1951 was runner-up for the Scottish. She played in the 1952 Curtis Cup side, and was a Scottish international in this period.

PENNINK, John Jacob Frank   England
b. Delft, Netherlands 1913

Frank Pennink accomplished the rare feat of winning the English Amateur in successive seasons, 1937 and 1938; and, equally rare, of being on a winning British Walker Cup team, the 1938 side. He also won the Royal St George's Challenge Cup that year; earlier he had taken the West of England Open Amateur. Three times an England international, he later was non-playing captain from 1959 to 1961. Later he become very much an insider in the golf establishment, serving on the Rules of Golf, Championship and Selection committees of the R & A. For the English Golf Union he has been chairman of Selectors and president, and also on the Executive Committee of the European Golf Association. A notable golf architect, he has been involved in the design of some 200 courses in 30 countries in the last 25 years or so; he has made changes to the championship courses of Royal Troon and Royal St George's, and assessed the changes necessary at Royal Birkdale to prepare it for the 1983 Open.

PERKINS, Tegwen (later Thomas)   Wales
b. Cardiff 1955

Tegwen Perkins set a couple of firsts for a Welsh player. She was the first, in 1974, to win a Curtis Cup place, and two years later became the first Welsh woman to win all six matches in the home

Tegwen Perkins

year, and also took the British Amateur, beating Roger Wethered 6 and 4 in the final. By this time few would have disputed that he was the best amateur in Britain. In the rest of the 1928 season he had less enjoyable experiences. In the Walker Cup in August at the Chicago GC he and Dr William Tweddell were dismissed by Jesse Sweetser and George von Elm by 7 and 6, and the following day Perkins met Bobby Jones in the top singles, no doubt striving for a better result. Jones beat him by 13 and 12! However, Perkins was by no means done for. At Brae Burn he became, with Harold Hilton, the only British player at that time to reach the final of the US Amateur; but there he found Bobby Jones in wait once more. Jones, then engaged in his sequence of five wins from 1924 to 1930, this time won 10 and 9. Perkins turned professional in the USA, and in 1932 was shot through the thigh when some gangsters used him as a shield in a shoot-out with the police. The same year in the US Open at Fresh Meadow, he had rounds of 76, 69, 74, 70 to lead Gene Sarazen by 5 strokes after two rounds, but Sarazen finished 70, 66 and left Perkins in joint second place with Bobby Cruickshank.

internationals. She played in the Curtis Cup from 1974 to 1980, taking 1½ points out of 3 on her first appearance and improving to 3 out of 4 on her next. Tegwen won the Welsh Girls' in 1970 at the age of 14 and has represented Wales in internationals at adult level since she was 16. In 1974 she was second in the British Ladies' Strokeplay, won the Welsh Ladies' in 1976 and 1967, and in 1980 took the Welsh Open Strokeplay. She won the 1973 Wills Matchplay, the 1977 Avia Foursomes, the Worplesdon Mixed in 1973 and 1978, was seven times Glamorgan champion between 1972 and 1981 and won the title of Daks Woman Golfer of the Year in 1976.

PERKINS, Thomas Philip   England
b. West Bromwich 1904

In 1921, at the age of 16, Phil Perkins won his first Warwickshire Amateur and then proceeded to extend the sequence to nine, which in fact was every entry he made. By 1927 he was English Champion and joint leading amateur in the Open. He was runner-up in the English the following

Phil Perkins

PEROWNE, Arthur Herbert — England

b. Norwich 1930

I first recall playing with Arthur Perowne in the 1946 Boys' Championship at Bruntsfield. Of a Norfolk family, he later became a farmer. By 1949, he was in the Walker Cup side and was chosen again in 1953 and 1959, but he was never a winner in foursomes or singles. He was also nine times an England international and played in the 1958 Eisenhower Trophy; at a vital point at St Andrews he had the following finish: 16th, birdie; 17th, 2-iron to 6 feet and another birdie; 18th, he went for a birdie putt boldly and missed the return. Great Britain and Ireland lost by 1 stroke. Perowne's one major championship success came in the 1958 English Strokeplay. He was a dominant figure on the East Anglian scene, winning the Norfolk Open in 1964 and the East Anglian Open in 1952, while he almost made the Norfolk Amateur his personal property, winning eleven times between 1948 and 1961, eight of these victories being consecutive from 1951. He won the Swedish Amateur title in 1974.

PERRY, Alfred — England

b. Coulsdon 1904; d. 1974

Alf Perry is one of a select band of only nine British golfers to have won the British Open since 1924, though his win came during the late 1930s, when there were usually few US entries. In 1935 Perry went round Muirfield in 69, 75, 67, 72; his 283 equalled the championship record and won him the title by 4 shots from Alf Padgham. Many still recall the apparently casual way in which he banged wood shots into the last two greens. In 1939 he might well have won again at St Andrews, but a last round of 76 dropped him to joint third. His grip was unorthodox, with the right hand well under the shaft, and he stood far from the ball but, as Bernard Darwin wrote: 'He wallops the ball with a gorgeous and whole-hearted confidence.' Perry reached the final of the PGA Matchplay in 1932, where he was beaten by Henry Cotton, and once played four tournament rounds at Wentworth in a damp autumn in under 70 each time, proof that such scoring is not only a modern phenomenon. In 1938 he had one of his most successful seasons, winning the *Daily Mail*, the *Yorkshire Evening News* and the Dunlop Metropolitan. He was chosen to play in the Ryder Cup for three matches in succession – in the years 1933, 1935 and 1937.

PETERS, Gordon Buchanan — Scotland

b. Barrhead 1910

Gordon Peters was a Scottish international between 1934 and 1938, and was also chosen for the 1936 and 1938 Walker Cup teams. In the first he halved his foursomes and lost his singles. At St Andrews in 1938, on a winning team, he won his foursomes and came home by 9 and 8 in the singles. He won the Glasgow Amateur in 1934 and the Tennant Cup in 1939.

PHILP, Hugh — Scotland

b. St Andrews 1782; d. 1856

The most famed name amongst early clubmakers, Hugh Philp was working in St Andrews early in the 19th century. Without doubt his speciality was the wooden putter and today these have a status like that of a violin by Stradivarius. A genuine Philp will fetch about £5,000 at auction – but beware of imitations. He helped to make hickory shafts popular, in preference to ash.

PICKARD, Kathleen Margaret (née Nichol) — England

b. 1938

Winner of the English Ladies' in 1960, defeating Angela Bonallack in the final, Margaret Pickard had been heavily defeated in the 1957 final by Jeanne Bisgood; she also reached the 1967 final, where she

Margaret Pickard

went down to Ann Irvin. She was seven times an England international between 1957 and 1969, a Curtis Cup team member in 1968 and 1970, and played three times in the Vagliano Trophy. She was, and is, a dominant figure in Northumberland (a strong golf region of England), winning the county title 14 times from 1956 to 1977 and again in 1982. She also took the Northern Ladies' in 1957 and 1958.

PIM, Dorothy: see Beck

PLATTS, Lionel   England
b. Sheffield 1934

One half of a famed money-match pairing with Hedley Muscroft in Yorkshire, Lionel Platts was amongst the 20 or so most successful British golfers from the early 1960s to the early 1970s, being seventh in the Order of Merit in both 1964 and 1965. In the latter year he won a Ryder Cup place at Royal Birkdale and was paired with Peter Butler throughout. In foursomes they lost to Boros and Lema by 1 hole and then halved twice with Casper and Littler. Platts then played two singles, losing to Julius Boros and beating Tommy Jacobs. He was perhaps at his best in matchplay; but he won the Assistants' Championship in 1961, the Sunningdale Foursomes in 1963, and also in that year the East Anglian Open. In 1964 he won his only major British event, the Braemar Tournament, a rarity in which players were limited to a choice of seven clubs. The following year he lost a play-off in the Swallow-Penfold and reached the final of the Matchplay Championship, losing to Neil Coles on the 19th. In 1971 he won the Portuguese Open. Other successes included the North of England title in 1970 and 1971 and the Wentworth Pro-Am Foursomes in 1969. He relished the psychological ploys of matchplay and one of his, to deter the opposition from gaining benefit from seeing what iron he had used, was to employ a set of irons which were all marked '3'.

POLLAND, Edward   Ireland
b. Newcastle (County Down) 1947

Since joining the European tour in 1968 Eddie Polland has always held a Top 60 place, with his best seasons coming from 1973 to 1976. He lay sixth in 1973 and was 13th in all the other years.

Eddie Polland

Polland is a short-game specialist, being rated highly for his short irons, chipping and putting. Fred Daly has gone on record to rate him as highly as Bobby Locke as a chipper and putter, but Irish favouritism may be showing here. Polland first won in 1971 and had added four more victories by 1980. These included a win in the 1975 Matchplay Championship and two Spanish Opens, 1976 and 1980, his second win being by the margin of 5 strokes. He was chosen for the 1973 Ryder Cup at Muirfield, where he lost in foursomes and four-balls and did not play in the singles. In other team events he has represented Ireland frequently in the World Cup and Double Diamond internationals. He has won several Irish events, including the 1974 Professionals' by 16 strokes.

Europe wins 5 (1971–80)
Europe money £145,187 (1968–82) (22nd all-time)

POOK, Elizabeth: see Chadwick

PORTER, Ruth (later Slark)　　　　**England**

b. *Chesterfield 1939*

Ruth Porter achieved one of the few 'maximums' possible in golf. In the first round of the 1963 British Ladies' she won her first-round match by 10 and 8. Good though her play was, her opponent can hardly have been in full fettle. Ruth Porter won the British Girls' in 1956, was a girl international from 1955 to 1957 and won the Scottish Girls' Open Strokeplay in 1958. In 1959 she won the English Ladies', defeating Frances Smith in the final; she won again in 1961 and 1965, and was runner-up in 1978. She was runner-up in the Australian Ladies' in 1963 and a Curtis Cup team member from 1960 to 1964, also playing in the World Team Championship from 1964 to 1966 and an England international ten times in the period 1959–78. In major competition she won the *Fairway and Hazard* Foursomes in 1958, the Astor Prince's in 1961, the Astor Salver in 1962 and 1963, the Roehampton Gold Cup in 1963, the Hovis Ladies' in 1966 and the Avia Foursomes in 1968. Particularly a force in golf in the South-West of England, she took the Gloucestershire Ladies' 14 times from 1957 to 1977 and the South-Western Ladies 13 times between 1956 and 1979.

POVALL, John K.D.　　　　**Wales**

b. *Cardiff 1938*

A leading Welsh player for many years, Povall made 18 successive international appearances from 1960 to 1977. In this same period he won the Welsh Amateur in 1962 and 1967, and was four times second. He won the Welsh Closed Open in 1962 and was top amateur in the 1962 Dunlop Masters. In this season, undoubtedly his best, he was also losing finalist in the British Amateur. The following year he was a reserve for the Walker Cup team. He later won the Welsh Strokeplay in 1970 and was second in 1974.

POXON, Martin Arthur　　　　**England**

b. *Tamworth 1955*

If making a first mark on the US Tour is difficult the European circuit is not very much easier. Poxon was a Walker Cup player in 1975, after having played golf for only four years, having won the

French Junior Matchplay in 1974 and been an international at youth level from 1974 to 1976 and full in 1975 and 1976. He then turned professional and finished 160th in the Order of Merit his first season, winning £120. He improved a little in the next few seasons but did not make the Top 60 until 1981, when he was 59th. His nearest approach to a win was in the 1981 Ivory Coast Open, which he lost in a play-off to Gordon Brand Snr.

Europe money £25,641 (1977–82)

PRICE, Elizabeth (later Fisher)　　　　**England**

b. *London 1923*

A Curtis Cup player between 1950 and 1960, Elizabeth Price built one of the best records to be established by a British woman, taking 7½ points of a possible 12. In one match at Muirfield in 1952, playing against Miss de Moss and 1 up with a few to play, she had the odd experience of being presented with a hole when the American, on the brink of taking it, produced two shanks and a fluff. Elizabeth Price came to the fore immediately after World War II, being defeated in the final of the English Ladies'; but she reached her peak in the 1950s. In this decade she twice again reached the

Elizabeth Price

English final, in 1954 and 1955, each time being defeated by Frances Stephens. She also three times reached the final of the British Ladies', losing to Frances Stephens again in 1954 and to Jessie Valentine in 1958. In 1959 came her last national final, in which she faced Belle McCorkindale and with two holes to play was 2 down. She squared the match and won on the first extra hole, thus thwarting Belle Robertson at the beginning of a 22-year quest for the British title. Elizabeth Price took two other national titles, the Danish in 1952 and the Portuguese in 1964, and had a host of victories in major amateur competition, which included the Astor Salver three times, the Spalding twice, the Kayser-Bondor, *Fairway and Hazard* and Central England Mixed Foursomes and the Roehampton Gold Cup. She won the South-Eastern Ladies' four times and the Surrey title on seven consecutive occasions. She was an England international from 1948 to 1960, turned professional for a few years from 1968 to 1971, and became a golf correspondent for the *Daily Telegraph*. As recently as 1982 she was one of the winning pair in the Central England Mixed Foursomes.

RAFFERTY, Ronan   Ireland
b. 1964

Among the youngest golfers to be listed in this book, Rafferty was in 1981 the most precocious Walker Cup player in history. By that time he had won the Irish, Ulster and British Youths' Championship in 1979; been a boy or youth international from 1978 to 1980; played against Wales at senior level in 1979; and in 1980 been a full Ireland international and represented Great Britain in the Eisenhower Trophy. In the last of these years he also won the Irish Amateur and tied for the English Strokeplay. Rafferty turned professional after the Walker Cup and failed by 1 stroke to secure his European Tour player's card at Dom Pedro and Quinta do Lago in Portugal, but then he did well enough in South Africa to qualify. During the 1982 season his performances at the age of 18 were good enough to suggest that he may well be a future star, though his swing shows a perhaps excessive Irish individualism. He was 48th on the money list. Near the end of the year he won the Venezuelan Open, putting together the very good scores of 66, 66, 70, 70.

Europe money £10,064 (1982)
Overseas wins 1 (1982)

RAVENSCROFT, Gladys (later Dobell)
England
b. *Rock Ferry 1888; d. 1960*

Winner of the British Ladies' in 1912, Gladys Ravenscroft reached the 1914 final also, where she went down to Cecil Leitch. In between she had accomplished the rare feat of becoming the US Champion as well. In the semi-final she defeated the 1913 British Champion, Muriel Dodd, and then beat Marion Hollins in the final. She was runner-up for the 1912 French Championship and in 1919 was beaten 10 and 8 by Cecil Leitch in the final of the English Ladies'. She was an England international between 1911 and 1930, took the Cheshire title seven times and was runner-up at the age of 61. She won the Veteran Women's in 1939.

RAWLINGS, Amanda   Wales
b. *Bargoed 1964*

A girl international from the age of 12, Mandy Rawlings was in the full Welsh team by 1978 and was also a Vagliano Trophy representative in 1981. She won the Welsh Girls' title in 1979 and 1981 and the Welsh Ladies' in 1980 and 1981, and was runner-up to her sister Vicki in 1982.

Ronan Rafferty

287

RAWLINGS, Victoria (later Thomas)   Wales
b. Northampton, England 1954

A Welsh girl international for five years from 1969, Vicki Rawlings won the Welsh Girls' in 1973 and had already taken the Glamorgan county title in 1970 and 1971, later to be repeated in 1979. Her later achievements came after a gap of some years: she won the Welsh Championship in 1979 and repeated this in 1982, the latter a good year for her as she also took the Welsh Open Strokeplay title (which she also won in 1981 and in which she was runner-up in 1980) and was runner-up for the Spanish Ladies'. She was awarded a Curtis Cup place. Amongst other achievements, Vicki Thomas was second in the 1979 British Amateur Strokeplay. A third sister, Kerri (later Bradley) is good enough to have been Welsh Junior Champion in 1975 and an international.

RAWLINS, Horace: see North America

RAY, Edward   England
b. Jersey 1877; d. 1943

Ted Ray, with Harry Vardon and Tony Jacklin, is one of only three British players to have won both the British and US Opens. He first came to the fore in 1903, when he reached the final of the Matchplay Championship, losing to James Braid. In this event he twice more reached the final, in 1911 and 1912, and was also twice a semi-finalist. By 1907 he was also making his mark in the British Open, in which he had the following record: 1907: 5th; 1908: 3rd; 1909: 6th; 1911: 5th; 1912: 1st; 1913: 2nd; 1920 3rd; 1925: 2nd. He did not at first concern himself with the US Open, but in 1913 he happened to be on a promotional tour of the US with Harry Vardon. The event was postponed to enable them to compete and the famous play-off over 18 holes between Harry Vardon, Francis Ouimet and Ray followed, with Ouimet the victor. Ray competed again at Inverness, Ohio, in 1920 with Vardon, who with a few holes to go seemed to have the title in his pocket. However, Ray won by a single stroke from Vardon, Jack Burke, Leo Diegel and Jock Hutchison. A remembered feature of that victory illustrates Ray's prodigious hitting: the 7th was a 334-yard hole with a chasm forming the dogleg. Ray attempted the 275-yard carry in all four rounds, made it, and birdied each time. At the time, his victory was not at all unexpected, though he is

Ted Ray

still the oldest man to win. However, it was not until 1965 that another foreigner, Gary Player, was to win, and the next Englishman was Tony Jacklin in 1970. Ray's win proved to be the last flicker of British dominance in golf. The features of Ray's game that were most remarkable were his long hitting, violent recovery play and good putting. When full out, he swayed into the ball and finished off balance, but he is said to have never relinquished the pipe between his teeth. He is also responsible for the sage advice to someone who asked him how to get more length: 'Hit it a bloody sight harder, mate!' He played in three matches against the USA: in 1921, 1926 and 1927, the last of these being the first Ryder Cup, for which he was captain. He was still winning as late as 1935 when, at the age of 57, he took the Herts Open, which he had won several times before.

REES, David James, CBE Wales

b. Barry 1913

With Abe Mitchell, Dai Rees is, most would agree, the best British player to fail to win the Open Championship, and he is certainly the best golfer Wales has produced. His best Open finishes were as follows: 1936: 11th; 1939: 12th; 1946: 4th; 1950: 3rd; 1951: 12th; 1953: 2nd; 1954: 2nd; 1956: 13th; 1959: 9th; 1960: 9th; 1961: 2nd. In a sense the closest Dai Rees came to winning was in 1946. At St Andrews that year, he recorded the lowest round of the championship, a second-round 67 and, with 75, 73 to add to this, went into the final round level with the eventual winner, Sam Snead. No one scored well the last round – Snead had a 75 – but Rees began very badly and played more steadily only when it was too late. He finished in 80. In both 1950 and 1953 he outscored the winner over two rounds, but both Locke and Hogan closed with 68s to win in comfort. In 1954 he was unfortunate. He produced scoring identical to Thomson in the first three rounds – 72, 71, 69 – and came to the last needing a par for a tie. He hit a good 4-iron to the green at Birkdale but it ran through and Rees could not get down in 2 strokes. His last chance came when he was 48. He went into the last round 1 behind Arnold Palmer and both finished in 72. Perhaps, then, his best performances came in the Ryder Cup and the PGA Matchplay, in his time the premier event after the Open. It was in this that he first made a name, reaching the final where he met E.R. Whitcombe, one of a famous trio of golfing brothers who had finished second to Walter Hagen in the 1924 Open at Hoylake. At lunch Rees was 5 down and with 12 holes to play was still 4 down, but he recovered to be all square after 29 and went on to win. He won again in 1938, this time against E.E. Whitcombe, son of E.R. In 1949 he won against Henry Cotton, and again the following year, beating Frank Jowle. He reached three more finals, losing to Max Faulkner in 1953, Peter Thomson in 1967 and Maurice Bembridge in 1969. These last two final appearances were truly remarkable for Rees was 54 and 56 years of age on these occasions, performances that rank extremely high amongst world achievements in late middle age. Dai Rees was always in the Great Britain and Ireland Ryder Cup team from 1937 to 1961. He began well by beating Byron Nelson in the 1937, but his most memorable peformance came in 1957 at Lindrick. Here, with Ken Bousfield, he was the only foursomes winner and then went on to demoralize Ed Furgol, 1954

US Open Champion, beating him by 7 and 6. The British team eventually won 7–4, their only victory since World War II. Rees also gave of his best in his last appearance in 1961, losing and winning in foursomes and beating Jay Hebert and Doug Ford in the singles, this at the age of 49. He was playing captain in the four matches from 1955 to 1961 and non-playing captain in 1967. No one else has been captain five times. Rees, at 5 feet 7 inches, is a little short for a top golfer, at least by today's standards. Early in his career he was famed for his putting, his long game being less reliable. Later he became a very straight hitter, adopting a wide stance and, most unusually, had all fingers of the right hand on the club, partly because he has small hands but also because he believes that the overlapping or interlocking grips do not suit everyone. On the backswing he allowed the shaft to slip into the slot between right thumb and forefinger and hit very firmly through the ball with the right. Having played his shot, Rees would then move off at high speed, usually talking at the same rate. So far it may

Dai Rees

seem that Rees was at his best in matchplay, but this is hardly so. At the age of 60 he tied for second place in the 1973 Martini and, in a good-class field, won the South of England PGA at the age of 62 in 1975. Among his other late achievements, he came second in the 1964 and 1965 Seniors and won in 1966. Earlier, he was leading money-winner in 1950, won the Vardon Trophy for the season's lowest stroke average in 1955 and 1959 and took the Dunlop Masters in 1950 and 1962. He won six national Opens, including the Swiss three times, won 20 British major tournaments and twice further afield, in Australia and New Zealand. He competed only a little in America, but he came third in the Los Angeles Open in 1947, and was similarly placed in the Hawaiian Open the same year. He represented Wales in the World Cup most years between 1954 and 1964 and in the Double Diamond internationals was still representing his country at the age of 63. For many years professional at South Herts, he is today still occupied with golf clinics in Britain and overseas and in journalism for *Golf Monthly*.

GB wins 21 (1936–62)
Europe wins 4 (1954–63)
Overseas wins 3 (1951–4)

RICHMOND, Maureen: see Walker

ROBB, Diane: see Frearson

ROBB, James   Scotland
b. Dunfermline 1878

James Robb was runner-up in the British Amateur in 1897 and 1900, being beaten by A.J.T. Allan and Harold Hilton respectively. However, he again reached the final in 1906, and this time won.

ROBERTS, Margaret Patricia   Wales
b. Haverfordwest 1921

Margaret Roberts enjoyed a remarkably long career at the top of Welsh golf, winning the Monmouth Championship in four different decades in the course of her 18 wins from 1947 to 1972. She also won the Welsh Ladies' in 1956, 1959, 1962 and 1963, and was six times runner-up. She played in the 1964 World Team Championship and for Wales every year but one between 1950 and 1970.

ROBERTSON, Allan   Scotland
b. St Andrews 1815; d. 1858

Undoubtedly Allan Robertson was the greatest player of his era; but he could not show this as today, by winning an Open Championship. The event had not begun: the reason for its foundation is often taken to be that it would settle who was the best player. With Robertson alive, there had been no doubt. Although his deeds are obscured by the mists of time, certain achievements have come down to us. He once, for instance, partnered 'Old Tom' Morris in a foursomes match played in three legs at Musselburgh, then St Andrews and finally at North Berwick. After Musselburgh they were 1 down, having lost by 13 and 12; they levelled at St Andrews and finally won at North Berwick, after being 4 down with eight to play. He and Tom were frequently partners in money matches but fell out for a time when Tom, who was an assistant of his at St Andrews, began making the newfangled gutta-percha ball, which Robertson considered a threat to his livelihood as he was a specialist in making featheries. Tom left for Prestwick, returning after Robertson's death, but they had continued to partner each other, probably never being beaten. Robertson was the first man to break 80 around St Andrews and, after the guttie had come to stay, may have been the first to realize the increasing importance of iron clubs with the new development and to use them for approach shots. One legend has it that he was never beaten in a singles; another that he seldom played in singles and that after Tom Morris had once beaten him in 1853 took care to avoid repeating the experience. He was buried in St Andrews Cathedral, where there is a memorial to him.

ROBERTSON, David M.   Scotland
b. Edinburgh 1957

Short, at 5 feet 6 inches, but strongly built, David Robertson had a glittering career in his mid teens. In 1972, for instance, while still 14, he won a match on the 13th of the British Amateur at Royal St George's, and was 8 under par at the time. The same year he won the Scottish Boys' title, winning the final by 9 and 8. He repeated that victory in 1974, winning this time by 6 and 5. He won the British Boys' in 1973 and British Youths' in 1974, and at full level was equal first in the Scottish Open Strokeplay, coming in with a 67 in the last round. In 1973 he was the first Scot to represent his country at boys', youths' and full international level, and this was repeated in 1974. On 9 December 1974, at 17, he turned professional. Virtually nothing has been heard of him since. He was 122nd in the 1977 Order of Merit, 134th in 1978, 156th in 1981 and 130th in 1982, with a stroke average of 77.57 and winnings of £232. His best performance is to tie for 17th in the 1977 Matchplay Championship.

ROBERTSON, Isabella, MBE (née McCorkindale)   Scotland

b. Southend, Argyll 1936

In 1981 Belle Robertson won the British Amateur on the 20th. She had been 5 up with five left to play and then her lead had crumbled away, but she came through in the end to be the oldest winner of the event. It was one which she had first lost in the final in 1959, the year her 1982 opponent, Wilma Aitken, had been born. Some years previously she had announced her retirement from competitive golf! However, it can hardly be said that Belle Robertson was a late developer, for she had reached the final of this championship in 1959, 1965 and 1970. In 1959 she lost to Elizabeth Price on the 37th, having seemed in control until then. She went down to Brigitte Varangot in 1965 at St Andrews and to Dinah Oxley by 1 down in 1970 at Gullane. In the Scottish Ladies' she was a more frequent finalist, the winner in 1965, 1966, 1971, 1972, 1978 and 1980 and losing at that stage in 1959, 1963 and 1970. She won the British Ladies'

Open Strokeplay in 1971 and 1972 and, after it became open to professionals also (from 1976), was second in both 1980 and 1981. Among many other achievements Belle Robertson has been six times a Curtis Cup player, won the Dunbartonshire Ladies' title every year but two from 1958 to 1969, the Scottish Ladies' four times, the New Zealand Matchplay in 1971 and such other titles as the Sunningdale Foursomes, the Avia Foursomes, the Helen Holm Trophy, the Players No. 6 Cup twice, and the 1982 Roehampton Gold Cup. She was also leading qualifier for the 1978 US Amateur, and established the remarkable record in 1981 of taking 3½ points out of 4 in the Vagliano Trophy and winning all six of her matches in the home internationals that year. She made what will probably but by no means certainly be her last Curtis Cup appearance in 1982 and won a singles and a foursomes, a very fair contribution in a British defeat of 3½ to 14½ at Denver, Colorado. She also played in the World Team Championship in 1982 to follow previous appearances from 1964 to 1968, in 1972 and in 1980.

ROBERTSON, Janette: see Wright

ROBSON, Frederick   England

b. Shotten 1885

Fred Robson was noticed in 1908, the year he was runner-up to J.H. Taylor in the Matchplay Championship and finished sixth in the Open. He came in fifth in 1910 and ninth in 1911. He did not reappear strongly until later in the 1920s when he finished joint second behind Bobby Jones in the 1927 Open. His opening 76 had left him 8 strokes behind Jones but he gained 4 strokes on him with a third-round 69. He was fourth to Hagen the next year. He continued to be a prominent player for some time longer, being a Ryder Cup player in 1927, 1929 and 1931; he had also played in the Great Britain versus USA match in 1926. He won both foursomes and singles in 1926, lost both in 1927, won his foursomes in 1929 but lost his singles to Horton Smith, and won his foursomes in 1931 but lost by 7 and 6 to Gene Sarazen in the singles. He was also a superb clubmaker and had a great reputation as a teacher, at one time being coach to the Walker Cup team.

Belle Robertson

RUTTLE, Maureen (later Garrett)   England
b. 1922

Maureen Ruttle's greatest achievement was to win the French Amateur in 1946. This she did by the remarkable margin of 13 and 11 in the final against Diana Critchley, British Champion in 1930 and still good enough after World War II to take the English title in 1949. She did not three-putt once throughout the championship, and when the French arrived to watch after lunch it was all over. Her father Major J.R.S. Ruttle, president of the English Golf Union in 1958 and originator of the famous 'bob a nob' scheme to help provide coaching for junior golfers, had ambitions for her to be a worldbeater. Maureen Ruttle was a successful figure in Middlesex golf in particular. She first took the county title in 1939, followed with another victory in 1953 and, with a late spurt of form, in 1973, when in her 50s. She was an England international four times in 1947 to 1953 and played in the 1948 Curtis Cup team. Later, as Mrs R.E. Garrett, she captained the winning Middlesex, England and Great Britain and Ireland teams in 1959 and in 1960, a year when she was Curtis Cup captain at Lindrick, the only time she captained a losing side. She again captained Middlesex, England and Great Britain in 1963. She became president of the Ladies' Golf Union in 1982. Late that year she received the Jones Award, which is given to a person of either sex considered to have given particularly distinguished service to golf. She is the first non-American woman to have been thus honoured.

SADDLER, Alexander   Scotland
b. Forfar 1935

During the 1960s Sandy Saddler assembled one of the best records of a British Walker Cup player. In the matches from 1963 to 1967 he won three singles, halved two and lost only once, to Deane Beman. Only 5 feet 4 inches tall and weighing about 130 lb, he became known to the press as 'the wee baker from Forfar' – not a title that he relished. Although Saddler's great determination showed itself at its best in matchplay, he won the Berkshire Trophy in 1962, and was runner-up in the Scottish Amateur in 1960. He played six times for Scotland and in the 1970s was non-playing captain of the Walker Cup team and for Scotland in the home internationals and Europe. He played for Great Britain in the 1962 Eisenhower Trophy, and once came close to winning a tournament with a strong professional entry when at Carnoustie he tied with John Panton on 283 and lost the 18-hole play-off by only 1 stroke.

SAUNDERS, Vivien Inez   England
b. Sutton 1946

After being a girl international from 1964 to 1967 Vivien Saunders hit the peak of her amateur career in 1966 when she reached the final of the British Ladies'; two years later she was in the Curtis Cup team. She turned professional in 1969 and shortly afterwards became the first European to qualify for the US Tour, in which she competed frequently with modest success for some years. In 1973 in Australia she won the Schweppes-Tarax and Chrysler Opens and in 1977 took the British Open after a tie with Mary Everard. Other successes include winning the Avia Foursomes twice – in 1967 and 1978 – the 1980 British Car Auctions event and the 1981 Keighley Trophy. She is well known as a golf journalist, often taking her own accompanying photographs, and contributes regularly to *Golf World*. She was a founder of the WPGA and its chairman in 1978 and 1979. She is author of *The Complete Woman Golfer* and *The Young Golfer*.

SAYERS, Bernard   Scotland
b. Leith 1857; d. 1924

Ben Sayers played in every Open Championship from 1880 to 1923; his best performances were to be runner-up in 1888 and third the following year. He was, at 5 feet 3 inches, one of the shortest of golfers – which made the cartwheels he performed across greens on holing important putts easier to carry out, if no less disturbing to opponents. He was much in demand as a teacher and travelled to both the USA and Monte Carlo, where he was an instructor of princes. From about 1875 he began to make golf clubs, and the firm at North Berwick continues today. Amongst the more famous implements he devised were the 'Benny', for approach shots; the 'Jigger', a chipping club; and the 'Dreadnought', a driver with a particularly large head. He was the originator of the saying 'It's no' possible but it's a fact', making the remark after he had been defeated on his home course, North Berwick, by Freddie Tait. He has the distinction of having played for his country at the venerable age of 56, in a match against England in 1913.

SCOTT, Lady Margaret   England

b. 1875; d. 1938

Lady Margaret was one of a highly talented golfing family: her brother Michael won the first Australian Open and the French, Australian and British Amateurs, while two other brothers contested the final of the Italian Amateur. She herself won the first three British Ladies' – and then married and retired. Her wins came in the years 1893–5; she is still, with Cecil Leitch and Enid Wilson, the only woman to have won three times consecutively. She was a long hitter for her era, probably as a result of having played with her brothers. Despite the encumbrances of leg-of-mutton sleeves and voluminous skirts, she had a huge backswing that travelled well past the horizontal – indeed the club shaft almost touched her back.

SCOTT, the Hon. Michael   England

b. London 1878; d. 1959

One of a successful golfing family, Michael Scott had a sister who won the first three British Ladies Amateur titles; his brother Osmund was British Amateur runner-up in 1905; and another brother, Denys, was a good player. Michael lived for some time in Australia and there won the Amateur Championship in 1905, 1907, 1909 and 1910; he also won the first Open, in 1904, by 8 strokes, and in 1907. During his second win he should strictly, according to the R & A, have been disqualified for driving from outside the tee markers. The Royal Melbourne club felt that he had derived no advantage; they were perhaps influenced by the fact that this time too Scott had finished 8 strokes ahead. In 1910 he returned to Europe. He was leading amateur in the British Open in 1912 and 1922, won the French Amateur in both these years, and was second in the 1911 Irish Open. He played in two Walker Cup teams, 1924 and 1934 (at the age of 55!), and in the first of these showed his mettle by beating Jess Sweetser 7 and 6 in the singles and in foursomes defeating W.C. Fownes and Bobby Jones. He reached the semi-finals of the British Amateur in 1920, but his most famous achievement was to become the oldest winner of the British Amateur at Hoylake in 1933, defeating Dale Bourn in the final by 4 and 3. He had had to face George Dunlap, the formidable US Walker Cup player, in the semi-final, but had convincingly beaten him 5 and 4. By this time he was a short hitter but proved very adept at keeping the ball in play.

SCOTT, Sydney Simeon   England

b. Armathwaite 1913

Lacking power, Syd Scott was an exceptionally good player of short irons. A career highpoint was his joint second place at the 1954 Royal Birkdale Open, when he finished 1 stroke behind Peter Thomson. Scott had middle rounds of 67, 69. He won the German Open in 1955 and the Portuguese in 1956, the Sunningdale Foursomes in 1955 and the Leeds Cup four times – the last of these events is said to be the oldest continuing professional competition in Britain, and dates from 1902. He played in the 1955 Ryder Cup, losing both his matches. He was professional at Carlisle City and Roehampton for many years. In 1964 he won the British Seniors, and was beaten by Sam Snead for the World title. He is now retired.

SCRUTTON, Philip F.   England

b. 1933; d. 1958

Phil Scrutton won the English Open Strokeplay in 1952, 1954 and 1955, the first to do so three times; he also won the Berkshire Trophy from 1950 to 1952. Considered a much better player in strokeplay than match events, he was chosen for the 1955 and 1957 Walker Cups, but he lost all the matches in which he was involved. He was killed in a car crash after playing at Sunningdale. In 1959 the Scrutton Jug was presented in commemoration. It is awarded to the player with the best combined aggregate in the English Strokeplay and Berkshire Trophy, the events in which he had done so well in his short career.

SEWELL, Douglas N.   England

b. Woking 1929

An excellent short-iron player and putter, Doug Sewell would have been good enough to have won the Open with another 25 yards on his drive. He turned professional in 1960 after winning the English Strokeplay in 1957 and 1959 and the English Amateur in 1958 and 1960. Beside these, in 1959 he won the Sunningdale Foursomes and the Scrutton Jug, and in 1960 the *Golf Illustrated* Gold Vase. As a professional his best performance was to be joint winner of the 1970 Martini. He was also successful in the 1968 Wentworth Pro-Am Foursomes, and twice won the West of England Professional title. He has for many years been professional at Ferndown in Dorset.

SHADE, Ronald David Bell Mitchell, MBE
Scotland

b. Edinburgh 1938

Ronnie Shade's initials and his consistency with the driver gave rise to his nickname 'Right Down the Bloody Middle'. He had a long and successful career as an amateur before turning professional in 1968. For ten years he was the best Scottish amateur and proved it by winning his national title five years in a row, from 1963 to 1967, in the course of his reign winning 44 consecutive matches. He was also runner-up in the 1966 British Amateur, losing the final to Bobby Cole. He was a Walker Cup stalwart in four matches (1961–7), losing both on his first appearance, winning both singles in 1963, winning in two foursomes and one singles in 1965 and finally winning and halving in foursomes and losing both singles in 1967. In other team events Shade was in the Great Britain Eisenhower team four times, from 1962 to 1968, and was individual winner in 1966 and a Scotland international in 1957–68. He had previously won the Scottish Boys' in 1956, and took the Scottish Open Amateur Strokeplay in 1968 and was leading amateur in the 1966 British Open, being among the leading players after two rounds with a start of 71, 70. As a professional his mechanical, 'in pieces' swing continued to be successful and his 1969 win in the Carrolls tournament was the last by a first-year professional until Gordon Brand Jnr repeated the feat in 1982. Shade was 20th in the Order of Merit in 1969, 14th in 1970 and remained in the Top 60 until the mid 1970s. His other tournament successes included wins in the 1970 Scottish Professional and the Mufulira Open in Zambia in 1975. He also represented Scotland in the World Cups from 1970 to 1972 and in the Double Diamond internationals from 1971 to 1975. He has also won numerous Scottish events.

SHEPPERSON, Alec E. England

b. Sutton-in-Ashfield 1936

Alec Shepperson was beaten finalist in the 1952 British Boys' Championship, but won the following year. He won the 1957 President's Putter and was second in the English Amateur Strokeplay in 1958 and 1962. He has won the Nottinghamshire Amateur four times and the county's Open twice, and was an England international from 1956 to 1962. He played in two Walker Cup teams, 1957 and 1959, halving in foursomes the first year and losing

in foursomes in 1959 but beating Tommy Aaron in singles. The demands of a business career cut short his golf achievements.

SIMPSON, Jack Scotland

b. Earlsferry

One of a golfing family, Jack Simpson won the 1884 British Open at Prestwick by 4 strokes from Willie Fernie and Douglas Rolland. His brother Archie was joint second the following year and again in 1890.

SKERRITT, Patrick Joseph Ireland

b. Lahinch 1930

One of eight brothers, three of whom became golf professionals, Paddy Skerritt was a good rhythmic striker but a relatively poor putter. His one major success was his win in the 1970 Alcan International. He also won the Irish Matchplay that year, the Irish Native Professional in 1977, and the Seniors in 1980. He has always made playing golf seem a carefree matter.

Europe wins 1 (1970)

SLARK, Ruth: see Porter

SMITH, Alfred Edward England

Smith is the joint record holder for a low round over a course of par 70 or more. On the first day of 1936 he played round his home course, Woolacombe, 4,248 yards, in 55, having four 2s and seven 3s. On the homeward half he scored 2, 3, 3, 3, 3, 2, then had a 'disastrous' 5 but pulled himself together to hole in one on the last for 26 back. His record may be considered inferior to Homero Blancas's 55 in 1962 over a course measuring a little over 5,000 yards. Today, of course, neither course would be rated as par 70.

SMITH, Frances, OBE (née Stephens)
England

b. 1924; d. 1978

A key British Curtis Cup player in the years 1950 to 1960, the most successful period for British teams, Frances Smith established arguably the best record of all time by a British player. In singles she was unbeaten in five matches and won four of them. In her first match the British team scored only 1½

Frances Smith

points, with Frances Smith winning her foursome with Elizabeth Price, and in her singles she was 3 down with three to play against Dorothy Germain Porter but still managed a half. Muirfield in 1952 saw the first ever victory by a Great Britain and Ireland team. On the losing 1954 team Frances Smith holed a putt of about 20 feet on the last green to beat Mary Lena Faulk. The year 1956 saw one of the most closely contested of all Curtis Cup matches: in the last and decisive match Frances Smith faced Polly Riley, who was also undefeated in Curtis Cup encounters. Frances secured a 4-up lead early on but was all square at lunch. In the afternoon, with about seven holes to play, it was clear that the destiny of the cup depended on the Riley-Smith match. Frances went 1 up on the 15th; Riley squared on the next; both were a breath short with their putts for wins on the next, and on the last hole Frances Smith hit a 5-iron a few yards past the hole and won with a 4 to a 5 for her match and the Curtis Cup. This situation almost repeated itself in 1958 at Brae Burn, with Frances Smith facing Polly Riley in the final match and needing victory to halve the match and retain the Curtis Cup. Frances came to the last hole 1 up and took the final hole. This was the first time that any British Ryder, Walker or Curtis Cup team had not been defeated in

America. It was also the last time that a British Curtis Cup team did not lose. As the leading English player in the immediate post-war years, Frances Smith had a very fine record in both the British and English Amateur for several years. She won the British title in 1949, lost the 1951 and 1952 finals and then defeated Elizabeth Price in 1954. She won the English title in 1948, 1954 and 1955, and was runner-up in 1959. Years past her best in 1970, she finished second in the British Ladies' Strokeplay. She won the French Championship in 1949. Something of Frances Smith's consistency can be seen by her dominance in Lancashire. There she took the county title from 1948 to 1955 and again in 1959 and 1960, while she was almost equally effective in the *Daily Graphic* tournament, winning from 1946 to 1950 and in 1953; in the Worplesdon Mixed Foursomes she was four times in the winning pairing. At the time of her death she was president of the English Ladies' Golf Association.

SMITH, William Dickson   Scotland
b. Glasgow 1918

In 1945 Captain W.D. Smith won the Indian Amateur Championship, defeating I.S. Malik in the final by 6 and 5. Malik was later to prove himself one of the very best Indian amateurs, being runner-up on four more occasions and winning four times. Little more was heard of Smith for nearly a dozen years until he reappeared in the late 1950s. He became a Scottish international in 1957 and played four more years. His lifetime performance was to finish fifth in the 1957 Open at St Andrews with 71, 72, 72, 71, compared to the 69, 72, 68, 70 of the winner (Locke). No amateur has since equalled that performance. He played in one Walker Cup, at Muirfield in 1959. There he faced Jack Nicklaus in singles and lost. Smith won the Scottish Amateur in 1958 and the Portuguese in 1967 and 1970.

SMYTH, Desmond   Ireland
b. 1952

After being an amateur international Des Smyth joined the European Tour in 1974 and there served a long apprenticeship. After five years he had totalled only about £6,000 in money wins, although in 1979 he had won the Matchplay Championship. A better year followed in 1980, when he won the Newcastle 900, the Greater Manchester Open and the Irish Dunlop successively. He had a consistent season again in 1981 and won the Coral Welsh Classic, moving from 10th to 8th in the Order of Merit, while he was 13th in 1982. In 1982 he was one of a group of players who were within sight of winning the British Open. He began 70, 69, which in some years would have given him the lead. Although it scarcely matched Clampett's 67, 66, he was at that point in third place. He followed with 74, 73 and finished fourth, 2 strokes behind Tom Watson, whom he had led into the final round. Usually an excellent putter, Smyth had been less sharp on the greens than he might have been. He was twice a Ryder Cup player, in 1979 and 1981. At the Greenbrier, White Sulphur Springs, in West Virginia in 1979, Smyth had the unusual experience of having a partner, Ken Brown, who seemingly would not speak to him. They lost to the Irwin–Kite pairing by 7 and 6. He later lost his singles to Hale Irwin by 5 and 3. In the 1981 match at Walton Heath Smyth won and lost in both foursomes and four-balls, and also lost his singles by 6 and 4 to Ben Crenshaw on the last day. Smyth 'sets the angle' early in his backswing and gets through to an exceptionally full 'inverted C' position on the follow-through. Possibly because of the early setting, he is one of the best mid-iron players on the European Tour, but less secure with woods.

Europe wins 4 (1979–81)
Europe money £132,051 (1974–82) (28th all-time)

SOULSBY, Janet England
b. Prudhoe 1964

One of the most promising prospects in British women's golf, Janet Soulsby has been filling all the hours of daylight at her home course, Prudhoe, near Newcastle, for some 10 years. By the age of 13, she was good enough for a place in her county team and was her club champion at 14. In 1979 she reached the semi-finals of the Girls' Championship and the finals the following year, when she was English Girls' Champion. In 1981 she won the English Under-23s, as well as the English Girls' where she had been runner-up in 1980; with victory in the British Ladies' Amateur Strokeplay, she became the youngest of either sex ever to take a British title. In 1982 she made her first Curtis Cup appearance and did better than most in a defeated, even humiliated, team. On the first day she halved her foursomes and won her singles, to provide the

only points gathered by Great Britain and Ireland, and on the second day she and her partner went down by only one hole in the foursomes and Janet lost by 2 and 1 in singles. In all, only two singles out of 12 were won by the British. She later reached the semi-finals of the US Girls'. She is considered by Henry Cotton to be one of the few women who hits the ball, rather than swings through it.

SPEARMAN, Marley (later Harris) England
b. 1928

Brawn is not all – or even very much of what goes to make up a talented golfer. The sense of balance that a dancer can bring to the game can be vital to the movement of the body in the hitting area. Perhaps Marley Spearman owed much to her background as a professional stage dancer – though she was never, as so often said, a Windmill girl but did appear at the Coliseum and the Adelphi, in

Marley Spearman

London. In 1961 and 1962 she achieved the rare feat of winning the British Ladies' consecutively, beating Diane Robb and Angela Bonallack. In 1963 she added the New Zealand Ladies' Strokeplay to her record, then in 1964 the English title. She was an England international every year from 1955 to 1965, twice represented Great Britain in the Commonwealth event and was three times a Curtis Cup team choice between 1960 and 1964. In important amateur tournaments she had six major victories in 1965: the Sunningdale and Casa Pupo Foursomes, the Roehampton Gold Cup, the Astor Salver, the Astor Prince's and the Hovis Ladies'. In other years she won the Spalding Ladies' (1956), the Astor Salver (1964) and the Astor Prince's (1964). She was one of the first British women to adopt stylish dress for golf, and learned the game quickly. Indeed, she early on asked to play in her husband's regular four-ball, saying: 'I learned how to play at Harrods yesterday.'

SQUIRRELL, Hew Crawford — Wales
b. Cardiff 1932

Hew Squirrell was a Welsh international for an extremely long run: 1955 to 1975, with just one year omitted. He won the Welsh Amateur five times, from 1958 to 1960 and in 1964 and 1965, and was also twice runner-up. On the British scene he won the Royal Mid-Surrey Antlers in 1959 and 1961 and the Hampshire Hog in 1961, and during this period was on the fringe of the Walker Cup team.

STEPHENS, Frances: see Smith

STEWART, Gillian — Scotland
b. Inverness 1958

In Scottish golf Gillian Stewart's successes began with the North of Scotland title in 1975, a success she was to repeat in 1978, 1980 and 1982. She won the Northern Counties in 1976, 1978 and 1982, the Scottish Ladies' in 1979 and the 1981 Helen Holm Trophy. In Britain as a whole she took the 1976 Girls' Championship and was runner-up for the 1982 British Ladies'. In team events she has represented Scotland in the home internationals from 1979 and in the Vagliano Trophy from 1979 to 1981. In 1980 she played for the first time in the Curtis Cup, in which she won the only singles she played. She was in the team again in 1982.

STOREY, Eustace Francis — England
b. Lancaster 1901

Renowned for his putting, Eustace Storey was runner-up to Sir Ernest Holderness for the 1924 British Amateur, and was a Walker Cup player three times from 1924 to 1928. In 1926 he played in the most remarkable final of the President's Putter against Roger Wethered: after playing six extra holes they were forced to call the match halved because of darkness. Storey was in winning partnerships for the Worplesdon Mixed Foursomes in 1938 and 1948, was leading amateur in the 1938 British Open and seven times an England international between 1924 and 1936.

STOUT, James Alfred — England
b. Whitehaven 1896; d. 1973

English Amateur Champion in 1928, beating the redoubtable Phil Perkins, Stout took part in the most remarkable of Walker Cup matches. In 1930 he stood 7 up against Don Moe with 13 to play. Moe won seven holes in succession and birdied the last hole to win by 1 up. Said Stout: 'That was not golf. That was a visitation from the Lord.'

STOWE, Charles — England
b. Sedgley 1909; d. 1976

Charlie Stowe was an artisan player from the Black Country in England, one of the few to be chosen for the Walker Cup team, for which he played in 1938, winning his singles and losing his foursomes. He also played in 1947 with the reverse result. He was an amateur international from 1935 to 1949. He was runner-up twice in the 1947 and 1949 English Amateur. In the British Amateur he reached the semi-finals twice, then was beaten by Frank Stranahan in the final of the 1948 event. He won the English Open Strokeplay in 1948 and 1953. Among his other achievements were eight wins in the Staffordshire Amateur and two, 1937 and 1949, in the Prince of Wales Challenge Cup.

STRATH, Andrew — Scotland
b. St Andrews, 1836; d. 1868

Andrew Strath had a good record in the Open Championship in his short career. In 1860 he was third, in 1863 fourth, in 1864 second, 2 strokes behind 'Old Tom' Morris, and then he won by 2 from Willie Park in 1865. He was fourth in 1867.

STRATH, David Scotland

b. St Andrews, 1840; d. 1879

Davie Strath was involved in the only 'walk-over' in the British Open. He came to the last two holes at St Andrews needing two 5s to win and on the 17th, thinking himself out of range, played to the green while players ahead were still putting out. His ball was prevented from going on the road. However, on the last, Strath took 6 and was tied with Bob Martin. A protest was made about the incident on the 17th and the committee decided that the 18-hole play-off should be played 'under protest'. Strath refused to play if the protest were not decided on first, with the result that Bob Martin walked the course and became the 1876 champion. Davie Strath was also third in 1870, second in 1872 and sixth in 1875.

STUART, Hugh Bannerman Scotland

b. Forres 1942

Hugh Stuart was Scottish Boys' Champion in 1959, and later a Scottish international from 1967 to 1976. He won the Scottish Amateur in 1972 and was runner-up in 1970 and 1976, and also twice won the North of Scotland title. He was three times a Walker Cup choice, having mixed fortunes. In 1971 he won all three of his matches, in 1973 lost three and won a singles, and in 1975 lost all three. He was chosen for the Eisenhower Trophy in 1972.

TAIT, Frederick Guthrie Scotland

b. Dalkeith 1870; d. 1900

Freddie Tait, a much loved golfer, was killed while leading a charge of the Black Watch during the Boer War. By that time he had established a formidable record in British golf. In 1890 at St Andrews he beat all previous amateur records with a round of 77 and went a giant leap further in 1894 with a 72. To the modern eye these scores may seem distinctly unspectacular, but it should be remembered they were done with a gutta-percha ball and inferior clubs and course maintenance. By way of comparison, when the Open was won at St Andrews by Hugh Kirkaldy, he did it with a pair of 83s and J.H. Taylor's winning rounds there in 1895 had 78s as his best rounds and an 86 as the worst. Freddie Tait won the British Amateur twice: first in 1896, when he beat Johnny Laidlay, John Ball, Horace Hutchinson and, in the final, Harold Hilton; and again in

1898. He won his two finals by 8 and 7 and 7 and 5. He was runner-up in 1899, losing to the great John Ball on the 37th, after he had been 3 up after 18 holes. In the British Open he was leading amateur in 1894, 1896 and 1899 and was third overall in 1896 and 1897. Freddie Tait was also a good rugby player and cricketer, and an expert rifle shot. His swing was long, seemed gentle – though he was a long hitter – and, in the manner of the day, he gripped well under the shaft with the right hand. He used the lofted putter that many favoured to deal with the rough and bumpy greens of his day.

TAYLOR, John Henry England

b. Northam 1871; d. 1963

A member of the Great Triumvirate with James Braid and Harry Vardon, J.H. Taylor – as he was always known – contrasted strongly with them. He neither hit with the savagery of Braid nor had the grace of swing of Vardon. He was, however, the best putter of the three and an exceptionally fine iron player, having special mastery of the mashie in

J.H. Taylor

approaching: he hit high or low, depending on the wind. He was much respected for his abilities in foul weather. Taylor's father died when he was an infant and Taylor left school at the age of 11 (but years later he wrote his own autobiography) and worked at Westward Ho!, the club where he was to be made president in 1957. In 1891, with a sovereign in his pocket, he went to Burnham in Somerset as greenkeeper and professional, and by this time he was a good golfer. The next year he beat Andrew Kirkaldy in a match, and shortly afterwards succeeded him as professional at Winchester. He played in his first Open in 1893, and led for a while. In 1894, the first time the Open was played outside Scotland, he was champion at Sandwich. He led after 36 holes and eventually won by 5 strokes, the first English professional to do so. The next year he won again at St Andrews, after an opening round of 86, by 4 strokes and had established himself as the best player in Britain. But there was a cloud on the horizon: Harry Vardon. On 14 May 1896 they met in a challenge match at Ganton, where Vardon was the professional, and Taylor was beaten 8 and 7. A month later they met again at Muirfield in the Open; this time Taylor led by 3 strokes going into the final round, with scores of 77, 78, 81. Although there was no par at the time, it should be thought of as about 78 or 79. Sandy Herd had one round in 72 and The Times commented: 'In the opinion of many authorities on the game it was considered very doubtful whether such a feat had ever been accomplished before.' Herd followed with an 84. Taylor finished with an 80, good for the time, but Vardon tied with his final 77. In the play-off Vardon held the lead most of the time, with Taylor fighting back, and eventually won by 4 strokes. Taylor won his third Open at St Andrews in 1900. Only the third man to break 80 in each round, he beat Vardon by 8 strokes, with the third member of the Triumvirate, James Braid, third, another 5 strokes back. That year while on a promotional tour to the US, Taylor and Vardon entered the US Open, and this time Vardon came through by 2 strokes, with the third-place man 7 behind Taylor. For the next several years James Braid became the dominant member of the Great Triumvirate, although Taylor was second four years consecutively from 1904 to 1907, having an almost unheard-of 68 in his final round at Sandwich in 1904 but still finishing 1 behind. At Deal in 1909 he produced the most consistent golf seen to that time in an Open: 74, 73, 74, 74. He beat Braid

by 4 and became the third of the trio to take the Open four times. It was perhaps the best period in his later career, for he also won the Matchplay in 1908 and the French Open in both 1908 and 1909. In the years that followed Vardon and Braid both won again. In the 1913 Open at Hoylake Taylor played poorly in the two qualifying rounds, needing a 6-foot putt in the end to qualify for the championship proper. He then began finely with 73, 75 to be 1 behind Ted Ray when a full gale got up for the 36 holes of the last day. One contender soared to an 89, yet still finished joint third. Ray was second with 81, 84 and Taylor gained 9 strokes on him that day to win by 8. The year 1914 saw the end of many aspects of British life, the Great Triumvirate among them. The Prestwick Open was their last as a major force in the game. In the final duel between Vardon and Taylor the latter held a 2-stroke lead going into the final round and on the 1st hole missed a short putt which would have had him 4 ahead. On the 4th he pushed his drive into a shallow burn and failed to get out at the first attempt, ending with a 7 to Vardon's 4. Taylor later said that on the next hole he could hardly hold his putter: 'For the remaining holes I played like a beaten man, as indeed I was.' By 3 strokes Vardon took his sixth Open, a record that has only been threatened by Thomson, Locke and, it could be, Tom Watson. When peace returned the Triumvirate were in their late 40s; with a few flickerings left in them. Taylor was sixth in the 1922 Open won by Hagen, though he led him by 1 stroke into the last round. He was fifth in 1924, again behind Hagen, whom he had led by 1 stroke after two rounds. He played in the 1926 Open, then announced his retirement at the age of 55. He continued to be active in golf, however. He had been in at the founding of the PGA in 1901, and served as both captain and chairman. He played in the first Great Britain versus USA match in 1921, and was a winning Ryder Cup captain in 1933. In 1949 he was made an honorary member of the R & A and when he finally retired to his native Northam in 1957 in his late 80s, he was made president of the Royal North Devon Golf Club. It is an irony that James Henry Taylor might never have been a professional golfer at all. He was rejected in turn by Army, Navy and police on account of flat feet and poor eyesight. Bernard Darwin wrote of his tireless work to improve the lot of professional golfers that it 'turned a feckless company into a self-respecting and respected body of men'.

THIRLWELL, Alan   England
b. Newcastle 1928

A superb striker of the ball, Alan Thirlwell was held back from higher achievements by a less effective short game. He was an England international from 1951 to 1964 and a Walker Cup choice in 1957. He won the English Amateur in 1954 and 1955 and again reached the final in 1963, when his superior play through the green was nullified by Michael Bonallack having a near-miraculous day in chipping and putting. In the same championship in 1969 Thirlwell beat Bonallack, bringing his run of success to an end. He twice reached the final of the British Amateur, losing to Joe Carr in 1958 and to Trevor Homer in 1972. Among many other successes Thirlwell won the County Champion of Champions in 1962 and was in the winning pairing of the Wentworth Pro-Am Foursomes three times. He won the Northumberland Amateur four times and the Northumberland and Durham Open in 1960. He is now secretary of Formby GC.

THOMAS, David C.   Wales
b. Newcastle, England 1934

For a spell perhaps the longest straight driver in the world, Dave Thomas twice came very close to winning the Open. In 1958 several players came to the last hole at Royal Lytham with a chance to tie or win, but only Thomas and Thomson emerged to tie on 278. In the 36-hole play-off that followed, Thomson scored 68, 71 to Thomas's 69, 74. His second near miss came in 1966 when he finished 69, 69 to be joint second with Doug Sanders, but 1 behind Jack Nicklaus. One of the early British players to compete fairly frequently in the US, he was not particularly successful, but was once second in the St Paul Open and won a qualifying competition for the 1964 US Open. Tales of his long hitting were legion. During a practice round for the 1967 Hoylake Open he drove level with the 2nd green, a distance of some 420 yards. The one great weakness in his game was thought to be the short pitch from around 50 yards, unfortunately one of the most vital to good scoring in golf. He played in the Ryder Cup in 1959 and from 1963 to 1967; his record was: singles, a half in four matches; four-balls, 1 point from 6 possible; foursomes, 4 points from 7 possible. He also represented Wales 11 times between 1957 and 1970. Dave Thomas won three national Opens, the Belgian, French and Dutch, and ten events on the

British mainland, including the 1963 Matchplay. He also won twice in New Zealand. He withdrew from tournament golf in the early 1970s, mainly as a result of eye and back trouble.

Europe wins 14 (1955–69)
Overseas wins 2 (1958–9)

THOMAS, Tegwen: see Perkins

THOMAS, Victoria: see Rawlings

THOMSON, Hector   Scotland
b. Machrihanish 1913

British Boys' Champion in 1931, Hector Thomson later won the Irish Amateur in 1934 and 1935, the Scottish in 1935 and the British Amateur in 1936, beating Jim Ferrier of Australia in a close-fought final. He was a Scottish amateur international from 1934 to 1938 and a Walker Cup team member in 1936 and 1938. He lost both his matches in 1936 but in the winning 1938 team first won in foursomes and then beat Johnny Goodman 6 and 4 in singles. He turned professional in 1940, won four Scottish titles and was leading overseas player in the 1953 Tam o' Shanter. He later got a job as a club professional in an exotic location not usually associated with golf – Athens.

THOMSON, Muriel Natalie   Scotland
b. Aberdeen 1954

A girl international from 1970 to 1973, Muriel Thomson played for the full team in 1974–8 and progressed to play in the 1978 Curtis Cup and World Team Championships. Individually, she won the Helen Holm Trophy in both 1975 and 1976, was runner-up for the 1977 Scottish Ladies' and won the 1978 Canadian Foursomes. She turned professional in 1979 and the following year won three events and topped the WPGA Order of Merit. She won another event in 1981.

TOLLEY, Cyril James Hastings, MC   England
b. London 1895

After spending 13 months as a prisoner of war, Cyril Tolley proved himself an all-round sportsman at Oxford by winning his blue in three sports. Indeed he considered himself more a cricketer when he won the British Amateur in 1920. He beat

Bob Gardner of America on the first extra hole at Muirfield, having been 3 up with four to play. The following year he won the Welsh Amateur, and repeated the victory in 1923. Playing to the same standard as a leading professional, Tolley took the French Open twice, in 1924 and 1928, and added his second British Amateur in 1929. In the same event one of the classic matches of all time followed when he met Bobby Jones, seeking the first leg of his Grand Slam, in 1930. In strong winds, the match was very close throughout, Jones winning after a stymie on the first extra hole. Tolley reached the semi-final on two other occasions, the most remarkable coming as late as 1950; when he was 54. He beat Joe Carr in the quarter-finals and was then eliminated by the eventual champion, Frank Stranahan. His game had lasted so well because of his full, rhythmic and powerful swing, which had enabled him on occasion to drive to the green of both the last at St Andrews and the first at Troon, holes of over 350 yards. Among his other tournament feats were six major amateur events and a host of others. He was an England international between 1921 and 1947 and played in the Walker Cup, or its earlier equivalent, seven times between 1921 and 1934. He was captain of the R&A from 1948 to 1949 and served on R&A committees. He was Walker Cup chairman of selectors in 1938 and 1947.

TORRANCE, Sam   Scotland
b. Largs 1953

Sam Torrance has a great appetite for tournament golf. He usually plays the maximum of events in Europe and then seeks out competition in Africa, the Far East and South America. He joined the European Tour in 1972 and that year won the Under 25 Matchplay and a non-tour event, the Radici Open, in Italy. He made the Top 60 comfortably in 37th place and was named Rookie of the Year. He retained his place every year after, making real progress after about three years when he won the Zambian Open and took the Martini International and the Piccadilly Medal in 1976 to be third in the European Order of Merit. He did not quite sustain that form in the years that followed, though he was 19th every year from 1978 to 1980, adding the 1979 Colombian Open and the 1980 Australian PGA. In 1981 he made his best effort in a major championship when, after a hole in one near the end, he appeared certain of being top British

player; but then he took a 6 on the last for fifth place. He did, however, take the Irish Open by 5 strokes and finished sixth in the Order of Merit, which assured him of his first Ryder Cup place. The following year he emphasized his position as a leading British player with a consistent season during which he dominated the European Open, seemed to have it won with 30 to the turn at Sunningdale but was then caught by Manuel Pinero on the final nine. He compensated a little later by winning the Spanish and Portuguese Opens comfortably, to be third in the Order of Merit, about £1 behind Sandy Lyle. Sam Torrance is a long hitter and one of the best bunker players in Europe.

Europe wins 6 (1972–82)
Europe money £214,925 (1972–82) (9th all-time)
Africa wins 1 (1975)
Australia wins 1 (1980)
South America wins 1 (1979)

Sam Torrance

TOWNSEND, Peter Michael Paul   England
b. Cambridge 1946

As an amateur, Peter Townsend quickly established one of the best reputations as a winner in post-war British amateur golf. In both 1962 and 1964 he was British Boys' Champion and added the Youths' title in 1965. In 1966 he won the English Strokeplay, and in the years 1965–6 won seven major amateur titles. He was chosen for the 1965 Walker Cup team and was a hero of the tied match, winning both his foursomes and beating Billy Joe Patton in singles, but on the final afternoon he was one of the six British losers. Townsend turned professional in 1966 and his progress was watched with the keenest interest, for he was then perhaps the most promising recruit since World War II. He went off to blood himself in South Africa and soon found himself incapable of breaking 90, probably because many amateurs attempt to alter their style and mental approach to tournament golf. Townsend then perhaps made things worse by modifying his swing. His results were hardly better when he returned to Britain: he won £99 in the season. However, he did win the Dutch Open. In 1968 he fared dramatically better and shot up to sixth place in the Order of Merit, winning the Young Professionals' Championship and the PGA Closed Championship, and established himself as an international player by scoring 75, 69, 69, 73 in the Alcan Golfer of the Year to finish second to Gay Brewer. In Australia he won the Western Australian Open. Townsend's ambitions were pitched high: he set his sights on the US Tour. He qualified; his results were mixed, though he had three top 10 finishes and won some £21,000. At this point in his career judges were rating his eventual prospects higher than those of Tony Jacklin, though that was to change when Jacklin won the Open. Eventually Townsend decided that his prospects were better in Europe and thereafter played full-time this side of the Atlantic, though continuing to compete overseas. He was fifth and fourth respectively in the 1971 and 1972 European Order of Merit, winning the 1971 Swiss Open (with a third round 61), which was to prove his last victory in Europe, though he could claim seven wins worldwide in his first five professional years. In this period he was twice a Ryder Cup player, in 1969 and 1971. He had a splendid beginning at Royal Birkdale in the tied 1969 match, taking both foursomes the first day and a four-ball the next morning, but then lost in the afternoon four-ball and in the singles. He lost in each of the four matches he played in 1971. After 1972 Townsend remained in the European Top 60 from 1973 to 1981, although he enjoyed only two years of high standard: 1974, when he was ninth, and 1979 at 14th. He earned no more Ryder Cup places and was not chosen for other internationals after 1974. However, he did have quite frequent overseas successes, recording wins in Africa and South America. Perhaps during this later phase his best performance was to win the 1978 Moroccan Grand Prix, the only time this has been done by a British player. This year was in fact arguably his best, for he took four events in all.

Europe wins 5 (1967–71)
Europe money £113,173 (1967–82) (31st all-time)
South America wins 4 (1969–78)
Africa wins 3 (1976–8)
Australia wins 1 (1968)

Peter Townsend

TUCKER, William Iestyn — Wales

b. Nantyglo 1926

A stalwart of Welsh international teams, Iestyn Tucker holds the record number of consecutive appearances in 1949 to 1972. He played again in 1974 and 1975. Tucker won the Welsh Amateur in 1963 and 1966 and was six times runner-up, including 1976, when he was 49. The same year he won the Welsh Strokeplay. His other achievements include winning the Duncan Putter five times and the Monmouth Amateur 16 times, including 12 consecutive from 1952 to 1963. He once had a medal round of 59.

TUPLING, L. Peter — England

b. Sheffield 1950

Peter Tupling won the 1967 Boys' Championship and in 1969 was an England and Walker Cup international. In the latter he lost to Dick Siderowf in singles but won a foursomes in partnership with Michael Bonallack. The same year he was leading amateur in the British Open and turned professional. In February 1981 he set the world record for a 72-hole tournament with 255, beating Mike Souchak's 257 set in the 1955 Texas Open. Tupling did it at the 6,024 yard Ikoyi course near Lagos in the Nigerian Open with rounds of 63, 66, 62, 64; yet even this kind of scoring did not give him an easy victory. Bill Longmuir twice did 62 and finished with a last nine holes in 29, but Tupling birdied four of the last five holes to win. Golf records can be misleading and Tupling's remarkable score must be seen in the light of Ikoyi being a short course with 'greens' of oil-bound sand, which are easier to read, and putt more consistently. In his years on the European Tour Tupling's best finish was 17th in 1974, when he was second to Tommy Horton in the Penfold tournament. He has been in the Top 60 from 1970 to 1974 and in 1981, and played for Great Britain and Ireland in the 1978 PGA Cup match against the USA. He was second in the 1970 Wills tournament and the 1971 Kenya Open, and in 1972 led the British Open after one round with a 68, remaining in contention for two more rounds until a final 81 dropped him down the list. He gave up a club professional's job in Boldon, Co. Durham, to concentrate on tournaments, and is now sponsored by an African airline.

Africa wins 1 (1981)
Europe money £38,312 (1970–82)

TWEDDELL, Dr William, MC — England

b. Whickham 1897

Amateur Champion in 1927, William Tweddell again reached the final in 1935 where there awaited the ominous figure of Lawson Little, who had won the previous year's final with awesome power and precision that had led to a still-record 14 and 13 victory. Tweddell was outgunned by far from the tee but was only 3 down with 10 to play and eventually lost only on the last hole. Tweddell played in the 1928 Walker Cup match, when he lost twice, and was non-playing captain in 1936. He was also four times an England international and captain of the R & A from 1961 to 1962. His achievements as a player were of great merit, especially considering that he was a full-time doctor with very limited time for playing golf.

UZIELLI, Angela (née Carrick) — England

b. Swanton Morley 1940

Runner-up in the 1976 English Ladies' to Lynne Harrold, Angela Uzielli had her greatest success the following year when she reached the final of the British Ladies' and defeated Vanessa Marvin 6 and 5. She has also won the Astor Salver four times (1971, 1973, 1977 and 1981), the Roehampton Gold Cup in 1977 and the Avia Foursomes in 1982. She has been Berkshire county champion in the successive years 1976–81 and an England international from 1976 to 1978. A late developer, she was named Daks Golfer of the Year in 1977 and played in the 1978 Curtis Cup. With her mother Peggy Carrick she has won the Mothers and Daughters Foursomes 11 times since 1965 while her mother, twice an England international, has been 11 times Norfolk champion.

VALENTINE, Jessica, MBE (née Anderson) — Scotland

b. Perth 1915

Jessie Valentine had a career at the top of British women's golf that lasted over 30 years. It began with victory in the 1933 British Girls', and three years later she made the first of a record seven Curtis Cup appearances. On the first occasion she played a vital role in Great Britain's halving the match. She holed a putt of some length on the last green to win her match by 1 up. In 1937 she won her first major title, the British Ladies', the first of a record time-span of wins. In 1950 she was beaten finalist to the Vicomtesse de St-Sauveur, but in the 1955 final she defeated Barbara Romack 7 and 6. Two years later she fell to Philomena Garvey in the final, but in 1958 won for the last time against Elizabeth Price. At the time she was, at 42 years 3 months, the oldest to win. Belle Robertson has since bettered the achievement. A dominant figure in Scottish golf, she took the title first in 1938 and had other victories in 1939, 1951, 1953, 1955 and 1956. She was twice runner-up for both British and Scottish titles. She won two other national titles, the New Zealand Ladies' in 1935 and the French the following year, defeating Pam Barton on the 37th in the final. Amongst other tournament successes she won the East of Scotland four times, the Spalding in 1957, the Kayser-Bondor in 1959 and 1961 and the Worplesdon Mixed Foursomes three years in a row (1963–5), in partnership with J.E. Behrend. She was a Scottish international in the years 1934–58, a sequence that ended only because she turned professional in 1959, one of the earliest British players to do so.

VARDON, Harry   England
b. Grouville, Jersey 1870; d. 1937

British Open Champion: 1896, 1898, 1899, 1903, 1911, 1914
US Open Champion: 1900

Harry Vardon's childhood in the Channel Isles gave him limited opportunity to play golf, and he would never have become one of the greatest of golfers but for the fact that his brother Tom went to England. By the age of 20 Vardon had played the game only two or three dozen times, usually on public holidays, but his brother was earning money at the game so Vardon took a club professional's job at a nine-hole course, Ripon in Yorkshire. He soon moved to Bury St Edmunds and came to fame as professional at Ganton. Vardon played his first Open in 1893 to no great effect, but he was fifth the following year. In 1895 he led after the first round, but finished in ninth place. Nevertheless, his time was at hand. Taylor was the biggest name in the land, having set out as an Englishman to beat the Scots at their own game, and had won the Open in 1894 and 1895. About a month before the 1896 Open, the Ganton members raised the money for a challenge match between the two. Vardon won by 8 and 6. And so to Muirfield for the Open. There he began with an 83, to trail Taylor by 6 strokes, and he was still 3 behind with a round to go. They

finished tied and Vardon went on to win the play-off over 36 holes. By the turn of the century his reputation was established as the greatest of the Great Triumvirate – the trio of himself, Braid and Taylor – for he had won twice again, and consecutively, in 1898 and 1899. In 1900 he was second. During an almost year-long tour of the US he won the Open there as well. Even more remarkably, he is said to have lost only one exhibition game in the time he was in the USA. Challenge matches and exhibition matches were very much a feature of the playing professional's year at that time. Tournaments, except on a local level, scarcely existed in either Britain or America, and a man's reputation rested squarely on what he did in the Open Championships and in matches. Vardon was second in the 1901 Open and again the following year when the winner, Sandy Herd, used a wound-rubber ball for the first time – only one was available. In 1903 he was champion again, this time with his brother Tom second, but 6 strokes behind. This period, 1896 to 1903, saw Vardon at his greatest. Thereafter he suffered from tuberculosis, and some have traced the decline in his putting to that cause. In later years Vardon's putting was to seem bad enough to make it seem impossible that a man so afflicted could be a major golfer. Gene Sarazen, seeing him in the 1920s, thought him the worst putter he had ever seen, and said: 'He didn't three-putt, he four-putted.' However, this was Vardon in decline, and suffering from what today would be called the twitch, but which he referred to as 'the jumps'. He recommended putting in the dark as a cure. Vardon was probably as good a putter as anyone in his best years and, until past 50, remained a good long and medium-length putter; but after the turn of the century he became less sure on the short ones. Notwithstanding, even during his first 1896 win The Times was moved to comment: 'In putting he seemed very weak.' In any case it was not Vardon's putting method that demanded attention, but his play through the green. Technically he was one of the game's great innovators. When he came to prominence the ideal swing was long, with a tendency to flatness, and the aim to hit a low ball. Vardon showed that an upright swing and a high ball worked as well and, when he became the great player of his era, he was also the model that others copied. At his first appearances it was thought there was too much of a 'lift' in the backswing but either this was modified or the universal adulation his success aroused caused this to be seen as the norm. Expert and spectator opinion alike was that this was the most graceful and easy swing that golf had yet seen. It was achieved by means of a very full shoulder turn but, at variance with modern methods, an equally full hip turn so that at the top of the backswing Vardon's back was square to the hole, and in effect he swung around a right leg that was as straight as a post. Of course, the Vardon grip in name derives from him, though he was not the originator – probably Johnny Laidlay, a gifted amateur, was, and J.H. Taylor was winning Opens with the overlapping little finger before Vardon arrived. But it was Vardon who was imitated. Earlier the majority had played with all fingers on the club, sometimes with a small gap between the two hands, and the shaft, particularly with the right hand, was held in the palm. Vardon believed that the club should be held firmly (very easy for him as he had enormous hands) but that the right-hand grip should relax on the backswing to allow free wrist movement at the top of the swing. He had a

Harry Vardon

moderately flying right elbow and a bent left arm on the backswing. Taylor called the result 'the finest and most finished golfer that the game has ever produced'. During his 1903 Open win Vardon had felt so ill that he believed he would not be able to finish, and shortly afterwards entered a sanatorium where he was to spend further time in the ensuing years. However, he continued to play golf, although far less effectively. From 1904 to 1910 he failed to win the Open, third in 1906 being his best placing, but he continued to feature quite strongly in each championship. In 1911, in a very close-fought championship, he led after three rounds but faltered to an 80 in his last round – still good enough to tie with the Frenchman Arnaud Massy. Vardon was champion again when Massy conceded on the 35th hole of the play-off. The following year he was second to Ted Ray, after he had closed with the very good score of 71, and in 1913 there came the dramatic three-way play-off at Brookline for the US Open between Ray, Vardon and the young American, Francis Ouimet, which the last won. The 1914 Open was played as war loomed, shortly after the assassination of the Archduke Ferdinand at Sarajevo. At Prestwick Vardon won by 3 strokes over J.H. Taylor to become the first man to win the Open six times – and still the only one, a record threatened in modern times only by the dominance of Peter Thomson in the 1950s. When the war ended Vardon was approaching 50 and did not feature again in the British Open except for eighth place in 1922. His last real stand came in the 1920 US Open at Inverness. He began 74, 73, 71, to lead Ted Ray by 2 strokes, and a representative of the new generation, Leo Diegel of the USA, by 1. In the final round he played steadily to the turn and after a birdie on the 11th, 41 strokes for the rest of the round would have seen him champion. But then a gale rose, strong enough for Vardon to need four strokes to reach the next green. The shots slipped away fast as he next missed a short putt and then three-putted three greens in a row, followed by a shot into a brook later. He finished in 78, a score which did not compare badly with most of those in contention but good enough only for joint second place behind winner Ted Ray. Beside his swing the feature of Vardon's play that was most noted was accuracy. There was the often-repeated story that he could not play the same course twice in a day because he would find himself in the divots he had taken in his morning round (a story spoiled by the fact that Vardon did not take divots, preferring to shave the turf). All his contemporaries agreed that he seldom missed fairways and was outstanding with his fairway woods. Today, as the majority of players hit irons into the par 5s, such excellence would count for little, but in Vardon's time it would be normal to be playing a wood for the second shot at holes over, say, 350 yards. In effect the brassie became an approaching club. Vardon was said to be able to fade his shots in consistently to a few feet from the flag. In view of Harry Vardon's consistency and accuracy it is only appropriate that in both Britain and Europe a Vardon Trophy should be awarded for just that: the year's lowest stroke average.

VARDON, Tom — England

b. Grouville, Jersey 1872

Although Tom Vardon's deeds were overshadowed by his brother Harry's to the extent that he is seldom mentioned, he was a good player. In 1903 he finished second in the Open, behind his brother;

Tom Vardon

was fourth the following year, this time a stroke in front; and came joint third in 1907. Perhaps his outstanding feat was to reach the final of the 1905 PGA Matchplay, where he was beaten by James Braid.

VAUGHAN, David — Wales

b. St Helens 1948

David Vaughan turned professional in 1965, and in 1971 won the Under 23 title. He was in the European Tour Top 60 from 1971 to 1975, and had an extremely consistent year in 1972 to finish 11th in the Order of Merit. He was third in the Benson and Hedges that year, but perhaps his finest performance was his joint seventh in the 1972 Open, when he finished with rounds of 70, 69. He has represented Wales, and in the 1980 World Cup led after the first round.

WAITES, Brian — England

b. Bolton 1940

Brian Waites is very much an oddity in European tournament golf: he did not became a substantial money-winner until he had reached an age at which most golfers are thinking of retiring. From 1966 to 1973 he won less than £3,000 from tournaments. He was a club professional making occasional appearances and not really feeling he was good enough to compete full-time. For a few years thereafter he continued in the same way, and did not make the Top 60 until 1977; then in 1978 he won the Tournament Players' Championship and was 13th in the Order of Merit. In 1979 he won the Kenya and Mufulira Opens and was 20th in the Order of Merit, his best performance in Europe coming in the Tournament Players' Championship, in which he came home second behind Michael King. He achieved the same result in this event in 1981 when, after a last-round 62 from Brian Barnes, he lost the play-off to him on the fourth extra hole. He just missed a Ryder Cup place, to go with his PGA Cup appearances in 1973, 1974, 1975, 1976 and 1979 against the USA, but he finished in 11th Order of Merit position. In 1982 he won twice in Zambia and on the European Tour won the Car Care Plan International at Moor Allerton, finishing 14th on the money list. It was his good form in the PGA Cup matches that mainly convinced Waites that he had the game to compete in tournament golf full-time; but he still retains the security of his club job, which he has held since 1969 at Hollinwell. A very fast backswing is a feature of Waites's game, as is his straight driving; he is also a very reliable short putter.

Africa wins 4 (1979–82)
Europe wins 2 (1978–82)
Europe money £142,754 (1966–82) (26th all-time)

WALKER, Carol Michelle   England
b. Alwoodley 1952

One of few British players to qualify to play the US Tour, Mickey Walker had her best US season in 1976 when she finished 42nd in the rankings with $15,011 and came close to a tournament win, her scores of 69, 70, 74 in the Jerry Lewis Muscular Dystrophy Classic leaving her tied with Sandra Palmer, JoAnne Carner and Mary Lou Crocker. Sandra Palmer won the play-off. She had originally qualified for the Tour in 1974 but with winnings of only $838 during the season had to re-qualify and did so, leading the qualifiers by 9 strokes. She now plays the British WPGA Tour, is a leading player and has won some tournaments; but she has not capitalized on the brilliant promise of earlier years. The best player in Britain and a potential world beater in the early 1970s, she lost her game and has yet fully to regain it. She won the 1980 and 1981 WPGA Matchplay and the 1982 Sunningdale foursomes, and was second in the 1979 British Ladies' Open. Mickey Walker was a girl international from 1969 to 1971, and in 1970 was runner-up in the English Girls' title and also in the British Girls'. The following year, at 18 years 6 months, she became the youngest winner in modern times of the British Ladies', beating Beverly Huke, herself only 20 at the time. That same year she won the French Open Under 22 Championship. Her achievements in 1972 were at an even higher level. She again won the British Ladies', this time facing Claudine Cros in the final, was second in the British Ladies' Strokeplay and won the Hovis Ladies'. Internationally she took the Portuguese Ladies' and the Costa del Sol tournament and in America won the Trans-Mississippi, by this victory becoming the first British player to win a major US title since Pam Barton won the US Women's Amateur in 1936. In the Curtis Cup she showed she was fit to rank among the best in the world when with Mary McKenna she won in both foursomes, and in singles halved with Laura Baugh and beat Jane Bastanchury Booth. She was Daks Woman

Golfer of the Year and won the Golf Writers' Trophy. The following year, Mickey Walker took the English Ladies' yet again, beating Carol Le Feuvre by 6 and 5 in the final, the Avia Foursomes, Spanish Ladies' and was runner-up for the British Ladies'. In the late summer she turned professional.

WALKER, James   Scotland
b. Bartonholm 1921

Jimmy Walker won the Scottish Amateur in 1961 and the same year reached the final of the British Amateur, where he was defeated 6 and 4 at Turnberry by Michael Bonallack. He played in the Walker Cup that year; he had previously been selected in 1959 but had to withdraw after a car crash. He lost both his matches. He got to the semifinals of the 1960 British Amateur. Walker was a Scottish international from 1954 to 1963, and won the West of Scotland title in 1954.

WALKER, Maureen (later Richmond)   Scotland
b. Kilmacolm 1955

A girl international from 1969 to 1973, Maureen Walker won the Scottish Girls' title three times in 1970, 1971 and 1973, and the British Girls' in 1972. She was a Scottish international from 1972 to 1978 and played in the 1974 Curtis Cup, winning in foursomes and singles the first day and losing in both the second. She was selected for the 1974 World Team Championship but was unable to accept because of studies.

WARD, Angela: see Bonallack

WARD, Charles Harold   England
b. Birmingham 1911

When Charlie Ward won the *Daily Mail* Victory tournament at St Andrews in 1945 it was both his first major victory and the first post-war event. The odd repercussion was that he was late back to his RAF camp at Wallingford, and having been busy winning a golf tournament was not taken as an excuse: he was confined to barracks as a punishment! He was one of the leading British players from that time until the early 1950s and won the Vardon Trophy twice, in 1948 and 1949. Otherwise his most notable victory was in the 1949 Dunlop Masters. He won ten titles in all, a considerable achievement in days when there were relatively few tournaments annually. He had a good record in the Open Championship for a few years after the war, being joint fourth in 1946, sixth the following year, joint third in 1948, fourth in 1949 and third in 1951. He played in the Ryder Cup team from 1947 to 1951 but with little success. He won the Seniors in 1965, losing to Snead for the world title. Charlie Ward was short and lacked power, but made up for his lack of length off the tee by concentrated short-game practice. He was particularly good with the wedge from 50 yards in and also, unusually, a specialist at chipping with a 4-iron.

GB wins 10 (1945–56)

WATSON, Charlotte: see Beddows

WAY, Paul   England
b. 1963

A Walker Cup player in 1981, Paul Way won his place by virtue of his victory in the English Strokeplay event. He turned professional towards the end of the year and was eighth in the Cacharel World Under 25 Championship. In his first full European season he proved himself to have a highly promising future, making the Top 60 with ease in 30th place and winning the Dutch Open after a fine finish of 67, 65.

Europe wins 1 (1982)
Europe money £17,250 (1982)

WEETMAN, Harry   England
b. Oswestry 1920; d. 1972

Harry Weetman was a major figure on the British golf scene from the late 1940s to the early 1960s, attracting much attention because of his ferocious hitting, which was balanced by a natural and excellent putting stroke. Together they brought him many tournament successes. He was particularly formidable in matchplay, winning the PGA Championship in 1951 and 1958 and being beaten finalist in 1956, 1959 and 1960. Partly on the strength of this performance he was chosen for the Ryder Cup team for every match from 1951 to 1963. In the series he had a fairly poor record, never being in the winning pair in foursomes or fourballs; but he had a particularly famous victory in one singles when, at Wentworth in 1953, he stood 4 down with six to play against the most feared

Harry Weetman

opponent on the US team, Sam Snead, yet won by 1 up. Snead contributed to his own defeat by hitting into trees; it was his only Ryder Cup loss in singles. Not until his last match in 1963 did Weetman win another singles, when he beat Julius Boros but lost to him later in the second singles match. In strokeplay events he was twice a winner of the Dunlop Masters, in 1952 and 1958; won the Vardon Trophy for low stroke average in 1952 and 1956; and four times took the Penfold tournament. He was for long a leading British hope in the Open, his best results being sixth in 1951 and 1964 and fifth in 1955. Not only his play but his sometimes fiery temperament attracted publicity, as when he declared he would not play again under the captaincy of Dai Rees, when dropped for the 1957 Ryder Cup singles (but later he did!). At various times he was warned, fined and suspended by the PGA. He still holds the record for the lowest round on a course over 6,000 yards in Britain, with a 58 over Croham Hurst in 1956. Tragically, he was killed in a car accident in 1972.

WETHERED, Joyce (later Heathcoat-Amory)　　England

b. 1901

Joyce Wethered is one of a considerable number of women golfers who have much benefited from playing with their brothers. It seems to have the effect that the ladies become used as a matter of course to seeing a golf ball struck hard and try to emulate, rather than make just a gentle swing at the ball – as many women club golfers do to this day. In Joyce's case she was taught by her brother Roger from the age of 17 during family holidays at Royal Dornoch and, as he was a top amateur, had the experience of playing often with good men players. She later felt that, having been used to being outdriven (though not outplayed), play against women seemed easier. In 1920 she decided to enter the English Championship at Sheringham 'just for fun' and to keep a friend company, expecting to get one enjoyable round of golf out of the experience. However, round succeeded round and eventually she found herself in the final against Cecil Leitch, unquestionably the finest British player at that time, it seemed, with the recent record of having won the British, French and English titles in 1914 and retaining each when they were next held after World War I. At 29, she was at her peak, while Joyce Wethered was 19. At lunch Cecil Leitch had established a comfortable 4-up lead, and then seemed to put the match beyond doubt by winning the first two holes after lunch. But then came a swing: Joyce Wethered produced a string of 3s and went into the lead with four holes to go, winning 2 and 1. That was probably the closest Joyce Wethered came to losing any match in the English

Joyce Wethered

Championship. She was to play in the event four times more, and in the finals her highest winning margin was 12 and 11 and the lowest 7 and 6. Her record shows that between 1920 and 1924 she played 33 matches and won them all. Her record in the British Amateur Championship was scarcely inferior. In 1921 she reached the final but lost to Cecil Leitch (the same happened in the French equivalent that year). Thereafter she crushed Cecil Leitch by 9 and 7 in the 1922 final, lost in the semi-finals the following year and again won in 1924 and 1925, in the latter year defeating Cecil Leitch in a closely fought final on the first extra hole. Joyce Wethered then retired from championship golf but in 1929 returned, mainly because the venue was St Andrews and she wished to play there. Again she reached the final, where her opponent was the greatest America had to offer, Glenna Collett. It was indeed a historic match, establishing who was the best player in the world. Glenna went to the turn in 34 to be 5 up but was pulled back to a 2-up lead by lunch, after which Joyce Wethered played at her finest and not only pulled back but led by 4 up. Glenna Collett then produced a couple of 3s to halve the margin, but in the end lost by 3 and 1. This was Joyce Wethered's last entry in a British Amateur; her final record was: matches played 38, won 36. She never thereafter contested another championship, though she played an international against France in 1931 and in the 1932 Curtis Cup. Like Jones, she had retired with no more worlds left to conquer. She found the strain considerable, and preferred to play golf for fun rather than glory anyway. She did, however, continue to play in the Worplesdon Mixed Foursomes for many years and won the event eight times between 1922 and 1936 with seven different partners; in 1948 she brought her husband, not a player of the highest calibre, through to the final. In 1935, times being hard, she forfeited her amateur status by playing an exhibition tour in the US, during which the other players were usually Gene Sarazen, Horton Smith and Babe Didrikson. The main interest was in seeing how Joyce compared with the long-hitting Babe. She is said to have outscored her by several strokes a round, and in 52 matches broke course records 18 times. Undoubtedly the overall standard of women's golf has risen enormously since World War II, particularly under the competitive influence of the US Tour, but two supreme players and judges, Bobby Jones and Henry Cotton, have rated her highly enough not to speculate on whether or not she was the best woman golfer ever, but to suggest that she might have been the best of either sex. Jones once commented that he had never felt so outclassed as after a round with her, and Cotton examined her game in some detail. He concluded that her length off the tee was comparable to a scratch male player; her fairway woods were as straight as the short irons of most professionals; her chipping and putting exemplary; and the strongest feature of her game was the pitch and run with mid irons. He felt she had superb touch and that Harry Vardon was the only player who equalled her in straightness.

WETHERED, Roger Henry   England
b. Maldon 1899

One of the best known British amateurs of the 1920s and 1930s, Roger Wethered reached his greatest achievement in tying for the 1921 British Open with Jock Hutchison at St Andrews. There followed the famous story that Wethered professed doubt as to whether he could stay for the 36-hole play-off: he had promised to turn out for his village cricket team. He was persuaded that playing for the Open title would justify his gaffe of not appearing for his village, but was then beaten 159–150. In the championship proper he had begun 78, 75, which put him not far behind the leaders, but closed with fine rounds of 72, 71 (both new St Andrews amateur records), against Hutchison's 79, 70. In one round, having walked up the fairway to study the line of a shot, he trod on his ball on returning for a 1-stroke penalty. It is said that, but for that misfortune, he would have won the Open. This, of course, is highly speculative, for the incident may even have made him play with increased determination. In 1923 he won the British Amateur by a comfortable margin. He reached the finals in 1928, losing to Phil Perkins; and again in 1930, where he met Bobby Jones who then took the first leg of his Grand Slam. Roger Wethered was frequently an erratic driver and this was the main reason why he did not achieve other comparable successes, for his iron play was very highly rated and he was also a good putter. He represented Great Britain against the USA in 1921, 1922, 1923, 1926, 1930 and 1934 and was an England international every year from 1922 to 1930. He won the President's Putter six times, and four other major amateur events, and was elected captain of the R & A in 1946. His sister is the great Joyce Wethered.

WHITCOMBE, Charles Albert   England
b. Burnham 1895; d. 1981

One of a trio of talented golfing brothers, Charles was considered the best of them by most of his contemporaries although, unlike Reg, he did not win the Open Championship. Dai Rees went further than this, judging him to be the straightest hitter he had seen – and he had seen players from 1935 or so to the present day. Rees also rated him extremely high as a striker. Charles Whitcombe had a very long career. He played in the Open before World War I, and also qualified for the Matchplay Championship at that time. Between the wars he frequently contended for the Open, coming in the top 6 six times between 1922 and 1937, third in 1935 being his best finish. His highest tournament achievements were his two victories in the PGA Matchplay in 1928 and 1930 and, perhaps, the 1930 Irish Open. In all from 1924 to 1939 he won nine major tournaments, and also the West of England Professional in 1921, 1924 and 1929. He played in every Ryder Cup team from 1927 to 1937, having a 50% success rate, and was captain in 1935 and 1937 and non-playing captain in 1947. He won the first Vardon Trophy for low stroke average, presented in the year of Harry Vardon's death, 1937. This outstanding player had only one weak feature in his game: unreliable putting.

Roger Wethered

WHITCOMBE, Ernest Edward   England
b. West Flagg 1913

The son of one of the Whitcombe brothers, E.R., Ernest Edward turned professional in 1928 but was prevented from reaching a higher standard by lack of power, although he was an excellent putter. His best achievement was reaching the final of the 1938 Matchplay Championship, where he lost to Dai Rees. He also won the East Anglian Open three times between 1953 and 1964.

WHITCOMBE, Ernest R.   England
b. Burnham 1890; d. 1971

Like his brother Charles, Ernest played in both the Open and Matchplay before World War I. He won the Matchplay in 1924 and again reached the final in 1936, when he established a commanding lead over Dai Rees but still lost. Rees thus beat father and son (E.E.) in finals a couple of years apart. Whitcombe came once very close indeed to an Open Championship. In 1924 Walter Hagen had to match par over the closing holes at Hoylake to win, and few thought he would be able to do it. Ernest Whitcombe finished second, 1 behind Hagen but 2 ahead of Macdonald Smith. He figured again in 1927, finishing joint fourth but 8 behind Bobby Jones, who dominated the championship that year from start to finish. Ernest won the Irish and Dutch Opens in 1928 and the 1930 French Open. He was also a Ryder Cup choice in 1926, 1929, 1931 and 1935. In 1935 he won in foursomes against Olin Dutra and Ky Laffoon. His partner was his brother Charles, the only time brothers have played together in a Ryder Cup match.

WHITCOMBE, Reginald Arthur   England
b. Burnham 1898; d. 1958

One of the Whitcombe brothers, Reg was for most of his career considered the inferior of Charles, but he reached his peak in the late 1930s, when about 40. In 1937 he led the Carnoustie Open with a round to go but was overhauled by Henry Cotton, and finished second. In 1938, in fine weather, he began at Royal St George's with two 71s. On the final day the gales were of legendary force. J.J. Busson, who had led with 71, 69, soared to 83, 80, yet this was still good enough for a tie for fourth place. Reg Whitcombe had 75, 78 and was Open Champion by 2 strokes. The following year he tied

for third place. He never played in a Ryder Cup team but was chosen for the 1939 event, not played because of the outbreak of World War II. Among other successes Reg won the 1936 Irish Open and the West of England title seven times. He later became professional at Parkstone in Dorset.

WHITE, Jack   Scotland
b. Pefferside, North Berwick 1873; d. 1949

Jack White enjoyed a good run in the Open Championship at the turn of the century. He was runner-up to Harry Vardon in 1899, fourth in 1900, sixth in 1901 and third behind the Vardon brothers in 1903. Eventually he won at Sandwich in 1904. He accomplished the rare feat of scoring lower in each round – 80, 75, 72, 69 – to win by 1 stroke from James Braid and J.H. Taylor, one of only three players to intrude on the dominance of the Great Triumvirate between 1898 and 1911. White's score of 296 was the first time 300 had been broken for the four rounds and remained a record until Braid's 291 in 1908. Jack White was a nephew of Ben Sayers and was professional at Sunningdale for a quarter of a century. He played eight times for Scotland.

WHITE, Ronald James   England
b. Wallasey 1921

At the age of 17 Ronnie White won the Carris Trophy and went on to captain the England Boys' team, on which he played from 1936 to 1938. Then came World War II. After it he was for a short while incomparably the finest English amateur but, as a busy solicitor, was fairly soon lost to competitive golf at a high level. It is interesting to wonder what he might have achieved as a full-time professional. He won the English Amateur in 1949 and was runner-up in 1953 to Gerald Micklem. He took the English Strokeplay in 1950 and 1951. In 1961, he was top amateur in the Open; by that time it had become unusual for him to appear at that level. He made several Walker Cup appearances from 1947, in which year he won in both foursomes and singles. In 1949 he won his foursomes in partnership with Joe Carr and went on to defeat Willie Turnesa by 4 and 3 in the top singles. Those two points were the only ones secured by the British team! In 1951 he halved in the foursomes and again took his singles; in 1953 he at last lost a match, in foursomes, while again winning his singles against Dick Chapman. In 1955 he lost a singles, to Harvie

Ward, a meeting of two giants of the amateur game. Ronnie won the R & A British Seniors in 1978 and 1979. He is the author of *Golf as I Play It*.

WHITEHEAD, Ross   England
b. Sutton 1934

Ross Whitehead reached the final of the 1962 Matchplay Championship, where he was beaten by Eric Brown. His major tournament success was in the 1972 John Player Trophy. He was also twice in winning pairings of the Sunningdale Foursomes, and once in the Wentworth. He was British Assistants' winner in 1962.

WHITLOCK, Susan: see Hedges

WILCOCK, Peter   England
b. St Annes on the Sea 1945

Peter Wilcock reached his peak in the early 1970s and was in the top 35 from 1970 to 1973; his best years were the last two, when he was 17th and 16th in the Order of Merit. He won the 1972 Italian BP Open, and in 1973 was joint second in the Martini and reached the semi-final stages of the Matchplay. He represented England in the World Cup that year. Wilcock accomplished the odd and extremely rare feat of having two holes in one during the 1974 Penfold tournament.

WILL, George Duncan   Scotland
b. Ladybank 1937

George Will was Scottish Boys' Champion in 1955 and took the British title two years later, along with the Fife Amateur and the Gleneagles-Saxone. He then turned professional and the following year, 1958, won the Northern Open. During National Service he twice won the Army Championship. Will played full-time tournament golf from 1960 and finished six times in the top 20 of the Order of Merit between 1964 and 1971, with a best placing of fifth in 1964. He himself thought that his greatest problem was to be able to put four good rounds of golf together and that this failing limited his tournament successes; nevertheless he won the 1964 Smart Weston and the 1965 Esso Golden, among others. He was chosen for the Ryder Cup side in 1963, 1965 and 1967, and represented Scotland in the World Cup three times. In the 1968 Open he had a particularly odd round of 80 at

Carnoustie: out in 33, back in 47! In more recent years Will has captained the PGA Cup team. He is known as a grower of prize roses.

WILSON, Enid   England
b. Stonebroom 1910

All the highest achievements of Enid Wilson were packed into the late 1920s and early 1930s. She first attracted attention when she took the 1925 British Girls'. She was runner-up in the 1927 English Ladies' before taking her first national title in the same event the following year; she won again in 1930 – by 12 and 11 in the final. Enid Wilson had reached the semi-final of the British Ladies' in 1927, 1928 and 1930 but in 1931 she won, then in the next two years joined Lady Margaret Scott and Cecil Leitch as the only players to win it three times consecutively. Her winning margins in each final were conclusive. She also made serious attempts to add the US Championship. She reached the semi-final in 1931 and in 1933 was qualifying medallist with 76, then the record, and again reached the semi-final, where she was put out by the eventual champion, Virginia van Wie. Enid Wilson was for very many years golf correspondent for the *Daily Telegraph*.

WOLSTENHOLME, Guy: see Australia & New Zealand

WOOD, Norman   Scotland
b. Prestonpans 1947

Norman Wood was a golfer who turned professional in 1965 and made steady progress to be a player of some significance and a Ryder Cup choice. Then his form fell away. His most notable achievement came in 1972: a win in the Italian Open by 2 strokes at Villa d'Este with rounds of 65, 69, 68, 69. It was a breakthrough that he was unable in the end to consolidate. In 1973 he tied for the Singapore Open but lost the play-off to Ben Arda. However, he won the Jamaican Open that year. In 1974 he finished second in the Australian Open to Gary Player. Earlier in his career he had won the Scottish Assistants' in 1968 and the Scottish Coca-Cola Tournament in 1969 and 1970. He was in the Top 60 of the Order of Merit from 1971 to 1976, and in 1975 achieved his best placing at 18th. That year he was in the Scotland World Cup pair and the

Ryder Cup, beating Lee Trevino in the singles. He later moved to Barbados and is now the professional at the Royal Guernsey club.

Europe wins 1 (1972)
Overseas wins 1 (1973)

WOOSNAM, Ian   Wales
b. 1958

By the end of the 1981 season in Europe this 5-foot 4-inch, stocky and powerful young golfer stood 104th on the money list. He had won the 1979 Under 23 Matchplay and been chosen for his country in the 1980 World Cup (but Wales has a very limited pool of players to choose from). He then went off to that very useful school for aspiring players, the Safari Circuit in Africa, and finished third in the money list. He had been fourth in the Kalahari Classic, second in the Ivory Coast Open and had lost a play-off for the Nigerian Open. But such a measure of success in Africa is by no means always – or even often – followed by comparable success on the more competitive European Tour. However, Ian Woosnam had good early-season results in 1982, finishing joint second in the Italian Open and later coming fourth in the Dutch Open – thanks to an old driver he picked up for £17. He really attracted attention during the Benson and Hedges at Fulford, York, when he had four 71s, finishing joint second. He had birdied the 16th and 17th in his last round to stand on the last tee with

Ian Woosnam

Greg Norman, level with Graham Marsh and Bob Charles, both needing to hit the last green, a par 5 but in range, in two. Norman did, while Woosnam pushed his second into the grandstand and could not get down in two from the free-drop zone. The following week he was at Crans-sur-Sierre for the Swiss Open and began with a pair of 68s followed by a 66, which led the American Matt Runge by 2 strokes. Bill Longmuir then put in a final 66 to catch Woosnam's 70, but the Welshman won the play-off for his first major tournament victory. It brought his August winnings to about £20,000 and pushed him into the top 10 in the money list. Late in the season he came second in the Spanish Open and won the World Under 25 by 5 strokes. In 1982 he won £38,820 and was eighth on the money list. Woosnam has built a record of solid achievement in a very short period of time, and is regarded as one of the best prospects in Europe.

Europe wins 1 (1982)

WRIGHT, Janette Sneddon (née Robertson)
                                                  Scotland
b. Glasgow 1935

Winner of the British Girls' in 1950, Janette Wright was to be Scottish Champion in three different decades, taking the event from 1959 to 1961 and in 1973; she was also runner-up in 1958. She appeared many times for Scotland between 1952 and 1973 and was four times a Curtis Cup choice between 1954 and 1960. Among other successes she won the Kayser-Bondor Foursomes twice and the Worplesdon once. She took the Lanarkshire championship six times consecutively from 1954 to 1959, the West of Scotland Ladies' three times and the North on one occasion. Her daughter Pamela is a promising player.

WRIGHT, Nancy (née Cook)   Wales
b. Hale 1917

A Welsh international in five different decades, her first appearance was in 1938 and her last in 1973. She won the Welsh Ladies' in 1953, 1954, 1955, 1958, 1965 and 1967, and was four times runner-up. She played in the 1964 World Team Championship. Runner-up to the same opponent four years consecutively for the Caernarvonshire and Anglesey Ladies' from 1949 to 1952, she won the event eight times and won the Caernarvonshire District 17 times.

EUROPE

ABREU, Francisco   Spain

b. Santa Cruz, Tenerife 1943

'Tito' Abreu may well be the only professional golfer of substance who was also a wrestling champion: he won the Greco-Roman championships of the Canary Isles. Not surprisingly, Abreu is a very powerful golfer indeed, but his achievements have been hindered by a lack of ambition, for he has largely confined himself to continental European golf. Here he has had occasional successes during the period when he was reckoned to be the longest hitter in Europe. In 1973 he took the German Open by 2 strokes from Dale Hayes and was 12 under par in doing so. Three years later he was 13 under and took the Madrid Open by a highly unusual 9 strokes. Competing seldom in Britain, he was nevertheless in the Top 60 each year but one between 1973 and 1979. Easily his best position came in 1977, when he was ninth.

Europe wins 2 (1973–6)
Europe money £49,115 (1971–80)

ADO, Jean-Baptiste   France

b. 1913

This massive and friendly Basque became more famous for his personality and his past than for his golfing achievements. For the record, he was winner of the French Native Professional title in 1951, but what is remembered is a gentle man walking the fairways of the 1950s, rolling his own cigarettes as he went. Gentle? On the golf course, yes; but as a member of the French Resistance there are stories of his having strangled Germans with his bare hands. After his arrest during the war he was shot by a firing squad and left for dead. His jaw was broken and several teeth were shot out but he survived. In common with several other long hitters he preferred using a woman's driver – in this case a Jean Donald model – and his style was to take a great lunging swing at the ball. He won little money in golf and is said to have gambled away whatever he won.

ANGELINI, Alfonso   Italy

b. 1918

Despite the loss of toes through frostbite on the Russian Front during World War II, Angelini established himself as the best Italian golfer for many years, winning the Italian Native Championship 12 times between 1947 and 1969. This portly but handsome man owed a great deal to an excellent putting stroke. Angelini never won his own Open, though once tying and losing the play-off to Ugo Grappasonni, but did take five other national Opens. He was also second in the Seniors in 1972. He used frequently to play with the wife of ex-King Leopold of the Belgians, the Princesse de Rethy, who would encourage him by giving him different amounts of money for various scores. On one occasion Alfonso asked what a 64 would be worth. An Alfa Romeo, said the Princess. He got it.

BALBUENA, Salvador   Spain

b. Torremolinos 1949; d. 1979

Balbuena developed great length from a short backswing. In 1976 he took his first important event, the Portuguese Open, and was second in the French Open that year. In 1977 he won the Moroccan Grand Prix against top-class opposition, though in a restricted field. He was in the European Top 60 from 1976 to 1978, with a best placing of 20th in 1976, a year in which he represented continental Europe against Britain in the Hennessy Cup. He died suddenly on the eve of a tournament in 1979. Most of his fellow Spaniards withdrew in tribute; but, more imaginatively, Severiano Ballesteros continued and donated his prize money to Balbuena's widow.

BALLESTEROS, Manuel   Spain

b. Pedrena 1949

Elder brother of Severiano, Manuel has now been eclipsed by him; yet at one time it was thought that the younger brother 'would never be as good'. Manuel turned professional in 1967, but he has yet to win an important tournament. However, he has several times finished well in the Order of Merit: 20th in 1972, 25th in 1975, 31st in 1976 and 21st in 1978. His best performances have been to lead the 1975 PGA most of the way (Arnold Palmer surged through to win in the last round) and to record rounds of 66, 67, 65 to start the Swiss Open before fading to a 73 and second place in 1971. In 1974 he tied with Peter Oosterhuis for the El Paraiso Open and lost the play-off. He has also represented Europe against Great Britain.

Europe money £68,941 (1971–82) (54th all-time)

BALLESTEROS, Severiano   Spain

b. Pedrena 1957

Severiano is nephew of the once leading Spaniard Ramon Sota, which might have been taken as a sign of things to come. He arrived at overnight stardom

Seve Ballesteros

on the best stage the world of golf has to offer: the British Open Championship. The year was 1976, the place Royal Birkdale. He was just 19 years old. He began with a 69, and not a few were asking who he was. He followed with another, and by now there was some measure of agreement as to how his name should be pronounced. There followed a 73, and the teenager was going into the last round with a lead of two over Johnny Miller, with Nicklaus five shots in arrears. Ballesteros held his own for the early holes of the final round, but from the 6th onwards began to slip. After eleven holes he was 5 behind and out of it. It had begun to seem that Ballesteros would now finish no better than about fifth, but he finished in a flourish of birdies and even an eagle, at the last playing a deft chip and run and holing a putt which enabled him to tie with Nicklaus for second place. Although an overnight success, he had already achieved a little before this Open: 26th in the 1975 Order of Merit and in 1976 a fifth place in the Portuguese Open, sixth in the Spanish, eighth in the French. Now he began to believe he was a major golfer. In the Scandinavian Open he was third after a last-round 66 and again third the following week in the Swiss. Ten days later at Zandvoort he took his first tournament, the Dutch Open, and became the youngest player to win a European Tour event. A week later and he was third in the German Open. In the late autumn he took the Lancôme at St-Nom-la-Bretèche by 1 from Palmer, having five birdies on the last nine to do so. He had ended the European season with the Vardon Trophy and a money-winning record for the European circuit. In America, teamed with Manuel Pinero, he won the World Cup for Spain. In 1977 he widened his range internationally, taking six events, three in Europe, one in New Zealand and two in Japan, including the Open, a feat he was to repeat the following year when he won seven events, including the Greater Greensboro', his first US win. In both years on the European Tour he was the undisputed number one. A much quieter year followed in 1979 with only two wins; but one of these was the British Open, in which he became the first player from the continent of Europe to win for 72 years. The manner of that victory was memorable. Before play began at Lytham, the experts were unanimous that at least one fancied player, Ballesteros, had no chance. The rough at Royal Lytham was testing enough to subdue Severiano, who had a well-deserved reputation for being wild off the tee. He continued to be wild, hitting only a couple of fairways in the final two rounds and finding a host of bunkers. At the end of it all, he reckoned he had been down in two from sand no fewer than 15 times. He had opened with a 73 and followed with a 65. In this second round he was out in 33, but the last five holes into a north-westerly wind were felt to be crucial. True par for the day was 4,5,4,5,4. Ballesteros recorded 3,3,4,3,3. The next day, he had a 75 but, most importantly, lost no ground to Hale Irwin. With a round to go, Ballesteros was 2 behind Irwin, 1 ahead of Nicklaus and Mark James and 2 ahead of Rodger Davis and Ben Crenshaw. These seemed the players who would contest the final stages, and so it proved. Irwin was quickly accounted for as Ballesteros began 2,4 against Irwin's 3,6, and the year's US Open Champion came in eventually with a 78 in sixth place. He had perhaps been worn down by matching his meticulous play against the élan of the Spaniard. The last holes were a riotous progress as Ballesteros hit and surged eagerly after his ball. On the 13th he went for the green with his driver on this 339-yard hole but was bunkered. Down in two more, it was still a birdie. On the 16th, he found a car park, but sent his recovery to 15 feet and holed the putt. He had a 3-stroke advantage on Crenshaw and Nicklaus. After parring the next (again he was bunkered) almost anything would do as long as he didn't hit it far right. Severiano compromised and hooked it left, played short of the green with a 5-iron, ran it up to 3 feet and holed the putt. He was Open Champion by 3, and the youngest since Tom Morris. Americans had been a touch slighting about Severiano's abilities and possibly resentful of a man who would play only occasionally on the US Tour. In April 1980, he began the US Masters with a round of 66, which tied him for the lead, and then went 3 ahead with a second round of 69. A third-round 68 saw him 7 ahead, and the usually closely contested Masters was becoming a procession. After nine holes in the last round he was no less than 10 ahead. Ballesteros was putting some of this down to a new swing. It was a little shorter and flatter, there was less wrist break and the ball went in more predictable directions. Be that as it may, Ballesteros's game suddenly came apart. He three-putted the 11th, took 5 on the par-3 12th after being in water and played a miserable iron shot to the 13th that again was in water. In three holes he had dropped 5 shots and Gilbert, Newton and Green were all playing excellent last rounds. Severiano then played the last five holes in 1 under par, to

finish in 72 and become the youngest Masters winner ever – and by 5 shots. He then returned to Europe and won three events in the season. This victory made Ballesteros the most marketable commodity in world golf and caused a somewhat troubled season for him in 1981. Under the rules of the European Tour, Ballesteros did not qualify to be paid appearance money, and with fewer restrictions elsewhere he stayed away from the European circuit for most of the season. In what remained after he came back, he returned the lowest stroke average at 69.62 and won £65,928. He was not selected for the Ryder Cup, mainly a political decision, though there were some who argued that Severiano was not a particularly good matchplayer. This claim was put to the test in the 1981 World Matchplay event at Wentworth. In his first match he despatched Hale Irwin by 6 and 4, and then he annihilated Greg Norman by 8 and 6. He then had to play Europe's number one for the year, Bernhard Langer. The 'Who's best in Europe' argument on this occasion went by 5 and 4 in the Spaniard's favour and gave him the title. In 1982 he won the Madrid and French Opens and finished equal third in the US Masters. Despite not being at his best he was still good enough to repeat his World Matchplay victory, first beating Clampett and Wadkins, and then Sandy Lyle in a close finish when he holed a 10-yard putt on the first extra hole.

Europe wins 20 (1976–82)
Europe national Opens 10 (1976–82)
Europe money £388,242 (1974–82) (1st all-time)
Japan wins 4 (1977–81)
Australasia wins 2 (1977–81)
US wins 2 (1978–80)
Africa wins 1 (1978)
World money $1,727,824 (1974–82) (20th all-time)

BARRIOS, Valentin   Spain
b. *Madrid 1942*

Beginning his sporting career as a bullfighter, Barrios later became one of the best continental European golfers of the late 1960s and early 1970s. He took first place in the Continental Order of Merit in 1967, 1969 and 1973, winning the 1971 Madrid and Bergamo Opens, the 1972 Algarve Open and the 1973 Lancia d'Oro. In this last year he was also second to Jacklin in the Italian Open and to Miller in the Lancôme. In 1972, with Angel Gallardo, he won the Nations Cup for Spain. A very strong man,

Barrios was one of the longest hitters in Europe and has hit a measured drive of 568 yards. However, this was as part of a publicity stunt for a new type of golf ball, and the fairway used was in fact an aircraft runway. He is now professional at Moraleja, Madrid.

BERNARDINI, Roberto　　　　Italy
b. *Rome 1944*

Only the second continental European to win a US Tour card, Bernardini won his national PGA in 1967, 1968, 1973 and 1975 and also the 1971 Italian BP Open. He was arguably the best Italian player for several years, but then, despite having both power and touch, he faded. He could have been the Ballesteros of Italy.

BEVIONE, Franco　　　　Italy
b. *1922*

The best Italian amateur for many years, Franco won the Italian Closed Amateur Championship twelve times between 1940 and 1971. He also took the Open three times and the Swiss and Scandinavian titles. The brother of Isa Goldschmid (née Bevione), he was also twice selected to represent Europe against Great Britain. Bevione lacked style but was a fierce competitor with nerves of steel.

BEVIONE, Isa:　see Goldschmid

BIELKE, Count Gustav Adolf　　　　Sweden
b. *1930*

As a junior the Count won the Junior national championships of his own country, and also of Belgium, Germany, Italy, Norway and France. He later won the Swedish Open Amateur in 1951, the Closed in 1956 and the Open Strokeplay in 1958 and 1961. He was 28 times an international from 1950 to 1965, and twice was chosen for his country in the World Cup and for Europe against Great Britain.

BOYER, Auguste　　　　France
b. *Cagnes-sur-Mer 1908*

Competing seldom in Britain, Auguste Boyer can be considered the leading continental European between the wars. Outstanding in the short game, he took 18 national Opens in this period.

BOYKIN, Gerda:　see North America

CALERO, Manuel　　　　Spain
b. *Barcelona 1952*

A Hennessy Cup player in 1978, 1980 and 1982, Calero has yet to win on the European Tour. He came closest in 1982 when he tied with Antonio Garrido for the inaugural Tunisian Open but lost the play-off. On that circuit he has improved considerably in the last few years, finishing 21st in the 1980 Order of Merit and 24th the following year. He was second in the 1980 Swiss Open after a closing 65. He had his best year to date in 1982 at 15th in the money list and winnings of almost £30,000, and was often challenging for the lead.

Europe money　£87,458 (1973–82) (42nd all-time)

CANIZARES, José Maria　　　　Spain
b. *Madrid 1947*

Since 1980, Canizares has been one of the most consistent achievers in European golf. He was seventh in the Order of Merit in 1980 and tenth in 1981. This level of performance made him one of the first Continental players to earn a Ryder Cup place in 1981. He first appeared on the European Tour in 1971 and secured his first win in the 1972 Lancia d'Oro. Despite this early success Canizares did not get into the Top 60 in Europe until 1974. Although he remained there securely for several years, he did not make a big splash until 1978 and the Swiss Open. In that event he concluded his second-round 67 with five consecutive birdies and the next day went out 4, 3, 2, 3, 3, 3, 2, 3, 4. That was 27, which equalled the nine-hole world record jointly held by Mike Souchak from the 1955 Texas Open and Andy North from the 1975 BC Open. Canizares had also set a new world record – including the previous day's concluding five – of 11 birdies in sequence plus an eagle for good measure. It is a record that could last longer than most. Despite this he did not win the event, falling to third place with a last-round 74, 10 strokes worse than he had managed as result of that dazzling sequence. In 1980 he won twice, and both, unlike the Lancia d'Oro, were major events, the Avis-Jersey Open and, late in the season, the Bob Hope British Classic. In 1981 he won again – the Italian Open. Of these wins, the Hope was his best: he started the last round 7 behind the leaders but a closing 64 won him the event when others faltered at the end. Another low score came in the 1982 Hennessy Cognac Cup, when he broke the Ferndown record with a 62. He has become an extremely consistent player, as he proved once again in the 1982 World Cup in which he formed one of the winning pair with Manuel Pinero.

Europe wins 3 (1980–81)
Europe money £159,380 (1971–82) (17th all-time)

CASERA, Aldo — Italy
b. San Remo 1920

Casera had a quick, agitated swing but was a superb striker of a golf ball except on the greens, where he became subject to the yips. He represented Italy in the Canada Cup and won the Italian Closed Professional title in 1948, 1949 and 1956. He also took the Italian Open in 1948 and the Swiss Open in 1950. He was for many years professional at Monza.

CHARBONNIER, Carole — Switzerland
b. Jadonville, Congo 1956

Carole Charbonnier won the Zambian Amateur title in 1972 and 1973 and then went on in 1975 to be Junior Champion of France, Spain and Switzerland. Later, in 1977, she won both the Open and Closed titles of Switzerland. She qualified for the US Tour in 1980 but ill health has impeded her progress. She was second in the 1982 Mary Kay Classic, 1 behind Sandra Spuzich, and won some $40,000 that year.

US money $44,988 (1980–82)

de la CHAUME, Simone Thion (later Lacoste) — France
b. Paris 1908

Thion de la Chaume was the first overseas player to win the British title, doing so in 1927, having been defeated in the semi-finals the previous year by Cecil Leitch. Three years earlier she had also been the first foreigner to win the Girls' event. She continued to be a dominant force in French women's golf up to World War II, taking the Closed title in 1929 and 1930 and again from 1936 to 1938 while she took her national Open title six times in 1926 beating Cecil Leitch and in 1927 winning the final by 15 and 14. She married French tennis champion René Lacoste, and their daughter

Catherine became a greater player than her mother. When she won the British title in 1969 this produced the only mother–daughter combination to have done so. Thion took part in a famous exhibition match in 1938 in which she, Joyce Wethered and Enid Wilson matched their best ball against Henry Cotton. He won.

CROS, Claudine (later Rubin) — France
b. Paris 1943

An early developer, Claudine Cros first won the French Ladies' Open Amateur at the age of 17 and remained one of the top trio – herself, Catherine Lacoste and Brigitte Varangot – for about a dozen years. She took the French title again in 1968 and was runner-up to Brigitte Varangot in 1961 and 1962. She won the French Closed in 1964 and 1965, beating Varangot this time in one of the finals and Lally St-Sauveur in the other. She was runner-up in 1962, 1963 and 1970, losing to Brigitte Varangot on each occasion. So far then Varangot had the edge, and the same was true in the British Ladies', in which Claudine twice was a finalist. In 1968 Varangot beat her on the 20th. In 1972, Michelle Walker beat her by 2 up. Claudine took the German title in 1961 and from 1964 to 1972 was a member of the French World Team Championship squad. On the winning team in 1964 with Lacoste and Varangot, she had a 68 in 1972 to equal the lowest recorded up to that time. A little later she played for a time as a professional in Japan in order to raise the level of her game. It was certainly a boost for women's golf to have three French players active at the same time. Claudine Cros was especially attractive, her simple, rhythmic style and her elegance on and off the course being a joy to watch. She came from a golfing family and her brother Patrick was an excellent player, winning the French Amateur in 1963 and the Closed title three years running, from 1963 to 1965. Another brother, Jean-Pierre, won the Closed title in 1959.

CROS, Patrick — France
b. 1939

The famous brother of the famous Claudine Cros, Patrick three times won the French National Amateur Championship – from 1963 to 1965. He was also twice runner-up. He won the French Amateur in 1963 and was runner-up in 1966.

DALLEMAGNE, Marcel — France
b. Port Marly 1898

The best French golfer of the 1930s, and very highly thought of by Henry Cotton, Marcel Dallemagne took his national Closed title five times in 1930, 1932, 1935, 1937 and 1939 and the national Open from 1936 to 1938. He competed frequently in the British Open and was joint fourth in 1934 behind Henry Cotton and joint third to Alf Padgham in 1936. He won the Belgian Open in 1927 and 1937, the Italian in 1937, the Dutch in 1933 and the Swiss in 1931 and 1937. He reached his peak as World War II approached but was approaching 50 when it ended and, not surprisingly, played no further part in competitive professional golf.

DASSU, Baldovino — Italy
b. Florence 1952

Dassu won the British Open Youths' in 1970, and shortly afterwards turned professional. His first three seasons were promising rather than successful, and then he missed 1974 through national service. In 1975 he had his third Top 60 season, but still had not earned as much as £2,500 in a single season. 1976 went much the same way until he was a late qualifier for the Dunlop Masters at St Pierre, Chepstow. He opened up with a 66, followed by a pair of 68s. Only Hubert Green, 4 behind, was still in touch. It was, however, felt that the seasoned American would catch him in the final round. Green made a strong attempt, closing with a 66 to follow his third-round 65 but it was not quite enough: Baldovino had a 69 and a 1-stroke win. His next event was the Italian Open, about three weeks later towards the end of October, at Is Molas, Sardinia. Dassu began 71, 71 over this long and testing course and closed 69, 69. Of the top 50 finishers in the event, there were just five scores to break 70. Dassu won very comfortably indeed by 8 strokes. These twin victories in the dog days of the golfing year had catapulted Dassu to the top of European golf and ninth place in the Order of Merit for 1976. Apart from wins in the Italian Native Professional Championship, an event obviously of limited field, Dassu has not won since and has returned to the kind of placing he was getting in the Order of Merit before his miracle month, in the Top 60 but seldom finishing in the top group for a tournament. An exception came in the 1979 PGA at St Andrews. In foul weather on the last day he faced a pitch to the dreaded 17th with a lead of 1 stroke. Dassu over-allowed for the strength of the wind and hit his shot through the green and on to the road. From there he took four more to get down. He finished equal second, behind Vicente Fernandez. He is holder of the European single-round record with a 60 in the third round of the 1971 Swiss Open.

Europe wins 2 (1976)
Europe money £68,872 (1971–82) (55th all-time)

van DONCK, Flory — Belgium
b. Tervueren 1912

The best Belgian player ever, van Donck is also in the highest class of continental European players and was a great force on the European and British circuits, especially in the 1950s. From 1949 for 11 years he only twice finished out of the top 10 in the British Open and was second in both 1956 and 1959, 3 behind Peter Thomson on the first occasion and 2 behind Gary Player's first major championship-winning score. He was also twice runner-up in the British PGA Matchplay, beaten by Fred Daly in both 1947 and 1952. During his career van Donck won no less than 26 national opens; mostly in continental Europe and took five events on the

Flory van Donck

British circuit. He won the Dutch Open five times, beginning in 1936, and the Belgian professional as a matter of course. His best season was probably 1953, a year in which he took the Vardon Trophy for lowest stroke average. In 1979 he was the oldest player, at 67, appearing in the World Cup and was making his 19th appearance at this time, having been individual winner as far back as 1960. Despite a rather high, squeaky voice, the courtly and elegant van Donck had a great following among women spectators. His swing was rhythmic and his putting quirky: the toe of the putter was in the air in Aoki style.

Europe wins 31

DORRESTEIN, Jan　　　　　Netherlands
b. Soest 1945

Flat lands do not appear to favour the emergence of golfers of quality but for a few years Dorrestein showed promise. After turning professional in 1966, Dorrestein took his own native title in 1970 and 1971, was a World Cup player from 1970 to 1973, and won the Kenya Open in both 1970 and 1973 against strong fields. In the European Order of Merit he was 35th in 1972, then 32nd and 44th. He played for Europe in the 1973 Double Diamond International and for the Continent versus Great Britain in 1974. Shortly after, he disappeared from the tournament scene.

FIGUERAS-DOTTI, Marta　　　　Spain
b. 1957

In 1982, against all the best European professionals and some overseas players, Marta Figueras-Dotti crowned her amateur career by winning the British Ladies' Open at Royal Birkdale. She led by a stroke from Jenny Lee Smith, the year's leading money winner in Europe. Later in the season, she was second to Juli Inkster in the World Women's Amateur Team Championship, four strokes behind. These achievements set her firmly amongst the best amateurs in the world. Earlier, Marta won the Spanish Girls' title in 1975 and 1979 and the Juniors' in 1978, and was runner-up for the Spanish Ladies' in both 1977 and 1978. In 1979, she won the Amateur Championships of three countries: Spain, France and Italy, and also took the Sherry Cup, while in 1980 she was joint second in the British Ladies' Amateur Open Strokeplay and finished low amateur in a US LPGA event. In 1981,

she was runner-up in the Canadian Amateur. Many of these successes were achieved while she was a medical student.

FORSELL, Liv:　see Wollin

GALLARDO, Angel　　　　　Spain
b. Barcelona 1943

The best of three golfing brothers, Angel turned professional at the age of 19 and began to play in major events in 1965, taking the Portuguese Open in 1967 and adding his own national title in 1970. In Britain he has always competed spasmodically and his only win has been in the 1969 Sumrie Four-ball. Another success was also achieved with a partner: with Valentin Barrios the Marlboro Nations Cup was won for Spain. Perhaps his finest victory was the 1971 Mexican Open, in a field that included such US stars as Lee Trevino. His last win came with the 1977 Italian Open, which contributed to his finishing tenth in that year's Order of Merit, much his best placing so far.

Europe wins 4 (1967–77)
Europe money £47,335 (1965–82)
Overseas wins 1 (1971)

GARAIALDE, Jean　　　　　France
b. Abowve, Basses-Pyrenées 1934

Turning professional in 1952, it was not many years before Jean Garaialde had established himself as the best French golfer and indeed achieved almost total dominance in his homeland. In 1957 he won the French Native Open for the first time and won it a further 15 times by 1975. His achievements were similar in the French PGA, which he took 17 times between 1960 and 1977. It can be claimed that for two decades he was France's premier golfer, a fact further illustrated by well over 20 appearances in the World Cup. So far, of course, all this illustrates is that Jean was a very big fish in a small golfing pond; but his performances in the British Open in the early 1960s add to his reputation: 12th, 9th and 13th in successive years. His peak came at the end of the 1960s, and in 1969 he became the first Frenchman to take his own Open for 22 years. In that same year he won two other national titles, the Spanish and the German, the latter a victory he repeated a year later. Also in 1970 he came out on top after a long tussle with

Jack Nicklaus in the Volvo tournament in Sweden, winning by 2 strokes. His appearance in the 1982 World Cup was his 25th and a record. Later in the year he announced his retirement.

GARRIDO, Antonio   Spain
b. Madrid 1944

Antonio is the most un-Spanish golfer of them all. In his play, there is no suggestion of the dash of a Ballesteros and he far more resembles a dour Yorkshireman or someone mainly concerned to keep the ball in play and make the Top 60 on the US Tour. In 1976, for instance, he did not once miss a cut in a tournament, and he played a spell of 81 tournaments up to 1980 during which he only three times failed to make money. More known for finishing second, in the top 10 or at least 'in the money', Garrido does have victories to his credit. He took the Spanish Open in 1972, the Madrid Open and the Benson and Hedges in 1977 to be third in the Order of Merit, and is the first winner of the Tunisian Open (1982). His play through the green is his main strength, for he is one of the best strikers on the current European tour and an extremely straight hitter; but his putting is by no means in the same class. With Severiano Ballesteros he made history in 1979 by becoming the first Continental player to represent Great Britain and Europe against the United States in the Ryder Cup. In the same year, partnered by Manuel Pinero, he took Spain to third place in the World Cup. His best scoring feat came in the 1976 German Open when he recorded opening rounds of 66, 66, 63 and led by 5, but he fell away a little in the final round with a 72 to finish second.

Europe wins 4 (1972–82)
Europe money £147,489 (20th all-time)

GARRIDO, German   Spain
b. Madrid 1948

Brother of Antonio, German won the first Madrid Open in 1968, a victory he repeated against a strong field in 1973. He also pushed Tommy Horton into second place in winning the 1972 Portuguese Open. In more recent years, little has been heard of him.

Europe wins 3 (1968–72)

GOLDSCHMID, Isa (née Bevione)   Italy

As a brother-and-sister combination perhaps ranking only below the Wethereds (Joyce and Roger), Isa was Closed Champion of Italy no fewer than 21 times, starting in 1947, her last victory coming in 1974. She won this title 15 times consecutively from 1953 to 1967! Isa was almost as effective in her national Open amateur, winning ten times between 1952 and 1969. She also won the French title when past her best, in 1975, and the Spanish in 1952. In Britain she took the Kayser-Bondor in 1963 and twice reached the final of the Worplesdon Mixed Foursomes. Isa was a member of the Italian team in the World Team Championship from the first event in 1964 until 1972, and in the Vagliano Trophy every year from 1959 to 1973. Her international career dates back to 1950.

Isa Goldschmid

321

GRAPPASONNI, Ugo   Italy
b. 1922

One of the best Continental golfers during the years shortly after World War II, Ugo took his national Open in 1950 and 1954 and his country's Closed title on four occasions. He also won the Dutch, French and Swiss titles, the latter on two occasions.

LACOSTE, Catherine (later de Prado)   France
b. Paris 1945

René Lacoste was a US Forest Hills Champion at tennis and his wife, as Thion de la Chaume, won the British Ladies' title in 1927. The daughter they produced was perhaps for a few years the foremost woman golfer in the world, motivated at least in part by not wishing to be thought just 'a daughter of the Lacostes'. Catherine grew up competitively in a hard school. Although France is not renowned as a golfing country, she has produced a steady flow of top women players and as Catherine grew to maturity she faced, amongst others, the Vicomtesse de St-Sauveur — still formidable though towards the end of a long career — Claudine Cros and Brigitte Varangot. The last of these established some dominance over her, beating her in the finals of the 1965 and 1966 French Open Amateur and in the latter year also for the Closed title. By this time, however, Catherine Lacoste had established herself as a player of world stature, for she had tied for first individual in the Women's World Amateur Team Championship, and in 1967 she overwhelmed Brigitte Varangot by 8 and 6 in the final of the French Open Amateur. She then went to America and after a 70 in the second round established a 5-stroke lead in the US Women's Open. At a later stage she increased the lead to 7 and, even though she faltered towards the end, came home eventually with 294, winner by 2 strokes. At 22 years 5 days she was the youngest player to win the title and, with Fay Crocker of Uruguay, one of only two foreigners to do so. More significant still, she was, and is, the only amateur to do so. In 1968 she took the French Closed title again and was individual winner in the World Team Championship, having been third in 1966. Her greatest year, despite this record of achievement, was still to come. In 1969 she swept all before her: the French Open and Closed and the British title, and then in the final of the US Amateur she beat Shelley Hamlin by 3 and 2 to become one of only three women to win both

British and US titles the same year. She then married and announced her retirement from international competition. Later she was to return and, though no longer a dominant force, still won the French Open Amateur in 1970 and 1972, for a total of four wins. In 1974 her 71 was the lowest round in the World Team Championship. Among other successes Catherine Lacoste won the Spanish Ladies' in 1969, 1972 and 1976, the US Western Amateur in 1968, the Astor Trophy with a round of 66 at Prince's Sandwich in 1966, and the Hovis at Moor Park in 1969 by 15 strokes. She was a very powerful player, one of few women to be able to master long irons.

LACOSTE, Thion: see Chaume

de LAMAZE, Henri   France
b. Trelissac 1918

De Lamaze was incomparably the finest French amateur of his generation — a long generation at that. Here is his sequence in the French Native Amateur: 1947–51, 1953, 1955–8, 1961–2, 1966 and 1971 — 14 wins in all, the last at the age of 53. His record was scarcely inferior in the French Open Amateur, with eleven wins: 1947–50 and 1954–60. Lamaze also took the French Open three times, in 1952, 1956 and 1959, and was top amateur eight times. Outside France his best achievement was to take the Spanish Open in 1955 and to reach the semi-finals of the British Amateur in 1966, the first Frenchman to get that far. He also won the Spanish Amateur three times, the Italian twice and the Portuguese and Belgian once each. He gained a reputation for gamesmanship, and some felt he needed to win at all costs.

LANGER, Bernhard   West Germany
b. Anhausen, Bavaria 1957

In September 1980 during the Hennessy Cup matches at Sunningdale, Langer picked up an Acushnet Bull's Eye ladies' putter. He liked the feel of it and had the grip thickened a little. He began to feel more confident in his putting. At the time he had been playing quite well, having taken fifth place in the European Open a week or so before and a 13th in the Swiss Open just before that. Previously there was a 43rd in the German Open, a 16th in the Irish, and 18th in the Benson and

Bernhard Langer

Hedges, an eighth in the Dutch Open. These were the events that followed the British Open, after which he had accumulated only £3,260 during the European season. But putting had remained a weak link in his game, which otherwise combined length and straightness from the tee and excellence with irons. Langer's putting had once been very bad indeed. He had been known to hit the ball twice, to knock a 2-foot putt convulsively 4 feet past or twitch the ball well wide of the hole. Langer describes the feeling as intense pressure in the hands and 'like some other being had taken me over'. This is similar to all the classic accounts of the feeling, from Vardon through Hagen and Jones down to Snead and Hogan. The player is confident and smooth with his long putts, but once the hole looms under his nose he makes a nice little practice movement with the club before he gets down to the real thing – and then follows that moment when the nerves take charge, usually just a few inches away from striking the ball. At best there's a check or unwanted acceleration of the stroke. At worst

players have been known to jerk their ball clear off the green. There is no known permanent cure. Snead was a sufferer as a young man and they returned when he was not confident – he even yipped the last putt that by chance went in and gave him a 59 at the Greenbrier in 1959. He and others have found temporary solace from a new method or a new putter, while some walk quickly up to their ball and give it a tap while on the walk, thus not giving the nerves the chance to take over the stroke. At his worst Langer in an earlier series of Hennessy matches (1976) had been conceded not even the shortest putts and had missed most of those. But the £5 second-hand Bull's Eye seemed to be the cure. He played well in the Hennessy and then went off to Moortown and had a 64 and a 65 to finish joint second in the Tournament Players Championship; then opened 66, 67, 67 in the Bob Hope before a final 71 dropped him to fifth place, 2 behind the winner, Canizares. He next became the first German to win a European Tour event, the Dunlop Masters. And, wonder of wonders, he did it with his putter. Langer had rounds of 70, 65, 67, 68, taking 29, 25, 26 and 30 putts in each. The total of 110 is said to be a European Tour record. He beat Brian Barnes by 5 and Nick Faldo by 8 and then went off to St-Nom-la-Bretèche near Paris to come in third in the Lancôme. In two months he had won over £28,000, and after the end of the European season he won the Colombian Open by 6 and finished second in the World Cup. Germany had a golfer of world stature where previously she had never had a moderate touring professional; Langer had his 'Bull's Eye', and the yips were gone. Perhaps. Things went better still in 1981. In Europe he competed in 17 events, finished in the top 10 on 14 occasions, was in the first five 11 of those times, was runner-up six times and won twice. His worst finish was 21st. All this was consistency of the same order that Tom Kite was producing in America. He had become the first German to take his country's Open with rounds of 67, 69, 64, 72 and had led throughout. That followed closely his 73, 67, 70, 70 in the British Open at Sandwich which left him in second place, 3 ahead of Floyd and James but 4 behind Bill Rogers. Shortly afterwards he was second in the Benson and Hedges by one to Tom Weiskopf, who had been aided by a rather too strong iron shot that scuttled into the hole for an eagle. He then won the Bob Hope with rounds of 67, 65, 68 in the rain-shortened event to be 5 clear of the field. Only in the World Matchplay did he show feet of clay when Severiano Ballesteros, keen to show who was best in Europe, beat the two challengers, Greg Norman and Langer, by wide margins. Otherwise, Langer was number one, with prize money totalling £95,990, some £40,000 ahead of Nick Faldo and the best stroke average except for Ballesteros, who had competed far less frequently. He had made his first appearance in the USA at the World Series at Firestone, had shared the lead after one round and been 1 behind after two with a 68, 69 start before dropping to equal sixth place. In 1982 the yips returned, though by no means in an extreme form. Nevertheless Langer was to be seen on the courses of Europe trying a smooth practice stroke but being far more tentative for the real thing. The condition was seen at its worst during the PGA Championship at Hillside. Langer was playing well enough to have won by several strokes. Ironically, his companion in the last round was Tony Jacklin, himself no stranger to feelings of acute unease and distaste when surveying putts of all lengths. After missing birdie chances throughout the event Langer eventually gave Jacklin a helping hand to the title by four-putting the 16th, going behind when Jacklin birdied the 17th and then on the last negating his 'shot of the season', a long bunker shot from a downslope, by missing another putt. To add a final irony, Langer had been using his Bull's Eye less often, while Jacklin was delighted with a new acquisition. As Henry Longhurst once wrote: 'Once you've had 'em, you've got 'em.'

Europe wins 5 (1979–82)
Europe money £194,271 (1976–82) (11th all-time)
Overseas wins 1 (1980)

MASSY, Arnaud   France
b. Biarritz 1877; d. 1958

Although players from America, South Africa and Australia have dominated the British Open for the past 60 years it was Arnaud Massy who was the first non-Briton to win, and the only Continental European until Severiano Ballesteros in 1979. Massy's victory came at Hoylake in 1907, when he beat J.H. Taylor by 2 strokes, with Tom Vardon a further 3 behind. He had finished fifth two years before at St Andrews, sixth at Muirfield in 1906 and later, in 1911, tied with Harry Vardon at Sandwich. In the 36-hole play-off Massy conceded after the 35th hole when he had taken 148 to Vardon's 143. Undaunted, he returned to France to

Arnaud Massy

take the French Open for the third time by 7 strokes over Ted Ray and 9 over Harry Vardon. He won the French Open four times between 1906 and 1925 and was three times runner-up, also taking the French Native title in 1925 and 1926. Massy also won the Belgian Open in 1910 and the Spanish Open in 1911, 1927 and 1928, the last occasion at the age of 51. Possibly the greatest French golfer ever, Massy was a Basque. He was wounded at Verdun in World War I.

MIGUEL, Angel   Spain
b. Madrid 1930

With his brother Sebastian, Angel was a forerunner of the large numbers of very good Spanish golfers, and was perhaps just the better player of the two. Both were slim, elegant swingers who would have made much money in the richer European tournament scene of today. Angel's record in Britain included three victories between 1964 and 1966, the Spanish Open in 1961 and 1964, the Mexican in 1959, the Argentine in 1962, the Dutch in 1965, the Portuguese three times, and the 1956 French Open. Perhaps his greatest achievement was to be individual winner in the 1958 World Cup and to share the second team position with Sebastian. He also performed well in the Open Championship, though never coming within sight of winning, his best placing being eighth in 1964; oddly, he came equal 14th with his brother in 1961. On the European Tour he once had the second most consecutive birdies – seven – in the 1960 Daks tournament. He is now professional at Los Monteros on the Costa del Sol.

Europe wins 10 (1954–66)
Overseas wins 2 (1959–62)

MIGUEL, Sebastian   Spain
b. Madrid 1931

Although he was a good competitor in Britain, Sebastian's successes were mainly gained on the Iberian peninsula. Here he won the Portuguese Open in 1959, the Spanish in 1954, 1960 and 1967 and the Spanish professional four times. He was a consistent performer in the British Open and four times came in ninth or better, sixth in 1967 being his best placing. Later he became professional at Andalucia on the Costa del Sol.

Europe wins 4 (1954–67)
Overseas wins 1 (1959)

PALLI, Anne-Marie   France
b. Ciboure 1955

One of the best present-day French players, Anne-Marie Palli won the French Closed title successively from 1972 to 1974 and again in 1976. She reached the final of the Open in 1973, being beaten on the 37th by Brigitte Varangot, but won in 1977 against the Swiss player, Marie-Christine de Werra. She also took the Spanish title in 1974, the Dutch in 1975, the 1972 World Junior Championship and the 1973 British Girls', and was twice French Junior winner. Eventually turning professional, she qualified for the US Tour in 1979, but lost her place in 1981. She was the leading money-winner on the mini-Tour in 1982 and requalified for the full US LPGA Tour in 1983.

PINERO, Manuel   Spain
b. Puebla de la Calzada 1952

At 5 feet 7 inches one of the shorter European golfers, Manuel Pinero made rapid progress at the beginning of his professional career, taking the Spanish PGA in both 1972 and 1973. By 1974, he was 22nd in the European Order of Merit and had won his first major victory, the Madrid Open. Since that time, he has been well up in the order, only once slipping to 30th. He was fourth in 1976 and 1977, and fifth in 1981 and 1982. His form fell away in the period 1978–80, though not severely, but it returned the following year. Pinero is a relatively short hitter with a round, quick swing. He is extremely determined, and one of the best putters in Europe. His consistency is well illustrated by the fact that during the 1976 season he was never out of the top 11 in any tournament, won the Swiss Open, and then with Severiano Ballesteros went on to win the World Cup. In that event in 1979 he and Antonio Garrido finished third. In other team events, he has represented Europe in the Hennessy Cognac Cup since 1976, and was one of three Continental Europeans to qualify for the 1981 Ryder Cup team. In the Walton Heath match he lost in his foursomes then, paired with Bernhard Langer in the four-balls, went on to beat Floyd and

Manuel Pinero

Irwin and lose to Nicklaus and Watson. He won his singles against Jerry Pate by 4 and 2. Pinero's best victories to date are in the 1977 PGA Championship and the 1982 European Open at Sunningdale, which Sam Torrance seemed to have won with nine holes to play. However, Pinero went out in 33 and came back in 30 to win. Later the same year, in a sadly debased World Cup in Acapulco, he was in the winning Spanish pair with Canizares and also took the individual title, by 1 stroke from Bob Gilder and Canizares. He was one of the four-ball with whom Bing Crosby played his last round.

Europe wins 8 (1974–82)
Europe money £221,527 (1972–82) (7th all-time)

de PRADO, Catherine: see Lacoste

RUBIN, Claudine: see Cros

St-SAUVEUR, Lally Vicomtesse de (née Vagliano, later Segard)   France
b. 1921

Lally St-Sauveur had a competitive golf career which lasted about 30 years, resulting from a long, lissom swing, perfect grip and an attacking mentality. She first came to the front of women's golf before World War II, when she won the British Girls' title in 1937, was for three years a French international and won the French Closed on the first of six occasions in 1939. After the war, she swept all before her on her national scene, winning the Open title in 1948 and from 1950 to 1952 and the Closed in 1946, from 1949 to 1951 and in 1954. As late as 1964 and 1967 she reached the final of the latter event. In Europe, she also won the Swiss title in 1949 and 1965, the Luxembourg in 1949, the Italian in 1949 and 1951 and the Spanish in 1951, while her international career was interrupted only by the war, lasting from 1937 to 1965. In Britain, she won the Worplesdon Foursomes (1962), Kayser-Bondor Foursomes (1960) and Avia Foursomes (1966). However, her greatest achievement came in 1950, when she beat Jessie Valentine by 3 and 2 in the final of the British Ladies'. Under her chairmanship the first Women's World Amateur Team Championship was held, in Paris in 1964 and won by France. Thereafter the World Amateur Golf Council assumed responsibility for the event.

SCHLEEH, Gerda: see Boykin, North America

SEGARD, Lally: see St-Sauveur

SOTA, Ramon   Spain
b. Pedrena 1938

Today Ramon Sota is in danger of being more well known as the uncle of Severiano Ballesteros than as what he was: in his best years a leading Continental European golfer. He began to play in the same part of Spain as Ballesteros and similarly emerged from purely local competition with an excellent short game; but, unlike Ballesteros, he was relatively weak on the long shots. However, once he saw what was demanded in the wider golf world he raised his standards. In 1963 he took both Spanish and Portuguese Opens, and by 1971 had added six more European national titles and the 1965 Brazil Open. In the 1965 Masters, his sixth place was the highest at that time achieved by a European golfer. In 1971 he was the top player in Continental Europe and achieved a distinction of a less welcome kind. Always a slow player, in Britain he became the first player to be penalized by the PGA for that reason. Sota was tenth in the Order of Merit that year. There are few valid comparisons to be made between English and Continental European golfers of his generation, for most of them seldom crossed the Channel in either direction to compete.

Europe wins 8 (1963–71)
Overseas wins 1 (1965)

SWAELENS, Donald   Belgium
b. St-Martens-Latem 1935; d. 1975

After Flory van Donck, Don Swaelens was the best Belgian player to emerge after World War II, representing his country some 15 times in the World Cup. In 1967 he won three tournaments on the Continent, the Ramstein, Evian and German Opens, and he and Ian McDonald beat myself and Harold Ridgley in the Gleneagles Foursomes. Although Continentals tended to play less in Britain during his best years, Swaelens was as high as 15th in the Order of Merit in both 1973 and 1974, the latter performance being that year the best by a Continental player, while he was also second in the European Order of Merit in 1973. His best performance in Britain was to be joint second in the 1973 PGA, and he was joint seventh in the 1974 British Open with an equal best last-round score of 69. Perhaps he was consistent rather than a likely tournament winner, and this consistency was

Don Swaelens

shown in his last season when he finished in the top seven of the French, Dutch, British, German and Swiss Opens and the Martini International.

Europe wins 3 (1967)

von SZLAVY, Erzsebet   Hungary
b. Budapest 1902

Undoubtedly the best Hungarian woman golfer ever, Erzsebet took her national title almost automatically between the wars. From 1922 to 1939 she won 15 times. However, she did not entirely restrict her competition to her own country, and also won the German title once and the Czechoslovak and Austrian four times each.

TOUSSAINT, Philippe   Belgium
b. Brussels 1949

After being runner-up in his own national Amateur and winning the 1969 Italian, Philippe Toussaint turned professional and joined the European Tour in 1971; but he won only about £700 in his first three seasons. In the 1974 Benson and Hedges he played steady golf for three rounds and then produced a 7-under-par 64 first to tie with Bob Shearer of Australia and then win on the first extra hole of the play-off. Although he has great talent Toussaint never threatened to win another tournament, though he twice more made the Top 60. He no longer plays on the European Tour.

Europe wins 1 (1974)

VAGLIANO, Lally: see St-Sauveur

VARANGOT, Brigitte   France
b. Biarritz 1940

With Claudine Cros and Catherine Lacoste, Brigitte Varangot formed one of a great trio of French women golfers in the 1960s, good enough indeed to win the Women's World Amateur Team Championship the first time it was held in 1964. Brigitte played six times in the event in all. Brigitte could be seen at the age of 17 moving seductively around the course, usually with a Gauloise between her lips, when she won the British Girls' title from Ruth Porter at North Berwick. A year later she again reached the final, this time losing. She won the French equivalent three times in a row and first took the French Closed title in 1959, winning three consecutively from 1961 to 1963 and again in 1966 and 1972. She also reached the final on five other occasions. She was just as formidable in the French Open Amateur, reaching the final every year between 1960 and 1967 and winning five of those eight finals, including three consecutive ones from 1964 to 1966. She was a beaten finalist in 1970 and won for the last time in 1973. In Britain she took the Open three times: 1963, 1965 and 1968, beating Philomena Garvey, Belle Robertson and Claudine Cros in the finals.

WHALEN, Gerda: see Boykin, North America

de WIT, Gerard   Netherlands
b. Wassenaar 1918

In his home country Gerard de Wit was formidably successful, winning the Dutch Closed title 14 times and the Professional the same number. Against international fields in the Dutch Open he did not once succeed but was a runner-up on five occasions, three of those after a play-off. He was a frequent competitor in the British Open.

WOLLIN, Liv (née Forsell)   Sweden
b. 1945

The best Swedish player in recent years, Liv Wollin won the Scandinavian Open Amateur in 1963, 1964, 1965, 1967, 1970, 1971 and 1972, and the Swedish Closed in 1963, 1964, from 1966 to 1969, 1972, 1973, 1976 and 1980. Also during the 1960s, she won the 1967 Portuguese title and reached the semi-final of the British Ladies'. She took the Swedish Open Strokeplay in 1971, 1972, 1977 and 1979 and the Moroccan in 1972.

AUSTRALIA & NEW ZEALAND

BACHLI, Douglas W.   Australia
b. Victoria 1922

Doug Bachli is surprisingly the only Australian to have won the British Amateur title. This he did in 1954 when he beat Bill Campbell in a run of 22 wins in sequence which included play in the Commonwealth Tournament of that year. He was a member of the Australian winning team in the 1958 Eisenhower trophy and took his own country's amateur title in both 1948 and 1962. His many wins in Australia include the Victoria and Queensland state titles, which he won three times each.

BALL, Edward   Australia
b. Sydney 1939

A member of the Australian World Team Championship team and Australian champion in 1960, Ted 'Cricket' Ball turned professional the following year. In 1962, he won the Queensland Open but 1964 was his biggest year. He won the Singapore, Sydney, Tasmanian and New South Wales Opens and the Wills Classic in New Zealand. Playing with Arnold Palmer during that year's Australian Open he astonished the great man by being 5 under par for the first five holes played. He represented Australia in the World Cup that year. In 1965 he won the Lakes Open but thereafter things went a good deal less well. Eventually Ted left tournament golf for a while, taking a job on a prawn boat fishing out of Cairns to the Gulf of Carpentaria. The first day out he broke his wrist. His form eventually returned to some extent and he was later to win the 1972 South Australian Open, the 1974 Wills Masters and New South Wales Open in a year when he again represented Australia in the World Cup, the 1975 Indian Open and the 1977 Papua New Guinea Open. His most recent victory has been in the 1980 New South Wales PGA. His burning ambition is to organize a charity golf match played over one hole – from one side of Australia to the other!

BORTHWICK, Patricia   Australia
b. New South Wales 1928

A superb player of long irons, Pat Borthwick won the Australian Ladies' four times: in 1948, 1949, 1953 and 1956. She took to golf originally because her parents felt that the surfing she loved was too dangerous. She toured the British Isles twice and South Africa once. It is claimed that the Slazenger B51 golf ball was named after her.

CHARLES, Robert James, OBE   New Zealand
b. Carterton 1936

Bob Charles has achieved two enviable all-time firsts: he is the most successful New Zealand golfer and also the only left-hander ever to have been recognized as of genuine world class. He is also first-class in another field – it would be difficult to put the case that there has ever been a better putter than Bob Charles. He won just one major championship and it has sometimes been said that he did that with his putter. At Royal Lytham and St Annes in 1963, while producing rounds of 68, 72, 66, 71, he averaged 30 putts a round. This was good enough to tie with US player Phil Rodgers. In the 36-hole play-off he moved 3 strokes ahead of Rodgers in the morning round, using only 26 putts, and completed his task in the afternoon, winner by 8 clear shots, this time taking 31 putts. There were many other occasions when Bob Charles's putter seemed invincible, and it is worth singling out just a few. In the 1969 World Matchplay at Wentworth he began with a 65 in the morning against Maurice Bembridge to be 7 up, and coasted to victory in the afternoon. Against Tommy Aaron in the semi-finals he first produced a 66 to Aaron's 67 and then raced away in the afternoon to a 9 and 7 win after six birdies in 11 holes. His opponent in the final was Gene Littler, himself one of the best putters around, who had just knocked out Gary Player with a 65 that included seven 3s in a row. The two were all square after 18 holes and in the afternoon Charles began to fall behind. Then on the 26th, 27th and 28th holes he holed from 40, 25 and 50 feet, and again from 30 feet on the last so that the match could go into extra holes. Thereafter Bob hardly needed his putter, knocking a 4-iron to 30 inches on the first hole. There have been not a few players who seem scarcely ever to miss short putts and others who have been able almost inevitably to coast the long ones up to the holeside before appearing far less sure at the finishing touches (of the latter, Sam Snead and Jack Nicklaus are examples). But Bob's abilities were well balanced. In his best years, which lasted about a dozen seasons, he seemed never to miss from about 5 feet down and expected to hole most of the 8- to 10-footers. From longer distances he usually left the ball dead. It was these talents that once enabled him in 1972 to play 11 rounds consecutively before three-putting, and in the 1966 New Zealand Open to need just 24 putts in his first round before eventually setting the championship record of 265. A left-hander at golf always looks at least a little odd, one reason why few have ever conceded that there was much to admire in the Charles long game. True, he is a relatively short hitter, and has been known to advise spectators to watch someone else when he has been striking badly, but he has normally been adept at keeping the ball in play, rather like Bobby Locke in his aim to keep out of trouble through the green and thereafter let his putter do the talking. Bob Charles's first significant victory was in the

Bob Charles

1954 New Zealand Open, which he won as an amateur, but he continued in his job as a bank teller. It was not until 1960 that he took the plunge of turning professional and, because of the limited competition opportunities in his own country, was soon an international golfer. He first competed in Europe in 1961, the year he first won the New Zealand PGA, and was quite successful. Never playing a complete season, and in some years not playing at all, he had taken his career earnings to £169,330 by the end of 1982. His most important achievements, other than those already mentioned, were to win both the John Player Classic and the Dunlop Masters one after the other in 1972. He also twice finished in second place in the 1968 and 1969 British Opens. In 1968 he came 2 strokes behind Gary Player with a poor final round of 76. The next year he opened 66, 69 to lead Tony Jacklin by 3, but a third-round 75 was too much to carry forward and he followed Jacklin to a 2-stroke win. In his peak years, Bob Charles concentrated on the US Tour and lived in the USA. He joined the Tour in 1962 and his first victory came with the 1963 Houston Open. His finest victory was in the 1968 Canadian Open. He made the Top 60 over the periods 1963–5 and 1967–71, and again in 1974. He topped $70,000 in 1967, 1968 and 1970. His Houston win made him the first left-hander ever to win on the US Tour. It is odd that golf's greatest left-hander is, in fact, not left-handed at all. He first swung a golf club at the age of five and stood up to the ball the way his parents did. In everything other than golf he is a natural right-hander. Although the 1963 British Open was to remain his only major championship success, he twice came third in the US Open (in 1964 and 1970), and was second in the 1968 US PGA, a total of three seconds and two thirds in championship golf. He won the New Zealand Open five times, the New Zealand PGA three times and the South African Open once. In 1982, at the age of 46, he seemed to be enjoying an Indian summer in England, coming second equal in the Benson and Hedges at York, third in the Bob Hope Classic and breaking 70 in all four rounds at Ferndown in the Hennessy Cognac Cup.

New Zealand wins 10 (1954–80)
Europe wins 8 (1962–74)
Europe money £169,330 (1961–82) (14th all-time)
US wins 5 (1963–74)
US money $533,615 (1962–81) (89th all-time)
South Africa wins 1 (1973)
World money $1,173,020 (1960–82) (41st all-time)

CRAFTER, Jane   Australia
b. Perth 1955

A professional since 1980, Jane Crafter won the Australian LPGA and topped the US 1981 mini-Tour money before qualifying for the full Tour. As an amateur she won the national titles of New Zealand in 1978 and 1979 and Belgium in 1980, and was runner-up in the 1977 Australian and 1980 Canadian Amateurs. She won the South Australia Strokeplay five times and the New Zealand once.

US money $9,088 (1981–2)

CRAMPTON, Bruce   Australia
b. Sydney 1935

The career of Bruce Crampton on the US Tour illustrates the rewards that persistence can bring. After winning the 1956 Australian Open he tried the British circuit briefly, but was critical of the way tournaments were run and moved to the US. That first year he won just $1,500 and the ensuing years were not much kinder to him: in his first five years he did not top $8,500. However, he earned the nickname of 'the Iron Man' because he played almost all the possible tournaments, some 30 a year, and once played 37 consecutively. Eventually, in 1961, he won, and the following year began to be a substantial money-winner. He was in the Top 60 from 1961 to 1975 and did not fall below 14th in the period 1968–75. His best placings were fifth in 1969, third in 1970 and second in 1973. Always a good putter, Crampton was for some time an unreliable driver, and it was that more than anything else which held up his progress. That overcome, he became known even more for his consistency than as a tournament winner, though he won a fair share, including three in 1965 and four in 1973. At his peak, 1968–75, he topped $100,000 each year and in 1973 went to $274,266. Twice he took the Vardon Trophy for the lowest stroke average, in 1973 and 1975. His first tournament win was the first by a non-American since 'Light-Horse' Harry Cooper in 1937. Crampton's record in the major championships was less impressive, and he was perhaps the best player of his time not to win one. He did come close: he was equal second in the 1972 Masters and twice second in the US PGA. In the US Open he had a fifth, a sixth and, in 1972, a second to Nicklaus. So in 1972 he was second in three of the four majors. In 1973, Crampton became only the fifth man to reach $1 million in winnings and the following year was fifth in all-time money winnings. Even now, several years after his retirement, he still ranks 17th. That 'Iron Man' nickname derived from more than the persistence of his tournament entries. On course he seldom said a word, and smiled even less often. Off course, he was a non-drinker and non-smoker. Yet, as he entered his 40s, some of the iron went. In 1976 his earnings dropped to $50,000. The next year, he won just $800, his health gave way, and he had the good sense to retire from competitive golf and go into the oil business.

US wins 15 (1961–75)
US money $1,374,294 (1957–77) (17th all-time)
Other wins 2
World money $1,499,554 (1953–77) (24th all-time)

CREMIN, Eric   Australia
b. Mascot, New South Wales 1914

Cremin was one of three early players – Ossie Pickworth and Norman von Nida were the others – who set Australia firmly on the golfing map. He confined his play mainly to Australasia but also helped in the development of the Far East circuit and occasionally played in Europe during the 1940s and 1950s. His best achievement was to win the 1949 Australian Open. He also took the Australian PGA in 1937–8, and in the years shortly after World War II, when it was still played as matchplay, he was runner-up no fewer than seven times including 1946–8 consecutively. In all it is estimated he won 32 events, including seven in 1951. He was active from the late 1930s to the early 1960s, and helped to smooth the way for the fine Australian players who followed him.

DAVIS, Rodger   Australia
b. Sydney 1951

Rodger Davis has a love-hate relationship with the Brabazon course at the Belfry, near Birmingham (which Dave Thomas and I designed). In the English Classic there in 1979 he began by holding the two-round lead, then plummeted to an 83. In 1980, the pattern was similar: a 69, 66 start was followed by an 81, then a 77 and only equal sixth place. In 1981 he began 70, 68 and again faltered in the third round, but this time only to a 74 and he still shared the lead with Gary Cullen and Stewart Ginn. He played steadily the last day and finished 2 ahead for his first and only win outside Australia.

He had 14 times been second since his win in the 1979 Victoria Open. This win helped him to 17th place in the 1981 Order of Merit, easily his highest placing. In 1979, however, he was on the edge of gaining an even more prominent name. He began 75, 70, 70 in that Lytham Open and with 5 holes to go in the final round led the championship. However, like several others, he then fell away and finished in 73, leaving Ballesteros champion and himself in fifth place. He represented Australia against Japan in 1980. Davis is a rather distinctive figure on the golf course, invariably wearing plus twos. Less well known is that his name is set in gem diamonds down the sides of the accompanying socks.

Australia wins 5 (1977–9)
Europe wins 1 (1981)
Europe money £67,350 (1977–82) (57th all-time)

DEVLIN, Bruce William   Australia
b. Armidale 1937

After more than 20 years as a formidable golfer, Devlin had become a little-known figure to the general public when he turned up at Pebble Beach

Bruce Devlin

for the 1982 US Open. He began with a 70 over the par-72 course to share the lead and then led by 2 after the second round, when he shot 69 with a birdie, birdie finish. Though he fell away to a 75, 74 final two rounds, that was still even par, a respectable 6 behind winner Tom Watson. In recent years, Bruce has been limiting his appearances and 'diversifying' into a golf-course design partnership based in Houston, Texas, and work for NBC TV. However, he has usually continued to win useful spending money and entered 16 tournaments in 1981. In 1980 he rated as the eighth best putter on the US Tour. Devlin first attracted attention as long ago as 1958, when he finished equal first in the Eisenhower Trophy individually and was a member of the winning Australian team at St Andrews. A year later he won the Australian Amateur and then the following year took the Australian Open as well. The latter experience persuaded him to turn professional, though he had to refuse an invitation to the US Masters that year because of lack of funds. For his first two seasons, Devlin played worldwide, winning the 1963 French and New Zealand Opens. Thereafter, he settled for the US Tour, with forays back to Australia, where he won often, including the 1969 and 1970 PGAs, and to Britain, where he won the Carling in 1966 and was the leading money-winner in Europe, and the 1970 Alcan, the last such event and worth $55,000. He took the latter at Portmarnock in Ireland by the margin of 7 strokes. With 1964 his first full-time year on the US Tour, Devlin was immediately a considerable money-winner (16th that season) and took the St Petersburg Open. The next year he finished sixth on the money list, his best placing and won twice in 1966. In 1970 he was 11th, winning over $100,000 for the first time, and was eighth in 1972, again topping $100,000, Thereafter he faded considerably, partly as a result of interests outside the Tour, especially in his Houston golf-course architecture partnership with Bob von Hagge. Another cause was that Devlin broke a favourite driver; he claims to have bought a hundred (including four specially made for him by Ben Hogan) since that time in search of its equal. He also became a great buyer of putters and has now a collection of about 70. By this time, he had established a reputation as being the third best non-American player ever on the US Tour – behind only Gary Player and Bruce Crampton. By the end of 1981 Devlin had competed 20 seasons in the US, had six times been in the top 16, had made the Top

AUSTRALIA & NEW ZEALAND

60 nine times and had been in the top 100 every season except two. At one point in 1965 he had played 36 consecutive tournaments winning money and in 1969 he won substantially on the US Tour and then departed for Australia to win three events inside five weeks. Devlin is one of the best players of modern times not to have taken a major championship, though he has come close. In the US Masters he came fourth in 1964, and in 1968 was again fourth after he had taken 8 on the 11th in the third round yet still finished in 69. He was 3 behind winner Bob Goalby. In 1972 he was fifth, while his best US Open performance was 6th in 1965. In 1980 he was made a Member of the Order of Australia.

US wins 8 (1964–72)
US money $894,189 (1962–82) (44th all-time)
Australasia wins 4 (1960–70)
Overseas wins 7 (1960–70)
World money $1,167,921 (1961–82) (43rd all-time)

DUNK, E. William   Australia
b. Gosford, New South Wales 1938

Since the advent of fast air travel, golf has become an international game. Many Americans and Japanese may still largely confine themselves to their own circuits but in Australia, with a limited circuit over a short season, the Cramptons, von Nidas, Thomsons, Grahams, Devlins and Normans have for long recognized that fame and fortune lay in Europe and America. Of their best players of the last four decades only Billy Dunk, a professional since 1955, has consistently stayed at home, despite three World Cup appearances – and paid the penalty in terms of world renown. He must be the best player of the last 20 years to be unknown to the great majority of golf followers, content to carve his niche in Australia, with occasional forays to New Zealand, the Asia Circuit or Japan. In Australia, he holds an estimated 75 course records and has won more than a hundred professional tournaments. Overseas, the 1963 Malaysian Open and the 1972 and 1975 New Zealand Open feature in his record. He led the world scoring averages in 1970 and holds the record for the lowest round in an Australian tournament, a 60 at Merewether on 15 November 1970, finishing with seven birdies in a row. He has been a dominant force in the Australian PGA. This he first won in 1962 and has repeated in 1966, 1971, 1974 and 1976. Only Kel Nagle, himself a stay-at-home until Peter Thomson persuaded him to venture overseas, exceeds that total, while Thomson himself won it only once in an equally long career. Billy Dunk has won some 11 Australian state titles, the last in 1981. It is now too late for hm to achieve anything of note outside Australia, but his wife did insist that he compete in the 1981 British Open. Although never in contention he had a 67, a round bettered only by Gordon Brand Snr, Jack Nicklaus and Brian Jones. At 5 feet 6½ inches he is on the short side for a leading player. His hobby is collecting wine.

FERRIER, James   Australia
b. Manley 1915

This 6-foot 4-inch Australian began by dominating golf in his homeland, four times securing the Amateur title between 1935 and 1939, and also taking the Open in 1938 and 1939. From 1931 he had also been second three times. Australian golfers at that time were operating in a small pond and, like others, Jim Ferrier decided to seek fame and fortune elsewhere. In 1940 he turned professional and went to the USA the following year. Earlier he had been to Britain, where in 1936 he was the first Australian to reach the final of the Amateur Championship, losing to a birdie on the last hole. In the same year he finished leading amateur in the Open. Ferrier's successes came more from the excellence of his putting stroke than from his overall game. His swing, for instance, was highly idiosyncratic, with a pronounced knee dip into the hitting area, caused by a knee injury. After a slow start on the US Tour while he acclimatized himself, Ferrier became a major Tour competitor from about 1944 onwards and remained so until his mid 40s. In the US Open he twice finished in the top half dozen; his one major win came in the 1947 US PGA when he defeated Chick Harbert in the final by 2 and 1. There is an apocryphal story that he was never asked to putt twice in that final: his pitching to the flag was so precise that his first putts were either in or dead. Thirteen years later he came second to Jay Hebert when the event had become strokeplay. However, it was a failure that brought Jim more fame than his successes. In the 1950 Masters he had 'only' to complete the back nine in 38 to win – and there are at least two good birdie chances on the par 5s. But Jim trailed in with a sad 41. On the 13th he hit into the creek and then dropped shots on four more consecutive holes. On the last six holes, in fact, there was a 7-stroke swing

Jim Ferrier

between him and the winner, Jimmy Demaret, an Augusta specialist, who recorded a 69. Jim finished second, and was equal third two years later. There was perhaps some consolation in his winning the Canadian Open later that year and repeating this the following year. This was in fact his peak period, for he was second in the money list in 1950, and in 1951 he took five events, three of these in a row, a feat that has been achieved by only ten others in US Tour history. He was in the Top 60 from 1944 to 1947, 1949 to 1954, 1956, 1960 and 1962.

US wins 21 (1944–61)
US money $183,798 (199th all-time)

GALE, Terry   Australia
b. 1946

Australia is a rather expensive country from which to assault the world golf tour and Terry has mostly confined his efforts to Australasia. He did, however, venture to Europe in 1979 and in just five events earned enough to push himself into 58th place in the Order of Merit. During the visit, he finished as high as 13th in that year's British Open. Between 1977 and 1979 he had four wins, three in Australia, and also won the Singapore Open in 1978. More recently, he took the 1982 New Zealand PGA, was second in the New Zealand Open and won the Air New Zealand Open.

GINN, Stewart   Australia
b. Melbourne 1949

Although mostly playing in Australia and the Far East, Ginn is a frequent, usually short-term, visitor to Britain, where he won the 1974 Martini. After turning professional in 1971 he topped the Australian Order of Merit two years later, but belied his promise by going into decline. The reason was an extremely destructive hook. However, he came back strongly in 1979, when he took the Australian and New South Wales PGAs and the New Zealand Open, the latter an event he also won in 1981.

GOGGIN, Lindy (née Jennings)   Australia
b. Tasmania 1949

One of the best Australian players for a good many years, Lindy Goggin took her national title in 1971, 1977 and 1980, and was runner-up in 1982. She was one of the celebrated Australia team that took the 1978 World Team Championship by 1 stroke, and has been an international since 1970. In 1981 she became the first Australian to reach the final of the US Amateur, where she faced the defending champion, Juli Inkster, without much doubt the world's leading woman amateur. Lindy won the 16th to go 1 up but then was rushed to defeat as Juli Inkster birdied the last two holes to win – they were the only birdies either player had in the match. In the semi-finals, Lindy Goggin was 4 down with eight to play and then won the next five holes, eventually taking the match by 1 up. Lindy Goggin once won the Tasmanian Amateur seven days after leaving hospital following the birth of one of her children, and has won that title about a dozen times.

GRAHAM, Anthony David   Australia
b. Windsor, New South Wales 1946

Even today, the Australian golfer must venture overseas if he is to win both fame and fortune, and David Graham is truly an international golfer although he has long since been US-based, having qualified to play that Tour in 1971. Graham has won in Mexico, Japan, Australia, Thialand, New Zealand, South America, Britain and South Africa, besides taking seven events on the US Tour. He has steadily come to be considered a major golfer. In 1979 he became the first Australian since Peter Thomson to take one of the four major championships. In the US PGA of that year, over one of the most testing courses in the USA, Oakland Hills, he opened 69, 68, 70, and in his final round came to the 459-yard last hole needing a par 4 for a 63, which would have equalled Bruce Crampton's 1975 record. Graham pushed his tee shot and then took one club too many for his shot to the green and finished through the back. His chip to the flag finished only on the fringe and he then chipped 5 feet past and missed the putt. He was then left with a testing downhill putt to tie Crenshaw's score, but he managed it. In the sudden-death play-off, Graham had to hole from 25 feet and 10 feet to save himself, but then birdied the 3rd to be champion. Two years later came his greatest achievement. At Merion in the US Open he began 68, 68, 70, a score that left him 3 behind George Burns. In the final round Burns began consistently to put his tee shots in the left rough and Graham steadily overhauled him. I consider that his final round of 67 was the finest exhibition of consistent striking I have yet seen. Not once did he fail to hit a green in regulation strokes and only once did he miss a fairway. He won by 3 strokes over George Burns and Bill Rogers, the first non-American to win since Tony Jacklin in 1970. Graham has taken two other titles that rank only a little below the major championships: the 1976 World Matchplay at Wentworth, which he took with a series of stupefying putts from Hale Irwin, and the 1977 Australian Open. Graham is fairly graceless in style. As he sets up to the ball there is very much the impression of a machine being aligned for action. The head is tucked into the hunched-up shoulders, he has rather straight legs and the right wrist is notably arched. Even his walk is rather stiff. But it all works very effectively indeed. He is a good thinker about the game and has carried this over into golf-club design. Unlike other major players, if a club is said to include his thoughts it really does, and a few years ago he worked on the clubs that eventually bore the Nicklaus imprint. Rather a hard and sometimes bitter man, he was perhaps tempered by early disagreements with his father who said he would never speak to him again if the young Graham left school to become a professional golfer. David did leave, and they are said not to have met since. For a good many years now David has centred on the US Tour, playing away only in a handful of selected events, and on that Tour he has four times passed $100,000, on three of the occasions also passing $150,000. His best placing on the money list was in 1976 when he took two events and came eighth and he has been in the Top 60 every year from 1972 except for 1973. In 1981 he was 13th for his highest money total of $188,286. In 1982 he won $103,616 without a win but in France took the Lancôme Trophy for the second successive year at the end of the season. Graham did not play in the Australian Open at the end of 1982 because of a disagreement about appearance money.

US wins 7 (1972–81)
US money $1,132,498 (1971–82) (28th all-time)
Overseas wins 17 (1970–82)
Europe money £98,921 (1972–82) (37th all-time)
World money $1,753,762 (1969–82) (19th all-time)

GRESHAM, Anthony Y.   Australia

In 1982 Tony Gresham announced his retirement from international competition, during which he had seven times represented Australia in the World Team Championship. In this series his greatest achievement was to win the individual title at Buenos Aires in 1972. With rounds of 70, 69, 73, 73 he beat Ben Crenshaw by 2 strokes. Against professional fields, he had won the Opens of South Australia and New South Wales and took the 1979 Australian Amateur. He also won the 1980 French Amateur, and in 1981 reached the semi-finals of the British. Gresham has been outstanding as a chipper and putter and would have made his mark as a professional. He began the 1981 Victoria Open with 69, 66, though he eventually finished well down the field.

HAMMOND, Dame Joan   Australia
b. Sydney 1912

Although far more famed as operatic and concert soprano than golfer, Joan Hammond owed some opportunities in singing to golf. After she had won three New South Wales women's titles and had represented Australia in international matches against Great Britain and New Zealand, the Australian LGU raised money so that she could follow musical studies in Austria and Italy during the 1930s. Dame Joan later repaid her debt by giving concerts to help finance overseas trips by Australian women golfers.

HICKEY, Marea: see Parsons

JENNINGS, Lindy: see Goggin

KENNEDY, Edwina   . **Australia**
b. 1959

Three times Australian Junior Champion and a runner-up for the Australian title, Edwina Kennedy had the greatest moment of her career in 1978 when she reached the final of the British Ladies'. There after a very close-fought match she beat Julia Greenhalgh by one hole to be the first Australian winner. Later in the year she was with Lindy Goggin and Jane Lock in the Australian team which won the World Team Championship. She also won the Canadian title in 1980 by 11 strokes with scores of 72, 72, 72, 71. She is physically extremely powerful.

KIRKWOOD, Joseph H.   **Australia**
b. 1897; d. 1970

Joe Kirkwood earned more fame as a trick-shot artist than as a top golfer, and once holed in one after hitting his shot from a watch face. During 1937 and 1938 he embarked on a world tour with Walter Hagen for a series of exhibition and challenge matches, enlivened by his trick shots. He also toured with Gene Sarazen. He was the first man to make big money without many tournament victories. As a golfer Kirkwood first came to the fore by winning both the Australian and New Zealand Opens in 1920, and the following year in Canada came joint second in the Canadian Open. Playing in the US, he won the 1922 North and South and had three wins in 1924. Although he never succeeded in making much of an impression in the US Open, he did better in Britain. After a sixth in 1921, he was fourth at Troon in 1923 despite having a 79 and 78 amongst his scores, and was fourth equal behind Jones at St Andrews in 1927.

KOLB, Jan: see Stephenson

LISTER, John Malcolm   **New Zealand**
b. Temuka 1947

The US Tour is an unrelenting test of golf. Consider the case of John Lister, one of the best golfers New Zealand has produced in 20 years and one who devotes most of his competitive time to the US, where he plays very nearly full time. In the four years 1978 to 1981 he won some $53,000 and played well over 400 rounds of golf to do so. From 1980 to 1981 he entered 42 tournaments, won money on six of these entries and totalled just over $6,000 in the two years. Yet in 1978 and 1980 he averaged under 73 per round and that was good enough to bring in only $50,000 or so, while in 1981 he travelled the length and breadth of the USA to play in 23 tournaments and only once received a cheque for the trouble. It was for $1,300, which would just have covered his week's expenses. During 1982 he decided to return to New Zealand. Before choosing to concentrate on the US Tour John Lister had been, and continued to be, successful on the local scale. He was second in the 1969 New Zealand Open, won the country's PGA in 1971, 1976 and 1977 and took the Garden City Classic four years in a row, from 1972 to 1975. In Europe he won the Piccadilly Medal in 1970 and en route to the Ulster Open equalled the 54-hole record at Shandon Park with 194. He was a World Cup player in 1969, 1971 and 1972. Lister qualified for the US Tour in 1970 and his best year was 1976, his only breakthrough into the Top 60 when he was 54th and won the Quad Cities Open. In 1982 he decided to leave the US Tour.

New Zealand wins 7 (1972–7)
Europe wins 2 (1970)
US wins 1 (1976)
US money $253,959 (1970–82) (169th all-time)

LOCK, Jane, MBE   **Australia**
b. Melbourne 1955

After being dominant in the Victoria Junior Championship and three times Australian Junior title holder from 1973 to 1975, Jane Lock was Australian Women's Champion in 1975, 1976 and again in 1979. She had perhaps her most dramatic experience in the World Amateur Team Championship of 1978. With all depending on her, she was 8 over par with four to play. She then eagled the 15th and parred in. On the last she was some 20 yards from the hole in 2 strokes and needed to get down in two more if Australia were to win. She did, eventually holing a 3-foot putt. In 1979 she was finalist for the British Ladies' and in 1980 was runner-up for the French title, winning the Astor Salver in Britain. She won the Canadian the following year, after which she turned professional. In 1981 she won the Australian Women's Open, and has now taken the plunge and competes on the US Tour.

US money $8,961 (1982)

Graham Marsh

MARSH, Graham, MBE — Australia

b. Kalgoorlie 1944

Graham Marsh was a mathematics teacher at the time when he finished runner-up in the 1967 Australian Amateur and won the West Australian title. He then decided to try professional golf; he still had the teaching profession to fall back on. He was to become one of the most successful golfers ever internationally. In 1977, for instance, he proved himself on the US Tour by winning the Heritage Classic and being 22nd on the money list, while he also recorded victories in the Philippines, Japan, England and France. He won $275,000 worldwide. Marsh's first professional win came in New Zealand in 1970 and he then followed with a win in his European debut, the Swiss Open. The next year he added India to his bag and in 1972 had his first Japanese event; in that country by 1982 he had won 21 times, easily a record for a non-Japanese player. He was the Asia Circuit number one in 1972 and 1973. It could almost be said of Graham Marsh that he was so successful elsewhere that he did not need to 'prove' himself by competing in the USA. However, he did so, though after his 1977 triumphs and two more quite successful campaigns, he now plays there little. Marsh's reputation suffers a little from the fact that he has been more successful in Japan than anywhere else and there is little press attention in the West to

happenings either there or on the Asia Circuit. Yet only in the USA can competitive standards be said to be clearly higher. Marsh has for long been a major player in Europe, where in recent years he has been accustomed to appear for a relatively short time, win £20,000 or £30,000, and then depart with a couple of new titles or high-place finishes. Oddly, he has been relatively unsuccessful in his own country and, until 1982, he had only a Western Australia Open win to show for his efforts. However, 1982 saw a breakthrough with wins in the South Australia Open and the Australian Masters, an event of increasing prestige. The one remaining gap in his record is that he has yet to take a major championship, his nearest approaches being the 1981 European Open and the World Matchplay. In 1973 he reached the final, and in a dramatic match was not defeated until the 40th hole as Gary Player saved himself with a sequence of excellent bunker shots. Marsh was there again in 1977, this time defeating Ray Floyd by 5 and 3. Marsh is an intelligent, sensitive and withdrawn man and his play reflects these characteristics. He sets himself for each shot with great care to align all the moving parts correctly, and then hits the ball neatly. He strikes firmly, but without ever suggesting that the procedure is other than meticulously controlled, while on the putting greens his demeanour changes little whether the ball goes in or lips out. In all this he is in strong contrast to his equally famous brother, Rod Marsh, for many years the Australia wicketkeeper, who gives the impression at least on the field of being flamboyant, raucous and aggressive. Graham is a model professional. Latterly he has added to his burden by becoming involved in golf politics. Soon, inevitably, the strains of this, of competition, and of endless world travel (as his statistics show, he is one of the most international of golfers) will get through to him, and he may already be on the decline, though he won the Australian PGA late in 1982. Graham Marsh is one of the few Australian golfers to have been rewarded for his services to golf with the MBE.

Japan wins 21 (1977–82)
Europe wins 10 (1970–81)
Europe money £193,198 (1970–82) (12th all-time)
Asia wins 7 (1971–77)
Australia wins 4 (1976–82)
US wins 1 (1977)
US money $199,386 (1977–82) (184th all-time)
World money $1,867,709 (1970–82) (16th all-time)

MASTERS, Margaret Ann   Australia

b. Swan Hill, Victoria 1934

Five times winner of the Victoria Junior Championship, Margee Masters added the national event in 1955 and the following year the New Zealand Women's Open. In 1957 she won the South African Amateur, and in 1958 the Australian title. In her home state she took the championship consecutively from 1959 to 1963, and also won the 1960 New Zealand Strokeplay Open, was runner-up for the Australian title in 1962 and took the Canadian Ladies' in 1964, thus completing a slam of national titles of four different major golf countries. With few worlds left to conquer she joined the US Tour in 1965, probably a little past her best, and was Rookie of the Year. Late or not, she was in the top 20 from 1965 to 1971, with a best place of tenth in 1967. Thereafter, she continued to play into the 1980s, remaining in the Top 60 until 1976. Margee used to travel with two poodles, Mateus and Lancer. She was a top swimmer at school.

US wins 2 (1967–8)
US money $112,220 (1965–80)

NAGLE, Kelvin David George   Australia

b. Sydney 1920

Kel Nagle was an extremely late developer, all his most memorable achievements coming at a time when most tournament players are thinking of a peaceful retirement. His first success of note came in the Australian PGA of 1949, after turning professional in 1946. Little followed this and Nagle disappeared for some time, leaving behind him the

Kel Nagle

reputation of his being a very long hitter and a poor putter. When he re-emerged he was an excellent putter and, with a burly, simple swing, not particularly long off the tee but undeniably straight. He still confined his competitive play to Australasia, where he was at his most effective in New Zealand. He won the New Zealand Open seven times between 1957 and 1969, the last three years consecutively, and has taken the New Zealand PGA the same number of times, his last victory coming in 1975 at the age of 54. Part of the explanation of his skills lasting into late middle age is that Nagle is fortunate in actually enjoying competition, while to most professionals it is an almost unbearable stress that has to be tolerated and can be borne only until the nerve bank is exhausted. Nagle was persuaded to try his luck in Britain in the early 1950s, but at this time he had little or no success, and his appearances on the world stage were rare. However, in 1954 and again in 1959 he paired with Peter Thomson to win the Canada (World) Cup. Thomson again argued that his game was good enough to take on anyone and Nagle was at St Andrews for the Centenary Open in 1960, the year that Arnold Palmer made his dramatic first appearance. Thomson, a St Andrews specialist, instructed him in its subtleties and, with Nagle's starting price at 35–1, put money on him to win. Kel Nagle's opening rounds of 69, 67 left him 2 strokes behind Roberto de Vicenzo but the Argentinian then fell away to a 75 and Nagle went into the afternoon's final round 2 ahead of Vicenzo and, as was to prove more significant, 4 ahead of Arnold Palmer, who a few weeks before had charged through the US Open field at Cherry Hills with a last-round 65 to win. The climax came on the last two holes. As Nagle faced a 10-foot putt on the 17th green, a 2-stroke lead in hand, a roar came from the last green. Palmer had birdied to finish in 68. Nagle now had to hole his putt and par the last to win. He did just that. Nagle continued thereafter for several years to feature strongly in the British Open. He was fifth the following year, and at Troon in 1962 was the only player to threaten Palmer's dominance of the championship. He came in 6 behind but 5 clear of the rest of the field. In 1963 he was fourth, in 1965 fifth and 1966 again fourth. He continued to feature well up the field until after 1971, the year he finished 11th at the age of 50. Now a Senior, he won the 1971 British title, scoring 62 in the last round to do so; then he beat Julius Boros 4 and 3 in America for the World title. He won the British event in

1973 and in the USA was beaten by Sam Snead only on the 41st hole. In 1975 he again took both titles. Nagle had earlier competed in the USA, finishing 22nd in the 1964 money list and winning the Canadian Open. In 1965 he came very close to adding the US Open to his record, tying with Gary Player and losing the play-off. Nagle was above all an extremely steady player, bolstered by the excellent putting of his mature years. He seldom lapsed into the high 70s, though there was one occasion – the 1968 Alcan – when he had a 105 in the second round. On his score card, Christy O'Connor had written in Nagle's nine-hole total of 34 in the space reserved for Nagle's score on the 9th and the rules dictated that it had to stand after Nagle had signed his card as correct. From being a stay-at-home, Nagle became a truly international player, winning in Australia, New Zealand, Canada, France, Britain, the USA and Sweden.

Australasia wins 21 (1949–76)
Europe wins 10 (1960–71)
US wins 1 (1964)
US money $112,762

NEWTON, Jack   **Australia**
b. *Sydney 1950*

The 1975 British Open at Carnoustie set Tom Watson on his way to become a great player. In his victory Watson enjoyed two vital pieces of 'luck', a long putt on the 72nd hole and, in the play-off, a chip in for an eagle. The sufferer was Jack Newton, who had given his best performance in a major championship. He had begun 69, 71 and then broke the course record with a 65, which equalled the championship record. Bobby Cole led him by 1 going into the final round with Miller 1 behind Newton and Watson 2. Newton had been putting very well indeed, he thought as a result of a Nicklaus tip to let forearms dominate the stroke. With four holes to go he had a 2-stroke lead and was 1 under par for the round. He then took three to get down from just off the green, dropped another shot on the 16th and made his fatal error on the 17th. Possibly not noticing a change of wind, he used a 2-iron to clear the Barry Burn when a wood was called for. He cleared the Burn but was on the bank slope with no hope of reaching the green on the 454-yard hole. He had now to birdie the last, as had Watson, to win. In the event, he had a long putt for the Open but came up short. The play-off was closely contested, though Watson took an early 2-

stroke lead. Newton fought back and on the par-5 14th was dead in three, the point at which Watson chipped his eagle. Nevertheless, the pair were all square on the last tee but Newton bunkered his shot to the green and did not get his bunker shot close. Newton had been born with great sporting talents, being chosen for Australian Schoolboys at both cricket and rugby. Deciding to concentrate on golf after a rugby injury, he is perhaps the best cricketer among today's professional golfers. He also qualified as a PE teacher. At golf he won some 30 amateur competitions and reached the semi-finals of the 1969 Australian Amateur before he turned professional in 1971. As an Australian golfer of ambition must, he went on the international scene and has competed extensively in Australia, New Zealand, Africa, Europe, Japan and the USA, having successes everywhere. However, he has not become quite the top player that once seemed likely because of his good all-round game and powerful driving. For a while, he was a leading player in Europe, being second in the money list in 1973 and producing superb golf in the 1974 Match-play when he was 36 under par for the 107 holes he played. Before beating Cesar Senudo in the final, he demolished the defending champion Neil Coles by being 10 under par for the 13 holes he needed before victory came. In 1972 he won the Dutch Open and the Benson and Hedges Festival successively. In America Newton had one good short run in 1980, though the result this time was only two second places. At the Greater Greensboro', he came in behind Craig Stadler, and the next week in the Masters he was again second, with Ballesteros totally dominant. Newton had long wanted to play the US Tour if he could earn enough elsewhere to be secure without the need for a sponsor. His US results have been only moderate in the years 1977–82, but he has suffered injuries. He has won once – the Buick Open in 1978 – and made the Top 60 in 1980, a year in which he was also leader of the Australian Order of Merit; but he played 20 tournaments in 1981 for only 173rd place on the money list. Newton may now be fading, having not really made the best of his talents, and his two major championship performances and victory in the 1979 Australian Open may prove the high-points of his career. At the end of 1982 he decided to abandon the US Tour, intending to return to European competition.

Australasia wins 5 (1972–9)
Africa wins 3 (1974–6)

Europe wins 3 (1972–5)
US wins 1 (1978)
US money $191,898 (1977–82) (191st all-time)

von NIDA, Norman George   Australia
b. Strathfield 1914

Norman von Nida came into golf from the ranks of the caddies. In 1929 he announced himself to the touring Walter Hagen with the words 'I am the best caddie in Brisbane.' 'OK, son,' said Hagen, 'then you and I are a pair because I am the best golfer in Brisbane.' Von Nida first attracted attention by winning the Queensland Amateur at the age of 18 in 1932. Shortly afterwards he turned professional, making a living mainly by money matches with wealthy amateurs and challenge matches with visiting US golfers. He took the Queensland Open in 1935, beating Jim Ferrier by 2 strokes, and the New South Wales the following year. In his career he was to total 17 state titles. With limited opportunities in Australia he tried the embryo Far East circuit and won a couple of tournaments. He went to the USA to try his luck in 1939, but the outbreak of war forced his return home. He had been runner-up for the Australian Open that year. In 1946 he arrived in Britain with £17 in his pocket and a month to go to the first tournament. Immediately among the money-winners, von Nida finished the season in joint second place with £1,330. The following year he set several records. He is still the only player since the war to have won three tournaments in a sequence of four, and to have won four of the first six in which he played. By the end of the season he had won or tied first seven times and beat the previous money record by some £750 with his total of £3,263, though this seems little enough today. In the Open Championship that year he shared the lead after three rounds; but Fred Daly, in the best of the weather, came through to win with von Nida tied for sixth. His Vardon Trophy-winning stroke average of 71.25 set the record. Von Nida was never again so dominant in Britain but he continued highly successful, finishing third in the 1948 Open and winning the Dunlop Masters that year. He shot a 63 at Sunningdale. He took three other tournaments, and his last British first place came in 1951. In Australia he won the PGA four times between 1946 and 1951 and the Australian Open in 1950, 1952 and 1953, on the last occasion closing with a 65 to beat Peter Thomson. A short man, usually topped with a beret, von Nida was a colourful and outspoken figure. Often in the news, he had no high opinion of the press, whose coverage of him was sometimes unfavourable. During one of his occasional forays to the USA much talk resulted from an incident in the 1948 Lower Rio Grande Valley Open. Playing the first hole with von Nida, US Ryder Cup player Henry Ransom attempted to knock in a putt of an inch or two one-handed – and missed. He later insisted that he had taken just two putts and after the round punched the Australian, who insisted that three putts had been taken. The local sheriff eventually pulled them apart and Ransom was both disqualified and banned for three months. But the press blamed von Nida. Although he weighed just 9 stone and stood 5 foot 6 inches, he was not a short hitter, making up for lack of height by a wide and long swing and very full shoulder turn and, like Gary Player, hitting very hard. He was a great player of bunker shots and a straight hitter, deciding against the current USfashion of learning to play with either fade or draw. His putting was good on occasion, but normally his scores were made on good play through the green. He is said to have snapped more than one putter in anger and to have once thrown one over the railway at Southport and Ainsdale. Once past 40 von Nida decided that his putting nerve and general concentration had gone, and from 1963 he cut down his appearances; yet as late as 1978 he was seen in competition, putting with a driver in one tournament as cure for a problem on the greens. He won a host of tournaments in Australia which cannot be counted as of full status, including the New South Wales Open four times. In semi-retirement 'the Von' became very generous with his time in encouraging young Australian golfers, including Peter Thomson, Bruce Crampton, Kel Nagle, Bruce Devlin, David Graham and Greg Norman. Although his career was highly successful there is little doubt that World War II deprived him of almost half his peak years; yet he still ranks in the top half dozen of post-war Australian golfers.

GB wins 12 (1946–51)
Australia wins (major) 8 (1946–53)
Asia wins 2

NORMAN, Greg   Australia
b. Mount Isa 1955

Greg Norman did not play golf until the age of 17, and then became a scratch golfer in under two years. Things came similarly easily to him after he turned professional in 1976, his first tournament win in the West Lakes Classic in Australia coming in only his fourth tournament entry with a 10-stroke lead after three rounds. Late the same year he was chosen for the Australian World Cup pair after he had played just six professional tournaments. Norman von Nida commented that he was better than two other precocious golfers, Peter Thomson and Gary Player, had been at the same age. Norman soon won a reputation for savage hitting, and Tom Weiskopf was to rate him as the longest straight hitter he had seen. In the 1981 US Masters he hit one drive of 340 yards and averaged 275, while in the 1979 Australian Open he had a $100-a-hole side bet with Fuzzy Zoeller on the longest drive and came through easily. For some years, however, it was felt by many that a weakness in his game was that he hit too many shots full out and did not pay enough attention to the short game. Von Nida worked on his approaches from 50 yards in and bunker play, while Norman has in recent years paid more attention to his putting, with good results. In 1977 he came to Europe for the first time and finished 20th in the Order of Merit, taking one event, the Martini. In 1978 he added a Fiji win to the New South Wales Open but did not win in Europe, though he moved up to 15th place in the Order of Merit. He topped the Australian Order of Merit that year. He again won the Martini in 1979 and also took the Hong Kong Open. More important, he had completed his apprenticeship and was about to become a major player: with Ballesteros, he became a man of star quality, producing his first overwhelming performance in the French Open where, with scores of 67, 66, 68, 67 for 268, he won by 10 strokes. Then, in the Scandinavian Enterprises Open, he began with a 76, followed with 66, 70 and then came through the field with a last-round 64, when only three others in the field broke 70. At the end of the European season, in the World Matchplay, he took a good lead away from Nick Faldo and won on the 38th, then beat Bernard Gallacher and finally Sandy Lyle – who was leading money-winner that year, while Norman was second. He then went home to take his most prestigious tournament to date, the Australian Open. In 1980 he topped the Australian Order of Merit. In 1981 he won £27,000 in an 18-day spell. First he took the Martini – mainly because he covered the 17th and 18th at Wentworth, both par 5s, in 4, 3 to beat Bernhard Langer by 1 stroke –

went on to a fourth-place finish in the PGA and then in the Dunlop Masters at Woburn had a 68, 66, 67 finish for a 4-stroke win. Although he played only nine tournaments he finished fourth in the Order of Merit. The only real disappointment came in his defence of the World Matchplay, when Severiano Ballesteros proved for at least one day who was number one in Europe, beating Norman by 8 and 6. Norman had by this time won two 'near' majors, the 1980 Australian Open (next year he was second) and the 1980 World Matchplay, but he has produced relatively little in the four majors. His best performance came in the 1981 US Masters where, on his first appearance, he finished fourth, with scores of 69, 70, 72, 72. He had held the joint lead after the first round and was second and third in the succeeding rounds. In 1982 he became one of only two players to win the Dunlop Masters title in successive years, one of his most dominant performances. Scoring 68, 69, 65, 65, he finished 17 under par and won by 8 strokes. Two other wins followed in the State Express Classic and the Benson and Hedges. In both he showed how good his nerve is by holding on at the Belfry to par the last hole, the most testing on the course, and later

Greg Norman

having a birdie on the last at Fulford. Despite a restricted European schedule, he finished leading money-winner with £66,405. During the season he had shown improved putting, and also that he had lost none of his length, for he once hit the green at a 371-yard hole with a 3-wood and at 281 yards had the longest average on the European Tour. He was also best at hitting greens in regulation. Norman now bases himself in the USA and intends to concentrate on the US Tour while also playing selected events in Europe, Australia and the Far East. He has a formidable record of international successes behind him and appears to have the nerve necessary to take a major championship. He is also one of few crowd-pleasers in present international golf, able to chat affably to spectators whether things are going well or ill. He is both an excellent competitor from the front and able to come through with a strong last round.

Europe wins 10 (1977–82)
Europe money £41,938 (1977–82) (6th all-time)
Australia wins 5 (1976–81)
Asia wins 3 (1977–9)

OWEN, Simon   New Zealand
b. 1950

'One crowded hour of glorious life is worth an age without a name', said Sir Walter Scott, and Simon Owen may well agree. His crowded hour came at the 1978 British Open. He began 70, 75 and then had a 67. This equalled the best round of the championship and put him 1 behind the leaders. He was paired with Jack Nicklaus the final day and did not falter under the pressure, having five 3s in a row from the 8th and taking the lead when he chipped in on the 15th. However, on the 16th there followed a sand-iron shot that pitched perhaps a yard too far and then bounded 25 yards through the green. Owen failed to get down in 2; Nicklaus birdied. Later he dropped another shot to finish in second place with Kite, Crenshaw and Floyd. At the end of the season he showed that this result was no mere flash in the pan when in the World Matchplay he beat Andy North, Severiano Ballesteros and Graham Marsh before going down to Isao Aoki in the final. Owen turned professional in 1971 and won the Fiji Open in 1972, following with his own country's PGA in 1973, a win he was to repeat in 1978. He first competed in Europe in 1974, finishing 11th in the Order of Merit and winning the German Open, while in 1976 he won the

Simon Owen

Double Diamond Individual and the New Zealand Open. In 1978 he came 16th in the Order of Merit. Since then, his form has fallen away, something he ascribes in part to his favourite driver having been stolen in 1978. He represented New Zealand in the 1973 and 1976 World Cups and was for a while New Zealand's best player, a position regained by Bob Charles in 1982.

Europe wins 2 (1974–6)
Europe money £81,064 (1974–82) (45th all-time)
Overseas wins 4 (1972–8)

PARSONS, Marea (née Hickey)   Australia
b. Gosford, New South Wales 1945

After being twice Australian Junior champion, Marea Parsons won the Australian Women's in 1964 and 1969, and also took the New Zealand title on her 19th birthday in 1964. In 1969 she won the South African title, en route beating Sally Little in the semi-finals. She played three times in the World Team Championship and in 1968 was runner-up for the individual title.

PERCY, Judith   Australia
b. Assam, India 1925

Judith Percy won the Australian title in 1954, 1960 and 1962; the six-year gap came when she gave up the game from 1955 to 1959 in order to concentrate on running the family farm at Toowoomba. She played in internationals against South Africa and New Zealand and in the Commonwealth event, and in 1950 reached the semi-final of the British Ladies' where she lost to the eventual champion, the Vicomtesse de St-Sauveur.

PHILLIPS, Frank   Australia
b. Moss Vale 1932

A mighty hitter, Frank Phillips was overshadowed by such contemporaries as Peter Thomson, Bruce Crampton and Bruce Devlin. He was also troubled by eyesight and back problems. However, he twice took the Australian Open, in 1957 and 1961, and on the latter occasion his 275 was the second lowest score recorded. Phillips confined himself mainly to Australasia and the Far East. He won the New Zealand PGA in 1955, the Singapore Open in 1961 and 1965 and the Hong Kong Open in 1966 and 1973, the latter his seventh Asian win. He was four times runner-up for the Australian PGA. He retired from tournament golf in 1977, becoming a Sydney professional.

PICKWORTH, Horace Henry   Australia
b. Sydney 1918; d. 1969

Ossie Pickworth came too early for the big money but was a dominant figure on the Australian golf scene for some ten years after World War II. In 1946 he took his first Australian Open title, beating his coach, Jim Ferrier, in a play-off which prevented Ferrier from winning a record three in a row. This was a record Pickworth was himself to take, for he added further victories in 1947 and 1948, when he beat Jim Ferrier in a play-off again. He won once more in 1954, and announced his retirement from competitive golf after finishing second in the 1957 event. He won the Australian PGA in 1947, 1953 and 1955 and was beaten finalist in 1951. He also won six Ampol events and four state Opens. A superb putter, he once played that other master on the greens, Bobby Locke, at the par-73 Royal Melbourne course in a match in which Locke went round in 65 but was bested by a Pickworth 63. Pickworth seldom ventured overseas but did come

to Britain in 1950, when he finished third in the Order of Merit, won the Irish Open, tied for the *Daily Mail* tournament and played in Australia's first World Cup team. His fairway wood play was very highly rated, Henry Cotton thinking him the best in the world. He had a curious dip of the knees coming into the ball, which he felt helped to keep the hands low through the hitting area and beyond.

PULZ, Penelope   Australia
b. Melbourne 1952

An Australian international and later winner of four Australian professional events, Penny Pulz joined the US Tour in 1974. Since 1975 she has had high tournament finishes each year and has been in the Top 60 from 1975 to 1981, her best years being 1978–81, with a career-best tenth in the money list in 1978 with $71,011. In 1979 she had her only Tour victory in the Corning Classic.

US wins 1 (1979)
US money $285,343 (1974–82) (33rd all-time)

RATCLIFFE, Noel   Australia
b. 1945

Noel Ratcliffe did not turn professional until later than most, in 1974, having represented Australia at amateur level in the 1972 Eisenhower Trophy. He had a good year in 1976, winning the Huon Open in Papua New Guinea. The next year he won the South Australia Open and came to Europe. He had little success that year, but in 1978 finished 11th in the Order of Merit when he won the Belgian Open as result of a last-round 66 when 6 out of the lead. He was joint second in the Benson and Hedges to Lee Trevino after a play-off. His scores at Fulford were 69, 69, 69, 67. He was less successful in the following seasons, his best performance coming in the 1981 Martini International, for which he had to pre-qualify. He led into the last round, but finished third. He qualified for the 1983 US Tour.

Europe wins 1 (1978)
Europe money £51,336 (1977–82)
Overseas wins 2 (1976–7)

SHANKLAND, William   Australia
b. Sydney 1907

As an Australian international footballer Bill Shankland toured Britain in 1929, and came back to play rugby for Warrington. Eventually, his wife insisted he try a less bruising sport, and Bill Shankland became a very effective professional golfer, with some good performances in the Open to his credit. He was joint third in 1939, fourth in 1947, when his last-round 70 was the best produced by contenders, 11th in 1949 and 6th in 1951. He won the *Yorkshire Evening News* in 1945 and 1947, and the 1948 Leeds Cup. A man of strong opinions, he persisted for some time in putting with an implement that resembled a car starting-handle, and at Potters Bar GC both advised and clashed with the young Tony Jacklin. He played in many charity exhibitions during World War II. Now retired, he plays frequently at Parkstone.

SHAW, Andrew J.   New Zealand
b. Troon, Scotland 1898

Emigrating to New Zealand after World War I, Andrew Shaw became the best player in that country during the years between the wars. In days of easier international travel he would probably have established a worldwide reputation. He won the New Zealand Open in 1926, 1929, 1930, 1934

Bob Shearer

and 1936, in 1930 by no less than 18 strokes. In the New Zealand Professional he was equally dominant, winning in 1928 and 1929 and from 1931 to 1934. During world tours by Gene Sarazen and Walter Hagen he beat them both.

SHAW, Robert   Australia
b. Sydney 1944

Bob Shaw won the 1968 New Zealand PGA and then had a very successful season in Continental Europe, winning the Spanish Open, losing a play-off for the Dutch and finishing second and fifth in the German and French Opens. He then qualified for the US Tour. He never made the Top 60 but won the 1972 Tallahassee Open, the Florida Open in 1976 and 1977 and the 1976 Jamaican. Eventually he returned to Australia and won the 1980 West Lakes Classic. He was fourth in the Order of Merit that year, and tenth in 1982. In 1978, playing with Greg Norman, he suggested a $50 side bet for birdies with triple for eagles. With his next shot Norman holed the 2nd at Pacific Harbour, Fiji, in one to be $150 to the good. Shaw was one of the best strikers in the world, but lacked discipline.

US wins 1 (1972)
US money $77,068 (1969–78)
Overseas wins 2 (1968)

SHEARER, Robert Alan   Australia
b. Melbourne 1948

Bob Shearer is a golfer who has had to struggle. He won the Victorian Boys' Championship at the age of 15 and took the Australian Amateur title in 1969. The following year he turned professional, but it was some time before he began to be a winner with the 1974 Chrysler Classic and Tasmanian Open. At much the same time his effectiveness in Europe increased, for in 1974 he rose to 21st place in the Order of Merit and the following year won the Madrid Open and the Piccadilly Medal, rising to second place in the Order of Merit; he also won again in Australia. In 1976 he won once in Australia and once in New Zealand, qualified for the US Tour and played little in Europe, though doing well enough to take 17th place in the Order of Merit. He found the US Tour a difficult proposition and won only $4,000, but has since concentrated on playing that Tour and in Australia and New Zealand. In 1977 he topped his home country's Order of Merit and won twice, while in the US he made the Top

60 both in that and in the following year; but for the next three seasons he fell well out of the Top 60 and totalled only some $74,000. He did, however, win the 1978 New Zealand Open and the 1980 Gold Coast Classic. Then in the 1981–2 Australasian season he had a spurt of form, winning the New Zealand Open again, and he dominated the Air New Zealand Open. Beginning with a 63, he added three more sub-70 rounds and came home with an 8-stroke margin. He later won in Wellington as well, and topped the Australian Order of Merit. With his confidence renewed, he then had easily his best US season. He won the Tallahassee Open with a birdie, birdie, eagle, par finish, was sixth in the Byron Nelson Classic, second in New Orleans and nearly won in Houston, but lost a play-off. In that tournament he had seemed in command, beginning 69, 67 and then having birdies on eight of the first 15 holes in the third round and completing it in 64, good enough for a 5-stroke lead into the final round, where he drifted to a 75. His results later that year in the USA were not as good, but he won well over $100,000 in 34th money place for the year. Shearer has suffered ill health, particularly in 1980 when he was troubled by pancreatitis and low blood sugar. He has also been dogged by the yips, but a reverse-hand grip brought about at least a temporary cure. He won the New South Wales Open late in 1982 and the Australian Open.

Australasia wins 14 (1974–82)
Europe wins 2 (1975)
US wins 1 (1982)
US money $306,822 (1976–82) (144th all-time)

SMITH, Marilyn J.　　New Zealand
b. Lower Hutt 1952

Known as 'M.J.', partly to avoid confusion with the great American player Marilynn Smith, she won the New Zealand Junior three times between 1968 and 1972, and the national strokeplay title in 1972. She then turned professional and was leading money-winner on the Australian Tour the following year, and also took second place in the Japan Open. In Australia she had four wins and nine seconds in 19 tournaments. Since then M.J. has played the US Tour with reasonable success. She was in the Top 60 in 1976, 1977, 1978 and 1980, with 42nd in 1977 and 43rd for $33,720 in 1980 her best seasons. She finished second to Jan Stephenson in the Sun City Classic in 1982.

US money $138,843 (1974–82)

STANLEY, Ian　　Australia
b. Melbourne 1948

A powerful player, Ian Stanley earned a reputation for 'always coming second'. During the second half of the 1970s he is said to have finished in this position about 20 times. One of these was in the 1974 Australian PGA, in which he tied with Billy Dunk and lost the play-off. He has also been an occasional winner, taking the 1975 Queensland Open, being joint winner of the 1975 Martini and winning the 1976 South Seas Classic, the 1979 Victorian PGA, the 1980 Geraldton Open and the 1981 Traralgon Classic. He played the European Tour in the 1970s and was in the Top 60 every year from 1972 to 1976, 27th in 1975 being his best ever finish.

STANTON, Robert James　　Australia
b. Sydney 1946

Bob Stanton turned professional in 1965 and the following year won both the German Open and the Australian Dunlop, beating Arnold Palmer in a play-off. The following year he joined the US Tour and was in the Top 60 in 1969 and 1970. At that point he had twice been second and twice third, and reached 34th place on the 1970 money list. Thereafter his form declined abruptly from 1971 to 1973, when he averaged only a little over $4,000 a year. He revived a little in 1975 but has since dropped out of the US Tour.

US money $210,000 approx. (1966–75)

STEPHENSON, Jan (later Kolb)　　Australia
b. Sydney 1951

Current achievements indicate that Jan Stephenson may be the best Australian woman player ever, and that in a country where standards are very much on the rise. She came to prominence very young, winning the New South Wales schoolgirl championship from 1964 to 1969 and then the Junior Championship from 1969 to 1972. She had also taken the Australian Foursomes at the age of 15, and the New South Wales Women's twice. She represented Australia against New Zealand in 1970. Turning professional in 1973, that year she won the Australia LPGA and four other events, including closing with a 64 to take the Lady Tarax. In 1974 Jan Stephenson went to the USA and was immediately successful, finishing 28th in the

Jan Stephenson

money list her first year. She was Rookie of the Year. However, for some time her sex appeal received rather more attention than her golf, as was also the case with Laura Baugh. She has refused offers to pose for both *Playboy* and *Penthouse*, compromising by appearing topless in the French magazine *Oui*. Much comment was caused in 1981 when she appeared in a photograph which her fellow Tour player Jane Blalock called 'quasi-pornography' in *Fairway*, a publication of the US LPGA. Little was revealed to public gaze but she was reclining on an unmade bed. Jan Stephenson has commented: 'I'm not ashamed of my body and if I feel like flaunting it I'm going to.' Certainly this has done no harm at all to US gates, for she is undoubtedly the leader among players whom the public wants to look at rather than appraising the quality of their golf. But Jan Stephenson is also in the highest class as a golfer despite that fact being obscured by her other publicity in earlier Tour years. After her first season she improved modestly in 1975 but made a big advance in 1976, when her stroke average was 73.38, she won the Sarah

Coventry and Birmingham Classics and was eighth on the money list. The following year she won the Australian Open after a play-off with Pat Bradley, reduced her stroke average to a very good 72.52 on the US tour and was 11th on the money-list, though without another win. Since then she has been consistently successful, always in the top 15 except in 1980, when back trouble limited her entries and effectiveness. In 1981 she became one of the top group of players. In fifth money-list place she won three times, including a major championship, the Peter Jackson Classic at Quebec. She began 69, 66 and finished 72, 73, holing a putt of 4 or 5 yards to win by 1 stroke from Nancy Lopez and Pat Bradley. Another win was in the Mary Kay Classic, in which she gave probably her finest scoring performance. With 65, 69, 64 she won by 11 strokes from Sandra Haynie, while her 198 total broke the record by 2 for a 54-hole tournament. Her prize money for the year of $180,528 in the USA, was added to by her victory in the 'Women's World Championship' in Japan. Jan Stephenson's 1982 was a little troubled. She was fined $3,000 for playing in Japan when expected to play in the USA, and was involved in a complicated personal lawsuit. Nevertheless she produced another major championship-winning performance to take the LPGA, her 69, 69, 70, 71 giving her a 2-stroke margin over JoAnne Carner and making her, with Chako Higuchi and Sally Little, one of three non-Americans to win the title. The following week she won the Lady Keystone to be ninth in the money list at the time, and won $133,212 on the US Tour for the year. At the beginning of 1983 she had played 191 tournaments without missing a cut.

US wins 9 (1976–82)
US money $657,595 (1976–82) (15th all-time)

THOMSON, Peter W., CBE   Australia
b. Melbourne 1929

The best Australian golfer ever, Peter Thomson, with five, has the most victories in the British Open since the days of Vardon, Taylor and Braid. He won it three times consecutively from 1954 to 1956, a feat only previously achieved by 'Young Tom' Morris, when standards can hardly have been comparable. His main rival during these years was Bobby Locke, and they were similar in some ways. Neither was a long hitter, and both were more interested in keeping the ball in play, using a 3-wood from the tee with frequency. If Locke was a far better putter and chipper, Thomson was competent enough there and the better long-iron player. Both had superb judgement of distance and the run of the ball, which made them at their best on running linksland courses. His first tournament win came in the 1950 New Zealand Open, a victory he was to repeat on no less than eight occasions, and he took his own national title the first of three occasions the following year. In 1951 he came to Britain, the scene of his finest achievements, for the first time and finished sixth in the Open. His record in the next several years was as follows: 1952: 2nd; 1953: 2nd; 1954: 1st; 1955: 1st; 1956: 1st; 1957: 2nd; 1958: 1st. Thereafter he did not feature strongly for some years but returned to winning ways in 1965. After a long battle with Tony Lema he came through to record his fifth victory. This was almost the last time he featured among the contenders, though he scored well in 1969, finishing 3 strokes behind Tony Jacklin in third place. Thomson's victory in 1965 was specially relished by him because a full US entry was assembling each year by this time; that had hardly been the case during the 1950s, though there had been a strong international field. He had been advised to prove his greatness by playing the US Tour but did so only intermittently, for his low, running style of play was not suited to lush US courses. Indeed he recorded only one victory over there, in the 1956 Texas Open; it was in the same year that he gave his best performance in a US Open, finishing 4 strokes behind Cary Middlecoff in fourth place. The next year he was fifth in the Masters. He was particularly effective as a golfer in Britain, arguably the most successful tournament competitor since World War II. Apart from the Open, he won 20 other tournaments, including the Matchplay Championship four times, the Dunlop Masters twice and the 1967 Alcan International. He played in this last event because he had not qualified for the Alcan Golfer of the Year. His winning score was 2 better than Gay Brewer's in the main event. When he won the 1962 Martini at St Andrews his score of 275 betters what has ever been achieved in an Open Championship over the course by 3 strokes. In more recent times, it can be compared to Nicklaus's winning 281 in 1978. Thomson never felt that golf was all, or even most of, life, and he is said not to have relished the company of fellow professionals, many of whom he found limited in outlook and conversation. To some extent he preferred his own company, or that of people outside golf, or perhaps

a book, the theatre, a museum. He also became involved in golf 'politics' and was a strong influence in the development of the Asia Circuit, in which he competed consistently and with great success. He wished also to see a world golf tour come about, and was successful to the extent that it is certainly now possible for a professional to move from continent to continent and compete at a high level for 12 months of the year. Thomson made golf look a simple game, partly because he stood to the ball briskly and without obvious complicated adjustments to the mechanism, and struck without notable effort. He gripped the club very lightly, believing that the grip naturally tightened as the player came into the shot. There was considerable lateral sway in the backswing and a hip-slide into the ball. Faults were that he allowed the club to slip in the right hand and sometimes his head turned towards the target too early. He believed that touch and judgement were worth far more than power. He announced his retirement from tournament golf after the 1979 Australian Open. Since then he has occupied himself mainly with golf architecture; presidency of the Australian PGA; journalism;

Peter Thomson

Odyssey, an organization concerned with drug addicts; and politics. He stood in the Victorian State elections and came fairly close to winning a seat. Thomson was made an honorary member of the R&A in 1982. He appears on the US Senior Tour occasionally.

Europe wins 26 (1954–72)
Europe money £71,400 (50th all-time)
Australasia wins 19 (1950–72)
Asia and Japan wins 11 (1954–76)
US wins 1 (1956)

VINES, Randall Colin   Australia
b. Queensland 1945

This very good Australian golfer would probably have enjoyed even more success had he enjoyed competitive golf but found it a considerable strain on his stomach, and generally on his 10-stone frame. However, he was successful for a while, particularly on the Asia Circuit where he was a particularly consistent money-winner and took the 1968 Thailand and Hong Kong Opens successively. In Europe he won the Côte Basque and Swiss Opens in 1967, the latter with scores of 67, 68, 69, 68. In 1968 it was claimed, incorrectly, that his winning margin of 17 strokes in the Tasmanian Open was a tournament record. Vines began with an unpromising 77 but followed with 65, 67, 65 to leave Walter Godfrey far behind. In his last round he was seven under par in one five-hole spell: birdie, birdie, albatross, birdie, birdie. Perhaps his outstanding achievement was to win the Australian PGA in the successive years 1972 and 1973. He left tournament golf to be professional at Helensvale, Queensland.

WHITTON, Ivo Harrington   Australia
b. Melbourne 1893; d. 1967

A very important figure in early Australian golf and later in administration, Ivo Whitton won the Australian Amateur in 1922 and 1923 and was also twice runner-up. More at home in strokeplay, he did even better in the Open, winning it in 1912, 1913, 1926, 1929 and finally 1931, when he beat the young Jim Ferrier by 1 stroke. He also won nine state amateur titles. He once had what must be a record handicap of plus eight.

WOLSTENHOLME, Guy England & Australia
b. Leicester, England 1931

Guy Wolstenholme has had three careers: first as one of the best British amateurs, then as a successful tournament professional, and finally as a Senior. He first came to the fore as a boy international from 1946 to 1948 and was a full England international from 1953 to 1960, a period during which he was perhaps the best English amateur, following the virtual retirement of Ronnie White. Wolstenholme won the English Amateur twice, in 1956 and 1959, and the English Strokeplay in 1960, being also twice second in this event. He won the German Amateur in 1956 and six major amateur events, including the Berkshire Trophy three times. He was twice in the Walker Cup team, in 1957 and 1959. He won his singles the first year but was beaten 9 and 8 by Harvie Ward in 1959. In 1960, when he was top amateur and finished sixth in the Open Championship with rounds of 74, 70, 71, 68, he turned professional. He was 16th in the Order of Merit the following year. He had eight other placings in the top 25 up to 1970, with 11th in 1966 and ninth the year after being his most successful. He played for England in the 1965 World Cup (and was to be an Australia international in 1971). The 1963 Jeyes was his first major tournament victory and he did it in style: by 12 strokes. Later he won the 1966 PGA Closed title. Wolstenholme won three national Opens, in Kenya, Denmark and Holland, the first two in 1967 and the Dutch in 1969. In the mid 1960s he made his home in Australia and took three Australian state titles, two New Zealand tournaments and one in Japan. As a Senior he has won the 1981 Australian title and tied with Christy O'Connor in Britain in 1982, losing the play-off. He also competes successfully in the USA, and came close to winning in 1982.

Australasia wins 5 (1968–76)
Europe wins 5 (1963–9)
Japan wins 1 (1969)

SOUTH AFRICA

BAIOCCHI, Hugh   South Africa
b. Johannesburg 1946

After winning the 1968 Brazil Amateur and his own country's title two years later, Hugh turned professional at the end of 1971. After a quiet first year, in which he did respectably in Europe, he had his first win in the Western Province Open and took a further event on the South African circuit. Later he took the Swiss Open. Since that time, while Hugh has seldom attracted close attention, he has compiled a very consistent record, winning every year up to and including 1980. His consistency in 1973 in Europe took him to third place in the Order of Merit and he bettered that in 1977 with second place. This was the year when he had possibly his most prestigious victory, the PGA Matchplay Championship, though the South African Open the following year may well be his proudest achievement. He has won four European national titles, the Swiss Open twice.

South Africa wins 9 (1973–80)
Europe wins 5 (1973–79)
Europe money £164,015 (1972–82) (16th all-time)

BAKER, Vincent   South Africa
b. Durban 1946

Having been good at soccer and an excellent tennis prospect, Vince Baker took up golf at the age of 16 and later decided to make that, rather than tennis, his career. He improved up to the 1973 season when he tied for second place to Bob Charles in the South African Open, and then in Britain produced a last round of 64 in the Benson and Hedges Festival which took him past leader Dale Hayes. That year he finished 31st in the Order of Merit. Since then he has not reproduced similar form, though he did finish 26th in the Order of Merit in 1978 and was equal second in the Italian Open.
Europe wins 1 (1973)
Europe money £25,950 (1971–9)

BLAND, John   South Africa
b. Johannesburg 1945

In 1981 John Bland tied with Gary Player and Warren Humphreys for the South African Open. After an 18-hole play-off Bland and Player were still level, with Gary eventually winning in extra holes. Bland's other successes in South Africa include five wins, one of these the 1977 PGA, a year in which he finished top of the South African Order of Merit and won three times. Before this Bland had seldom competed in Europe and on his few appearances had won less than £200 in total, but, once into his thirties, he became a much improved player blessed with a smooth putting stroke and a generally excellent short game. From 1977 to 1982 Bland has not finished worse than 45th in the European money list, and his best placing came in 1980, when he was 11th, winning £27,945. In that year he produced some of his best golf in the Benson and Hedges Festival. Beginning 73, 69 he lay 13 strokes behind Graham Marsh but finished 65, 67. When he holed a pitch shot on the 12th hole in the final round he had caught Marsh but the Australian produced a couple of birdies over the closing holes to regain his lead, with Bland finishing second.

South Africa wins 5 (1970–79)
Europe money £108,828 (1970–82) (33rd all-time)

BREWS, Sidney F.   South Africa
b. Blackheath, England 1899; d. 1972

Sid Brews compiled a remarkable record of longevity by winning the South African Open in four different decades. In all he won eight times and also took the South African PGA six times within a similar period. Particularly remarkable was the fact that he won both in 1952, when he had reached the age of 53. In all Brews is estimated to have won nearly 50 important tournaments, by no means all of these in South Africa. He also, for instance, won a couple of times in the US in the mid 1930s and won five European Opens. No one was considered his equal on the South African scene until the emergence of Bobby Locke in the late 1930s, but Brews continued to be successful even after Locke's appearance. Possibly his finest hour was in the 1934 British Open. After two rounds Brews was 6 behind the man eventually to finish third and was 15 behind Henry Cotton. In the third round he picked up 1 on Cotton and in the last a further 8. Not, of course, enough, but he had outscored the champion over the last three rounds and finished firmly in second place.

BRITZ, Tienie   South Africa

b. Johannesburg 1945

Winner of six tournaments in South Africa, including the 1970 and 1971 PGA, Britz has won only once overseas, the 1977 German Open. He has competed regularly in Europe during the 1970s and early 1980s and is a frequent money-winner though very seldom in the limelight. Since 1971 he has been seven times in the Top 60 and easily his best year was 1977, when he finished 19th in the Order of Merit. Solid rather than spectacular, he is an excellent putter, as are so many South Africans. He has represented South Africa in the World Cup and in 1972 finished third in the individual placings.

South Africa wins 6 (1969–72)
Europe wins 1 (1977)
Europe money £70,281 (1971–82) (52nd all-time)

COLE, Robert E.   South Africa

b. Springs 1948

At the age of 15 Bobby Cole was national Junior Champion and Transvaal Amateur winner. Three years later he finished second in the English Amateur Open Strokeplay and set a record in the British Amateur at Carnoustie. His victory at the age of 18 years 1 month equalled the achievement of John Beharrell 10 years earlier. The following year he became the youngest player, amateur or professional, to survive the halfway cut in the Masters. Later, he finished first in the US Tour qualifying competition. Thereafter there was less glory for Bobby Cole. Although he has passed $300,000 on the US Tour, in his 1968–82 spell, only once has he made the Top 60 and has just one victory to his credit – the 1977 Buick Open. Besides that victory, perhaps his best achievements in

North America have been an equal third place in the 1974 US PGA and third in the 1973 Canadian Open. In South Africa, Cole has been more successful, winning 12 times and taking his national Open in 1974 and 1981. He was also instrumental in South Africa's World Cup win, taking the individual title. Cole has always been thought to have a superbly lissome swing, one of the best in world golf, and Gary Player has called him golf's longest hitter, pound for pound. Cole himself ascribes some of his troubles to his swing: lissome it may be, but he has felt that there is some looseness on the backswing. Although seldom competing in Britain except for appearances in the Open, Cole played strongly in 1974, finishing seventh, and then in 1975 began 72, 66, 66 at Carnoustie, which gave him a 1-stroke lead going into the final round. Throughout the final day he was in contention but eventually came in with a 76 and third place behind the Watson/Newton play-off. In 1980 he married Laura Baugh, a leading US woman golfer (and the leader in terms of endorsements).

South Africa wins 12
US wins 1 (1977)
US money $371,274 (1968–82) (121st all-time)

Bobby Cole

FOURIE, John   South Africa
b. Pretoria 1936

A late recruit to the professional game – he did not give up his amateur status until the age of 34 – John Fourie was perhaps finally persuaded to make the change when he won the 1970 South African Dunlop Masters by 6 clear strokes. Previously he had not had a particularly successful amateur career, but he had been runner-up in the South African Amateur Championship the year before. Into the professional game he took a superb putting stroke, which has in large measure been responsible for his successes. These include five wins in South Africa and one in Europe, when he took the Callers of Newcastle tournament in 1977. Though he competes little in Europe now, he has four times been in the top 30 in the Order of Merit with best placings of 19th in 1975 and 18th in 1977. Probably his most unfortunate experience was to have the Spanish Open snatched from his hands in 1975 when Arnold Palmer eagled the final hole.

HAYES, Dale   South Africa
b. Pretoria 1952

In 1981, Dale Hayes announced that he had had enough of tournament golf and henceforward would concentrate on the less stressful life of a South African club professional. At only 29 he felt burned out. Hayes grew to near greatness in the early 1970s with one of the shortest and fastest swings ever seen on a golf course. He always appeared to be hitting the ball as hard as possible, which is perhaps one reason for his achieving slightly less than had been forecast for him. He was a most notable young amateur, winning the South African Strokeplay title twice, the Scots and German Amateur and the World Junior. In 1970 he finished second in the individual rankings in the Eisenhower Trophy. He then turned professional. Quickly he won his first tournament in South Africa, then won in Brazil and Europe also, where he took the Spanish Open at the age of 18, as precocious a talent as the Ballesteros of 1976. Although 1972 was a quiet year for him, in the three European seasons that followed he finished fourth, second and first in the Order of Merit, winning the Vardon Trophy in 1975. He had by this time won a dozen tournaments. In 1976, when he became both South African Open and PGA Champion, he answered the call of America because he needed to prove himself against the best. For 1976

and 1977 he concentrated on the US Tour and was relatively unsuccessful, though he did finish equal second in the 1977 Florida Citrus Open. Back in Europe again, Hayes finished second in the Order of Merit and won both the Italian and French Opens. In the latter, at La Baule, he had rounds of 66, 69, 67, 67 for a total of 269, perhaps his best performance ever in a tournament. This left him 11 strokes ahead of Severiano Ballesteros and 14 ahead of those in third place. Since that year Hayes has had one more victory – in the 1979 Spanish Open. In 1980 he fell from fourth to 16th place in the European Order of Merit.

South Africa wins 10 (1971–6)
Europe wins 6 (1971–9)
Europe money £156,978 (1971–82) (18th all-time)

HENNING, Harold   South Africa
b. Johannesburg 1934

In 1955 the young Henning (known as 'Horse' on the circuit) gave Gary Player his first tournament victory – Player beat him in the final of the Egyptian Matchplay Championship at the Gezira club. Twenty-six years later, Henning was saying

Harold Henning

'I've a great future behind me' – just after taking the 1981 Dutch Open, at the age of 46. As these results perhaps indicate, Henning has played all over the world, relying for the cornerstone of his game on superb putting. Although not consistently a player on the US Tour, he won the 1966 Texas Open and a year later finished 21st on the US money list. He was in the top 50 seven of the eight years he played in Europe in the period 1961–79, and in 1963 had the most enjoyable experience of being handed the then vast sum of £10,000 for a hole in one at Moor Park during the Esso Golden tournament. He has won five events in Britain and eight Continental Opens amongst his accredited 54 wins worldwide, of which most have been in South Africa. When he won the US Tallahassee Open he produced the startling finish of birdie, eagle, birdie. A frequent player for South Africa in the World Cup, he won it with Gary Player for South Africa in 1965, when the event meant far more than it does to the major golfing nations today. Besides his Continental Opens, Henning was twice third in the British Open, in 1960 and 1970, and won the South African in 1957 and 1962, thus breaking Player's almost total dominance in the event. He has also four times won the South African PGA, from 1965 to 1967 and again in 1972. This record shows that Harold Henning could with justification claim to be the third best South African golfer ever, after Locke and Player.

South Africa wins 39
Europe wins 13
Europe money £47,830 (1961–82)
US wins 2

LEGRANGE, Cobie   South Africa
b. Boksburg 1942

Cobie Legrange was not a golfer who lasted any too well. In 1964 he looked a future world-class player. He took two events in Australia, one in New Zealand, one in South Africa and one in Britain, the Dunlop Masters. But he was a particularly intense player and suffered one of golf's most painful ailments: the difficulty of taking the clubhead away from the ball. In 1969, when he again took the Dunlop Masters, at a point when he was 6 ahead after three rounds, he developed a stop in his backswing about an inch away from the ball and two more stutters on the rest of the way back. For many, a pause before beginning the backswing (which with Nicklaus was once an age) may indi-

cate that the player is waiting to feel 'right' for the stroke; for others the delay is really caused by fears of what is going to go wrong once the player commits himself to it. Most golfers suffer from this – it is often called 'choking' – but Legrange had it worse than almost any other professional. Nearly all his successes came when he had the problem reasonably under control, in the period from 1964 to 1969. After this he won only twice, in 1970 and 1974.

Africa wins 12 (1964–74)
GB wins 4 (1964–9)
Australasia wins 3 (1964)

LEVENSON, Gavin Neal   South Africa
b. Johannesburg 1953

After winning the 1978 French and Rhodesian Amateurs and playing for his country as an amateur Gavin Levenson turned professional in 1978 and had immediate success by finishing second in the South African Open. Since then he has played the South African and European circuits. He qualified for the US Tour for 1981 but failed to hold his card. His best performance was in the 1979 Belgian Open, in which he led, or joint led, all the way with scores of 68, 71, 68, 72 and won by 3 strokes from Michael King, Nick Faldo and Bobby Cole. In 1982 he again played the US Tour with more success. The pronounced leg action in his swing has given him the nickname 'Legs'.

Europe wins 1 (1979)
US money $33,303 (1981–2) (282nd all-time)

LITTLE, Sally: see North America

LOCKE, Arthur D'Arcy   South Africa
b. Germiston, Transvaal 1917

In the 1946–7 season Bobby Locke played a 16-match series in South Africa against Sam Snead, who was most surprised that Locke never seemed concerned where the flag was: he just put his ball on the green and holed the putt. Locke won 12 matches, Snead two. The experience had the effect of damaging Snead's own putting, so that he fell out of the top half dozen in the US Tour for the first time in his career. Locke had been advised to try himself in the USA by Walter Hagen in the late 1930s, and now he decided to go. In 1947 he arrived in time for the US Masters and came in

14th. Some US professionals who had watched him on the practice ground at Augusta felt that that was the best he could hope for. His swing was far too long and the clubhead too far right at the top; his wrists were floppy; and 'The guy duck-hooks all his shots.' Locke went on his way and won the Carolinas PGA, which he followed rapidly with the Houston Invitational, then third in the Texas Open. An encounter with Ben Hogan came in the *Philadelphia Inquirer* Open, Locke managing a swing of 7 strokes in the third round and going on to win yet again. He then completed a sequence of four wins in five entries with the Goodall Round Robin. He followed with a couple of thirds, one of which was in the US Open, and then took the Canadian Open. George May offered him what was then the very substantial sum of $5,000 to compete in his Tam o' Shanter tournament; Locke won that too, and another $7,000. In his two remaining Tour events Locke was first and second, and finished second on the money list in his short season. Locke, not surprisingly, returned for more in 1948, winning three times. The most notable was his dismissal of the field in the Chicago Victory National Championship by 16 strokes, the largest margin in US Tour history and beating a mark of 14 set by Hogan in 1945 and Johnny Miller's 1975 win in the Phoenix Open. Locke won three times in 1949 and once in 1950. In this latter year in the Tam o' Shanter, he tied Lloyd Mangrum with four birdies in the last five holes, needing four long putts to do so, and then took the play-off 69–73. This was worth $50,000 in prize money to Locke, and there was also a contract for 55 exhibitions at $1,000 each with an option to double the number. The tournament was therefore worth the then vast sum of $160,000. In the meantime he had been banned by the US PGA from competing in their tournaments, which Gene Sarazen called: 'The most disgraceful action by any golf organization in the past 30 years'. Contempt for Bobby Locke's style had turned to terror of his competitive successes. However, the experience soured Locke's attitude to the USA, where he competed little thereafter, preferring the warm appreciation he received in Britain and Europe. By the age of eight Bobby Locke had been a 14 handicap player and by the age of 18 was playing off plus 4. He had also acquired the discoloured putting blade with a hickory shaft that he used all his golf career. He took the South African Boys' in 1931 and in 1935 won the Amateur and Open Championships of

South Africa when just 18. If the putter was one turning-point in Locke's development, his 1936 visit to Britain was another,: he realized that he was a short hitter, being outdriven by some 35 yards by British professionals. At the time Locke played with fade and considered that everything about the golf swing must be relaxed and even loose. He did not wish, therefore, to hit harder; instead he must learn to draw his shots. The eventual result was the Locke trade mark of aiming further right than any golfer of stature before or since and floating it back in. He did not become a truly long hitter, but his ball rolled much further. By the time World War II came, Locke, who had turned professional in 1938, had won the South African Open five times, the Amateur twice, the PGA three times, had held ten South African state championships and had also begun to win overseas. In 1938 he won the Irish and New Zealand Opens, and the Dutch Open in 1939. The 10-stone stripling then went off to fly over 100 missions in Liberator bombers over the Mediterranean. For two and a half years he did not touch a golf club; then he returned to golf in 1946 as the portly figure of about 14 stone soon to be so familiar in Britain, Europe and the USA. He continued to dominate in South Africa, and won three tournaments in Britain and was joint second in the Open. Two years later at Sandwich he took it as his first major championship, beating Irishman Harry Bradshaw by 12 strokes in a 36-hole play-off. He won again at Troon in 1950, setting a new championship record of 279 with rounds of 69, 72, 70, 68, finished fifth the next year and at Royal Lytham in 1952 had his third victory, this time with the ominous name of the young Peter Thomson 1 stroke behind. From 1954 to 1956 Thomson won three in a row, with Locke once second, 1 stroke behind, and once fourth. Then in 1957, when thought past his best, he made a final surge at St Andrews. With rounds of 69, 72, 68, 70 he equalled his 279 Open record and beat Thomson by 3 strokes. After the match a brief controversy arose. On the last green Locke had marked his ball a couple of putterheads' distance from his line, to allow space for a fellow competitor to finish off his round. Locke then forgot to replace his ball and himself putted out. No one noticed at the time: it was spotted on news film. Would Locke be disqualified as the laws might demand? The R & A met, decided that Locke had derived no benefit, and the result stood. It was, however, nearly the end of Locke's days as a major championship golfer. He

Bobby Locke

OOSTHUIZEN, Andries   South Africa
b. Pretoria 1953

At the British Open at Carnoustie in 1975 there was some confusion among the press at the similarity of names between Peter Oosterhuis and Andries Oosthuizen, compounded by the fact that both were strongly in contention. Oosthuizen began 69, 69, 70. He shared second place after two rounds and was 1 shot behind the eventual winner, Tom Watson, with a round to go. Few scored very well on the final day, particularly Oosthuizen, who came in with a 78 in joint 12th place. However, it had been a glittering start to a career that had begun with his being South African Amateur Champion in 1973. He turned professional and in 1974 was 63rd in the European Order of Merit, improving to 14th in 1975 and then falling to 42nd in 1976. Little has been heard of him since, though he showed some revival of form in the South African season of 1981–2.

PLAYER, Gary Jim   South Africa
b. Johannesburg 1935

British Open Champion: 1959, 1968, 1974
US Masters Champion: 1961, 1974, 1978
US Open Champion: 1965
US PGA Champion: 1962, 1972
South African Open: 13 wins
Australian Open: 7 wins
World Matchplay: 5 wins

Only the first four of those listed rank as major championships, and in these Gary Player's nine victories rank him level with Hogan and John Ball, and behind only Nicklaus, Jones and Hagen. However, his more than 120 tournament successes worldwide rank behind only Snead and de Vicenzo. Player, as a South African, had to be a world traveller to find fame and fortune, and he has almost certainly covered more miles in pursuit of golf than any other golfer. His normal year has been to compete in Australia, South Africa and the USA in particular, with forays to Europe and South America – there are few golfing countries indeed where he has not played. Player has ascribed his success to various causes: Norman Vincent Peale's *The Power of Positive Thinking*; not smoking or drinking alcohol, tea or coffee; eating bananas and wheat germ; self-hypnosis; wearing black clothing to absorb the strength of the sun; press-ups, running and other exercise; and, most of all, practice.

won two British events the same year, and finally the Transvaal Open of 1958. What were the features of an ability that brought more than 80 wins? From the tee there was the slow, hooking flight that usually found the fairway. Into the green he had superb feel for distance: if he missed the green he was usually pin high, and from there he was probably the best chipper in golf for a good many years. He was also a pitching master, that feel for distance again paying dividends. His putting stance was a little unusual, for he stood with his feet together and the left foot advanced well in front of the right. He then took the putter back on an inside line, regarding cut on a putt as anathema. From there, some Americans claimed he hooked the ball into the hole. This is not a serious possibility, but certainly his putts seemed struck particularly caressingly, and to roll on and on when it had looked inevitable that they would stop short. He spent some time on long putts pacing the green in stately manner, trying to assess the pace of the surface. He was then just about the best there was at coasting the ball to the holeside or at holing the middle distance ones. Locke himself declared that he was not a good short putter – but then he left himself few to deal with.

South Africa wins 38 (1935–58) (amateur and professional and including state Opens)
GB wins 18 (1938–57)
US wins 15 (1947–50)
Europe national Opens 5 (1939–54)
Other overseas wins 5 (1938–55)

As a teenager Player spent most of the hours of daylight on the course, the most beneficial results probably being that he became a very good judge of distance, reader of greens and arguably the best bunker player there has yet been. All this did not give him a good swing, and I remember thinking when he first came to Britain in 1955 that his stance was faulty, his left hand grip too 'strong' and his swing too flat. When one well-known British professional was asked his opinion by Player he advised him to go back to South Africa and get an honest job. Player took his first title in 1955, the Egyptian Matchplay, then the British Dunlop and the South African Open in 1956. He was on his way, already nearing the high status that was to last for more than 20 years. In 1957 he paid his first visit to the USA and sat at the feet of Hogan, who also thought his swing too flat, and he won the first of many Australian tournaments, the PGA, beating Peter Thomson in the final. The next season he won his first Australian Open and his first in the USA, the Kentucky Derby Open. He was an established international player, with wins in four continents. There followed his first major championship: he came through the field with a last-round 68 to take the British Open at Muirfield. Before the 36 holes of the last day he had been 8 strokes behind the leader, a good illustration of one of his characteris-

tics: he never gives up and has won many tournaments from positions that others would have thought hopeless. In 1961 he had a very good year in America, becoming the first overseas-based player to be leading money-winner, with $64,540, and won the Masters, with Ballesteros, still the only foreigner to do so. The finish was dramatic: Player was bunkered by the last green but got down in two. Moments later, Palmer was in the same position, needing to get down in three to tie – and took four. He was to have his revenge the next year, when he beat Player and Finsterwald in a play-off. Later in the same season Gary Player added his third major championship, the US PGA, again the first overseas golfer to do so. The punishing world schedule continued. In 1965 he became one of four golfers (Nicklaus, Sarazen and Hogan are the others) to win all four major championships when he won the US Open at Bellerive after a play-off with Kel Nagle. He was the first overseas player to win the US Open since Ted Ray in 1920. He was now established, with Nicklaus and Palmer, as one of 'the Big Three'. His prime ambition now was to do the slam of four majors all over again. In 1968 he added a win in the British Open at Carnoustie, after a rousing contest with Jack Nicklaus in the final round, and in his best year to that date won seven times in Britain, America and South Africa, including demonstrating his dominance in matchplay by taking the Piccadilly World Matchplay for the third time. It was in this event that he had in 1965 made the best-known recovery of all time, one that he said 'contains my whole life story'. In the 36-hole match he was 7 down with 17 holes to play, got it back to 3, lost another hole and with three still to play was still 2 down. Player won the 34th, holed a 3-yard putt on the next to avoid losing the match and birdied the last to draw level. On the first extra hole he went ahead for the first time since the 11th tee and was into the final, which he won, beating Peter Thomson. His great 1968 season had come when there were many to say that he was beginning to slide from his 'Big Three' position. In 1974 more people were saying that, yet in terms of major championships it was his best season, the only time he has won two the same year. It began at the US Masters. After two rounds he lay 5 behind Dave Stockton and also behind such golfers as Tom Weiskopf, Hale Irwin, Jack Nicklaus, Hubert Green and Frank Beard. He then had a 66 to pull himself back among the leaders. With nine holes to go, in the final round, some eight players were still in

Gary Player

with a chance before Gary settled it on the penultimate hole when he hit his approach shot to within inches. He won by 2 from Stockton and Weiskopf. That year the big ball was compulsory in the British Open for the first time at Royal Lytham. In strong winds he began 69, 68, to lead Peter Oosterhuis by 5 strokes and came home with a winning margin of 4 over the Englishman. At the end of the year he recorded the lowest score in a national championship in the course of winning the Brazilian Open. This was his card: 3, 4, 3, 3, 4, 2, 3, 3, 4 (29); 2, 4, 3, 4, 4, 4, 2, 4, 3 (30). During the season he reached 100 victories worldwide. By common consent he was golfer of the year. By 1978 he had not won another tournament in the USA, though he had recorded a sequence of three consecutive wins in the South African Open and in 1977 won the World Cup individual for the second time. At Augusta in the US Masters he began by playing very well indeed through the green but with ineffective putting, still unconvinced that his change from a jabbing movement to a stroke was fully effective. He had rounds of 72, 72, 69 to be 4 behind Rod Funseth and Tom Watson and 7 behind Hubert Green. For the first nine of the final round he made some progress on the leaders, having three birdies but dropping a stroke on the 7th. He was out in 34 and then put in one of the most dramatic finishes recorded in a major championship. He parred only three holes; the rest were all birdies, climaxed by a 15-foot putt at the last to set a 277 target. One by one the pursuers failed, Green missed a short putt to tie, and Player had his third Masters and ninth major championship. His 64 equalled the Masters record. The following week he was at the Tournament of Champions. He began with rounds of 70, 68, 76 and was again 7 strokes behind the leader, Severiano Ballesteros, with 69, 65, 73. Player produced a 67, while Ballesteros collapsed to 79; he was first by 2 strokes. And so to the Houston Open where he began 64, 67, 70 for a 3-stroke deficit before his closing 69 gave him a 1-stroke victory and made him only the 11th man to win three US PGA events in a row. Even then he was not done, for the following week at New Orleans he began 69, 67, 69 to share the lead; but this time he sagged in the last round and came in fifth. In terms of money won on the US Tour, 1978, with $177,000, was his best and he finished ninth on the money list, one of nine times he has been in the top 9. From 1961 to 1965 he was seventh or better, fifth in 1969 and 1971 and seventh in 1972. Seven times he has

topped $100,000, and he has been 20 times in the Top 60. Although never playing the US Tour full-time, he has built easily the most successful record there of an overseas player. At 5 feet 7 inches Player has always lacked the length to be a world-beater but has surmounted the obstacle by striving for enough length to reach the par 5s in two. He has done this by a relentless pursuit of strength and physical fitness and by hitting more full-out than perhaps any other great golfer – he seldom looks perfectly balanced at the end of the drive. Thereafter, his short irons are particularly crisp and accurate, his bunker play unexcelled and he is still one of the most successful putters. Most important of all, however, is his mental toughness and will to win. As one professional said: 'Why is Gary such a success? Oh, he just likes beating people.'

Australia wins 30
US wins 21 (1958–78)
US money $1,671,137 (1957–82) (10th all-time)
World wins over 120 (1955–82)
World money $2,887,820 (1953–82) (4th all-time)

SEWGOLUM, Sewsunker South Africa
b. Durban

Very much an oddity as a golfer, Sewgolum was the only successful golfer to play all shots with a grip in which his left hand was positioned below the right. He was a very good putter. He won the Dutch Open in 1959, 1960 and 1964; but at home his appearances were much restricted by apartheid, for he was of Indian parentage. He often played in Europe, where he was popular with the tournament crowds partly because of his charm but mostly because of the novelty value of his strange grip.

SHEARD, Alison Irene South Africa
b. Durban 1951

The best South African amateur woman golfer after the departure to the USA of Sally Little, Alison won the South African Ladies' from 1976 to 1978, and also the Strokeplay title in 1974, 1975, 1976, 1978 and 1979. She was runner-up to Cathy Panton for the 1976 British Ladies', and in 1979 won the British Women's Open as a professional in the year that she was leading money-winner on the British circuit. Since 1980 she has tried the US Tour, finishing 91st and 96th in her first two years and 99th in 1982.

US money $27,128 (1980–82)

SUNDELSON, Neville   South Africa

Neville Sundelson was a leading South African amateur of the early 1970s, packing considerable achievements into a small space of time. He won his national Amateur in 1972, but perhaps his best year was 1974. Then he was second in the South African Amateur, won the South African Open Strokeplay, was top amateur in his Open, was second in the French Amateur and won the English Open Strokeplay.

TAYLOR, Reginald Carden   South Africa

In a long career as a top amateur Reg Taylor won the South African Open in 1954, a time when Bobby Locke was the strongest force in South African golf. He won his country's Amateur in 1956 and was runner-up in 1968. In Europe he won the Belgian and German Amateurs in 1958 and the French in 1970. He also won the Canadian Amateur in 1962.

TSHABALALA, Vincent   South Africa
b. 1941

A Bantu, Tshabalala took a trip to Europe in 1976 financed by Gary Player, and probably surprised even his mentor by winning the French Open. With scores of 69, 70, 66, he lay three behind the late Salvador Balbuena with one round to go but, finishing in 67, won by 2 strokes. Later that year he was chosen for the South African World Cup pair but refused to play, believing that this would countenance apartheid. His entry for the South African Open was later rejected.

VERWEY, Robert   South Africa
b. 1941

The son of Jock Verwey, who was winner of the South African PGA twice in 1948 and 1949, Bobby Verwey has confined most of his play to South Africa; but he played in Britain in the early 1960s, returning to make the Top 60 on the European Tour in 1978 and 1979. In 1978 he represented South Africa in the World Cup, but in 1981 he was banned from tournaments for two years for allegedly moving his ball marker nearer to the hole. His sister Vivienne is married to Gary Player.

WALKER, Arthur   South Africa
b. Johannesburg 1929

When Arthur Walker won the English Amateur in 1957 there was some adverse comment because of his South African accent. However, he was qualified by his English parentage. He also reached the semi-final of the British Amateur in 1957 and won the South African Amateur in 1959, being second in both 1956 and 1958. He is the holder of many South African province titles.

WATSON, Denis Leslie
Zimbabwe & South Africa
b. Salisbury (now Harare) 1955

Denis Watson, now based in South Africa, is a possible future star who has made considerable progress in the 1980s. After turning professional in 1975 he had little success for a while. He began appearing in Europe in 1978. In his first two seasons he did not make the Top 60, but he entered it at 35th in 1980, with three finishes in the first six. He was also second in the South African Order of Merit that year, while in 1981 he won the Asseng Champion of Champions event there. After his moderate European success he decided to try the US Tour, and qualified for the 1981 season. In 13 entries he won nearly $50,000 to be 87th on the money list, with a stroke average about 2 below what he had last managed in Europe. In 1982 he became a tournament contender in the US, finishing joint second in the Tallahassee Open and reaching a play-off stage in the Bay Hill Classic with Jack Nicklaus and Tom Kite. On the first extra hole he was nearest, but it was Tom Kite who holed from off the green to win.

South Africa wins 1 (1981)
Europe money £19,232 (1978–80)
US money $108,243 (1981–82) (234th all-time)

WESTBROOK, Terry
Zimbabwe & South Africa
b. Johannesburg 1938

Winner of the 1971 Natal Open and the 1972 Schoeman Park Open, Terry Westbrook played in Europe with some success in the early 1970s, finishing 50th in the 1972 Order of Merit and 37th the following year.

AFRICA

CULLEN, Gary   Kenya & England

b. *Nairobi, Kenya 1954*

Gary Cullen divides his time in a pleasant way, living and playing the European circuit in summer and then moving to Kenya in the winter, where he is attached to the Karen Golf Club. In the period 1977–81 his placings in the Order of Merit ranged between 39th and 48th, but he cannot be said to have made any great progress during that period. He remains a player unable to put four consecutive rounds together. An example was his play in the 1978 British Open. After two rounds he lay just 1 off the lead after a second-round 67 (this won him the Tooting Bec Cup for the lowest round by a British player) but he then soared to a 79, followed by a 73 for 34th place. One of his best performances

Simon Hobday

came the same year, when he tied for third place in the French Open at La Baule. He was 32nd on the 1982 money list, his best performance being second place in the Sanyo Open in Spain, in which he was only a stroke behind Neil Coles with rounds of 71, 68, 64, 64.

Europe money £72,495 (1974–82) (49th all-time)

HOBDAY, Simon F.N.   Zimbabwe

b. *1940*

In 1956, Lady Eden felt that the Suez Canal was flowing through the drawing-room of 10 Downing Street. Simon Hobday must have felt similarly plagued by UDI and the civil war in Rhodesia: the more money he won in Britain, the harder the Bank of England froze it. There was some relief in 1979 when he won the Madrid Open worth £5,500, for at least this money was not frozen by the Bank of Spain. At last he had some spending money in addition to the £15,000 in winnings resting untouched in a Jersey bank. Perhaps Hobday needs spending money more than most for he has a reputation for open-handedness and roistering. Be that as it may, his path through life has not been smooth. Once a farmer in Zambia, he was given 48 hours' notice to leave the country, so loaded up a couple of furniture vans and set off forthwith for a new life in Salisbury (Harare) as a car salesman. As a golfer, Hobday did not mature until into his 30s, when his first victory was a significant one: the 1971 South African Open. Thereafter, he began coming over to Europe, but had very little success in the period 1970–72 (£1,052) and little more over the next couple of years. During 1975 his form improved, and in 1976 he came to the fore in the German Open. Beginning the last round 5 behind, he came through the field to the championship with a 66. He was on his way, and finished the season at tenth in the Order of Merit. In the period 1975–9 Simon was always in the top 30, and became an increasingly popular tournament figure, his willingness to indulge in banter and repartee during play in strong contrast to the often sullen or agonized faces around him. The year 1979 was a good one for him, with the Madrid victory to add to two in Africa the previous season, and he finished 11th in the European Order of Merit. In 1980 he won the Zimbabwe-Rhodesia Open, and the ICL International in South Africa a year later. Hobday is particularly good with his mid-irons.

Africa wins 5 (1971–81)
Europe wins 2 (1976–9)
Europe money £71,282 (1970–80) (51st all-time)

JOHNSTONE, Anthony   Zimbabwe
b. 1956

A relative newcomer to the European Tour, Tony Johnstone finished 32nd in the 1981 lists and came close to winning a tournament, the 1981 Swiss Open. After rounds of 69, 69, 71, 68 he tied with Manuel Pinero and Antonio Garrido at Crans-sur-Sierre, but lost the play-off to Pinero. He is known on the Tour as 'Elvis' because of his body movement during address. He was 42nd on the 1982 money list.

Europe money £28,005 (1980–82)

McNULTY, Mark William   Zimbabwe
b. Bindura 1953

Mark McNulty topped the South African Order of Merit in the successive seasons 1980–81 and 1981–2. In the latter season he was especially impressive, winning four of the last five events and over £35,000. He then set out to seek fame and fortune on the US Tour, where his white 'Bobby Locke' cap is reviving anxious memories for the US professionals of a certain age. McNulty competed in Britain and Europe from 1978 to 1981, and his swing made a particularly good impression. He was always comfortably in the Top 60 with a best placing of 17th in 1980 for £23,089, and won twice, including the 1980 German Open. He is now doing well on the US Tour (90th in the first year), and has the technique and will to be a top tournament player.

South Africa wins 4 (1981–2)
Europe wins 2 (1979–80)
Europe money £63,020 (1978–82) (58th all-time)
Asia wins 1 (1980)
US money $50,322 (1982)

PRICE, Nick   Zimbabwe
b. Durban, South Africa 1957

It comes to few golfers to have a major Open championship within reach: Nick Price experienced the feeling at Troon in 1982. He began 69, 69 to be 5 behind Bobby Clampett's 67, 66. Thereafter both faded, but Price much less so than Clampett's collapse to 78, 77. After the third round Clampett was still 1 ahead of Price, a lead that evaporated when Price birdied the 1st and then holed a putt from well off the green to lead the championship. After 7 holes he led by 3 strokes, but ahead of him Tom Watson was making up ground that was eventually to prove decisive, hitting a 3-iron on the par-5 11th hole to 4 feet and holing the putt to draw level. Price proved by no means done for, birdies following on the 10th, 11th and 12th to lead Watson by 3. He then dropped a shot on the 13th but really lost the Open on the 15th. Here he put his second shot in a bunker, hit the bank in front of him from the sand and played his little pitch shot well short of the flag. It added up to a 6, and he now had to par the last three to tie. A missed putt from 7 feet on the 17th meant that he had to birdie the last to tie. Price then hit a horrid drive but an equally good iron to the green and putted dead. With Peter Oosterhuis, he finished second. In 1974 Price won the World Junior Championship in America. Later, as a professional, he finished second in the 1978 Dutch Open and the following year in Europe reached the final of the PGA Matchplay, losing only to a birdie on the last hole. In 1980 he produced his best performance to that time, winning the Swiss Open with a. score of 267, the season's lowest in Europe, by 6 strokes. He had six other finishes in the top 10 to be 14th in the Order of Merit. In 1981 he won the South African Masters, but was less successful in Europe, second place in the Dutch Open being his best finish while he fell to 38th in the Order of Merit. Back in Africa, he won the Vaal Reefs Open in 1982. He has represented South Africa in the World Cup and was 22nd on the 1982 European money list. He then qualified for the 1983 US Tour.

South Africa wins 2 (1981–2)
Europe wins 1 (1980)
Europe money £79,485 (1978–82) (46th all-time)

WATSON, Denis: see South Africa

WESTBROOK, Terry: see South Africa

ASIA

AOKI, Isao   Japan
b. Abiko, Chiba 1942

Unorthodoxy used to be the norm in golf. Think of Sarazen's strange grip; the swaying lunge at the ball of Walter Hagen; the huge loop and lash of James Bruen's swing; even the excessive hip turn of Harry Vardon. The swarm of golf instruction books, strips and films and the proliferation of good golf coaching has meant in recent decades that the unorthodox have been told not to do it that way and in the main they have probably heeded the advice. No one seems to have put Aoki right and what we now have is one of the most unorthodox talents ever seen on the world stage. Attention has largely centred on the odd sight of his putter head with heel on the ground, toe pointing skywards and the ball burrowing into the hole. His full swing is equally rare: a casual flicking movement at the ball

Isao Aoki

that apparently owes more to wrists than anything else and thus contradicts all the sages' words about full shoulder turns, driving leg action and the like. Aoki's level of unorthodoxy would usually have meant a short reign at the top followed by oblivion as his youthful reflexes waned. In Aoki's case the reverse happened: he did not become a major player until he was thirty. In 1973 he was first in the top 4 on the Japan Tour and has remained there. He was leading money-winner in 1976 and from 1978 to 1980, earning nearly $300,000 there in 1980. In two years, 1972 and 1978, he had six wins. Between 1971 and 1982, he has recorded 39 wins on the Japan Tour, including the Japan Matchplay four times and the Japan PGA twice. Oddly, he has yet to take the Japan Open, though he has twice been third and three times second, twice losing by just one stroke. In 1979 he lost a play-off for the title. Although only making brief raids out of his own territory, Aoki took the World Matchplay in 1978 and was runner-up the following year. In the 1978 British Open he led at one stage but eventually finished seventh to Nicklaus after closing rounds of 73, 73. He repeated this placing the following year. In 1980 at Muirfield he equalled Mark Hayes's Turnberry 63, which had set an Open record. Perhaps his greatest achievement has been in a championship he did not win: the 1980 US Open. Aoki opened 68, 68, 68, and that still equals the US Open 54-hole record. Aoki then had a 70 in the final round, but it was not good enough to win. Nicklaus had the same score after 54 holes and a 68 in the last round, perhaps his greatest achievement. Nevertheless, Aoki's 274 broke the previous 72-hole record and earned him a substantial sum as a special prize from a US golf magazine.

Japan wins 39 (1971–82)
Japan money ¥320,000,000 (1973–80) (1st all-time)
Overseas wins 1
US money $77,412 (1981–82) (256th all-time)
World money $2,244,467 (1969–82) (12th all-time)

ARDA, Ben   Philippines
b. 1930

Nicknamed 'the Toy Tiger', Arda is the winner of some seven events on the Asia Circuit, the 1969 Indian Open and three events in Japan, including the 1973 Open. He has won his own national Open twice and has been second three times. He was third in 1979 at the age of 49. He is the best golfer yet produced by the Philippines.

AYE, Mya   Burma
b. 1940

An Asia Circuit player since 1960, he has since then been Burma's only tour player and the only top-class player the country has produced. He won the Philippine Masters in 1979 and in the same year the Japan Pepsi-Wilson. In 1975 he took the Shizuoka Open, and the Indonesian Open in 1976, a year in which he came fourth in the Japan Open. His most recent success has been in the 1981 Singapore Open, an event in which he was second the previous year.

HIGUCHI, Hisako Matsui   Japan
b. Tokyo 1945

Although she has never played the US Tour full-time Chako Higuchi has established perhaps the highest reputation of any Japanese woman player outside her own country. She had won three Japan Open or PGA titles by the time she made her first US appearance in 1970. The following year she finished second in the Heritage Open and had two second places in 1973. In 1974 she won the Japan LPGA Classic and in 1976 a US Tour event, the Colgate European Open at Sunningdale, with rounds of 68, 74, 68, 74 which left her 6 strokes clear of the field. In 1977 she won the US LPGA by 3 strokes from Pat Bradley, Sandra Post and Judy Rankin, and in 1981 she took the Pioneer Cup. She was 10th in the US money list in 1976 and 18th in 1977, while in 1979 she won some $25,000 in only six events, with a stroke average of just over 72, one of the best of the season. In Japan, Chako won the LPGA a record nine times (seven being consecutive from 1968 to 1974) and the Open eight times (five times consecutively from 1970 to 1974). She was 11 times leading money-winner on the Japan Tour, including every year from 1968 to 1976. There is little doubt that she is the best woman player yet produced by Japan, although Ayako Okamoto has now taken over as the Japanese number one. Chako has a highly unusual swing which features a flying right elbow and a sway to the right on the backswing, her head moving about a foot. Nevertheless she is highly consistent and could undoubtedly have been more of a major figure in world women's golf had she competed more frequently outside Japan. It is said that the odd swing derives from Japanese professional Peter Nakamura, for whom she used to caddie.

US wins 2 (1976–77)
US money $209,100 (1970–82) (49th all-time)
Total wins 59

HSIEH Min-Nan   Taiwan
b. 1940

A dominant Far East player during the 1970s, Hsieh was leading money-winner on the Asia Circuit three times: 1971, 1975 and 1977, and in all totted up some 20 victories. In 1979 in Japan he won the Japan PGA, reached the final of the matchplay event and tied for the Tohuka Classic. He finished sixth in the Order of Merit. As an amateur he won the individual title in the Eisenhower Trophy, and as a professional had the same result in the World Cup.

KUO Chie-Hsiung   Taiwan
b. 1940

Top of the Asia Order of Merit three times – 1974, 1975 and 1978 – Kuo once won over $100,000 in five weeks, primarily by winning the Japan Open, the Jun Classic and the *Golf Digest* tournament. In 1975 he became one of only three players to win three events on the Asia Circuit, and when he took the Dunlop International in Japan his 265 total included a 64. In the same year he also won the Indonesian Open.

LU Hsi-Chuen   Taiwan
b. 1943

After an amateur career in which he won 13 titles, he turned professional in October 1978 for the Asian season and very soon had become one of very few players to win three times on the Circuit. After six months as a professional he had won $43,000. He later won the 1981 Malaysian Open. At 5 feet 5 inches he is distinctly on the short side for a golfer.

LU Liang-Huan   Taiwan
b. Taipei 1936

'Mr' Lu, as he was known during his major effort for the 1971 British Open at Royal Birkdale, had rounds of 70, 70, 69, 70 but lost by 1 stroke to Lee Trevino. During the championship he did not once have a 6 on his card. He endeared himself to the spectators by politely taking off his hat in salutation. Consolation for his narrow defeat came a week later when he recorded 262 in the French Open, with middle rounds of 63, 62, and won. A year later he was in the winning Nationalist China team in the World Cup. He had represented his country as early as 1956 in the Canada Cup at Wentworth, but his first important victory came in 1965, when he won the Philippines Open. In 1974 he became one of three to have won three times on the Asia Circuit. Mr Lu has won a host of minor tournaments (about 50 is one estimate), and has eight major Asia wins to his credit. He incurred an unusual penalty in 1979. Playing in the Japanese Dunlop International, he rolled his ball into the hole by hand after missing a putt. There was a rule in force prohibiting retaking putts during the event and he received a 2-stroke penalty for 'practising'. He now owns a large hotel in Taiwan.

MIZRAHIE, Barbara: see North America

MORIGUCHI, Yuko   Japan
b. Toyama 1955

A professional from 1975, Yuko Moriguchi has won 21 Japanese events and was in the top six money-winners from 1977 to 1982. She qualified for the US Tour in 1981, winning the qualifying competition by 7 strokes. She won four events in Japan in the 1982 season.

US money $26,624 (1981–2).

NAKAJIMA, Tsuneyuki   Japan
b. 1955

The youngest player, at 18, to take the Japanese Amateur title, Nakajima turned professional three years later in 1976 and had three victories both that year and the following, when he was third in the Japanese money list and took the PGA Championship. The following year two disasters that befell him attracted wide coverage. At Augusta in the US Masters he ran up the unlikely score of 13 on the 13th hole, and a couple of months later at St Andrews in the British Open was in contention when he found himself in the greenside bunker on the Road Hole. Endeavouring to play the necessary shot – one that would only just clear the lip and trickle to the holeside – Nakajima was not on the green until his fourth attempt and ran up a 9 to put himself out of contention. A par on the hole might well have seen him battle out the finish, as his score of 70, 71, 76, 71 testifies. Nakajima announced his intention to play a considerable number of US Tour events in the 1983 season.

OHSAKO, Tatsuko   Japan
b. Miyazeki 1952

Winner of 21 Japanese events, Tatsuko Ohsako has played several tournaments a year in the USA since 1978. Her best performance was to win the 1980 Mazda Japan Classic. In that year she was leading money-winner and won the Japan LPGA Championship. She was among the top 5 money-winners on the Japan Tour from 1975 to 1982. At the Sun City Classic in 1982 she set an unofficial US Tour record, with 55, for the most consecutive holes without a bogey.

US wins 1 (1980)
US money $61,939 (1978–82)

OKAMOTO, Ayako   Japan
b. Hiroshima 1951

Winner of more than $300,000 in Japan and over 20 tournaments, Ayako Okamoto in 1982 became the second Japanese (after Chako Higuchi) to win a US event when she beat Sally Little in a play-off for the Arizona Copper Classic, which was her 21st professional win in a career that began in 1975. She had been third in the Japan money list in 1979 and 1980 and first in 1981. On the 1981 US Tour, she played in just seven events in her first year (she won eight Japanese events), was in the top 20 on four occasions and won $14,000, good enough to encourage her to make a more prolonged effort in 1982. By early April, she stood eighth in the US money list. Other high placings during the year included third in the Olympic Gold and two second places in the WUI Classic and the World Championship of Women's Golf, when she came in 5 strokes behind JoAnne Carner at the peak of her game. She is one of the longest hitters on the Japanese Tour, and it will be interesting to see how

Ayako Okamoto

she fares when fully acclimatized to the US scene if she continues to make a major effort there. Apart from her eight victories in Japan in 1981, she set records for both stroke average (72.56) and annual money winnings ($130,000). She was also second six times and was among the top 10 in a remarkable 26 of 28 events entered. A former left-hand softball pitcher, she represented Japan at that sport in 1972. She was the 1979 Japan LPGA Champion, winning at 17 under par. Her 1982 US winnings of $85,267 were a record for a 'visitor' to the US Tour.

US wins 1 (1982)
US money $99,414 (1981–2)

OZAKI, Masashi   Japan

The popularity of golf in Japan can almost be called a legacy of General Douglas MacArthur and the post-war US occupation, though it should be remembered that the game had enjoyed some popularity in pre-war times, the Open having begun in 1927. But a former baseball player, 'Jumbo' Ozaki, contributed much to the boom because, in a nation of predominantly small people, he was the first outstanding player who was also a long hitter. Until the late development of Isao Aoki, Ozaki was the outstanding Japanese player during the 1970s, winning some 41 tournaments including the Open and PGA; twice he had five wins in a season, 1979 being his first season without a win in nearly a decade. He has played overseas occasionally and was eighth in the 1973 US Masters and 14th and 10th in the 1978 and 1979 British Opens. He was leading money-winner five times: from 1971 to

1974 and in 1977. He won nearly 50 million yen in both 1973 and 1974 and, with 10 wins in 1972, set the Japanese record for the most wins in a year. Ozaki also holds the four-round scoring record, 265 at Hiroshima in 1971.

World money $1,251,115 (1982) (39th all-time)

SUGIHARA, Teruo   Japan
b. 1938

Teruo Sugihara joined the Japanese circuit in 1958 and in 1962 took his national Open. He was a major player throughout the 1960s and 1970s with approaching 40 career victories. Playing the Asia Circuit more occasionally, he won the 1969 Hong Kong Open.

World money $727,049 (1958–80)

SUGIMOTO, Hideyo   Japan
b. Ito 1938

A leading Japanese player during the 1960s and early 1970s, Hideyo Sugimoto won his country's Open in 1964 and 1969, having turned professional in 1959. On the Asia Circuit he won such events as the Taiwan, Philippine and Malaysian Opens. In the 1966 World Cup at Tokyo, he came to the last hole, a par 3, needing just a 4 to take the individual title; but he had a 5 and went on to lose the play-off to the Canadian George Knudson.

SUZUKI, Norio   Japan
b. 1951

A leading Japanese player by the end of the 1970s, Suzuki had accumulated over a dozen wins in his career and was second on the Japanese money list in 1980.

TU Ai-Yu   Taiwan
b. 1954

Playing only some half dozen events on the US Tour annually, Tu Ai-Yu has averaged about $13,000 a season between 1977 and 1981, having qualified for the Tour as medallist. She came close to the Rookie of the Year award her first season and her best performance has been a tie for second place in the 1978 Mizuno Japan Classic. She won the 1975 Philippine and Hawaiian Opens and was once second in the Japan Open.

US money $67,274 (1977–81)

SOUTH & CENTRAL AMERICA

ACOSTA, Ernesto Perez   Mexico

As an unknown player on the world scene, Acosta caused more than a little surprise when he took the World Cup individual prize in 1976. Since then he has achieved little, and it seems that this success may have been the result of one of those weeks when all the putts go in.

BERTOLACCINI, Silvia   Argentina & USA
b. Rafaela, Argentina 1950

Silvia Bertolaccini won her national women's title in 1972 and the Colombian in 1974. She then decided that her future was in professional golf and that this meant moving to the USA. On the US Tour from 1975, she finished 45th in her first year and for the next four years was always in the top 18, and she won over $50,000 in each of the years 1977–9. Her standards have fallen away a little since then though she has remained in the top 50. She has won the Colgate Far Eastern twice (1977 and 1979) and another tournament in 1978. Silvia is a long hitter who likes to play with draw, and equalled the US Tour record of 29 for nine holes in 1979.

US wins 3 (1977–9)
US money $336,937 (1975–82) (25th all-time)

CERDA, Antonio   Argentina
b. 1921

During the 1950s Tony Cerda was the dominant Argentine player, his record of success not inferior to Roberto de Vicenzo's. He took his national Open in 1948 and 1956, the German Open in 1951 and 1952, the Spanish in 1950, the Dutch in 1956, when he also won the Italian title, the Jamaican in 1955 and the Mexican in 1958. In 1953 he won the individual title in the World Cup and the following year helped Argentina to second place in the team event. Between 1951 and 1957 he was always in the first eight of the British Open and twice came within sight of winning. In 1951, he was overhauling the eventual winner, Max Faulkner, until he took 6 on Royal Portrush's 14th hole. He recorded 74, 72, 71, 70 to finish 2 behind Faulkner but 3 ahead of the third-place man. Two years later, he finished 4 behind Ben Hogan, accompanied in second place by Frank Stranahan, Dai Rees and Peter Thomson. Cerda was an excellent putter and in his long game had a strong tendency to hit low, intentionally half-thinned shots – in wind, a good way to keep the ball in play.

Tony Cerda

CROCKER, Helen Fay — Uruguay & USA
b. *Montevideo, Uruguay 1914*

Descended from the captain of a New England whaler who settled in Montevideo and built a golf course, Fay Crocker must also have owed much to her father, who won the Uruguayan Amateur no fewer than 37 times. She was to make a similar habit of it, taking the women's equivalent 20 times and the Argentine title 14 from 1932 to 1953. In times of slower international travel, she did not compete frequently outside her normal hunting grounds, but she did reach the quarter-finals of the 1950 US Amateur, losing on the 27th hole, a record for extra holes played. Nearer home, by 1953 she had won nine of the last 11 Argentine Amateurs played. Nearing the age of 40 she turned professional and went to the USA to play and test herself against the highest competition. In 1955 she won three events, one of these being the Open. In high winds she came in 4 strokes ahead of Louise Suggs and Mary Lena Faulk. Among other achievements in top events, she was second in the 1957 Tam o' Shanter, third in the 1958 US Open and second in the 1958 US LPGA, 6 strokes behind Mickey Wright. On the US Tour as a whole she had two wins each in 1956, 1957, 1958 and 1960, the last at the age of 46. At the time of her US Open victory she was the first foreigner to win and, at 40 years 11 months, the oldest.

US wins 11 (1955–60)

FERNANDEZ, Vicente — Argentina
b. *Buenos Aires 1946*

Vicente is one of those golfers who, in the way they set up a shot, put you in mind of a mechanical device being readied for use. In his style there are none of the supposedly carefree ways of South America. Rather, he appears to be getting all the bits and pieces of his action into their correct positions and alignments. But this 5-foot 7-inch man, who has one leg shorter than the other as a result of a pre-natal accident, is undeniably a very effective golfer indeed; very straight as a hitter and an excellent putter. These are perhaps the two most important qualities for success in professional golf. Vicente is very much a world golfer, though his main achievements have been in Europe and South America, where one could argue a case that he is the number one golfer. In 1976 he also qualified for the US Tour but had little success and is now content with other pastures. After winning his national Open in 1968 and 1969, a success he repeated in 1981, Vicente's first international success was in winning the 1970 Dutch Open. From that time, although he has by no means played the full schedule, Vicente has consistently been quite prominent in Europe, has four times been in the top 20, and had his lowest round of 62 in the 1971 French Open. He has won two tournaments in Britain. Both were spectacular. After three rounds in the 1975 Benson and Hedges Festival at Fulford, York, he was no fewer than 19 under par, and won with a tournament record score of 266 – but his finest hour was yet to come. In the 1979 PGA Championship at St Andrews he began 71, 70, 72, which put him right up with the leaders (as Nick Faldo faded after an opening 65, 70), and then faced a full gale in the final round. Only Gary Player, Ray Floyd and Neil Coles can be said to have mastered the conditions, scoring 71, 71, 72 respectively, but these had set out fairly well back in the field. Vicente went round in 75, which compared well with the high 70s and early 80s that were being recorded by other contenders. His round is especially memorable for the way he and Baldovino Dassu played the dreaded 17th Road Hole. Vicente hit his second well left of the green, then played a deft pitch and holed the putt for his par. Dassu was short in two, and then made too much allowance for the wind and whacked his third shot well past the green and on to the road. He then took four more to get down. Four to Vicente, seven for Dassu, who with Player finished equal second just a shot behind. In South America Fernandez is a big fish in a relatively small pond – one where the big names turn out quite frequently but never in full force. In the 1978–9 season, however, he played in 11 tournaments, won seven of them and was three times second, a run that even de Vicenzo has not rivalled. He temporarily left the 1982 European Tour because of the Falklands War.

Europe wins 3 (1970–79)
Europe money £101,171 (1971–82) (35th all-time)
Overseas wins 5 (1968–82)

GONZALEZ, Jaime — Brazil
b. *São Paulo 1954*

Son of Mario, Jaime represents his country in the World Cup and obtained his US Tour card in 1979, having turned professional in 1977. He has also competed on the European Tour and made the Top

60 in 1979 when closing rounds of 67, 66 in the Benson and Hedges International brought him a third-place finish. He was 44th in 1982, when he won £10,406 in the season.

GONZALEZ, Mario   Brazil
b. São Paulo 1923

The best player in his homeland from the mid 1940s for at least a decade, Mario dominated both amateur and professional championships during that period. He took the Brazilian Amateur first in 1939 and won ten times more up to 1949, including five in a row from 1945 to 1949. During the same period he once took the Argentine Open, as an amateur, and the Amateur three times. Sometimes venturing overseas, he won the Spanish Open in 1947. In the Brazil Open he was eight times the winner, seven times in the period 1946–55 and then late on in 1969. He was a superb striker, particularly with the 1-iron; but his eventual downfall was his putting.

Mario Gonzalez

JURADO, José   Argentina
b. 1899

The best Argentinian during the 1920s and early 1930s, Jurado had taken his national title six times by 1931, the year of his greatest performance on the international scene. This was in the British Open at Carnoustie. In a high-scoring championship his 76, 71, 73 had him in the lead with a round to go – by 4 on Tommy Armour, eventual winner, and by 5 on Percy Alliss and Gene Sarazen and 3 on Macdonald Smith. He came to the last two holes needing a 4, 5 finish to win, but then topped a 4-iron into the burn virtually under his nose. He took 6 and then played the last hole safely through wrong information when he should have gone for the green in two. His 6, 5 finish brought him in 1 stroke behind Tommy Armour in second place. Jurado had only been 1 stroke behind Hagen after three rounds at Sandwich three years earlier, but took 80 in the last to finish tied for sixth place, a finish he also achieved in the 1932 US Open.

de LUCA, Fidel   Argentina
b. 1921

Fidel de Luca may have become the oldest player to win an important event when he took the Brazil Open in 1979 at the age of 58. He had previously won it in 1956. He also won the Argentine Open three times: 1954, 1960 and 1961. He competed in Europe during this period, where we knew him affectionately as 'Fred Luca' or 'Filthy' (lucre).

POSE, Martin   Argentina
b. 1911

A leading Argentine golfer for many years, Martin Pose won his national Open in 1933, 1939 and 1950. He also took the Brazil title in 1945. He had a successful season in Europe in 1939 when he won the French Open and came fifth in the British Open, his total including a penalty shot for grounding his club on the grass verge by the wall beyond the road on the 17th at St Andrews – with only one hole to play.

REGALADO, Victor   Mexico
b. Tijuana 1948

Regalado represented Mexico in 1968 and 1970, won his national amateur title the latter year and turned professional. In Mexico, he later won the

Victor Regalado

PGA in 1978 and the Mexican Masters in 1972 and 1973, but he has principally been a US Tour player since 1973, and is based in San Diego, California. After a poor first season he won the Pleasant Valley Classic in 1974 and was 39th in the money list. Since then, he has won once again, the 1978 Quad Cities; and was in the Top 60 from 1976 to 1979, with 38th in 1977 being his best placing. He represented Mexico in the 1979 World Cup.

US wins 2 (1974–8)
US money $500,219 (1973–82) (95th all-time)

de VICENZO, Roberto   Argentina
b. Buenos Aires 1923

The greatest golfer to emerge from South America, Roberto de Vicenzo turned professional in 1938 on the advice of Paul Runyan. With the passing of time he came to be recognized as one of the best strikers golf has seen. He had begun in golf as a *lagunero* ('pond boy'), a sort of caddie's assistant used by them mainly to retrieve golf balls from inaccessible or unattractive places; but at the age of 21 in 1944

he won the Argentine PGA and Open. He won that PGA another six times by 1952 and the Open a total of nine times, his last win coming in 1974 when he was past 50. The saga of Jack Nicklaus's numerous high finishes in the British Open is well known, and a similar story can be told of Roberto from the late 1940s. In 1948 he was joint third, and the following year third again, 2 behind in Locke's first championship, while in 1950 he was second, again 2 behind Locke. In 1953 he was level with Hogan with a round to play but fell back to 5 strokes adrift and sixth place. In 1956 he was again third, despite a third round of 79. In the centenary Open of 1960 he began with a pair of 67s to lead the field but fell away to another third with closing rounds of 75, 73. He was third yet again in 1964, Lema's year, and fourth the following season. Putting had been, as always, Roberto's main problem. When level with Hogan in 1953, for instance, he claims to have gone out for his final round knowing he was going to lose it on the greens, while in his best chance, 1960, he had followed his 67, 67, start by missing a very short putt at the very beginning of the last day. The other problem was that his great length from the tee and drawn shape of shot sometimes ran out of fairway and the draw sometimes became a hook. Around 1964 he changed his grip to combat the hook so that the shaft of the club lay across the left hand, and worked at pulling the clubhead into the ball. He also eliminated most wrist movement in putting, which made him more confident. By 1967 Vicenzo had won some 30 national titles around the world and about 130 tournaments; but he had still not won a major championship, and felt his chances of doing so were slipping away as the years advanced. At Hoylake he began 70, 71 and although he was high up the field, few rated his chances. That changed after his third-round 67, which gave him a lead of 3 on the defending champion, Jack Nicklaus; 2 on Gary Player, with whom he played the last day; and 4 on the new British hope, Clive Clark. Of these only Nicklaus gained ground on the last day. Vicenzo began a little shakily but good chips to save par on the 3rd and 4th seemed to steady him, while ahead Nicklaus was not holing the birdie putts he needed to catch Vicenzo. Vicenzo finished with three superb tee shots, the first across the out of bounds on the 16th, and he followed with vast drives that left him with 9-iron shots to the greens. At 44 years 93 days he had become the oldest Open Champion of modern times; only 'Old Tom' Morris had won at a greater age. It was one of the most popular of all victories. In 1968 the final day of the US Masters was also his birthday. He began it 2 strokes behind Gary Player and 1 stroke behind Ray Floyd, Don January, Frank Beard, Bruce Devlin and Bob Goalby. That altered considerably on the first hole, where Vicenzo hit a 9-iron into the green and holed out for an eagle 2. The next, a par 5, he birdied comfortably and then had a tap-in putt for a birdie on the next to be 4 under par for the three holes. He had one more birdie to the turn to lead Devlin by 1 and Goalby by 2. His next birdie came on the 12th and he also birdied the 15th and 17th, dropping a shot only at the last. Goalby had made up ground on the second half with some good play of his own so it was a 66 for him, a 65 for Roberto and a tie. Or was it? Roberto seemed to have signed his card for a 65 but his individual hole scores amounted to 66. His playing partner, Tommy Aaron, had written in a 4 instead of the birdie 3 on the 17th. Despite the fact that his shots on that hole had been seen by thousands on course and millions on TV, and that Aaron fully agreed he had made a mistake, a player is responsible for checking his own card. Goalby became champion. 'What a stupid I am,' said Roberto. His loss made him more friends around the world than even he had had before and his behaviour in disappointment was a model. He went away and won the Champions International instead, but it had been his last close approach to a major championship. Vicenzo had first played in the USA in 1947, winning nine events during his spasmodic appearances there and first appeared in Britain in 1948, winning the North British Harrogate that year. From that time he became an international traveller and accumulated the Open Championships of Britain, France (three times), Germany, Spain, Holland, Belgium, Brazil (five times), Chile, Uruguay, Colombia, Mexico, Panama – the list is longer than for any other golfer, for he is estimated to have won 39 national championships

Roberto de Vicenzo

and some 165 tournaments in all. Among his outstanding achievements are World Cup performances. With Antonio Cerda, the first event of all was won in 1953 and he won the individual title in 1962 and 1970, on the latter occasion with a record 269. He represented Argentina about 20 times in the event. In his Senior years Roberto took the 1974 US and World Seniors and won the US Seniors Open in 1980. He has announced his retirement more than once, but as late as 1979 tied for the Brazil Open.

US wins 9 (1951–68)
US money $188,292
Total wins 165–230 (various estimates)

INDEX

A

Aaron, Tommy (Thomas Dean) 11
Abreu, Tito (Francisco) 314
Acosta, Ernesto Perez 363
Adams, Jimmy (James) 203
Adams, Lynn 11
Adams, Sam 12
Ado, Jean-Baptiste 314
Ahern, Kathy (Katherine) 12
Aitken, Wilma 203
Albers, Roberta 12
Alcott, Amy 12
Alex, Janet 13
Alexander, Skip (Stewart) 13
Allan, Dr Jack (A.J.T.) 203
Allen, Donald 13
Allin, Brian 13
Alliss, Percy 204
Alliss, Peter 204
Anderson, Jamie (James) 205
Anderson, Janet: see Alex 13
Anderson, Jean: see Donald 234
Anderson, Jessie: see Valentine 303
Anderson, Willie (William) 13
Angelini, Alfonso 314
Anstey, Veronica: see Beharrell 209
Aoki, Isao 359
Archer, George William 14
Arda, Ben 360
Armour, Tommy (Thomas Dickson) 15
Armstrong, Wally (Walter) 16
Ashby, Harry (Harold) 205
Ashley, Jean 16
Attenborough, Michael F. 205
Auchterlonie, Laurence 205
Auchterlonie, Laurie 16
Auchterlonie, Willie (William) 206
Austin, Debbie (Deborah) 16
Austin, Michael Hoke 16
Aye, Mya 361

B

Bachli, Doug (Douglas W.) 328
Bailey, Diane: see Frearson 242
Baiocchi, Hugh 348
Baird, Butch 16
Baker, Vince (Vincent) 348
Balbuena, Salvador 314
Balding, Al (Albert) 17
Balfour-Melville, Leslie 206
Ball, John, Snr 206
Ball, John, Jnr 206
Ball, Ted (Edward) 328
Ball, Tom (Thomas) 207
Ballesteros, Manuel 315
Ballesteros, Severiano 315
Bannerman, Harry 207
Barber, Jerry 17
Barber, Miller 17
Barber, Sally 207
Barnes, Brian 207
Barnes, Long Jim (James M.) 18
Barnett, Pam (Pamela) 18
Barr, Dave (David) 18
Barrett, Sharon 18
Barrios, Valentin 316
Barron, Herman 19
Barrow, Barbara 19
Barton, Pam (Pamela) 208
Bastanchury, Jane: see Booth 26
Bauer, Alice 19
Bauer, Marlene: see Hagge 75
Baugh, Laura Zonetta 19
Baxter, Rex 20
Bayer, George 20
Bean, Andy (Thomas Andrew) 20
Beard, Frank 20
Beck, Dorothy 209
Beck, John Beaumont, MC 209
Beddows, Charlotte 209
Beharrell, John Charles 209
Beharrell, Veronica 209

Bell, Peggy (Margaret Anne) 21
Beman, Deane R. 21
Bembridge, Maurice 209
de Bendern, Count John 210
Benka, Peter 210
Bentley, Arnold Lewis 210
Bentley, Harry (Harold Geoffrey) 210
Berg, Patty (Patricia Jane) 22
Bernardino, Roberto 317
Berning, Susie (Susan) 23
Bertolaccini, Silvia 363
Besselink, Al (Albert Cornelius) 23
Bevione, Franco 317
Bevione, Isa: see Goldschmid 321
Bielke, Count Gustav Adolf 317
Bies, Don (Donald William) 23
Billows, Ray (Raymond E.) 24
Bisgood, Jeanne Mary 210
Bishop, Stan (Stanley E.) 24
Blackwell, Ted (Edward B.H.) 210
Blair, Major David Arthur, MBE, MC 211
Blalock, Jane 24
Blancas, Homero 24
Bland, John 348
Bolt, Tommy (Thomas) 25
Bonallack, Angela 211
Bonallack, Michael Francis, OBE 212
Bonallack, Sally: see Barber 207
Boobyer, Fred (Frederick) 213
Boomer, Aubrey B. 213
Booth, Jane 26
Boros, Julius Nicholas 26
Borthwick, Pat (Patricia) 328
Bourassa, Jocelyne 26
Bousfield, Ken (Kenneth) 213
Boyer, Auguste 317
Boykin, Gerda 27
Boyle, Hugh 213
Bradley, Pat (Patricia) 217
Bradshaw, Harry 214
Brady, Mike (Michael Joseph) 27
Braid, James 214
Brand, Gordon, Snr 216
Brand, Gordon, Jnr 216
Breer, Murle 28
Brewer, Gay 28
Brews, Sid (Sidney F.) 348
Briggs, Audrey 216
Britz, Jerilyn 29
Britz, Tienie 349
Brodie, Allan 217
Brooks, Andrew 217

Brown, Audrey: see Briggs 216
Brown, Mrs Charles S. 29
Brown, David 217
Brown, Eric Chalmers 217
Brown, Ken (Kenneth) 217
Brown, Pete (Peter) 29
Brown, Stuart 218
Browne, Mary Kimball 30
Bruce, Louise: see Parks 141
Bruen, James 219
Bryant, Bonnie 30
Budke, Mary Anne 30
Bulla, Johnny (John) 30
Burfeindt, Betty (Elizabeth) 31
Burke, A.J. 31
Burke, Billy (William) 31
Burke, Jack, Snr 31
Burke, Jack, Jnr 31
Burke, John 219
Burkemo, Walter 31
Burns, George, III 32
Burrows, Gaylord 32
Burton, Dick (Richard) 219
Bussell, Alan Francis 219
Busson, John Joseph 220
Butler, Peter 220
Byers, Eben M. 32
Byman, Bob (Robert) 32
Byrd, Sam (Samuel Dewey) 33

C

Cadden, Suzanne 220
Caldwell, Ian 220
Caldwell, Rex 33
Calero, Manuel 317
Callison, Carole Jo 33
Campbell, Bill (William Cammack) 34
Campbell, Dorothy Iona 33
Campbell, Joe (Joseph) 34
Campbell, Tommie (William Thomas) 221
Campbell, Willie (William) 220
Canizares, José Maria 317
Caponi, Donna 34
Carner, JoAnne 35
Carr, Joe (Joseph Benedict) 221
Carr, Roddy (Roderick J.) 222
Carrick, Angela: see Uzielli 303
Casera, Aldo 318
Casper, Billy (William Earl, Jnr) 35

Caygill, Alex (Gordon Alexander) 222
Cerda, Tony (Antonio) 363
Cerrudo, Ron (Ronald) 37
Chadwick, Elizabeth 222
Chambers, Doris Elaine, OBE 222
Chapman, Dick (Richard Davol) 37
Chapman, Roger 222
Charbonnier, Carole 318
Charles, Bob (Robert James), OBE 328
de la Chaume, Thion (Simone Thion) 318
Cheney, Leona 38
Cheney, Mary Bea: see Porter 146
Cherry, Don (Donald R.) 38
Christmas, Martin J. 22
Clampett, Bobby (Robert Daniel) 38
Clark, Clarence 39
Clark, Clive Anthony 223
Clark, Gordon James 223
Clark, Howard K. 224
Clark, Judy (Judith) 39
Clarke, Doug (Douglas) 39
Cochran, Bob (Robert E.) 39
Coe, Charlie (Charles Robert) 39
Colbert, Jim (James Joseph) 40
Cole, Bobby (Robert E.) 349
Cole, Laura: see Baugh 19
Coles, Janet 40
Coles, Neil, MBE 224
Collett, Glenna 40
Collins, Bill (William) 41
Commans, Ron (Ronald R.) 41
Compston, Archie (Archibald Edward Wones) 225
Congdon, Chuck (Charles W.) 42
Conley, Peggy Shane 42
Connachan, Jane McGrath 226
Conner, Frank Joseph 42
Conrad, Joe (Joseph W.) 42
Coody, Charles Billy 42
Cook, John H. 226
Cook, John Neuman 43
Cook, Nancy: see Wright 313
Cooper, Harry E. 43
Cooper, Pete (Peter) 44
Cornelius, Kathy (Katherine) 44
Cosh, Gordon B. 226
Cotton, Henry (Thomas Henry), MBE 227
Couples, Fred (Frederick Stephen) 44
Courtney, Chuck (Charles) 45
Cowan, Garry 45
Cox, Bill (William James), OBE 229
Cox, Simon 228
Cox, Whiffy (Wilfred H.) 45

Craddock, Tom (Thomas) 229
Crafter, Jane 330
Crampton, Bruce 330
Crawford, Jean: see Ashley 16
Crawley, Leonard George 229
Creavy, Tom 45
Creed, Clifford Ann 45
Cremin, Eric 330
Crenshaw, Ben Daniel 45
Critchley, Bruce 229
Critchley, Diana: see Fishwick 241
Crocker, Helen Fay 364
Crocker, Mary Lou 47
Cronin, Grace: see Lenczyk 107
Cros, Claudine 318
Cros, Patrick 318
Crosby, Bing (Harry Lillis) 47
Crosby, Nat (Nathaniel) 47
Cruickshank, Bobby (Robert Allan) 48
Cudone, Carolyn 49
Cullen, Betsy (Elizabeth) 49
Cullen, Gary 356
Cummings, Edith 49
Cunningham, Gordon 230
Cupit, Jacky D. 49
Curl, Rod 49
Curtis, Donald Allen 230
Curtis, Harriot 49
Curtis, Margaret 50

D

Dabson, Kim 230
Dalgleish, Colin 230
Dallemagne, Marcel 319
Daly, Fred (Frederick) 230
Daniel, Beth (Elizabeth Ann) 50
Daniel, Mary Lou: see Crocker 47
Darben, Althea: see Gibson, 68
Darcy, Eamonn, 231
Darwin, Bernard, CBE 232
Dassu, Baldovino 319
Davies, E.N. 232
Davies, John C. 232
Davies, Richard D. 51
Davies, William Henry 233
Davis, Rodger 330
Dawson, Peter 233
DeArman, Marlene: see Floyd 63
Decker, Anne: see Quast 148

Deeble, Peter George 233
DeFoy, Craig Bryan 233
Deighton, Dr Frank William Gordon 234
Demaret, Jimmy (James Newton) 51
Denenberg, Gail: see Toushin 178
Dent, Jim (James L.) 51
Derouaux, Cathy: see Reynolds 152
Devlin, Bruce William 331
Dickinson, Gardner 52
Dickson, Bob (Robert B.) 52
Didrikson, Babe: see Zaharias 199
Diegel, Leo 52
Diehl, Terry (Terrence Jeffrey) 53
Dill, Mary Lou 53
Dill, Terry (Terrance) 53
Dobell, Gladys: see Ravenscroft 287
Dod, Lottie (Charlotte) 234
Dodd, Muriel 234
Donald, Jean Macalister 234
van Donck, Flory 319
Dorrestein, Jan 320
Douglas, Dave (David) 54
Douglas, Findlay S. 54
Douglass, Dale 54
Downes, Paul 235
Drew, Norman Vico 235
Dudley, Ed (Edward Bishop) 54
Duncan, George 235
Duncan, Colonel Tony (Anthony Arthur), OBE 235
Dunk, Billy (E. William) 332
Dunlap, George T., Jnr 55
Dunn, Tom (Thomas) 236
Dunn, Willie (William), Snr 237
Dunn, Willie (William), Jnr 55
Dutra, Mortie (Mortimer) 55
Dutra, Olin 55

E

Edgar, John Douglas 237
Edwards, Danny (Richard Dan) 55
Edwards, David Wayne 55
Egan, H. Chandler 56
Eggeling, Dale 56
Ehret, Glo (Gloria Jean) 56
Eichelberger, Dave (Martin Davis) 56
Elder, Robert Lee 57
von Elm, George 57
Elson, Pip (Philip) 238
Englehorn, Shirley 58

Espinosa, Al (Albert R.) 58
Evans, A.D. 238
Evans, Chick (Charles, Jnr) 58
Evans, Duncan 238
Everard, Mary, 238
Ewing, Reginald Cecil 239

F

Fairfield, Don (Donald) 59
Faldo, Nick (Nicholas Alexander) 239
Fallon, Johnny (John) 240
Farrell, Johnny (John J.) 59
Faulk, Mary Lena 59
Faulkner, Max 240
Fazio, George 59
Fergon, Vicki 59
Fergus, Keith Carlton 60
Ferguson, Bob (Robert) 241
Ferguson, Marjory 241
Fernandez, Vicente 364
Fernie, Willie (William) 241
Ferraris, Jan (Janis Jean) 60
Ferree, Jim (Purvis Jennings) 60
Ferrier, Jim (James) 332
Fetchick, Mike (Michael) 60
Fezler, Forrest Oliver 60
Figueras-Dotti, Marta 320
Finsterwald, Dow Henry 61
Fiori, Ed (Edward Ray) 61
Fischer, John William 62
Fisher, Elizabeth: see Price 286
Fishwick, Diana Lesley 241
Fitzsimmons, Pat 62
Fleck, Jack 62
Fleckman, Marty 63
Fleischer, Bruce 63
Flenniken, Carol: see Sorenson 169
Floyd, Marlene 63
Floyd, Ray (Raymond Loran) 63
Ford, Doug (Douglas) 64
de Forest, John: see de Bendern 210
Forsell, Liv: see Wollin 327
Foster, Martin 241
Foster, Rodney 241
Fought, John Allen 65
Foulis, James 242
Fourie, John 350
Fowler, Marjory: see Ferguson 241
Fraser, Alexa: see Stirling 172

Frearson, Diane Jane 242
Funseth, Rod 65
Furgol, Ed (Edward) 66
Furgol, Marty 66

Guilford, Jesse C. 72
Guldahl, Ralph 72
Gunderson, JoAnne: see Carner 35
Gunn, Watts 72

G

Gadd, Bert (Herbert) 242
Gale, Terry 333
Gallacher, Bernard 242
Gallardo, Angel 320
Garaialde, Jean 320
Garbacz, Lori 66
Gardner, Bob (Robert A.) 66
Gardner, Bob (Robert W.) 66
Garner, John R. 243
Garrett, Maureen: see Ruttle 292
Garrido, Antonio 321
Garrido, German 321
Garvey, Philomena 243
Geiberger, Al (Allen Lee) 67
Germain, Dot (Dorothy) 67
Ghezzi, Vic (Victor) 68
Gibson, Althea 68
Gilbert, Gibby (C.L., Jnr) 68
Gilder, Bob (Robert Bryan) 68
Giles, Vinny (Marvin, III) 69
Ginn, Stewart 333
Glutting, Charlotte 69
Goalby, Bob (Robert) 69
Goggin, Lindy 333
Golden, Johnny 70
Goldschmid, Isa 321
Goldsmith, Brenda 70
Gonzalez, Jaime 364
Gonzalez, Mario 365
Goodman, Johnny (John) 70
Gourlay, Molly (Mary Perceval), OBE 244
Graham, Cathy: see Sherk 161
Graham, David (Anthony David) 333
Graham, Jack (John) 244
Graham, Lou (Louis Krebs) 70
Grappasonni, Ugo 322
Gray, A. Downing 71
Green, Charlie (Charles Wilson) 244
Green, Hubert Myatt, II 71
Greenhalgh, Julia 244
Gregson, Malcolm 244
Gresham, Tony (Anthony Y.) 334
Grout, Jack 71

H

Haas, Fred (Frederick) 72
Haas, Jay Dean 73
Hagen, Walter Charles 73
Hagge, Marlene 75
Hahn, Paul 76
Haliburton, Tom (Thomas Bruce) 245
Hallberg, Gary George 76
Halldorson, Dan (Daniel Albert) 76
Hamilton, Bob (Robert) 76
Hamlin, Shelley 77
Hammond, Dame Joan 334
Hancock, Phil (Philip Ransom) 77
Hanson, Beverly 77
Harb, Helen: see Hicks 82
Harbert, Chick (Melvin R.) 77
Harbottle, Pat: see Lesser 107
Hardy, Carol: see Mann 119
Harley, Katherine: see Jackson 94
Harmon, Claude 77
Harney, Paul 78
Harper, Chandler 78
Harris, Labron, Jnr 78
Harris, Marley: see Spearman 296
Harris, Robert 245
Harrison, Dutch (Ernest Joseph) 78
Hatalsky, Morris 79
Havers, Arthur Gladstone 245
Hawkins, Fred (Frederick) 79
Hayes, Dale 350
Hayes, Mark Stephen 79
Hayes, Patty (Patricia) 80
Haynie, Sandra 80
Heafner, Clayton 81
Heafner, Vance (Clayton Vance) 81
Heard, Jerry Michael 81
Heathcoat-Amory, Joyce: see Wethered 309
Hebert, Jay 81
Hebert, Lionel 82
Hedges, Peter J. 245
Hedges, Susan 246
Henning, Harold 350
Henson, Dinah: see Oxley 280
Herd, Fred (Frederick) 246

Herd, Sandy (Alexander) 246
Herron, Davy (S. Davidson) 82
Hetherington, Jean Clara 246
Hezlet, May 246
Hickey, Marea: see Parsons 341
Hicks, Betty (Elizabeth) 82
Hicks, Helen B. 82
Higgins, Pam (Pamela Sue) 82
Higuchi, Chako (Hisako Matsui) 360
Hill, Carolyn 82
Hill, Cynthia 82
Hill, Dave (James David) 83
Hill, Mike (Michael) 84
Hill, Opal 84
Hilton, Harold Horsfall 247
Hinkle, Lon Currey 84
Hinson, Larry 85
Hiskey, Babe (Bryant) 86
Hitchcock, Jimmy (James) 247
Hoad, Paul 248
Hobday, Simon F.N. 357
Hoch, Scott Mabon 86
Hogan, Ben (Benjamin William) 86
Holderness, Sir Ernest William Elsmie 248
Hollins, Marion 90
Holmes, Jean: see Hetherington 246
Holtgrieve, Jim (James) 90
Homer, Trevor Walter Brian 248
Hood, Vince (Vincent) 248
van Hoose, Myra 90
Horne, Reg (Reginald W.) 248
Horton, Donna; see White 193
Horton, Tommy (Thomas) 249
Howell, Henry Rupert 249
Hoyt, Beatrix 90
Hsieh Min-Nan 360
Hudson, John 250
Huggett, Brian George Charles, MBE 250
Huish, David 250
Huke, Beverly Joan Mary 251
Humphreys, Warren 251
Hunt, Bernard John, MBE 251
Hunt, Geoffrey Michael 252
Hunt, Guy L. 253
Hunt, Noel 253
Hunter Willie (William Irvine) 90
Hurd, Dorothy: see Campbell 33
Hutcheon, Ian C. 253
Hutchinson, Horace (Horatio Gordon) 253
Hutchison, Jock 90
Hyndman, Bill (William, III) 91

I

Ingham, Mike (Michael B.) 253
Ingram, David 254
Inkster, Juli 91
Inman, Joe (Joseph Cooper) 92
Irvin, Ann Lesley 254
Irwin, Hale S. 92

J

Jack, Reid (Robert Reid) 255
Jacklin, Tony (Anthony), OBE 255
Jackson, Bridget (Barbara Amy Bridget) 257
Jackson, Hugh 257
Jackson, Katherine 94
Jacobs, John Robert Maurice 257
Jacobs, Tommy (K. Thomas) 94
Jacobsen, Peter Erling 94
Jaeckel, Barry 94
Jagger, David 258
James, Mark 258
Jameson, Betty (Elizabeth) 95
Jamieson, Andrew 260
Jamieson, Jim (James) 95
January, Don 96
Jenkins, Tom (Thomas Wayne) 96
Jennings, Lindy: see Goggin 333
Jessen, Ruth (Mary Ruth) 97
Job, Nick (Nicholas) 260
Johnson, Howie 97
Johnston, Bill (William) 97
Johnston, Jimmy (Harrison R.) 97
Johnstone, Ann Casey 97
Johnstone, Tony (Anthony) 358
Jones, Bobby (Robert Tyre, Jnr) 98
Jones, Ernest 260
Jones, Grier Stewart 97
Jowle, Frank 260
Joyce, Joan 97
Jurado, José 365

K

Kabler, Carole: see Callison 33
Kazmierski, Joyce 100
Keiser, Herman 101
Kennedy, Edwina 335

Kertzman, Karolyn 101
Kelley, Michael John 260
Kidd, Tom 261
Kimball, Judy (Judith Ann) 101
King, Betsy (Elizabeth) 101
King, Michael 261
King, Sam (Samuel Leonard) 261
Kinsella, Jimmy (James J.) 262
Kirby, Dorothy 101
Kirk, Peggy: see Bell 21
Kirkaldy, Andra' (Andrew) 262
Kirkaldy, Hugh 262
Kirkwood, Joe (Joseph H.) 335
Kirouac, Martha: see Wilkinson 194
Kite, Tom (Thomas O.) 101
Klass, Beverly 103
Knight, Nancy: see Lopez 112
Knudson, George 103
Koch, Gary Donald 103
Kocsis, Chuck (Charles R.) 104
Kolb, Jan: see Stephenson 344
Krantz, Mike (Michael) 104
Kratzert, Bill (William Augustus, III) 104
Kroll, Ted (Theodore) 105
Kuo Chie-Hsiung 360
Kyle, Alex (Alexander Thomson) 262

L

Lacy, Arthur J. 262
Lacoste, Catherine 322
Lacoste, Thion: see de la Chaume 318
Laffoon, Ky 105
Laidlay, Johnny (John E.) 263
de Lamaze, Henri 322
Langer, Bernhard 322
Langley, John D.A. 263
Large, Bill (William) 263
Lassen, E.A. 263
Lauer, Bonnie 106
Laupheimer, Mary: see Everard 238
Lees, Arthur 263
Lee Smith, Jenny (Jennifer Constance) 264
Legrange, Cobie 351
Leitch, Cecil (Charlotte Cecilia Pitcairn) 264
Lema, Tony (Anthony David) 106
Lenczyk, Grace 107
Leonard, Stan (Stanley) 107
Lesser, Pat (Patricia Ann) 107
Levenson, Gavin Neal 351

Levi, Wayne John 108
Lewis, Bob (Robert) 108
Leitzke, Bruce Alan 108
Lindstrom, Murle: see Breer 28
Lister, John Malcolm 335
Little, Lawson (William Lawson) 110
Little, Sally 109
Littler, Gene (Eugene Alex) 111
Llewellyn, David J. 265
Lloyd, Joe (Joseph) 112
Lock, Jane, MBE 335
Locke, Bobby (Arthur D'Arcy) 351
Longhurst, Henry Carpenter 265
Longmuir, Bill (William) 265
Lopez, Nancy 112
Lott, Lyn (Clinton Lynwood, III) 113
Lotz, Dick (Richard) 113
Low, George 113
de Luca, Fidel 365
Lucas, Laddie (Percy Belgrave), CBE, DSO, DFC 265
Luckhurst, Terri: see Moody 127
Lu Hsi-Chuen 360
Lu Liang-Huan 361
Lundquist, Dale: see Eggeling 56
Lunn, Bob (Robert) 113
Lunt, Michael Stanley Randle 266
Lye, Mark Ryan 115
Lyle, Sandy (Alexander Walter Barr) 266
Lyon, George S. 115

M

McAllister, Susie (Susan) 114
McClelland, Doug (Doublas W.) 267
McClure, Jean: see Hetherington 246
McCorkindale, Belle: see Robertson 291
McCready, Max (Samuel Maxwell) 268
McCullough, Mike (Michael Earl) 114
McCumber, Mark Randall 114
McDermott, Johnny (John J.) 114
Macdonald, Charles Blair 115
McEvoy, Peter 268
Macfarlane, Willie (William) 115
MacFie, Allan F. 268
McGee, Jerry Lynn 115
McIntire, Barbara Joy 115
McKenna, Mary 268
Mackenzie, Ada 116
McKinlay, Sam (Samuel Livingstone) 269

M'Lean, Jack 269
McLendon, Mac (Benson Rayfield) 116
McLeod, Freddie (Frederick Robertson) 116
McMahon, Suzanne: see Cadden, 220
McMullen, Kathy 117
McNamara, Tom 117
McNulty, Mark William 358
McSpaden, Jug (Harold) 117
Madill, Maureen Elizabeth Jane 269
Mahaffey, John Drayton 117
Maltbie, Roger Lin 118
Manero, Tony 118
Mangrum, Lloyd Eugene 118
Manley, Norman 119
Mann, Carol 119
Marchbank, Brian 269
Marks, Geoff (Geoffrey C.) 269
Marr, Dave (David) 120
Marsh, Dr David Max 270
Marsh, Graham, MBE 336
Marston, Max (Maxwell R.) 120
Marti, Fred (Frederick) 120
Martin, Bob (Robert) 270
Martin, Jimmy (James) 270
Martin, Kathy (Katherine) 120
Martin, Steve (Stephen W.) 270
Martin-Smith, Eric 270
Marvin, Vanessa Price 270
Mason, Carl 270
Massengale, Don (Donald) 120
Massengale, Rik (Richard Gregg) 120
Massey, Debbie (Deborah) 120
Massy, Arnaud 324
Masters, Margee (Margaret Ann) 337
Maxwell, Billy Joseph 121
Maxwell, Robert 271
Maxwell, Susie: see Berning 23
Mayer, Dick (Alvin Richard) 121
Mehlhorn, Wild Bill (William E.) 122
Melnyk, Steve (Steven Nicholas) 122
Melton, Nancy: see Lopez 112
Melville, Janet Kay 271
Menne, Bob (Robert) 122
Metz, Dick (Richard) 123
Meyers, Pat (Patricia) 123
Micklem, Gerald Hugh 271
Middlecoff, Cary 123
Miguel, Angel 324
Miguel, Sebastian 325
Millensted, Dudley 271
Miller, Allen 124
Miller, Johnny (John Laurence) 124

Miller, Lindy Ray 125
Miller, Sharon Kay, 126
Mills, Mary 126
Mills, Peter (Ralph Peter) 271
Milne, Willie (William T.G.) 272
Milton, Moira: see Paterson 282
Mitchell, Abe (Abraham) 272
Mitchell, Bobby (Robert Wayne) 126
Mitchell, Jeff (Jeffrey Keith) 126
Mizrahie, Barbara 126
Moffitt, Ralph Lawson 273
Monti, Eric 126
Moody, Orville Cleve 126
Moody, Peter Henry 273
Moody, Terri, 127
Morey, Dale 127
Morgan, Gil (Gilmer Bryan) 127
Morgan, John 273
Morgan, John Llewellyn 274
Morgan, Wanda 274
Moriguchi, Yuko 361
Morley, Mike (Michael E.) 128
Morris, J.O.F. 274
Morris, Old Tom (Thomas, Snr) 274
Morris, Young Tom (Thomas, Jnr) 275
Morrison, John Stanton Fleming 275
Morse, Cathy (Catherine) 128
Mosey, Ian 275
Moxness, Barbara 128
Mudd, Jodie (Joseph Martin) 128
Munson, Edith: see Cummings 49
Murphy, Bob (Robert J.) 128
Murray, Ewen 276
Murray, Gordon H. 276
Murray, Stuart W.T. 276
Muscroft, Hedley 276

N

Nagle, Kel (Kelvin David George) 337
Nakajima, Tommy (Tsuneyuki) 361
Nelford, Jim (James Cameron) 129
Nelson, Byron (John Byron) 129
Nelson, Larry Gene 131
New, Beverly Jayne 277
Newell, Betty: see Hicks 82
Newton, Jack 338
Nichol, Margaret: see Pickard 284
Nichols, Bobby (Robert Herman) 131
Nicklaus, Jack William 132
von Nida, Norman George 339

Nieporte, Tom 135
Norman, Greg 340
Norman, Moe 135
Norris, Tim (Timothy Garrett) 136
North, Andy (Andrew Stewart) 136

O

O'Brien, Kyle 136
O'Connor, Christy, Snr 277
O'Connor, Christy, Jnr 278
Ohsako, Tatsuko 361
Okamoto, Ayako 361
O'Leary, John 278
Oliver, Ed 136
O'Meara, Mark Francis 137
Oosterhuis, Peter A. 278
Oosthuizen, Andries 353
Orcutt, Maureen 137
Ouimet, Francis de Sales 137
Owen, Simon 341
Oxley, Dinah 280
Ozaki, Jumbo (Masashi) 362

P

Padgham, Alf (Alfred Harry) 280
Page, Estelle Lawson 138
Palli, Anne-Marie 325
Palmer, Arnold Daniel 138
Palmer, Johnny (John) 141
Palmer, Sandra Jean 141
Panton, Cathy (Catherine Rita) 281
Panton, John, MBE 281
Park, Mungo, Snr 281
Park, Mungo, Jnr 282
Park, Willie (William, Snr) 282
Park, Willie (William, Jnr) 282
Parks, Louise 141
Parks, Sam (Samuel McLaughlin, Jnr) 141
Parsons, Marea 341
Pate, Jerry (Jerome Kendrick) 142
Paterson, Moira 282
Patton, Billy Joe (William Joseph) 143
Pavin, Corey 143
Peck, Michael 143
Peete, Calvin 143
Penna, Tony (Antonio) 144
Pennink, Frank (John Jacob Frank) 282

Percy, Judith 342
Perkins, Phil (Thomas Philip) 283
Perkins, Tegwen 282
Perowne, Arthur Herbert 284
Perry, Alf (Alfred) 284
Peters, Gordon Buchanan 284
Pfeil, Mark Glenn 144
Phillips, Frank 342
Philp, Hugh 284
Picard, Henry G. 144
Pickard, Margaret (Kathleen Margaret) 284
Pickworth, Ossie (Horace Henry) 342
Pim, Dorothy: see Beck 209
Pinero, Manuel 326
Platt, Woody (J. Wood) 145
Platts, Lionel 285
Player, Gary Jim 353
Pohl, Dan (Danny Joe) 145
Polland, Eddie (Edward) 285
Pook, Elizabeth: see Chadwick 286
Pooley, Don (Sheldon George, Jnr) 146
Porter, Dot: see Germain 67
Porter, Mary Bea 146
Porter, Ruth 286
Pose, Martin 365
Post, Sandra 146
Postlewait, Kathy 147
Pott, Johnny (John) 147
Povall, John K.D. 286
Powell, Rene 147
Poxon, Martin Arthur 286
de Prado, Catherine: see Lacoste 322
Prentice, JoAnn 147
Pressler, Leona: see Cheney 38
Preuss, Tish (Phyllis) 147
Price, Elizabeth 286
Price, Nick 358
Pulz, Penny (Penelope) 342
Pung, Jackie (Jacqueline) 148
Purtzer, Tom (Thomas Warren) 148
Pyne, Julie Stanger 148

Q

Quast, Anne 148

R

Rafferty, Ronan 287

Ragan, Dave (David William) 149
Rankin, Judy 149
Ransom, Henry 149
Rassett, Joe (Joseph) 150
Ratcliffe, Noel 342
Ravenscroft, Gladys 287
Rawlings, Mandy (Amanda) 287
Rawlings, Vicki (Victoria) 288
Rawlins, Horace 150
Rawls, Betsy (Elizabeth Earle) 150
Ray, Ted (Edward) 288
Rees, Dai (David James), CBE 289
Regalado, Victor 365
Reid, Mike (Michael Daniel) 150
Reinhardt, Alex (Alexandra) 151
Renner, Jack 151
Renner, Jane 151
Revolta, Johnny 151
Reynolds, Cathy (Catherine) 152
Richmond, Maureen: see Walker 307
Ridley, Fred 152
Riegel, Skee (Robert Henry) 152
Riley, Polly Ann 152
Ritzman, Alice 152
Rizzo, Patti (Patricia) 152
Robb, Diane: see Frearson 242
Robb, James 290
Robbins, Hillman 153
Roberts, Margaret Patricia 290
Roberts, Sue (Susan) 153
Robertson, Allan 290
Robertson, Belle (Isabella), MBE 291
Robertson, David M. 290
Robertson, Janette: see Wright 313
Robson, Fred (Frederick) 291
Rodgers, Phil (Philamon Webster) 153
Rodriguez, Chi Chi (Juan) 153
Rogers, Bill (William Charles) 154
Romack, Barbie (Barbara Gaile) 155
Rosburg, Bob (Robert) 155
Ross, Alex (Alexander) 155
Roth, Nancy: see Syms 176
Rubin, Claudine: see Cros 318
Rudolph, Mason 156
Runyan, Paul Scott 156
Ruttle, Maureen 292

S

Saddler, Sandy (Alexander) 292
St-Sauveur, Lally Vicomtesse de 326

Sander, Anne: see Quast 148
Sander, Bill (William Knox) 156
Sanders, Doug (George Douglas) 157
Sanders, Gary 156
Sarazen, Gene (Eugene) 158
Sargent, George 159
Saunders, Vivien Inez 292
Sayers, Ben (Bernard) 292
Schlee, John 159
Schleeh, Gerda: see Boykin 27
Schroeder, John Lawrence 160
Scott, Lady Margaret 293
Scott, the Hon. Michael 293
Scott, Syd (Sydney Simeon) 293
Scrutton, Phil (Philip F.) 293
Segard, Lally: see St-Sauveur 326
Semple, Carole Keister 160
Sewell, Doug (Douglas N.) 293
Sewgolum, Sewsunker 355
Sfingi, Beverly: see Hanson 77
Shade, Ronnie (Ronald David Bell Mitchell), MBE
    294
Shankland, Bill (William) 343
Shaw, Andrew J. 343
Shaw, Bob (Robert) 343
Shaw, Tom 160
Sheard, Alison Irene 355
Shearer, Bob (Robert Alan) 343
Sheehan, Patty (Patricia Leslie) 160
Shepard, Alan B. 161
Shepperson, Alec E. 294
Sherk, Cathy (Catherine) 161
Shute, Denny (Herman Densmore) 161
Siderowf, Dick (Richard L.) 161
Sieckmann, Tom 162
Sifford, Charlie (Charles) 162
Sigel, Jay 162
Sikes, Dan 162
Sikes, Dick (Richard H.) 162
Simon, Judy: see Kimball 101
Simons, Jim (James B.) 163
Simpson, Jack 294
Simpson, Juli: see Inkster 91
Simpson, Scott William 163
Skala, Carole: see Callison 33
Skerritt, Paddy (Patrick Joseph) 294
Slark, Ruth: see Porter 286
Smith, Alex (Alexander) 163
Smith, Alfred Edward 294
Smith, Frances, OBE 294
Smith, Horton 164
Smith, Macdonald 164

Smith, Marilyn J. 344
Smith, Marilynn Louise 165
Smith, Wiffi (Margaret) 165
Smith, William Dickson 295
Smith, Willie (William) 165
Smyth, Des (Desmond) 295
Snead, J.C. (Jesse Carlyle) 165
Snead, Sam (Samuel Jackson) 165
Snead, Ed (Edgar Morris) 168
Solomon, Beth (Elizabeth) 168
Somerville, Sandy (Charles Ross) 168
Sorenson, Carol 169
Sota, Ramon 326
Souchak, Mike (Michael) 169
Soulsby, Janet 296
Spearman, Marley 296
Speer, Roberta: see Albers 12
Spuzich, Sandra Ann 169
Squirrell, Hew Crawford 297
Stacy, Hollis 169
Stadler, Craig Robert 170
Stanley, Ian 344
Stanton, Bob (Robert James) 344
Stephens, Frances: see Smith 294
Stephenson, Jan 344
Stewart, Gillian 297
Stewart, Marlene 171
Stewart, Payne (William Payne) 172
Still, Ken (Kenneth Allan) 172
Stirling, Alexa 172
Stockton, Dave (David) 172
Stone, Beth (Elizabeth) 173
Storey, Eustace Francis 297
Stout, James Alfred 297
Stowe, Charlie (Charles) 297
Stranahan, Frank R. 173
Strange, Curtis Northrup 174
Strath, Andrew 297
Strath, Davie (David) 298
Streck, Ron 174
Streit, Marlene: see Stewart 171
Stuart, Hugh Bannerman 298
Suggs, Louise 175
Sugihara, Teruo 362
Sugimoto, Hideyo 362
Sullivan, Mike (Michael James) 175
Sundelson, Neville 356
Sutton, Hal 175
Suzuki, Norio 362
Swaelens, Don (Donald) 326
Sweeny, Bob (Robert), DFC 176
Sweetser, Jess W. 176

Syms, Nancy 176
von Szlavy, Erzsebet 327

T

Tabor, Vicki 177
Tait, Freddie (Frederick Guthrie) 298
Tapie, Alan Francis 177
Taylor, Frank M. 177
Taylor, J.H. (John Henry) 298
Taylor, Reginald Carden 356
Tewell, Doug (Douglas Frederick) 177
Thirlwell, Alan 300
Thomas, Dave (David C.) 300
Thomas, Tegwen: see Perkins 282
Thomas, Vicki: see Rawlings 288
Thompson, Leonard Stephen 177
Thomson, Hector 300
Thomson, Jimmy (James) 177
Thomson, Muriel Natalie 300
Thomson, Peter W., CBE 345
Thorpe, Jim (James Lee) 177
Tolley, Cyril James Hastings, MC 300
Torluemke, Judy: see Rankin 149
Torrance, Sam 301
Toski, Bob 178
Toushin, Gail 178
Toussaint, Philippe 327
Townsend, Peter Michael Paul 302
Trahan, Sam 178
Travers, Jerry (Jerome Dunstan) 178
Travis, Walter J. 179
Trevino, Lee Buck 179
Tshabalala, Vincent 356
Tu Ai-Yu 362
Tucker, Iestyn (William Iestyn) 303
Tupling, Peter L. 303
Turnesa, Jim (James) 181
Turnesa, Joe (Joseph) 182
Turnesa, Willie (William P.) 182
Tweddell, Dr William, MC 303
Twitty, Howard Allen 182

U

Updegraff, Dr Ed (Edgar R.) 182
Urzetta, Sam 183
Uzielli, Angela 303

V

Vagliano, Lally: see St-Sauveur 326
Valentine, Jessie (Jessica), MBE 303
Valentine, Tommy (Thomas Ervin) 183
Varangot, Brigitte 327
Vardon, Harry 304
Vardon, Tom 305
Vare, Glenna: see Collett 40
Vaughan, David 306
Venturi, Ken (Kenneth) 183
Verwey, Bobby (Robert) 356
de Vicenzo, Roberto 366
Vines, Ellsworth 184
Vines, Randall Colin 347
Voigt, George 184

W

Wadkins, Bobby (Robert Edwin) 185
Wadkins, Lanny (Jerry Lanston) 184
Waites, Brian 306
Walker, Arthur 356
Walker, Cyril 185
Walker, Jimmy (James) 307
Walker, Maureen 307
Walker, Mickey (Carol Michelle) 307
Wall, Art (Arthur J.) 185
Ward, Angela: see Bonallack 211
Ward, Bud (Marvin Harvey) 186
Ward, Charlie (Charles Harold) 307
Ward, Harvie (E. Harvie) 186
Washam, Jo Ann 187
Watrous, Al (Andrew Albert) 187
Watson, Charlotte: see Beddows 209
Watson, Denis Leslie 356
Watson, Tom (Thomas Sturges) 188
Way, Paul 308
Weaver, DeWitt 190
Weetman, Harry 308
Weibring, D.A. (Donald Albert) 191
Weiskopf, Tom (Thomas Daniel) 191
Welts, Anne: see Quast 148
Weslock, Nick 192
Westbrook, Terry 356
Westland, Jack (Alfred John) 193
Wethered, Joyce 309
Wethered, Roger Henry 310
Whalen, Gerda: see Boykin 27
Whigham, Henry James 193

Whitcombe, Charles Albert 311
Whitcombe, Ernest Edward 311
Whitcombe, Ernest R. 311
Whitcombe, Reg (Reginald Arthur) 311
White, Donna 193
White, Jack 311
White, Ronnie (Ronald James) 311
Whitehead, Ross 312
Whitlock, Susan: see Hedges 246
Whitton, Ivo Harrington 347
Whitworth, Kathy (Kathrynne Ann) 193
van Wie, Virginia 194
Wilcock, Peter 312
Wilkinson, Martha 194
Will, George Duncan 312
Willing, Dr Oscar F. 194
Wilson, Enid 312
Wilson, Peggy (Margaret Joyce) 195
Wininger, Bo (Francis G.) 195
de Wit, Gerard 327
Wollin, Liv 327
Wolstenholme, Guy 347
Wood, Craig Ralph 195
Wood, Norman 312
Woosnam, Ian 313
Worsham, Lew (Lewis Elmer) 196
Wright, Janette Sneddon 313
Wright, Mickey (Mary Kathryn) 196
Wright, Nancy 313
Wynn, Bob 198
Wysong, Dudley 198

Y

Yancey, Bert (Albert Winsborough) 198
Yates, Charlie (Charles Richardson) 199
Young, Donna: see Caponi 34

Z

Zaharias, Babe (Mildred Ella) 199
Zarley, Kermit Millard 201
Ziegler, Larry (Lawrence Edward) 201
Zoeller, Fuzzy (Frank Urban) 202
Zokol, Richard 202

PHOTOGRAPHIC
ACKNOWLEDGMENTS

BBC Hulton Picture Library: 229

Peter Dazeley: 19, 38, 80, 83, 85, 102, 108, 144, 146, 157, 170 left, 174, 181, 198 right, 202, 216, 225, 239, 254, 259, 277, 279, 315, 321, 336, 345, 349, 354, 359

David Evans: 184

The Ladies' Professional Golf Association: 12, 109, 152, 362

Bert Neale: 16, 21, 22, 29, 43, 57, 67, 73, 76, 86, 89, 93, 103, 104, 106, 111, 118, 121, 142, 149, 154, 171, 182, 193, 198 left, 199, 201 left & right, 204, 211, 212, 214, 218, 221, 223, 227, 231, 232, 234, 240, 242, 245, 252 left & right, 255, 256, 258, 261, 264, 266, 273, 281, 284, 285, 286, 289, 295, 296, 308, 309, 319, 325, 327, 329, 337, 340, 341, 350, 353, 363, 365, 366

The Professional Golf Association: 236, 298, 305, 346

Phil Sheldon: 11, 14, 17, 24, 32, 35, 36, 46, 50 right, 61, 64, 70, 75, 96, 105, 112, 124, 128, 131, 133, 140, 141, 160, 167, 170 right, 175, 187 left, 188, 191, 203, 249, 250, 268, 283 left, 287, 291, 301, 302, 313, 323, 331, 343, 357, 367

The United States Golf Association: 15, 25, 28, 30, 41, 44, 48, 50 left, 53, 54, 58, 68, 74, 79, 91, 95, 99, 114, 116, 122, 130, 137, 138, 145, 151, 158, 164, 173, 176, 179, 186, 187 right, 195, 196, 197, 206, 208, 215, 219, 247, 274, 283 right, 288, 306, 310, 324, 333